STANDARD HISTORY
OF
KNOXVILLE, TENNESSEE

A reproduction of a book originally published in 1900,
William Rule, editor.

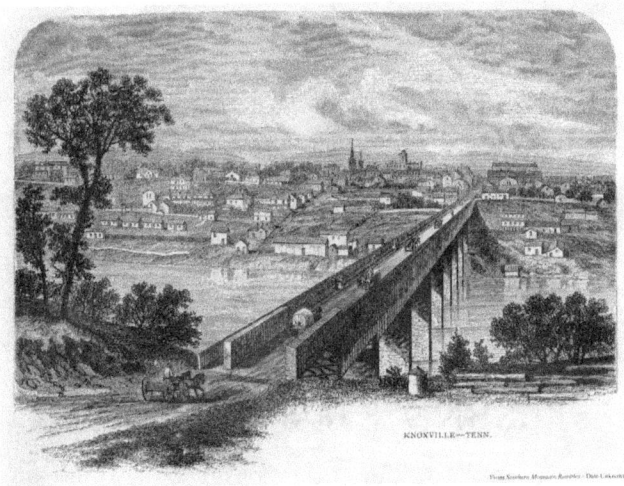

This version created by Charles A. Reeves, Jr.
With the Index courtesy of Steve Cotham,
The Calvin M. McClung Historical Collection,
Knoxville, TN

©2009
Charles A. Reeves, Jr.

Produced By:

Charles A. Reeves, Jr.
Technical Illustration & Publishing
Specializing in Cartography and Genealogy

10812 Dineen Drive   (865) 966-5768
Knoxville, Tennessee 37934-1809
e-mail: reevesca@tds.net
Home Page: http://www.ReevesMaps.com

ISBN 978-0-9800984-9-5

The image on the title page is from *Southern Mountain Rambles,*
publication date unknown.
It can be seen in greater detail following page 148.

INTRODUCTION

I will admit to mixed emotions about reproducing this book, in light of the fact that it has been reproduced before, although I do not know how often nor the date(s). In addition, complete texts of it are on the Internet, both in the form of scanned images of each page, and a transcription of the contents. A CD is also available in PDF format. But I do hope there are still folks out there who like books they can hold in their hands and in which they can mark references. Hopefully the inclusion of a complete Index (see Acknowledgements below) and a few old engravings (see Additional Illustrations below) will also add interest.

ACKNOWLEDGEMENTS

Mere words cannot express how much I am in debt to Steve Cotham and others at the Calvin M. McClung Historical Collection in Knoxville, TN for providing a copy of an Index to this book. The value it adds is beyond measure for those doing research on the City. Readers will note that it is extremely thorough, encompassing some 170 pages at the end of the book. I make no claim of having anything to do with its creation, other than correcting some minor errors, and formatting it for this book. The creation was entirely theirs, and it must have required a sizeable effort.

Charles A. Reeves, Jr.
July 31, 2009

ADDITIONAL ILLUSTRATIONS

Note: The illustrations/photographs in the original book do not have page numbers. I followed that convention, with the illustrations inserted after the page numbers given in the table below. They are all from publications in the private library of Charles Reeves, Jr.

Description	Page No.
Blockhouse - Knoxville, 1793 (also depicted on the cover)	38
South-Western Knoxville, 1861	86
The City of Knoxville, 1881	88
Scenes around Knoxville, *Harper's Weekly*, 1887	90
Knoxville, showing the Bridge, date unknown	148
Rockwood, TN Iron Furnace, date unknown	188
Marble Quarry, *Harper's Weekly*, 1887	204
"The Suck," date unknown	276
Aerial Cable Car Across the River, *Scientific American*, 1894 (two pages)	302
Charles W. Dabney, Jr., 1892	368
University of Tennessee Professors, 1892	368
Buildings at The University of Tennessee, 1892	378

STANDARD HISTORY

OF

KNOXVILLE, TENNESSEE

WITH FULL OUTLINE OF THE NATURAL ADVANTAGES, EARLY SETTLEMENT, TERRITORIAL GOVERNMENT, INDIAN TROUBLES, AND GENERAL AND PARTICULAR HISTORY OF THE CITY DOWN TO THE PRESENT TIME

EDITED BY

WILLIAM RULE

GEORGE F. MELLEN, Ph. D., AND J. WOOLDRIDGE

COLLABORATORS

PUBLISHED BY

THE LEWIS PUBLISHING COMPANY

CHICAGO

1900

PREFACE.

IN undertaking his part in this work, the Editor was prompted chiefly by his desire to see prepared and published a "History of Knoxville," a city that has a history full of interest. It may be that inaccuracies will be seen, though in the preparation of the matter much painstaking, conscientious labor has been given; but if there are such they can be corrected only by publicity. In any event it may be confidently claimed with this work before him the task of the future historian of Knoxville will be rendered much easier. It may be explained that the matter for most of the chapters was written early in 1898, since which time some changes have occurred that are not noted; but none of sufficient importance to mar the value of the book.

The only chapter written by the Editor is that on the Knoxville Press, embracing a period of more than a hundred years. Much of the information concerning the history of the press of Knoxville for the first half century was derived from an address delivered by Colonel Moses White before the Tennessee Press Association. For some valuable information concerning the first newspaper published in Knoxville in the state, not heretofore printed, indebtedness is acknowledged to Dr. George F. Mellen, of the University of Tennessee. The facts concerning the Presbyterian Witness were furnished by Mrs. Andrew Blackburn, widow of the editor of the Witness, through Hon. Will A. McTeer, of Maryville, Tennessee.

In the chapter on the Bench and Bar, much of the matter was prepared by Mr. Joshua W. Caldwell, as his work on the Bench and Bar of Tennessee was very largely drawn upon for a history of the courts, and for the personal mention of most of the prominent lawyers and judges of the past. This was

PREFACE.

especially the case with regard to the sketches of Archibald Roane, Thomas L. Williams, John Williams, Hugh Lawson White, Robert J. McKinney, Connolly F. Trigg, Thomas C. Lyon, James W. Deaderick, William-Henry Sneed, Horace Maynard, Thomas A. R. Nelson, Willie Blount, Alfred Caldwell, Richard G. Dunlap, John Baxter, Joseph Anderson, Thomas Emmerson, L. C. Houk, Ebenezer Alexander, Spencer Jarnagin, George Andrews, Edward Scott, Pleasant M. Miller, William B. Reese, and Jacob Montgomery Thornburgh. The chapter, however, was not written by Mr. Caldwell, but by Mr. J. Wooldridge, who was also the writer of all the other chapters, except that on the press, and those hereafter mentioned. The value of the work has been enhanced by the kindly assistance of a great many Knoxville citizens, who have furnished information, their number being too large to render giving individual names practicable. Chapters II., III., IV., V., VI., VII. and VIII. were written by George F. Mellen, Ph. D., Professor of American History, University of Tennessee. THE EDITOR.

CONTENTS.

Chapter I.
NATURAL ADVANTAGES.

Resources of the Surrounding Country—All Tributary to Knoxville—Boundary of the County—Topography—Geology and the Geological Character of the Surface in Relation to Agriculture and Horticulture—Great Improvements in Methods of Cultivation—Coal, Iron, Brick Clay and Other Mineral Products—Mountain Gaps and Their Utility—Water Supply—Mineral Springs—Climate—Temperature Throughout the Various Seasons—Railroads........................9

Chapter II.
INITIAL MOVEMENTS TOWARDS SETTLEMENT.

Domain of Cherokees—Approach of Hunters, Trappers and Explorers—Immigration—Gradual Withdrawal of Indians—Treaties—Fort Stanwix—Hard Labor—Lochaber—Purchases of Watauga Association—Jacob Brown and Richard Henderson—Treaties of Long Island; of Holston, Dumplin, Coytoy, and Hopewell—Westward Movement 29

Chapter III.
EARLY SETTLEMENT.

Conditions in the West—Germ of Knoxville—White's Fort—North Carolina Grants—Explorations of James White—Fixed Settlement—Topography—Growth—New Stations or Forts—Roads—Cession of Territory to United States—Blount Appointed Governor—His Character—Appointments—Relations of Whites and Indians—Treaty of Holston—Provisions and Results............................37

Chapter IV.
FOUNDING OF KNOXVILLE.

Date of Founding—Confusing Statements of Historians—Articles of Agreement Between Proprietor and Commissioners—Original Drawers of Lots—Act Establishing Knoxville—Blount's Arrival—Named in Honor of General Henry Knox—Reasons......................46

Chapter V.
UNDER TERRITORIAL GOVERNMENT.

Establishment of Knox County—Officials Appointed—First Lawyers—County Roads and Buildings—Commercial Growth—Pioneer Merchants—Hostelries—Occupations—Postal Facilities—Army Post—Relations of Citizens and Soldiers................................54

CHAPTER VI.

INDIAN TROUBLES.

Indian War Imminent—Conditions in the West—Indian Atrocities—Policy of Blount and the National Government—Threatened Attack on Knoxville—Preparation of Whites—Pioneer Character—Stephen Foster's Account of the Massacre at Cavet's Station—Sevier's Successful Raid..61

CHAPTER VII.

TERRITORIAL LEGISLATURE.

Hamilton District—Sufferings from Indians—Appeals for Succor—Elections to Territorial Legislature—Preliminary Session—Spirit of Legislators—Active Measures for Resistance to Indian Depredations—First Regular Session—Acts Touching Education and Taxation—Act Preparatory to Organization of the State—Constitutional Convention 72

CHAPTER VIII.

LIFE OF THE PEOPLE.

Population—Interest in Education—Early Teachers—Samuel Cornik—His School—Blount College—Presbyterian Church Organized—Printing Press—Literary Effort—Books—Physicians—Amusements—Darker Phases—Strong Elements of Character................79

CHAPTER IX.

MUNICIPAL AFFAIRS.

First White Settlement—Original Capital of Tennessee—Incorporated in 1815—Looking for Railroads—Gas Lights Introduced—Extension of Corporate Limits—First Steam Fire Engine—Market Established—Fire Department Created—Water Works—System of Sewers—Names of Mayors—Paving Streets and Building Bridges—List of Postmasters—Three Municipalities Consolidated................87

CHAPTER X.

MILITARY HISTORY.

Early Indian Wars—Col. John Williams' Regiment—The Mexican War—Volunteers for Both the Union and the Confederate Service—Sanders' Raid—Knoxville Receives Gen. Burnside—Is Besieged by Gen. Longstreet—A Sanguinary Battle—Fort Sanders—Knoxville Pension Agency—In the Spanish War—Warm Welcome to Returning Volunteer Soldiers 148

CONTENTS.

Chapter XI.
MANUFACTURING INTERESTS.

Some of the Earlier Industries—Cotton Once a Staple Crop—S. T. Atkin, One of the Pioneers in Manufacturing—Growth and Multiplication of Industries—Extensive Marble Industries—Iron Mills—Brookside Cotton Mills—Knoxville Woolen Mills—Furniture—Telephone System 194

Chapter XII.
COMMERCIAL MATTERS.

First Stores Established—Growth as a Commercial Center—Unusually Large Jobbing Business—Some of the Largest Establishments in the South—The Territory Covered—Wholesale Trade Amounting to More Than $50,000,000 Annually—The Coal Trade, its Growth—Chamber of Commerce—Great Fire............................226

Chapter XIII.
BANKING.

First Bank Established 1811—State Bank Organized—Some of the Private Banks—The First National Bank in 1864—Other National Banks—Clearing House Association—Building and Loan Associations in the Hands of Receivers—Insurance Companies.........250

Chapter XIV.
TRANSPORTATION.

Charles McClung, the Pioneer Road Builder—Stage-Coach Lines—Progress in Turnpike Roads—The Tennessee River and Tributaries—First Steamboat at Knoxville—Railroad Building—The East Tennessee and Georgia and the East Tennessee and Virginia Roads—The Great Southern System—Roads to Atlanta and Cumberland Gap—Bridges—Street Railways 271

Chapter XV.
THE PRESS.

The Gazette, Knoxville's First Newspaper—The Register and Its Long Life—The Plebeian, Knoxville's First Daily—Brownlow's Whig and Its Remarkable Career—Recent Ventures in Knoxville Journalism—The Chronicle—The Press and Herald—The Tribune—The Journal and Tribune—The Afternoon Sentinel—The Church Newspapers..311

Chapter XVI.
EDUCATIONAL MATTERS.

The Schools of a Century Ago—Rev. Samuel Doak, the Pioneer—Interest Manifested by Governor Blount—Blount College, Now the University of Tennessee—Knoxville Female Academy—Hampden Sidney Academy—Organization and Success of City Schools—University School—Knoxville College for Colored Students—Tennessee Medical College 344

CHAPTER XVII.

CHURCH HISTORY.

The Pioneer Presbyterians—Rev. Samuel Doak—Knoxville's First Church—Early Methodists—Bishop Asbury's First Visit—First Baptist Organization—Good Works of Rev. Samuel Carrick—Rev. Isaac Anderson—Knoxville Churches Grow and Multiply—Many Large and Flourishing Churches Now in the City....................414

CHAPTER XVIII.

THE BENCH AND BAR.

THE COURT OF THE WATAUGA ASSOCIATION.

First Court in Tennessee—First Court in Knoxville, 1792—The Courts of Knox County and Judges who Held Them—Courts of Chancery—Clerks of the Courts—Sketches of Members of the Knoxville Bar in the Past Hundred Years...466

CHAPTER XIX.

MEDICAL HISTORY.

Knoxville's Medical Men Have Honored Their Profession—Dr. J. C. Strong—Fathers Followed by Sons in the Profession—Ramsey the Historian—Sketches of Knoxville Physicians, Past and Present—Some Disastrous Epidemics—Cholera in 1854—Organization of Medical Societies 501

CHAPTER XX.

PUBLIC INSTITUTIONS.

Provisions Made for the Treatment of Insane Persons—Lyon's View Hospital—School for Deaf Mutes—Lawson McGhee Library—Margaret McClung Industrial Home—St. John's Orphanage—New City Hospital—Home for the Friendless—Other Charitable Institutions—Woman's Building..535

CHAPTER XXI.

SOCIETIES.

Tennessee's First Masonic Lodge—Grand Lodge Organized—First Lodge at Knoxville in 1800—Chapter and Templar Masonry—Three Score Years of Odd Fellowship—Various Other Society Organizations 556

CHAPTER XXII.

CEMETERIES.

The Oldest, That of the Presbyterians—Gray Cemetery—The Confederate or Bethel Cemetery—The National Cemetery—Soldiers' Monument—Catholic Cemetery—Woodlawn Cemetery—The Hebrew Cemetery 582

HISTORY OF KNOXVILLE, TENNESSEE.

CHAPTER I.

NATURAL ADVANTAGES.

Resources of the Surrounding Country—All Tributary to Knoxville—Boundary of the County—Topography—Geology and the Geological Character of the Surface in Relation to Agriculture and Horticulture—Great Improvements in Methods of Cultivation—Coal, Iron, Brick Clay and Other Mineral Products—Mountain Gaps and Their Utility—Water Supply—Mineral Springs—Climate—Temperature Throughout the Various Seasons—Railroads.

IN enumerating the natural advantages of a city like Knoxville, it is necessary to allude with greater or less fullness to the resources of the surrounding country, for under the conditions of modern civilization these resources are very largely tributary to the city's requirements. And it will be found also necessary to extend inquiry even beyond the limits of Knox county, for at the present time the resources of the country, because of the facilities for transportation offered by the numerous and increasing railways, are carried from immense distances.

Knox county was taken in 1792 from territory then comprised in Greene and Hawkins counties, and named in honor of Henry Knox, Secretary of War in the cabinet of President Washington. The building up of a town where Knoxville now stands was immediately begun. As thus established and named, Knox county extended far beyond its present boundaries, which embrace about five hundred and seventy-three square miles. The county is unusually irregular in shape, no two of its boundary lines being of equal length and only two of them being parallel, the latter being along Bays Mountain and Flint Ridge. The boundaries of the county were shaped in the first place by the long straight ridges traversing it in parallels from northeast to southwest, these ridges giving direction to all its natural water courses; and they have to a considerable extent determined the natural products of the soil and the character of the inhabitants; for it has always been held by philosophical writers upon historical and ethnological subjects that the topography, soil and climate of a country have a wide and far-reaching effect, if not a controlling one, upon the people themselves, and their institutions, second, only even if second, to that of their government itself. And some say that the people will be free that live in a mountainous country.

The long, straight ridges mentioned, although so nearly parallel in direction and uniform in outline, differ greatly in their geological structure; and as the soil in the valleys comes originally from the rocks and depends mainly upon the wearing and washings from the mountain sides, that soil naturally varies as greatly as does the geological structure of the mountains themselves. From an elevated point of view Knox county appears to be divided naturally into what is called by Prof. Safford, in his Geological Survey of the State, the Ridge or Valley region, and the Knobby region, the latter lying southeast of the Tennessee river and the French Broad, and the former embracing the remainder of the county, about four-fifths of its entire area. The topography of the county lying to the southeast of the French Broad, mentioned above, while somewhat of the same nature as that of the entire valley region, is yet broken up by short spurs of hills running nearly at right angles to the longer ridges, which gives the country the appearance of large and irregular groups of hills, which rise to a height of from two to four hundred feet above the average elevation of the surrounding country. The tops of these hills are somewhat rounded, and are separated from each other by ravines, long, narrow, deep and winding, which taken altogether give the country in the vicinity of Knoxville an appearance peculiarly its own. The sides of these hills in many cases are too steep for successful cultivation, but the soil of the valleys is especially rich, and yields excellent returns even to fair cultivation, while in former years the hillsides as well as the valleys were covered with heavy forests of white oak, maple, hickory, poplar and other varieties of trees, and are still partially so covered.

In former years, while primitive methods in agriculture, as in other departments of industry, prevailed from the necessities of the situation, the productiveness of the soil was utilized only to a limited extent; but in more recent times the practices of farming have largely improved, and perhaps in few portions of the country do these modern methods prove more beneficial to the entire community, including the agricultural classes themselves, than to those in the immediate vicinity of Knoxville.

A cursory glance at the geological formation of this portion of Tennessee shows that the prevailing outcropping rock is limestone. It has been described as a "red, ferruginous, sandy limestone," and Prof. Safford says that it is interstratified with calcareous shale and flaggy limestone. There are large quantities of iron imbedded in this rock, and as a natural result there are also large quantities of this same mineral in the soil; but up to the present time no process has been discovered by which this mineral can be extracted either from soil or rock with profit. The chief value of the rock, therefore, lies in its utilization as building material and as flagging stones. But it is and has long been well known that the soil of limestone countries is especially adapted to the growing of wheat and other cereal crops, and, though in the vicinity of Knoxville the soil is inclined to toughness in its structure, is of a dark red or brownish color, bears deep plowing and requires to be thoroughly worked; yet all this is immensely to the benefit of the agriculturist, and when well underdrained it yields excellent crops of wheat, oats and corn, and is also capable of being well set with grass and clover. While in earlier years the market crops consisted mainly in fowls, eggs, feathers, beeswax, ginseng, a few pelts and now and then a young beef, at the present time all the great variety of a prosperous agricultural community finds its way to the excellent markets of the city of Knoxville, the demands of such a city, which is much wealthier than in former years, having had their effect upon what the farmers raise.

In a general way it may be stated that the varied resources of the great East Tennessee valley are all tributary to Knoxville, this valley being one of the most beautiful and prosperous in the state, and within its limits are embraced nearly all of the agricultural resources of East Tennessee. It is one of the eight natural divisions of the state, and is bounded on the southeast by the Unaka chain of mountains and on the northwest by the Cumberland mountains or table land. To the northeast it is continuous with the Valley of Virginia and to the southwest it extends into Georgia and Alabama. This Valley of Tennessee is therefore but a portion of that great natural highway which extends from the Susquehanna river in Pennsylvania to the Coosa and Black Warrior rivers in Alabama, which highway furnishes easy communication between New England and the Middle States and the great Southwest. This highway is now traversed by several lines of solid railway track throughout its entire length, which connect the resources of the Southwest with the capital and industry of the Middle and New England States, the benefits of which connection are largely felt by the city of Knoxville, situated as it is almost midway along the railways in the Valley of East Tennessee and near the head of navigation of the Tennessee river. This valley in its southwest course enters Tennessee obliquely from the northeast, but soon turns with a graceful curve toward the south and crosses the southern boundary of the state in almost a southerly direction. And toward this southern boundary line the mountain ridges that inclose the valley approach each other to within a distance of less than thirty-five miles. The area of the valley is about 9,200 square miles, considerably more than one-fifth of the entire area of the state, and it includes all of the following counties: Hancock, Hawkins, Grainger, Union, Jefferson, Knox, Roane, Meigs, and Bradley, besides most of Sullivan, McMinn, and portions of Blount, Bledsoe, Anderson, Carter, Cocke, Johnson, Greene, Washington, Monroe, Sevier, Polk, Claiborne, Rhea, Hamilton, Sequatchee and Marion. This valley, taken all in all, constitutes the most interesting portion of East Tennessee, and also of the Appalachian range that lies within the state.

The Tennessee river, originally named the Holston, to the mouth of Little Tennessee, enters Knox county near its northeastern corner and in a remarkably tortuous and serpentine course flows through it a little to the west of south until it approaches the south corner of the county, when it turns to the westward and then, having made a wide curve, again flows to the south and passes out of the county, at about the width of the county westward from its point of entrance. By these many windings a large part of the county is made up of rich valley lands, which are well watered and drained, much to the benefit of the owners of the lands, and the great value of the valley lands is only equaled by that of the many tributaries that enter it in its tortuous course. These tributaries are swift and clear streams, rising either within or without the county, and flowing through long, narrow valleys, and are in their turn fed on either side by numerous branches which largely increase their volume before they reach the main river. Upon many of these several creeks there were in former days, to a greater extent than at the present time, numerous sawmills, which reduced the forests to lumber of various kinds and shapes, that found ready sale in the markets of the towns and cities of the state, and also on the farms, as the farmers gradually supplanted log houses and barns with those of timber and lumber.

Flint Ridge, sometimes called Chestnut Ridge, constitutes the northwest boundary line of the county. The former is the older name and describes the principal characteristic of the crest of the ridge, this crest being composed of chert, or flint-like quartz or hornstone, much resembling true flint. The main ridge extends from Virginia into Georgia. On the eastern and southern side of this ridge lies Bull Run Valley, one of the long valleys of the state, which also extends from Virginia into Georgia, taking different names in different parts of its extent. In Knox county it takes the name of Bull Run, from the creek that flows through it, and which empties into Clinch river. This valley contains a large quantity of rich farming lands. It is abundantly watered and was at one time heavily timbered. This valley is bounded on the east by Copper Ridge, which in its turn bounds Beaver Valley on the west, this latter valley being one of the most fertile in the county. Hinds' Valley lies between Beaver and Black Oak ridges, the lower half of which in Knox county, is watered by Hickory creek, which flows into Clinch river. Grassy Valley, bounded by Black Oak and Webb's ridges, is of much importance from an agricultural point of view, much more so than Poor Valley, which comes next. But Knoxville Valley exceeds in importance any of the others, it being in fact the valley of East Tennessee.

The rocks within this valley are of the Nashville and Trenton limestone, which yields a dark, friable and fertile soil; and as all the creeks emptying into the Tennessee on its right bank flow through this valley, and as the Tennessee itself washes its entire eastern side, it is more abundantly watered than are all the other valleys of the county. Added to all these natural advantages is the artificial advantage of the East Tennessee, Virginia and Georgia railroad, which runs along the bed of the valley, furnishing rapid transportation and communication to and between the various towns and cities along its course and to the farmers throughout the entire length of the valley. To all of these things may be attributed the rapid and substantial growth of the city of Knoxville.

In connection with what may be stated on the subject of coal, it must be noted that the rock formation in the vicinity of

Knoxville is much older than the carboniferous strata. In fact the Knoxville strata belong to the very oldest of the stratified rocks, viz.: the Potsdam or Primordial group, as classified by Prof. Dana. The layers of rock constituting the Knoxville group are immediately upon the metamorphic or azoic rock, and belong to the very lowest of the Lower Silurian age. After their formation came the Upper Silurian, the Devonian and the Sub-Carboniferous, before any coal was formed. The Lower Silurian embraces three great groups of rocks, viz.: the Ocoee conglomerate, the Chilhowee sandstone, and the Knox group, the latter group being also divided into three formations, viz.: the Knox sandstone, the Knox shale and the Knox dolomite.

The coal measures consist of a series of sandstones, shales and stone coal, interstratified, and range from 200 to 2,500 feet in thickness. In the flat top of the Cumberland tableland the sandstones and shales form the cap of the two Short mountains in Cannon county; the sandstones and shales of the outliers in Overton and Fentress, and the same formations are on the top of Lookout mountain, Walden's Ridge and Racoon mountain. Coal is also found in Scott, Cumberland, Van Buren and Grundy counties.

Of the Knoxville group the most valuable rocks are the sandstones, which are interstratified with hard shales, the shales and sandstones being of many different colors, such as brown, red, chestnut, buff, gray, etc., and many of the iron ore deposits of the eastern counties rest upon the several divisions of the Knox group.

The Knox shale is a very important formation, and is often interstratified with thin layers of blue limestone, yielding the finest specimens of oölitic limestone to be found anywhere in the state. This shale, between Knoxville and Clinton, gives us Poor Valley, Hinds' Valley, Bull Run Valley, and Wolf Valley, and in the Knoxville shale valleys are located some of the finest farming lands in this portion of the state, the limestone contributing largely to the strength and fertility of the soil, and some of the iron ore banks are located on this shale.

But the Knox dolomite is the most important and massive of the three divisions of the Knox group, the thicker layers being often worked into millstones, and in the upper strata of this division there are cuts of dull, variegated dolomite, which are worked as marble and used as building material. In color it is light gray, variegated with brownish red clouds, and it is rather fine grained.

In addition to this variety of marble there are in the Knox group many iron ore banks, which contain two species of ore, viz.: limonite and hematite. Any of the strata of the Knox group will under certain conditions yield limonite, and limonite banks occur in all the mountain counties from Johnson to Polk. Hematite is found in the shale layers from one to two feet thick in Carter county, and there occur in this division also jasper and chalcedony. Iron pyrites is also found in the Knox group, usually associated with galena and blende. Carbonate of lead is also found in some localities, as also is the black oxide of manganese. Besides the above are found heavy spar, fluor spar, calcite and quartz.

The Knox dolomite and the Knox shale give some of the finest farming lands in East Tennessee, and are therefore of special interest to the agriculturist and to the inhabitants of cities, the aggregate area in East Tennessee of the farming lands based on the Knox group being far larger than that of the same lands based on the Nashville and Trenton groups.

But marble being one of the most noted products of the state, deserves a more particular description than has thus far been presented. And this description will be best given in the language of a pamphlet published in 1869, entitled "Facts and Figures Concerning the Climate, Manufacturing Advantages, and the Agricultural Resources of East Tennessee," printed by T. Haws & Co., Knoxville. Following is a quotation from that pamphlet:

"There is great interest attached to the marble of East Tennessee. In the columns and balustrades which largely contribute to adorn the state capitol at Nashville and the national capitol at Washington may be seen specimens of the fine quality of our variegated marble. We have in East Tennessee the variegated fossiliferous, the grayish fossiliferous, magnesian, black breccia conglomerate varieties. The first species is found in quantity in Grainger, Jefferson, Roane, Knox, Monroe, Meigs, McMinn and Bradley counties. There are two varieties of this species. The one is an argillaceous limestone, little fossiliferous, of a dull, brownish red and sometimes greenish, and receives a smooth, fine polish. The other is par excellence the marble of East Tennessee. It is a highly fossiliferous, calcareous rock, has a bright ground of brownish red colors which are more or less freely mottled with white and gray fleecy clouds and spots. This variety is found in large quantities in Knox, McMinn and Hawkins counties. Quarries are being worked in each of these counties and shippers find a ready sale for all they can ship to the eastern markets. A block of the light mottled strawberry variety was sent from Hawkins county to the Washington monument. This block attracted the attention of the building committee of the extension of the national capitol, who, although they had specimens before them from all parts of the Union, decided in favor of and used the marble from East Tennessee. The marble used in the Tennessee capitol was taken from Knox county. A large quantity from the same quarry was used in ornamenting the Ohio state capitol. One bed of grayish white lies near Knoxville, which is 375 feet thick; ninety feet of which, near the base of the bed, is massive white marble. The remainder contains more or less of the reddish points which make it variegated, the mottling consisting of fossil, corals and crinoids. On the French Broad river five miles east of Knoxville is a bluff of a beautiful light variegated marble which could be worked with little expense. Black marble is found in some localities in the extreme eastern part of the state. The whole extent of country between the Cumberland

and Smoky mountains is underlaid with the marble formation, and geologists have long looked upon this region with peculiar interest."

Zinc is also abundant in East Tennessee, there being a fine bed of this mineral in Knox county, as well as at Mossy creek, and there are large quantities of limestone interspersed with the marble beds.

But the greatest interest must always attach to the supply of coal, for as the great industries of the world largely support the civilization of the age, so does the consumption support most if not all of the great industries of the world. And so far as Tennessee is concerned most of the coal in the state is confined to the eastern portion, and in the main is limited to the Cumberland mountains and their cognate ridges. And while in some cases this coal is properly bituminous, yet in most cases it is semi-bituminous. Prof. Safford says, "Our coal in good quality and in beds thick enough to be profitably worked, is at least equal in the aggregate to a solid stratum eight feet thick and co-extensive with the tableland, and hence to 4,400 square miles." If the entire area of the state be taken at 42,000 square miles, which is nearly correct, then the coal area, if evened up to a thickness of eight feet, would occupy somewhat more than one-tenth of the entire area of the state. And as the amount of coal within the state when the first settlers arrived, about 1760, was in the neighborhood of 35,000,-000,000 tons, considering a cubic yard equal to a ton, and if at one time in the dim recesses of the past the entire state were underlaid or overlaid with coal, as it may have been, it is easy to see what a prodigious waste of valuable material nature has made in the denudation of such a large portion of the state, whereby somewhere near 320,000,000,000 tons of coal have been washed off into the Gulf of Mexico and the Atlantic Ocean.

In 1865 Mr. S. W. Ely, an experienced geologist from Ohio, made a report to a certain company by which he was employed, in which he said:

"In truth this inestimable mineral is so liberally deposited in the structure of the Cumberlands, that it would tax the imagination to comprehend the quantity. I trust the time is near at hand when Cincinnati and Louisville and the interior towns of Kentucky will seek in the coal of your Scott county lands, an article which exceeds in purity and other excellent qualities any I have ever seen from the bituminous fields of the North."

Since this report was made, the Knoxville and Ohio railroad has opened up the coal beds of Anderson county, which are within a distance of thirty miles of Knoxville, and from these Anderson county coal fields, coal has since been shipped not only to Knoxville, but also to many other towns and cities, both east and west, as to Nashville, Memphis, Atlanta, Augusta and Macon.

The counties in which coal is found are the following: Anderson, Bledsoe, Campbell, Claiborne, Cumberland, Fentress, Franklin, Hamilton, Marion, Morgan, Overton, Putnam, Rhea, Roane, Scott, Sequatchie, Van Buren, Warren, White. Only a small portion of this vast territory has as yet been developed, as previous to the war there were but few railroads anywhere near the coal, but since then many railroads run in all directions from Knoxville, connecting with the Cincinnati Southern, the Louisville and Nashville, opening up new fields in all directions.

Besides the other minerals mentioned there are copper, lead, silver and gold, though the last two metals do not exist in very large quantities. Gold is found in Monroe, Blount and Cocke counties, in the former county a man in mining it being able to earn about $1 per day.

The iron of the state of Tennessee exists in three distinct regions, as follows: The Eastern region, the Dyestone region and the Western region. It is with the two former only that Knoxville is especially interested. In the Eastern region the iron ore is classified as limonite, or brown ore; hematite, or red ore, and magnetite, or magnetic ore. In the Dyestone region, which skirts the eastern base of the Cumberland Tableland, or Walden's ridge, the ore is fossiliferous.

Limonite is the great ore of the Eastern region, and consists of iron, 59.92 per cent; oxygen, 25.68 per cent, and water, 14.40 per cent. Hematite consists of iron, 70 per cent, and oxygen, 30 per cent, and magnetite iron, 72 per cent, and oxygen, 27.6 per cent. Dyestone is a variety of hematite, and, as its name implies, is used much for coloring.

In Campbell county, according to Prof. Safford, there is a remarkable bed of fossiliferous ore, where, "owing to the great number of minor folds or wrinkles in the rock, the ore layer is repeated a great number of times, and crops out in numerous parallel bands for a distance of five or six miles; many of them being from twenty inches to three feet thick. In some places it is six feet thick. The Knoxville and Ohio railroad passes through this iron region. Coal also abounds in vast quantities in the Elk Fork valley. There is a similar deposit of iron and coal at Wheeler's Gap, also on the railroad."

The following extract from an iron manufacturer's communication to an association interested in the extent of iron in East Tennessee, made previous to 1869, is of peculiar value in this connection:

"Within eight miles of Knoxville are abundant beds of iron, and within twenty miles there is a body of iron said to be nearly equal in quantity to the Iron Mountain of Missouri, and of precisely the same quality. * * * No country of the world furnishes mineral wealth more convenient in locality, superior in quality, greater in variety, or easier of access than are our vast deposits. Almost every county possesses a wealth of iron sufficient to enrich a state or pay the debt of a nation, and the facilities for manufacturing are as great as the mineral is abundant. Convenient water power, an unlimited supply of timber and bituminous coal, cheap food and cheap labor, furnish all the facilities for producing iron cheaply and in unlimited quantity. A distinguished iron manufacturer from New York gave it as his opinion that iron could be made by charcoal at one of the mines of East Tennessee and hauled ten miles to the railroad at one-half the cost of producing a similar article in the North. If that can be done with charcoal ten miles from a railroad, what shall be said of mines equally rich and exhaustless lying where the railroad track cuts the ore-bed and where coal banks are as abundant as the iron?

"Along the line of the Knoxville and Ohio railroad, not fifty miles from Knoxville, are numerous properties now offered for sale at moderate prices where iron and coal lie side by side in limitless quantities and surrounded by beautiful forests of choice timber, with lime and sandstone, fire clay and water power close at hand, all waiting, as they have waited for ages, for the magic touch of industry, to convert them to use. In some localities these iron beds are pierced for the first time by the cuts on our railroads; and yet, such is the blindness of our present policy that we bring from beyond the Atlantic the iron rails to construct a railroad upon our own iron beds! More than two million of dollars have been sent out of East Tennessee since the war, for iron and iron wares that should have been produced at home. With such a fact before us there can be no question of a home market for all we can produce. The foundrymen of Knoxville have, until the present time, been compelled to purchase iron brought from Scotland to produce a single mixture for soft, light and thin castings. There are numerous places in East Tennessee where similar iron could be produced profitably at less than the cost of this freight alone, saying nothing of the price of the iron.

"The iron of Carter county has borne a reputation for nearly seventy years unsurpassed by any in the United States for toughness and adaptability to any use. The castings of this iron will bend before breaking, and car wheels made of it have worn more than twelve years on our railroads. And yet there is not a blast furnace in operation in that county at this time, and we import from abroad at vast expense the iron that might be obtained from these mines at one-third the price we are now paying. The Tellico Iron Works of Monroe county, more celebrated than those of Carter, with iron equal in quality and much greater in quantity, have been idle for years, producing nothing."

At the time the above was written there were two furnaces in Greene county carried on by northern companies, and one then recently established by Gen. J. T. Wilder in Roane county, that were in quite active operation, producing three times the iron that was being produced by all the old furnaces in East Tennessee.

When all things are taken into consideration, it may be stated with a good deal of positiveness, that Knoxville is as well situated for manufacturing as any city in the Southern states, except possibly Birmingham, Ala. And in some respects it is better situated than this fine Alabama city. The climate, as shown in this chapter, is most emphatically a temperate one, and it is naturally perfectly healthful. If disease at any time prevail it is because of unsanitary conditions which come about through oversight, or neglect, and which can always in a short time be completely removed.

Provisions are abundant and average in price about the same as in other cities in the country. East Tennessee, as has been shown, is a grass growing, grain growing and cattle raising country. Iron and coal are abundant and within easy reach, by means of the great systems of railroads centering in Knoxville, an outlet being supplied in every direction. By means of both railroads and the numerous streams which flow from all parts of the mountainous country timber is easily brought to Knoxville, and there is an almost inexhaustible supply of all kinds, such as white and yellow pine, red, white and black oak, black walnut, hickory, chestnut, yellow poplar, red and white cedar, ash, locust, cherry and hemlock.

Brick clay is also abundant throughout East Tennessee.

One of the most important questions asked by an emigrant

to a new country is as to its climate. Is it hot or cold, wet or dry, and is it or is it not subject to extremes of heat or cold, dryness or moisture? The entire history of migratory movements shows that in the main they are made along parallels, either of latitude or of temperature, and not along meridians. Most if not all of the writers on the climate of East Tennessee agree in placing it midway between the two extremes of northern cold and southern heat, and thus well adapted to health and industry. Of East Tennessee Knoxville is almost in the geographical center and is nearly 1,000 feet above the sea, and thus while considerably further south than Ohio its climate does not vary much from that of the latter state. Altitude is one of the elements that determine the climate of a country, the rate of decrease in temperature being one degree for every 300 or 350 feet of elevation, or, according to Prof. Henry, one degree for every 333 feet. As Knoxville is nearly one thousand feet above the sea its average temperature is three degrees below what it would be if on a level with the ocean. The average annual temperature of Knoxville is about 57 degrees, while that of Middle Tennessee is about 58 degrees and that of West Tennessee about 60 degrees. Then, too, the force of the winter winds from the west and northwest is greatly broken by the Cumberland mountains, and the winters are thus rendered comparatively mild and pleasant. Swamps and stagnant pools are almost unknown in this portion of the state, and hence the region of Knoxville is entirely exempt from fever and ague. The mountain air is pure and wholesome, the elevation of the country preserves it always from the encroachments of yellow fever, and the emigrant to this region no matter whence he comes, whether from the Eastern, Western or Southern states, or from Norway, Italy or France, finds himself upon his arrival already acclimated to the eastern part of Tennessee.

According to the records preserved by Prof. Safford in his Geological Survey of the state the average temperature of Knoxville for 1852 was 55.67 degrees; for 1854 it was 57.67

degrees, and for 1856 it was 57.75 degrees. The mean heat of summer along the parallel traversing the middle of the state ranges from 74 degrees in East Tennessee to 77.5 degrees in West Tennessee. The winter and summer temperatures of Knoxville for the years 1852, 1854 and 1855 together with the average winter and summer temperatures for those years, were as follows:

1852, winter, 39.28 degrees; summer, 70.87 degrees.
1854,   "   37.76   "   "   75.85   "
1855,   "   38.40   "   "   74.09   "
Average "   38.48   "   "   73.60   "

From the Meteorological Record kept by the East Tennessee University for January, 1868, the following statistics are derived:

Mean temperature for the month, 35.05 degrees; coldest day, the 30th; average for the 24 hours, 20.16 degrees; warmest day, the 7th, average for the 24 hours, 52.86 degrees; the extreme temperatures for the year 1868 were 14 degrees and 92 degrees, and the mean temperature for the year was 60 degrees.

During January, 1869, there were fifteen days on which plowing could have been carried on, and every day of the month was fit for outdoor work. There were but few days during the entire year which by reason of either heat or cold, were unfit for ordinary outdoor work upon the farm or elsewhere. East Tennessee occupies a happy mean in climate between the two extremes of heat and cold and in all the elements that constitute a pleasant and healthful climate there is scarcely a place between the two great oceans on the east and on the west, or between British America and the Gulf of Mexico, that will bear comparison with this region.

During the eight years immediately preceding 1881 the mercury descended below zero only three times, viz.: in January, 1877, in January, 1879, and in December, 1880. In the same eight years the mercury reached 100 degrees but once.

During three years of the eight it did not go above 95 degrees, the average temperature for the eight years being 57.8 degrees. The mean summer temperature was 73 degrees, and the mean winter temperature, 40 degrees. The average maximum temperature was about 91 degrees and the average minimum temperature about 2 degrees.

The following table shows the annual mean temperature, the highest and lowest temperatures, the annual mean relative humidity and the total annual rainfall for Knoxville for eleven years, 1871 to 1881, inclusive:

Year.	Annual Mean Temperature.	Highest Temperature.	Lowest Temperature.	Annual Mean Rel. Humidity.	Total Annual Rainfall.
1871	58.0	95.5	6.0	71.1	48.22
1872	55.0	94.0	1.0	69.8	44.66
1873	56.5	92.0	6.0	70.5	59.25
1874	57.7	97.0	11.0	70.4	58.38
1875	55.5	94.0	2.0	71.7	73.87
1876	55.7	96.0	6.0	70.0	41.19
1877	57.0	95.0	14.0	68.0	54.35
1878	57.6	97.0	6.0	68.2	47.76
1879	58.8	100.0	3.5	65.5	48.95
1880	58.5	96.0	5.0	70.1	52.54
1881	58.6	100.0	9.0	70.4	46.67

The following table shows the average temperature for each month during the years 1881 to 1898, inclusive:

Years.	Jan.	Feb.	Mar.	Apr.	May.	June.	July.	Aug.	Sept.	Oct.	Nov.	Dec.
1881	36	42	44	55	64	74	78	77	74	64	48	44
1882	43	49	53	61	64	73	72	73	69	63	48	35
1883	39	46	45	59	65	74	76	73	70	63	48	41
1884	30	47	50	55	67	72	75	73	72	65	46	40
1885	35	34	43	58	65	74	77	75	69	54	47	49
1886	38	37	48	59	69	72	75	75	71	58	46	39
1887	37	49	49	58	70	74	79	75	70	57	47	39
1888	40	46	47	62	65	73	76	74	64	52	48	37
1889	41	39	49	60	63	69	76	71	65	53	46	52
1890	49	52	45	60	65	75	75	72	69	54	44	41
1891	40	47	46	60	63	75	72	73	67	57	43	36
1892	35	45	46	58	65	74	74	71	68	56	46	40
1893	30	44	48	53	64	73	76	74	71	56	43	40
1894	44	41	44	58	65	75	74	74	72	52	47	39
1895	36	51	48	54	63	74	72	77	69	56	50	39
1896	40	41	45	64	72	73	76	75	72	63	50	42
1897	36	46	53	59	63	75	77	75	72	63	50	42
1898	43	39	55	53	70	77	78	78	73	58	44	38

The following table shows the highest, lowest and mean

elevation of the barometer at Knoxville for the years 1881 to 1898, inclusive:

Years.	Highest.	Lowest.	Mean.
1881	29.56	28.45	29.07
1882	29.60	28.49	29.08
1883	29.64	28.51	29.08
1884	29.60	28.47	29.05
1885	29.57	28.36	29.04
1886	29.64	28.33	29.05
1887	29.57	28.46	29.07
1888	29.53	28.54	29.07
1889	29.58	28.40	29.07
1890	29.56	28.52	29.09
1891	29.65	28.44	29.08
1892	29.52	28.39	29.68
1893	29.71	28.37	29.04
1894	29.53	28.44	29.07
1895	29.79	28.53	29.06
1896	29.66	28.16	29.08
1897	29.56	28.53	29.04
1898	29.62	28.42	29.04

The following shows the rainfall for the years 1881 to 1898 inclusive: 1881, 45.67 inches; 1882, 66.36; 1883, 52.67; 1884, 62.53; 1885, 54.70; 1886, 61.45; 1887, 42.98; 1888, 53.03; 1889, 47.73; 1890, 49.59; 1891, 46.61; 1892, 44.62; 1893, 43.42; 1894, 37.44; 1895, 38.75; 1896, 44.95; 1897, 52.95; 1898, 42.79.

The presentation of averages, however, does not always give a clear idea of what a climate really is; hence a few statistics regarding the extreme low temperature at Knoxville since the establishment of the weather bureau may prove of interest, if not of value. The lowest temperature during that period was on January 10, 1884, when the mercury registered 16 degrees below zero. Perhaps the most remarkable period of cold weather ever experienced at Knoxville since the establishment of the weather bureau was during the week beginning on Sunday, February 12, 1899. On that day the mercury went down to 6 degrees above zero; on Monday it went to 9 degrees below zero, and on Tuesday morning, February 14, it fell to 10 degrees below zero, and at that particular time Knoxville was the coldest place reported in the United States.

Four great gaps in the mountains furnish available outlets for railroads, and determine the direction of commerce and travel toward distant parts of the country. The gaps in the French Broad in the Alleghanies on the east, of the Emory river in the Cumberland range on the west, determine the direction of an east and west line from the coast of the Atlantic to the Cincinnati Southern railroad, and the Emory Gap, the Careyville Gap in the Cumberland range on the north, and the gap of the Little Tennessee in the Alleghanies surely determine a north and south line, connecting with the Georgia system of railroads and with the southeastern seaboard towns.

Knoxville lies where all these lines must meet and intersect each other. It is also on the Tennessee river, which is for several months in the year navigable for steamboats of considerable size. Knoxville is also on the East Tennessee, Virginia and Georgia railroad, which connects the great northeast with the great southwest, and could not be better situated for communication with all parts of the country. There must have been much of the fortuitous in the selection of this site for a city, for it was impossible for any one responsible for the selection of the location to have foreseen the vast uses to which these gaps in the mountains could be and would be put; there being then no such thought as that railroads would at some day find their way through them.

In this connection it may be well to note the distances from Knoxville to some of the principal cities of the north and south: To Louisville and to Cincinnati, 266 miles; to Cincinnati via Emory Gap, 300 miles; to Norfolk, 539 miles; to Port Royal, 378 miles; to Norfolk via Asheville, 578 miles; to Wilmington, N. C., 487 miles; to Charleston via Augusta, Ga., 404 miles, and to Port Royal via Augusta, 378 miles. The latitude of Knoxville is 35 degrees 56 minutes and its longitude is 85 degrees 58 minutes.

The water supply of this region is ample and pure. From every vale and mountain side there are many clear springs, numbering thousands in the aggregate, which pour forth their cooling streams, and there are in some places mountain torrents foaming over rocky beds and leaping over precipices; beautiful brooks winding slowly through fertile fields, and larger streams filled not only with clear water, but also with fish of various kinds, among them the trout. All along many of the streams is excellent water power which can never fail, and which in time must be utilized to drive machinery of various kinds, and to develop electricity in a much cheaper way than by steam, especially when the price of coal shall have advanced by the introduction of more and larger manufacturing establishments and a denser population, thus increasing the demand for fuel all over the south. There are also many mineral springs, some of which are known throughout the country, and in the vicinity of which have been built up what are now famous summer resorts, where even in the summer months the mercury does not rise much above seventy degrees, and where the nights are, in the hottest weather, delightfully cool. At some of these places fires in the grates are welcome throughout the entire year.

CHAPTER II.

INITIAL MOVEMENTS TOWARDS SETTLEMENT.

Domain of Cherokees—Approach of Hunters, Trappers and Explorers—Immigration—Gradual Withdrawal of Indians—Treaties—Fort Stanwix—Hard Labor—Lochaber—Purchases of Watauga Association—Jacob Brown and Richard Henderson—Treaties of Long Island; of Holston, Dumplin, Coytoy, and Hopewell—Westward Movement.

KNOXVILLE at present is the commercial center of an extensive territory, limited practically by the same boundaries which correspond to those of the Cherokee nation of Indians about the middle of the eighteenth century. Her commercial travelers visit southwestern Virginia, western North Carolina, northwestern South Carolina, northern Georgia, northeastern Alabama, and eastern Tennessee. The domain included the head-waters of the streams in the divisions of the states named, comprehending the mountains of the lower Appalachian system. Not all of this immense tract was occupied by them, nor was it unclaimed by other nations. While not formidable claimants, the Six Nations, Shawnees, and Delawares asserted their rights to a portion of it.*

Prior to the explorations of the first hunters and trappers and to the establishment of the first forts in eastern Tennessee, movements and negotiations had been begun which were to continue until, ultimately, this nation of intrepid warriors was removed west of the Mississippi river. The conflicts between neighboring tribes, the ravages of disease, particularly the smallpox, and other causes led to such diminution of the population of the Cherokees that at the time of the ingress of the explorer they were ill prepared to resist the onflowing tide of immigration, soon to set in by reason of his description

---

*Charles C. Royce: The Cherokee Nation of Indians, 141, in report of Bureau of Ethnology, 1883-'84.

of the beneficence and prodigality of nature in the region beyond the Alleghanies. Whether actuated purely by love of sport and adventure, as Dr. Thomas Walker, Wallen, and their hunting parties, or by a combined quest for land and game, as Daniel Boone and Henry Scaggins, or by motives of discovery and permanent habitation, as James Smith and James Robertson, or by the spirit of trade and commerce, as James Adair and John Findley, each returning individual and company or party gave such glowing accounts of the luxuriance of forests, fertility of the soil, abundance of game, freshness and purity of the waters, richness of pasturage, and exemption from external interference as to stimulate an immediate movement into the trans-Alleghany country for fixed settlement.

The starting point in the settlement of Tennessee is the cabin of William Bean, built in 1769 near the junction of Watauga river and Boone's creek in upper East Tennessee. From this point it is interesting to note the tide of immigration as it surged forward from Virginia and the Carolinas over the mountains into the valleys beyond. Like the impetuosity of the mountain torrent it continued its onward course, brooking no opposition and overcoming every obstacle. The checks it received were momentary, only serving, as it were, to gather renewed force for the occupancy of wider bounds. It is the beginning of a thrilling and marvelous history. Therein are crowded within the space of a quarter of a century deeds of heroism and daring, experiences of hardship and suffering, records of success and triumph that enkindle ancestral pride and foster patriotic devotion. What booted it that the Indian claimed it as his hunting ground, employed his lazy existence in darting over the hills in pursuit of game and skimming in his light canoe over the sparkling streams, or indulged his savage nature in banishing or exterminating those of his own blood? The pioneer regarded it a struggle of intelligence and civilization with ignorance and barbarism. He was willing, personally or through his governmental agents, to give the Indian in presents, money or other equivalent the value set by him upon his claims, though he himself had little or no respect for such claims. Perhaps his opinion touching these claims was best expressed in the policy of the mother-state, North Carolina, who "considered in all her provincial and state acts that the pretended title of the Indians was mere moonshine. It never was anything more."*

In the uneven contest it was not difficult to forecast the trend and outcome of events. Like the melancholy theme running through the chorus of Greek tragedy or the sad fate that pursued the fortunes of the house of Atreus, the dark, ominous clouds of extermination and expatriation lay across the pathway of the Cherokee. In treaty-making councils, in battles in the open or under cover, or in hand-to-hand conflicts, he was no match for his pale-face brother. The prophetic lament of Oconostota at the treaty of the Sycamore Shoals, the sullen protest of Old Tassel at Coytoy, the splendid generalship of Dragging Canoe at Island Flats, the strategy and cunning of Old Abraham at the Watauga fort, and the perfidious daring of John Watts in the threatened attack on Knoxville—all these availed nothing. The hand-to-hand fight of John Sevier and the "brave" at Boyd's creek, of Moore and the chief at Island Flats, and of Hubbard and Untoola near Citico tell the same story.

Trained in the school of self-help, along with self-defence, the step to self-government was an easy one for the pioneer to take. The Watauga Association and the state of Franklin were but movements created by imminent perils and unlooked-for emergencies. With the influx of large bodies of settlers, many of them representing disorderly elements of society, and with almost impenetrable forests, impassable mountains, and great distances separating them from the home government, and that government lukewarm in its interest and

---

*Opinion of Judge John Haywood in Cornet vs. Winton's Lessee; 2 Yerger's Tennessee Reports, 156.

indifferent to appeals for protection, it was natural that in the then western wilds the settler should seek to throw around himself every safeguard. That he was not a separatist in spirit is shown by his gallant stand and signal success at the battle of King's mountain during the Revolutionary war, and later by his loyalty to Washington and the Federal government, when his appeals for permission to assume the offensive against the Indian invader and marauder were constantly refused.

In the chain of events leading up to the dispossession of the Cherokees from the territory embracing Knoxville treaty negotiations form important links. These treaties have a chronological sequence in importance and character, and might be divided into three classes according to the objects had in view by the framers, or their agents. The first had to do with alliances, the second with alliances and the acquisitions of territory, and the third with the acquisitions of territory. Every treaty had in view the cultivation and maintenance of peaceful relations. The treaty relations of the Cherokees with the English colonial governments began as early as 1721, when the province of South Carolina, to protect her frontiers against French territorial encroachments, entered into a treaty of peace and commerce. Nine years later North Carolina pursued the same course. For years these treaties were observed, and harmonious relations existed. However, upon the outbreak of the French and Indian war, the Carolina governors sought to strengthen the alliance, to secure safety to the frontier. Fort Loudon, the first habitation of the Englishman in Tennessee, was built accordingly, in 1756. Thus far except the relinquishment of claims to lands to which the Catawbas had a better title, no portion of their lands had been given up by the Cherokees.

The acquisition of territory from the Cherokees began with the almost contemporaneous treaties of Fort Stanwix and Hard Labor in 1768. By these treaties a small strip of territory within the present limits of Tennessee was acquired, beginning thirty-six miles east of Long Island on the Holston river. Even while these treaties were in course of negotiation, white settlers were invading territory beyond the bounds to be agreed upon in treating. This brought about an immediate subsequent treaty and the adjustment of a new boundary.* These encroachments occasioned the treaty of Lochaber two years following in South Carolina, which brought the confines thirty miles down the Holston, to a point six miles east of Long Island. The next cessions of territory are in the nature of leases, out of deference to the inhibitions of George III., in 1763, and are made to the Watauga Association and to Jacob Brown for stipulated amounts of goods. Three years afterwards, in 1775, for additional remuneration these become in fee simple the property of the lessees. These acquisitions include all the waters of the Watauga river, part of those of the Holston to a point near the mouth of Cloud's creek, and those of the Nollichucky to the mouth of Big Limestone creek. The same year Brown adds to his purchase the lands on both sides of the Nollichucky below the Big Limestone's mouth to the mouth of Camp creek, a distance of ten miles down the river. Richard Henderson's purchase by treaty in 1775, by the deed known as the "Path Deed," acquired the lands north of the Holston beginning near the mouth of Cloud's creek and extending up that stream to the Virginia line. These purchases taking place in March, 1775, it will thus be seen that at the outbreak of the Revolutionary war, all that now embraces Sullivan, Johnson and Carter counties, much of Washington, and some of Greene, Hawkins and Unicoi counties had been wrested from the Cherokees.

The next treaty, in 1777, known as that of the Long Island of the Holston, was more in the nature of a peace treaty and brought little additional territory. By its terms some parts of Brown's line were adopted and on the Holston, lands as far

---

*Ramsey, Annals of Tennessee, 77.

down as the mouth of Cloud's creek were ceded.* This and its companion treaty of Dewitt's Corners in South Carolina gave great offence to the Chickamauga contingent of the Cherokees, and led to their removal to the region where they founded near and below Chattanooga of to-day the five Lower Towns, which for seventeen years were a constant menace and annoyance to the settlements. The thorough chastisement administered to the Cherokees by the Christian, Rutherford and Williamson expeditions from Virginia, North Carolina, and South Carolina respectively, produced a temporary respite from Indian assaults, but an arbitrary act of the North Carolina legislature in 1783 brought a renewal of bitterness and jealousy. Without the concurrence of the Indians or consultation with them, North Carolina had by this act extended her western boundaries to the Mississippi river, while reserving to the Indians that portion of the state in which were their towns, cultivated fields, and the territory adjacent. It will be seen later how this act was a factor in the settlement of Knoxville.

In 1785 the independent state of Franklin, arrogating to herself all the rights and dignity of a duly constituted commonwealth, invited the Cherokees to a treaty, to be held at the mouth of Dumplin creek on the north side of the French Broad river. In return for large cessions of territory south of the Holston and French Broad rivers extending to the ridge dividing the waters of Little and Little Tennessee rivers, the Franklinites made promises of "compensation in general terms."† The same year at Coytoy another treaty between the same parties took place which conveyed to Franklin all the lands sold by North Carolina and entered on the west side of the Holston river. Though protesting that they knew nothing of such sales Old Tassel and Hanging Maw yielded, after "a straight talk" on the part of the Franklin commissioners

---

*Ramsey. 173.

†Ramsey, 299.

threatening extirpation.* These two treaties involved the cession of most of Knox county. Those settling, therefore, on lands then ceded did so in good faith, not only having land warrants purchased from North Carolina by authority of her legislature, but also the sanction of the state of Franklin. However, the treaty of Hopewell, the first entered into between the United States and the Indians and negotiated the latter part of November, 1785, gave an abrupt check to the lawful possession of the territory by its restoration to the Indians, though it came too late to stem the tide of immigration that had gone in and possessed the land. The settlers "had done expanded," as many as three thousand of them being in the fork of the Holston and French Broad rivers. This treaty ignored the act of the North Carolina legislature and the treaties of the state of Franklin, but reaffirmed Henderson's purchase, inasmuch as he was dead, and the commissioners had in their possession the deeds showing the lands of the purchase. It left the dividing line practically where it was fixed in 1777 by the Long Island treaty. The commissioners reserved to the Holston and French Broad settlers, who were too numerous to remove, right of occupancy and freedom from molestation until that tract in dispute should be adjudicated by Congress. This treaty was not signed without the solemn protest of North Carolina through its agent, William Blount, who was present with delegated powers. This, the first appearance of this gentleman in active espousal of the cause of the frontiersman, was an earnest of the distinguished part he was to take in upholding and guarding their interests, as will be seen, at a later date. Such an act, he maintained, was an infringement upon the legislative rights of the state, which had granted these as bounty-lands to the officers and soldiers in the Continental line of that state in payment of services rendered in the Revolutionary war.

A knowledge of the occurrences and conditions antecedent

---

*Ramsey, 344-346.

to the settlement of Knoxville is necessary to explain many subsequent events in her history, yet these were but repetitions of the struggle that had been going on from the first occupancy of American soil. They exhibit the ceaseless westward movement of the pioneer, the reluctant yielding of his land on the part of the Indian, and the bitter animosity produced by the clashing of two ideas or forces contending for supremacy, one little removed above brute instinct, the other dictated by intelligent foresight.

CHAPTER III.

EARLY SETTLEMENT.

Conditions in the West—Germ of Knoxville—White's Fort—North Carolina Grants—Explorations of James White—Fixed Settlement—Topography—Growth—New Stations or Forts—Roads—Cession of Territory to United States—Blount Appointed Governor—His Character—Appointments—Relations of Whites and Indians—Treaty of Holston—Provisions and Results.

IN 1786 the first habitation was erected on the present site of Knoxville. At the time affairs in the West were in a state of deep ferment and grave uncertainty. Indeed, such was the condition all over the country. Congress was impotent, the states keeping their best statesmanship at home and sending to the national legislature their less experienced and distinguished sons. The Hopewell treaty was proving a futile compact, the whites continuing to settle upon lands declared thereby to be in Indian territory. The North Carolina party within the bounds of the state of Franklin was now making itself felt in rending the refractory state, and restoring her to the bosom of her mother. The wily Wilkinson was employing his cunning arts and seductive speech to dismember Virginia by the separation of Kentucky, and to identify the latter's fortunes with Spanish interests. It remained to be seen whether the machinations of Spain to sever the West from her Eastern connections were to prove abortive when prospects of extermination and of closing the Mississippi river to traffic were held out to the settlers and when such robust spirits as James Robertson were yielding to the blandishments of the neighbor on the southwest.

The germ of Knoxville lay in White's Fort, which was founded by Col. James White upon the extreme border land of the Indian country. He had entered the region thereabout as payment for his services in the Revolutionary war. To reward the valor and heroism of her officers and soldiers in that war, North Carolina gave of her immense domain westward large grants of land for their services, reserving only as hunting grounds for the Cherokee Indians the region included within the Tennessee, French Broad, and Big Pigeon rivers, east to the North Carolina line and south to that of Georgia.* Immediately after the passage of this act by the North Carolina legislature, in 1783, James White, in company with Robert Love, F. A. Ramsey, who was a practical surveyor, and others, began an exploration to select the most advantageous regions open for the location of land warrants. This party, beginning its work on the French Broad river not far from where Newport now stands, followed its valleys southwestward to the mouth of Dumplin creek, where they crossed over into the lands lying between the French Broad and Holston rivers. Crossing the Holston several miles above the present site of Knoxville and entering Grassy valley, they examined the lands adjacent to the Holston as far as its confluence with the then Tennessee river, opposite the present Lenoir City, thus passing through the territory which was to include the future Knoxville.† It is maintained that this exploration was continued as far down the river as Southwest Point, now Kingston.‡

With the passage of the act of the North Carolina legislature in May, 1783, for the sale and disposition of western lands and with the entry of much of these by May, 1784, in the land office at Hillsboro, the strong tide of emigration from North Carolina poured into what is now Tennessee, thus counterbalancing that influx of population which had hitherto flowed from Virginia. Returning to his North Carolina home Col. White made preparation to move. In 1784 he went to Fort Chiswell, Virginia, where he made a crop. By 1785 he had settled in the new territory and was sitting in the councils

---

*Haywood, History of Tennessee, 121. Reprint.
†Ramsey, Annals of Tennessee, 278.
‡Sketch of Knoxville, in Art Work of Knoxville, 2.

Blockhouse Erected on the Site Now Occupied by the Courthouse

From a Painting by Lloyd Benson

This image from an old post card, "Knoxville in 1793, cor. Gay and Main Streets."

of the state of Franklin.* His temporary abode was four miles above the junction of the Holston and French Broad rivers, where he remained only one year. In 1786, joined by an old neighbor and fellow-soldier, James Connor, likewise of Rowan, now Iredell, county, North Carolina, he moved thence, following the water courses downward, and established himself on the north bank of the Holston below the confluence of the two rivers. Here, several hundred yards from the river, he built his cabin and fort. Beauty of situation, availability of water power, proximity to numerous springs, and other natural advantages rendered the spot peculiarly attractive. The first clearing, according to tradition, was on ground that now includes the site of the First Presbyterian church, though the monarch trees near by would seem to question the correctness thereof. The cabin, one and a half or two stories high, was erected north of the clearing, between the present Union and Commerce streets. Having regard to the purposes of defence, it stood at one corner on a quarter of an acre of ground quadrangular in shape. Three other cabins not so pretentious occupied the other angles, and were connected therewith by heavy stockades eight feet high, provided with port-holes well arranged for defence.† More recent writers upon local history disconnect the fort or blockhouse and the cabin, placing the former on or between the sites of the Palace Hotel and the Hampden Sydney School and the latter on the present site of Mrs. Jane Kennedy's residence, just back of the Imperial Hotel. The L of this residence is thought to be the original cabin, weatherboarded in later years.‡

A study of the topography of this site will serve to show how admirable for defence was the location and how wise the judgment that dictated the selection. Half a mile apart, on the east and west respectively, First and Second creeks so flowed as to make an almost perfect parallelogram, while the

---

*Ramsey, Annals of Tennessee, 295.
†Ramsey, Annals of Tennessee, 374.
‡J. W. Caldwell, History of Knoxville, in East Tennessee, Historical and Biographical, 455. Sketch of Knoxville, in Art Work of Knoxville, 2.

ground sloped towards each stream in regular descent; on the north were abrupt hills and on the south was the river reached through the narrow gorges of the creeks or over abrupt precipices. On two sides, then, the approaches were exceedingly difficult, while the elevations on the other two gave a commanding sweep of vision and a decided advantage of position. Apart from its strategic importance and its natural resources, its location almost midway between the then extreme outposts of the population included within the present Tennessee was fortunate for its future. It was, so to speak, an unconscious prophecy of the place it was to occupy in subsequent years when, in 1789, upon the election of John Sevier to Congress, the certificates of the returning officers were brought to the house of James White for comparison by the Clerk of the Superior Court of Washington District, who for the convenience of the counties in Miro District attended at that place.*

In tracing the historic incidents leading up to the foundation of Knoxville the embryo is found in the unpretentious cabin and strong personality of James White. A settlement beginning with the simplest means of livelihood and the crudest conditions of life, where bread depended upon the pounding of corn and the supply of meat upon unerring marksmanship, where the ranger and the scout betook themselves in safety to recount adventurous scenes and hairbreadth escapes, where the immigrant paused to consider the inducements for permanent habitation or to rest his travel-weary cavalcade, it has grown to assume the position and dignity of a cultured, prosperous, and populous city. If James White had not been the father of his distinguished son, Hugh Lawson White, if he had not been throughout his career a useful pioneer, a brave soldier, a patriotic citizen, and a faithful public official, thereby winning an enduring fame, he would deserve it as the founder of a city which has enriched the state and the nation, not only by its contributions of material wealth and

---
*Ramsey. Annals of Tennessee, 433.

prosperity, but also by its illustrious array of business men, ministers, journalists, scholars, jurists and statesmen.

The years intervening between the establishment of White's Fort and the formation of the "Territory of the United States South of the River Ohio," 1786 to 1790, were full of keen interest to the settlers. Despite Indian depredations and murders, the conflicts of state and national authorities, internal dissensions and factional differences, the settlement of James White continued to grow until by the time Governor William Blount had fixed upon it as the seat of territorial government it had become a somewhat densely populated community. The year 1786 was particularly favorable for growth, bringing comparative freedom from Indian incursions and outrages in view of the concessions made by the Hopewell treaty. The immigrant profited by it and swelled the increasing tide of population or pushed on beyond. In view of its urgent necessity Col. White erected on the creek just east of the fort a small tub mill, the infant industry of Knoxville. The same year that saw the building of White's Fort, John Adair's station was established five miles northeast, as a supply store for the Cumberland guards who were entrusted with the safe conveyance of settlers through the wilderness to the Cumberland settlements. Stations were founded further westward in rapid succession, so that by 1787 the cutting and opening of a wagon road by way of Campbell's station and the lower end of Clinch mountain to the Cumberland country, became a matter of legislation on the part of the North Carolina legislature. The next year James Robertson announced through the columns of the North Carolina State Gazette the new road open for service.* This road seems, however, for several years to have been suited only for pack trains.† The stir and bustle of life around White's Fort was further accentuated by the presence of soldiery, the growing hostility and wanton

---
*Ramsey, 503, 505.
†Roosevelt, The Winning of the West, Vol. IV., 111; The American Historical Magazine, Vol. II., 60.

outbreaks of the Indians being checked only by the prospect of sudden invasion and the wreaking of speedy vengeance.

A step of far-reaching consequence to the young settlement was now taken. In 1789 North Carolina, as payment of all obligations incurred in the Revolutionary war, which were to be assumed by the general government, ceded to the United States all right and title to the Tennessee country. In the spring of 1790 the transfer was completed. While James White is justly regarded the father and founder of Knoxville, by his side as the next most conspicuous figure in her early history stands William Blount, commissioned governor of the "Territory of the United States South of the River Ohio" by Washington on June 8, 1790. Blount, from the largeness of his ideas and the wisdom of his policy, may be termed appropriately the Pericles of Tennessee. His appointment was an auspicious event for Knoxville, as subsequent events proved. A man of broad sympathies and tolerant views, of extensive legislative experience, of distinguished lineage, of courtly manners and large hospitality, of rare skill in the arts of diplomacy, he possessed pre-eminently the qualifications for the high office he was selected to administer. There was the additional recommendation that he came from the state which had just ceded the territory, and had enjoyed such opportunities for contact with frontiersmen and study of their difficulties as gave him the practical knowledge required for dealing intelligently with the delicate problems involved. Joined with his duties as governor was the superintendency of Indian affairs in the territory.

The governor reached the scene of his new labors October 10, 1790, fixed his temporary capital at the house of William Cobb in the fork of the Holston and Watauga rivers, and proceeded at once to the discharge of his official duties. After the appointment and commissioning of officers for Washington and Miro districts, one of the first and most delicate tasks imposed upon him was the arrangement of a treaty with the Cherokee Indians. The issues at stake involved the welfare and security of all those inhabitants in the fork of the Holston and French Broad rivers, south of the same streams and Big Pigeon, and northwest of the Holston. Their numbers ran up into the thousands. The Hopewell treaty had given umbrage to the whites and little satisfaction to the Indians. It brought, therefore, no cessation of hostile feelings, marauding expeditions, and murderous attacks. Proclamations of congress and threats of the Secretary of War proved unavailing to check the onward flow of immigration and encroachment upon lands guaranteed by treaty rights. Expeditions into the Indian country and summary punishment by burning villages, devastating crops, and capturing women and children served only as a temporary barrier to the retaliatory measures inspired by Indian cunning and venom. On their part, as has been shown, the settlers claimed the land under acts of the North Carolina legislature and treaties of the defunct state of Franklin, which they deemed duly constituted authorities.

After repeated efforts, involving the sending of various representatives among the Indians to enlist their interest and to counteract the malign influence of mischief-makers on the frontier and in the nation, and after changes of date and location, Governor Blount succeeded in assembling the chiefs for council at a point four miles below the confluence of the Holston and French Broad rivers on the present site of Knoxville.

An account of this treaty has been left*, which enlivens greatly the dreary details of Indian treachery and white aggression. The picture drawn is suggestive of some mediaeval court where the feudal lord is surrounded by his vassals to witness some feat of skill, to attend some council of his Witenagemot, to make some application of the ordeal, or to receive some embassy from a foreign court. The locality, which is near the foot of the present Central avenue, is a sylvan retreat where the rippling waters of First creek go to lose themselves in the outspreading bosom of the

---
*Ramsey, 555.

Holston river, and where the gently sloping hillside forms a natural amphitheater for the eager spectators. Beneath a monarch of the forest, seated in his chair of state, clad in the splendid paraphernalia of a high-ranking military officer, the governor waits to give audience to the representatives of the Cherokee nation. James Armstrong, otherwise "Trooper" Armstrong, who knew the etiquette of European courts, is the master of ceremonies. As the chiefs are introduced to him by an interpreter, he in turn, age taking precedence, presents them to the governor. A crowd of twelve hundred Indians, braves, women, and children gaze on the scene, while a large company of the whites of the neighborhood lend their presence to the occasion. The chiefs sit around in silent dignity, the speaker alone rising to present their cause to the presiding officer upon his bidding them to unfold their grievances. Thus far this was the great event of Gov. Blount's administration. It was to impress the Indians with some idea of the power, splendor, and majesty of the government under which he held sway, while the absence of the agents and implements of war signified to them its friendly and peaceful intentions.

After a seven days' conference, ending July 2, 1791, the treaty was signed by William Blount for the United States and by forty-one chiefs for the Cherokee nation of Indians. On October 26, 1791, President Washington laid before the senate the papers relative to the treaty for advice as to ratifying them. On November 9 following, Senator Hawkins from committee reported back to the senate their approval of the terms of the treaty, which now, as far as the authorities at the capital were concerned, meant the restoration of peace and friendship between the Cherokees and the United States. The treaty's material provisions were assurances of mutual friendship, the acknowledgment of the protectorate of the United States, the mutual surrender of prisoners, the designation of boundary lines and the guarantee of valuable goods and an annuity in consideration of the extinguishment of Indian claims, the unmolested navigation of the Tennessee river and use of a road connecting Washington and Miro districts, provision for the punishment of criminals, notification of any designs detrimental to the welfare of the United States, and material aid in the fostering of industrial pursuits among the Indians on the part of the United States.* By this treaty the lands on the south side of the Holston river, opposite Knoxville, were ceded.

When it is recalled that the treaty, in reality, did not strengthen the bonds of friendship between the two nations, that strained relations and frequent outbreaks continued unabated, that it required seven days of patient negotiation to bring about any agreement, that the point of dispute, the ridge separating the waters of Little and Tennessee rivers as a dividing line, remained undetermined for some years, and that a delegation of Indian chiefs without the consent or knowledge of Blount visited Philadelphia and extorted larger gifts of goods and bounties from the national government, one is disposed to question the efficacy of the governor's tactics and diplomacy on this occasion.

---

*Royce, The Cherokee Nation of Indians, 158, 159.

CHAPTER IV.

FOUNDING OF KNOXVILLE.

Date of Founding—Confusing Statements of Historians—Articles of Agreement Between Proprietor and Commissioners—Original Drawers of Lots—Act Establishing Knoxville—Blount's Arrival—Named in Honor of General Henry Knox—Reasons.

KNOXVILLE was founded and named in 1791. The constitution of the United States had been in operation three years; Washington had been president two years; and William Blount had been governor of the territory south of the River Ohio one year. The year is significant as that which saw the passage of the first internal revenue bill, the establishment of the United States Bank, and the differentiation of two great political parties based on principles outlined and advocated respectively by Hamilton and Jefferson.

February, 1792, has been accepted generally as the date of the establishment and laying off of Knoxville, but as to the exact time much confusion exists. The two oldest and most widely known historians of the state, Haywood and Ramsey, make contradictory statements, each in his own work. Speaking of the Knoxville Gazette, Haywood calls attention to the name and date of the paper, alleging, however, that "Knoxville was not laid off till February, 1792."* Farther on, citing the act of the territorial legislature establishing Knoxville, he says, "which had been laid off by Col. James White in the year 1791."† Ramsey, speaking of the Gazette, says: "In February of the next year (1792) Knoxville was laid off by Col. White," yet farther on he says: "Some of the lots were sold in 1791, but no considerable improvement was commenced until February of 1792, when several small buildings

---

*History of Tennessee, 272.
†Page 336.

were erected."* The semi-centennial of Knoxville was celebrated February 10, 1842, the date having been arbitrarily fixed. On this occasion the late Dr. Thomas W. Humes was the orator. In the appendix to his published address is a letter from Hugh Dunlap to E. G. Eastman, then editor of the Knoxville Argus, in which he says: "I am the only màn, whom I know to be alive, who was living there when the lots were laid off. * * * In February, 1792, Col. Charles McClung surveyed the lots and laid off the town. I do not recollect on what day of the month. It excited no particular interest at the time."†

The oldest extant authorities on this subject are the Knoxville Gazette and the published acts of the territorial legislature. These say specifically and unequivocally that the town was laid out in 1791. As documents of historic importance and unique interest both are given in their entirety. The Gazette, in its issue of December 17, 1791, has this notice or advertisement:

"KNOXVILLE, October 3, 1791.

"Articles of agreement made and concluded on this third day of October, 1791, by and between James White, proprietor of the land *laid* off for the town of Knoxville, of the one part, and John Adair, Paul Cunningham, and George McNutt, commissioners appointed in behalf of the purchasers of the lots in the town of Knoxville, of the other part, all of Hawkins county and Territory of the United States of America South of the River Ohio, WITNESSETH that the said James White do bargain and sell to the subscribers for lots in the said town, 64 lots, each containing one-half acre square, reserving 8 lots which are not to be loted for. The said town to be loted for and drawn in a fair lottery by the said commissioners in behalf of the subscribers, on the third of October aforesaid; and further, the said James White doth hereby bind himself, his heirs, executors, administrators, and assigns to make or cause to be made, a good and sufficient title for each

---
*Annals of Tennessee, 558.
†Address, 91, 92.

lot to the person drawing the same, as soon as payment is made, agreeable to the terms of sale of said lots. And we the commissioners aforesaid, do covenant and agree in behalf of the said purchasers, to superintend the drawing of the tickets for the said lots and that we will do equal justice between the parties, without fear or affection to any, whether present or absent. And the said James White doth agree that all the lands lying between the said town and the river, one pole in breadth along the river bank excepted, and all the land between the town and the creek, as far as the southeast corner of Broad street, with a street thirty-three feet wide around the remainder of the town, shall be commons for the said town. And further that the lots for which payment hath not been made agreeable to the articles of sale of the said lots, shall be for the use of the said James White, he, when selling them, binding the purchasers to abide by the rules and regulations which shall be made by the aforesaid commissioners. And the said commissioners shall have power to act, and to regulate all matters respecting the said town, until an act of assembly shall be made for the rules and regulations thereof. And further, it is agreed that any person refusing to comply with the rules for building and other necessary expense, shall pay to the said commissioners a sum not exceeding five dollars for such refusal made. The fines shall be collected and applied to the use and benefit of said town.

"In witness whereof, we have hereunto set our hands this third day of October, 1791.

Teste:
CHARLES McCLUNG,
JAMES COZBY.

JAMES WHITE,
JOHN ADAIR,
PAUL CUNNINGHAM,
GEORGE McNUTT.

James White, 1.
James W. Lackey, 2.
His Excellency William Blount, 3.

James Armstrong, 4.
William Davidson, 5.
Andrew and J. Belfour, 6.
John Hays, 7.

Thomas Amis, 8.
Jacob Brown, 9.
James Knox, 10.
James Richardson, 11.
William Boyd, 12.
Thomas Amis, 13.
James Hodges, 14.
Hon. Judge Anderson, 15.
John Gehon, 16.
Ignatius and J. Chisholm, 17.
John Carter, 18.
James Cozby, 19.
Thomas King, 20.
Rev. Mr. Carrick, 21.
Jacob Carper, 22.
John Love, 23.
John Owens, 24.
James Greenway, 25.
Jacob Carper, 26.
George Roulstone, 27.
Reserved Lot, 28.
Reserved Lot, 29.
Andrew and J. Belfour, 30.
John Rhea, 31.
Matthew A. Atkinson, 32.
Rev. Mr. Carrick, 33.
John Stone, 34.
Hon. Judge Campbell, 35.
Reserved Lot, 36.
Reserved Lot, 37.
Samuel Hannah, 38.
Jacob Carper, 39.
George Roulstone, 40.
Andrew Green, 41.
John Adair, 42.
William Lowry, 43.
Nathaniel Cowan, 44.
Samuel McGaughey, 45.
William Henry, 46.
William Cox, 47.
John Chisholm, 48.
John King, Sr., 49.
Lewis Newhouse, 50.
Peter McNamee, 51.
Nicholas Perkins, 52.
Daniel Hamblin, 53.
John Hackett, 54.
Jacob Carper, 55.
Robert Legitt, 56.
Adam Peck, 57.
David Allison, 58.
James and W. Lea, 59.
John Troy, 60.
William Small, 61.
Hugh Fulton, 62.
James Miller, 63.
Thomas Smith, 64.

"We, the commissioners, do certify that the above names are set opposite to the numbers agreeable to the lottery as they were drawn.

"JOHN ADAIR,
"PAUL CUNNINGHAM,
"GEORGE MCNUTT."

"N. B.: Those persons who subscribed for lots are desired to pay the purchase money immediately, otherwise their subscription will be deemed void, and the lots disposed for the benefit of the proprietor."

The act for establishing Knoxville was passed by the territorial legislature in September, 1794, and is as follows:

"An act for establishing Knoxville, on the north bank of Holston, and immediately below the second creek that runs into Holston on the north side, below the mouth of French Broad river, and for appointing commissioners for the regulation thereof.

"Whereas, In the year one thousand seven hundred and ninety-one it was found expedient to establish a town on the north bank of Holston, immediately below the second creek that runs into the north side of the same, below the mouth of French Broad, Governor Blount having determined to fix the seat of government on the said spot; and, whereas, a town was accordingly laid out by James White at the above described place, and called Knoxville, in honor of Major General Henry Knox, consisting of the necessary streets and sixty-four lots, numbered from one to sixty-four, as will more fully appear, reference being had to the plat of the said town.

"Section 1. Be it enacted by the governor, legislative council and house of representatives of the Territory of the United States of America South of the River Ohio, That a town be established on the above described spot of ground, which shall continue to be known as heretofore, by the name of Knoxville, in honor of Major General Knox, consisting of the necessary streets and sixty-four lots, from number one to sixty-four, agreeable to the plan of the said town, made in the year one thousand seven hundred and ninety-one.

"Sec. 2. And be it enacted, that Colonel James King, John Chisholm and Joseph Greer, Esquires, George Roulstone and Samuel Cowan be and hereby are appointed commissioners of the said town, with power to regulate the same, and, if necessary, with the consent of the proprietor, to enlarge it.

"Sec. 3. And be it enacted, That a correct plan of the said town as originally *laid off* in the year one thousand seven hundred and ninety-one, be made by the commissioners, and lodged in the office of the register of the county of Knox for the benefit of all persons concerned, with their names as commissioners subscribed thereto. And that it be the duty of the said commissioners to designate the first and second corners by the fixture of a stone or stones at each corner, at least eighteen inches in the ground and six above, and to use good care that the same be not removed or defaced."*

That the lots drawn passed to the ownership of those whose names are opposite is evidenced by conveyances in the first volume of deeds in the office of the Register of Knox county. There one will see that James White on July 16, 1792, conveyed lots 21 and 33 to Samuel Carrick for the sum of eight dollars per lot. That building had begun in and about Knoxville in 1791 may be learned from a letter of Governor Blount to James Robertson, written from the house of William Cobb on January 2, 1792, wherein he says: "Mrs. Blount and two of my sons are here, and here we shall stay until the first of March and then move down to Knoxville. The reason we do not move sooner my houses there are not done."†

The name Knoxville was applied to the place before it was laid off. Governor Blount, in a letter to James Robertson dated September 3, 1791, says: "I shall be living at Knoxville by the 10th of December at farthest."‡ That the destined position of the place was already recognized is shown by the fact that George Roulstone, while publishing the first issues of his paper at Rogersville, in 1791, called it the "Knoxville Gazette." The distinction of naming Knoxville in honor of General Henry Knox, Washington's Secretary of War, is ascribed by Phelan** to James White, by Marcus J. Wright††

---

*Laws of the State of Tennessee published by George Roulstone, 39.
†American Historical Magazine, Vol. I, 281.
‡American Historical Magazine, Vol. I, 192.
**History of Tennessee, 149.
††Life and Services of William Blount, 12.

and by Roosevelt‡‡ to William Blount. Whether the name was bestowed as an expression of gratitude for services rendered to his country or as a compliment to a cabinet officer may never be known, but the fact suggests an interesting bit of history which may offer some explanation. General Knox, the year before the administration of Governor Blount began, unqualifiedly and bitterly censured the settlers upon Cherokee lands. Touching their encroachments he expressed himself in vigorous language, characterizing the settlement of the lands as a gross violation of treaty rights, and suggesting the application of extreme penalties to uphold the authority of congress, which had been exposed to ridicule and contempt. He speaks of the "disgraceful violation of the treaty of Hopewell with the Cherokees as a direct and manifest contempt of the authority of the United States" and "of the lawless whites" who "render the promises of the government imbecile unless that government asserts its authority." He urges that a garrison of five hundred soldiers should be stationed within the territory assigned to the Indians to protect them against such ravages and encroachments as had been practised.* Later, in January, 1791, in communications to the president and laid before congress, General Knox, asserting that no partial measures would be adopted in dealing with the frontiers, said that favors granted to the other parts should likewise be granted to "the exposed parts of the Cumberland settlements, and the settlements lying upon, and between, the Holston and French Broad Rivers."† Relative to the frontiers, in the same communication he says: "The population of the lands lying along the Western waters is increasing rapidly. The inhabitants request and demand protection; if it be not granted, seeds of disgust will be sown; sentiments of separate interests will arise out of their local situation, which will be cherished either by insidious, domestic, or foreign emissaries.

---

‡‡Winning of the West, Vol. IV, 106.
*American State Papers. Indian Affairs. Vol. IV, 53. 54.
†Same, 107.

It, therefore, appears to be an important branch of the administration of the general government to afford the frontiers all reasonable protection, as well in their just rights as against their enemies."* Still later, on February 22, 1792, writing to Governor Blount, he says: "But, if the hostile Indians should, after having these (peaceful) intentions of the government laid fully before them, still persist in their depredations on the frontiers, it will be considered as the dictate of humanity to endeavor to punish, with exemplary severity, so incorrigible a race of men, in order to deter other tribes, in future, from a like conduct."†

It was not in keeping with the rugged, Scotch-Irish character of James White to be eager or disposed to name his town in honor of a man who had not refrained from the use of harsh language and opprobrious epithets in speaking of his settlement in common with others, whereas it was like the tactful course of William Blount to gain if possible the favor and consideration of the Secretary of War, and to bring him to a better understanding of the needs and difficulties of the Tennessee settlers. As Knoxville was founded and named in 1791, so it may be safe to maintain that the naming of it was the act of William Blount.

---

*American State Papers. Indian Affairs, Vol. IV, 113.
†Same, 252.

CHAPTER V.

UNDER TERRITORIAL GOVERNMENT.

Establishment of Knox County—Officials Appointed—First Lawyers—County Roads and Buildings—Commercial Growth—Pioneer Merchants—Hostelries—Occupations—Postal Facilities—Army Post—Relations of Citizens and Soldiers.

AFTER Governor Blount's decision to fix the seat of the territorial government at Knoxville, and the laying out and sale of lots, the next most important step in its development was the establishment of Knox county, with courts of pleas and quarter sessions to be held at Knoxville. This was done by ordinance of the governor on June 11, 1792, Charles McClung and James Mabry being designated as commissioners to run and mark certain boundaries. It brought an array of court officers and lawyers to the young town, either as permanent inhabitants or frequent visitors. Five days after the passage of the act a bench of fifteen justices of the peace, commissioned by the governor, had the oath administered to them by the Hon. David Campbell, one of the territorial judges. The other officers were Charles McClung, clerk; Thomas Chapman, register, and Robert Houston, sheriff. The first court, by proclamation of the sheriff, met at the house of John Stone on July 16, 1792, and was attended by the following justices: James White, who was appointed chairman; Samuel Newell, David Craig, and Jeremiah Jack.

The lawyers admitted to practice in this primitive court were Luke Bowyer, Alexander Outlaw, Joseph Hamilton, Archibald Roane, Hopkins Lacy, John Rhea, and James Reese, to which list was added some months later the name of John Sevier, Jr. Most of these played a conspicuous part in the affairs of state. Alexander Outlaw was a state-maker and a legislator, Joseph Hamilton had an honorable career,

Archibald Roane became governor of Tennessee, John Rhea was a member of congress for eighteen years, and James Reese was a member of the second Franklin convention. Some of these enjoyed the best educational advantages of their day. Roane and Hamilton were educated at Liberty Hall, the germ of Washington and Lee University, under William Graham, a Princeton graduate, and Rhea was reputed a graduate of Princeton College. They were likewise the fosterers of education; otherwise the following facts prove that college trusteeships were empty compliments: Roane and Hamilton were simultaneously charter trustees of three colleges, Blount, Greeneville, and Washington, while Rhea was likewise of Washington and Greeneville.

The court took immediate steps to make Knoxville accessible to all portions of the county by opening roads and highways, a wise measure which the present generation has sought to improve upon by the construction of thoroughfares that are models. Alexander Cunningham was granted permission to keep a public ferry at his landing opposite Knoxville, and south, across the Holston, roads were laid out leading to Col. Alexander Kelly's mill and to David Craig's on Nine Mile creek, north to the ford of the Clinch river, west to Campbell's station, and east to the mouth of French Broad river.*

The next note in this forward movement might indicate progress or retrogression; it is in the form of a protest demanding a better jail, and emanates from the sheriff. The court accordingly appointed commissioners to contract for the erection of a jail, whose "dimensions were sixteen feet square, the logs to be a foot square, the lower floor to be laid of logs of that size, to be laid double and crosswise, the loft also to be laid with logs, and covered crosswise with oak plank, one and a half inches thick and well spiked down."† Likewise to meet the ends of justice, at the same time, January 26, 1793. the court authorizes the same commissioners to let contract for

---
*Ramsey, 568.
†Ramsey, 569.

building a courthouse. Two months before this the governor and territorial judges, Campbell and Anderson, had passed an act authorizing the courts of the several counties to levy taxes for the repairing or building of court-houses, prisons and stocks and for other expenses incurred. The occasion of the act was the removal of the expressed doubt whether the courts of pleas and quarter sessions, acting under the laws of North Carolina, had authority to levy taxes for the purposes named. The tax was not to exceed fifty cents on each poll and seventeen cents on each one hundred acres of land.

Knoxville was now beginning to enjoy a veritable building and commercial growth. Governor Blount built his first cabin on a knoll between the University hill and the river, which was reached from the town by a winding road along the river. Soon afterward he built a more commodious residence on what was later the residence lot of S. B. Boyd, Esq. "The mansion stood near the center of the lot—was finished with some taste, and the grounds were better improved than any other in town."* Like the courthouse of modern days at the small county seat, his office became the center around which clustered the business houses of the place. Merchants advertised their stores with reference to their proximity to the governor's office, which stood just to the side of his residence on State street, not far from the corner of State and Front streets.

The pioneer merchants were Nathaniel and Samuel Cowan and Hugh Dunlap, the latter occupying one of the government "shanties" erected at the time of holding the treaty of Holston, the former being on the corner of State and Front streets, opposite Chisholm's tavern. These were speedily followed by others, as the wave of migration moved westward and Governor Blount's capital became more of an assured fact. Some of them, from the upper towns, Jonesboro and Rogersville, retained at these places their interests before committing themselves fully at Knoxville. James Miller, while merchandising

---

*Ramsey, 560.

at Rogersville, advertised to open store at John Adair's in Grassy Valley, but two weeks later decided to open at Knoxville on June 1, 1792.* Miller was an enterprising man, having made the first attempts to raise silkworms in the territory and, as a merchant, anticipating the wholesale trade by advertising that he would make a "great allowance to those who buy and sell again." Nathaniel and Samuel Cowan continued their business at Jonesboro. The next merchants to arrive, if the order of their advertisements in the *Gazette* indicate priority, were S. Duncan and Co., in December, 1792; John Sommerville and Co. in February, 1793, and Titus Ogden in February, 1793. Charles McClung in December, 1792, offers "first-rate powder for sale at house which Col. White formerly lived in near Knoxville. $1.00 per lb., for which good merchantable corn will be received at 1-3 of a dollar per bushel, delivered at my house."†

Some of the advertisements in the *Gazette* forcibly remind one of modern methods. S. Duncan and Co. give notice that they are going to leave Knoxville and, therefore, offer liberal inducements to customers. Six months afterwards they are advertising new stock. J. Sommerville and Co. have a display advertisement filling two columns, ending it, however, with notice that no credit will be allowed. Other merchants of the territorial epoch were James Ore, Samuel Miller, associated with James Miller, and King and Crozier. Soon after beginning business Titus Ogden died, lamented as a useful and exemplary citizen. As witness from the state of North Carolina he had been present at the Holston treaty in 1791, and was paymaster of troops and of Indian annuities. Goods were bought in the markets of Philadelphia and Baltimore and, brought overland, involved time, labor and expense. Hugh Dunlap, in the letter already mentioned, says: "I left Philadelphia with my goods in December, 1791, and did not reach Knoxville until about the 1st of February, 1792."

---

*Knoxville Gazette, May 19 and June 2, 1792.
†Knoxville Gazette, December 1, 1792.

At the outset the taverns begin to do a thriving business, as many as four houses of entertainment being advertised by John Chisholm, Alexander Carmichael, John Wood, and Peter McNamee. Other occupations also receive encouragement, inasmuch as jewelers, tanners, tailors and the butcher acquaint the public with their willingness to serve them, while well-diggers and tanners are advertised for and promised "good encouragement."

With increasing business and population there came a demand for postal facilities. In the early part of 1792 a rumor was current that a continental post would run between Richmond and Knoxville beginning on June 1st the same year.* This, it seems, did not materialize, as later, in October, John Chisholm advertised in the *Gazette* that he would establish for the sum of $250.00 a postal service to include Jonesboro and Abingdon, Virginia, and to return by Sullivan courthouse and Rogersville to Knoxville, making the circuit in twenty-one days. This scheme must have fallen through, for in November of the same year Roulstone and Co., of the *Gazette* advertise a post from their printing office every other week, to leave the next morning after publication of the paper and to make all the county towns in Washington District and Abingdon, Virginia. Again, there are proposals advertised to carry mails between Knoxville and Abingdon once in two weeks. These efforts show the urgent necessity of a regular mail service. Accordingly, in 1795 the national government gave Knoxville a bi-monthly mail, with George Roulstone as postmaster, which relieved somewhat the pressing necessity for an improved service. By Knoxville came all mail for the West and much for the East. Hitherto letters and papers had been committed to the care of travelers and emigrants, who upon arrival opened their wallets and distributed their charge to eager crowds, always glad to confer such favors gratuitously. Important government correspondence was conveyed by volunteer expresses, who received as pay for their services about $1.00 per day.

---

*Knoxville Gazette, February 25. 1792.

Knoxville then, as she aspires to be now, was an army post, which meant much to the life and business of the town. Though John Adair's house had first been named as a depot of supplies, later it was found better to make Knoxville the place for the rendezvous of troops and the depository of arms and supplies. In 1793 Capt. Carr with a company of United States troops came and began the erection of a barracks for his men, which occupied the site of the present courthouse. This building extended from Main street towards the river, and was a two-story structure, the upper story projecting two feet on every side beyond the lower as a means of defense. Portholes on every side and even in the floor of the upper story added to the completeness of the defense, while the felling of trees within gunshot prevented the approach of an assailant.* The *Gazette*† mentions with genuine pride the arrival of William Rickard's troops from Salisbury, North Carolina, who, after a long and tedious march, entered the town with a movement bespeaking the order and discipline of war-worn veterans. The columns of the paper for almost a twelve-month, with each issue, bear the name of Commander Rickard, either advertising for deserters, clashing with the merchants of the town, officiating on the Fourth of July celebration, or giving notice forbidding the citizens from having anything to do with his soldiers without written orders. Hugh Dunlap says in the letter hereinbefore quoted that Carr was arrested by his lieutenant, Rickard, for drunkenness a few months after their arrival, and resigned his office through chagrin at the efforts of his subordinate officer to supplant him. Daniel Smith, the territorial secretary, writing to the Secretary of War, July 19, 1793, mentions a Capt. Kerr, in command of regulars, to whose care he intended to entrust a number of families removing to the Cumberland country.‡ It is evident that in the dim past of Knoxville the soldier was

---

*Dr. Humes, Semi-Centennial Address. 59: Goodspeed. History of Tennessee, 840.
†March 9, 1793.
‡American State Papers. Indian Affairs, Vol. IV. 464.

sometimes an element of disorder and confusion. Nathaniel and Samuel Cowan advertise that they will expect captains of militia as security for goods sold to the soldiers, to pay if the soldiers do not discharge their obligations.* On the other hand Rickard publishes this notice:†

"I do once more forbid the inhabitants of this town and vicinity from having any dealings with the soldiers of my company, without permission in writing from the commanding officer, as they not only involve themselves in difficulty thereby, but also injure the public service. I have been informed that some persons in the country have purchased articles of the soldiers, such as part of their regimentals, public axes, etc. Purchasers are invited to bring all such soldiers to headquarters.

"WILLIAM RICKARD, *Commanding Officer,*
"*12th Company, 3rd Sub-Legion.*
"Camp New Boston, near Knoxville."

---

*Knoxville Gazette, May 4, 1793.
†Gazette, January 2, 1794.

CHAPTER VI.

INDIAN TROUBLES.

Indian War Imminent—Conditions in the West—Indian Atrocities—Policy of Blount and the National Government—Threatened Attack on Knoxville—Preparation of Whites—Pioneer Character—Stephen Foster's Account of the Massacre at Cavet's Station—Sevier's Successful Raid.

THE presence of regular troops and organized bodies of militia indicated the tension of relations between Indians and settlers. The year 1793 was one of excitement and constant anxiety. In 1792 there were ominous events and influences. With the intelligence of St. Clair's defeat in the Northwest, the dissatisfaction over the treaty of Holston, and the increasing thirst of young braves for plunder, carnage, and prestige, the frequency of murders and depredations became noted. The restraint imposed by the national government upon the military organizations that guarded the frontier, to act only on the defensive, and the toleration of the frontiersmen under great provocation served to invite attack and molestation rather than to encourage peace and friendship. Notwithstanding the fact that Governor Blount had been invited by the Cherokee chiefs, Hanging Maw, John Watts, and others, to meet them in conference at Coyatee, whither he repaired to be greeted with distinguished honors in the presence of two thousand Indians and to be received with protestations and manifestations of peace and good will, still the great scalp dance in the Lower Cherokee towns, participated in by Cherokees, Creeks, and Shawnees, was a surer prophecy of what was in store for the struggling settlements along the Holston and Cumberland rivers. The successful intercepting of Capt. Samuel Handley and his company of forty-two men near Crab Orchard by a party of these Indians, his capture and the discomfiture of his men, gave renewed confidence in the plans of extermination.

With the immediate danger of a protracted and destructive Indian war there came to the governor grave and delicate responsibilities. The young government at Philadelphia was not yet secure in its domestic or foreign policy. Important negotiations were pending, which if disturbed or thwarted meant untold detriment and disaster to the South and West. It was yet in the minds of many an open question whether the vast region of country drained by the Mississippi river eastward should belong to Spain or the United States, or should become part of a great southwestern empire. The free and unobstructed navigation of the Mississippi was likewise an unsettled question of gravest concern to the settlers. It required all the arts and refinements of diplomacy to forego the commission of a blunder, which might prove fatal to the welfare of the young nation trying her unpracticed hand upon an effete monarchy. The policy of Spain was, after supplying the Indians with guns and ammunition, to incite them to attacks upon the American settlements and thus to foment a war of extermination: that of the United States was with rum and presents to cultivate the friendship of the nations and thus to preserve intact all that territory ceded by the treaty with Great Britain in 1783, which included the domain inhabited principally by the Cherokees, Chickasaws, Creeks, and Choctaws. A statement of these facts is necessary to appreciate the causes of the Indian troubles which, in the East, centered around Knoxville, but fell most heavily upon the Cumberland settlements in Middle Tennessee. They serve also to explain, without excusing it, the indifference of Congress to making a wise provision for the defense of the Holston and Cumberland settlers against Indian forays.

The increasing atrocities of Indian bands, emboldened by fortuitous circumstances, brought the settlers to the verge of despair. With grim determination they resolved to visit upon their foes death and destruction, regarding neither age, sex nor faction. Governor Blount sent to the places of their uprising or rendezvous Sevier or White or some other influential man of the settlements, and for a time quelled the spirit of revenge and insubordination. However, the killing of the friendly Chickasaw, John Morris, while a guest at the governor's home in Knoxville, the invasion of John Beard and his one hundred and forty followers, against orders, of the Upper Cherokee towns, and the killing of Hanging Maw's wife and other kindly disposed Indians, and Col. Doherty's invasion of the Indian country when ordered positively to desist, show the utter desperation to which these men were goaded. The failure of court-martial proceedings further testified to the common impulse by which they were moved.*

On the other hand, the government and Governor Blount were unceasing in their efforts to placate the Indians and to preserve peace and friendship. Early in the year the Secretary of War wrote to the governor urging him to visit the seat of government with representative chiefs of the nation, promising an abundant supply of such articles as they and their nation may require.† After repeated urgings the governor failed to induce them to accompany him, and yet went on with the hope of settling controversies and removing all uneasiness. In his own home he entertained with lavish hospitality for eight or ten days Unacata, a Cherokee chief, when at the end of this entertainment he came to the conclusion that the chief had all the while acted the part of spy. When Morris was killed, either by mistake for a Cherokee or through the wanton conduct of some disorderly person, he caused him to be buried with military honors, walking with the dead man's brother among the chief mourners, and later soothed the injured feelings of the living by "pretty liberal presents."‡ When the uprising at Gamble's station took place, threatening instant invasion of the Indian country, he dispatched Lieutenant Kelly, then Col. James White, to the scene to urge

---
*Ramsey, 568.
†American State Papers. Indian Affairs, Vol. IV, 429.
‡American State Papers, 435.

acquiescence in the terms of the Holston treaty, and then betook himself to the spot. The solicitude expressed in these words indicates the gravity of the situation: "I can truly say, my feelings were never more agitated than they were on this occasion. I considered my reputation as an officer, in great measure, the reputation of the country over which I had the honor to preside, and my prospects of returning peace, all at stake upon the event."*

The most romantic episode in these troublous times was the threatened attack of a combined force of Cherokees and Creeks, variously estimated from nine to fifteen hundred warriors, on Knoxville in the fall of 1793. For a time after the treaty of Holston, it will be recalled, there was a cessation of violent outbreaks; but here and there sporadic assaults marked by an occasional murder or some theft of horses showed that beneath the formality of peace lay the smouldering embers of irreconcilable race hatred. Sufferings from Indian cunning, treachery, vindictiveness, and atrocity had placed the settlers on their guard. In the midst of apparent security, every means of defense was employed to ward off sudden onslaughts and to guarantee personal safety. The cabin was so constructed as to be impenetrable to shot from without, while portholes commanding all sides guarded the approaches. Scouts patroled the woods to discover any lurking enemy; the workman in the field kept his rifle near at hand to offer resistance if molested, and wives and daughters learned the arts of war, becoming skilled in the moulding of bullets and the use of the rifle. All, trained to be ready for any emergency, were inured to hardship and became sharp-witted and keen-sighted in the hour of danger. Their readiness for combat, their presence of mind in imminent peril, their endurance of privation, produced a type of manhood and womanhood nowhere excelled in annals that extol magnanimous souls and preserve courageous deeds. Whether it be James Cozby, to protect his home besieged by twenty warriors, giving stentorian orders

---

*American State Papers, 455.

to an imaginary platoon of soldiers and thus striking them with terror and thwarting their purposes; or Margaret McEwen, when Houston's station is attacked by a band of one hundred assailants, taking the bullet moulds and placing therein the shapeless lead fired from Indian guns into the fort, remoulding it and bidding her husband: "Here is a ball run out of the Indians' lead; send it back to them as quick as possible. It is their own; let them have it in welcome;" or Mrs. Gillespie when her defenseless home is entered and her sleeping infant marked for slaughter, rushing to the door and shouting in pealing tones to her husband and others as if hard by, "White men, come home! come home, white men! Indians! Indians!" or Mrs. Campbell, when her husband and his helper, ploughing side by side, are shot at by cowardly foe, taking down the rifle from the rack, barricading the door, and waiting at the portholes to receive the ruthless invader; or Andrew Cresswell and his wife, when their humble cottage is threatened and retreat is possible, resolving that they will hold the house until the Indians take them out; or Samuel Handley, when bound to the stake a ready sacrifice to Indian ferocity defying his captors to shoot him as a brave man deserves, and upbraiding them as merciless cowards;* or Mrs. George Mann, when her husband has fallen a victim to the brutal instincts and malignant hate of the foe, in defense of her home and little ones, sending a ball through the body of the first Indian who forces an ingress and wounding another and thus rescuing herself and household†—these and multiplied examples like these attest the material out of which heroic pioneer characters were made.

The chief source of authority for an account of this attack is an essay of Professor Stephen Foster, of East Tennessee college, read before the Knoxville Lyceum and published in the Knoxville Register, September 21, 1831. Any history of Knoxville is incomplete that does not recount this intended

---

*American Historical Magazine, Vol. II, 88.
†Thomas W. Humes, Semi-Centennial Address, 56.

attack. Because of its historic value and to give wider circulation to so noteworthy a contribution to Knoxville history, the entire article is given.

MASSACRE AT CAVET'S STATION, SEPTEMBER 25TH, 1793.

"On the road from Knoxville to Major Joseph Martin's is passed Joseph Lonas' on the creek, the formerly celebrated Cavet's station. This Cavet's station was nothing but the log-house dwelling of a family of thirteen persons in the days of Indian havoc and bloodshed. It is eight miles below Knoxville and seven miles above Campbell's station. This latter station was one of the chief forts of the country, containing as many as twenty families, and assuming an air and attitude of defense which inspired courage within itself, and extended to the savages that prowled around it a salutary respect for the prowess of its interior.

"In 1793 a party of Creeks and Cherokees, from 900 to 1,500, crossed the Holston with the design of burning and sacking Knoxville. They halted upon the question. 'Shall we massacre the whole town or only the men?' The Hanging Maw was a leading man in the councils of his people. His opposition to the scheme of an indiscriminate massacre was strenuous and weighty. Another circumstance is here related. Van, Cherokee chief, possessed a little captive boy, that was riding behind him. Doublehead became envious at this sight, and picked a quarrel with Van, and to satiate his malice, killed the little boy with a sudden stab of his knife. The animosity of these chiefs added hindrance to delay. And before the plan of procedure could be satisfactorily adjusted, it was found to be too late to arrive at Knoxville before daylight.

"Then to avoid an entire failure of their enterprise, they repaired to Cavet's, as affording the readiest and easiest prey. This establishment they reduced to ashes. Its thirteen tenants were slaughtered except one. Cavet himself was found butchered in the garden. Several bullets were still lying in his mouth, having been put there by himself for the convenience of speedily loading his gun. The day of this slaughter was the 25th of September.

"In the meantime intelligence of the contemplated attack had arrived at Knoxville, and given to the minds of its citizens that impulse which is only to be looked for on great occasions, when the dignity of a single heroic conception is enough to consecrate danger and death. The number of fighting men in Knoxville was forty. But it was thought preferable to combine this force, and to risk every life in a well-concerted effort to strike a deadly and terrific blow on the advancing enemy, at the outskirts of the town rather than stand to be hewed down in its center by the Indian tomahawk.

"Gen. James White was then advanced a little beyond the prime of manhood, of a muscular body, a vigorous constitution, and of that cool and determinate courage which arises from a principle of original bravery, confirmed and ennobled by the faith of the Bible. He was the projector and leader of the enterprise. Robert Houston, Esq., from whose verbal statements the substance of much of this narrative is copied, was of the age of twenty-eight, and was a personal actor in the scene.

"It was viewed to be manifest by those who were acquainted with Indian movements, that the party would come up the back way near the present plantations of Mrs. Luttrell and Henry Lonas, rather than the straighter way now traveled by the stage. The company from Knoxville accordingly repaired to a ridge, on that road, which now may be inspected about a mile and a quarter from Knoxville. This ridge is marked by the irregular and shelving rocks of the road, which passes over it.

"On the side of this ridge next to Knoxville, our company was stationed at the distance of twenty steps from each other, with orders to reserve their fire till the most forward of the Indian party was advanced far enough to present a mark for the most eastern man of our party. He was then to fire.

This fire was to be the signal to every man of our own to take aim with precision. This would be favored by the halt thus occasioned in the ranks of the Indians. And these latter, it was hoped, astonished at the sudden and fatal discharge of thirty-eight rifles extended over so long a line, would apprehend a most formidable ambuscade, and would quit all thought of further aggression, and betake themselves to the readiest and safest retreat.

"But to provide for the worst, it was settled beforehand that each man upon discharging his piece, without stopping to watch the flight of the Indians, should make the best of his way to Knoxville, lodge himself in the blockhouse then standing at the present mansion of Mr. Etheldred Williams, where three hundred muskets had been deposited by the United States, and where the two oldest citizens of the forty, John McFarland and Robert Williams, were left behind to run bullets and load.

"Here it was proposed to make a last and desperate struggle; that, by possessing every porthole in the building, and by dealing lead and powder through it to the best advantage, they might extort from an enemy nearly forty times their number, a high price for the hazard of all they had on earth that was dear and precious. There were then two stores in Knoxville, Nathaniel Cowan's and James Miller's.

"Though the practical heroism of this well-concerted and thus far ably conducted strategem, in consequence of the sudden retreat of the enemy, was not put to the test of actual experiment, yet an incident fraught with so much magnanimity in the early fortunes of Knoxville should not be blotted from the records of her fame. It is an incident on which the memory of her sons will linger without tiring, when the din of party shall be hushed and its strife forgotten. Those men of a former day were 'made of sterner stuff' than to shirk from danger at the call of duty. And it will be left to the pen of a future historian to do justice to that little band of thirty-eight citizens, who flinched not from the deliberate exposure of their persons in the open field, within the calculated gunshot of fifteen hundred of the fleetest running and boldest savages.

"This expedition on the part of the Indians, though in its issue abortive by their divided councils, was marked with singular daring and despatch. They knew that Col. Sevier with a detachment of four hundred mounted riflemen, ready to ravage their territory, had recently left Knoxville and lay at that moment at Ish's station on the south side of the river, about ten miles from Cavet's; that a respectable force lay in garrison at Campbell's station, and that the above-mentioned forty men were at Knoxville. Here then were three points from which, at a moment's warning, they would be assailed from three different directions at once. But they had formed their plan, that by a movement too quick for discovery and by a ridge not commonly traveled by our warriors, they would pass the forces at Ish's and Campbell's stations, seizing the favorable moment of the absence of Sevier's troops, to fall upon Knoxville entirely unexpected, scalp the inhabitants in their beds, pillage the only two little stores in the place, and in the light of its blazing ruins, make off with their booty, divided into two or three parties, to elude pursuit, prevent delay and make good their escape.

"The above-mentioned disagreement between their principal chiefs, by the loss of a single hour, like the counsel of Hushai in Absalom's rebellion, frustrated the whole project, divested this band of its martial prowess, and sent it skulking on the shameful butchery at Cavet's station.

"The circumstances of this massacre will strikingly illustrate the Indian mode of warfare, a singular union of cunning, deceit and atrocity, without concert of action or unity of plan. For at the beginning of the attack Cavet's house contained three fighting men. These plied their rifles with such coolness and dexterity that two Indians lay dead and three were wounded. The Indians then made a temporary halt from the fury of their onset, and employed Bob Benge, a man of mixed blood, who spoke English, to offer to the garrison terms of surrender.

These were very favorable, namely, that their lives should be spared and they exchanged for as many Indian prisoners then among the whites. No sooner were these terms accepted and the prisoners beginning to leave the house, than Doublehead and his party fell upon the men and put them to death. He treated the women and children with barbarous indelicacy and then killed them. John Watts, who was the main leader of the expedition, interposed and saved one of Cavet's sons, and poor Benge, who first proposed the conditions of surrender, was all the time striving, to no purpose, to check the murderous atrocities of Doublehead.

"How different this confused havoc from the measured discipline of the Roman legion where to fight 'extra ordinem,' as Sallust says, that is to overstep the battle line and to fight alone in front of it, was an offense to be punished with capital severity.

"When the Indians had accomplished this inglorious deed, they made for a well known house on Beaver creek, twelve miles from Knoxville, now owned by Mr. Callaway. That house had been occupied by Mr. Luke Lea's father. That gentleman, from an apprehension of danger, had removed his family to the present residence of Col. Miller Francis, only a week previous to this terrible morning, and thus happily saved them from becoming the victims of Indian fury. Some of their bed clothes were still left in the house, and the wheat stacks standing by the barns and stables. The whole was soon a heap of ashes.

"The Indians retreated with characteristic speed and address. They sought the fastness of Clinch, and by a brisk march they were soon beyond the reach of immediate danger. Danger awaited them still. In three weeks they were bearded out of their own den by Sevier's invasion."

Having summoned reinforcements for immediate pursuit, the dashing and knightly Sevier was soon on the trail of the murderers. The restrictions against carrying the war into the enemies' country were removed by the territorial secretary,

Daniel Smith, and Sevier, infusing his own impetuous courage into the spirits of his men, with the speed and fury of the hurricane, struck such blows with torch and sword as to cause a sudden cessation of Indian hostilities. The campaign, extending as far down as the present site of Rome, Georgia, is memorable as his last and one of his most effective. Knoxville was relieved; the gallant soldiery returned with the small loss of three men; Sevier was to enter upon the larger field of civil affairs and administrative duties.*

---

*Humes, Address, 38, 39; Ramsey, 588, 589.

CHAPTER VII.

TERRITORIAL LEGISLATURE.

Hamilton District—Sufferings from Indians—Appeals for Succor—Elections to Territorial Legislature—Preliminary Session—Spirit of Legislators—Active Measures for Resistance to Indian Depredations—First Regular Session—Acts Touching Education and Taxation—Act Preparatory to Organization of the State—Constitutional Convention.

GOVERNOR BLOUNT, on March 13, 1793, established a third judicial district, calling it Hamilton in honor of Alexander Hamilton, Secretary of Treasury in Washington's cabinet. It comprised the counties of Knox and Jefferson, and its courts were to be held in April and October of each year in Knoxville. At the sitting of the October court, in 1793, the grand jury of the district issued an address to the governor upon his return from Philadelphia. Therein they express in most cordial terms an appreciation of his work and services in behalf of the territory over which he presided, but lament its sufferings from the atrocious conduct of the Indians and hope for a speedy recognition of its needs and a declaration of war to prevent further outrages. At the same time they remind him of the fact that their numbers had reached five thousand free male inhabitants, which warranted by congressional ordinance the organization of the territorial legislature. This address, dated at Knoxville, October 17, 1793, is signed by James Roddye, foreman, Joshua Gist, Adam Meek, Samuel Wear, John Adair, Adam Peck, James Hill, John Blackburn, George McNutt, John Kean, William Donaldson, Garret Fitzgerald, William Lea, Thomas McCulloch and Jeremiah Jack.*

As the initial movement towards the formation of a ter-

---

*Knoxville Gazette, November 23, 1793.

CHARLES McCLUNG.

ritorial legislature this document possesses a unique interest. In so far as his authority lay, ever alert to the reasonable demands and evident interests of the people, Governor Blount without delay ordered an election of representatives on the 22d and 23d of December, 1793.* Col. Alexander Kelly and Capt. John Beard, both tried Indian fighters, were elected to represent Knox county. With the election returns all in, the governor on January 1st following called the legislature to convene at Knoxville on the fourth Monday of February. In session, religious services marked the beginning. The Rev. Samuel Carrick, at the time pastor of the Presbyterian church in Knoxville, having offered prayer, preached a sermon from this text: "In hope of eternal life, which God, that cannot lie, promised before the world began; but hath in due time manifested his word through preaching, which is committed unto me according to the commandment of God our Savior. Titus 1: 2, 3." At the outset steps were taken for the organization of a duly-constituted law-making body by recommending to congress ten men, from whom were to be selected five as members of the legislative council, the upper house by provision of the ordinance of 1787. In the matters of election and selection Governor Blount carefully abstained from interference by suggestion or recommendation. He says: "I call the persons elected to represent the several counties together at so early a period that the nomination of counsellors may be before Congress in the present session, otherwise there could not be a general assembly in the territory until after the next session of congress. Who shall be counsellors I don't care. provided they have ability to do their duty."† This was another exhibition of that sound judgment and wise policy he had displayed when he took charge of the affairs of the territory, selecting for office men in accord with the wishes of the people.

---

* Haywood, 312.
† Letter to James Robertson, January 19, 1794, in American Historical Magazine, Vol. III, 283.

Much has been said and made of the earnest men who participated in the Watauga Association, the Cumberland Compact, and the state of Franklin, and of the measures and principles they advocated. Their deeds and deliberations have been far and widely heralded, but not so much is written of this first legislative council in Tennessee, which, acting under duly authorized calls, entered with patriotic zeal and intelligent foresight into the consideration and adoption of such laws as concerned the immediate pressing and undeniable needs of their constituents. Still the question of all-absorbing public interest was the hostile attitude and violent outbreaks of the Indians. For months previous this editorial paragraph had been running through successive issues of the *Gazette:* "The Creek nation must be destroyed! or the southwestern frontier, from the mouth of St. Mary's to the western extremity of Kentucky and Virginia will be incessantly harassed by them. *Delenda est Carthago!*" Accordingly the first utterances upon assembling were appeals to the governor and to congress to aid in the suppression of the murders, robberies, cruelties and indignities by which their lives and interests were constantly imperiled. Deeming themselves almost a merciless and helpless prey to the ferocity of their enemies, yet without the abandonment of hope, there is a touching and melancholy pathos in this description of their suffering: "Scarcely is there a man of this body but can recount a dear wife or child, an aged parent or near relation, besides friends, massacred by the hands of these bloodthirsty nations, in their houses or fields; nor are our friends and neighbors less miserable. They, too, can enumerate the suffering of equal calamities."* The appeal to congress was not without some tangible results. A committee, in their report upon the memorial, expressed deep sympathy with the petitioners and their objects, and recommended measures for the immediate pursuit and punishment of the Indians. The house of representatives approved and ordered

---

*Haywood, 315.

a bill, but it finally failed. However, through an organized medium, congress had been reached and enlightened.†

Having finished such business as could properly come before it at this preliminary session, the legislature was prorogued by the governor to meet on the fourth Monday of August, 1794. In the meantime congress nominated the legislative council, and President Washington commissioned the following: Griffith Rutherford, James Winchester, John Sevier, Stockley Donelson and Parmenas Taylor. In the legislature there was but one lawyer, William Cocke, in the lower house. It is fair to presume that the absence of lawyers in this and the state's first legislature may be attributed to that antipathy to and distrust of the legal profession manifested ten years before in the Houston draft of the Frankland constitution, a section of which excluded attorneys at law from becoming members of the legislature.

The first regular session of the legislature met August 25, 1794, and continued to September 30, 1794. Deducting five Sundays, it was in session thirty-two working days and passed twenty-three acts. At once rules, some of them quaint, were adopted, committees appointed and bills introduced. In the constituting of committees the names of the Knox county representatives do not appear, they on the third day of the session as officers of the militia having been granted leave of absence to go on a scouting expedition against the Cherokee Indians. The first act proposed and passed reflects the wisdom and beneficence of the body, being one to establish Greeneville college. The acts of greatest local interest were the establishing of the town Knoxville and of Blount college, and of the office of public printer to be filled by George Roulstone, editor of the Knoxville Gazette. Other acts affected more or less directly local interests and welfare. Governor Blount was assiduous in his attention to the wants of the law-makers and generous with his advice. The most elaborate and most important act of the session, that establishing the courts and

---
†Haywood. 329.

regulating them, was a measure drafted by him, a deed which received the hearty thanks of the legislative body. The bill which provoked most discussion and elicited a wide divergence of views was the tax bill, the leading point at issue being whether lands should be taxed at twelve and a half, eighteen or twenty-five cents per hundred acres. The council supported the first, then the second, and finally acceded to the demands of the house, which championed the last. Besides land, other sources of revenue or subjects of taxation were free males and male servants between the ages of twenty-one and fifty years, all slaves between ten and fifty years of age, all stud horses and all town lots, "a rather queer combination," according to Theodore Roosevelt.*

As evidence of the diligence and fidelity of these public servants the fact is mentioned that many of their sessions began at seven o'clock in the morning, and that the two houses on one occasion met for conference at four o'clock in the afternoon. The meeting place for conference was the court house, a one-story building about thirty feet long and twenty-five feet broad, which afforded the only available room in the town sufficiently large for a joint session. The legislative council met either in the barracks or the house of John Stone; the house met sometimes in another room of the barracks or at Carmichael's tavern. In the settlement of the expenses incurred ten dollars were allowed John Stone for the use of his room, and five dollars to James White for the court house.†

The legislature adjourned to meet by the governor's call, on the first Monday in October, 1795. Rapidly changing conditions, the growth and prosperity of the territory, the successful invasion of the Lower Cherokee towns and the disastrous destruction of Nickojack and Running Water, the effectual suppressing of Indian expeditions, the growing feeling of security,

---

*Laws of the State of Tennessee, published by G. Roulstone in 1803, p. 29; Roosevelt, Winning of the West, Vol. IV, 112.
†Ramsey, 630, 635.

the flush state of the treasury, and the belief that, with the dignity of statehood, the people through their representatives in congress might enjoy greater benefits—these made the movement for admission into the Union a common impulse. Governor Blount gave his cordial sanction to the movement and contributed his personal efforts and influence to this end. Instead of waiting the appointed time for the second session of the legislature, he summoned it to convene on June 29, 1795.

The most important measure under consideration was the passage of an act for the enumeration of the population, to ascertain whether there were as many as sixty thousand inhabitants to meet the requirements for the organization of a state government. The bill passed with one dissenting vote. This session was brief, extending to July 11th. Only fourteen acts were passed, among them one being for the establishment of Blount county taken from the territory of Knox county. The tax rate was lowered, even going so far as to accept the contention of the legislative council at the former session, that land should be taxed twelve and a half cents per hundred acres. In fact, everything taxable was cut in half.

In accordance with the act of enumeration a census was ordered by the governor and taken by the sheriffs in their respective counties. By November 28th all returns were made, and the governor announced to the President the result. The population, 77,262, was found to exceed greatly the required number. There were nine thousand voters and sixty-five hundred of these expressed preference for the organization of the state. Wherefore Governor Blount issued a proclamation calling upon each county to choose in December five delegates to a constitutional convention, called to meet in Knoxville on January 11, 1796. Elections were held, Knox county sent a delegation composed of William Blount, James White, Charles McClung, John Adair and John Crawford, the delegates met and drafted a constitution characterized by Thomas Jefferson as the least imperfect and most republican of any of the constitutions adopted up to that time.* After some delay in congress, caused by political jealousy, on June 1, 1796, Tennessee was admitted into the Union, with its capital at Knoxville.

---

*For a full account of the work and proceedings of the constitutional convention, see Caldwell's Constitutional History of Tennessee, 73-108; paper on the "Constitutional Convention of 1796," by Edward T. Sanford, Esq., in Proceedings of the Bar Association of Tennessee, 1896, 92-148.

CHAPTER VIII.

LIFE OF THE PEOPLE.

Population—Interest in Education—Early Teachers—Samuel Cornik—His School—Blount College—Presbyterian Church Organized—Printing Press—Literary Effort—Books—Physicians—Amusements—Darker Phases—Strong Elements of Character.

THE early history of Knoxville is, for the most part, the history of Indian hostilities and governmental beginnings. Having followed as minutely as the sources permit its military and political history, it remains to look at that side of the people's life which indicates most accurately the present status and determines most largely the future. This involves their interest in education, religion and literature, their social intercourse and their mode of life.

One has but to note the constituent elements of a population to determine its interest in matters of education. Knox county, like the remainder of East Tennessee, having been settled largely by Scotch-Irish Presbyterians, who fostered education along with religion, the school house sprang up by the side of the house of worship, and the rudiments of knowledge were inculcated with the principles of religion. At the outset the interests of education suffered materially from the fact that communities were sparsely settled, from the dangers of Indian attacks, from the necessities imposed by pioneer life when the boys had to hew down the forests and till the soil, and the girls attend to the spinning wheel, loom and other domestic duties. "Go to school half the year and work the other half," was the rule governing school attendance. The character of instruction was as a rule quite indifferent. Some of the teachers were of the itinerant class with no thought of permanency, some intemperate and ill-humored, who chastised unmercifully and injudiciously, while others were devoted to their work and spent their lives in the cause. Governor John Reynolds of Illinois, who spent his early childhood in the vicinity of Knoxville prior to the removal of his family to that state, has left this testimony to the types of teachers and methods of instruction then employed: "I was sent to school at a tender age. My first teacher was a cross, ill-natured Irishman, as unsuitable a character as can be well imagined to have the charge of a young and diffident child. I was often severely chastised, though I had not intentionally committed any fault. The scholars soon learned to detest him and learned little else. The unjust severity with which I was treated made the very name of school odious to me. My next teacher was a just and kindhearted man, who was much esteemed by his pupils. Under his tuition I became fond of going to school, and improved rapidly. I attended these schools in 1794-95."*

As far as the record goes, the two earliest known instructors in or around Knoxville were the Rev. Samuel Carrick and Governor Archibald Roane, and the first pupil Hugh Lawson White, distinguished names in the annals of the state.† The Memoir states that when young White was fifteen years of age, in 1788, he was studying the ancient languages under the tutorage of these teachers, Samuel Carrick being a young Presbyterian minister and Archibald Roane a young barrister. The pioneer teacher of Knoxville then was the Rev. Samuel Carrick, who settled in the vicinity of the place in 1791. Mr. Carrick had visited this portion of the country in 1787, and it is maintained by some that he became a resident within the present limits of Knox county the next year. However, his dismissal from Hanover to Abingdon Presbytery, and his resignation of the trusteeship of Liberty Hall academy in 1791 fix this year as that of the removal.‡ He took charge of Leb-

---

*Life and Times of Governor John Reynolds, 12, 13. Governor Reynolds returned in 1810 to Knox county to pursue his studies under the Rev. Isaac Anderson at old Union academy, on the present Washington pike, where he was a schoolmate of Sam Houston.

†Nancy Scott, Memoir of Hugh Lawson White, 9.

‡Dr. James Park, Address upon the Centennial Anniversary, of the First Presbyterian Church, Knoxville, 12; General Catalogue of Washington and Lee University, 37.

anon church in the Fork and taught in connection with his pastorate. His home was fixed on a farm four miles northeast of Knoxville, at the west end of the present county bridge over Holston river. Here, in December, 1792, he planned an institution of large scope and pretensions. It was to be opened on January 1, 1793, at his "seat" and under his direction, wherein should be given a "competent introduction to Latin and Greek languages, attention being particularly given to grammatical construction, pronunciation, the design and connection of each author; the English language grammatically, applying the rules in reading, parsing, correcting and composing; the liberal arts and sciences, viz., geography, logic, natural and moral philosophy, astronomy and rhetoric. The seminary will open two sessions in the year, continuing five months each. The terms will be $7.00 per scholar for each session, paid at entering. Beginners in Latin will be admitted at the beginning of the session only, which will be the first of January and the first of July annually."†

The next and the most important and far-reaching step in the educational beginnings of Knoxville was the already mentioned establishment of Blount college, now University of Tennessee.§ The first president was the Rev. Samuel Carrick.

The first and only church organization prior to 1796 was the First Presbyterian church, organized in or before 1793. The Rev. Samuel Carrick, as mentioned, in February, 1794, delivered before the territorial legislature a discourse which was subsequently published and advertised as preached by the "pastor of the church in Knoxville."* The congregation worshiped either in the court house or in the barracks, as they continued to do for some years. The original bench of elders was composed of James White, John Adair and George Mc-

---

†Knoxville Gazette, December 1, 1792.
§For full particulars of the history of this institution see Moses White, Early History of the University of Tennessee; T. C. Karns, History of the University of Tennessee in Merriam's Higher Education in Tennessee: Edward T. Sanford, Blount College and the University of Tennessee.
*Gazette, April 10, 1794.

Nutt.† The foundation of this congregation, built upon a quickened conscience and an unswerving faith, has left its enduring impress upon the community.

The presence of the printing press encouraged immediately literary effort and production. Published discourses by the Revs. Samuel Carrick and Hezekiah Balch were announced for sale in the columns of the *Gazette*. The controversial spirit, so characteristic of the people at a later stage of their history when political and religious divisions arose, manifested itself at the outset. Correspondents signing their names "Trenck," "The Reviewers" and "Amicus," fulminated their views through Roulstone's bi-monthly organ and sparred at each other with incisive pen. The first effort or attempt at anything of a permanent nature and value was put forth by William Tatham, who first appears upon the stage of Tennessee history as one of the commissioners of the Watauga Association and the clerk of the court or committee of five. Later he was associated with Spruce McCay and William R. Davie, Esquires, in the land warrant business. He is best known by his famous "Fiat justitia" promulgation—a protest against the selfish policy of Joseph Hamilton, James Reese, Archibald Roane, Hopkins Lacy and S. Mitchell, lawyers constituting the Knoxville bar, who advertise that they will enter into no suit unless paid therefor in advance.* Influenced by his interest in the welfare of the southwestern country whose cause he had early espoused, anxious to remove all impressions prejudicial to the truthful history and real status thereof, and wishing to introduce strangers to a knowledge or better conception through maps and correct accounts, he proposed to write the history of its rise and progress from the first settlement or lease from the Indians and to illustrate it by maps. Making Knoxville his headquarters, he eagerly sought all data in the way of history and geography.‡ The arrival of Col. Tatham was

---

†Dr. James Park, Centennial Address, 17.
*Gazette. March 23, 1793.
‡Gazette. November 3, 1793.

heralded by Roulstone with his accustomed enterprise and enthusiasm. The editor said: "Col. Tatham, we are happy to say, has arrived with a large amount of geographical materials and fixed his office in this town. This gentleman has been at considerable pains and expense to perfect a map of the southern states, which is now far advanced, and will be shortly completed. This work is fully descriptive of the country, and very neatly executed. Col. Tatham has also engaged, under the patronage of his excellency Governor Blount, to bring forward a map of the rising territory, for which purpose he is about surveying the rivers, roads, etc.

"We need not inform our fellow-citizens how much their prosperity will be enhanced by this careful work. It is therefore hoped that those who possess partial surveys or drawings of any part of the country will furnish them for the use of this undertaking, and that the respective surveyors and others, who possess personal information, will cheerfully contribute their aid."* If anything ever came of this highly commended venture, the muse of history has thrown the mantle of oblivion over it.

The tastes of the reading public are best indicated by the advertisements appearing from time to time in the *Gazette*. Samuel and Nathaniel Cowan offer for sale the following: Hervey's Meditations, Wilson's works, Marshall's works. Bibles, Testaments, spelling books, hymn books, primers, Philadelphia Harmony, Buchan's Family Physician. Titus Ogden advertised at his store on State street copies of Iredell's Revisal of the Laws of North Carolina and Martin's Justice. Roulstone & Co. offer for sale Toplady's Translation of Zanchi on Predestination.

No community is complete in equipment that does not have its physicians for the body as well as for the soul. Dr. James Cozby was the pioneer doctor of the vicinity of Knoxville, administering antidotes against disease and performing operations of surgery. About the middle of May, 1794, Dr. Thomas

---

*Gazette, March 23, 1793.

McCombs tenders his professional services to the people of Knoxville, bespeaking a share of their patronage and basing his claims upon the long studies and careful training he had enjoyed in the Atlantic states under eminent practitioners, and upon fidelity to his profession. He proposes to keep on hand a large assortment and supply of genuine medicine, as if there were adulterated medicines in those good old days.* In the summer of the same year Dr. Robert Johnston advertises, and only a few months afterwards calls for a settlement of bills and accounts.

With the seriousness and earnestness crowded into their lives, the first settlers were not without the means and occasions of amusement. Corn huskings, house raisings, log rollings, quiltings and dances made up largely the sports of the country people, while balls, receptions, Fourth of July celebrations and school exhibitions furnished those of the town. Mary Grainger Blount, the accomplished wife of the governor, was in all these the center of attraction, and her entertainments were the models after which others were patterned. The gay uniforms of young officers, the rich silks of young maidens, the flare of multitudinous lights from candelabra, and the soul-stirring music of fife, bugle, drum and violin throw a glamour of romance over the scene.

An account of the Fourth of July celebration in 1793 has been left, which offers a pleasing view of the festivities indulged in on that occasion. At two o'clock in the afternoon the federal troops under the command of Capt. Rickard paraded before the public and fired the federal salute. The handsome appearance of the company and the thorough execution of the evolutions made a great impression. At four o'clock the citizens of the town partook of an elegant banquet, after which toasts were drunk as follows:

1. The day. 2. The illustrious chief magistrate of the United States. 3. The Honorable Secretary of State. 4. The Honorable Secretary of War. 5. The Honorable Secretary of the

---

*Knoxville Gazette. May 8, 1794.

Treasury. 6. The Honorable Judges of the Supreme Court of the United States. 7. His Excellency William Blount. 8. The Honorable Secretary Smith. 9. The Honorable Judges of the Southwest Territory. 10. The Ministers of Spain and America, who have opened up the navigation of the Mississippi. 11. Gen. Wayne and his Army. 12. Piamingo and the Chickasaw Nation. 13. May the wisdom and humanity of the General Government soon put an end to the distresses of our fellow-citizens of the frontier. 14. The virtuous but unfortunate LaFayette, may he be restored to freedom and America. 15. The friends of freedom, who are this day assembled to celebrate the glorious epoch of our liberty. "In the evening Mr. Rickard's company were under arms; they were drawn up in a grove near the encampment, where they fired a *feu de joie,* which, from the darkness of the evening and the judicious manner in which the company was disposed, produced a most pleasing effect; after which there was a display of fireworks, from an elegant colonnade in front of Mr. Rickard's marque."*

Another favorite source of amusement was the exhibition given by the students, boys and girls, of Blount college. It must be recalled that this was long before the era of stump speaking and political campaigning, so that every gathering of the kind was a strong social bond and provided an excellent opportunity for social intercourse. An open space, in the rear of the barracks and included in its grounds, was the scene of festivities. From a platform, whose sounding board was one side of the building, the youthful declaimers, orators and composers, presented in formal phrase to the audience by Mr. Carrick, poured forth upon waiting ears rhythmic melodies, stirring eloquence, descriptive effusions and moral essays. The interspersing of booming cannon and martial music added to the enthusiasm of the occasion.† To appear creditably before his hearers was the crowning ambition of the young participant, while their applause and commendation made him the

---

*Knoxville Gazette, July 13, 1793.
†Dr. Humes, Semi-Centennial Address, 60.

hero of the hour, the pride of his home, and the joy of his master.

It would be misleading to leave the impression that there were no darker sides or pictures to this pioneer life. That there were miscreants and stirrers-up of strife, brawls and dissensions goes without saying. Some of these were inexcusable, some ludicrous. Like John Overton, founder of Memphis, James White was troubled with depredations upon his timber lands, and repeatedly warned the culprits with threats of prosecution. The following incident shows that advantage was taken sometimes when least expected, and that the dissentients aired their grievances through the public print. Capt. Parmenas Taylor, one of the legislative council, returning from a campaign with John Sevier, left his horse, suffering from foot evil, at the home of his friend, Capt. A. Bird. There the animal was left from October, 1793, to April following, when a board bill was presented to Taylor for $80, though the horse was valued at $100. Upon protest Bird abated $50, whereupon Taylor "submitted a statement to the candid public to judge of the *righteousness* of the charge."*

The murderous career of the Harpes, who plied their bloody vocation towards the end of the period under survey, forms as dark a picture as the annals of demoniacal fury and bloodthirsty malice unfold.

Glancing back over the trend of events from the beginnings of Knoxville to the time of Tennessee's admission to the Union, its growth and development, it will be seen, depended upon those factors which lie at the basis of national wealth and prosperity—a sturdy manhood and a courageous womanhood, flinching not in the presence of dangers and obstacles, but keeping in view one undeviating purpose, the redemption of the soil from barbarism and the dedication of effort to the upbuilding of a strong and enduring social fabric.

---

*Gazette. May 8, 1794.

South-western view of Knoxville.

The view shows the appearance of Knoxville, descending the hill on the old country road in front of the University. Part of Cumberland-street is seen on the left; Main-street on the right; the Cupola of the Court House in the central part; Hampden Sidney Academy on the extreme left; the Female Institute on the right.

From: *Our Whole Country: Or The Past and Present of the United States. Historical and Descriptive*, 1861. John W. Barber and Henry Howe.

CHAPTER IX.

MUNICIPAL AFFAIRS.

First White Settlement—Original Capital of Tennessee—Incorporated in 1815—Looking for Railroads—Gas Lights Introduced—Extension of Corporate Limits—First Steam Fire Engine—Market Established—Fire Department Created—Water Works—System of Sewers—Names of Mayors—Paving Streets and Building Bridges—List of Postmasters—Three Municipalities Consolidated.

IN 1790 North Carolina ceded to the national government, which cession was finally accepted, the territory which now composes the state of Tennessee. In May following congress passed a law for the government of the territory southwest of the River Ohio, which law or ordinance followed the general lines of the famous ordinance of 1787, with this difference that North Carolina made the cession conditional upon the non-passage of any law tending to emancipate the slaves, which doomed the great Southwest to suffer from negro slavery, and as one of its remote results brought on the war of 1861-65.

William Blount of North Carolina was appointed governor of the new territory and at once proceeded to his new home. The town of Knoxville was soon afterwards selected as the capital, where Governor Blount built a good house, which had a lawn in front. The two districts into which the territory was then divided were named Washington and Miro (Mero), John Sevier being appointed brigadier-general of the former, or Eastern district, and James Robertson of the latter or Western district.

Early in 1791 Governor Blount entered into a treaty with the Cherokee Indians or with their principal chiefs and hundreds of their principal warriors, meeting on the Holston, and there in consideration of an annuity of $1,000, afterwards increased to $1,500, these Cherokees surrendered all their claims to the various tracts of land for which they had claimed under former treaties. This treaty with the Cherokees in connection with a treaty made with the Creek Indians the previous year, extinguished the Indian title to all the lands in Tennessee, with the exception to some lands in the western part of the state, still held by the Chickasaws, and thus the whole of East Tennessee came into possession of the whites.

One of the taverns of those early days in Knoxville advertised its rates as follows: One shilling for breakfast, one shilling for supper, and one shilling and sixpence for dinner. Board and lodging by the week was two dollars, and board alone, nine shillings.

White's Fort, as this place was called before it was named Knoxville, was the center of the settlement here. The treaty ground was at the foot of Water street. Knoxville was laid off in February, 1792, by Col. James White, the town consisting of the necessary streets and sixteen squares, four squares each way, and each square containing four lots. These sixteen squares were bounded by the following streets, as they are to-day: Church street on the north, Front street along the Holston river on the south; Crooked or Walnut street on the west, and Water street running along First creek on the east. A portion of the lots within these boundaries was sold in 1791, and after the laying off of the town in 1792 small buildings were erected, and lots were designated by the proprietor for county purposes. Temporary buildings for a court house and jail were erected, the court house being on the lot adjoining and west of the residence of S. R. Rogers. The jail was constructed of logs one foot square laid down close together, and the floor and loft were of similar materials. It was inclosed with long palisades driven deeply into the ground and sharpened at the top. The building was about sixteen feet square and stood near the spot formerly occupied by the Bank of East Tennessee at the corner of Gay and Main streets.

Barracks were erected and extended from Gay to Prince street and embraced the entire front of that square on Main

From *Frank Leslie's Illustrated Newspaper*, March 12, 1881

TENNESSEE.—THE CITY OF KNOXVILLE, THE GREAT IRON CENTRE, AS SEEN FROM THE UNIVERSITY GROUNDS.—FROM A SKETCH BY WALTER GOATER.

street. This building was made of logs notched closely together, and though an extensive was not an expensive structure. Being constructed as it was it was secure as a defense against small arms. The second story projected two feet beyond the first on every side, so as to prevent the application of fire in case of a siege. Portholes were left in both stories at suitable distances, and the entire area around the building was cleared of trees as far as a rifle would carry a ball, not even a stump being left large enough to protect the body of an enemy. In 1793 the first government troops were stationed in Knoxville. The barracks referred to above stood where now the court house stands.

The first lots improved were those nearest the river in the southeast corner of the town, but it was not until 1794 that the trees were cut down from the lots afterward owned by Capt. Crozier east of Gay and north of Cumberland street. Crozier's corner was then considered out of town. The cabin of Gov. Blount was on the knoll between the university and the river. Afterward a more suitable residence location was selected by him, on the lot afterward owned by Judge Boyd. The mansion stood near the center of the lot, the grounds being quite extensively improved. The governor's office was immediately between his own residence and Chisolm's tavern, the pioneer tavern of the place. Col. McClung's clerk's office was on the corner afterward known as Craighead's. Nathaniel Cowan's house was on the corner of Water and River streets. Stone's tavern was on the property known as Park's corner, and Joseph Greer resided on the lot afterward owned by S. R. Rogers.

The approach to Knoxville was at first along the deep hollow or ravine which reached Cumberland street before its junction with Main, in front of where stood the residence of Major Swan.

When the legislature adjourned in 1794 the two houses concurred in a resolution allowing James White five dollars for the use of the court house during the session of the assembly. The following quotation is from Ramsey, pages 638-9: "Among other acts of a local character (passed at the session of October, 1795), was one for establishing Knoxville. It was at that time the seat of the territorial government, and so continued to be during the existence of that organization. It became the seat of government of the state of Tennessee and so continued to be for many years after. Kingston, Murfreesborough and Nashville were its successors for several years, when in 1817 Knoxville again became the seat of government, but for the last time. The sudden flood of emigration toward the West had carried with it the center of population beyond the Cumberland mountains, and with it the seat of government. The scepter had departed from her; but time and change and progress cannot deprive her of her ancient honors, nor make her less venerable for the proud associations that cluster around her early history. Here Squollecuttah, Kunokeskie, Nemtooyah, Chuquilatague, Enolchi, Talohtuski and other chieftains of the Cherokee nation met Governor Blount for council, smoked the pipe of peace and formed the treaty of Holston; here the pious White was joined in the wilderness, lived his life in patriarchal simplicity and unostentatious usefulness; here died the founder of Knoxville and his memory is here embalmed in the affectionate remembrance of a succeeding generation. Here the infant government of the territory was cradled and afterward in its youth was nurtured by the paternal care of Blount, Anderson and Campbell. Here, too, the sages and patriots of 1794 met and deliberated and made laws. Here, too, was born the infant Hercules, since become the giant Tennessee. Tennessee looks back to Knoxville and recognizes her as the home of her youth and the fond center of her heart's recollections."

On November 28, 1795, Governor Blount certified to the legislature a schedule of the inhabitants of the territory, the enumeration having been taken with a view of ascertaining whether there were people enough within the territory for the formation of a state. Knox county in that schedule is credited

KNOXVILLE, TENNESSEE
And its surroundings
To accompany the article, "The Industrial South," in the May 7, 1887 issue of "Harper's Weekly"
Drawn by Charles Graham

with inhabitants as follows: Free white males sixteen years and upward, including heads of families, 2,721; free white males under sixteen, 2,723; free white females, including heads of families, 3,664; all other free persons, 100; slaves, 2,365; total number of inhabitants, 11,573; voting for the formation of a state government, 1,100; against it, 128.

On the same day the governor issued a proclamation providing for elections to be held in each county, at which five delegates to a constitutional convention were to be elected from each of the eleven counties of the state, to convene at Knoxville January 11, 1796. The delegates from Knox county were William Blount, James White, Charles McClung, John Adair, and John Crawford. The session began next day with prayer by the Rev. Mr. Carrick, and on the committee to draft the constitution were William Blount and Charles McClung, the latter being chairman of the committee. The draft of the constitution was read at the secretary's table January 27, and passed unanimously February 6, 1796. This year Knoxville contained forty houses and a population of 1,200. The next year the place was selected as the county seat.

Knoxville remained the capital of the state until 1811, and was again for a short time the capital in 1817, in which year the last session of the legislature was held within its limits. In the early days of its history, Knoxville was the home of many of the prominent men of the young state, such as William Blount, James White, John Sevier, Andrew Jackson and Davy Crockett. To the pioneers of the state this city was the distributing point for all kinds of goods and supplies, and it has since remained the recognized center of trade for not only the greater part of East Tennessee, but also for territory beyond the limits of the state, and it is now also the educational and religious center of a territory far larger than East Tennessee.

"The original block house was situated on the square on which the present court house stands, but a little further to the north. The second story overhung the first, and there were projecting abutments at each corner.

"It was in the second story of this block house that the first legislature met while Knoxville was the capital of the territory. The senate met in the upper story of a log house, afterward weatherboarded, belonging to Charles McClung, and standing immediately south of the old Webb brick house on the corner of Water and Cumberland streets. Water street having since borne the name of Crozier street and now Central avenue. This old house of Mr. Webb's was the first brick house built in Tennessee, and the pioneers had much amusement in witnessing the efforts to make a house out of 'daubs of mud.' The second brick structure in Tennessee was the house used by Joseph L. King as a dining room immediately beneath the present opera house. The next brick house in Knoxville was built by James Park, and is now the residence of Judge Temple. On this house was employed William Morgan, of Masonic notoriety, Morgan being discharged because of alleged unsatisfactory work. He then went to Madisonville, where he published his original exposition of Masonry, but later went to New York state and ultimately disappeared, some say in the waters of Lake Ontario.

"The first United States troops that came to Knoxville were under the command of Lieut. Edmund P. Gaines of the United States army, and camped at Cantonment Springs, a few miles east of Knoxville, where Dr. Fayette Rogers had some years ago a fish hatching establishment. Lieut. Gaines married Barbara Blount, the red-headed daughter of Governor Blount."*

On October 17, 1797, the legislature passed an act for the regulation of Knoxville, and John Adair, Paul Cunningham and George McNutt were elected commissioners. These same commissioners had been in their respective offices for several years, and were in all probability the first commissioners of the town. On August 1, 1794, they leased to Samuel Cowan a piece of land "lying and being as follows: adjoining Water street and exactly opposite lot No. 1 and lot No. 16, between

---

* W. A. Henderson.

them and the river, the property of said commissioners, given to them by James White, agreeable to a copy of an obligation inserted in the 4th number of the Knoxville Gazette, December 17, 1791, and leased for ninety years from August 1, 1794, for and in consideration of one cent to said commissioners in hand paid, and to their successors yearly every year on the first day of January each year throughout the entire period of ninety years."

This land or lot lay on the side of the hill and was bounded as follows: "Beginning at a cedar post, and running thence south 35 degrees east six and a half poles to a locust stake; thence south 55 degrees west fourteen poles to a locust stake; thence north 35 degrees west six and a half poles to a locust stake, and thence north 55 degrees east to the beginning."

The curious minute is then recorded in the council proceedings that "The lease says 93 roods, as well as the plat, instead of 2 roods and 13 poles, an error of 22 acres, 2 roods and 27 poles." As it is clear that the plat of ground leased, being 6½ rods one way and 14 rods the other, contains just 91 roods, or square rods, or 11 square rods more than half an acre; how the error above mentioned, of 22 acres, 2 roods and 27 poles, was made would seem extremely difficult of explanation.

Under an act of the legislature passed October 29, 1801, the following persons were appointed commissioners of the town, the appointment being made January 2, 1802: Jenkins Whiteside, Pleasant M. Miller, John Crozier, Francis May and Patrick Campbell. On January 4, all being present except Mr. Whiteside, they were sworn into office by Robert Craighead, justice of the peace for Knox county. Pleasant M. Miller was chosen chairman and George Roulstone, clerk. In 1803 town lots were taxed $2 each, and parts of lots in proportion. Each white poll was taxed seventy-five cents and each black poll $1.50.

In 1809 the Knoxville water works were incorporated and

pure spring water from McCampbell's springs was brought to the city by means of logs bored through the center and laid along Tazewell pike.

On October 27, 1815, an act was passed by the legislature incorporating the inhabitants of the town of Knoxville, and on January 13, 1816, the first meeting of the board of aldermen was held in the court house of the county. The members of this first board under this act were Thomas Emmerson, Thomas McCorry, Rufus Morgan, James Park, Thomas Humes, James Dardis and John M. Cullen. James Park, being a justice of the peace, swore in the other members, and then James Dardis swore in Mr. Park. Thomas Emmerson was elected mayor; Anderson Hutchinson, recorder, and David Nelson, high constable, and John M. Cullen was appointed treasurer. William Park, John Crozier and Calvin Morgan were appointed assessors, and the tax on real property was fixed at one-fourth of one per cent. Each white and slave poll was taxed $1; retail merchants were required to pay $5; retail licenses were $5; tippling shops had to pay $5 and billiard tables $20.

On February 20, 1816, Rufus Morgan, James Dardis and Thomas Humes were appointed to contract for and superintend the erection of a market house, which was to be 26 feet long and 18 feet wide. This market house was finished in the following December, and Thursdays and Saturdays were designated as market days. This market house stood on what was then called Market street, now Main street, midway between Prince and Walnut streets, the latter being then known as Crooked street. The house stood until 1823, when it was sold and removed.

In June, 1817, $340 was appropriated for the improvement of the streets; $120 to be expended on Cumberland street, $80 on State street, $60 on Water street, and the rest on other less important streets. In February, 1822, a fire company was organized with Calvin Morgan as captain and John Boyd, Carey Thatcher, David Campbell and William Park, lieutenants. An ordinance passed at this time required every owner of a dwelling, office or store to provide a leather bucket. At the next meeting Thomas Aiken and James Hickey were appointed night watchmen, whose duty it was made to patrol the streets and to call the hour and the state of the weather at the end of each hour.

In 1826 a systematic effort was made for the first time to improve the streets of Knoxville. All free inhabitants and slaves of the description subject by the laws of Tennessee to work on the public roads (except students in East Tennessee university) were required to work on the streets four days during each year, or pay seventy-five cents forfeiture for each day's failure. The city was at this time divided into three wards; the first ward being that portion of the city east of State street and extending north to the boundary street of the town, which is now Clinch street; the second ward included that portion of the town lying between the first ward and Prince street, extending north to College street, and the third ward embraced the remainder of the town west of the second ward. Overseers of the streets for each ward were appointed, their duties being the same as those of overseers of highways. An ad valorem tax on real estate was levied and the moneys thus raised on any street were to be expended on that particular street; moneys raised on corner lots to be expended equally on the contiguous streets. Street commissioners were appointed to disburse the moneys appropriated for the respective streets. The property owners on Main street petitioned the board of aldermen to double their taxes for street improvement!

In January, 1839, the citizens of Knoxville for the first time elected their mayor, that officer having previously been chosen by the aldermen from their own number. At this election W. B. A. Ramsey was elected, receiving forty-nine votes to forty-eight cast for James Park.

About this time it was thought that Prince street would be the principal thoroughfare of the city, and that State street would be a very important one; but by 1852 Gay street had captured about three-fourths of the trade, and it was then determined to permanently improve this street.

In 1837 and 1838 the subject of water works occupied a great deal of attention in the board of mayor and aldermen. Messrs. Oldham and Moseley offered the site of their factory for a site for such works for $1,500, the board offering the bonds of the city for $1,000 bearing interest, and the bonds then held by Mr. Kennedy as they stood. In March, 1838, correspondence was opened with Albert Stein looking to his engagement as engineer to superintend the erection of the contemplated works, and he was thus engaged. On November 24 the proposition of Mr. Kennedy and Mr. Morgan was accepted, and the mayor ordered to have the premises surveyed, and was authorized to execute the bonds of the city for the payment to Mr. Kennedy, to the amount of $6,500, due six months after date, and to execute a bond of the city for $1,000 to Calvin Morgan, payable twelve months after date, and also an obligation to furnish a hydrant within fifty feet of the reservoir to be used by Mr. Morgan exclusively for domestic purposes, in payment for a piece of land two hundred feet square, for a site for the proposed reservoir. December 31 Capt. S. S. Thatcher was appointed to superintend the removal of Mr. Kennedy's dams on First creek. On January 26, 1839, sealed proposals were called for for furnishing 160 tons of cast iron pipe for the water works. On March 30, 1839, the mayor was authorized to execute the bonds of the corporation for $6,500 to the trustees of the East Tennessee college to run fifteen years, with interest payable semi-annually, for the purpose of taking up the bonds previously issued to Mr. Kennedy in payment for a site for the water works.

In the early days, when Knoxville had no fire engine, the method of extinguishing fires was exceedingly primitive, and interesting to the present age. The fires were put out as best the people could manage with buckets and single-handed means. About 1821 every head of a family in town was required to procure a leathern bucket, holding two gallons, which was so prepared as to be water-tight, and afterward each family was required to own two such buckets. In 1822 the entire male population between the ages of fifteen and fifty was organized into one grand fire company, with suitable officers. The first fire engine brought to town was very small, and had no hose, but had a nozzle about eight feet long. Through this nozzle the water was thrown up from a reservoir, which the owners of the buckets had to keep full. When an alarm of fire was given every owner of a bucket rushed to the scene, together with the women and children of his family, and the men formed themselves in a line on one side of the streets from the creek to the fire, the women and children forming another line on the other side of the street. Buckets full of water were then passed up from the creek on the side lined up with men and down the other side to the creek through the hands of the women and children. This old engine thus supplied with water lasted until the war, when it was destroyed together with many other things and institutions peculiar to this section of the country. Two hand fire engines were purchased in the year 1859, and volunteer fire companies were organized.

On January 13, 1846, an ordinance was passed providing for the election of a tax collector and treasurer, whose duty it should be to collect the taxes due to the corporation and to disburse the funds that might be in the treasury, and that said tax collector and treasurer should also act as recorder, and that for his services as recorder he should receive $20. On the same day Hiram Barry was elected tax collector, but Mr. Barry resigned on the 27th of the same month, David A. Deaderick being elected in his place. It was also ordained at this time that license to sell spirituous or vinous liquors within the corporation should be the same sum that was then payable to the state, as per the act of January 23, 1846.

May 13, 1846, the recorder was ordered to make out a list of property within the corporation subject to pay tax to the state, and that an ad valorem tax of one-half of one per cent upon all real property be levied, and that the tax on each free poll should be $1 and that licenses be issued to merchants and others upon their payment of the taxes imposed by ordinance of April 14, 1838.

July 16, 1846, the mayor of the town and I. P. N. Craighead were appointed a committee to secure the construction of a suitable house for the fire engine.

In 1850 it became necessary to exercise control over market wagons coming into town from the country, and an ordinance was therefore passed requiring the town constable to arrange these wagons on the west side of Gay street, extending from the corner of Main as far west as the wagons thus arranged would extend.

The board of health for 1850 was appointed March 22, as follows: William J. Baker, B. R. Strong, John W. Paxton, William Palmer, J. M. Welcker, George McFarlane and R. D. Jourolmon. On April 19 the board required all persons who had not been vaccinated to be vaccinated.

July 5, 1850, the mayor and the board of aldermen passed a resolution to the effect that the recorder call the citizens of each ward together in a meeting at the courthouse in order that another effort might be made to organize a fire company in the town, and on the 10th of the same month it was ordained that in case of the failure to raise sufficient means by taxation to complete the improvements on the streets then in progress, bonds of the corporation of the denomination of $500, payable in twenty-five years, be issued to the extent that such improvements might require, provided that not more than $10,000 in the aggregate should be issued, and that the bonds issued should bear interest at the rate of 6 per cent per annum.

August 7, 1850, the people were notified that on the 17th of that month an election would be held for the purpose of ascertaining whether the mayor and the board of aldermen should go into the erection of waterworks for the town.

October 3, 1850, the engineer of the city was instructed to ascertain by survey the corporation boundaries, beginning at the junction of Main street with Second creek, and ending at the north boundary of said corporation, and also to ascertain whether Mrs. J. H. Kennedy's kitchen was within the limits of the corporation. On the 5th of that month the engineer, Albert Miller Lea, reported that in accordance with the above resolution he had examined the limits of the corporation on the southwest and northwest, and had to report: 1. That all the houses along and near Second creek from the bridge on Main street to the head of Bosworth's dam, were clearly within the limits of the city. 2. That the northwestern line of the city, assuming the width of the street on the northwest side of the Second Presbyterian church lot at the minimum width of even thirty-three feet, runs near the mouth of the ravine which passes through what is called "William's Grove," passes very near to the front wall of the residence of the Rev. Mr. Myers, cutting off his front yard, and thence crossing the field of Calvin Morgan, cuts Gay street near the south edge of a clump of plum trees, and passing on leaves off G. M. Hazen's lot to the south, and passes through an apple tree some thirty feet to the north of the extreme northern corner of the kitchen belonging to the residence of Mrs. Jane H. Kennedy, and strikes Water street near an oak which is said to be the corner of a lot belonging to the corporation.

On February 21, 1851, the mayor and board of aldermen passed the following preambles and resolution:

"Whereas, The East Tennessee and Virginia railroad and the East Tennessee and Georgia railroad are each under contract for a considerable portion of their respective lines and at no distant day will be united at Knoxville, thereby affording one great line of railroad from the northeast to the southwest, and

"Whereas, It is desirable that the precise localities of their respective depots at Knoxville be fixed upon and known at as early a day as may be, therefore

"Resolved, by the mayor and aldermen of the city of Knoxville, that the respective presidents of said railroads be and they are hereby requested to take the necessary measures to fix and establish permanently and definitely the locations of their said depots at Knoxville at as early a day as they may deem practicable."

Following up this question of the railroads coming into Knoxville it will be interesting to note the course of the mayor and board of aldermen and the people themselves with reference to the issue of bonds, to aid in the construction of the roads. On March 24, 1852, a resolution was adopted to the effect that a committee of two be appointed to inquire whether or not it would be expedient to submit to the voters within the corporation a proposition made on the part of the East Tennessee and Virginia Railroad company to the corporate authorities of the town to subscribe for stock in said railroad company, and to issue coupon bonds in payment of said stock, etc. Aldermen Rodgers and Coffin were appointed the committee.

On April 3 a town meeting was held to consider the question of subscribing to the capital stock of the aforesaid company it was determined to hold an election at the court house to determine the question, $50,000 worth of bonds being the amount under consideration, and at this election there were cast in all 85 votes, of which 59 were for the bond issue and 26 against it. These bonds were to run not less than thirty nor more than forty years, and the railroad company was to pay the interest on them semi-annually until the completion of the road, and if on the completion of the road the company had not used the bonds it was to have the privilege of returning those unused. These conditions were not satisfactory to the company, and it therefore declined to accept the bonds. The corporation thereupon considered itself released from any further obligation with reference to the bonds.

On March 26, 1853, an election was held for the purpose of ascertaining the sense of the voters upon the proposition to subscribe $50,000 to the bonds of the Knoxville and Lexington railroad company, the result being that ninety-two out of ninety-three votes were cast in favor of the bonds. This railroad is now the Knoxville and Ohio. On October 4, 1856, it was voted to increase the amount taken in the stock of this company to $100,000. This increase was effected by diverting the amount, $50,000, from the amount voted on April 26, previous, namely, $100,000, toward or for the erection of waterworks for the city. The vote on April 26 was 58 in favor of the waterworks bonds, and on October 4, on the diversion of $50,000 to the railroad, was 144 in favor and 26 against. This railroad was then called the Knoxville and Kentucky railroad.

On January 16, 1852, it was resolved by the mayor and board of aldermen that a number of negro slaves, not to exceed fifteen, should be hired to work on the streets of the town until December 25, next ensuing, on the conditions that the white employer of the slaves should clothe, board and lodge them, pay their doctors' bills and take care of them in sickness, losing the time any slave should be sick.

On February 20, 1852, it was resolved by the mayor and board of aldermen that if a slave should within the limits of the town empty any slop or other pot liquor upon the guttering or upon the streets of said town, or should empty such slop or other filth so that the same should run into the gutter or streets, such slave should for every such offense receive not less than five nor more than fifteen stripes on his or her back by one of the town constables, unless the white person in whose employ such slave might be should pay a forfeit of one dollar in lieu of said stripes.

In 1851 an ordinance was passed requiring the sidewalks on Main and Gay streets to be eleven feet wide, while those on other streets were required to be four and a half feet wide. In 1852 Gay street had become the principal street of the town and it was resolved that this street should be macadamized and permanently improved as soon as Main street was completed to the east side of Gay street, and beginning on the south side of Main street, extending the permanent improvement on Gay street at least as far as the north side of Cumberland street, a suitable number of hands to be kept employed in the extension of the Main street improvement to its western terminus.

In 1853 William G. Swan and Joseph A. Mabry presented to the town the lot on Market square on which the market house now stands, on the condition that the city would erect a suitable market house by the first of January, 1854. This liberal proposition was accepted and a contract made with Newman & Maxwell to build the house. This new market house was opened for the first time on January 31 (Tuesday), 1854. Upon the institution of this market house the city council passed an ordinance inflicting a fine of $5 in case any two or more persons should combine to raise the price of any article in the market, or to prevent any article being sold below any particular price.

In 1853-54 Gay and Prince streets were paved with river rock, or boulders, or, in other words, with cobblestones, and these cobblestones are now the foundation upon which rests the macadam afterward placed upon Gay street.

July 2, 1852, upon receipt of the tidings that Henry Clay was dead, a full meeting of citizens responded to the call of the mayor, George M. White, of which meeting Hon. William B. Reese was chairman. A committee of nine was appointed, consisting of Col. John H. Crozier, Samuel B. Boyd, George M. White, John M. Welcker, William J. Baker, Dr. F. A. Ramsey, W. G. McAdoo, W. C. Kain, and James W. Campbell, which committee reported a series of resolutions expressive of the sense of the meeting upon the loss of so great a man. Following is a portion of the language used: "As the melancholy tidings have sped from point to point, from man to man, that Henry Clay is dead, every heart has bowed in sadness at the thought. All have ceased for a while in the toils and cares of life, to pay a moment's adoration to the virtues of the dead; the hammer of the artisan, the shuttle of the weaver, the axe of the woodsman, have stopped suddenly in their course, paying instinctive homage to the American statesman. A nation mourns the loss of its greatest orator, and one of its most profound and sagacious statesmen and purest patriots. Let the people's tears bedew his grave; a nation's affection cherish his memory. The name and fame of Henry Clay belongs now, not to parties of the day, but to the memory of his country; they are blazoned on its proudest pages and are linked with the most important epochs of his country's greatness and renown."

On February 9, 1854, it was resolved that State street be opened to the northern boundary of the corporation.

February 16, William M. Churchwell and William G. Swan were granted the exclusive right to light the city with gas and supply it with water or either, the gas works being required to be in operation within eighteen months, the mayor and aldermen of Knoxville as a corporate body to be supplied with as much gas as they might require at no greater price per cubic foot than was then being paid by the city of Nashville. On April 1 it was ordained that when the above-named gentlemen had expended twenty per cent of the cost of the waterworks the city would issue ten per cent of the cost in bonds, and so on, until the works were completed, the parties erecting the waterworks to mortgage them to the city and after their completion these parties should invest ten per cent of the profits therefrom in the bonds of the city or of the county or state, to be used as a sinking fund for the payment of the bonds issued to them on the construction of the works.

On the 19th of April, 1855, the board of health called the attention of the authorities to the Flag Pond on the northern limits of the city as a fruitful source of disease, suggesting that it be drained and its marshy bed be covered over with a stratum of clay two feet thick; that the drain leading from Gay street down Cumberland street east to First creek be abated, and that the drain from the Coleman House be also abated as a nuisance.

On July 27, 1855, a most curious regulation of the liquor traffic was adopted, it being deemed necessary to the good order and quiet of the town to require the sale of spirituous and vinous liquors to be regulated by the recorder, he being given authority to close all saloons whenever he might deem it necessary to so close them, notice being given to each saloon-keeper in writing by the marshals of the town. The recorder was authorized to keep the saloons closed so long as he might deem it necessary. This same regulation was again adopted in 1858.

The corporate limits of the city have been several times extended. In 1856 they were extended and there were then four wards. In 1858 there were five wards, and in 1868 East Knoxville, which had previously existed as a separate corporation, was taken in.

On February 19, 1859, two fire engines were purchased from William Wilson of Baltimore for $1,200 each, these engines reaching the city about March 18. On January 7, 1860, an election was held for mayor of the city at large, and two aldermen from each of the five wards, resulting in the election of James C. Luttrell as mayor. The vote cast in the five wards for Mr. Luttrell was 155, and for the other two candidates, 126.

The rates of taxation for the last two years before the breaking out of the war of the rebellion, 1859 and 1860, as established by the board of aldermen, were as follows: On each $100 worth of real estate, or less, $1; on persons engaged in speculating and dealing in slaves, by purchase or sale, for the license, $20, and at the end of the year fifteen cents on each $100 in excess of an aggregate capital of $13,333.33, provided that the entire tax should not exceed $100; wholesale and retail merchants paid the same for license and the same aggregate amount of tax, as slave dealers; and also commission merchants; receiving and forwarding merchants paid a license fee of $25; auctioneers paid a license of $20, and a tax of fifteen cents on each $100 worth of goods sold, but not to exceed $100; confectioners paid a license of $20 and their tax was the same as that of wholesale and retail merchants; brokers paid a license of $200; note-shavers paid a license of $30; the owner of a four horse omnibus paid $50; of a two horse omnibus, $25; of a four horse hack, $30; of a three horse hack, $25; of a two horse hack, $20; theater license was $50 per year, and every keeper of a Jenny Lind table or billiard table paid $50 per year. Other kinds of licenses were imposed, but these will serve to indicate the range of prices.

On April 3, 1860, it was ordered that two large cisterns be built, one at the corner of Gay and Cumberland streets and the other at the corner of Gay and Main streets.

On May 11, 1860, $25,000 of the $50,000 subscribed to the Knoxville and Kentucky railroad was paid over to the proper officers of that company, security being taken for the proper disbursement of the money for the construction of the road. On June 21, 1861, the remaining $25,000 was paid over to the president of the company, Joseph A. Mabry.

April 12, 1861, Williamsburg was opened up to travel and traffic, the boundaries of this portion of Knoxville being West Boundary street and Second creek, and Main street and the Tennessee river.

April 13, 1866, a committee consisting of Aldermen Powell, Hudiburg and Newman was appointed to confer with a similar committee appointed by the county court at its last previous quarterly session, with reference to the establishment of a workhouse, for the joint use of the city and county. This committee reported on the 28th of September, 1866, that the joint committee had unanimously decided in favor of the workhouse, but that they had not agreed upon who should control the labor of the convicts. A committee was therefore appointed by the mayor to act for six months in conjunction with a similar committee to be appointed by the county, the joint committee to have control of the labor of convicts for that length of time. The committee on the part of the city consisted of Messrs. Hudiburg, Wilson and Newman.

The proceedings of the mayor and board of aldermen with reference to the purchase of the first steam fire engine ever bought by the city are interesting. On September 27, 1867, a number of citizens agreed in writing to take a certain amount of scrip of the city of Knoxville, payable July 1, 1868, and drawing six per cent interest, and receivable for taxes for the year 1868, the money to be used by the city in the purchase of a steam fire engine, twelve hundred feet of hose and a hose carriage, the entire amount to be raised to be $8,250, the scrip to be delivered December 1, 1867. The engine had already been purchased by the city council, provided the necessary funds could be raised by the issue of scrip, the company furnishing the engine to take half its pay in scrip, and the citizens to take the other half. Following are the names of the firms and individuals that subscribed for the city scrip. Cowan, McClung & Co., $1,000; Barry & McDaniel, $500; John S. Van Gilder, $100; Peter Kern, $150; C. M. McGhee, $500; William Rule, $100; Coffin, Wilson & Martin, $200; W. W. Woodruff, $100; Henry Ault, $100; James R. Cocke, $100; Rayl & Boyd, $300; M. D. Bearden, $100; Staub & Co., $400; Victor Burger & Son, $100; George M. White, $200; John R. Beaman, $200, and George M. Beaman, $200; total amount, $4,250.

November 8, 1866, Alderman Kennedy suggested that a name should be selected for this new steam fire engine before it left the factory of Silsby & Co., and the name selected be engraved upon it. This suggestion meeting with favor, the name "J. C. Luttrell" was chosen by the city council, and it was engraved on the engine, which arrived in Knoxville on or perhaps a day or two previous to January 10, 1868. Between this date and January 13 the engine was tested, found satisfactory, and on this latter date was paid for by the council.

On June 7, 1867, a committee was appointed, consisting of A. S. Hudiburg, S. B. Newman and L. C. Shepard, to draft a plan for a building to be erected at the north end of the market place that would answer for the meetings of the city council, recorder's office, etc. June 21 this committee reported that they had "pretty much agreed upon a plan for a building."

and they were then authorized to contract with some responsible person to erect it on the plan they had adopted. This building was erected during that and the succeeding year. It was a two-story brick, about forty feet square, and had suitable rooms in it for the purposes for which it was designed, and a room below for the fire engine.

The erection of a United States building was begun in 1869 under the superintendency of J. H. Holman, with A. B. Mullett as supervising architect and George W. Ross as disbursing agent. The building is entirely of marble, and though not large, is yet one of the most substantially constructed buildings anywhere to be found. It was completed in 1873 at a cost of $392,000. It is three stories high, the lower floor being occupied by the postoffice, the second floor by the office of the pension agent, district attorney and clerks of the circuit and district court, and the third by the courtroom and rooms for judges and juries.

On March 30, 1868, a committee appointed to assess taxable property for the year reported a very considerable increase over 1867, the increase in real estate being from $1,565,868 to $1,952,775. There were on the tax list 150 dogs and 147 pianos. On this same day the track of the East Tennessee and Virginia railroad was made the dividing line between the fourth and fifth wards.

January 4, 1869, an appropriation was made by the city council of $15,000 for the establishment of a library in the agricultural college, the first $5,000 to be paid when the college should be permanently established in Knoxville, and the remaining $10,000 in two equal annual payments immediately afterward. An attempt to secure the diversion of this donation from the library to general purposes did not succeed.

January 9, 1869, the legal debts of East Knoxville were adopted by the city of Knoxville and on November 19 following the streets and alleys then laid out through what was called the McMullin property were adopted.

March 25, 1870, the council ordained that inasmuch as the

108 HISTORY OF KNOXVILLE, TENNESSEE.

floating debt of the city amounted to about $40,000, and had become troublesome, the bonds of the city should be issued to the amount of $13,300 and that scrip should be issued to the amount of $20,000, payable in one, two, three, four and five years, the bonds and scrip each to bear six per cent interest. On the same day the city was divided into eight wards, as follows:

First Ward.—Beginning at the southeast corner of Gay and Cumberland streets, thence with Cumberland street and Rutledge pike to the corporation line; thence with the corporation to the river; thence with the river to where the line of Gay street extended would strike it, and thence with Gay street to the place of beginning.

Second Ward.—Beginning at the southwest corner of Gay and Cumberland streets; thence with Cumberland street to Second creek; thence with Second creek to Holston river; thence with Holston river to where the line of Gay street extended would strike it, and thence with Gay street to the beginning.

Third Ward.—Beginning at the northeast corner of Gay and Cumberland streets; thence up Gay street to Clinch street; thence with Clinch street to the corporation line; thence with said corporation line to Rutledge pike; and thence with Clinch street to the beginning.

Fourth Ward.—Beginning at the northwest corner of Gay and Cumberland streets; thence up Gay to Clinch street; thence with Clinch street to Second creek; thence with Second creek to Cumberland street; and thence with Cumberland street to the beginning.

Fifth Ward.—Beginning at the northeast corner of Gay and Clinch streets; thence with Gay street to Vine and Mabry street to the corporation line; thence with the corporation line to Clinch street; and thence with Clinch street to the beginning.

Sixth Ward.—Beginning at the northeast corner of Gay and Clinch streets; thence on Gay street to Vine and Academy streets to the East Tennessee and Georgia railroad; thence with the railroad to Second creek; thence down Second creek to Clinch street, and thence with Clinch street to the beginning.

Seventh Ward.—Beginning at the northeast corner of Water and Mabry streets; thence with Water street to Crozier street; thence with Crozier street to the corporation line; thence with the corporation line to First creek; thence down First creek to the corporation line at the bend of First creek; thence with the corporation line to Mabry street, and thence with Mabry street to the beginning.

Eighth Ward.—Beginning at the northwest corner of Vine and Water streets; thence with Water to Crozier street; thence with Crozier street to the corporation line; thence with the corporation line to Second creek; thence with Second creek to the East Tennessee and Georgia railroad to Academy street; thence with Academy street to Vine street, and thence with Vine street to the beginning.

It was also ordained on the same day that there should be elected two aldermen from each ward.

April 3, 1870, Alderman Howell moved that the compensation which had been paid the aldermen for some years past be paid to them for 1870, this resolution or ordinance being adopted by the following vote: Lewis, Bearden, Shepard, McLemore, Glass, Sullivan, Howell and Payne, eight for it, and the following six against it: Atkin, Mitchell, Swan, McCampbell, Munson, and Stephenson.

On the 22d of the same month the mayor, John S. Van Gilder, in a somewhat elaborate message vetoed the ordinance upon the principle that the mayor and board of aldermen were dedicated to "retrenchment and reform," and to administer the affairs of the city without compensation, fear or favor, making the offices which they held offices of honor instead of profit, and that owing to the embarrassed condition of the treasury of the city they were to endeavor to serve the public faithfully and use every effort to improve the condition of the finances of the corporation. He said:

"At our first meeting it was unanimously agreed to cut off all perquisites of office and to let all fees go into the treasury, which has produced a good effect in a just observance of the law of equity and impartiality. In former times a public office was a place of honor as well as profit; but in later times they have become places of profit and speculation; hence the reckless extravagance of public funds, the utter disregard of the private rights of the tax-paying community. I find that by the records since the city was incorporated until the last three years no alderman was allowed compensation unless for extraordinary services rendered, and, as a chief principle, excepting large cities, where their entire time is necessary, is it customary for the office to be one of public trust and confidence. At a regular meeting in January, 16 members present, 2 absent, a tie vote was made, creating the casting vote upon me. I then decided no compensation. At the last meeting it was brought up for repeal. The two absent members being present, voted on each side, making the whole board a tie on the record; but by the absence of some without notice it was carried, and being a personal matter entirely of the members, justice requires this explanation on my part."

On April 23, 1838, an interesting ordinance was passed for regulating business matters on the Sabbath day. It was to the effect that no steamboat or other boat should load or unload at the wharves on the river; that wagons should not load or unload merchandise on the streets; that no person should disturb any religious congregation; that no person should keep open a grocery, confectionery, or other place of business; that no one should give away or sell spirituous liquors; that no one should cut any timber either with ax or saw, nor should any laborer or merchant exercise his ordinary functions on that day. But masters of steamboats might, in case of necessity, obtain permission from the mayor or any two aldermen to load or unload their boats. Any slave violating this ordinance was subject to a punishment of from five to twenty-five stripes on the back, unless his or her master, owner or overseer should promptly pay the fine, which might be imposed in any amount not to exceed fifty dollars.

On June 17, 1870, a petition signed by a number of the citizens of Knoxville was presented to the mayor and board of aldermen, asking that the above ordinance be so modified as to permit the selling of cakes, confectioneries, ice cream, soda water, fruits and tobacco, which petition was referred to a committee consisting of B. J. Stephenson and S. D. J. Lewis, for investigation and report, and they reported that "in their judgment it is a first-rate document, and one which every good citizen should cheerfully obey. We would not dot an 'i' nor cross a 't' in the law." This report was adopted by the board. But on July 15, 1870, an ordinance was adopted by the mayor and board of aldermen repealing a portion of the above so-called Sunday law, this repealing ordinance being to the effect that all laws prohibiting the delivery of ice and milk, or prohibiting butchers from conveying their meat to their stalls on Sunday for Monday morning's market, provided the same were done in a quiet and orderly manner, at reasonable hours, were repealed.

The fire department was created November 18, 1870, not that there had been no fire companies before that time, for there had been several companies that had rendered the people of the city excellent service. The advent of the first steam fire engine has already been referred to. By this ordinance of November 18, 1870, the entire fire department of the city was brought under one head and thus made more effective in case of large fires. By it the office of chief of the fire department was created, the chief being allowed two assistants, named first and second assistants. These three officers were to be elected annually by the mayor and aldermen, and they were to serve without compensation. The chief and his assistants were to be and to be recognized as the head of the fire department during the time of any fire, and the captains and foremen of any companies or hook and ladder companies should defer to the chief and his assistants; afterward no fire company was to consist of more than fifty persons, and the engineer of the steam fire engine was to be elected by the board of mayor and aldermen, and should continue in office during their pleasure.

On August 25, 1871, when the sale of the Knoxville and Kentucky railroad was imminent, the mayor and the members of the finance committee were appointed a committee to confer with the officials of Knox and Anderson counties, and if possible prevent the loss of the stock in said railroad being lost. The sale occurred at Nashville a short time afterward, and the mayor received the thanks of the board of aldermen for the prompt action he had taken, which resulted so favorably to the city.

On May 30, 1873, the board of mayor and aldermen ordained that bonds should be issued to the amount of $125,000 for the purpose of establishing a system of waterworks, provided the citizens at an election to be held should approve. This election came off on June 12, and resulted in a vote being cast in favor of the works of 205 and against them of 191.

Early in 1873 Mayor Rule caused the erection of a house in a retired spot outside the limits of the city, to be used as a smallpox hospital, and ordered the removal of all persons afflicted with that disease to be removed thereto, appointing Dr. Swan M. Burnett to take charge of the hospital. He also appointed a board of health, with Dr. F. K. Bailey as health officer.

On December 15, 1873, a proposition was made to the "United States" to unite in the construction of a sewer along Prince street from the custom house or government building down to the river, the sewer to be 14x21 inches in diameter, to be egg-shaped, and about 1,900 feet long, except that a sewer previously built by the city from the north side of Front street south to the wharf should be connected with the proposed sewer and made a part thereof, the city to pay $772 toward the construction of the new sewer. On the next day this proposition was accepted on the part of the United States by Gen. J. H. Holman, superintendent of construction.

On February 6, 1874, an ordinance provided for the election of a city physician, at an annual salary of $300, and on the same day the board elected Dr. A. B. Tadlock to that position. On March 6, 1874, an ordinance providing that the mayor should receive for his services $1,000 for the year 1874 was passed, which also provided that each alderman should receive $75 per annum. Dr. Tadlock resigned as city physician May 5, 1876, and was succeeded by Dr. S. B. Boyd, on the 19th of the same month. John M. Brooks was elected chief of the fire department February 19, 1875, and resigned that position January 23, 1876, being succeeded by William Coffman.

July 31, 1875, the board of mayor and aldermen took appropriate action regarding the death of Andrew Johnson, eulogizing him as a man of the people, as against being a partisan.

After repeated attempts to secure the construction of a bridge across the railroad tracks at the foot of Gay street, an effort was made in 1876 which was a success. Then the East Tennessee, Virginia and Georgia railroad company offered to pay $5,000 toward the construction of such a bridge, and a contract was made with the Louisville Bridge and Iron Co., on September 25, to build such a bridge as was needed for $13,030, the bridge to consist of four spans, each $42\frac{1}{2}$ feet, two spans, each 80 feet, and two spans $56\frac{1}{2}$ feet in length. On the west side was to be a foot-walk six feet in the clear, and the carriageway was to be twenty feet in the clear. The city set the masonry pedestals on which rest trusses and iron piers, and the entire structure was completed by January 1, 1877.

The proceedings of the board of mayor and aldermen in securing the construction of a reservoir and establishing a system of waterworks is of more than passing interest, hence some considerable space is devoted thereto. On April 11, 1879, a proposition was received by J. J. Fitzpatrick and W. B. McDonough to establish such a system in Knoxville, this proposition being submitted to a special committee of four aldermen and eight citizens, afterward, however, the mayor was added to the committee so as to make the number thirteen. The aldermen appointed on this committee were Scales, Allison, Lyon and Sullivan, and the private citizens, Samuel McKinney, Joseph Jaques, J. B. Hoxsie, John S. Van Gilder, W. W. Woodruff, E. J. Sanford, Charles J. McClung, and George W. Albers.

On June 6 this committee reported through Alderman Scales, chairman of a sub-committee, that the Tennessee river was a good, unfailing and healthful source of supply, all that was necessary being a reservoir of sufficient capacity to allow the water to settle after being pumped into it. Two sites were under consideration—Mabry hill and Fahnestock hill, the former being 132 feet above the junction of Gay and Clinch streets, and the latter 97 feet above said junction. Fahnestock hill, 300x220 feet, could be obtained together with a right of way to the river and a station on the river bank for $3,100, while Mabry hill, 300x100 feet, together with right of way and station for pumping station on the bluff, would cost about $8,000. Mabry hill was 263 feet above the Tennessee, while Fahnestock hill was only 228 feet above it. Mabry hill would allow the tapping of the river above White Spring branch, the other site below that branch, and it was thought that on the whole Mabry hill would effect a saving to the city through the greater effectiveness of the fire department because of the greater pressure it would give.

The result of the discussions and reflections on the whole subject was that the board of mayor and aldermen would, provided a two-thirds vote of the qualified voters would give their consent thereto at a special election to be held for the purpose, issue $75,000 in city bonds, for the purpose of constructing the works. This decision was arrived at on June 6, 1879, by a vote of eleven for the bonds to four against them, but even these four were in favor of the works, only preferring some other means of securing their erection. On the same day a standing committee on waterworks was appointed, consisting of Aldermen Scales, Sullivan, Allison and Lyon, and Citizens Col. A. Terry, Charles J. McClung and Peter Kern, and on the 20th of the same month a board of waterworks trustees consisting of five citizens was provided for and appointed to have full control of the erection of said works, the members of the committee being Peter Kern, Charles J. McClung, S. B. Boyd, Peter Staub and Adrian Terry. Afterward Mr. McClung and S. B. Boyd declined to serve, and their places were filled by the appointment of Samuel McKinney and John S. Van Gilder.

The election to determine the sense of the voters was held on June 28, 1879, resulting in a vote for the bonds of 387 and against them of 170, more than a two-thirds vote in the affirmative.

August 7 the board of waterworks trustees, named above, reported that they had made an agreement with Moses Lane of Milwaukee, and were awaiting his report on the comparative advantages of the two sites, Mabry hill and Fahnestock hill, before making a final selection of a site for the reservoir and route to the river, etc. Moses Lane soon afterward made an elaborate report, which it is not deemed necessary to present here in full, showing to the trustees all the elements of advantage possessed by the Fahnestock hill over the Mabry hill, and favored the construction of a reservoir on the former, together with a standpipe thirty feet above the water level in the reservoir thus constructed. The elevation of the two hills, according to Mr. Lane was: Mabry hill, 263 feet above the Tennessee at low water, and of Fahnestock hill, 228 feet, the difference in the height to which the water would have to be pumped if Mabry hill were selected tending largely to determine him in favor of the lower hill. Fahnestock hill was therefore unanimously selected by the board.

It had already been determined that the income from the waterworks should be divided into three parts—one part to be devoted to the running expenses of the works themselves; a second part to be devoted to paying the interest on the bonds, and the third part to be set aside as a sinking fund to pay off the bonds. On September 12, 1879, a waterworks sinking fund board of trustees was appointed, consisting of Peter Staub for three years, Peter Kern for two years, and H. B. Branner for one year. On September 26 John S. Van Gilder resigned from the construction trustees and was succeeded by H. B. Branner. And on this same day the committee reported that they had made a contract with Messrs. McDonough & Co. for the erection of the waterworks, the price to be paid being $64,000, either in money or bonds of the city.

But notwithstanding the making of this contract there was difficulty ahead not then foreseen. On April 9, 1880, Samuel McKinney, chairman of the waterworks commission, stated that in accordance with instructions received from the council the commissioners had employed eminent counsel in the persons of Judge George Andrews, Judge H. H. Ingersoll, and Judge J. B. Cook, the latter of Chattanooga, to pass upon the validity of the waterworks bonds, the issue of which had been provided for, and that these gentlemen had made an exhaustive investigation of the whole matter. The conclusion to which they had arrived was as follows:

"We are of the opinion that the statute under which the bonds are to be issued is valid under the constitution of the state, and that the two-thirds vote given for the issuance of the bonds is sufficient if the election had been held upon sufficient notice to authorize their issue. We think, however, that by reason of the failure to give the full notice of ten days as required by the statute, the election as actually held was void, and that the bonds would be void in the hands of any person taking them from the city with notice of that fact, and that while the bonds would be valid in the hands of an innocent purchaser without notice, any tax-payer might upon promptly filing a bill for that purpose, have the issuance of the bonds enjoined by the courts."

On June 3, 1881, it was ordered that the $75,000 worth of

bonds which the board had on hand, but which had not been filled out, were ordered burned, and they were afterward thus destroyed.

Captain John M. Brooks, a member of the waterworks commission, then reminded the council that his commission were without funds and without authority, and said he thought the people should have another opportunity of voting on the question. Alderman McCroskey thereupon offered a series of preambles and resolution to the effect that inasmuch as the preceding proceedings had failed because of their irregularity, therefore there should be issued $100,000 in bonds for the object sought, provided the people at an election held for the purpose, should approve, and April 24, 1880, was chosen as the day on which the people should again express their will and pleasure on the subject.

On February 13, 1880, a resolution was introduced to the effect that for the year 1880 the salary of the mayor should be $300, and that of each of the aldermen $50. This resolution was vetoed by the mayor, who was in favor of the mayor of the city and the councilmen serving without any compensation for that year. A resolution was almost immediately introduced by Alderman Atkin protesting against the vetoing of the resolution granting compensation, which was as follows:

"That it is the sense of this board of mayor and aldermen that the mayor of this city is devoid of the power to veto any of the proceedings of this council, and we hereby protest against the assumption of the power by H. B. Branner, mayor, and it is further resolved that the recorder is hereby required to obey the instructions of this board at its last meeting in reference to the payment of any bills or salaries at that meeting."

This resolution was declared by the mayor to be out of order, and upon an appeal from the mayor's decision, Aldermen Atkin, Burger, Boyd, Caldwell, Dickson, Irwin, Hudiburg, McAffry, McCroskey and Michaels voted in favor of the appeal, while Aldermen Allison, Hockenjos, McLemore,

Murphy, O'Connor and Sullivan voted nay. Not having received a two-thirds vote the appeal was lost.

On September 10 following this same matter came up again, and a resolution was adopted allowing the mayor $1,000 for the year and each alderman $75, no protest being made, except that four of the aldermen voted against the resolution, seven voting for it.

The subject of waterworks still occupied the attention of the people and of the board of mayor and aldermen, notwithstanding the bad luck and failures to which the cause had been doomed in the past, and on May 6, 1881, the mayor, Peter Staub, delivered an address to the council in which he stated that inasmuch as it was not desirable for the city to undertake the building of a system of waterworks, he thought the privilege of constructing such a system should be granted to some private company, and suggested that he be authorized to appoint a committee to receive bids and to report from time to time. A special committee was therefore authorized and appointed, consisting of Messrs. Nelson and McLemore, but Mr. McLemore, not wishing to serve, Alderman Brooks was appointed, the two members thus appointed to act in conjunction with the mayor; but at length, on June 20, the committee consisted of Peter Staub, the mayor, and Thomas A. R. Nelson and John M. Brooks. They reported bids from Charles E. Robinson of New York and from R. D. Woods & Co. of Philadelphia, the latter firm agreeing to erect waterworks according to the specifications of Moses Lane for $95,000. Then a proposition made by Charles E. Robinson and H. A. Church was read and an agreement made between these parties and the city attorney was approved by the board by a vote of 11 to 4, and the mayor and recorder were authorized to sign the contract by a vote of 13 to 2. Next, on October 1, 1881, still another contract was submitted by F. M. Lawrence of Red Bank, N. J., and William Runkle of New York, which the committee recommended for adoption, the citizen members of the committee, J. A. Rayl and J. W. Gaut, being satisfied with it, and thereupon the following resolution was adopted:

"Whereas, The special committee on waterworks have received a proposition from F. M. Lawrence and William Runkle; therefore be it resolved that the mayor and recorder be and they are hereby authorized to execute a contract as soon as the said contractors shall have signed the same."

Then on December 30, 1881, came a suggestion which resulted in the successful construction of a system of waterworks which had so long and so persistently been sought, this suggestion being in the form of an application to the board of mayor and aldermen by several of the citizens for a charter for the Knoxville Water Company, who stated that neither Mayor Staub nor any of the applicants, except Mr. Lawrence, the contractor, had a particle of interest financially in the matter. The mayor and the recorder were then required to sign the charter of this company and to affix the official seal of the corporation. The Knoxville Water Company, on July 1, 1882, gave bond in the sum of $25,000 to construct a system of waterworks in accordance with the plans and specifications of Moses Lane, to be completed within twelve months, this plan contemplating the use of eight and a half miles of pipes to weigh 1,221 tons, and the system to supply 2,000,000 gallons of water each twenty-four hours. The president of the Knoxville Water Company at that time was S. E. Cooke, and the secretary, A. Barton. The city agreed to pay at the rate of fifty dollars per year for each hydrant that it used.

August 8, 1884, a board of health was established by ordinance to consist of one lawyer, one commercial man and three physicians, regular graduates in medicine. The members were to be selected by the city council, and to serve one for one year, one for two years, one for three, one for four and one for five years, afterward one member to be appointed each year.

Among other things this board was required to keep an

accurate record of the births, including color, sex, date of birth, etc., and the same particulars in regard to deaths.

March 6, 1885, an ordinance was adopted establishing a paid fire department, which was to consist of one engineer, one stoker, one foreman, and two pipeman, who were to be elected immediately and afterward annually forever. The wages of these different members were then fixed as follows: Engineer, $75 per month; foreman, $50 per month; stoker, $40 per month, and pipemen, $40 each per month. D. Newman was elected engineer; William Newman, stoker, D. A. Smith, foreman, and Alexander Flennikin and John Moxley, pipemen.

January 26, 1886, it was ordained that in addition to the officers prescribed by the new charter there should be a chief of police, one first and one second lieutenant, and eighteen patrolmen, to be elected by the board of public works, as prescribed by the charter, they to hold office during the pleasure of the board appointing them. Under this new charter the board of public works also had the authority to appoint a market master, and a watchman and janitor. The volunteer fire department was to receive such compensation for their services as they and the board of public works could agree upon.

On July 6, 1888, it was determined to erect a new city hall, to cost $14,000, including the heating apparatus, and on July 19, there was appropriated toward the cost of this new building, $14,117. This new city hall was erected at the north end of the market house, and the first meeting of the board of mayor and aldermen was held therein on March 29, 1889.

The necessity for a system of sewers in Knoxville was apparent long before the establishment of such a system was practicable. Sewers are useless without water, and hence before water works were established it would have been useless to build sewers. But at length, after many attempts and many failures, water works were constructed in 1882 and the year following, and in 1884 it became possible to look forward to a thorough sewer system with a reasonable hope of success in the near future.

A few of the steps leading up to this success may be of historic interest. April 18, 1884, the board of health urged upon the board of mayor and aldermen the construction of such a system of sewers as the city needed, which they said the coming use of water from the water works would soon demand. On September 18, 1885, Judge H. H. Ingersoll called the attention of the board of mayor and aldermen to the fact that every day increased the necessity for the establishment of a system of sewers, a portion of which he thought should be constructed at the earliest practicable moment from the railroad down Crozier street to the river and from the railroad down Second creek to the river. Judge Ingersoll suggested the use of pipes or mains twenty inches in diameter, while Dr. S. G. Brown thought these mains should be at least thirty inches in diameter.

On January 21, 1887, Col. J. W. Gaut urgently advised the council to build the sewers required, and on the same day the passage of an act by the legislature permitting the issuance of bonds for the purpose was recommended, subject to the will of the people of Knoxville, to be determined at an election to be held for that purpose.

On July 5, 1889, M. E. Thompson was granted the right to lay a sewer main at his own expense from the corner of Crozier street and Fifth avenue to the river, along Crozier street said main not to be less than twenty-four inches in diameter, and to be laid under the direction and supervision of the board of public works and a competent sanitary engineer, who was to be selected by the board, this sanitary engineer being required to make a complete survey and plan of sewerage for the entire city, of which the above-mentioned line permitted to be laid by Mr. Thompson to be a part of the city's system.

On February 14, 1890, a committee consisting of John S.

Van Gilder, W. W. Woodruff, J. L. Cooley, L. H. Middleton, J. C. White, John Dempster and Matthew McClung was appointed to supervise the engineering and other work necessary to commence the work of establishing such a system of sewers as should be adopted. On March 8, 1890, the board of public works was requested to correspond with sanitary engineers of high reputation with the view of ascertaining the approximate cost of making a thorough and complete survey of the entire locality and of preparing plans for the best system of sewers for the whole city.

January 30, 1891, the mayor informed the board that the bill providing for an election at which the qualified voters of Knoxville might express their desires on the question of sewers had passed both branches of the legislature. This bill was approved by the governor on the 31st, and the election was held under the provisions of this bill on July 16, 1891, resulting in the casting of 1,220 votes, 1,000 of which were in favor of issuing bonds for sewers and 220 against such issue. The amount of bonds voted was $500,000, of which $250,000 were to be used in constructing sewers, $125,000 for the building of bridges and $125,000 for the improvements of the streets.

On July 8, 1892, the office of sewer engineer was created by the board of mayor and aldermen, the ordinance creating the office being vetoed by Mayor Thompson on the ground of economy, and passed over the veto. The salary of this officer was at first fixed at $1,200, but was afterward raised to $1,500, which increase was likewise vetoed by Mayor Thompson for the same reason, and was likewise passed over the veto. W. B. Crenshaw was elected to the office of sewer engineer. On July 20, 1892, there was appropriated for the construction of sewers $208,455.02, as follows: For first section sewer, $100,288.12; for second section sewer, $89,403.65; for sewer in the tenth ward, $8,763.25; and for preliminary survey, $10,000. In October, 1893, after the sewer system had been constructed the following summary of the cost of the same was spread upon the minutes of the council: First creek main sewer, $87,527.97; first creek lateral sewer, $57,751.20; second creek main sewer, $54,864.20; second creek lateral sewer, $31,298.00; engineering, $12,899.21; total cost, $244,340.69, from which was to be deducted for not plastering the main sewer, $750, making the net cost, $243,590.69.

Comparisons were made of cost of sewer systems with Memphis and Louisville, as follows: Memphis system, 53.74 miles, cost $8,132.92 per mile; Louisville, 23,096 lineal feet of brick sewer, the size corresponding as nearly as possible with the size of the main sewers in Knoxville, cost $198,364.17, or $8.59 per lineal foot; while 17,558 lineal feet of main sewer in Knoxville cost $142,410.72, or $8.11 per lineal foot.

On April 10, 1891, an act was passed extending the limits of the city of Knoxville so as to include the following territory:

Beginning at a point in the eastern boundary of the city in the center of the culvert of the East Tennessee, Virginia and Georgia railroad where said railroad crosses First creek; thence southwardly following said corporate line down the course of First creek to a point in the bend of said creek where the present corporation line leaves said creek; thence with said corporation line southeastwardly to a point where it crosses the boundary line of the property of Joseph W. Sneed and the McCammon tract; thence northwardly with the said line of Sneed and McCammon and with the line between the Mabry tracts, known as the Mount Isabella tract and Susan Nelson and Mabry's addition on the west and the McCammon tract, known as Chilhowee park and the Saxton tract on the east; in a general northerly course crossing the Dandridge pike to Nelson street; thence eastwardly with the county road, which is the eastern extension of Nelson street, parts of which are now known as Orange street and Cavalier street, to the southeast corner of the State Fair Grounds, now known as the Thompson & Strong addition; thence northwardly to the eastern boundary of the said Thompson & Strong addition; thence northwardly with the eastern boundary of the said Thompson & Strong addition to the eastern boundary of the street in said addition down to the Corso; thence with the eastern boundary of the same northwardly to Cherry street as laid off in the Cold Spring addition to Knoxville; thence with said Cherry street still northwardly to the northern boundary of the said Cold Spring addition to the County road, known as the "Hardin Hill road;" thence with the said road eastwardly and then northwardly to the center of the East Tennessee, Virginia and Georgia railroad, and then with said railroad in a general westward direction to the place of beginning.

The territory inclosed within the limits above mentioned became the tenth ward of the city.

Following is a list of the mayors of Knoxville, together with the periods during which they severally served: Thomas Emmerson, January 1, 1816, to January 1, 1818; James Park, January 1, 1818, to January 1, 1822; W. C. Mynatt, January 1, 1822, to January 1, 1824; James Park, January 1, 1824, to January 1, 1827; W. C. Mynatt, Joseph C. Strong, January 1, 1828, to January 1, 1832; Donald McIntosh, January 1, 1832, to January 1, 1834; Solomon D. Jacobs, 1834 to 1835; W. C. Mynatt, 1835-36; James King, 1837; W. B. A. Ramsey, January 1, 1838, to January 1, 1840; Samuel Bell, January 1, 1840, to January 1, 1842; Gideon M. Hazen, 1842; Matthew M. Gaines, 1843; Samuel Bell, January 1, 1844, to January 1, 1846; Joseph L. King, 1846 to 1847; Samuel B. Boyd, January 1, 1847, to January 1, 1852; George M. White, January 1, 1852, to January 1, 1854; James C. Luttrell, January 1, 1854, to January 1, 1855; William G. Swan, January 1, 1855, to November 1, 1856; James H. Cowan, November 1, 1856, to January 1, 1857; Samuel A. White, January 1, 1857, to August 1, 1857; Thomas J. Powell, August 1, 1857, to January 1, 1858; James M. White, January 1, 1858, to

May 1, 1858; A. M. Piper, August 1, 1858, to January 1, 1859; James C. Luttrell, 1859 to 1868; M. D. Bearden, January 1, 1868, to January 1, 1870; John S. Van Gilder, January 1, 1870, to January 1, 1873; William Rule, January, 1873, to January 1874; Peter Staub, January, 1874, to January, 1876; Daniel A. Carpenter, January, 1876, to January, 1878; Joseph Jacques, 1878; Samuel B. Luttrell, January, 1879, to January, 1880; H. B. Branner, 1880; Peter Staub, 1881; Reuben S. Payne, 1882; William C. Fulcher, January, 1883, to January, 1885; James C. Luttrell, Jr., January, 1885, to January, 1887; Martin J. Condon, January, 1888, to January, 1890; Peter Kern, January, 1890, to January, 1892; M. E. Thompson, January, 1892, to January, 1896; S. G. Heiskell, January, 1896, to January, 1898; William Rule, January, 1898, to January, 1900.

At the last election held for mayor and alderman in Knoxville in January, 1898, William Rule was elected by a vote of 1,554 votes over S. G. Heiskell, then mayor of the city, who received 1,246 votes, and also over Edwin R. Wade, who received 747 votes, the total vote for mayor being 3,547.

The successful candidates for aldermen in the several wards were as follows: First ward, Robert E. McMillan; second ward, H. M. Aiken; third ward, George W. Brown, fourth ward, W. H. Gass; fifth ward, Joseph M. Trigg; sixth ward, Samuel E. Cleage; seventh ward, O. T. Smith; eighth ward, Charlton Karnes; ninth ward, A. D. Waltz; tenth ward, J. C. Sterchi, and eleventh ward, J. W. Saylor.

Sanford N. Littleton was elected chairman of the board of public works. The associate members are John L. Hudiburg and Thomas Munsey.

C. C. Nelson, who had served the city as recorder and treasurer since 1880 was elected again by the board of aldermen, and is now the incumbent of the two offices, and is under the city charter ex officio justice of the peace.

The city attorney is T. L. Carty; city engineer, W. A. Gage

since March 23, 1898, and the city physician, Dr. H. P. Coile.

The present status of the board of health is as follows: On September 16, 1898, there was appointed a board of health of the city of Knoxville, which has for its object the protection of life and the care, promotion, preservation of the health of the people, and has advisory sanitary jurisdiction of the city and for one mile beyond the city limits; and during the prevalence of pestilential, contagious, infectious or epidemic diseases it may extend its jurisdiction to a distance of ten miles beyond the limits of the corporation. The board consists of six members, one of whom must be a lawyer, one a commercial man, three of them physicians, and the other is the city physician. The three physicians are required to be graduates of medicine and residents of Knoxville, and the city physician is the secretary of the board of health, serving without extra salary other than that received as city physician. The office of health officer was on the same day abolished, the patrolmen of the city being required to act in that capacity, each in his respective beat, and the associate members of the board of public works were required to be present, one each week on alternate weeks, at the office of the city physician during regular office hours to receive the reports of the patrolmen. The members of the board of health appointed November 18, 1898, were as follows: Dr. J. M. Black, H. J. Kelso, J. H. Kincaid, H. W. Hall and S. P. Fowler.

The charter of the city of Knoxville, under which its government is now conducted, was enacted by the legislature of the state June 10, 1885. The first paragraph reads as follows: "The inhabitants of the city of Knoxville, Tennessee, within the present boundaries of said city, embracing nine wards as at present constituted, are hereby constituted a body politic and corporate, by the name and the style of the board of mayor and aldermen of the city of Knoxville."

Section 3 of said charter provided that: "The corporate

authorities of said city of Knoxville shall be vested in the board of mayor and aldermen, a board of public works and such officers as may be appointed or elected in pursuance of law. The board of mayor and aldermen shall be composed of nine aldermen, who shall be elected for a term of two years at a general election by the qualified voters of the said city, each of the nine wards electing by its qualified voters one alderman, that person being elected who shall receive the largest number of votes."

The compensation for the services of the mayor was fixed at $1,000 per year, and could not be changed during his term of office. By section 24 of this charter the board of mayor and aldermen were prohibited from levying in any one year "for any and all purposes, ordinary and extraordinary, a higher rate of tax than 1 1-4 per cent of the assessed value of the taxable property within its limits."

Section 30 of the charter provided that there should be a board of public works composed of three persons, one of whom should be elected by the people and serve four years, the other two to be nominated by the mayor and confirmed by the board of aldermen, one to serve two years and the other four years, and each two years thereafter one member of the board should be similarly nominated and confirmed. The salary of the chairman of the board was fixed at $1,800 and those of the associate members at $600.

Sections 63 and 64 provided that there should be a board of education to consist of five members, not members of the board of mayor and aldermen, who should be elected by said board of mayor and aldermen from the citizens and qualified voters of the town, by ballot, each member of the board of education to serve five years.

This charter also provided for the election of a board of public works, the chairman of which was to be elected by the people, to hold office for the term of four years, with two associate members to be appointed by the mayor, who should also have a tenure of four years, except one of the first should hold only two years, so that one associate member should thereafter be chosen every two years. At the first election held under this charter, in 1886, Col. Isham Young was elected chairman of the board and he held the office until August, 1889, when he lost his life in a railroad accident. The first associate members were Peter Kern and Col. Adrian Terry. At the biennial election in 1890 John Gleason was elected chairman; in 1894 Reps Jones and in 1898 the present incumbent, Sanford N. Littleton, with whom the associate members are John L. Hudiburg and Thomas Munsey.

The original contract between the city of Knoxville and the Knoxville Gas Light Company was made in 1855, and was to continue in force forty years. The gas supplied to the city was to be as good as that furnished upon the streets and to the citizens of Nashville by the Nashville Gas Company. This contract remained in force until 1883, when on account of the many improvements made in the methods of manufacturing gas the officials of the city of Knoxville demanded that the Knoxville Gas Light Company should grant a reduction in the price of gas. Gas could be made in 1883, these officials claimed, at least fifty per cent cheaper than in 1855. In 1885 the city officials made an investigation, finding that the price of gas was still too high and secured another reduction, a new contract being entered into, but afterward the gas being manufactured by a cheaper process was not of such great illuminating power.

In 1886 a contract was entered into between the city and the electric light company by which the latter agreed to light the city for $10,000 per annum, a saving of $4,000 per annum, or of $36,000 for the remaining part of the gas company's contract. This was not done, however, until the company had given bonds to the city to guard against loss that the latter might sustain in litigation over the breaking of the gas company's contract. Arrangements were, however, made with the gas company by which the company agreed to permit the displacement of its gas lights on Gay street, the Market Square and the Custom House Square with electric lights, and this displacement occurred only after correspondence with various electric lighting companies in different cities of the North.

The officers of the Knoxville Gas Light Company at the present time are as follows: R. R. Swepson, president; L. H. Spilman, vice-president, elected in 1898, succeeding Dr. A. D. Leach; E. H. Saunders, secretary and treasurer, succeeding R. C. Jackson soon after Mr. Jackson's death; Robert Young, superintendent since 1895. The works of this company from the time of its organization in 1855 down to 1888 were on the bank of the Tennessee river near the foot of Locust street; but in this latter year, on account of the encroachments the city was making in its growth in the vicinity of the works, new works were erected on Jacksboro street near Munson street. Here the company has two gas holders, or reservoirs, only one of which is now in use, this one having a capacity of 350,000 cubic feet. The price of gas to consumers has been reduced at different times, beginning at $5 per 1,000 cubic feet, then being reduced to $2.50, and in 1885 to $1.50, for lighting purposes, while for cooking purposes the price is $1 per 1,000 cubic feet. Gas is now used for lighting purposes by about 2,000 patrons of the company, and for cooking purposes by about 600 patrons.

The Knoxville Water company was organized December 26, 1881, and application for a charter made by the following gentlemen as incorporators: Peter Staub, J. M. Brooks, F. M. Loweree, Joseph T. McTeer, Hector Coffin, Alvin Barton and H. H. Ingersoll.

In June, 1882, the Knoxville City Water company, composed of F. H. McClung, W. W. Woodruff, S. B. Luttrell, James D. Cowan, C. J. McClung, M. L. Ross, John S. Van Gilder, C. M. McGhee and George W. Ross was organized, and this company, as well as the Knoxville Water company and J. A. Cloud & Co., submitted bids for the construction of water works for the city.

On June 16, 1882, the proposition of the Knoxville Water company was accepted, which was in part that the system of works should have a capacity and quality of machinery and material equal to that contemplated by the specifications of Moses Lane as supplemented by S. H. Lockett, the reservoir to contain 3,200,000 gallons of water; the company to establish seventy-five hydrants, sixty-three of which were to be located at points indicated in the Lane plan, and twelve on the line of new mains and points designated by the city, twenty of them to have double nozzles; the supply of water to be at least 2,000,000 gallons of water every twenty-four hours. The city was to pay $50 as rental for each hydrant.

In February, 1894, the Knoxville Water company began making important improvements, then greatly needed, including the standpipe now on Reservoir hill, which is eighty-five feet high and thirty-two feet in diameter, and the large filtration plant. The filtration house is a brick structure 60x112 feet in size, and contains a high service pumping engine and boilers, and also the filters. This improvement was made because the company had agreed to furnish North Knoxville with filtered water, and the intention was to give filtered water to the entire city. The standpipe cost about $15,000; the filter plant building about $18,000, and the machinery itself nearly $20,000, the entire cost of the improved filter plant being nearly $100,000. It was finished in September, 1894. In August, 1894, the company began making extensive improvements at the pumping station on the river bank, increasing its size to about double what it was before, and putting in a new 4,000,000 gallon pump and a new intake. During this same year and 1895 the company also relaid a large part of its pipes in the city, and added eight or ten miles of pipes. Since the beginning of 1894 the entire system has been made new, except the reservoir. There are now from forty-five to fifty miles of mains, ranging in size from twenty inches down to three inches, this being the smallest pipe now used. The company rents to the city at the present time (February, 1899) 214 hydrants at a cost to the city of $10,128 per year. The president of the company is William Wheeler of Boston, Mass.; secretary, E. T. Sanford of Knoxville; treasurer and general manager, Elbert Wheeler of Boston, Mass.; and superintendent, Frank C. Kimball, of Knoxville.

The Lonsdale-Beaumont Water company was incorporated in 1892, the charter members being D. S. McIntyre, C. H. Hudson, W. M. Baxter, D. T. McIntyre and H. P. Coile, and was organized with H. P. Coile, president; C. H. Hudson, vice-president, and D. S. McIntyre, secretary and treasurer. Its authorized capital stock was $100,000. The purpose of the organization was to supply water to West Knoxville and other territory, and in furthering this purpose the Tillery spring was purchased, located at the head of Third creek. Afterward the company secured perpetual leases of other springs in the same locality and also valuable springs at the head waters of Third creek, from which latter springs alone the system has been supplied so far. The first to be used was the Griffin spring, four miles from the city, and later the famous Blanc spring, 3,000 feet above the Griffin spring, was added to the system. These two springs furnish the water supply to West Knoxville, including such prominent institutions as the University of Tennessee, and also the Southern car shops, Lonsdale, Knoxville college, and the Knoxville woolen mills.

The springs were at first thoroughly cleaned out and walled up by heavy stone masonry and then capped over, so as to prevent the admission of any contaminating substance. From these springs the water is piped four and a half miles to an impounding reservoir situated on the Clinton pike and the K. C., G. & L. railway, and excavated in solid rock. It is fifty-three feet in diameter and twenty-two feet deep. The pumping station is located at the reservoir, the pump being a Dean duplex capable of pumping 2,000,000 gallons every twenty-four hours. The water is pumped three-fourths of a mile into a standpipe seventy feet high and twenty-five feet in diameter located on Beaumont ridge, two miles north of Fort Sanders. The system consists of seventeen miles of pipe ranging from two to twelve inches in diameter, and has a pressure capable of throwing five fire streams to an average height of 120 feet in West Knoxville, rendering the use of fire engines unnecessary in that part of the city. The officers of this company at this time are W. S. Shields, president; Alexander McMillan, vice-president; and H. W. Lyman, secretary and treasurer.

The first steam fire engine brought to Knoxville was the J. C. Luttrell, No. 1, in 1867, a brass Silsby engine, not now in use. While not the first in the southern states, yet it was near the first, Augusta, Ga., Macon, Ga., and Memphis, Tenn., having had steam fire engines of this make about one year earlier. The next steam fire engine bought was the Alexander Allison, in 1876, which is now at the Central Market station, and is known as engine No. 2. The third was bought in 1893, and is named the M. E. Thompson, located at the Central station on Commerce street, between Gay and State streets, at which station, besides the engine company, there is also a hook and ladder company, and a 65-foot extension ladder.

The fire department is now officered as follows: V. F. Gossett, chief; Capt. W. H. Salmon, assistant chief, and captain of the hook and ladder company, with five men under him; A. G. Bayless, captain of engine company No. 3, at the Central station, with seven men under him; John B. Hawkins, captain of engine company No. 2, at Central Market station, with six men under him. Herman Schenk is the city electrician.

On March 16, 1888, a contract was made with the Gaynor company of Louisville, Ky., for putting in a complete fire alarm system for the city. At first there were to be forty-five stations and the price $7,500. At the same time a fire brigade station was located in North Knoxville. The work of erecting the poles for the fire alarm system began January 24, 1889. This system was in use until 1897, on August 27 of which year the board of mayor and aldermen accepted a new and much improved system. This was the new Gaynor six-circuit repeater, and the Gamewell six-circuit automatic standard combination repeater and storage battery board, the apparatus consisting of one complete chloride accumulator storage battery plant of 100 cells with the necessary shelves or cabinet; one six-circuit combination slate base switch board containing the necessary rheostats, lamps, meters, galvanometers, switches, etc. The price for putting in the entire system was $3,000, of which $2,200 was paid in cash and the old system turned in for $800. Knoxville was the second city in the southern states to adopt this system, Houston, Texas, being the first. The six-circuit automatic switch board put in here was the first of that size in the United States. It has given complete satisfaction and is as near perfection as such things can possibly be.

In 1891 the Fifth avenue bridge over the Knoxville & Ohio railroad was constructed, the contract for its construction being let on January 8 to the King Iron & Bridge company. The city appropriated $5,200 toward the payment for the land condemned, the entire cost of the bridge being $14,835 outside of the masonry. The span of the bridge is 480 feet, the first span being 117 1-4 feet; the second 103, the third 80 feet. The first trestle is 110 feet, and the trestle on the Branner street end 70 feet. The bridge is of the Pratt truss pattern, the roadway is twenty feet wide and the foot-walk eight feet wide.

The following bridges over First creek were built in 1892, the contracts for them being let on April 29, that year: Oak street, Church street and Hill street. The Oak street bridge was let to the Groton Bridge company for $21,000; the Church street bridge to the King Iron & Bridge company for $13,450, and the Hill street bridge to the same company for $19,150. For the Oak street bridge the masonry cost

$6,793 and the superstructure $530, making the total cost of the bridge $28,323; for the Church street bridge the masonry cost $4,459 and the superstructure $795, making the total cost of this bridge $18,704, and for the Hill street bridge the masonry cost $5,451 and the superstructure $630, making the whole cost of this bridge $25,231.

Knoxville had no good streets prior to 1893, though some of them had been macadamized for several years. After long consideration and investigation as to the success met with in other cities with brick pavement, it was decided to put down pavements of this kind on a portion of the streets. It is not to be denied that so thoroughly had the city authorities become satisfied that great expectations were entertained with respect to this kind of pavement, and on August 25, 1893, Miss Mary Gaines, a granddaughter of the then oldest living ex-mayor of the city, M. M. Gaines, laid the first brick in the sand on Gay street near Main. Previous to the laying of this first brick, however, there were interesting preliminary exercises. Mayor M. E. Thompson announced that these exercises would begin with prayer, which prayer was delivered by Rev. Dr. James Park. Then followed an oration by Walter M. Cocke, a prominent young Knoxville lawyer. The oration having been delivered, Mr. Gillespie, general manager of the paving company, handed the first brick to Miss Gaines, who laid it in the sand. By night of that day about one-half the block on Gay street from Main to Cumberland street had been laid.

When this brick paving began the old stone pavement had to be taken up. It consisted of cobble stone, and was put down in 1848 under the direction of Albert Miller Lea, a professor of mathematics and a civil engineer. Mr. Lea paved the wharves and Prince street up to Main. The work was continued on other streets in the old city, and on Gay street up to 1852.

On November 20, 1893, a contract was let to John Shea for paving Market Square, which was completed by January,

1894, at a cost of $12,118.42, and at that time Crozier street from the railroad north to Depot street was nearly complete, and Commerce street from Gay street to the Palace Hotel was under contract.

The following extract from the message of Hon. William Rule, mayor of Knoxville, is of interest, as showing the financial condition of the city on January 6, 1899, the day on which the message was read:

"The bonded indebtedness of the city now amounts to $1,128,600. On $292,600 of that amount the city is paying interest at the rate of six per cent. On $34,000 the rate is four per cent, and on the remainder, $962,000, the rate is five per cent. The annual interest now being paid out of the city treasury on this bonded indebtedness is $67,016.

"The floating debt, including $10,000 recently appropriated for the maintenance of the schools, and estimating some minor judgments rendered against the city in the courts, is $86,566.06, the annual interest on which, at the rate of six per cent would be, in round numbers, $5,200. This added to that on the bonded debt will make the interest charge against the city to be provided for in the budget of the next fiscal year $72,216.

"Of the floating debt here mentioned, $56,766.06 was handed down to us as a legacy from the old municipalities, as follows:

Old Knoxville	$43,124.11
West Knoxville	9,953.25
North Knoxville	3,688.70
Total	$56,766.06

"In addition to this the floating debt has been increased during the fiscal year by items over which the present board of mayor and aldermen had no control, as follows:

The J. W. Sneed judgment	$15,500
Bill of Gaynor Fire Alarm Co.	1,700
Sundry court judgments	1,700
Total	$18,900

"It thus appears and is a fact that outside the judgments rendered by the courts for which this board is not responsible, and which were in a measure unavoidable, and, excepting the loan for the public schools, the present city council has increased the floating debt only about $500."

Following is a list of postmasters at Knoxville with the dates of their appointment, kindly furnished upon request by J. L. Bristow, fourth assistant post-master general: George Roulstone, April 1, 1795; John Crozier, August 30, 1797; Lewis P. Roberts, December 3, 1838; James W. Campbell, March 26, 1841; Samuel W. Bell, January 18, 1845; James C. Luttrell, June 26, 1849; John E. Helms, April 5, 1853; Felix W. Earnest, February 21, 1856; George W. Harris, July 27, 1857; J. F. J. Lewis, March 8, 1858; Charles W. Charlton, May 3, 1859; James C. Luttrell, July 20, 1861; James Rodgers, April 9, 1869; William Rule, March 14, 1873; Oliver P. Temple, October 21, 1881; James M. King, October 19, 1885; John L. Hudiburg, April 9, 1889; J. W. Gaut, February 16, 1894, and William L. Trent, February 23, 1898.

The report of the Knoxville postoffice, as completed November 3, 1898, for the fiscal year ending June 30, 1898, was as follows: Receipts for July, 1897, $6,262.34; for August, $5,821.11; September, $5,964.23; October, $7,156.85; November, $6,140.04; December, $6,755.26; January, 1898, $6,881.72; February, $6,049.73; March, $6,716.27; April, $6,180.37; May, $6,301.37; and June, $5,903.51; total amount received, $76,132.80, or an average monthly receipt of $6,344.40.

Up to near the beginning of the civil war the growth of the town was rather slow, and its intercourse with the world outside of the mountain ranges plainly in view in all directions was necessarily limited. But in 1856 the first railroad reached the town from Georgia, and in 1857 railroad connections were made with the state of Virginia. But the civil war for a time put an end to progress in this direction, and during the war much of the town was destroyed by fire. The battle of Fort Saunders, fought on Sunday morning, November 29, 1863, in which nearly 1,000 lives were lost, was one of the most severe of the war, when the time it lasted is taken into account. And during the period of reconstruction the growth of the city was also necessarily slow, and yet many of the soldiers of both Federal and Confederate armies, delighted with the climate and other features of this region, settled down here and have since made it their permanent homes. In 1865 there were but 4,000 inhabitants in the city; in 1870 there were 8,000; in 1880 there were 10,000; in 1890 there were 22,535 within the city proper, and when the population of the suburbs is added there were over 40,000. In 1898 there are 50,000, of whom about one-fifth are negroes, this being a smaller proportion than is found in any other southern city.

EAST KNOXVILLE

Was incorporated by an act of the legislature passed February 22, 1856, and was bounded as follows:

Beginning at the mouth of First creek in the Holston river; on the line of the corporation of the city of Knoxville; thence up the meanders of said river to the mouth of Samuel McCammon's spring branch; thence up said branch, including his spring, and from thence in a direct line to the lower end of the Bell place on First creek, the line of the corporation of Knoxville, and thence down said creek with the corporation line to the place of beginning; provided that the corporation of East Knoxville shall not be responsible for the keeping up of the bridges, but the same shall continue county bridges as heretofore, unless the said corporation shall otherwise agree with the county court to take charge of said bridges.

This act provided for the division of the corporation of East Knoxville into three wards, and for the election by the qualified voters of a mayor and for two aldermen from each ward. William Swan, William F. Seav and James Rodgers, or any two of them, were authorized to make the division into wards, which they did. According to this charter an election for mayor and six aldermen was held on the second Saturday of March that year, and was to be so held each succeeding year. In 1856 the mayor elected was William Swan, and the aldermen were as follows: First ward, James Rodgers and Samuel Morrow; second ward, W. G. Brownlow and S. S. Thompson, and third ward, James O. Patton and J. B. G. Kinsloe.

William Swan was elected mayor in 1857 and also in 1858; James Rodgers in 1859, resigning in October of that year, William Craig being elected to fill out the unexpired term; Mr. Craig was elected in 1860; W. G. Brownlow in 1861; William Craig in 1862, 1863 and 1864; John S. Van Gilder in 1865 and 1866; M. L. Hall in 1867 and S. H. Smith in 1868, serving until the annexation of East Knoxville to Knoxville in January, 1869.

William F. Seay was recorder and treasurer of East Knoxville during the existence of that corporation.

On October 29, 1868, a called meeting of the board of mayor and aldermen of East Knoxville was held for the purpose of discussing the propriety of annexation to the city of Knoxville, at which were present S. H. Smith, mayor, and Aldermen Foster, Burger, Householder, Stephenson and Johnson. M. D. Bearden, mayor of Knoxville, was present and made a speech on the subject in favor of the annexation, and extending the boundary of Knoxville so as to include East Knoxville. This step was finally approved and the two corporations merged into one.

The last meeting of the board of mayor and aldermen of East Knoxville was held January 5, 1869, at which there were present the mayor, S. H. Smith, and Aldermen Childress, Stephenson, Burger, Dozier, Foster and Johnson. The mayor stated that inasmuch as in a few days the corporation of East Knoxville would cease to exist, he thought it best for the board to bring their business to a close, and on motion it was ordered by the board that inasmuch as the property of the corporation had been listed for twelve months on

March 8, 1868, and that only ten months in the year would expire before it would have to be listed again, therefore

Be it Resolved, That all uncollected taxes be reduced one-sixth, and that all persons who had paid their taxes should have refunded to them one-sixth of what they had paid.

A contract made some time before with William Hays to excavate and macadamize Water street from Main street near M. J. Childress's residence to the Holston river was reported by the street committee by H. Foster, chairman, this contract having been entered into October 28, 1868. This was the last entry made on the records of East Knoxville.

On October 19, 1894, a communication was received from each of the two outlying corporations, North and West Knoxville, with reference to the consolidation of the three corporations, and Knoxville, favoring such consolidation, appointed as her two commissioners Judge Joseph W. Sneed and John S. Van Gilder. The legislature of the state on April 2, 1897, passed an act providing that the three cities might become one if they so desired, but this act also provided that an election should be held within four months from the time of its approval, at which the people should have the right to choose between consolidation and remaining as they were, separate cities. This election was held in all three cities on the same day, July 23, 1897, with the result that there were cast in Knoxville 699 votes for consolidation, and 35 against it; in North Knoxville, 154 votes for it to 87 against, and in West Knoxville 142 votes for it to 6 against it, making in all 995 votes for to 183 against consolidation.

NORTH KNOXVILLE

Was incorporated under an act of the legislature of the state attested by John Allison, secretary of state, January 16, 1889. A meeting was held February 4, 1889, of citizens in this portion of what is now Knoxville to effect the organization of the government of North Knoxville, an election having been held, at which the following officers were elected: L. A.

Gratz, mayor; and A. W. Anderson, S. A. Caldwell, W. E. Moses, O. T. Roberts, W. O. White and J. W. Ward, aldermen, the number of votes cast at this election being 239. Following is the act of incorporation referred to above, showing the boundaries of the territory included in North Knoxville:

"Be it known that the city of North Knoxville, Tennessee, situated in Knox county, state of Tennessee, and beginning at the eastern side of the right of way of the East Tennessee, Virginia and Georgia railroad where it intersects with the corporate limits of the city of Knoxville, Tenn.; thence with said eastern line of said right of way to its intersection with Ricker street; thence with the center of said Ricker street to its intersection with Pearson avenue; thence with the center of Pearson avenue to its intersection with the east line of the right of way of the Knoxville, Tazewell and Jacksboro turnpike; thence in a direct line north 83 degrees west to the center of Morse street; thence with the center of Morse street in a southwesterly direction to the boundary line between the Second and Twelfth Civil districts of Knox county; thence with the said boundary line to the northern boundary line of the corporation of the city of Knoxville, Tenn.; thence with said boundary line of the said city of Knoxville, Tenn., to the beginning, is hereby duly and legally incorporated, and as such is entitled to all the benefits and is subject to all the responsibilities of the laws of the state applicable to municipal corporations."

The offices of recorder and treasurer were combined, and Robert Irwin elected thereto, and A. M. Burns was elected policeman, afterward called marshal, each of these two officers to receive forty dollars per month. February 12, 1889, the tax upon each $100 worth of taxable property for the unexpired portion of that year was fixed at seventy-five cents and poll tax at $1 per year.

As no modern corporation can carry on its improvements and conduct its business without borrowing money, so North

Knoxville, on April 13, 1889, submitted the question to the legal voters at an election held that day as to whether they would authorize the issuance of $100,000 in bonds for the improvement of the streets, etc., the result of the election being that 159 votes were cast, 156 of which were in favor of the issuance of the bonds. On May 4 following an ordinance was passed providing for the issuance of the bonds, which were to run thirty years and bear interest at the rate of five per cent. On May 11, a contract was entered into with McDonald, Shea & Co. to grade the streets at certain prices; for instance, solid rock excavation cost the corporation 75 cents per cubic yard, loose rock 35 cents, and earth 17 cents per cubic yard.

In many instances corporations in issuing bonds meet with unforeseen difficulties, and North Knoxville was no exception to the rule. The sale of its bonds having been effected, the purchasers declined to take them for the reason that although the assessment of property within the corporation had been fixed by law on January 10, 1889, yet the assessment was not actually made until some time in June, and the election authorizing the issue of the bonds was held in April. In order therefore to enable North Knoxville to sell her bonds, another election was necessary to be held after the actual assessment of the property. This election was therefore held August 22, 1889, resulting in the casting of 199 votes, of which only three were cast against the issue of bonds. The assessment made in June showed that there was in the corporation of taxable property $1,020,550, and under the law they could borrow not over ten per cent of this valuation, hence the issuance of $100,000 in bonds was clearly within the law.

A chemical fire-engine was purchased and paid for, after being submitted to a severe test on September 21, 1889.

On February 3, 1890, the city engineer submitted a report as to the amount of work done on the streets and the cost for the previous nine months, which was in substance as follows: That there had been graded 40,380 lineal feet of streets, in doing which there had been excavated 126,861.1 cubic yards of stone and earth, besides other work, all at a cost of $26,883.01.

February 8, 1890, the finance committee reported that the receipts of the corporation had been up to that time $126,804.78, and the disbursements $93,167.27.

On February 1, 1890, L. A. Gratz was re-elected mayor, and the following aldermen were elected: O. T. Roberts, A. W. Anderson, W. O. White, T. P. Roberts, John Shea and W. E. Moses for the first, second, third, etc., districts, respectively. L. A. Gratz was again elected mayor in 1891 and 1892, this year by 137 votes, as against 70 votes cast for W. A. Wray. In 1893 W. L. Welcker was elected mayor, and served continuously in that office as long as North Knoxville existed as a separate corporation. Robert Irwin continued to serve as recorder and treasurer until his death in August, 1894, when he was succeeded by W. E. Moses, who held that office until the consolidation of the corporations. On February 20, 1892, the finance committee reported that for the three years of the existence of the corporation the receipts had been $138,318.73.

In 1892 by a vote of the people of North Knoxville the council was authorized to issue $75,000 in bonds for street improvements, and for a sewer system, but later, when the question of consolidation with Knoxville had been settled, the mayor of North Knoxville, Hon. W. L. Welcker, in an address to the council, advocated the repeal of the ordinance by which such issue had been authorized, for the reason that the city of Knoxville would have no right to either issue the bonds or expend the money, which recommendation was complied with.

October 6, 1894, a resolution was adopted by the mayor and aldermen of Knoxville inviting North Knoxville and West Knoxville to unite with Knoxville in one corporation, and stating that as such consolidation could not be effected without the consent of the legislature, a fair and just plan of union should be prepared and submitted to the legislature for its approval; and also suggesting a consolidation commission be appointed by each of the three corporations to consist of seven members, two of them from each of the three corporations, and one to be chosen by these six from the ex-tenth ward. North Knoxville agreed to this proposition, only modifying it in such a way as to require that one of the two members from each city should be the city attorney of said corporation, in order that the legal questions involved might be thoroughly understood by the consolidation commission, and named the Hon. W. L. Welcker as one of her commissioners. The city of Knoxville appointed Hon. Joseph W. Sneed and John S. Van Gilder as her two commissioners. All of this matter, however, had to be submitted to the people, and hence on July 23, 1897, an election was held in North Knoxville as well as in the other corporations, to determine whether the people were willing to consolidate their three cities in accordance with the provisions of the act of the legislature providing therefor; the result being as given on a preceding page.

On July 26 the mayor and aldermen of North Knoxville resolved that inasmuch as the act providing for consolidation had in every particular been complied with that the said act had therefore become effective for the consolidation of the three corporations at the time specified therein, viz.:

On January 18, 1898, a statement was presented to the board of aldermen showing that the cash receipts of the corporation from February 13, 1897, to January 1, 1898, had been $26,255.54, and there was on hand $732.16. The property of the corporation, according to the inventory presented, among other things of less value, consisted of one steam road roller, worth $1,800; school buildings and city hall, $15,000; lots, $6,000; school furniture, $2,750; furniture in the large building, $1,000, and electrical and physical apparatus, $150; total, $26,750.

The last meeting of the board of aldermen of North Knoxville was held January 21, 1898, and consisted of two sessions, one in the afternoon, the other in the evening. After receiving the finance committee's report, and adopting a resolution approving of the official conduct of the recorder and treasurer, W. E. Moses, and of the marshal, W. T. Farmer, as faithful, sober, energetic and efficient officers, the council adjourned sine die. The minutes were then signed by the following members, who were present: W. L. Welcker, mayor; W. R. Carter, James A. Hensley, David T. McMallin and George W. Peters, aldermen.

WEST KNOXVILLE

Was incorporated March 8, 1888, the territory included being bounded as follows: In the twenty-fourth civil district, beginning on the Tennessee river at the mouth of Second creek; thence up said creek with the east bank thereof to Asylum street; thence westward with Asylum street to the East Tennessee, Virginia and Georgia railroad; thence westward with said railroad to where it crosses Crawford's branch; thence south with said branch to Third creek; thence down Third creek to the Tennessee river, and thence up said river to the place of beginning.

The incorporation was decided on by the people at an election held March 3, 1888, at which there were cast 231 votes, 165 of which were in favor of the incorporation. The movement for incorporation, however, began on January 21, 1888, when notice was given that application for a charter would be made, those signing this notice being as follows: W. W. Woodruff, W. H. Simmonds, George Andrews, J. M. Thornburg, John Marshall, M. L. Ross, W. P. Smith, James M. Meek, A. G. Scott, R. F. Galyon, W. H. Collett, W. H. Salmon, S. R. Ogden, W. B. Henderson, S. H. Johnson, G. W. Searle, and G. L. Maloney. At the election held on March 3, the following gentlemen were chosen as mayor and aldermen: J. W. Yoe, mayor; F. K. Huger, M. L. Ross,

E. H. Flenniken, Frank Barker, W. P. Smith and R. Z. Roberts. The first meeting of the board of mayor and aldermen was held at the school house on Altavia street, March 28, 1888. At this meeting an organization was effected, and on April 9, A. G. Scott was elected recorder and treasurer, and John M. Luttrell, marshal. April 26, the name of Kingston Pike was changed to Cumberland avenue. August 3, J. G. McClannahan made a report to the board that the number of inhabitants in West Knoxville was 1,520, and that the number of school children was 532, of which number there were 481 white children and 51 colored.

In December, 1888, "Payne Circle" was offered to the corporation as a public park, and after some preliminary matter had been satisfactorily arranged the "Circle" became the property of the city of West Knoxville, January 4, 1889.

The first movement looking toward the improvement of the streets, alleys, etc., was made March 23, 1889, when an election was ordered to determine whether the voters would authorize a bond issue of $75,000 for such purpose, the election being held April 5 following, with the result that there were cast 200 votes for the issue of the bonds and none against such issue. On April 4, 1890, a contract was entered into with Thomas P. Wells for such excavation as might be necessary in the work of grading the streets, the several prices being as follows: For earth excavations, 17 cents per cubic yard; for loose rock, 35 cents, and for solid rock 65 cents. For hauling more than 500 feet Mr. Wells was allowed 1 1-2 cents per cubic yard for each additional 100 feet. On the same day the finance committee reported that the receipts of the city for the year ending March 15, 1890, had been $93,290.30, and that the expenses had been $68,035.50, leaving a balance on hand of $25,254.80. The indebtedness of the city was $75,000, less $500 in the hands of the sinking fund commission.

The work of giving West Knoxville a sewerage system was one of the most important undertaken by the board of mayor and aldermen during the existence of the corporation. It was begun in 1893, and on October 5, 1894, the sewer commission made a report to the board that there had been laid in the streets of the corporation 20,328 feet of sewers. On November 5, 1894, there had been laid 33,372 feet, twenty-eight siphons had been put in, eighty-eight manholes built and 212 house connections made. December 7, 1894, the city engineer, J. C. Wright, reported that in West Knoxville there had been laid pipe of all sizes the following lengths: Of 12-inch sewer pipe, 855.5 feet; of 10-inch sewer pipe, 1,581.6 feet; of 8-inch sewer pipe, 16,528.8 feet; of 6-inch sewer pipe, 15,493.3 feet; of 12-inch iron pipe, 204 feet, and of 8-inch iron pipe, 96 feet; total feet, 34,755.2, or 6.58 miles. He said that the sewer system was sufficient for a city of 40,000 people.

On October 11, 1894, an agreement was made between Knoxville and West Knoxville that the latter corporation might make connections with the Second Creek main sewer at Asylum street, at Clinch street and at Main street, on the condition that West Knoxville pay to Knoxville $3,000, which should become the property of the city of Knoxville in case the two corporations should be consolidated on or before January 1, 1896, otherwise the money should be expended in the improvement of the streets of West Knoxville.

The votes cast in the several divisions of the present city, Knoxville, North Knoxville and West Knoxville, have been given in other connections, and the date upon which the consolidation took place.

The mayors of West Knoxville were J. W. Yoe from the organization of the board of mayor and aldermen, March 28, 1888, until his death, September 9, 1895; M. L. Ross from that time until January, 1897, and J. S. Monday from January, 1897, until the consolidation. The recorder and treasurers were as follows: A. G. Scott, from the time of organization until 1891; W. B. Henderson, until 1892; W. W. Morrison from April 11, 1892, until June, 1893; A. G. Scott, from June, 1893, to 1895, and W. W. Morrison from 1895 to 1897, and John M. Luttrell from March, 1897, until the time of consolidation. The marshals of the corporation were John M. Luttrell, J. R. Johnson, W. P. Wardrope and J. R. Curtis.

The last meeting of the board of mayor and aldermen of West Knoxville was held January 24, 1898, at which time the final reports of the recorder and treasurer and of the several standing committees were made. Mayor J. S. Monday thanked the aldermen, who at the time were J. W. Crudgington, H. W. Hall, A. C. McNulty, A. J. Miller, Jacob Staub and J. C. Sterchi; recorder and treasurer, John M. Luttrell; marshal, J. R. Curtis; patrolman, G. W. Roberts, city physician, Dr. J. P. Hood; members of the board of health, Dr. E. C. Deaderick and W. H. Salmun; and sinking fund commissioner, Fred D. Griffith, for their uniform kindness, courtesy and assistance rendered him in the performance of his duties as mayor, and then declared the council of West Knoxville adjourned sine die.

CHAPTER X.

MILITARY HISTORY.

Early Indian Wars—Col. John Williams' Regiment—The Mexican War—Volunteers for Both the Union and the Confederate Service—Sanders' Raid—Knoxville Receives Gen. Burnside—Is Besieged by Gen. Longstreet—A Sanguinary Battle—Fort Sanders—Knoxville Pension Agency—In the Spanish War—Warm Welcome to Returning Volunteer Soldiers.

THE part played by the people of Tennessee in wars with Indians made necessary by the occupation of the territory by white men and through the misinterpretation and misunderstanding of treaties, has been sufficiently set forth in earlier chapters in this work. It remains therefore necessary to deal with the wars that came subsequently, that is, with the "second war for independence," the Indian wars caused thereby, the war with Mexico, the war of the Rebellion and the war with Spain.

No sooner had war with England become imminent in 1812, than that country sent emissaries among the Indians to the south of Tennessee for the purpose of engaging them as allies in her cause, which was a part of her policy as to all the Indians on the southern, western and northwestern settlements of the United States. At length the massacre at Fort Mimms thoroughly aroused the people of this state, and they with alacrity sprang to arms. This massacre occurred August 30, 1813, and the legislature almost immediately authorized a call for 3,500 troops to join the 1,500 already in the field. An appropriation was also made of $300,000 for defraying the expenses of the war. Governor Blount commissioned General Cocke to command the troops furnished by East Tennessee, and General Jackson those from what is now Middle Tennessee. With his accustomed energy General Jackson was soon in the field, and established a camp which he named Fort Deposit, but on account of low water

KNOXVILLE—TENN.

From *Southern Mountain Ramblers* · Date Unknown

in the upper branches of the rivers in East Tennessee the supplies from that part of the state, which were in great demand, were long delayed, causing some disappointment and bitterness. While awaiting these supplies the General wrote letters to Governor Blount and General White, urging the utmost dispatch in having them forwarded. The battle of Talladega was fought December 8, 1813, without the co-operation of General Cocke or General White. the latter being, however, within twenty-four miles of Jackson's camp at Fort Strother, resulting in great loss to the Indians. General White joined General Jackson at Fort Strother on the 13th of the month.

After considerable severe fighting between General Jackson and the Indians he was reinforced in March, 1814, by 2,000 men from East Tennessee under command of General George Doherty, and also by a regiment from the same portion of the state commanded by Colonel John Brown. A terrible battle was fought in a bend of the Tallapoosa river, called from its shape Tohopeka, meaning horseshoe, in which the Indians lost more than 700 men, and then, after almost continual wars with the Indians up to 1836, volunteers were called for in June of that year, the apportionment of Tennessee being 2,000 men. Of the troops from East Tennessee, which rendezvoused at Athens, R. G. Dunlap was elected brigadier-general, and the last fighting done by soldiers from Tennessee in these Indian wars was at the battles at the Wahoo Swamp, November 18 and 21, 1836, though the wars themselves can not be said to have come to an end before 1842.

Of the soldiers that went from Knox county, for it would be impracticable to distinguish between those that went out from the city of Knoxville and those that went from the county, were those of the Thirty-ninth Regiment United States Volunteers, of which John Williams was the colonel; and which by June 18, 1813, had in its ranks about 600 men. Thomas H. Benton was the lieutenant-colonel, and Lemuel

P. Montgomery, major. The captains of the several companies were as follows: Samuel Bunch, who afterward became colonel of a regiment of militia in General White's brigade; James Davis, John Jones, John B. Long, John Phagan, Thomas Stuart and William Walker. Some of the first lieutenants were as follows: David Lauderdale, David McMillen, Nathaniel Smith, Guy Smith, A. Stanfield, and J. O. Tate, while the second lieutenants were Andrew Greer, N. Dortch, M. W. McClellan, M. C. Molton, Simpson Payne, R. Quarles, and J. K. Snapp. The third lieutenants were as follows: Dicks Alexander, A. G. Cowan, Joseph Denison, R. B. Harvey, Joseph S. Jackson, Ellis Thomas and T. B. Tunstall. One of the ensigns was Sam Houston.

Colonel Williams, after the return of Judge Hugh L. White from a visit to General Jackson, decided to go at once to the assistance of that general, reaching him March 1, 1814, and on the 27th of that month participated in the battle of Tohopeka. In this battle Major Montgomery was killed, and Sam Houston severely wounded. The regiment remained in the Creek country until after the signing of the treaty of peace and was mustered out June 15, 1815.

This brings us down again to 1836, when a company was recruited to serve two months as militia in the Seminole war. The captain of this company was Dr. James Morrow; first lieutenant, Samuel B. Kennedy; and second lieutenant, Thomas C. Lyons. The regiment to which this company was assigned assisted to remove the Cherokee Indians to the west of the Mississippi river, and Lieutenant Lyons was promoted to a position on the staff of General Wood.

In the war with Mexico Knox county bore no inconsiderable part. Upon the declaration of war by President Polk, the appointment of Tennessee was made 2,000 men, but it was finally decided to accept 1,600 infantry and 800 cavalry. The people throughout the state were exceeding anxious to enlist. The state was divided into four military districts: one in East Tennessee, two in Middle and one in West Tennessee.

From East Tennessee went the Knoxville Dragoons, organized June 10, 1846, with William R. Caswell, captain; Samuel Bell, first lieutenant; Calvin Gossett, second lieutenant, and James Anderson, third lieutenant. This company went to Memphis, and there became a part of the Second Regiment Tennessee Volunteer Cavalry, of which J. E. Thomas was colonel; R. D. Allison, lieutenant-colonel; and Richard Waterhouse, major. The first and second regiments were with General Taylor at Matamoras, and soon afterward found the hot weather and general climatic conditions extremely prejudicial to health, and in fact they suffered much more from these than from the bullets of the Mexicans. The two regiments participated in the battle of Monterey September 21, 1846, the city surrendering on the 25th. Of the 350 men in the charge, 105 were lost, the killed numbering 26, wounded 77, and the missing 2.

Both Tennessee regiments were then assigned to General Pillow's brigade, which on December 14 started for Tampico on the way to Vera Cruz, reaching the latter place on March 9, 1847. On the 22d the siege guns opened on Vera Cruz, the bombardment continuing until the 27th, the city of Vera Cruz and the strong castle of San Juan de Ulloa surrendering on the 29th. The Tennessee regiments then went with General Scott to the City of Mexico, fighting the battle of Cerro Gordo on the way, on April 18, 1847, and losing in all 79 men, all but eight of them from the Second Cavalry. Their time of service having expired, they were then sent to New Orleans and mustered out.

A call was then made for two additional regiments from Tennessee, the Third and Fourth, and for a battalion of six companies, known as the Fourteenth. Two companies of the Fourth regiment were raised in Knox county, one commanded by Capt. Parsons the other by Capt. Jordan T. Council. Of this latter company the first lieutenant was Tazewell Newman; the second, Joseph H. Crockett; the third, Thomas McAffry, and the orderly sergeant, James Henderson. The company was ordered to Memphis, and there became company D, Fourth Tennessee infantry, with Richard Waterhouse, of Rhea county, colonel; J. D. Swan, lieutenant-colonel, and McD. J. Burch, major.

But the greatest event in the history of Tennessee, as of the Union at large, was the war of the Rebellion. Because of the peculiar condition of society in the eastern part of the state, only one in twenty of the population being slaves, the stronghold of the Unionists was in East Tennessee. And this was true even after the firing on Fort Sumter, this fact being due in large part to the attitude assumed by such leaders as Andrew Johnson, T. A. R. Nelson, William G. Brownlow, Horace Maynard, Connolly F. Trigg, Oliver P. Temple, and others who, though of less prominence, were yet of equal patriotism. These men and such men as these did all in their power to prevent Tennessee from seceding from the Union. The first great movement that distinguished East Tennessee from the rest of the state in this matter was made in May, 1861, on the 30th of which month there assembled at Knoxville five hundred delegates from all portions of East Tennessee, in pursuance of the following call, the meeting being held in Temperance Hall:

"The undersigned, a portion of the people of East Tennessee, disapproving of the hasty and inconsiderate action of our general assembly, and sincerely desiring to do, in the midst of the trouble which surrounds us, what will be the best for our country, and for all classes of our citizens, respectfully appoint a convention to be held in Knoxville on Thursday, the 30th of May inst.; and we urge every county in East Tennessee to send delegates to this convention, that the conservative element of our whole section may be represented, and that wise and judicious councils may prevail—looking to peace and harmony among ourselves.

F. S. Heiskell.	John Williams.	W. H. Rogers.
John J. Craig.	S. R. Rogers.	John Baxter.

Dr. W. A. Rogers.   O. P. Temple.   W. G. Brownlow.
John Tunnell.   C. F. Trigg.   C. H. Baker.
David Burnett.   And others."

After prayer by Rev. Thomas W. Humes, Hon. Thomas A. R. Nelson was made permanent chairman and John M. Fleming secretary; the chairman and General Thomas D. Arnold delivered addresses, and a general committee was appointed representing most of the counties in East Tennessee, of which Connolly F. Trigg was chairman, and the convention adjourned until next day. At this time a report of the general committee was presented, debated and adopted. This report consisted of a long preamble and twelve resolutions, the principal ones of which were as follows:

"First. That the evil which now afflicts our beloved country in our opinion is the legitimate result of the ruinous and heretical doctrine of secession; that the people of East Tennessee have ever been and we believe still are opposed to it by a very large majority.

"Second. That while the country is upon the very threshold of a ruinous and most desolating civil war, it may with truth be said, and we protest before God, that the people (so far as we can see) have done nothing to produce it.

"Sixth. That the legislature of the state, without first having obtained the consent of the people, had no authority to enter into a 'military league,' with the 'Confederate States,' against the general government, and by so doing to put the state of Tennessee in hostile array against the government of which it then was and still is a member. Such legislation in advance of the expressed will of the people, to change their governmental relations, was an act of usurpation and should be visited with the severest condemnation of the people.

*   *   *   *   *

"Eighth. That the general assembly in passing a law authorizing the volunteers to vote wherever they may be on the day of election, whether in or out of the state, and in offering to the 'Confederate States' the capitol of Tennessee, together with other acts, have exercised powers and stretched their authority to an extent not within their constitutional limits, and not justified by the usages of the country."

* * * * *

"Tenth. That the position the people of our sister state of Kentucky have assumed in this momentous crisis, commands our highest admiration. Their interests are our interests. Their policy is the true policy, as we believe, of Tennessee and all the border states. And in the spirit of freemen, with an anxious desire to avoid the waste of the blood and treasure of the state, we appeal to the people of the state of Tennessee, while it is yet in their power, to come up in the majesty of their strength and restore Tennessee to her true position."

The convention adjourned to meet at the call of the president.

Andrew Johnson then followed with an able address in favor of the Union. A large number of these resolutions was printed and distributed throughout the state, but the tide of secession in Middle and West Tennessee was so strong that it was impossible to check its progress. It was so strong, in fact, that many ardent and able Union men were carried away with it, and became the most powerful advocates of the destruction of the Union. At the election held on June 8, 1861, there were cast in East Tennessee against secession 32,962 votes, while the entire number cast in the state against this doctrine was only 47,274. And it is somewhat remarkable that the number of soldiers furnished to the Union army by East Tennessee should be almost precisely the same, viz., 31,092.

Three days after this election was held Judge Nelson issued a call for the East Tennessee convention to meet on the 17th of the month at Greeneville, which convention was attended by delegates from all the counties in East Tennessee except Rhea. It remained in session four days. At this convention a declaration of grievances was adopted and a series of resolutions similar to those already quoted as having been adopted at the Knoxville convention. The third resolution entire was as follows:

"Third. That in order to avert a conflict with our brethren in other parts of the state, and desiring that every constitutional means shall be resorted to for the preservation of peace, we do therefore constitute and appoint O. P. Temple of Knox, John Netherland of Hawkins and James P. McDowell of Greene, commissioners, whose duty it shall be to prepare a memorial and cause the same to be presented to the general assembly of Tennessee, now in session, asking its consent that the counties composing East Tennessee and such counties in Middle Tennessee as desire to co-operate with them, may form and erect a separate state."

The fourth resolution provided for an election to be held in the counties of East Tennessee and such adjacent counties of Middle Tennessee as might desire to unite with East Tennessee, at which election delegates should be chosen to meet in convention at Kingston at such time as the proper officer of the convention should select, and in the sixth resolution it was provided that Knox county should be represented by three delegates, Washington, Jefferson and Greene two each, and all the other counties one each.

There were published in pamphlet form 20,000 copies of the proceedings of this Greeneville convention, the same pamphlet containing the proceedings of the Knoxville convention. Brownlow's Knoxville Whig, which had a large circulation in East Tennessee, was a powerful influence in favor of the Union cause, and taking all things into consideration, it was seen by the Confederate authorities and those favoring secession that nothing but military force could accomplish anything in East Tennessee toward suppressing the

Union sentiment existing there, stimulated and maintained as it was by such men as Judge T. A. R. Nelson, Connolly F. Trigg, Oliver P. Temple and William G. Brownlow.

The unconquerable Union sentiment thus existing in the eastern part of the state did much to prevent and delay the organization of regiments to aid the Confederate cause, and several of the young men favoring this cause, anxious to enter the field, went down into Georgia and united with the first regiment raised in that state. But as it was seen by the secession leaders to be necessary to suppress the Unionists who would, if left to follow out their own will and policy, destroy communication between Virginia and the states southwest of Tennessee, the old fair grounds two miles west of Knoxville were converted into a camp for such secession companies and regiments as might be organized in East Tennessee. On May 29, the Third (Confederate) Tennessee regiment, made up mainly from citizens of Monroe county, which was strongly secession, was organized, and soon afterward the Fourth and Nineteenth regiments were also organized. On July 26, General Zollicoffer reached this camp and assumed command of the Confederate forces in East Tennessee, remaining in Knoxville until the following September, when he went to Cumberland Gap, leaving Col. W. B. Wood in command of the camp at the fair grounds. November 15, Col. Wood was succeeded by General W. H. Carroll, with General G. B. Crittenden as division commander, who also had his headquarters at Knoxville.

The first company organized in Knox county for service in the Confederate army was Company E, Nineteenth Tennessee infantry, which was in May, 1861, with the following officers: Dr. John Paxton, captain; John Miller, first lieutenant; George Boyce, second lieutenant; L. B. Graham, third lieutenant; Samuel Hamilton, orderly sergeant. In 1862 this company was reorganized and then had officers as follows: W. W. Lackey, captain; S. Abernethey, first lieutenant; H. A. Waller, second lieutenant; J. L. Waller, third lieutenant. Captain Lackey was killed at the battle of Chickamauga, September 19, 1863, and was succeded as captain by Second Lieutenant H. A. Waller. The Nineteenth regiment was organized at the fair grounds near Knoxville, June 10, 1862, by the selection of the following officers: D. H. Cummings, colonel; F. M. Walker, lieutenant colonel; A. Fulkerson, major; V. Q. Johnson, adjutant; J. D. Taylor, quartermaster; H. M. Doak, sergeant major; J. E. Dulaney, surgeon, and Rev. D. Sullins, chaplain.

While Company E, of the Nineteenth infantry mentioned above as the only company raised in Knox county that joined that regiment, yet there was a considerable number of residents of Knox county that joined the Fourth infantry, of which the colonel was W. M. Churchwell, and also the Thirty-first, commanded by Col. William Bradford. Of this latter regiment James W. Humes was lieutenant colonel and James White, sergeant major, both of whom were from Knoxville.

Of the Sixty-fifth Tennessee infantry, Company D was partially recruited at Knoxville in May, 1862, by Captain A. A. Blair. The remainder of the company was raised in Washington and Hawkins counties. The officers, aside from the captain, were J. R. McCallum, first lieutenant; J. W. Carter, second lieutenant; J. L. Wilson, third lieutenant, and R. N. McCallum, orderly sergeant.

Quite a number of men went from Knoxville and Knox county into the First and Second Tennessee cavalry. The First Tennessee cavalry was organized at first at Knoxville in August, 1861, as "Brazleton's Battalion," and then consisted of seven companies commanded by Lieutenant Colonel William Brazleton, with William Bradford as major. In the spring of 1862, when the battalion was reorganized, James E. Carter became lieutenant colonel and Alonzo Bean, major. Afterward at Murfreesboro the battalion was recruited to a full regiment, with James E. Carter, colonel; Alonzo Bean, lieutenant colonel; Alexander Goforth, major, and J. D. Carter, adjutant. The only company in this regiment from

Knox county was Company E, of which the captain was John Jarnagin. After seeing service in various parts of the state, it participated in the siege of Knoxville under Gen. Longstreet, and remained with him during his stay in East Tennessee.

In the Second Tennessee cavalry the greater portion of the men from Knox county were in Company I, of which the captain was N. C. Langford.

Besides the infantry and cavalry mentioned above there were recruited in Knox county for the Confederate service four batteries of light artillery. One of these batteries was organized in the spring of 1861 by H. L. W. McClung; E. S. McClung was the senior first lieutenant; Alexander Allison, junior first lieutenant; William Lewis, senior second lieutenant. The battery of this company consisted of four smooth-bore six-pounders and two twelve-pounder howitzers.

Burrough's battery was organized in June, 1861, by W. H. Burroughs, who was elected captain; James C. Luttrell, first lieutenant; G. A. Huwald, junior first lieutenant; J. E. Blackwell, senior second lieutenant, and J. J. Burroughs, junior second lieutenant.

Kain's battery was organized in March, 1862, with W. C. Kain, captain; Thomas O'Connor, senior first lieutenant; Hugh L. White, junior first lieutenant; James Newman, senior second lieutenant, and W. C. Danner, junior second lieutenant.

Huwald's battery was organized later with G. A. Huwald, captain; G. B. Ramsey, first lieutenant; William Martin, second lieutenant, and Charles McClung, third lieutenant.

As has been stated elsewhere, most of the Union regiments and companies from East Tennessee were organized in Kentucky from bands of refugees who went to that state for the purpose of being thus organized, because they could not well be organized at home. And it necessarily happened that very few companies were organized wholly from any one county. Of the First Tennessee cavalry Company C was composed mainly of men from Knox county. This company was organized with James P. Brownlow, captain, who, upon becoming lieutenant colonel, was succeeded by M. T. Burkhart; and upon the promotion of Capt. Burkhart to major of the regiment, the command of the company devolved upon Elbert J. Cannon. The last captain of the company was Jacob K. Lones, who was commissioned in December, 1863. John Roberts and James H. Smith were successively second and first lieutenants. The entire number of men in the company was 122, of whom forty-one were killed or died of wounds or disease.

There was also a considerable number of men from Knox county in the Second, Third, Fourth and Ninth cavalry regiments.

The First Tennessee cavalry was organized at Camp Garber, Ky., March 1, 1862, as the Fourth Tennessee infantry, and remained an infantry regiment until November 1, 1862, when it was transferred to the cavalry arm of the service. The first officers of this regiment were as follows: Robert Johnson, colonel; James P. Brownlow, lieutenant colonel; James O. Berry, major, and John Hall, adjutant. When it became a cavalry regiment, M. T. Burkhart became major and was succeeded in this office by William R. Tracy. In the summer of 1863, Russell Thornburgh and Calvin M. Dyer successively became majors, and both of them subsequently became lieutenant colonels. Henry G. Flagg and Burton Smith were also promoted to the rank of major, the former in August, 1863, and the latter in July, 1864.

The Third and Sixth regiments of infantry were also composed largely of men from Knox county and the county was well represented in the First, Second and Eighth regiments. The companies in the Third Tennessee infantry, organized in part or in whole from Knox county men, were D, F, H and I.

Company D was organized February 10, 1862, with John O'Keefe, captain; W. C. Robison, first lieutenant; S. L. King, second lieutenant, and W. C. Brandon, orderly sergeant.

Company F was organized with J. L. Ledgerwood, captain; James Clapp, first lieutenant; C. Rutherford, second lieutenant, and C. Zachary, orderly sergeant. Of company H, J. W. Adkinson was captain; J. G. Roberts, first lieutenant, and W. W. Adkinson, second lieutenant. Not long after the organization J. G. Roberts became captain and E. C. Roberts first lieutenant. Company I was organized with E. D. Willis, captain; W. L. Ledgerwood, first lieutenant; J. H. Ellis, second lieutenant, and R. Bince, orderly sergeant. Afterward by promotion W. L. Ledgerwood became captain; J. H. Ellis, first lieutenant, and J. C. Bayless, second lieutenant.

The Sixth Tennessee infantry was organized almost wholly from Knox county, all but Companies E and F. Company E was from Claiborne county and Company F from Campbell county. Company A was organized with A. M. Gamble, captain; Thomas D. Edington, first lieutenant, and V. F. Gossett, second lieutenant. In August, 1862, Captain Gamble was promoted as major, the inferior officers being regularly advanced, W. W. Dunn becoming second lieutenant. Company B was organized with Spencer Deaton, captain; James M. Armstrong, first lieutenant; Thomas A. Smith, second lieutenant, and William D. Atchely, orderly sergeant. In May, 1864, James M. Armstrong became captain of the company. Company C was organized with Rufus M. Bennett, captain; John P. Barger, first lieutenant; William L. Lea, second lieutenant, and Joseph A. E. Blang, orderly sergeant. In March, 1863, Lieutenant Lea became captain, and was killed August 6, 1864, being succeeded as captain by Adam T. Cottrell. G. L. Maloney was made first lieutenant and James M. Berry, second lieutenant. Company D was organized with M. D. Bearden, captain; S. L. Gilson, first lieutenant; Thomas Parham, second lieutenant, and William N. Price, orderly sergeant. In January, 1863, James H. Coleman became first lieutenant and was succeeded in July, 1864, by J. L. Turner. F. B. Nickell becoming second lieutenant. Company G was organized with Francis H. Bounds, captain;

A. E. Murphy, first lieutenant; A. M. Cate, second lieutenant, and Ignaz Fanz, orderly sergeant.

The officers of this regiment were as follows: Joseph A. Cooper, colonel; Edward Maynard, lieutenant colonel; William C. Pickens, major; D. W. Parker, adjutant; William Rule, commissary sergeant, and T. T. Thornburgh, sergeant major. In August, 1862, A. M. Gamble became major and in 1863 William Rule adjutant.

Of the Seventh Tennessee mounted infantry, one company was organized in Knox county with Charles W. Cross, captain; T. L. B. Huddleston, first lieutenant; S. D. Webster, second lieutenant, and E. E. Longmire, orderly sergeant.

On July 10, 1861, Judge T. A. R. Nelson issued a proclamation for an election to be held August 31, at which delegates were to be chosen as provided by the convention which had met at Greeneville, but this election was not held. At an election held during the first week in August, Horace Maynard, T. A. R. Nelson, and G. W. Bridges were elected representatives to the congress of the United States, and Judge Nelson, a few days afterward, while on his way to take his seat in congress, was arrested in Lee county, Virginia, and taken to Richmond, where he was paroled and sent home. Mr. Bridges was also arrested, in Morgan county, but was released on taking the oath of allegiance to the Confederate States.

Meantime, during the summer and fall of 1861, the Unionists were organizing themselves into companies and regiments, and preparing for active service in defense of the government to which they owed allegiance. In some localities this was done openly because of the prevailing Union sentiment, but in other places this organizing and drilling had to be carried on in secret. Many of them then sought opportunity to enlist in Federal regiments by making their way into Kentucky, where they were organized into regiments.

On October 11, the Thirty-seventh (Confederate) regiment was organized with Moses White, colonel; H. P. Moffet, lieutenant colonel, and W. M. Hunt, major. But it was so difficult to supply this regiment with arms that on December 9, 1861, of the 771 men belonging thereto only 200 had arms of any kind, and many of these were wholly unfit for use. On December 10, Gen. Carroll, with his brigade, was ordered to join Gen. Zollicoffer, but could not move until the close of the month. When he did go away, Major G. H. Monserrat was left in command at Knoxville. In March, 1862, Gen. E. Kirby Smith took command of the department of East Tennessee, with his headquarters at Knoxville for a short time. During the autumn of 1862 and the winter succeeding the post at Knoxville was under the command successively of Gen. J. P. McCown, Gen. Sam Jones and Gen. Maury, partially unavailing efforts being made in the meantime to enforce the conscription act. From April 27, 1863, to the following September, Gen. S. B. Buckner was in command at Knoxville.

This town, on account of its position among the mountains, was to a considerable extent inaccessible to the Federal forces, and it remained uninterrupted until the summer of 1863. Gen. William P. Sanders, while serving as chief of cavalry, department of the Ohio, made a raid into East Tennessee, as if for the capture of Knoxville, leaving Kentucky June 14, with 1,500 men, composed as follows: First Tennessee mounted infantry, 700 men; Forty-fourth Ohio mounted infantry, 200 men; One Hundred and Twelfth Illinois mounted infantry, 200 men; Seventh Ohio cavalry, 150 men; Second Ohio cavalry, 150 men; First Kentucky cavalry, 100 men, and one section of Konkle's First Ohio artillery.

This expedition entered East Tennessee at Wartburg, where it captured a small Confederate force and destroyed some supplies. Passing by Kingston and London, they being too strongly fortified for successful attack, it first struck the railroad at Lenoir's, where it captured another small force and began the work of destroying the railroad, tearing up gaps one mile apart all the way up to Knoxville, reaching the outskirts of this place on the 19th of the month. It drove in the Confederate pickets and threw the town into great consternation, as Gen. Buckner had just gone away to Big Creek Gap with all the available men in the city with the exception of the Fifty-fourth Virginia and the Sixth Florida. There was great hurrying to and fro to secure volunteers to man the small number of guns that were picked up from various parts of the town. But eight pieces of cannon were got ready for action, manned by convalescents and citizens. These guns were posted on College hill, on Mabry's hill and on Summit Hill, but the Union forces made no attack on the city, and there was only a little firing between the pickets of the two opposing detachments, this being at 2 a. m. of the 20th. At 8 o'clock, however, Gen. Sanders' men approached the town from the north, as if they intended to make an attack. Col. Haynes, Confederate commandant of the place, in the absence of Gen. Buckner, with a section of Wyly's battery, opened fire upon the Union forces as they closed in on the town north of the railroad shops, the Unionists taking shelter in the houses and sending forward sharpshooters to pick off the artillerists. At the same time the Union artillery opened fire at a distance of 800 yards on the Confederate batteries on Summit hill, killing Col. Pleasant M. McClung and Lieut. Fellows.

After a brief show of force, General Sanders withdrew and moved off toward Strawberry Plains. As he moved up the valley he laid waste the railroad, took a number of prisoners at New Market, destroyed the bridge at Mossy Creek, and then turned north to escape a superior force, which he had reason to fear would cut him off. He reached Kentucky on the 24th of the month, having destroyed the railroad at intervals from Lenoir's to Mossy Creek. During his next visit to Knoxville he lost his life.

On September 3d the advance portion of Gen. Burnside first entered the place, the general himself following the next day and establishing his headquarters in a house afterward occupied by the Journal newspaper, on Gay street. On October 22, 1863, the rumor was in circulation that Gen. Longstreet was on his way up the Tennessee valley from the vicinity of Chattanooga, and in order to meet this supposed movement, Gen. Burnside sent the greater part of his forces from Knoxville to Loudon. At Loudon he awaited the coming of Longstreet, who did not leave Chattanooga until November 4. Burnside's army consisted of the Ninth corps, commanded by Gen. Potter, and composed of two divisions commanded respectively by Gen. Hartranft and Gen. Ferrero; the Twenty-third corps, composed of two divisions, commanded respectively by Gen. White and Gen. Hascall, and a body of cavalry under Gen. J. M. Shackleford, numbering in all about 10,000 men.

Upon the appearance of Gen. Longstreet, Burnside's forces were arranged about as follows: The Ninth corps at Lenoir's, where a pontoon bridge had been thrown across the river; White's division was on the north side of the river at Loudon, and other portions of the Twenty-third corps were at Knoxville under command of Gen. John G. Parke. Burnside's chief of staff, Gen. Sanders, was in command of a division of mounted infantry and cavalry south of the river, not far from Rockford, and there were detachments at Maryville, Kingston and other places.

Longstreet's army consisted of Gen. Hood's, McLaws' and Wheeler's divisions, and two battalions of artillery commanded respectively by Col. Leyden and Col. Alexander, the entire strength of his army being about 20,000 men.

Gen. Wheeler, on the 13th of the month, with three brigades of cavalry, captured the detachment at Maryville and made an attempt on the heights south of Knoxville, but was here repulsed by Gen. Sanders after a fierce encounter. Thereupon he marched down the river to reunite his forces with the main army, which had thrown a bridge across the river at Huff's Ferry. The day before this capture of Maryville, Charles A. Dana, assistant secretary of war, and Col. Wilson, of Gen. Grant's staff, paid a visit to Burnside, and upon consultation it was determined to hold Knoxville at all hazards and Kingston also, if it did not involve too much loss. The next morning Burnside began to withdraw his forces from their position in front of Longstreet and soon after daylight on the 15th had his entire army moving toward Lenoir's, where two days' rations were issued and the army went into camp for the night. On the 16th Longstreet made a savage attack on Burnside at Campbell's station, but although gallant charges were made, he was compelled to retire. In this battle the Union loss was in killed, 26; in wounded, 166, and in missing, 57. The loss of the Confederates was in all probability fully as large.

Gen. Burnside, relieved of the pressure caused by this attack, began his retreat toward Knoxville, and although the night was very dark and the roads extremely heavy, he reached his destination by daylight next morning. Chief Engineer O. M. Poe had already selected the lines of fortification and the work of intrenching immediately began. Ferrero's division was posted on the west side of the city, and extended from the river to where the railroad crosses Second creek; Hartranft's division was on the north, extending from Second to First creek, along Vine street; and White's division was on the east, from First creek to the old glass works, and was strengthened by a portion of Hascall's division. Artillery was placed on all the hills on and within these lines, and a portion of the artillery supported Cameron's brigade of the Twenty-third corps, occupying the hills south of the river, across which a bridge had been thrown.

On the morning of the 17th, in order to delay as much as possible the approach of Gen. Longstreet, who was advancing by the Kingston pike, the cavalry of Gen. William P. Sanders was dismounted and sent out to meet him four or five miles from the city. The entire day was spent in skirmishing with McLaws' division, which was in the advance. Sanders slowly falling back and McLaws advancing until night, when Sanders made a determined stand about 500 yards above the house of R. H. Armstrong, where a line of defense, consisting of rails and rifle pits, was constructed, extending from the railroad to the river. McLaws occupied a line parallel to this line of Gen. Sanders, and just in front of the Armstrong house.

During the next day Gen. McLaws made strenuous attempts to force back the Union line, which was stubbornly defended because of the necessity of gaining time to strengthen the works around the city, every hour, according to Engineer O. M. Poe, being worth the addition of 1,000 men to the defense. But notwithstanding the resistance which he met, Gen. McLaws was so determined in his attack that about three o'clock in the afternoon he succeeded in breaking it down, and Gen. Sanders rode forward to direct the retreat. When Sanders had reached a point near the center of his line and immediately in its rear, he was so conspicuous an object on his snow-white horse that he was shot by a sharpshooter concealed in the Armstrong residence, and fell to the ground mortally wounded. He was promptly carried into the city and taken to the Lamar house, where he died at eleven o'clock next day, having been baptized one hour previously by Rev. J. A. Hyden, of the Methodist Episcopal church, and by moonlight in the evening of the 19th he was buried in the yard of the Second Presbyterian church, in the presence of Gen. Burnside and officers of the Union army, the services being conducted by Rev. Thomas W. Humes. After the fall of Gen. Sanders the command devolved upon Gen. Wolford, who succeeded in withdrawing his forces into the city, and Gen. Longstreet remained satisfied with the achievement of the day. Next day Gen. Longstreet's command was disposed for a determined siege, McLaw's division occupying the space between the railroad and the river; Hood's division that between the railroad and Clinton pike and Hart's completing the investment by extending from the Tazewell pike to the river on the east. During the next five or six days Longstreet was continually receiving reinforcements from Gen. Sam Jones, Gen. Jackson and Gen. "Cerro Gordo" Williams, and from the 18th to the 24th nothing was done except skirmishing and the making a few sallies from the Union lines for the purpose of destroying houses furnishing shelter for the sharpshooters of the Confederate army. The strengthening of the fortifications went steadily forward under the direction of Engineer O. M. Poe. First Creek was dammed at the Mabry street crossing, and Second creek at the railroad crossing, thus flooding the low ground along the railroad where "Flag Pond" had formerly been. And Fort Sanders, the name of which had been changed from Fort Buckner immediately after the killing of Gen. Sanders, was rendered practically impregnable by a deep ditch all round it, and in front of this ditch there was stretched a network of wires fastened to the stumps of trees which had been cut down for this purpose in part, these wires playing a very important part in the defense of the fort when the assault was finally made upon it.

On the night of the 24th Longstreet sent across the river near the Armstrong house a force of about 1,100 men, with the hope of carrying the heights south of the river, but this attempt was unsuccessful except as to the one hill below the university, which was captured and upon it placed a battery, which battery, however, was of little service in the siege. From this time on until the final attack was made on Fort Sanders but little was done except to make an occasional sortie for the possession of rifle-pits in front of the fort.

As is well known, the object of Gen. Longstreet was to starve the Union forces into surrender, in which he would certainly have succeeded had he cut off all the supplies from reaching the fort; but large quantities of provisions were continually brought down the Holston river from the vicinity of the French Broad under cover of the darkness and the fog, the river not being carefully guarded by the Confederate forces, and at the close of the siege, when the attack was made upon the fort, there were within the fortifications a sufficient supply to last the Federal army ten days. These supplies were freely furnished by the citizens in the immediate sections of the country, who were loyally disposed to the Government of the United States. It was therefore this faithfulness on the part of the people of East Tennessee that saved the city and caused its final abandonment by the Confederate forces. They were sent down the Holston by Captain Doughty and his company, who remained on the French Broad during the siege.

On November 28 Gen. Longstreet heard that Gen. Sherman was approaching the city for the relief of Gen. Burnside, and upon consultation with his officers determined that an immediate attack should be made upon Fort Sanders, in order to reduce it if possible before Sherman could reach the city. And on the morning of the 29th, which was Sunday, the attack was begun at daylight by three brigades of Gen. McLaws' division, composed of Mississippi, Georgia and South Carolina troops, a part of which force was the famous "Barksdale Brigade," but the obstacles in front of the fort were so numerous and so unexpected to the Confederate soldiers, especially the network of wire, the construction of which was suggested to the engineer by J. B. Hoxsie of Knoxville, that they were thrown into confusion. But notwithstanding the difficulties in the way three Confederate flags were planted upon the parapet, but the havoc caused in the assaulting column by the action of Lieut. Benjamin, who, taking the shells in his hand, cut the fuse to five seconds, lighted them with his cigar which he was smoking at the time, and threw them over the embankment into the heroic men struggling to scale the fortification, and thus caused them to fall back. Thus while the assault was most gallantly made it resulted in failure and the shattered forces had to be withdrawn. Longstreet soon afterward began a retreat up the valley to Morristown, and Gen. Burnside on the 12th of

December, having turned over the command to Gen. Foster, left the city.

Upon the arrival of Gen. Burnside in Knoxville the previous September, he appointed Gen. S. P. Carter provost marshal of East Tennessee, and in this position Gen. Carter remained until the close of hostilities.

Lieutenant-General A. P. Stewart, in his sketch of the Army of Tennessee, published in the Military Annals of Tennessee, by Dr. J. Berrien Lindsley of Nashville, says:

"The year 1863 had been a very eventful one. Vicksburg and Port Hudson had fallen, and the enemy were in possession of the Mississippi river. Gettysburg, perhaps the decisive battle of the war, had been fought and lost. The Army of Tennessee had retreated across the Cumberland mountains, had fought and gained the great battle of Chickamauga, and, as at Shiloh and Murfreesboro, had lost the fruits of victory and suffered the disaster of Missionary Ridge." In fact so full of events of great "pith and moment" was the year 1863, so actively engaged were the contending armies, and so poor were the means of communication, that little was known at the time, to the outside world, of the military movements and the great events that were transpiring in the Valley of East Tennessee. On September 3, 1863, Gen. Burnside reached Knoxville from Richmond, Ky., with an army of 20,000 men. Gen. Buckner, evacuating Knoxville, fell back to Loudon, and finally united with the Army of Tennessee, thus leaving upper East Tennessee virtually in possession of the Federal army.

"And after the signal but fruitless victory to the Confederates at Chickamauga, Gen. Rosecrans was relieved, and the Federal army at Chattanooga reorganized under Gen. Grant. On the 4th of November a council of war was called by Gen. Bragg, at which Generals Hardee, Breckenridge and Longstreet were present. Longstreet's campaign into East Tennessee was settled upon, and he received orders to begin his preparations, and on the same night the division of Gen.

McLaws was on the march. Part of Gen. Wheeler's cavalry corps, consisting of Armstrong's and Martin's divisions, accompanied the expedition. On the night of the 13th and 14th of November, Longstreet's corps crossed the Tennessee river at Huff's ferry, near Loudon, while Wheeler was sent with three brigades of cavalry to surprise a Federal cavalry force at Maryville, capture it, and then move to the rear of Knoxville and endeavor to gain possession of some of the heights on the south side, and hold until the arrival of the infantry; or, failing in this, to threaten the force at Knoxville, so as to prevent Burnside concentrating his forces against Longstreet before he reached Knoxville. Gen. Wheeler succeeded in surprising the force at Maryville; captured a part of it and dispersed the balance. He then moved on to Knoxville, and though he failed to get possession of any of the heights which commanded the town, created the diversion in Longstreet's favor. Longstreet moved slowly and cautiously but steadily forward. On the 16th he encountered the Federal force entrenched at Campbell's Station, and a severe fight ensued; the Federal loss being about three hundred and the Confederate loss one hundred and ninety-eight. During the night the main Federal forces were withdrawn into Knoxville and preparations for defense were pushed actively forward under the able direction of Capt. O. M. Poe, of the engineer corps. Longstreet closed in to the investment of Knoxville, but not without severe fighting. The Federal cavalry disputed every inch of ground. In a charge on the Federal lines on the 18th, the Confederates lost one hundred and forty men, and among the Federal slain was their gallant cavalry leader, Gen. Sanders. In his honor the name of Fort Loudon, which was built and named by Gen. Buckner during his occupancy of Knoxville, was immediately changed to "Fort Sanders," under which name it has gone into history. While Sanders on the Kingston road and Pennebaker on the Clinton road were disputing the advance of Longstreet, every available man in Knoxville was at work on the fortifications. Capt. Poe, in his report, says: "The citizens of the town and all contrabands within reach were pressed into service and relieved the almost exhausted soldiers, who had seen no rest for more than one hundred hours. Many of the citizens were rebels and worked with very poor grace, which blistered hands did not tend to improve." But as Capt. Poe says: "The hours in which to work, that the gallant conduct of our cavalry gave us, were worth to us 1,000 men each." Capt. Poe continues: "At daylight on the morning of November 19, our position had been much strengthened and we began to feel secure and confident." From this time until the final assault on Fort Sanders on the 29th, frequent, in fact almost constant skirmishes occurred; and as Gen. McLaws, in his report, says: "Sharpshooters, occupying rifle-pits between the main lines, were constantly exchanging shots whenever the slightest opportunity was offered by either party for even a chance hit; and they were in easy rifle range of each other." Artillery practice was kept up with more or less regularity from various points around the town. By the 28th there had been completed a continuous line of rifle-pits, connecting a series of strong earthwork forts. The forts were surrounded by deep, wide ditches. First and Second creeks were dammed so as to cover a mile or more of the valleys with water; and in front of Fort Sanders the saplings were cut down and the sharpened stumps converted into a veritable death trap. Telegraph wires were woven in and around the stumps, stretched tight and firmly fastened.

"On account of reports of a battle at Chattanooga there was a serious difference of opinion between Gen. Longstreet and Gen. McLaws as to the advisability of assaulting Fort Sanders. Gen. Longstreet, however, in his letter of November 28, settled the matter by saying: 'The assault must be made at the time appointed, and must be made with a determination which will insure success.'

"Gen. McLaws thereupon informed his brigadiers that the assault would be made at daylight the next morning. Sunday, the 29th of November, and the following orders were given for the assault:

" '1. A regiment from Humphreys' (Mississippi) brigade and one from Wofford's (Georgia) should be selected to lead in the assault. Wofford's regiment to lead the column composed of Wofford's brigade assaulting from the left, and Humphreys' regiment the column assaulting from the right, composed of two regiments of Humphreys' brigade, and three of Bryan's, following close on Humphreys as a reserve.

" '2. The brigades to be formed for the assault in columns of regiments.

" '3. The assault to be made with fixed bayonets and without firing a gun.

" '4. The assault should be made against the northwest angle of Fort Loudon.

" '5. The men should be urged to the assault with a determination to succeed, and should rush to it without halting, and, mounting the parapet, take possession of the work and hold it against all attempts to recover it.

" '6. That the sharpshooters should keep up a continuous fire into the embrasures of the enemy's works and along the fort, so as to prevent the use of their cannon, and distract, if not prevent, the fire from all arms.

" '7. Gen. Kershaw to advance to the assault on the right of the fort so soon as the fort was taken.'

"The commands selected for this terrible assault were made up of 'true and tried' soldiers. 'Theirs not to reason why, theirs but to do and die.' At 4 o'clock on the morning of the 29th, Gen. McLaws saw in the person to the formation of the assaulting column. The weather was bad, misty and freezing. A large number of the Confederates were barefooted and thinly clad. At last, as the first gray streaks of dawn announced the coming of the Sabbath morn, the booming of Confederate artillery gave the signal for the assault. Though 'cannon to the right of them, cannon to the left of them, cannon in front of them volleyed and thundered,' calmly but quickly with fixed bayonets and with the precision of dress parade, the assaulting columns moved through the mists of the early morning toward the bastions of the dimly outlined fort. The distance was short. The garrison was fully aware that the assault was to be made at daylight and every man was at his post. The embrasures of the fort bristled with twenty-pound Parrotts and twelve-pound Napolean guns, which had been double and triple shotted with shot and shell; and which, almost from the moment the columns moved, had full play upon them. Yet proudly, confidently, heroically and defiantly the gray, grim and grizzled veterans moved into the 'jaws of death.' Suddenly the head of the assaulting column was broken, the men pitching forward and falling over each other. They had struck the invisible telegraph wires stretched from stump to stump. The guns of the fort belched forth thunder and lightning into the disordered ranks. Quickly reforming under the galling fire, the Confederates rushed for the fort, when once again they halted. They had reached the deep, wide ditch about which they were misinformed, and over which they had no way to cross. Only for a moment they paused. Apparently endued with superhuman activity and determination they crossed the ditch, while volley after volley of artillery and musketry was poured into them from above, and while 'twenty-pound shells with fuses cut to explode them at twenty seconds were hurled from the fort into the living mass below.' Still onward was borne the cross of St. Andrews. The parapet was reached only to find it covered with ice. Undismayed the boys in gray attempted to scale the slippery sides. A few reached the top only to meet instant death or capture. Three times the cross-barred battle flag of the Confederates was planted on the parapet to float only for a moment. Col. Ruff, commanding Wofford's brigade, and Col. Thomas, his next in command, had been killed and the next in command wounded, and the brigade forced to retire. The assault had failed. Gen. McLaws, in his report, says: 'When it was seen that Wofford's brigade could not mount the parapet, Gen. G. T. Anderson's brigade of Hood's division came rushing to the assault in the same place where my command had attempted it, but was repelled at once and retired.' E. A. Pollard, the Southern historian, writing of the assault, says: 'Never, except at Gettysburg, was there in the history of the war a disaster adorned with the glory of such devout courage as seen at Longstreet's repulse at Knoxville.' The engagement lasted about twenty minutes. The Confederate loss, according to their official reports, was 129 killed, 458 wounded, 226 missing; total, 813. Georgia, Mississippi and South Carolina suffered most. Col. McElroy, of the Thirteenth Mississippi, was killed while leading the assault on the right. A few days afterward a Federal courier was captured, bearing an autograph letter from Gen. Grant to Gen. Burnside, informing him that three columns were advancing to his relief; one by the south side, under Gen. Sherman; one by Decherd under Gen. Elliott, and one by Cumberland Gap under Gen. Foster, and about the same time Wheeler's cavalry was ordered to rejoin Gen. Bragg's army, which had fallen back into Georgia, and Gen. Ransom had ordered two brigades of his cavalry, which had been operating around Knoxville, to rejoin him. Under these circumstances, believing it to be impossible to make a junction with Gen. Bragg, Gen. Longstreet concluded to withdraw in the direction of Virginia, and his orders to move were issued on December 2. On the night of the 4th the troops were withdrawn and the memorable siege of Knoxville was raised.

"In this short sketch it is impossible to mention, much less do justice, to the various commands engaged. While Knoxville was being besieged by Longstreet, the cavalry of Gen. Wheeler's and Gen. Ransom's commands were by no means idle. Almost daily encounters were had with the Federal troops in their efforts to prevent reinforcements or commissary stores from reaching Burnside's army, and the soil of East Tennessee drank deep of the blood of the brave and chivalrous troopers. The facts given in this sketch are taken mainly from official reports to be published in Vol. XXXI., Part I. of the 'Records of the War of the Rebellion.'"

With reference to the number of Confederate soldiers killed in the attack on Fort Sanders, it is altogether probable that the number given above (129) is considerably too low. Some time after the battle occurred Mr. S. T. Atkin went over the ground where these soldiers had been hurriedly buried, and seeing their bodies protruding from the ground, being rooted out and eaten by hogs, he suggested to a wealthy friend, whose name he prefers not to divulge, that they should be taken up and decently buried. This friend said to him that if he would have the work done, he (the friend) would pay the expense incurred. Mr. Atkin thereupon made a contract with James H. Renshaw, an undertaker, to make neat pine boxes to serve as coffins, and bury the dead in Bethel cemetery, and in due time Mr. Renshaw brought in his bill for $368, the price agreed upon having been $4 per corpse, which would make ninety-two buried in this way.

Besides these ninety-two there were buried immediately after the battle dead bodies to the number of 300, according to the present sexton of the Bethel or Confederate cemetery, thus making in all 392 that were killed in storming the fort.

Fort Sanders was a bastioned earthwork, built upon an irregular quadrilateral, the sides of which respectively, southern front, 125 yards; western front, 95 yards; northern front, 125 yards, and eastern front, 85 yards. The eastern front at the time of the attack was entirely open, the southern front was about one-half done, the western front was finished except cutting the embrasures, and the northern front was nearly finished. The bastion attacked was the only one completely finished. The fort was so constructed that apparently none of its guns protected this northwest corner, and Gen. Longstreet, noticing this fact, ordered the assault to be made upon it. No sooner, however, had he done this than the temporary embankments were removed and the guns inside the fort brought to bear with deadly effect upon the brave and determined men making the charge.

At the time of this assault there were within the fort Benjamin's battery, a part of Buckley's battery, a part of the Seventy-ninth New York infantry, four companies of the Second Michigan infantry, two companies of the Twentieth Michigan infantry, and one company of the One Hundredth Pennsylvania infantry, in the aggregate from 220 to 300 men. As to the losses sustained by each side, there are differences of statement, even in the official reports. Gen. Burnside on November 30, in his report, said that after the failure of the attack "we sent out a detachment to whom the rebels in the ditch surrendered, about 300 men and three stands of colors. Their killed and wounded amount to about 500, and our entire loss was about 20." Lieut. Benjamin, in command of a battery in the fort, in his report says: "We took about 250 prisoners, 17 of them commissioned officers, and over 200 dead and wounded lay in the ditch, among them three colonels." These were Col. Ruff, commanding Wofford's brigade which led the assault; Col. McElroy and Lieut.-Col. Thomas. Lieut. Benjamin also says that in the fort the loss was eight killed and five wounded.

According to Lieut.-Col. G. Moxley Sorrel, of Longstreet's army, the losses in that army on the 29th of November, in the assault on the fort, were as follows.

Brigade.	Killed.	Wounded.	Missing.	Total.
Anderson's	33	129	25	187
Wofford's	48	121	81	250
Bryan's	27	121	64	212
Humphrey's	21	87	56	164
Totals	129	458	226	813

One remarkable thing about this assault was that both Gen. Alexander and Gen. Longstreet thought there was no ditch in front of the fort, or at least no ditch that would interfere with the attack. Gen. Longstreet testified before the court martial that he had seen a man walk down the parapet across the ditch and up on the outside without jumping and without apparent difficulty, and some of the officers stated that they had seen dogs passing over the same ditch on the west side, hence the inference that even if there were a ditch in front of the fort it would in reality be no obstacle to an assault.

The spot where Gen. Sanders fell from his horse was marked by a common rough stone, and there was a solitary cedar tree standing near. This tree is still standing, about one-half mile east of the Armstrong residence.

For nearly twenty-five years the battlements of Fort Sanders stood out boldly against the sky, a monument to the bravery of the men in both armies; but by 1887 streets were run through the fortifications in both directions and beautiful homes began to be erected on either side of these streets. The same thing was then occurring or had occurred all over the South, and the old soldiers by this time began to remember the various battlefields on which they had struggled to the death with each other as only places where they had displayed their fortitude, heroism and genius, the fierce passions of the conflict disappearing even as did the forts and embankments temporarily thrown up to give a temporary advantage to the army acting on the defensive.

It is asserted by some people that Fort Sanders should be converted into a government park or fort. Its condition at the present time (December, 1898) is as follows: A street runs through the center of the fort, with three or four residences upon it, which would be available as quarters for officers. The long slope to the west and north, up which the Confederates made such a gallant charge, is still open country and the line of the fort is well preserved. By the natural growth of the city of Knoxville all of this long slope, containing nearly eighty acres of land, will be covered with residences should not the government of the United States soon take action. It would be eminently appropriate for the government to commemorate the storming and defense of Fort Sanders, for here was fought one of the most determined and important battles of the war, and East Tennessee should have a monument which should speak for all time of a completely reunited country.

General William P. Sanders, killed in this attempt to retard the progress of Gen. Longstreet toward Knoxville, was the only Union general from any of the southern states killed during the Civil war. He fell mortally wounded November 18, 1863, about one mile below or west of Knoxville. He was born in Kentucky and entered West Point from Mississippi in 1852, graduating from that institution in 1856. At San Diego, Cal., during 1856-57, he was lieutenant of dragoons and served in the Utah campaign from 1857 to 1861, in the latter year becoming captain in the United States cavalry in the defense of Washington, D. C. From August, 1861, to March, 1862, he was thus engaged, and from the latter date to the fall of 1862 he saw active service in the Peninsular campaign under Gen. McClellan. He was engaged in the Maryland campaign from September to November, 1862. On March 4, 1863, he became colonel of the Fifth Kentucky cavalry and joined in the chase after Gen. John Morgan during his famous raid. During September and October, 1863, he served as chief of the cavalry department of Ohio and was in command of a division of cavalry, Twenty-third army corps, from October 23 to November 18, 1863, the latter day being that on which he fell a victim to the enemy's bullets. On the day before he had been charged with the duty of delaying Longstreet's advance upon the city while the intrenchments about the city were being strengthened, and during the 17th and 18th his division held the enemy in check though hard pressed, but was driven in toward the close of the second day.

The battle thus fought in which General Sanders lost his life was fought almost entirely between southern troops, it being a clash between General Sanders' Kentucky division and Kershaw's South Carolina troops. Sanders' division was composed of the following brigades:

First brigade—First, Eleventh and Twelfth Kentucky cavalry.

Second brigade—Eighth Michigan cavalry and Forty-fifth Ohio mounted infantry.

Third brigade—Eleventh and Twenty-seventh Kentucky mounted infantry, Laws' howitzer battery and the Fifteenth battery Indiana light artillery.

Kershaw's command contained the Second, Third, Seventh, Eighth and Fifteenth South Carolina regiments and the Third battalion, all infantry.

Sanders' division was dismounted and posted in a transverse line across the hills from the railroad to the river immediately east of the Armstrong residence and one mile to the west of Knoxville. Sanders' men were not accustomed to fighting, but were well armed, some of them with the best rifles then known. Their stand was so stubborn that it required a strong display of force in infantry and artillery to drive them back.

General Longstreet in his official report says:

"The next day (18th) in riding to Gen. McLaws' front I found that the enemy's pickets occupied the same ground they had held the day before. Col. Alexander was ordered to use his guns against this defense. I finally ordered Gen. McLaws to order his troops to take this position."

The fighting was very sharp and well sustained on both sides. At 2 p. m. the Confederate forces moved their battery down to within 600 yards, but nevertheless the Union forces held their ground. The Confederates charged four lines deep to within twenty-five yards of the Union line, but were met with such a terrible shower of Minie bullets that it was impossible for them to make further headway. Four charges of this kind were made, each being repulsed. Longstreet says:

"Part of the troops moved up handsomely and got partial

possession; others faltered and sought shelter under a rise of ground. When Capt. Winthrop of Col. Alexander's staff approached the enemy and coming up in front of the line led the troops over the works, he had the misfortune to receive a severe wound."

The Forty-fifth Ohio was overpowered and driven from the field, perceiving which Capt. B. T. Thompson of the One Hundred and Twelfth Illinois ordered his men to fall back, that part of the Confederate line which had confronted the Forty-fifth Ohio passed around his right flank and came up in the rear of his position. After this there was sharp fighting in the vicinity of the Armstrong residence, and Capt. Thompson captured a colonel and a part of a regiment of Kentuckians.

One of the pleasant incidents in the history of Knoxville was the reunion of the veteran soldiers of both armies, which occurred on October 7, 8 and 9, 1890. Many were present from both North and South, and there were about 10,000 people in the city from Tennessee and Georgia. The Seventy-ninth New York volunteer infantry, otherwise known as the Highlander regiment, was represented by a large number of its survivors, and on account of its having borne a conspicuous part in the defense of Fort Sanders on that memorable November 23, 1863, was equally conspicuous on this re-union occasion. A welcoming address was delivered by Gen. R. N. Hood, which was happily responded to by Gen. William H. Gibson of Ohio. On the second day Hon. J. W. Caldwell delivered an address, as also did Mr. W. A. Henderson. An address prepared for the occasion by Gen. Longstreet was read by Hon. E. A. Angier, of Atlanta, Ga., Gen. Longstreet being unable to deliver it on account of a wound in the neck which he received during the war. A poem was read by Mr. J. R. McCallum, which was well received.

By an act of congress approved March 3, 1819, the secretary of war of the United States, under whose jurisdiction the payment of pensions was at that time, was authorized to appoint an agent, in addition to the one already appointed in Tennessee, for the purpose of paying such pensioners of the United States as resided in Eastern Tennessee. The precise date of the appointment of this additional agent can not be ascertained, but the records show that he began the payment of pensions September 4, 1819, and that he rendered his first account current, through the secretary of war, to the treasury department, December 31, 1819. The first pension agent was Mr. Luke Lea, who was then cashier of the bank of Tennessee at Knoxville. His successors have been as follows: Robert King, John T. King, William Lyon, John Cocke, Jr., David A. Deaderick, Isaac Lewis, Samuel Morrow, James E. Armstrong, John Caldwell, Daniel T. Boynton, Henry R. Gibson, Robert L. Taylor, Joseph H. Wagner, Daniel A. Carpenter, William Rule, Daniel A. Carpenter, and John T. Wilder, the latter of whom was appointed December 10, 1897, and is at present in office.

In connection with the statement which will be found in this chapter as to the amount of money disbursed from Knoxville to the pensioners of the various wars, the following information as to the numbers of these pensioners, classified in accordance with the wars on account of which they draw their pensions, will be found of interest:

Under the general law there were at the close of the fiscal year 1897-98, 9,599 invalids; 37 nurses, and 3,908 widows; under the law of June 27, 1890, 25,248 invalids, and 8,103 widows; on account of the war of 1812, 589 widows; war with Mexico, 2,881 survivors, and 2,850 widows; Indian wars of 1832-42, 1,624 survivors and 3,248 widows. On June 30, 1897, there were on the pension rolls in Knoxville 57,592 pensioners, and on June 30, 1898, 58,087.

The following statement of the disbursements by fiscal years from the Knoxville pension agency, was furnished by request to the writer of this chapter by the Hon. William Youngblood, Auditor for the Interior Department, Treasury Department, at Washington, D. C.:

"Statement showing the amount of money paid on account of pensions at the Knoxville, Tenn., Agency, during the fiscal years 1869 to 1898, inclusive.

Fiscal Years.	Amounts.	Fiscal Years.	Amounts.
1869	$ 326,355.53	1884	$2,815,612.72
1870	572,997.89	1885	3,214,278.63
1871	442,650.25	1886	3,397,011.36
1872	510,045.32	1887	4,161,745.88
1873	455,012.28	1888	3,901,978.67
1874	413,506.29	1889	4,070,189.74
1875	409,912.73	1890	4,743,603.41
1876	371,059.52	1891	5,482,196.82
1877	344,909.50	1892	6,870,276.52
1878	1,002,262.81	1893	8,324,748.00
1879	1,652,781.86	1894	7,745,817.55
1880	3,288,926.62	1895	7,647,587.00
1881	2,691,993.54	1896	7,427,514.44
1882	2,507,932.86	1897	7,828,709.79
1883	2,866,820.72	1898	8,082,496.80

Total.............$103,510,935.05"

The pension office at Knoxville pays out money to pensioners in the following states and territories: Tennessee, North Carolina, South Carolina, Georgia, Florida, Alabama, Mississippi, Louisiana, Arkansas, and Texas, and Oklahoma and the Indian Territory. There is paid to the employes in this pension office about $25,000, and supplies cost $2,000, thus $27,000 is spent in Knoxville on account of the office.

The primary cause of the war with Spain was her treatment of the Cubans, concentrating them in cities and towns and starving them into submission to tyrannical methods of government. The incentive cause was the blowing up of the United States battleship, Maine, in the harbor of Havana, February 15, 1898, the explosion causing the disaster being so tremendous as to shake the very city of Havana, and besides destroying the ship, killing 266 American sailors and marines. For while there were a few people in the United

States who actually believed that the explosion was the result of an accident interior to the Maine herself, yet the great majority quickly came to the conclusion, to which they still rigidly adhere, that the explosion came from the outside. A court of inquiry consisting of Captain Sampson, Captain Chadwick and Lieutenant Marix was appointed by Captain Sigsbee of the battleship Maine, and the people of the United States were requested by Captain Sigsbee to suspend judgment as to the origin of the disaster until this court of inquiry should have time to thoroughly investigate and make its report. The popular belief, however, was strengthened and intensified by the report of Diver J. W. Bonner, who went to Havana harbor February 23, worked on the wreck until February 28, and found that the forward turret of the ship had been thrown from the port side of the vessel backward a distance of seventy feet into the starboard superstructure, and that the ship's bottom on the starboard side had been thrown up and that it projected four feet above the surface of the water, which would have been impossible from an interior explosion.

A great tidal wave of patriotism swept over the country, which so acted on congress that on March 7 that body appropriated $50,000,000 to be used by the President of the United States at his discretion for the public defense, and while it was thought for a time that foreign nations would array themselves in support of Spain in case of war between that country and the United States, yet that fear soon vanished, especially when it became evident that England would remain steadfastly the friend of the latter country.

That war was inevitable became evident within one month from the blowing up of the Maine; but there was much disappointment upon the receipt of the report of the court of inquiry, for although it confirmed the popular belief in the exterior origin of the explosion yet it utterly failed to fix the responsibility therefor.

March 29 resolutions were introduced into congress providing for the recognition of the independence of Cuba, and there was much impatience manifested throughout the country because the President appeared to be opposed to warlike measures, but the people did not so fully understand the true condition of the army and navy as did the President. As in other states of the Union active preparations for war began in Tennessee in advance of the declaration of war by congress. In the month of March it was decided by the state authorities to increase the number of men in each company of militia to 100, and the militia was ready before April 1 to respond to any call that might be made upon them by President McKinley. In order to accommodate all such as might desire to enter the service of the state the Legion armory in Knoxville was kept open on Tuesdays, Wednesdays and Fridays of each week, and Major Ramage of the First battalion was anxious to enlist men enough to fill his companies, A and B, as soon as possible. March 31 an election of officers for company B was held, resulting in the election of W. H. Purple, captain; C. M. Dyer, first lieutenant; J. N. Day, second lieutenant. On April 11 President McKinley, by a message to congress, asked for the use of the army and navy to secure the termination of hostilities in Cuba, between Spain and the insurgents, which caused varied opinion and comment. April 19 both houses of congress passed resolutions demanding that Spain withdraw her land and naval forces from Cuba and Cuban waters, and directing and empowering the President to use the entire land and naval forces of the United States, and to call out the militia of the several states to such extent as might be necessary to carry these resolutions into effect. On April 18, the local troops of Knoxville and vicinity were in readiness to move, both those of the First battalion and of company C, unattached. The captains of these three companies were as follows: Company A, Mel. Brandon; company B, W. H. Purple, and company C, W. H. Brown. Rev. John H. Frazee was chaplain of the First battalion and Rev. M. D. Jeffries of company C.

Battery D of the Fifth United States artillery were the first troops seen in Knoxville after the trouble with Spain began. This was April 21, 1898, the battery consisting of seventy-five men and being on its way to Chickamauga. Battery F came next day, and afterward followed troops C, E, F, and G of the Third United States cavalry. The passing of these soldiers through the city raised the enthusiasm of the people to the highest state. April 21 came an order for the organization of a regiment in East Tennessee, and on the same day twenty young men from Carson-Newman college at Mossy Creek were admitted to company C. At this time came the news of the firing of the first gun of the war by Captain Washburn Maynard, second son of Hon. Horace Maynard. Captain Maynard being a Knoxville boy, born in that city in 1846, and entering the academy at Annapolis in 1865, graduating there in 1869. He made the first capture of the war, of the steamer Buena Ventura, with a cargo of 875,000 feet of lumber worth $10,000.

President McKinley issued his call for volunteers April 23, 1898, for 125,000 men, to serve for two years or during the war, unless sooner discharged. On the same day Adjutant General Sykes called out the entire national guard of the state of Tennessee, numbering 3,800 infantry and 200 artillery. The First battalion assembled at Pilgrim Congregational church Sunday, April 24, to listen to a sermon from their chaplain, Rev. John H. Frazee, and on the next day Captains Brandon and Purple were detailed as recruiting officers in order to fill up their respective commands. Finally on April 25 war was declared against Spain, by which the public mind was greatly relieved and satisfied that something was to be done that would redound to the honor of the country. On the same day an order was issued by Secretary of War Alger calling upon the several states for troops. Tennessee being required to furnish three regiments, and Nashville being designated as the rendezvous.

Recruiting troops in Knoxville was an easy matter, there

being more men applying for position in the several companies organized than they could hold. On the day of the declaration of war the two companies of the First battalion were filled, and there were men enough over to fill another company. A Legion Flag fund, started by Mrs. Mary Burns, was quickly raised to $87.50, and a committee appointed to oversee the matter of the presentation of the flag, which took place Wednesday morning, April 27. On the day previous company D from Elizabethtown and company K from Greeneville arrived in Knoxville, a large number coming in from Mossy Creek to join with company C. A meeting was held for the purpose of raising money with which to purchase blankets for the boys, $192.69 being quickly raised, and 160 men being supplied in this way. April 27 the inspection and examination of the recruits was begun in Knoxville, a corps of physicians volunteering for the purpose, consisting of Drs. William Bowen, J. F. Scott, John W. Carmichael, S. R. Miller and S. M. Miller. From the membership of company C, numbering 108 men, eighteen were rejected. The requirements were that each man must stand at least five feet four inches in height, weigh 128 pounds, have good eyes, good hearing, be temperate, have a minimum chest measure of thirty-four inches and a minimum chest expansion of one and a half inches. On April 28 a fund was raised quickly running up to $573.74 for the purchase of supplies for the soldiers, and on May 3 the companies of Major Ramage's command left Knoxville for Nashville. A war committee was selected, consisting of H. M. Branson, Jesse L. Rogers, Peter Kern, Daniel Briscoe, W. E. Gibbins, S. N. Littleton, N. B. Morrell, Edward Maynard and R. W. Austin, which did much and very efficient work during the continuance of the war.

Major Weeks, formerly Captain Weeks, of company D, which came in from Elizabethton, arrived in Knoxville May 12 to take charge of the recruiting and to raise if possible 100 men, as so many of those who had enlisted at first failed to pass the examination. The three companies that left Knoxville as above related became companies A, B and C of the Third Tennessee, and before the examination occurred this regiment contained 1,134 men. On the 17th of the month Major Weeks sent forward to Nashville fifty-three men, forty-seven others being sent from other portions of East Tennessee. Dr. William Bowen was appointed surgeon of this regiment, with Drs. G. C. Givens of Harriman and G. Manning Ellis of Chattanooga as assistant surgeons. This regiment was the first in the Southern States mustered into the service of the United States for the war. The regiment reached Chickamauga Park May 24th, 1898. The field and staff officers were J. P. Fyffe, of Chattanooga, colonel; D. M. Coffman, of Rockwood, lieutenant colonel; W. H. Brown and E. C. Ramage, of Knoxville, and Weeks, of Elizabethton, majors; E. A. Turner, Chattanooga, adjutant; Hart Reeves, of Huntsville, quartermaster; Rev. J. C. Wright, of Harriman, chaplain, and Dr. William Bowen, of Knoxville, major surgeon. The number of men in the regiment at that time was 1,005. Together with the First Vermont and Eighth New York, it was assigned to the Third brigade of the First division of the Third army corps. When the regiment was ready to be mustered it was found there were too many companies, and company E, recruited by Capt. S. E. Beyland, was disbanded, the men being assigned to fill out the quota of other companies. When company G was about to be mustered it was found one man short, when Beyland quietly took off his shoulder straps and took his place in the ranks as a private soldier. The next day he was appointed ordnance sergeant of the regiment.

The Fourth Tennessee volunteers was mobilized at Knoxville and was the first regiment mustered under the President's second call for volunteers in the Spanish war. Its colonel was George Leroy Brown, a regular army officer who for some time had been engaged as commandant of cadets at the University of Tennessee. Harvey H. Hannah, of

Oliver Springs, was lieutenant colonel and W. C. Tatom major of the Second battalion. Rev. R. N. Price, of Morristown, afterwards became chaplain. Company A was commanded by Capt. Walter M. Fitzgerald, and was made up in Knox and adjacent counties, his lieutenants being Thos. E. Matson, of Johnson City, and J. E. Stokely, of Jefferson county. Wm. A. Knabe, of Knoxville, was chief musician and Wm. H. Sanders first principal. The regiment was mustered July 13th, 1898, remained in camps here until November 28th, on which date it left Knoxville for Cuba, sailing from Savannah December 1st, landing at the port of Trinidad December 6th. It remained here, the regiment being divided and battalions being on duty at different points, until March 28th, 1899, when it sailed for Savannah on April 1st. The regiment was kept in quarantine until April 8th, and was mustered out at Savannah on the 6th day of May, 1899. A reception was tendered the regiment at Chilhowee Park, soon after its arrival, at which words of welcome were spoken, followed by refreshments prepared for the occasion by Knoxville ladies.

The Sixth U. S. volunteers, a magnificent regiment, was mobilized at Knoxville, and was largely a Knoxville regiment. Its commander, Col. Laurence D. Tyson, was a Knoxville man and had been a regular army officer. Andrew S. Rowan, the lieutenant colonel, was also a regular army officer. Paul E. Divine, of Tazewell, and Spears Whitaker, of North Carolina, were majors. Cary F. Spence was adjutant and Horace Vandeventer quartermaster, both Knoxville men. Among the other officers of the regiment were First Lieutenants Thos. A. Davis, Frank Maloney, J. Baird French, George F. Milton, E. R. Carter, Frank E. Murphy, and Second Lieutenants J. Welcker Park, Cornelius Williams and E. E. Houk. Cary F. Spence, Horace Vandeventer, Thos. A. Davis and Frank Maloney were each afterwards promoted to the rank of captain. A. M. Hall was promoted from quartermaster sergeant to second lieutenant, Shirley E. Spence

IRON FURNACES, ROCKWOOD, TENNESSEE.

From *Southern Mountain Rambles* - Date Unknown

from sergeant major to second lieutenant, and Alvin Barton from first sergeant company C to second lieutenant. Frank E. Murphy was made adjutant and afterwards quartermaster of the regiment. J. Baird French was commissioned adjutant and held that position when the regiment was mustered out. The regiment was mustered at Camp Wilder on the 15th day of July, 1898, by Lieutenant Vestal, of the 7th U. S. cavalry. July 30th it was ordered to Chickamauga Park, where it became a part of the Second brigade, first division, Third army corps. It left Chickamauga Park October 6th, 1898, for New York and sailed from there for Porto Rico on the 9th of October, arriving at San Juan October 15th. The regiment was then divided and was on garrison duty at various points in the northern half of the island, with headquarters at Arecibo. This duty was performed until February 12th, 1899, when the regiment was ordered to Savannah to be mustered out. The muster-out occurred at Savannah March 15th, 1899.

Gen. John T. Wilder, on a visit to Secretary of War Alger, June 20th, 1898, secured assurances that Knoxville would be made a camp site in the location of the camps for soldiers that were not sent forward to Cuba, or while they might be in waiting. Sites for the Fourth and Sixth regiments were selected June 22, that for the Sixth being on what was formerly Elmwood Park, two miles east of the city on the Park street short line, and consisting of seventy acres of land surrounded on three sides by woodland, and about fifty yards to the eastward was the site of the camp of the Fourth regiment, nearly south of the residence of N. S. Woodward, seventy acres of grass land and well drained. About 5,000 acres of land, partly covered with timber, was there available for a drill and parade ground. A pipe line was laid to the Knoxville water works through the camp, and there were pipes, four inches in diameter, from this main pipe through the center of the camp with hydrants where needed. The name given to this camp was Camp Bob Taylor, in honor of the governor of Tennessee.

June 29, the camp of the Sixth regiment was removed to the Lonsdale addition to the city, near the Southern railway shops, the new camp being named Camp Wilder, the Fourth regiment remaining at Camp Bob Taylor.

Brigadier General J. S. Poland of the Second division of the First army corps died at Chickamauga August 7, 1898. He was born at Princeton, Ind., October 14, 1836, and was a brave soldier of the Civil war. August 12, an armistice was declared between Spain and the United States, and on the same day Brigadier General McKee, accompanied by his staff officers, Major W. P. Kendall and Captain Alexander M. Davis, arrived in Knoxville for the purpose of looking over the ground at Camp Wilder and other places, with the view of finding a more healthful location for his command than that at Chickamauga. He visited Fountain City and Camp Bob Taylor, finally selecting Camp Wilder, and naming it Camp Poland, in honor of General Poland, who had died as related above. Lincoln Park was selected for a portion of his camp. August 23 the First Georgia regiment and the Thirty-first Michigan were in camp near the Brookside cotton mills. August 26 the One Hundred and Fifty-eighth Indiana came into this camp; August 27, the First West Virginia; August 28, the Sixth Ohio, and the Fourteenth Minnesota arrived; August 29, the First Pennsylvania, so that on September 1 there were in Camp Poland the Second Ohio, the Fourteenth Minnesota, the Thirty-first Michigan, the First Georgia, the One Hundred and Fifty-eighth Indiana, the Fourth Tennessee, the First Pennsylvania, the Sixth Ohio, and the First West Virginia, in all nine regiments, or nearly 9,000 men in camp in the immediate vicinity of Knoxville. All of the Second division of the First army corps were here, besides the Fourth Tennessee.

September 2 orders were received for mustering out the One Hundred and Fifty-eighth Indiana and the First Pennsylvania, the former regiment leaving for home on September

12 and the latter on the 15th. On this day arrived the Third North Carolina colored troops and the Sixth Virginia, also colored troops, arrived about the same time. The Fourteenth Minnesota left for home September 20. September 21 Secretary of War Alger reviewed the troops at Camp Poland, and on the 23rd the First Georgia left for Macon, Ga.

Brigadier General G. M. Randall arrived in Knoxville October 5 to take command of Camp Poland. October 6 Col. Tyson's regiment, the Sixth U. S. volunteers, passed through Knoxville on their way to New York, where they took passage on the 9th for Porto Rico. October 19 General Randall left for Athens, Ga., being succeeded in the command of Camp Poland by General McKee, who remained until October 27, when Colonel Kuert of the Second Ohio became commandant of the camp. On October 31 the board of commissioners appointed by the President to investigate the conduct of the war, arrived in Knoxville and began the inspection of the camps, leaving in the evening for Washington, having found the camps in first class condition. Those who took part in this inspection were Col. Charles Denby, Capt. E. P. Howell, ex-Governor E. P. Woodbury, Brigadier General John M. Wilson, General James A. Beaver, Major General Alexander McD. McCook, Richard Weightman, Lieut. Col. F. B. Jones, and Major Stephen C. Mills. General Simon Snyder took charge of Camp Poland November 5, relieving Colonel Kuert, of the Second Ohio, which regiment left for Macon, Ga., November 15. November 20 the Sixth Ohio was armed with the Krag-Jorgensen rifles. The Third North Carolina regiment left for Macon, Ga., November 22 and on the 30th of that month division headquarters were removed to Macon, together with company C of the Second Ohio. The Sixth Ohio left Camp Poland December 27, and the Thirty-first Michigan left on Monday, January 9, 1899, for Savannah, Ga., there taking passage for Cuba, and was the last regiment in Camp Poland to get away, thus leaving that camp entirely vacant, and wholly a matter of history.

Lieutenant-colonel Andrew S. Rowan of the Sixth United States Volunteers, Col. Tyson's regiment, joined his regiment in Porto Rico about the 20th of December, 1898, having previously been on detached duty.

The Division hospital, established early in the existence of Camp Poland, at Turner Park, was maintained until about February 10, 1899. It was of great benefit to the soldiers in the camp, an absolute necessity. Fifty of the sick soldiers in the camp were on November 21, 1898, taken to Fort Meyer, near Washington, D. C., the intention being then to discontinue the hospital as soon as possible. The number of deaths in this hospital between September 8, 1898, and January 17, 1899, so far as could be ascertained, was fifty-six, of whom there were twelve, six white and six colored soldiers, whose names do not appear on any record. Besides these there were two others, not enlisted men, that died, and one nurse, Sister Mary Elizabeth Flanagan, who belonged at Mt. Washington, Mo. On February 1, 1899, there were left but few patients in the hospital, all rapidly convalescing. Upon the closing of the hospital Major Kendall, surgeon in charge, reported to Macon, Ga., and Lieutenant King reported to his regiment in Cuba. The property was sold at public auction February 15, 1899.

By the 16th of January, 1899, it was known that the Third Tennessee was to be mustered out of the service, and preparations began to be made for giving the members thereof that belonged to Knoxville and vicinity a warm and appropriate reception. On the morning of the next day the committee appointed to make arrangements for such a reception, consisting of J. E. Chapman, W. R. Cooper, W. E. Gibbins, C. C. Howell and Rev. John H. Frazee, met in A. J. Albers' office and extended an invitation to the Daughters of the Revolution, Daughters of the Confederacy, Woman's Relief Corps and the Girls' Relief society to assist in preparing the reception and the banquet. The committee held meetings on the 19th and on the 20th, at the latter meeting deciding that every returning soldier should be presented with a badge, the badges to be procured and printed under the supervision of Dr. Frazee. All necessary committees were selected, the reception committee being composed of F. K. Huger, James Maynard, Peter Kern, Frank A. Moses, E. W. Crozier, S. G. Heiskell, J. W. S. Frierson, Gen. J. T. Wilder, Will D. Wright, Judge O. P. Temple and Dr. Charles W. Dabney. The mustering out of the regiment began at Anniston, Ala., January 30, and in the evening most of the men in companies A, D and F reached Knoxville, companies A and F being made up mostly of Knoxville Legion men, company D being from Elizabethton.

The reception took place Friday evening at 7:30 o'clock, in Market Hall, nearly 200 members of the regiment being present who belonged to Knox county. Lieutenant-Colonel D. M. Coffman and Chaplain J. C. Wright were also present, and notwithstanding a heavy rain was falling the hall was well filled. Music was furnished by Legion band and addresses were made by Major William Rule, Captain H. H. Taylor, Mrs. Charles A. Perkins, Hon. J. W. Caldwell, Lieut. Col. Coffman and others. The supper prepared by the ladies was well served, and taken all in all few if any happier events have occurred in Knoxville, it being an honor to the returning Third Tennessee and to all taking part in its preparation and conduct.

CHAPTER XI.

MANUFACTURING INTERESTS.

Some of the Earlier Industries—Cotton Once a Staple Crop—S. T. Atkin, One of the Pioneers in Manufacturing—Growth and Multiplication of Industries—Extensive Marble Industries—Iron Mills—Brookside Cotton Mills—Knoxville Woolen Mills—Furniture—Telephone System.

THE manufacturing interests of Knoxville are of late years becoming more important. This indicates a prosperous agricultural community in the immediate vicinity, widely extended exportations of manufactured goods and the growth of towns and cities, for it is only in a country where civilization is or is becoming complex that manufactures can flourish to any great extent.

Various industries were started as soon as Knoxville became a town. There were soon several blacksmith shops and there was also a goldsmith and jeweler, who in addition to what such a tradesman would carry on at the present day, advertised that he made "rifle guns in the neatest and most approved fashion."

One of the early industries of Knoxville was a tanyard, established in 1793, on Second creek by Lord & McCoy, and in 1795 a saddler's shop was established by John and Robert Hunter. In 1796 John Lavender opened a second shop of this kind. The number of tanyards gradually increased until in 1830 there were five: One owned by William Morrow on First creek where it is crossed by Cumberland street; one almost directly across the street, owned by John Webb; one owned by Robert Lindsey at the east end of Clinch street, and there was one on Second creek operated by Rutherford & White.

As it is perfectly natural to suppose, during the early history of the county and the city the early industrial establishments would be such as were needed to supply the means of existence and comfort, as the people had to live and to clothe and protect themselves from the elements. Grist and saw mills were much in demand, and during the first eighteen months after the county court was organized, permits for the erection of these kinds of mills were numerous. They were in all cases run by water power, which was then more commonly employed than now, when steam has taken possession of almost all kinds of industries and methods of locomotion, either directly or indirectly. Domestic manufactures were then numerous, though carried on on a much smaller scale than afterward; but now almost wholly superseded by much larger concerns.

In 1830, besides the five tanyards above mentioned, there were two spinning factories, ten wool carding machines, three saw mills, one brass foundry, six blacksmith shops, two cabinet makers, three hatters, six saddlers, eight shoemakers, one tinner, two coach makers and two wagon makers. The brass foundry was operated by William Morse, the foundry standing on Second creek near Churchwell street, and Mr. Morse also operated a spinning factory and a blacksmith shop. The other spinning factory was operated by Nathaniel Bosworth, a little higher up the creek, and here there were employed from fifteen to twenty hands. It remained in operation until 1838. William Oldham in 1833 built a cotton spinning factory, which was located on First creek between Church and Cumberland streets, the machinery for which Mr. Oldham hauled across the Cumberland mountains from Lexington, Ky. This mill was operated exclusively by water power. In 1838 the mill dams were destroyed by a freshet, and Mr. Oldham removed his machinery to Blount county.

It may be well to state that during the first twenty-five or thirty years of the history of Knox county, cotton was therein a staple crop. But it began to decline about 1820 and had entirely ceased by 1830. The first cotton gin about which anything is still remembered was erected by Calvin Morgan on Gay street near where the Insurance building now stands, and the second was built and operated on Second creek by Mr. McCulloch. The earliest wool carding machine in this vicinity was located on First creek about two miles above its mouth, set up by James Scott, and operated by him until the coming on of the Civil war. Another was run for a time near the site of Bosworth's factory, mentioned above.

In this connection it may be well to explain the decline of the water power, which up to 1838 was unusually abundant. Previous to that time the town was confined almost exclusively to the territory between First and Second creeks and the Flag pond and Holston river, and was almost entirely surrounded by water. Flag pond occupied the depression now occupied by the tracks of the East Tennessee, Virginia and Georgia railroad, now the Southern railway, and in 1838 the cutting down of the dams drained the ponds, and thus destroyed to a considerable extent the water power. Flag pond was looked upon for a number of years as a menace to the health of the town, and was frequently under the consideration of the board of health. On First creek, prior to the cutting down of the dams, there were three mill ponds within the space of half a mile, the upper one, known as White's pond, extending north and northeast for more than a mile. On Second creek there were two large ponds of this kind, and while the dams were afterward to some extent restored, yet there has not since 1838 been anywhere near as much water power. Since steam has been generally introduced water power is not so popular.

In 1838 a paper mill was erected at Middlebrook by Gideon M. Hazen and M. D. Bearden. It was about three and a half miles above the town, and was run about seven months in the year by water power, and the rest of the year by water and steam power combined. It was continued in operation until 1886, when the breaking of the dam caused its suspension.

In 1850 a small oil mill was built on Second creek by F. A. R. Scott. In 1851 Mr. Scott opened a tannery in connection therewith, and in 1853 sold the entire establishment to M. B. McMahan, who operated the tannery until 1860, when he was succeeded by an incorporated company. During the Civil war John S. Van Gilder, who was then largely engaged in the manufacture of boots and shoes, obtained control of the tannery, and was joined in 1865 by Mr. Scott. These two gentlemen continued to run it under the name of the Knoxville Leather company until 1890.

In 1853 the first large manufacturing establishment ever seen in Knoxville was started. It was a machine shop located at the corner of Broad street and the railroad and was erected by A. L. Maxwell, who came here from New York in 1852. This machine shop was erected for the purpose of supplying the iron work for bridges, which the firm of Maxwell, Briggs & Co., of which Mr. A. L. Maxwell was the senior member, was then erecting largely throughout the Southern states. The shop under consideration went into operation in 1853 with somewhat more than 200 hands. In 1855, finding that the bridge material could be more advantageously handled from Richmond, Va., an interest in the establishment was sold to some Vermont parties, and the Knoxville Manufacturing company was formed for the purpose of building engines, boilers, etc., which business was carried on until near the beginning of the war.

In 1852 a foundry and stove factory was erected on Second creek by Williams, Moffett & Co., near the site of the Knoxville Leather company's works, and this foundry carried on quite an extensive business for some time. In 1856 the establishment was transferred to Shepard, Leeds & Hoyt, who in 1854 had built a foundry and car works where the railroad shops now stand. The capital of this firm was about $20,000 and they employed some twenty hands. They were engaged in the manufacture of cars, car wheels, plows and agricultural implements generally. Later Mr. A. L. Maxwell purchased the interests of these gentlemen, and by 1861 had become the sole proprietor of the business, which he carried on until the siege of 1863, when the entire plant was destroyed by fire.

Clark, Quaife & Co. in 1867 erected a small foundry for the manufacture of stoves, hollow ware, etc., and later added thereto the manufacture of car wheels, becoming in 1873 the Knoxville Car Wheel company, with a capital stock of $57,000, and having as officers A. L. Maxwell, president, and Harvey Clark, secretary and treasurer. This company was located on Jacksboro street, and the manufacture of car wheels was for quite a number of years the exclusive business of the works. They purchased 30,000 acres of land in Carter county, which contained large quantities of brown hematite iron ore, known as among the best ores anywhere to be found. For the first eight or ten years of this company's existence the wheels turned out by them bore a reputation for excellence second to none made elsewhere in this country. In June, 1881, Charles H. Brown became secretary and treasurer, and in July, 1881, D. A. Carpenter became president, succeeding Mr. Maxwell, and being himself succeeded in the later eighties by Charles H. Brown, who remained president then during the company's existence. In 1883 a machine shop was added to the plant in Knoxville, and in 1886 the company making at this factory soft castings for cars, engines, gearing, pulleys, etc., with the view of enlarging and diversifying their product as much as possible, and of making the Knoxville Car Wheel works one of the leading industries in the land; but as additional money was needed to carry out this plan, a heavy mortgage was placed upon the property, and as it was at length found impracticable to manage the business, owing in part, perhaps, to the increasing stringencies of the times, the works ceased to operate, and the property was sold in the winter of 1898-99 in chancery court. Since then the buildings have been leased to and occupied by the Clark Foundry company, formerly located on Hardee street, the property of the latter being now occupied by the Knoxville foundry.

The Clark Foundry and Machine company was organized in 1881, with H. W. Clark president and Simpson Cornick secretary and treasurer. The works are located at the corner of Hardee and Hume streets, and make a specialty of mill machinery, though all kinds of machines and castings are made. The company employs about sixty hands and turns out about ten tons of finished product per day. At these works nearly all the work of the Knoxville division of the East Tennessee, Virginia and Georgia railroad is done. Mr. Clark has had many years of experience in his particular line, having learned his trade in his youth in one of the Northern states.

W. J. Savage began business in Knoxville in 1885 as a manufacturer of roller flouring mill machinery and marble mill machinery, on the Knoxville and Ohio railroad near the Knoxville Car Wheel works, but only in a small way, employing only six men. In 1889 he was succeeded by the Knoxville Supply company, composed of himself, Samuel Marfield and Henry Brandau, this company continuing the manufacture of the same line until 1892, in which year they were succeeded by the present firm, Savage & Tyler, composed of W. J. Savage and J. C. Tyler, the business being removed in 1893 to its present location on Cumberland street and Second creek. The company here continue to build roller mill machinery, setting up mills complete in several of the Southern states.

The Southern Car company was organized in 1881 with a capital stock of $50,000 for the purpose of manufacturing freight and mining cars of all kinds. The works were located on the East Tennessee, Virginia and Georgia railroad, just west of the city limits, and there were employed from 125 to 150 men. They manufactured from eight to ten cars per day, continuing the work in Knoxville until 1893, when they removed to Lenoir City, the name of the company at the same time being changed to the Lenoir City Car company.

S. T. Atkin, one of the earlier manufacturers of Knoxville, began business here as a tinner and stove man in 1844, and in 1860 purchased a saw mill which had been erected by Churchwell & Harris in 1854 or 1855. This mill he kept until 1867, having in the meantime bought other saw mills, being engaged in the meantime in the manufacture of sash, doors and blinds, and all kinds of woodwork. In the year 1862 he made a contract with the Confederate government to supply that government with all the iron he could make for two years; and as there were so many people dying and being killed he turned his sash, door and blinds establishment into a coffin factory, in this line having as a partner L. C. Shepard for about a year.

In 1863 the Federal army took possession of Knoxville, and his contract with the Confederate government became valueless, but upon the request of the Federal authorities Mr. Atkin made iron of various kinds, such as bar iron, horse shoes and wagon tires for them until 1865, when the war closed, and he sold his factory in 1866 to L. C. Shepard, H. S. Chamberlain, David Richards and others, and it became the property in 1868 of the Knoxville Iron company, a history of which is elsewhere printed in this chapter.

In the wood working department which was located on First creek, Mr. Atkin went on manufacturing lumber into various forms and also engaged in building houses, putting up more of this kind of buildings in the city than had any man up to that time, the houses built by him being both frame and brick. For the manufacture of brick Mr. Atkin had two or three brick yards, located at various points both inside and outside of the city limits. In the meantime, having a large amount of lumber on hand, Mr. Atkin engaged in the manufacture of furniture, lumber being quite low in price, and furniture being in demand. His furniture factory was located on Gay street between Main and Cumberland streets, extending back from Gay to State street. This line of manufacture he continued to carry on until 1887, when he turned the business over to his sons, F. S. and C. B. Atkin, each of whom is now engaged in a separate and distinct line of the business. Mr. Atkin himself then retired altogether from active business, except so far as the management of his own private affairs is concerned, with which he is still engaged.

S. T. Atkin sold his business to his sons March 3, 1886, they continuing the business under the name of S. T. Atkin & Co. about one year. From this time on until 1889 the two sons conducted the retail part of the business at the present location of Hall & Hawkins under the firm name of C. B. Atkin & Co., and the manufacturing portion of it under the name of F. S. Atkin & Co. In 1889 the brothers dissolved partnership, Frank S. Atkin taking the retail part and conducting it under his own name, C. B. Atkin taking the factory, continuing on in the manufacture of furniture but gradually changing to the manufacture of mantels. At first he was making about five per cent of his material into mantels, and the rest into furniture, while now the proportions are almost precisely reversed, the product of the factory consisting of five per cent furniture and ninety-five per cent mantels.

Mr. Atkin's factory consists of two three-story and basement buildings, and he has a large lumber yard, all on the old site, between Main and Cumberland streets, and extending from Gay to State. Here he employs about ninety hands, and the manufactured goods are sold in every state in the Union and are shipped to some foreign countries. The buildings now occupied are comparatively new, having been erected since the fire of 1893, which destroyed the old ones, and which was probably the largest fire in the history of Knoxville up to that time.

Frank S. Atkin & Co. established their present business in 1896, at the northeast corner of Gay and Church streets, the business consisting of the manufacture of hat racks, and the partner of Mr. Atkin being Samuel McKinney. Hat racks of all styles and sizes are made, and about thirty-five hands are employed, the products turned out being shipped to every state in the Union and to several foreign countries.

Frank H. Post & Co. The wagon and carriage works now owned and controlled by this firm were established in 1870 by S. T. Post, father of Frank H. Post, with only one employe, Mr. Post himself working at the forge. He afterward admitted his son to partnership under the name of S. T. Post & Son. A few years later they took in Mr. C. N. Simmons, and the firm name became Post, Simmons & Co., under which the business was carried on until 1886, when Frank H. Post bought the interest of Mr. Simmons and also that of his father, continuing the business in his own name until 1889, when he admitted Mr. R. A. Keller, the name of the firm for the next two years being Post & Keller. At the end of this time Mr. Post bought out Mr. Keller, and soon afterward admitted R. W. Barton, since which time the name of the firm has been Frank H. Post & Co.

The business carried on by this firm is that of manufacturing wagons, carriages and other vehicles, and has grown from the making of from two to three wagons and a small repair business until at the present time they are doing an annual business of about $10,000 in repair work and $20,000 in new work. They are doing a very wide range of work, consisting of farm and log wagons, moving cars, side seated passenger hacks, large and small transfer wagons, grocery and laundry wagons, delivery wagons, oil tank wagons, market garden wagons, spring wagons, buckboards, buggies, phaetons, and carriages. From thirty to thirty-five men are employed.

Sheridan & Quincy began the manufacture of wagons in Knoxville in 1885. Their shop at that time was on State street and was from the first well equipped with all necessary machinery. They made carriages as well as wagons, to the aggregate number of about 500 per year. In farm wagons their specialty was the "Dixie," very popular throughout the state and adjoining states. Both gentlemen were experienced workmen, learning their respective trades in Rochester, N. Y., Mr. Sheridan having charge of the wood and iron department and Mr. Quincy of the paint shop. Mr. Quincy retired from the business in the year 1892, since which time Mr. Sheridan has conducted the establishment himself. It was formerly located at 707 and 709 Central avenue, but now, as the Quincy Carriage Company, is located on Vine street.

The Knoxville Buggy Works were established in March, 1885, by C. Geiger and were managed by James A. Nisonger. The company was engaged in the manufacture of light wagons, buggies and carriages for the local trade. Later the proprietors of these works were T. T. Goodall & Co., who made an extension to the business, erected new shops and employed from twenty-five to thirty hands.

The Knoxville Ice Company's business was started in 1876 by J. C. Mustard, but only on a small scale and as an experiment. Mr. Mustard was so successful, however, that in 1881 the company above named was organized with a capital of $40,000. New buildings were erected, the most improved machinery obtainable was put in and other improvements made, with the view of making the business extensive as well as successful. The factory of this company is located at No. 204 Cumberland street, the works having a capacity of thirty tons per day, and the product being sold not only in Knoxville, but largely throughout East Tennessee. The water used in the manufacture of ice by this company is obtained from a large spring and is distilled before being frozen. The officers of the company at the present time are Peter Kern, president; Ignaz Fanz, secretary and treasurer, and Jackson L. Stewart, general manager.

The Crystal Ice company was organized in 1887 by Knoxville capitalists, and with a capital of $40,000. The works are located in North Knoxville and have a capacity of thirty-two tons per day. The water used by this company is obtained from the celebrated Moses spring, and the machinery is of the Columbus Iron works pattern. The officers are G. M. Harrill, president, and H. W. Lynn, secretary and treasurer. The works are located at the corner of Sixth avenue and Grainger street, and the office is at No. 315 Clinch street.

As has been elsewhere stated the marbles of Tennessee are remarkable for the fineness of their quality, and they are well known all over the United States. They are useful mainly for building purposes, for monuments and interior decorations. The marble business began in Hawkins county, extended thence into Blount county, then into adjoining counties, and finally to Knox county. The business so rapidly increased that in 1890 there were twenty-two quarries in operation and three large mills engaged in sawing and polishing the marble taken out. In 1892 the amount of business in this article reached nearly if not quite $1,000,000, the number of hands employed by the various firms was nearly 1,000, and the wages paid to them being about $375,000 per year. Marble is found along all the railroads running into Knoxville, and sales are held every year by the leading dealers, train loads being frequently made up for the larger centers of distribution.

The Knoxville Marble company was organized July 11, 1873, the members of the company at the time being William Patrick, president; George W. Ross, secretary and treasurer; James Patrick and J. H. Holman. This company purchased the old government quarry at the junction of the Holston and French Broad rivers, which they have operated ever since, where they now have three quarries on their sixty-five acres of land, where they employ regularly about seventy-five hands and take out each year about $100,000 worth of marble, which is of the finest quality. When polished it presents a most beautiful appearance and is used mainly for mantels and decorating purposes generally. The company runs four steam drills and two saw mills, each having two gangs of saws. The marble from these quarries is shipped to all parts of the

A MARBLE QUARRY NEAR KNOXVILLE, TENNESSEE.—DRAWN BY CHARLES GRAHAM AND JOHN DURKIN.—[SEE ARTICLE "THE INDUSTRIAL SOUTH." PAGE 239.]

country. In January, 1886, John M. Ross became president of the company.

J. J. Craig & Co. operate four marble quarries about five miles to the northwest of Knoxville, the business being established in 1886 by John J. Craig, the present senior member of the firm. Mr. Craig has been one of the most active in the development of the marble business of the city of Knoxville. This company organized the Great Southern Marble company, with officers as follows: John J. Craig, president; John J. Craig, Jr., secretary and treasurer; W. B. McMullen, general manager, and J. M. Edington, superintendent of quarries. This company was succeeded by the John J. Craig Company, of which John J. Craig, Jr., is president, and J. B. Jones, secretary and treasurer. The office of the company is at No. 47 Deaderick building.

The Phoenix Marble company was established in 1885 and incorporated with a capital stock of $20,000. This company operates quarries in Hawkins county, and a mill in Knoxville with three gangs of saws. At first the officers were John P. Beach, president, and Charles Pitman, secretary and treasurer.

W. H. Evans & Son established themselves in business in Baltimore, Md., in 1867, and built the Knoxville mill in 1886, the mill being 480x60 feet in size and three stories high. It is located on the Knoxville and Ohio railroad and just north of Munson street. It is equipped with twenty gangs of saws, turning lathes, and machinery complete for handling Tennessee marble for all purposes for which it is used and is considered the best equipped mill in the United States. This firm also operates two mills in Baltimore and are the largest importers of foreign marble in this country. They are prepared to make estimates and to contract for any known marble product, and all the three mills of the company are well equipped with the machinery needed in the business. This firm has furnished and set in place the interior marble work for most of the largest buildings in the country, for example the Italian marble in the new Congressional Library building in the city of Washington, the Tennessee and Italian marble in the Masonic Temple in Chicago, and in the Public Library in the same city, and also in any number of other buildings, public and private, throughout every state in the Union.

The mill in the city of Knoxville is under the management of J. E. Willard as superintendent, and there are here employed about 350 men the year round, they being engaged in quarrying the raw material and in finishing it and in many cases setting it in the buildings complete. The officers of this company are W. H. Evans, president; C. R. Evans, vice-president, and S. M. Wellner, secretary and treasurer.

The East Tennessee Stone and Marble company was incorporated in 1889, with the following incorporators: J. E. Hart, R. Z. Roberts, C. M. Funck and C. T. Stephenson, and was organized in 1890 with the following officers: J. E. Hart, president, treasurer and general manager; C. M. Funck, secretary. The mill is located at the junction of the K. C. G. & L. railroad and the E. T. V. & G. railroad, and it is here that the manufacture of marble and its finishing for interior decoration is carried on. There are two large buildings fully equipped with machinery of every description needed in the business, such as six gangs of saws, lathes, planers, and air tools. One hundred men are employed on the average, the marble being shipped to every state in the Union. Contracts are taken by this company for the finishing of buildings anywhere in the country, and their workmanship may be seen in some of the finest buildings in the land, notably in the Blackstone Memorial Library building in Branford, Conn., the third largest and finest library building in the United States, being surpassed only by the Congressional Library building at Washington, and the Public Library building at Chicago. Among the numerous buildings for which this company supplied the marble are the following: St. Nicholas Hotel in St. Louis, and the Chicago Historical Society's library building in Chicago. The officers at the present time are the same as at the beginning.

The Tennessee Producers Marble company has for several years been engaged in the production of marble of Tennessee. About ten years ago Mr. W. B. McMullen, who had for years been actively engaged in quarrying marble and in selling it, interested other parties and organized a stock company. The success resulting led to the re-organization of the company in 1894. Eastern capitalists becoming interested, and quickly perceiving the desirability of investment in the marble industry in Tennessee. A large factory and mill for sawing and finishing the product of the company's quarries were built, and now this is the largest in Knoxville of its kind, and the firm is engaged in shipping its marble in its rough and also in its finished state to all parts of the country. This marble is used for finishing the interior as well as the exterior of buildings and is now being shipped even to foreign countries.

This company has furnished the marble for the interior of the post office building in Washington, D. C., and several large buildings in the West. Their large plant was constantly busy during the years of the panic from 1893 to 1897, and it is equipped for a large increase in business, which the company believes is fast approaching. This company handles Tennessee marble exclusively, their quarries being situated in Knox, Blount and Hawkins counties, and they have such strong faith in the future of Tennessee marble that they urge its use in all cases in preference to foreign marble. In addition to their other lines they do a large business in cemetery lines. The mill is located on the Middlebrook street car line at the junction of University avenue and Seventeenth street. The present officers of the company are as follows: W. B. McMullen, president; E. R. Morse, treasurer, and B. L. Pease, superintendent.

The first attempt to manufacture iron and rolling mill products in Knoxville was made by the Confederate authorities during the Civil war, but from lack of skilled workmen this attempt was a failure. The machinery used in this attempt was confiscated at Loudon, Tenn., and moved to Knoxville. Soon after the occupation of the city by the Union army an attempt to operate this mill was made by H. S. Chamberlain, a quartermaster in the army, but his attempt was likewise a failure. After the close of hostilities John H. Jones, one of the owners of the mill, came to Knoxville and then a company was formed, composed of himself, S. T. Atkin, L. C. Shepherd and H. S. Chamberlain, the mill being put in operation by them. Soon afterward Mr. Jones sold his interest to D. and J. Richards and T. D. Lewis, men of extensive experience in the iron business, and a company was organized under the name of Chamberlain, Richards & Co. At first this company had considerable difficulty in carrying on their business, raw material costing a great deal and being hard to obtain. Coal was brought by them to Knoxville by boat in the winter season, and in the summer season by wagons, at a cost of fifty cents per bushel, that brought in the winter coming from Emory Gap, that brought in the summer from Winter's Gap. In 1867 a mine of coal was opened at Coal creek under the direction of D. Thomas, and in the fall of that year the first car load of coal was brought into Knoxville over the Knoxville and Ohio railroad.

The Knoxville Iron company was incorporated in 1868 with an authorized capital of $150,000, and was organized February 1 that year with the following board of directors and officers: H. S. Chamberlain, president; W. R. Tuttle, secretary; H. S. Chamberlain, treasurer, and Joseph Richards, general manager, the other directors being Daniel Thomas, David Richards, Thomas D. Lewis and William Richards. February 27, 1871, Mr. Chamberlain resigned as president of this company to accept a similar position with the Roane Iron company of Chattanooga, and on March 20 following the capital stock of the Knoxville Iron company was increased to $200,000. Up to this time the old buildings formerly in use by Mr. S. T. Atkin, elsewhere referred to as an iron manufacturer during the war of the Rebellion, were in use, but now a new building was erected, and in 1873 still another mill was erected to accommodate the growing business of the company. A nail factory was added in 1875, which was operated for several years, but is not now in use.

At the beginning of the company's existence the works were operated to manufacture finished bar iron, muck iron and a few sizes of round and square iron, only one train of rolls being in use. When the new mill was erected it included an eighteen-inch nail plate train, a sixteen-inch bar mill, and an eight-inch band mill. The nail factory contained forty-two nail machines and had an output of 70,000 to 75,000 kegs of nails per year. This factory was closed in 1890, and has not since been in use. A foundry and machine shop was decided upon in 1891. Within the last two years the mill has been limited to the production of bar iron of all kinds, from one-fourth inch to four and a half inch round and square; flats from five-eighths, No. 16, to 6x1½, graduating by ⅛ of an inch, light channel iron, other shapes and small "T" rails, for use in mines.

The mill is now equipped throughout with modern machinery, such as gas furnaces, gas producers, etc., by which the output of the works has since 1895 been increased about fifty per cent, and they now have a capacity of from 15,000 to 18,000 tons per year, of finished material. About 200 men are employed in the mill.

This company began mining coal in Anderson county in 1868, and continued operations at Coal creek until January 1, 1897. The mines were operated with free labor until July, 1878, when in consequence of strikes and other labor disturbances it was found necessary to employ labor that could be relied upon, hence the employment of convict labor in the mines, which was continued from July, 1878, to July, 1896. During this time the miners took exception to the use of convict labor and by force they were liberated twice, and it was necessary to station a military force at the mines to protect the company in the use of the state convicts, this standing army being present at the mines for eighteen months.

Since July, 1896, the company has again been employing free labor, and they are now the largest shippers of bituminous coal in this section of the country, their coal being shipped to all parts of Tennessee, North and South Carolina, Georgia, Virginia and Alabama, to an aggregate amount of from 200,000 to 250,000 tons. This company is the only one in the state using electricity in the mining of coal.

The officers of the company have been as follows:

Presidents—H. S. Chamberlain, elected in 1868; David Richards, in 1871; H. S. Chamberlain, in 1872; William S. Mead, in 1874; W. R. Tuttle, in 1875; James R. Ogden, in 1888, serving until his death in 1891; O. A. Brown in 1892, and the present incumbent of the office, W. P. Chamberlain, in 1895.

Vice-presidents—W. R. Tuttle, elected in 1872; W. S. Mead, in 1874; John B. Johnson, 1874; W. S. Mead, 1875; O. A. Brown, 1891; E. J. Sanford, 1892; T. I. Stephenson, in 1895.

Secretaries—W. R. Tuttle, elected in 1868; James B. Johnson, in 1872; W. S. Mead, 1873; James B. Johnson, 1874; W. H. Van Benschoten, 1874; W. S. Mead, 1880; O. A. Brown, 1886; T. I. Stephenson, 1891; O. A. Brown, 1895.

Treasurers—H. S. Chamberlain, elected in 1868; W. R. Tuttle, in 1871; W. S. Mead, 1874; O. A. Brown, 1886.

General Managers—Joseph Richards, elected in 1868; David Richards, in 1870, serving until 1875, when a committee was appointed to select the heads of the several departments. In 1895 T. I. Stephenson became general manager, and still holds the position.

This company has recently made a rich discovery in the coal field in the shape of a vein of coal of superior quality five and a half feet thick, a solid vein with rock above and below. Here there is no mining seam composed of slate, dirt, etc., but instead seams of cannel coal of such thickness as to amount to about one-third of the thickness of the entire vein, which renders the Cross Mountain coal particularly desirous for domestic purposes.

H. O. Nelsen manufactures iron and steel fences of all kinds, his works being located on the Maryville railroad track near Asylum street. Formerly they located at "Valley Forge," and are still known as the Valley Forge Fence works. In 1873 Mr. Nelsen moved to his present location, where he set up new machinery of a larger pattern, and increased the number of hands employed and the output from his works, which now amounts to about $60,000 per year. He is now devoting his energies to the production of wrought steel fences of various patterns and for all purposes, and has recently adopted new names for several of his leading styles of fence, as "Taylor," "Shafter," "Grant," "Sampson," "Lee," "Dewey," "Schley," "Hobson," etc.

Dempsters Machine shop is located at No. 114 East Main street, and was established in 1886 by James Dempster, who has manufactured a few engines, but found that manufacturing engines on a small scale did not prove profitable. He also in the past carried on the manufacture of machinery, steam pumps, etc., on a small scale, but has abandoned all kinds of manufacturing, and devotes his works and energies now exclusively to repairs. On the average he employs about four men in doing such repair work as comes to his shop. His is the old McClannahan mill, established many years ago, and which later became the property of Major R. R. Swepson, who owned it for some time and then sold it to the Champion Manufacturing company, which sold out to Mr. Dempsey in 1889, who, from the time he began in business in 1886, to 1889, was located near Nelsen's Valley Forge Fence works.

Fair, Day & DeKlyne's Foundry and Pattern shop, which is located on Jacksboro street beyond the Brookside mills, and close to the Knoxville and Ohio railroad, were established in 1880 by Fair & Day. In 1890 the works occupied about one and a half acres of ground on Second creek, which creek furnished them water power. Generally speaking Tennessee iron is used by these works, and about twenty-five men are employed. The product is principally house work, machine castings, hardware findings, fronts and grates. Sash weights are also made at these works. At present the name of the company is the Fair-Day Foundry company, the officers of which are David C. Richards, president; A. B. Day, vice-president and superintendent, and J. B. Fair, secretary and treasurer. The annual output of the works is about $30,000.

The Enterprise Machine works, situated on Chamberlain street near the brewery, were established in 1886 by D. C. Richards and Sons (W. P., A. T. and Roger P., the latter of whom died February 23, 1898). At these works are manufactured engines of all sizes from six up to 500 horse power, and both stationary and portable, heavy castings, hoisting machinery and derricks. Repairs of all kinds are made in these works, including the repair of locomotives, a new building having been erected for this special work during 1898. A new fourteen-foot boring machine was also put in during this year, which weighs twenty-eight tons, the cost of this machine being $4,000. Mr. Richards has been a resident of Knoxville since 1869, and is considered one of the most skillful and practical machinists in the place.

The Enterprise Foundry company was formed March 1, 1897, by R. R. Shipman, Calvin George and Len George, each of whom had at the time $33. They began in a small way in Skate's Furnace buildings, with the three men besides themselves, they being practical workmen and all taking hold with a determination to succeed. Their business grew so rapidly that it became necessary in April, 1898, to move to their present location, on the Knoxville and Ohio railroad, and nearly opposite the Brookside cotton mills. These buildings had been occupied by Roy & Armstrong. Here the business has grown far more rapidly than they at first dared to anticipate, and they now employ on the average twenty-four men, and are turning out about $2,000 worth of work per month. At first they made all kinds of shop castings, but have recently added a full line of stoves, five different kinds, the "Knoxville Dixie," every part of which is made in Knoxville, even to the nickel plating; the "Marble City," and three kinds of heating stoves, called the "Big Seven." They also make fire fronts and grate baskets. The machinery in this foundry is propelled by a twenty-five horse-power engine.

There have always been grist mills in Knoxville and its vicinity since Gen. James White erected his "tub mill" near the town. After his son, Moses White, built a mill on First creek near the crossing of Mabry street. John Craighead built a mill at the crossing of Main street, and about 1820 Rufus Morgan built one on the same creek. In 1830 there were three grist mills in Knoxville, all owned and operated by James and William Kennedy. And James Scott had a grist mill about two miles up the creek.

In 1855 a large steam flouring mill was erected on the site of the Knoxville rolling mill by M. N. Williams, but it was soon afterward burned down. It was succeeded by the Knoxville City mills, located on Broad street, and abandoned in 1880. In 1858 F. A. R. Scott and J. C. Deaderick erected on First creek what was for many years throughout this part of the South known as the "Trio Mill," which has been since then in continuous operation, and has for many years been as widely and well known for the many excellent brands of flour produced. The mill was remodeled in 1884, and fully equipped with the then latest roller process machinery. The most noted brands of flour manufactured at this mill are the "Magnolia," "Silver Leaf," "Choice," "Famous" and "Little Valley Family." One of the specialties of this mill is water ground corn meal, and other products used as feed, all of which are extensively sold throughout East Tennessee and surrounding states.

From 1877 to 1893 this mill was conducted by Scott,

Dempster & Co., but in the year last named Mr. Dempster retired, and from that time to 1895 it was conducted by Scott Bros. & Co., the firm consisting of James, David D., and F. A. R. Scott. Since 1895 it has been conducted by J. A. Scott under the name of the Scott Mill company.

The Peters-Bradley Mill company was incorporated in 1891 with a capital stock of $20,000, and the following officers: G. W. Peters, president; T. J. Bradley, secretary and treasurer. The business conducted by this company was started in 1867 by Mr. Peters, on First creek, at the old Scott mill, about one-fourth of a mile above the location of the present mill, which is on First creek just below Broad avenue, and Mr. Peters continued to run it alone until 1879, when the business was removed to its present location, and took into partnership with himself in 1885, Mr. Bradley, who remained in the business until 1894. The officers of the company at the present time are G. W. Peters, president and general manager; L. J. Kearns, secretary, and D. L. Ross, treasurer. The roller process was put into these mills in 1884, and they now have a capacity of seventy-five barrels of flour per day, besides grinding meal and feed. Both water and steam power are used to an aggregate of sixty horse-power. Twelve hands are given employment, and the company is one of the solid concerns of Knoxville.

The Lonsdale Mill company was incorporated May 28, 1890, the incorporators being W. B. Ragsdale, Leon Jourolmon, J. F. Ragsdale and E. L. Ragsdale. The purpose for which this company was incorporated was the manufacture of flour and other mill products. It was organized in 1890 with the following officers: President, Leon Jourolmon, and secretary, E. L. Ragsdale. The mill owned by this company is located two miles north of Knoxville on the Clinton pike, and is a four-story frame building above a basement, well-equipped with the latest roller machinery, with a capacity of 200 barrels of flour every twenty-four hours. The proprietors of the mill at the present time are T. S. Webb, Jr., and John

Dempster. The principal brands of flour made at these mills are the "Sunrise," and "White Rose."

The Knoxville City Mills company was incorporated in 1884 with a capital stock of $30,000, which was afterward increased to $100,000. The company erected a large flouring mill in 1885, having a capacity of 150 barrels of flour per day, which was increased in 1893 to 800 barrels per day. It is equipped with the most modern and finest machinery to be found in the country, and its products find sale throughout Tennessee, Kentucky, Virginia, North and South Carolina, Georgia, Florida and Alabama. An elevator with a capacity of 50,000 bushels of grain was erected in connection with the mill, but it was destroyed by fire in June, 1886. Later another elevator having a capacity of 75,000 bushels was erected, and in 1898 three steel elevators with an aggregate capacity of 100,000 bushels were built, so that at the present time the aggregate capacity of the four elevators is 175,000 bushels. The officers of this company are as follows: J. Allen Smith, president, and H. R. Goforth, secretary and treasurer.

The Brookside Cotton mills were incorporated in November, 1885, and the mills were put in operation in 1886. The capital of the company at first was $150,000, and it was increased in 1895 to $500,000. The building first erected was two stories high and 78x210 feet in size. This building was enlarged in 1895 to a length of 350 feet, the width remaining the same. Another building was also added which is one story high and 400x175 feet in size, which is devoted exclusively to weaving. At first there were 6,000 spindles, but in 1895, when the enlargement of the plant took place the number of spindles was increased to 21,000, and the number of looms was increased at the same time from 176 to 650. The products of these mills consist entirely of brown sheetings of a grade suitable for domestic and foreign trade, and the annual amount has increased from 3,000,000 yards per annum in 1886 and up to 1895, to 12,000,000 yards, the latter quantity being worth about $750,000. The officers of this company have been as follows: W. R. Tuttle, president and treasurer up to 1895, and president to 1898, in which year James Maynard was chosen president; treasurer since 1895, Justin E. Gale; secretary from the beginning, W. S. Mead. A fine stone office building was erected in 1890.

The Knoxville Woolen mills, one of the most substantial institutions of Knoxville, is the direct outgrowth of a single carding machine started twenty years ago in McMinn county, Tenn., by the present vice-president and general manager of the company, Mr. R. P. Gettys. From that small beginning the present Knoxville Woolen mills is indebted for its existence. At the time stated Mr. Gettys added first two looms, and finding that the product of his small establishment was easily disposed of, he added fifteen more looms and still later added other looms to the aggregate number of sixty-five, the location of this mill being at Sanford, McMinn county. It was then determined to remove to Knoxville, that being thought a better place for a mill, and in 1884, April 14, the Knoxville Woolen mills was incorporated by R. P. Gettys, E. J. Sanford, James D. Cowan, Charles J. McClung and C. M. McGhee, the purpose of the incorporation, as expressed in their application for a charter, being to manufacture raw material by the aid of machinery into woolen goods and fabrics at their mills, which they located in Knoxville at the intersection of the East Tennessee, Virginia and Georgia railroad and York street, the first mill of the present mammoth plant being erected in 1885. Additional capital was raised and the building up of the plant began and continued until at the present time the mills have a floor space of about four and a half acres, and in them about 600 hands find employment. The entire plant is alive with machinery and work connected with the enterprise, many thousands of yards of cassimeres and jeans being made daily, about one-half of the mills being occupied in producing each fabric. While Mr. E. J. Sanford is president of the institution the immediate management and operation of the mills is under the direct charge of Mr. R. P. Gettys, vice-president and general manager, and Mr. J. A. McKeldin, secretary and treasurer. These gentlemen have proved themselves to be the right men in the right places, and under them the institution is greatly prosperous.

The Knoxville Coffin company began business in a small way in 1884, and was incorporated in 1885 with the following officers: I. B. Ziegler, president; A. G. Mann, vice-president, and R. A. Keller, secretary and treasurer. Their factory was built on the Southern railroad near Sixth avenue. Here they have four buildings, two of them two stories high, the others one story high, and one of them being a steam dry kiln. The products of the factory, consisting of coffins, caskets and fine excelsior, are shipped to nearly every Southern state. The officers of the company at the present time are A. G. Mann, president; T. W. Keller, vice-president, and R. A. Keller, secretary and treasurer.

The Unaka Soap Company was incorporated in 1888 with a capital stock of $50,000 in shares of $100. S. B. Luttrell was president of the company, and W. H. Simmonds, secretary and treasurer. The factory is located near the Knoxville and Ohio railroad, opposite the Brookside Cotton mills. This company operated the factory until 1890, and from that time until 1894 it was idle. In this year Mr. J. A. H. Bell came into possession of the property, and has since operated the factory. There are two buildings here, one of brick, sixty feet square and two stories high, and the other a frame building 40x120 feet. The kinds of soap manufactured by this company are the "Red Cross," a fine grade of laundry soap; the "Best Yet," a cheaper grade of laundry soap; laundry chips, and a fine quality of toilet soap, called "Cocoa Castile." Of the laundry soaps the company makes about 1,200 boxes per month, and of the others a somewhat smaller quantity. S. A. Kidd has been foreman of this factory for the past two years.

The Southern Trunk company was incorporated under the laws of the state of Tennessee with a capital of $10,000, and organized November 1, 1897, with the following officers: W. C. Ingles, president; George M. White, secretary; D. W. White, treasurer, and Dr. A. P. White and S. H. McNutt the other directors. The company began business in East Knoxville on the day of organization, remaining there until July 1, 1898, when they removed to their present location on the southeast corner of Gay and Church streets. Here they manufacture trunks of various sizes, suit cases and traveling bags, employing from forty to fifty hands in the factory and three traveling salesmen. The business is now increasing quite rapidly, and the products of the factory find sale throughout all the Southern states.

The Whittle Trunk company was established in October, 1895, by R. D. Whittle and O. H. Whittle, and it was incorporated in December, 1896, with an authorized capital stock of $25,000, and with R. D. Whittle as president and Z. T. John as secretary and treasurer. The business consists of the manufacture of trunks and sample cases, and was located from the beginning until February 14, 1899, at 316-318 Jackson street. In July, 1898, the interest of the Whipples was purchased by J. G. Kincaid, who became president and manager of the concern, and still later the interest of Mr. John was purchased by John Bowman, of La Follette, at which time Mr. Bowman and J. G. and J. W. Kincaid became the proprietors. The business carried on was especially prosperous during the years 1897 and 1898, and until the fire of February 14, 1899, which caused the company a net loss of $4,000. At the present time, March 1, 1899, the plans of the company for the future have not been formulated, but they have a temporary office at 522 Gay street.

The Knoxville Brick company was organized August 31, 1888, the first board of directors being D. A. Carpenter, G. J. Kinzel, C. E. Lucky, R. M. Rhea and W. H. Simmonds. A farm of 750 acres was purchased at Powell station, and a committee appointed for the purpose purchased the necessary machinery for making brick. During the first year about

8,000,000 common brick were made, but since then different varieties of brick have been manufactured, viz.: common brick, red pressed, ornamental, buff and gray front brick, and vitrified roadway and sidewalk brick. The works now have a capacity of 135,000 brick per day, and when times are good there have been manufactured by this company from 10,000,000 to 12,000,000 brick per year. The officers at the present time are D. A. Carpenter, president; W. H. Fizer, vice-president; A. F. Sanford, secretary and treasurer, and the other members of the board of directors are E. J. Sanford, C. E. Luckey, R. M. Rhea and Matthew McClung.

The Jones Brick company was organized in 1890, by Reps Jones, president; W. L. Russell, secretary and treasurer, J. F. Pate, Bartow Smith and R. N. Hood. The company purchased twenty acres of ground immediately south of the Tennessee river at Knoxville, where they began making brick and carried the business on largely until the coming on of the panic of 1893, making from 7,000,000 to 8,000,000 brick per year. Since then, though the business has always been successful, it has not yet reached its former proportions, but the number manufactured now is about 3,000,000 per year. Both common and pressed brick are made by this company, the officers of which at the present time are J. R. McCallum, president, and J. W. McCallum, secretary and treasurer.

The New Knoxville Brewing company was organized as the Knoxville Brewing company in 1886, in which year their brewery was established with every necessary for a successful business. It is located at No. 613 McGhee street, at the corner of Chamberlain street, occupying a front on the latter street of 250 feet and on the former of 150 feet, and has an "L" extending 200 feet along Chamberlain street. The buildings consist of a four-story brick, comprising besides the brewery proper, a malt and bottling department, refrigerator cellars, stables, etc. Its refrigerator apparatus is of the largest pattern in the country, and the company purchases the finest malt and hops to be anywhere found either in this country or in Germany, and employs about forty hands, producing some 25,000 barrels of beer per year. The capital of the company is $50,000, and the officers are Mathew Senn, president; William Meyer, vice-president, and H. S. Mizner, treasurer, and A. A. Rothmann, secretary. The products of this brewery are shipped to all parts of East Tennessee, Southern Kentucky, North Georgia, North Carolina, South Carolina and Virginia. Two different brands of bottled beer are made here, viz.: "XX pale" and Export Lager. In 1896 an artesian well was drilled on the premises, 2,100 feet deep, with a capacity of 360 gallons per minute and a temperature of 58 degrees. The machinery is all of the most modern styles and patterns, the best that could be purchased, and is propelled by steam engines aggregating two hundred horsepower.

D. M. Rose & Co., who own one of the largest sawmills in operation in the vicinity of Knoxville, established themselves in this business in 1876, in Sevier county. In 1880 they removed to Knoxville, erecting a small mill on the south side of the Tennessee river, near the bridge. Since then their business has become very extensive and they now have a capacity of 50,000 feet of lumber per day. They are also engaged in the manufacture of sash, doors and blinds. The members of the company at the present time are Daniel M. Rose, Thomas H. Rose, John M. Pitner and William A. Pitner.

The Scottish Carolina Timber and Land Company was organized in 1888, with a capital stock of $1,000,000, and in 1889 completed a mill having a capacity of 50,000 feet of lumber per day. This mill was set up on the Tennessee river, a short distance below the Knoxville & Augusta railroad bridge, now the Atlanta, Knoxville & Northern. This company owned large tracts of timber in East Tennessee.

In 1873 Howe Brothers began the business of manufacturing furniture in Knoxville, continuing until 1876, when they were succeeded by William Caswell & Co. This firm carried on the business until 1880, when S. B. Boyd, proprietor of a carpet store, consolidated his business with that of the furniture manufacturing firm. Mr. Boyd's department became an extensive retail house furnishing establishment, and this arrangement lasted until 1886, when the partnership was dissolved, Mr. Caswell retaining the manufacturing department and Mr. Boyd his own peculiar line. The latter then associated with himself John M. Allen, R. J. Stevenson and S. B. Boyd, Jr., and carried on the business under the firm name of Boyd, Allen & Co.

The Standard Handle Company was incorporated in 1881 with a capital stock of $60,000. All kinds of handles are manufactured by this firm, hickory being the kind of timber mainly used. Formerly the officers of this company were Edward Nicoll, president; F. J. Leland, vice-president, and C. M. Woodbury, secretary and treasurer. At the present time the name of the company is the American Handle Company. F. J. Leland is president and general manager of this company.

The Barker Manufacturing Company was established in June, 1883, by J. H. and F. Barker, and was for some years extensively engaged in the manufacture of woodenware and handles. The officers were at first F. Barker, president; H. N. Saxton, Jr., secretary, and J. H. Barker, treasurer. This company went out of business in 1897, and Mr. Saxton, in company with C. Gustavo Schrader, is engaged in exporting lumber, under the name of Saxton & Co.

The Knoxville Box and Keg Company was established in 1872 by D. R. Samuel, who admitted his son, W. B. Samuel, to partnership in 1880. They manufacture packing boxes of all kinds, kegs, wagon felloes and wood specialties and novelties. Their building was afterwards destroyed by fire and the business was not resumed.

The Knoxville Furniture Company was incorporated in 1882, with a capital of $50,000, and was organized September 12, that year, having erected their building, a three-story frame, above a basement, in 1881. This building is on McGhee street, nearly opposite the brewery. The kinds of furniture made in this factory consist of bedroom suits and cabinet mantels, and the company employs in its factory and saw-mill at South Knoxville about 150 men. The furniture is made principally from oak timber and lumber, but some birch, especially curly birch, walnut and mahogany are used. The steam engine used in propelling the machinery is of 125 horse power. The officers of the company remain as at the time of organization, viz.: Thomas R. Price, president; H. S. Mizner, treasurer, and Abram J. Price, superintendent.

Cooley Bros., contractors and builders, have a planing mill located at No. 402 Chamberlain street, in which they employ about forty hands, including those engaged in their building operations, the number varying, however, according to the season of the year. They manufacture sash, doors, blinds, moldings, brackets, lath, shingle, flooring and other building materials, their factory being equipped with the most improved labor-saving devices.

The Hanna Manufacturing Company was organized in May, 1897, with the following officers: R. H. Hanna, president; J. T. Sienknecht, vice-president; J. W. McCallum, secretary and treasurer, and W. D. Trueblood, general manager. This company began manufacturing pants, overalls, etc., but in 1898 introduced the manufacture of a complete line of fine clothing, cassimeres and worsteds, being practically the first manufactory of the kind in the Southern states. Their building, a double front brick, two stories high, is located at 316 and 318 Depot street. They employ about sixty hands, and turn out about $50,000 worth of goods each year, which is increasing quite rapidly, so that the output is fifty per cent greater each month than in the corresponding month of the previous year. Their goods are shipped into the following states: Kentucky, Virginia, North and South Carolina, Georgia, Alabama and Mississippi, besides all parts of Tennessee.

The Marble City Fire Extinguisher Company began business in February, 1896. The company is composed of three brothers, John A., William J., and Benjamin F. Durham, and is a co-partnership. It is engaged in the manufacture of chemical fire extinguishers of different sizes, from a hand extinguisher, which a man can readily carry on his back, to a two-horse engine. The company in 1898 sold 1,850 of the hand extinguishers and 67 of the larger sizes. The smallest sized extinguisher holds twenty-six gallons and sells at retail for $12.50. The hand engine costs from $150 to $350; the one-horse engine, from $700 to $1,200, and the two-horse or 85-gallon double-battery chemical engine, $1,500. The smaller sizes are made of cold rolled copper, while the largest size is made of steel, except the wheels. One battery of this two-horse engine is charged while the other is playing on the fire. It carries a hose reel with seventy-five feet of hose, pick-ax, crow-bar, gong and ladders. This chemical engine is highly recommended by the chiefs of the Knoxville Fire Department, notwithstanding the fact that the city of Knoxville has never yet invested in a chemical fire extinguisher.

The Scates Furnace Company, as it now exists, was organized in 1897, though the business which they are conducting was established in 1883 by George R. Scates. This business is the manufacture of the Scates steel furnace for the heating of buildings by means of warm air. Of this steel furnace Mr. Scates is the inventor. Previous to 1883 Mr. Scates had had many years' experience in the furnace business in several of the Northern states and perceiving the great necessity and the demand for a warm air furnace superior to anything then in existence produced the furnace now being manufactured in Knoxville. The factory is located near the Southern railway, west of the Knoxville Woolen Mills, the building being owned by a number of Knoxville gentlemen, among whom are S. B. Luttrell, W. H. Collett, and Peter Kern, and is leased to the company. The patterns in this factory cost about $9,000, and of these patterns Mr. Scates was the patentee. In 1897 gentlemen from Pennsylvania and Chicago became interested in the business and a new company was formed, the officers of which are as follows: C. F. Van Dewater, president; J. L. Nelson, secretary; F. E. Fuller, treasurer, and G. R. Scates, superintendent. The furnace was patented January 23, 1883, and has been largely sold throughout the Southern states. The fire-box is lined on all sides with heavy fire-brick tile made for the purpose, and to a heavy steel gas-tight dome is attached a double horizontal steel radiator extending the entire length of the furnace on both sides and across in the rear of the dome. So long as the brick lining remains in its place it is impossible to burn out or even crack the steel fire-box. This furnace is manufactured in four sizes, adapted to all classes of buildings. The company also manufactures steel ranges in large numbers.

On February 4, 1899, a disastrous fire occurred at the factory, by which all the patterns for both range and furnace were destroyed, the loss to the company in patterns and otherwise reaching from $15,000 to $20,000. The foundry portion of the building was leased by the Scates Furnace Company to the Globe Foundry Company, composed of H. R. Wilhite and A. P. Patterson, who did all the foundry work for the Scates company. The loss of the Globe Foundry Company by this fire was about $500. The loss to the building was about $6,500.

In October, 1880, a company formed in New York established a telephone exchange in Knoxville with thirty-three subscribers, the system then used being known as the Law system and quite different from that now in use. This Knoxville exchange continued to be a small affair until it was purchased by the East Tennessee Telephone Company, which purchase was effected April 1, 1887, by O. F. Noel, of Nashville, the president of this company, which immediately began to make extensive improvements, the system being changed November 1, 1888, to the magneto system, which is in use at this time. July 1, 1891, the company had 405 subscribers.

and then the office was removed from the Sedgwick building to the present site on Summit Hill, No. 403 Vine street. On February 20, 1899, the company had 1,100 subscribers.

The long-distance telephone was put in in 1884, at which time the East Tennessee Telephone Company purchased a telegraph line of R. N. Hood, J. M. Greer and others, extending from Knoxville to Maryville. Since then this service has been largely extended, until at the present time Knoxville has communication with numerous towns in East Tennessee, among them being the following county seats: Athens, Chattanooga, Cleveland, Clinton, Dayton, Dandridge, Jallico, Jacksboro, Kingston, Loudon, Madisonville, Maryville, Morristown, Newport, Rutledge, Sevierville and South Pittsburg.

The managers of this company in Knoxville have been the following: Joseph C. Duncan, 1887 to 1888; Al. Cooper, a short time in 1888; A. P. Harrison, 1888-94; W. O. Rhode, 1894 to the present time.

The People's Telephone Company was established in 1894, with C. E. Lucky, president; W. L. Welcker, vice-president; Joseph C. Duncan, general manager and Elmer D. Ross, secretary and treasurer. These gentlemen still remain in office. This company has 800 subscribers in Knoxville and 150 outside of the city, these subscribers being located in many of the towns throughout East Tennessee. The office and exchange rooms of the company are in the Franklin building, at the northeast corner of Gay and Commerce streets.

CHAPTER XII.

COMMERCIAL MATTERS.

First Stores Established—Growth as a Commercial Center—Unusually Large Jobbing Business—Some of the Largest Establishments in the South—The Territory Covered—Wholesale Trade Amounting to More Than $50,000,000 Annually—The Coal Trade, its Growth—Chamber of Commerce—Great Fire.

IT WAS not long after the establishment of a town where Knoxville is now situated when several stores were started. The merchants obtained their goods in the great trade centers in the North and East, as in Baltimore and Philadelphia. These goods were transported in wagons to all the frontier towns. There was but little coin in the country and but few bank notes. Often the advertisements of these frontier merchants specified the kind of goods that would be taken for their merchandise, and also the different values at which these goods would be received. For instance, at the salt works located at Washington, Va., salt was sold at seven shillings six pence per bushel if paid for in cash or prime furs; at ten shillings per bushel if paid for in bear or deer skins, beeswax, hemp, bacon, butter or beef cattle; and at twelve shillings per bushel if paid for in country trade or in produce, as was usually the case. Stores advertised that they would take for such articles as were theirs for sale—cash, beeswax and country produce, tallow, hogs' lard, butter, pork, new feathers, corn, rye, oats, good horses, flax and "old Continental money," that issued by the Continental Congress, which had by that time depreciated wonderfully in value, and they also took certificates of indebtedness either of the state or the nation because of services performed against the Indians, and land warrants.

It would be impracticable to present a full list of all the

MARTIN L. ROSS.

various kinds of business men located in Knoxville, even down to the breaking out of the war; but a few of them, whose names are yet well remembered, are here given. The first merchants in this city were Samuel and Nathaniel Cowan, who were two of the five inhabitants of the place when it was laid out and named in 1792. Hugh Dunlap was another of the very early merchants, and Humes Fryar and Campbell Others.

In the year 1820 James H. Cowan, a nephew of Samuel and Nathaniel Cowan, the first merchants to do business in Knoxville, opened a store at the corner of Main and Gay streets, with a capital of $500. Mr. Cowan had not at that time attained his majority. In 1825 he formed a partnership with Hugh A. M. White. This partnership continued for five years. From 1830 to 1832 Mr. Cowan continued the business until 1832, when he entered into partnership with Mr. Perez Dickinson, his brother-in-law, who is yet living. Mr. Dickinson had come to Knoxville in 1830 from Massachusetts, to take charge of Hampden-Sidney academy.

This firm continued in business for forty-three years, until about the year 1875, when it sold out to Alvin Burton, who had been with the firm for many years. Cowan and Dickinson built the two-story double brick storehouse which still stands at the northeast corner of Gay and Main streets. Out of this firm grew the large wholesale house of Cowan, McClung & Co., established in 1858 by James H. Cowan, Perez Dickinson, Charles J. McClung and Frank H. McClung. This is still one of the leading wholesale houses in Tennessee, its members being Charles J. McClung, Matthew McClung, Robert M. Rhea and Jacob L. Thomas.

The first exclusively wholesale house in Knoxville was that of McClung, Wallace & Co., who began here in 1837, and carried on a comparatively large business, selling goods in East Tennessee, North Georgia and North Alabama. They continued in business until about 1850.

C. H. & D. L. Coffin began business in Knoxville about

1847, as wholesale and retail dealers and continued until some time previous to the war.

C. Morgan & Son began business in Knoxville in 1818, continuing until about 1835, at which time Franklin Morgan the junior member of the firm established a wholesale business in Nashville, which he carried on for about eighteen years. C. Morgan continued his business in Knoxville for some years after the son removed to Nashville.

C. J. McClung began business in Knoxville in 1849, as a retail dealer in merchandise, continuing until 1855, when he removed to St. Louis and there, with his brother, Frank H. McClung, became a member of the wholesale house of C. M. McClung & Co., remaining in St. Louis for three years, when he returned to Knoxville to become a member of the house of Cowan, McClung & Co.

James & Wallace Park were well-known business men in Knoxville before the war, successful, high-toned, and honorable in all respects. Their store was on the site of the present Flanders Hotel.

Col. John Crozier was likewise a well-known and highly-esteemed business man of the days before the war. He was the father of John H. Crozier and the grandfather of E. W. Crozier, publisher of the Knoxville Directory.

Walker, O'Keefe & Co. are also worthy of mention as wholesale and retail dealers in merchandise before the war, carrying on a profitable business for several years, closing out about 1855. Abner G. Jackson was also for many years a prominent retail merchant in the city.

Dr. James King was a dealer in groceries early in the history of the place. He owned a couple of steamboats, one of which was named the "Guide," with which boats he brought groceries to Knoxville from New Orleans. The "Guide" is remembered as a very pretty little boat. Dr. King's place of business was located on the southwest corner of Gay and Church streets, and there he built up a very prosperous trade. At the time of his death Henry Ault, father of the present cashier of the Merchants' Bank, purchased the stock of goods, and carried on the wholesale grocery business until his death, in 1875.

About 1840 Matthew McClung, Hugh L. McClung and William B. French went to Pittsburg for the purpose of building a steamboat, which they built at a cost of $15,000, and named her the "Harkaway." This boat they loaded with groceries, and came up the Tennessee river to the Mussel Shoals, where they had to wait for a rise of water, after which they came on up to Knoxville. Their warehouse was on the river bank, and they continued in business for some eight or ten years.

Later came James and William Williams, mentioned in the chapter on "Transportation," who carried on a large wholesale grocery business, and carried the United States mail on their steamboats between Knoxville and Decatur and also carried many passengers.

The wholesale grocery business in Knoxville is very extensive, especially when the aggregate amount of it is taken into account. Among the principal firms engaged in the business in the past and in the present may be mentioned the following: Borches & Co.; Dick, McMillan & Co.; Hazen & Lotspiech; Kaiser Bros.; Knaffl & Locke; W. B. Lockett & Co.; H. P. McMillan; McNulty Grocery Company, and M. L. Ross & Co.

McNulty & Borches was formerly one of the largest wholesale grocery firms in Knoxville. But besides groceries they carried also lines of dry goods, notions, boots and shoes, and carpets. The individual members of this firm were F. McNulty and Jacob W. Borches. They, however, at length dissolved partnership, and at the present time F. McNulty is proprietor of the McNulty Grocery Company, which carries on business at 402 Gay street, 226 Grand avenue, 801 Central avenue, and 802 North Broad street. The manager of the business is Howard O'Neal.

Jacob W. Borches & Co., the "Co." being Ben N. Donahue,

carry on a large wholesale grocery business at No. 103 Jackson street.

Coffin, Martin & Co. established themselves in business as wholesale grocers in Knoxville in 1867, the business afterward passing into the hands of Cone, Shields & Co. This firm carried a large stock of staple and fancy groceries and their trade extended to large distances in all directions from the city. J. S. Shields, once a member of the firm, which has passed out of existence, is now at the head of a firm which is engaged in the wholesale hat trade and is composed of J. S. Shields and Robert R. Swepson. This firm is located at 314 Gay street.

H. B. Carhart & Co., formerly carried on a wholesale grocery business which had been established in 1877 by Lewis & Carhart, this firm giving place in 1884 to the former firm, which was composed of H. B., W. B. and W. E. Carhart. This firm has been dissolved and now none of its members remain in Knoxville.

Williams & Zimmerman began business in Knoxville as wholesale grocers in 1870, and in 1880 were succeeded by Condon Bros., both of whom are still living in Knoxville—Michael J., who is now a railroad contractor, and Stephen P., who served a term as United States Marshal, under President Cleveland.

W. B. Lockett & Co. established themselves in business in Knoxville as wholesale grocers in 1883, at which time the firm consisted of W. B. Lockett, Sr.; W. B. Lockett, Jr.; R. S. Hazen and J. O. Lotspeich. At the present time the firm is composed of William B. Lockett, Edward Lockett and A. Percy Lockett. Their business is located at 107 Jackson street.

M. L. Ross & Co., wholesale grocers, began business as Carpenter, Ross & Co. in 1870. In 1879 they were succeeded by M. L. Ross and W. B. Lockett, the latter retiring in 1883, and being succeeded by S. B. Dow, so that at the present time the firm (January, 1899) is composed of Martin L.

Ross* and Samuel B. Dow, under the firm name at the head of this paragraph. They carry on a very large business and are located at No. 422 Gay street.

Knaffl & Locke (Rudolph Knaffl and E. C. Locke) engaged in business as wholesale grocers in 1881, in which year they succeeded Anderson & McNulty, who began business in 1876. Their extensive business is located at No. 125 Jackson street.

The Knoxville Provision and Sugar Company was established January 1, 1892, by Hazen & Lotspeich, Shields Bros., M. L. Ross & Co., H. B. Carhart & Co., W. B. Lockett & Co., Knaffl & Locke, and Smith & Bondurant, for the purpose of selling meats, lard and sugar at wholesale. Shields Bros. and H. B. Carhart & Co. have since withdrawn, the company otherwise remaining as at first. Their goods are sold mainly in Tennessee, Kentucky, North Carolina and Georgia, and their sales have amounted in one year to as much as $850,000. The location of the business is at 127-129 Jackson street.

Hazen & Lotspeich began business as wholesale grocers in 1888 and for a number of years were located at 206 Gay street. In 1895 they removed to their present location, 125 Jackson street, and their business is very extensive, covering Tennessee and the states adjoining on all sides. The firm is composed of R. S. Hazen and J. O. Lotspeich.

R. Knaffl, wholesale grocer and successor to Knaffl & Locke, a firm established in 1883, began by himself in June, 1897. Knaffl & Locke succeeded McNulty & Knaffl, a firm which was in business from 1880 to 1883. Mr. Knaffl's business extends throughout East Tennessee and the surrounding adjacent states and is very extensive.

The Knoxville Storage Company was established in 1895 in a building owned by B. L. Smith, by James A. Hensley and Mr. Smith, Mr. Hensley being the manager of the business. In the basement of this building, located on Jackson street.

---

*The death of Martin L. Ross occurred May 30, 1899.

and in the first two stories above the basement, the company stores commercial goods, and in the third story furniture and other household goods.

The business now conducted by the Sanford, Chamberlain & Albers Company was established in 1864 by E. J. Sanford & Co., the firm consisting of E. J. Sanford and Dr. O. F. Hill, located where the gas office is at the present time, and the business being both wholesale and retail. In 1865 this firm was succeeded by that of Chamberlain Bros. & Van Gilder, composed of H. S. Chamberlain, W. P. Chamberlain and T. I. Van Gilder. In 1866 this firm changed to Chamberlain & Albers (A. J.), the latter succeeding to the interest of Mr. Van Gilder. During this same year the old firm of E. J. Sanford & Co. resumed business in the building now occupied by S. B. Luttrell & Co. and in 1872 the two firms consolidated under the firm name of Sanford, Chamberlain & Albers, Dr. O. F. Hill and H. S. Chamberlain retiring. On January 1, 1897, the firm was incorporated under the name of The Sanford, Chamberlain & Albers Company, with E. J. Sanford, president; A. J. Albers, vice-president and general manager, and W. P. Chamberlain, secretary and treasurer, the stock in the company all being held by the parties mentioned. The annual amount of business, which consists in the wholesaling of drugs, amounts to from $200,000 to $300,000.

Chapman-White-Lyons & Company, wholesale druggists, were established in 1881 and incorporated under the above name in 1892. Mr. Chapman, the head of the company, was formerly in the wholesale grocery business, as a member of the firm of Carpenter, Ross & Co., the predecessors of M. L. Ross & Co.; Mr. Lyons was formerly a retail druggist, for several years in company with Judge D. K. Young of Clinton, Tenn., and Mr. White was formerly for several years in the wholesale tin and stove business. The company was incorporated with John E. Chapman, president; W. L. Lyons, vice-president, and W. C. Everett, secretary and treasurer.

At the present time the officers remain the same except that John C. Hickman is secretary and treasurer. From four to six traveling men are employed by this company.

The house of Daniel Briscoe, Bros. & Co. was established in 1882 by George & Briscoe. In 1886 the firm was composed of Daniel and P. J. Briscoe, R. R. Swepson, M. D. Arnold and S. C. Roney. At the present time the members of the firm are Daniel, Philip J., Philip J., Jr., and J. Earnest Briscoe, and Ralph H. Mountcastle. The business transacted by this firm aggregates about $1,000.000 per year, and they keep seven traveling salesmen on the road. Their stock is very extensive and well selected and consists of dry goods, boots and shoes and notions.

W. W. Woodruff & Co. is the oldest hardware house in Knoxville, the business having been established in 1865 by W. W. Woodruff, and on quite a small scale. At the present time the business aggregates about $500,000 per year. The firm is composed of Mr. Woodruff and William E. Gibbins, and the store, one of the finest in the state, is located at 424-426 Gay street.

S. B. Luttrell & Co. located at 613 Gay street, began business in Knoxville in 1871, and is one of the most substantial firms in the city. Without employing traveling salesmen they have a trade aggregating upward of $200,000 per year. The firm is now composed of Samuel B. Luttrell and James C. Luttrell.

In 1880 the firm of McClung, Powell & Co. succeeded to the hardware line of Cowan, McClung & Co., the new firm being composed of Calvin McClung, C. Powell, W. J. McNutt and A. Gredig. In 1884 this firm was succeeded by C. M. McClung & Co., consisting of C. M. McClung, W. B. Smith and W. B. Keener. They largely increased the business in the original line and also added thereto agricultural implements. The firm is now composed of Calvin M. McClung, Bruce Keener and Charles J. McClung, Jr., their business being located at 503-507 Jackson street.

The firm of McCorkle & Brown began business in 1869 and continued in existence about ten months, when George Brown become sole proprietor. The business consisted in wholesale dealing in hardware, seeds, implements and fertilizers. Judge Brown carried it on alone until his death, in 1892, when it passed into the hands of his children, John S. Brown, Mrs. L. B. Prosser and Mrs. M. L. Montgomery, who still carry it on under the name of George Brown.

The business now conducted by McClung, Buffat & Buckwell had its origin about 1875, when Mr. A. Gredig established a retail hardware business on Gay street. Continuing alone for three years he, in 1878, sold a half interest to J. H. Cruze, the style of the firm becoming Gredig & Cruze, as it remained until 1880, when Mr. Gredig sold out to Mr. Cruze, who carried on the business alone until 1886. At this time Mr. E. Buffat of Rogersville purchased half the business, the style of the firm then becoming Cruze & Buffat, and so continuing one year, when E. G. Buckwell was admitted to partnership and the firm became Cruze, Buffat & Buckwell. In 1894 Mr. Cruze sold his interest to C. M. McClung & Co., the firm then becoming McClung, Buffat & Buckwell, being incorporated under this name in 1897, with E. G. Buckwell, president; E. Buffat, vice-president, and J. C. Beck, secretary and treasurer. The present officers are E. Buffat, president; C. C. Cruze, vice-president, and J. C. Beck, secretary and treasurer. The business is now both wholesale and retail, hardware, agricultural implements and machinery and house furnishings, and amounts to about $100,000 per year.

McMillan, Hazen & Co. are the successors of R. S. Payne & Co. (F. McNulty), which firm began business in 1867 as wholesale and retail dealers in hats, but in 1869 boots and shoes were added. In 1875 Mr. McNulty bought the interest of R. S. Payne, and in 1876 Mr. Payne opened an exclusively wholesale boot and shoe house and a few years later admitted to partnership E. E. McMillan and Asa Hazen, and in 1883 the latter two gentlemen, together with M. S. McClellan, purchased the interest of Mr. Payne, the firm at this time becoming McMillan, Hazen & Co. Since 1897 this firm has been located at 122 Gay street, employing nine traveling salesmen and selling goods throughout Tennessee and the states adjoining. The present firm consists of the gentlemen named above and Reuben N. Payne.

Powers, Little & Co., wholesale clothing, established in 1892, are successors to Powers, Little & McCormick, who in 1888 succeeded Smith, Huddleston, Powers & Co., which latter firm succeeded Brock, Huddleston & Co., who began business in 1884 as retail dealers in clothing, continuing one year. Since January, 1896, Powers, Little & Co. have been located at 124 Jackson street. The business of this firm is very extensive, extending throughout Tennessee and the states adjoining and amounting to more than $250,000 per annum, seven traveling men being employed.

McTeers, Hood & Co., wholesale clothing, was established in 1884 by J. C. and C. E. McTeer, R. S. Payne, Charles Berger, and W. M. Hood. The first location of this firm was on Gay street, but later they erected their present large five-story brick building on the southwest corner of Commerce and State streets, at a cost of $60,000, and have been carrying on their business from this location since 1889. At different times J. T. McTeer and W. M. Hood purchased the interests of the other partners, and now are the sole proprietors. They keep on the road fourteen traveling salesmen, covering fifteen of the states of the Union, and their average sales amount to $750,000. The most prosperous year they have had brought their aggregate sales up to nearly $900,000.

The firm of Cullen & Newman began business in 1872, engaging in the wholesale china, glass and queensware business, and continued under this name until 1897, when they were incorporated under the name of Cullen & Newman Company. Their business consists in wholesale dealing in notions, millinery, houseware, table and pocket cutlery, jewelry, stationery, clocks, and all goods kept in a well stocked department store, no traveling salesmen being employed, but instead, catalogues to the number of 4,000 or 5,000 being sent out every sixty days.

Sterchi Bros. began business in 1889 on Vine street as retail dealers in furniture and carpets. In 1893 they removed to the Lawson-McGhee Library building, and afterward to the McNulty building, and in 1896 bought out the furniture business of King, Oates & Co., who were located in the McNulty building at Nos. 412-414 Gay street, where they are now located. At this time they became engaged in the wholesale trade and are still so engaged, selling wholly by catalogue, their trade extending throughout Tennessee, Kentucky, Virginia, North Carolina and Georgia. The firm now consists of J. C. and J. G. Sterchi.

Davis, Chumbley & Co. began business in 1890, under the firm name of J. T. Brownlee & Co., in 1893 the firm becoming Brownlee, Chumbley & Co., and in 1895 the firm became as it is now, Davis, Chumbley & Co. They deal exclusively in wholesale boots and shoes. The firm consists of J. L. Davis and J. F. Chumbley, the "Co." being merely nominal. Mr. Davis had previously been for twenty-five years engaged in the wholesale hat trade, as the head of the firm of J. L. Davis & Co.

Arnold, Henegar, Doyle & Co. began business in October, 1896, the firm consisting of M. D. Arnold, Edward Henegar, James S. Doyle, R. R. Swepson and I. E. Dooley, all of whom still remain in the firm. They are wholesale dealers in boots and shoes, employ from ten to twelve traveling salesmen, and have a business of nearly half a million dollars per annum. Their trade extends throughout Tennessee, Kentucky, Virginia, North and South Carolina, Georgia, Alabama and Mississippi, and they are located at No. 428 Gay street.

Brown, Payne, Deavers & Co. began business as wholesale dealers in dry goods, notions and furnishings, June 1, 1898, the members of the firm being T. G. Brown, R. S. Payne, Jr., J. L. Deavers, W. T. Kennedy, and N. W. Hale. They are all young men with the energy necessary to make their business a success, are located at Nos. 318-320 Gay street, and are selling goods throughout Tennessee, Kentucky, Virginia, North Carolina, Georgia and North Alabama, to the extent during the first year of their existence as a firm of about $350,000. The building in which they are located, a five-story structure, is exclusively occupied by them.

Cowan, George & Co. began business December 15, 1897, the members of the firm being James H. Cowan, S. H. George and Edgar and Albert George. Their business consists in the manufacture and sale of clothing, their trade extending throughout Tennessee, Kentucky, Virginia, North and South Carolina, Georgia and Alabama. They are located at 316 Gay street, occupying a four-story and basement building and also a building in the rear of this, extending back to State street, a three-story building, the two buildings having a floor space of about 30,000 square feet. This firm employs about 100 hands and carries on a very extensive business.

McArthur, Sons & Co., wholesale dealers in musical instruments, began business in Knoxville in 1889, Mr. F. E. McArthur being then the sole proprietor. He was then located on Gay street between Commerce and Vine streets. The house under its present name was incorporated July 1, 1898, with a capital stock of $25,000, and with F. E. McArthur, president; W. R. McArthur, vice-president, and A. M. King, secretary and treasurer. In August, 1896, they moved to their present location, 510-512 Gay street, where they have a fine large building, 50x150 feet in size and two stories high. They employ six salesmen on the road, and cover East Tennessee and the parts of states adjoining on all sides. The instruments sold by this firm are pianos and organs exclusively.

Samuel C. Roney began the shoe business in 1860, and for twenty years, 1866 to 1886, traveled throughout the South in the interest of a large shoe and leather company of New York city. In the latter year he came to Knoxville and became connected with the wholesale house of Briscoe, Swepson & Co., afterward Daniel, Briscoe & Co., remaining with them until 1894, when he organized the firm of Roney, Arnold & Co. From this firm he withdrew October 1, 1896, and soon afterward organized the Sam C. Roney Shoe Company, which is located on Gay street between Commerce and Vine streets, and which by means of about eight traveling salesmen covers the territory of Tennessee and states adjoining on all sides, and West Virginia.

Allen, Stephenson & Co. are successors to other firms in the same business, which has, however, been built up gradually from the time it was established in 1876 by Samuel B. Boyd, who began as a retail dealer in carpets. In 1880 the firm became Boyd & Caswell, and dealt in carpets and furniture. In 1886 it became Boyd, Allen & Co., and in 1891, Allen, Stephenson & Co. This firm now deals in carpets, furniture and house furnishing goods, their trade extending throughout East Tennessee, Kentucky, Virginia, and North Carolina. To the above lines they have recently added the manufacture and sale of the "indestructible bed springs."

S. H. George & Co. began business as wholesale dealers in hats in Knoxville in 1885, the pioneer house of the kind in the city. After several changes in the firm as to members and style it became Murphy & Robinson in 1896, as it remains. This firm now deals in hats and millinery, keeps five traveling men on the road, and covers Tennessee and the surrounding states. It is composed of G. W. Murphy and W. B. Robinson, the house being located at No. 420 Gay street.

Haynes, Henson & Co. composed of J. P. Haynes and J. A. Henson, established themselves in the wholesale boot and shoe trade in 1879. They are located at 312 Gay street, sell goods by means of about twelve traveling salesmen throughout Tennessee and the surrounding adjacent states, their business amounting to a little more than half a million dollars per annum.

The Greer Machinery Company began business in Knoxville in 1886, under the firm name of J. M. Greer & Co. (J. G. Duncan). Later the company was incorporated with a capital stock of $75,000, and with the following officers: J. M. Greer, president; John G. Duncan, vice-president; W. O. Greer, secretary, and O. Schmalzried, treasurer. The business transacted by this company is unusually extensive, covering East Tennessee, Kentucky, Virginia and West Virginia, and occasionally extending into other states. In 1898 it amounted to somewhat more than $225,000, one item alone being eighty-five complete threshing outfits, some of them steam and others horse-power. On February 14, 1899, their building on Jackson street west of Gay street was consumed by fire, but they immediately resumed business at 111 Jackson street, near Central avenue. The officers of the company at the present time are the same as above and with the addition of G. R. Moore, assistant treasurer. The surplus and undivided profits of this company for 1898 amounted to $16,000.

The Davies Furniture Company began business in Knoxville April 2, 1898, the company being composed of D. J. Davies, J. O. White and J. H. Spreen. They are located at 304 Gay street and deal in furniture, carpets, baby carriages and a general line of household goods, both at retail and at wholesale. Mr. Davies was formerly attorney-at-law. Mr. White connected with the Sun Life Insurance Company of Louisville, Ky., and Mr. Spreen a stock and grain broker of Cincinnati, Ohio. All are young and energetic men.

In 1889 the firm of Hooker, Littlefield & Steere was formed for the manufacture of confectionery. In 1892 Mr. Hooker withdrew and the firm became Anderson, Littlefield & Steere till 1895, when the present firm of Littlefield, Steere & Sanders was formed. Their factory and offices are located at 120 Gay street. They employ about 100 hands in the factory and keep four salesmen on the road. Their trade extends throughout the states of Tennessee, Kentucky, Virginia, West Virginia, North Carolina, South Carolina, Georgia and

Alabama, and amounts to over $1,000,000 annually. The members of the firm are H. E. Littlefield, A. H. Steere and W. C. Sanders, Jr.

Knoxville is a great center for the distribution of all kinds of goods, its trade extending to most parts of the Southern states, including Virginia, Kentucky, Tennessee, North Carolina, Georgia, South Carolina and Mississippi and Alabama. By the year 1892 Knoxville's wholesale trade had reached the grand total of $50,000,000, having increased to this amount from about $10,000,000 in 1880. During those twelve years the manufacturing carried on in Knoxville had most rapidly increased, having been in fact almost wholly created during that time. At the present time both the wholesale trade and the manufacturing business within the city and its immediate suburbs are much more extensive than they were in 1892. But in 1892 the grocery business amounted to about $5,000,000, the flour and provision business to about $1,500,000 and the manufacturing business amounted to about $10,000,000. The trade in these lines had increased about in the same proportion as the coal and iron business. The dry goods business then amounted to about $4,000,000, including the millinery and notion business. The agricultural implement trade, the clothing, boot and shoe trade, live stock, liquor business, marble and other numerous branches all had been unusually and gratifyingly prosperous during the twelve years before 1892. The number of wholesale houses in Knoxville was then about 100, this number including coal, marble and lumber dealers. Some of these also carried on a retail trade, and the number of exclusively retail houses numbered about 200. And there were in the aggregate about 225 manufacturing establishments in the city.

The coal business of Knoxville has become very extensive and important. Among the principal companies and firms at the present time engaged therein may be mentioned the following: The Black Diamond Coal Company, The Buck eye Coke Company, The Coal Creek Coal Company, The East Tennessee Coal Company, The Jellico Coal Mining Company, The Middle Ridge Coal Company, The Mingo Coal and Coke Company, The Whistle Coal and Coke Company, The Tennessee Coal Company and the Workingmen's Co-operative Coal Company.

It is believed that the first coal mining company organized in this city was the Knoxville Iron Company, in 1855, the members of which were John S. Moffett, John Shields, M. W. Williams, and A. L. Maxwell. This company brought coal from points down the Tennessee river from Knoxville in a small steamboat called the "Holston," but its operations were on a small scale and not of long duration.

In May, 1858, the Cumberland Mountain Coal and Land Company was organized with a capital stock of $1,200,000. the officers of which were at the time of organization G. B. Lamar, president; Thomas H. Calloway, treasurer; a Mr. Jackson, secretary, and the other members, Samuel Congdon. Thomas C. Lyons, C. M. McGhee, A. L. Maxwell, Robert Morrow, M. B. Prichard, Campbell Wallace, and Euclid Waterhouse. This company was reorganized in 1867 as the East Tennessee Iron and Coal Company, with C. M. McGhee, president. It had previously purchased large quantities of land in Anderson, Campbell and Scott counties, and now, as the East Tennessee Coal Company, the name being changed in 1876, owns 50,000 acres of land lying for thirteen miles along the Knoxville & Ohio railroad, containing the finest coal and the most accessible of any in this part of the state. The officers of this company at the present time are as follows: Evan J. Davis, president and treasurer; Frank C. Richmond, secretary, and W. T. Lewis, general manager. The office of the company is at 306 Union street, and the yard at the corner of Depot and Jacksboro streets. and the amount of coal handled each year amounts to about 100,000 tons.

The Coal Creek Mining and Manufacturing Company was

organized in 1868, with officers as follows: Henry H. Wiley, president, and Charles H. Bulkley, secretary. The capital stock at that time was $500,000, but before 1886 it was increased to $2,500,000, about three-fourths of which was owned in New York. The coal lands of this company consist of 240,000 acres, and are some of the finest coal lands anywhere to be found. In 1887 the officers were: E. J. Sanford, president; E. R. Chapman of New York, secretary and assistant treasurer, and W. P. Chamberlain of Knoxville, treasurer and assistant secretary. At the present time (1899) the oficers are: E. J. Sanford, president; C. H. Eicks of New York, secretary and assistant treasurer, and W. P. Chamberlain of Knoxville, treasurer and assistant secretary.

The Poplar Creek Coal and Iron Company was organized with a capital stock of $1,000,000. It owns a large tract of land, which it leases on royalty to operating companies. In 1887 its officers were E. R. Chapman of New York, president, and Thomas H. Heald of Knoxville, secretary. At the present time its officers are as follows: E. J. Sanford, president, and W. P. Chamberlain, secretary and treasurer.

The Coal Creek Coal Company was established in 1868 by E. C. Camp, M. C. and C. C. Wilcox, E. A. Reed, P. A. Mannier and S. S. Tuttle. The company is capitalized at $200,000 and operates two mines at Coal Creek, Tenn., from which it derives its name. At first the annual output of the company's mines was 30,000 tons of coal, but this has been gradually increased until at the present time it is shipping in the neighborhood of 200,000 tons per year. Major E. C. Camp, who is president of the company, has controlled its business since its organization, and H. N. Camp is secretary and treasurer of the company.

The Black Diamond Coal Company was organized in 1873, with T. H. Heald, president; E. C. Locke, secretary and treasurer, and W. J. Hornsby, W. S. Gears, and E. F. Wiley, directors. This company leases its mines from the Coal Creek Mining and Manufacturing Company, the mines being located at Coal Creek, Tenn. They have four mines equipped with steam and electric machinery, and have on their property about 25,000,000 tons of workable coal, the annual output being about 250,000 tons. The present officers are: T. H. Heald, president; W. F. Searle, secretary; and directors, E. C. Locke, W. J. Hornsby, E. F. Wiley, J. M. Andrews and T. H. Heald. The office of the company is at Knoxville.

The Proctor Coal Company was organized in 1887 by Dr. A. Gatliff, Hon. H. F. Finley of Williamsburg, Ky.; W. E. Grinstead and others, for the purpose of mining and shipping coal. The property of this company is in Whitley county, Ky., adjacent to the town of Jellico, Tenn., and comprises seven thousand acres of land, upon which is mined the famous Red Ash Jellico coal. The capacity of the mines is 250,000 tons per year and the product of the mines is shipped to Ohio and most of the Southern states. The Red Ash Jellico is a semi-anthracite coal, the hardest of the bituminous coals, a high grade domestic fuel and well adapted to storing and to the export trade. The general sales office of the company is in the Franklin building, Knoxville, and is under the management of J. L. Boyd. The other officers of the company are Dr. A. Gatliff, president and general manager; J. W. Siler, vice-president, and H. F. Finley, secretary and treasurer.

The Jellico Coal Mining Company was organized in 1888 by S. B. Luttrell, E. J. Davies, F. C. Richmond, Charles Ducloux, David Groves, D. D. Nicholas, Hywell Davis, Mrs. Jennie Williams, E. P. Lyman, John Morgan, R. G. Jones, Mary J. Brown, Carrie Brown, J. L. Williams, Francis Philip, William Thomas, J. Jenkins, D. Weiley Moore, T. R. Thomas, L. B. Welch, John Stone and W. L. Heath, and was officered by E. J. Davis, president; and F. C. Richmond, secretary and treasurer. Their object was to mine at and ship coal from Mountain Ash, Ky., where they purchased 2,500 acres of land in 1892. The capacity of their mines is from 60,000 to 100,000 tons per annum. The officers now are

E. J. Davis, president; Arthur Grove, secretary and treasurer, and John L. Wilson, general manager.

The Tennessee Coal Company was organized January 26, 1895, and purchased the mining plant and equipment of the Tennessee Coal Mining Company. The officers of the new company were S. P. Evans, president; D. B. Bean, vice-president and treasurer, and J. J. Reed, secretary, who continued in their respective offices until after the death of Mr. Evans, and on July 4, 1896, Mr. Bean was elected president; A. H. Bowling, vice-president, and J. J. Reed secretary. The property consists of about 1,000 acres of land, leased from the Coal Creek Mining and Manufacturing Company, and the output of the mines now is about 100,000 tons per year. It is located at Briceville, Tenn., where the plant of the company is one of the most modern in the state.

The Hywel-Davis Coal Company was organized in 1894, by Hywel Davis, B. Du Pont and Banner Coleman, and was incorporated in Kentucky with a capital stock of $50,000. The company leased the property of the Main Jellico Mountain Company, located in Whitley county, Ky., and consisting of 2,500 acres of land. From their mines they ship coal to most of the Southern states, and to Cincinnati, Ohio, and to Chicago, Ill., the annual output of the mines being about 85,000 tons per year. The present officers are T. C. Du Pont, president; Hywel Davis, general manager, and R. H. Gayle, secretary, treasurer and general sales agent. Their shipping point is Jellico, Tenn., and office in the Franklin building, Knoxville.

The East Tennessee Coal Company was organized in 1876, by E. J. Davies, Thomas C. Holloway, D. C. Richards, William Jenkins, Job Jones and Moses Jones, the first officers being Thomas C. Holloway, president; Job Jones, secretary, and E. J. Davies, general manager and treasurer. The object of this company was to mine coal and ship it from Careyville, where they had leased about 4,000 acres of land. In 1877 the company was incorporated with an authorized capital of $15,000. In 1879 they transferred their business to Coal Creek, where they had leased ten acres of good coal lands, and in 1882 they removed to Jellico, purchasing there about 2,500 acres of land, and there they are now mining about 75,000 tons of coal per year, the amount sometimes reaching 100,000 tons. Their vein of coal at this place is about three feet six inches thick, and the coal is considered as good domestic coal as there is on the market.

The officers of the company at the present time are E. J. Davies, president; F. C. Richmond, secretary and W. T. Lewis, general manager.

The Standard Coal and Coke Company was organized in 1882 by W. W. Woodruff, E. E. McCroskey, Joseph Chandler, J. F. McClure, and Lewis Tillman. They purchased about 5,000 acres of land in Campbell county, upon which they opened mines, which they operated until 1887. Russell A. Clapp at length became connected with this company in the capacity of secretary, treasurer and general manager, with office at Knoxville and in 1895 became president and treasurer of the company, with H. M. Wilson, secretary. On January 7, 1899, the property of this company was sold, the purchaser being James L. Breese of New York city, and on February 10, 1899, the Whistle Creek Coal Company was formed and purchased the property from Mr. Breese, who is now president of the company, J. G. Butterfield of New York city being secretary, and Russell A. Clapp, vice-president and treasurer, with his office in the Franklin building, Knoxville. The capacity of the company is 1,000 tons per day and its capital stock is $100,000. Coal from these mines is shipped all over the Southern states from Louisville, Ky., to Atlanta, Ga., to all points reached by the Louisville & Nashville and the Southern railway.

In February or March, 1870, a meeting of business men of Knoxville was held with the view of organizing a Board of Trade, at which a committee was appointed to report to a future meeting as to the practicability of organizing a board of trade. March 1, 1870, this special committee reported favorably to the project to a meeting held in Hoxie's hall, at which meeting a constitution and by-laws were adopted in which the organization was named the Knoxville board of trade, the object to be aimed at being the collection and recording of local and general statistical information relating to manufactures, trade, etc., that might promote the business prosperity of the city. About seventy members joined this board of trade, and on March 21 effected an organization by the election of Perez Dickinson as president; H. S. Chamberlain and S. B. Boyd, vice-presidents, and J. W. Gaut, secretary, and Henry Ault, treasurer. Among the first objects sought by this board of trade was the establishment of a custom house in Knoxville, and lower rates for the transportation of freight on the railroads. To secure better facilities for the bringing in and taking out of all kinds of goods, and passenger travel, has constantly been an object with the board.

In October, 1871, there was a reorganization of the board, forty-one members determining to be members of the new organization. November 2 officers were elected as follows: W. W. Woodruff, president; first vice-president, Henry Ault; second vice-president, J. W. Gaut; secretary, E. P. Bailey, and treasurer, Adrian Terry. September 10, 1872, W. W. Woodruff was re-elected president; Adrian Terry, first vice-president; Harvey Clark, second vice-president; W. P. Chamberlain, secretary, and Spencer Munson, treasurer. In 1873 J. W. Gaut was chosen president; W. O. White, first vice-president; R. P. Gettys, second vice-president; T. H. Heald, secretary, and A. J. Albers, treasurer. September 15, 1875, John S. Van Gilder was chosen president; L. C. Sheppard, first vice-president; J. D. Cowan, second vice-president; R. P. Gettys, secretary, and A. J. Albers, treasurer. In 1876 J. W. Gaut was elected president; W. J. Ramage, secretary, and A. J. Albers, treasurer.

From November 17, 1877, to January 2, 1883, no meetings were held by the board. On the latter date, a reorganization being determined upon, a new constitution was adopted and the following officers elected: W. W. Woodruff, president; S. B. Luttrell, first vice-president; M. J. Condon, second vice-president; N. S. Woodward, secretary, and W. P. Chamberlain, treasurer. In January, 1884, S. B. Luttrell was elected president; W. P. Chamberlain, first vice-president; J. Allen Smith, second vice-president; M. J. Condon, secretary, and Frank A. Moses, treasurer.

The Chamber of Commerce of Knoxville was incorporated April 21, 1887, the incorporators being Adrian Terry, W. R. Tuttle, M. L. Ross, J. W. Fletcher, and H. T. Ault. The objects for which this incorporation was effected were the same as those of similar bodies throughout the country, viz.: the promotion of the general material interests of the city, in the extension of its commerce, the encouragement of its manufacturers, the increase of transportation facilities, etc., these being within the purview of subsection 3 of section 7 of an act of the general assembly of the state of Tennessee, entitled an act to provide for the organization of corporations, passed March 19, 1875, and approved March 23, 1875, the said subsection in part reading: "The support of boards of trade or chambers of commerce and other objects of like nature."

Since this incorporation the officers of the chamber of commerce have been as follows: Presidents—Adrian Terry, 1887-1888; M. L. Ross, 1889-1892; A. J. Albers, 1895-96; M. L. Ross, 1897-99. (Note.—Mr. Ross died in May, 1899, and W. B. Lockett was chosen as his successor.)

First Vice-Presidents—W. R. Tuttle, 1887-90; J. C. Luttrell, 1891-94; T. H. Heald, 1895-96; E. C. Camp, 1897-98; B. R. Strong, 1898-99.

Second Vice-Presidents—M. L. Ross, 1887-1889; R. L. Teasdale, 1891-94; M. L. Ross, 1895-96; J. B. Pound, 1897; W. L. Trent, 1898-99.

Secretaries—J. W. Fletcher, 1887-89; J. W. S. Frierson,

1889-1891; W. J. Ramage, 1892-95; W. H. Kephart, 1896-97; H. M. Branson, 1897-99.

Treasurers—Frank A. Moses, 1889-94; D. B. Bean, 1895-96; John Rotach, 1897-99.

An event long to be remembered in the history of Knoxville was the "Big Fire" of April 8, 1897, in which property to the value of $1,152,250 was consumed and at least three persons lost their lives. The location of this fire was on the east side of Gay street between Commerce and Union streets. Not only were several business houses destroyed, but also the Hotel Knox, the names of three guests of this hotel who lost their lives being S. E. Williams of Springfield, Mass.; A. E. Weeks of Rochester, N, Y.; and G. W. Roberts of Pulaski, Tenn. Richard Hopkins of St. Louis, Mo., died of injuries received in jumping from the hotel.

The business houses destroyed were the Briscoe block, wholesale dry goods and notions; Sterchi Bros.' block, wholesale dealers in furniture and carpets; that of A. P. Lahr, retail dealer in dry goods; Marble City Hat Company, retail hatters; Murphy & Robinson, wholesale hatters; S. B. Newman & Co., printers and binders; Cullen & Newman, queensware; M. L. Ross & Co., wholesale grocers; W. W. Woodruff & Co., wholesale hardware, and Arnold, Hennegar, Doyle & Co., wholesale boots and shoes.

Within three days after the fire was extinguished most of these houses had secured temporary locations, and their representatives in the South and East were buying new goods, and within a year every building that was burned down, with one exception, was rebuilt. This exception was the building owned by Cullen & Newman and M. L. Ross. The new buildings thus erected on the site of the fire were all handsome ones except the McNulty building, which stands on the site of the Hotel Knox, in which the fire originated. The finest building of the whole is the Phoenix building, designed at first as a seven-story structure, but finally carried up only six stories. This is the highest building on Gay street, and, in fact, in the city of Knoxville.

For some time after the advent of railroads in the city its growth went on slowly. At the time when they appeared the principal busniess houses were on Gay street between Main and Church, and most of the dwellings were between the same two streets and the two creeks, First and Second. Coal has for many years been the base of business and industrial civilization, and when the coal mines were opened up by means of the railroads reaching to Knoxville then business began to improve and to expand; but when the railroad was carried through the Cumberland mountains, and thus through a number of coal fields, the business interests of Knoxville, feeling the impulse, began to show signs of an activity theretofore unknown to them. Manufacturing establishments then in existence became enlarged, and new establishments came in, and the area covered by the wholesale trade of the city was very greatly extended. Not only the whole of East Tennessee was reached, but also many of the surrounding states, especially those immediately adjoining the state of Tennessee, and even many of the Western and Southern states farther away.

CHAPTER XIII.

BANKING.

First Bank Established 1811—State Bank Organized—Some of the Private Banks—The First National Bank in 1864—Other National Banks—Clearing House Association—Building and Loan Associations in the Hands of Receivers—Insurance Companies.

THE history of banking in Knoxville is unusually interesting. The first bank established in the city was popularly known as the Bank of Tennessee, but its corporate name, the act of incorporation being passed November 20, 1811, was the "President, Directors and Company of the Bank of the State of Tennessee." This act of incorporation or charter provided that the capital stock should not exceed $400,000, the shares to be $50 each. Subscriptions were opened January 1, 1812, in Knoxville, and also in the following-named counties: Anderson, Blount, Carter, Campbell, Claiborne, Cooke, Bledsoe, Grainger, Hawkins, Jefferson, Greene, Rhea, Roane, Sullivan and Washington. To each of these counties 440 shares were assigned, and the state became a stockholder to the extent of $20,000, reserving the right to withdraw at the end of ten years. The subscriptions were payable in either silver or gold, and were divided into eight annual installments. As soon as $25,000 was paid in the stockholders met in Knoxville and organized, electing all of the officers, except one director, who was appointed by the governor to look after the interests of the state.

At this first election of officers Hugh L. White was chosen president, and Luke Lea, cashier. The first board of directors was composed of the following-named gentlemen: John Crozier, James Park, David Campbell, Calvin Morgan, John Hillsman, Robert King and James Dardis. The bank building stood on the northwest corner of Gay and Main streets, and there were branches of this bank in Clarksville, Jonesboro and Columbia. The smallest denomination of note from the establishment of the bank until 1815 was $5, but after that date bills of $1 could be issued. The charter of this bank extended for thirty years, but it continued in existence only until 1828, when it began to close up its affairs, which process continued for three years.

The next bank established in Knoxville was a branch of a bank established by an act of the legislature passed July 26, 1820, the act having been passed "to establish a bank of the State of Tennessee for the purpose of relieving the distresses of the community and improving the revenues of the state." The capital of this state bank was fixed at $1,000,000, in bills payable to order or bearer, to be issued on the credit and security of the borrower, the whole to be warranted by the state on the proceeds of the sales of public lands. To the branch of this bank established at Knoxville four-tenths of the capital stock was allowed, and there was an agency established in each county in the state which was formed prior to 1819. The principal reason for the establishment of this bank was the financial panic which occurred about that time, the first felt in the state, and the legislature was convened in extra session by Gov. McMinn for the purpose of providing some measure of relief. The president and the ten directors of this bank were elected by the legislature on joint ballot, and were instructed to put the bank into operation by October 15 of that year. They were to issue $500,000 in bills of denominations not less than $5 nor greater than $100, and afterward provision was made for the issuance of fractional notes to the amount of $75,000. According to the charter of this bank either the bank at Nashville or the bank at Knoxville, or both, together with their branches, could consolidate and incorporate themselves with the State bank, but this consolidation was never effected, the two banks mentioned being satisfied to remain independent of the State bank.

This State bank began business on the day fixed by the statute, and for a time was successful; but as it had so many agencies scattered throughout the State large amounts were lost through the defalcations of the county agents. Besides all this, the cashier of the main bank in Nashville in 1832 was found to have permitted overdrafts to friends and others to the extent of $80,000, the greater part of this being also lost, and on account of these various and extensive losses the governor of the state, William Carroll, in his message to the legislature in 1833, advised the closing of the bank, and in conformity with this recommendation the legislature at that session passed an act abolishing the bank and providing that its funds should be deposited in the Union bank, which had then recently been incorporated with a capital of $3,000,000, but which had no branch in Knoxville. Thus ended the second financial institution established in Knoxville. It was located at the corner of Crozier and Cumberland streets. James Campbell, or "Scotch Jimmy," as he was familiarly called, was its cashier. Its business was at all times quite limited.

Between 1850 and 1860 there was great activity in Knoxville in all departments of commercial and financial enterprise. The Bank of East Tennessee was chartered, this charter being obtained by Cowan & Dickinson, and sold by them to a Mr. Fiske of New Orleans. William M. Churchwell became the president of this bank in 1852, and under his management a system of wild speculation and over-issues was indulged in, and the bank ceased to exist in 1856. Samuel Morrow was cashier of this bank, and he, in connection with John Baxter, afterward established the Exchange and Deposit bank.

The Bank of Knoxville was organized in 1854 by John L. Moses, Joseph H. Walker and A. L. Maxwell. They in 1855 sold it to Hugh A. M. White and George M. White, who continued its business until near the beginning of the war, when they wound up its affairs.

The Farmers' bank was established in 1854 by Hugh L. McClung, who sold it to Shepherd & Wheless of Nashville. They continued it for a few years and then consolidated it with the Ocoee bank of Cleveland, Tenn., which in 1859 was purchased by John R., William A., George M., Joseph and Benjamin Branner, who removed it to Knoxville. Here they opened it in the building afterward occupied by the People's bank. Of the Farmers' bank John R. Branner was president and Joseph R. Mitchell, cashier. It continued in business until the breaking out of the war, and even afterward, but was wound up in the years immediately following.

The People's bank was established in 1865 by C. M. McGhee, John R. Branner, Thomas H. Calloway and Joseph R. Mitchell, the firm name under which the business was carried on being J. R. Mitchell & Co. In May, 1866, this bank was incorporated with a capital stock of $35,000, and with officers as follows: C. M. McGhee, president, and Joseph R. Mitchell, cashier. Later Mr. Mitchell became president and F. A. Moses, cashier. This bank had a prosperous career for some years, but at length, through misfortunes, its business had to be discontinued, and its affairs were wound up in 1892.

The First National bank was established in 1864, the principal movers in this enterprise being W. T. Perkins and Mr. Patterson of Cincinnati, and Perez Dickinson, Horace Maynard, William Heiskell and William G. Brownlow of Knoxville. It was organized by the election of Mr. Dickinson, president; Mr. Perkins, vice-president, and Mr. Patterson, cashier. The capital was $50,000, and it began business in the building which had been used by the old Bank of Tennessee, and which is now occupied by the Mechanics' National bank. Its business was always well managed, and its credit stood high all over the United States. One incident in connection with the history of this bank is especially worthy of note, that being the payment to the stockholders of their dividends in gold, while Mr. Dickinson was president. R. R. Swepson, who came to Knoxville from North Carolina, became president of this bank in 1868, succeeding Mr. Dickinson, and remained president during the remainder of the period of the bank's existence.

Mr. Patterson was succeeded as cashier by Rufus M. McClung, who continued in that position until the affairs of the bank were closed in 1872, it being in a certain measure then succeeded by the East Tennessee National bank.

The East Tennessee National bank was organized in July, 1872, and authorized to transact business under the National Banking law by John J. Knox, Comptroller of the Currency, in September following. The first board of directors was composed of the following gentlemen: Joseph R. Anderson, R. Love, Joseph H. Earnest, F. W. Taylor, William Brazelton, Joseph Jaques, Richard C. Jackson, J. A. Rayl, Samuel McKinney, F. H. McClung, J. W. Lillard, S. B. Boyd and J. E. Raht. The first officers elected were R. C. Jackson, president; F. H. McClung, vice-president; and William B. French, cashier. The bank began business in January, 1873, in the old First National Bank building, and was in a certain sense the successor of that bank, although its management was composed of entirely different men. Remaining in that building until 1885, it then removed to its present location at the southwest corner of Gay and Union streets. The presidents of this bank, succeeding Mr. Jackson, have been Joseph Jaques, from January, 1879, until December 27, 1882, R. S. Payne, until June 1, 1892; B. R. Strong, until June 1, 1894; and F. L. Fisher, from that date until the present time. The vice-presidents have been, besides Mr. McClung, W. W. Woodruff, from January, 1882, until 1884; R. S. Payne, January, 1884, to April, 1884; E. J. Sanford, April, 1884, to the present time. The cashiers, in addition to Mr. French, have been J. W. Lillard, June 18, 1873, to February 8, 1878; R. C. Jackson, from 1878 to 1883; J. L. Glover, from March, 1883, to August, 1883; F. L. Fisher, August, 1883, to June 1, 1894, and S. V. Carter, June 1, 1894, to the present time. The capital of this bank is $175,000; its surplus, $200,000; deposits, $1,000,000; and loans and discounts, $900,000. The directors of this bank elected for the year 1899 are as follows: E. J. Sanford, W. W. Woodruff, Daniel Briscoe, C. M. McClung, John McCoy, Adrian Terry,

H. S. Harris, Peter Kern, F. L. Fisher, C. M. McGhee and C. R. Love.

The Merchants' bank began business in July, 1881, under a charter granted to a corporation in 1869, which was never used and which this bank purchased. The officers elected were as follows: John S. Van Gilder, president; H. T. Ault, cashier, and Albert Van Gilder, assistant cashier, each of whom still retains his position. The paid-up capital of the bank is $100,000, and the business conducted is of a conservative character and at the same time as liberal as the rules of good banking will permit. In connection with the business of this bank are three striking features, viz.: It has never paid interest on deposits, has never re-discounted any paper, and has never borrowed any money. The bank is located at No. 516 Gay street, South.

The Mechanics' National bank was organized in 1882 with Thomas O'Conner, president; Sam House, cashier, and F. W. Armstrong, assistant cashier. It began business in the building then recently vacated by the East Tennessee National bank. September 15, 1882, E. J. Sanford was elected vice-president. The directors at this time were Thomas O'Conner, S. B. Luttrell, A. J. Albers, R. N. Hood, S. P. Evans, J. T. McTeer, M. L. Ross, B. R. Strong, J. W. Lillard, James M. Meek and Frank McNulty. The president, Thomas O'Conner, was killed October 19, 1882, and for a short time E. J. Sanford acted as president, being elected to that position October 23 and serving until 1883, when S. B. Luttrell became president, and has filled the office ever since. M. L. Ross became vice-president in 1883, and still remained in office until his death, May 30, 1899. Sam House was cashier until December 12, 1889, being then succeeded by the present cashier, E. G. Oates. W. B. Sullivan is assistant cashier. The capital of this bank is $100,000, the surplus $110,000, the deposits $500,000, and the loans and discounts $425,000. The bank is located at No. 612 Gay street, in the building formerly occupied by the old Bank of Tennessee and later by the East Tennessee National bank. During the war this building was occupied as an office by the provost marshal.

The Knoxville Banking Company was incorporated March 4, 1887, the incorporators being J. W. Hope, T. H. Heald, H. W. Lynn, R. Knaffle and Peter Kern. The object of the incorporators was the organization of a bank, and they were invested with the authority to couple with a general banking business a safe deposit trust company, by virtue of an act of the legislature passed March 19, 1875, and approved March 23, 1875, entitled an act to provide for the organization of corporations, and an act of the general assembly passed March 23, 1883, and approved March 28, 1883, entitled an act to amend an act entitled an act to provide for the organization of corporations, passed March 19, 1875. The organization of this bank was effected in January, 1888, the capital at the time being $25,000, and was opened for business in the February following. At the expiration of the first year of the bank's existence the capital was increased to $50,000, and in 1892 it had a surplus of $15,000. At the present time the capital is $50,000, the surplus and undivided profits $15,000, deposits $135,000, and loans and discounts $133,000. The officers of this company elected January 14, 1899, are as follows: W. H. Gass, president; J. W. Hope, vice-president; H. M. Johnston, cashier, and W. O. Whittle, assistant cashier. The directors are: C. R. McCormick, R. Knaffle, J. W. Hope, John W. Green, J. G. Hellner, H. M. Johnston and W. H. Gass.

This bank receives deposits of one dollar or more in its savings department, on which interest at the rate of three per cent per annum is allowed on sums not withdrawn, the interest being credited and becoming part of the principal at the end of each June and December.

Another feature of the business of this bank is this: In the savings department it makes loans on real estate at six per cent per annum, thus enabling those who desire to borrow small sums on good real estate security to do so, something which they have not heretofore been able to do.

The City National bank was chartered in 1888, the first board of directors being M. P. Jarnagin, James G. Rose, J. P. Haynes, John E. Chapman, J. T. Shields, Jr., James A. Anderson, R. F. Gaut, A. N. Strong and S. H. George. On January 12, 1888, an organization was effected with the following result: M. P. Jarnagin, president; James G. Rose, vice-president; and W. S. Shields, cashier. W. S. Shields became president in 1891, and still remains in that position. J. P. Haynes became vice-president in 1892. Edward Henegar became cashier in January, 1891, and was succeeded by the present cashier, William T. Marfield, in January, 1897. The bank began business with a capital of $100,000, paying no dividends for five years, at the end of which period the surplus of $100,000 was added to the capital, making it what it is at present, $200,000. Since that time fair dividends have been paid. The bank has always been a safe and conservative institution, has now a surplus of $30,000, carries deposits to the amount of $1,200,000, and is one of the strongest of the financial institutions of Knoxville. Its present board of directors is as follows: William S. Shields, S. H. George, D. K. Young, Edward Henegar, J. P. Haynes, J. T. Shields, Jr., John E. Chapman, J. A. Anderson and J. P. Powers The officers are as follows: William S. Shields, president; J. P. Haynes, vice-president, and William T. Marfield, cashier.

The Holston Banking and Trust Company was chartered January 17, 1890, by H. M. Aiken, R. M. Rhea, Anton Lobenstein, James L. Cooley and S. H. McNutt for the purpose of organizing and operating a bank in Knoxville. The capital was paid in instalments, the intention being that when $100,000 had been paid in the organization should be converted into a national bank. On October 26, 1891, this amount of capital had been paid and considerably more, the surplus being returned to the subscribers, and the Holston National bank was then organized with H. M. Aiken, president; H. S. Mizner, vice-president; and W. H. Geers, cashier. Mr. Aiken served as president until August 8, 1893, the vice-president then acting as president until January 9, 1894, when he was elected president, serving in that capacity until January 12, 1897, when Hu. L. McClung was elected and still remains in office. When Mr. Mizner was elected president, Jackson Smith became vice-president, and served until Mr. McClung was elected president, when he was succeeded by S. H. McNutt, who still fills the office of vice-president. Mr. Geers was cashier until April 8, 1892, and then after an interim of about six weeks Joseph P. Gaut was elected cashier on June 1, 1892, and still remains in office. This bank is located at No. 524 Gay street. Its capital remains at $100,000, its surplus is $20,000, deposits $250,000, and loans and discounts of $260,000. The present board of directors consists of Hu. L. McClung, John J. Craig, S. H. McNutt, James H. Cowan, A. D. Scruggs, D. A. Rosenthal, H. S. Mizner, John M. Allen and Jesse L. Rogers.

The Knox County Bank and Trust Company was incorporated August 25, 1890, the incorporators being J. C. Karnes, W. C. Karnes, C. Rutherford, J. E. Martin and J. C. Cawood, the purpose of the incorporation being the organization of a bank in the city of Knoxville, which was effected September 11, 1890, with A. Chavennes, president; C. Rutherford, vice-president; and Charles Karns, cashier. The bank opened for business October 7, 1890, in the Patterson block, at the junction of Central avenue and Broad street, remaining there until the expiration of a three years' lease, and then removed to its present location, No. 318 North Gay street. The only changes in the officers of this bank have been that James C. Karns became president in 1892 and E. H. De Pue vice-president in 1895, the cashier remaining the same. The capital of the bank at the beginning was $20,000, and at the present time it is $40,000; the deposits amount to $40,000 and the loans and discounts to $60,000.

The Third National bank was organized early in 1887 with the following officers: Gen. R. N. Hood, president; R. P. Gettys, vice-president; John A. McKeldin, cashier, and H. B. Branner, assistant cashier. It opened for business on Wednesday, July 6, 1887, in a building erected by Frank McNulty and Col. C. M. McGhee, on the east side of Gay street nearly opposite its present location. This first building was designed by Bauman Bros., architects, and the interior was furnished by Andrews & Co. of Chicago. It was destroyed by the great fire of April, 1897, the bank, however, having in the meantime erected for its own use the building now occupied on the west side of Gay street, No. 413, at a cost of $30,000. This also is a fine building, two stories high, though all in one story in the interior, and has marble counters, marble wainscoting, etc., and taken all in all is one of the finest buildings erected for banking purposes in the Southern states.

Gen. Hood served as president until January 1, 1889, when he resigned and was succeeded by F. W. Armstrong, Gen. Hood taking the vice-presidency, and F. W. Armstrong being also cashier. This arrangement lasted until September 1, 1889, when Gen. Hood again became president; H. B. Carhart, vice-president; H. B. Branner, cashier, and F. W. Armstrong, assistant cashier. Upon the death of Gen. Hood, in February, 1892, H. B. Carhart became president; H. B. Branner, vice-president; and F. W. Armstrong, cashier. In January, 1893, H. B. Branner became president; E. E. McMillan, vice-president, and F. W. Armstrong, cashier, which arrangement continued until the death of Mr. Armstrong in March, 1896, and in January, 1898, C. M. Cooley became cashier, the officers remaining as thus given.

The capital stock of this bank is $200,000; circulation, $45,000; surplus, $45,000; deposits, $609,000; and loans and discounts, $595,000.

The directors of this bank for the year 1899 are as follows: D. A. Mims, E. E. McMillan, J. Van Deventer, H. B. Lindsay, B. L. Smith, E. C. Camp, J. L. Thomas, W. R. Tuttle, Charles T. Cates, Jr., William S. Mead, W. P. Hood and Joseph Burger.

The Farmers and Traders' Bank, Safe Deposit and Trust Company was chartered March 6, 1891, by C. R. Love, George

M. Burdett, T. W. Keller, James F. Beals, M. A. M. Armstrong, C. W. Steele, J. L. Maxwell, Jr., and D. R. Samuel. In 1895 the officers of this bank were C. R. Love, president; D. R. Samuel, vice-president; and J. L. Maxwell, Jr., cashier. The Associated Banking and Trust Company was chartered August 3, 1892, by W. H. Geers, George W. McCally, William P. Hoskins, Tully R. Cornick and Charles Dawes, for the purpose of conducting a banking business in Knoxville. This latter bank was located at No. 313 Union street. By a consolidation of these two banks, the Union bank was organized November 1, 1895, the first officers of this bank being C. R. Love, president; W. H. Geers, vice-president; J. L. Maxwell, Jr., cashier, and the capital of the institution was $92,450. At the election held in October, 1896, W. L. Welcker was made president; C. R. Love, vice-president; W. H. Geers, cashier, and at the election in October, 1897, the only change made was in the office of vice-president, W. P. Flenniken being elected to that office. In October, 1898, W. H. Geers was elected president; Henry Hudson, vice-president, and Oscar M. Tate, cashier, being promoted from the position of assistant cashier and teller. The Union bank is located at No. 313 Wall street, and pays interest on time deposits.

The Market bank was organized in 1893, with George W. Albers, president; T. B. Cox, vice-president, and W. J. Carty, cashier. The authorized capital was $50,000, at which it still remains. The first directors were George W. Albers, T. B. Cox, W. J. Carty, L. W. Davis, John B. Carty, John W. Howell and Thomas L. Carty. This bank was located at No. 313 Union street.

The Clearing House Association of Knoxville was organized August 7, 1895, with Henry T. Ault, president; William S. Shields, vice-president, and E. G. Oates, cashier. The executive committee was composed of H. B. Branner, Frank L. Fisher and E. G. Oates. The business of the association is transacted at eleven o'clock, a. m., and its effect has been to aid in establishing Knoxville in the eyes of the country as a monetary center. For the first year of the existence of the clearing house the clearings amounted to $21,421,570.01; for the second year, $21,612,543.19, and for the third year, $24,887,786.91, the year ending August 31.

The Mechanics' Association was organized in 1870 for the benefit of the mechanics of the city, who were then comparatively few in numbers. In May, 1871, they gave an industrial exhibition lasting several days, which attracted considerable attention. On the 20th of that month Mr. W. H. Browning, architect of the Government building then being erected in Knoxville, delivered an address to the association, in which he ably presented to the members the benefits of co-operative building associations, and urged that as the mechanics were the bone and sinew of the country it was only proper that they should take their proper place in society, which they could best do through providing themselves with homes, and thus be independent of landlords. Associations of the kind had been successful in England and in the Northern states for years, he said, and there could be no reason why they should not succeed in the South. The association fixed the price of shares of stock and allowed their members to take out as many shares as they could pay for, the payments being made monthly. When $500 or $1,000 had been accumulated the money was sold at auction to the highest bidder, who would sometimes pay as high as twenty-five per cent for the money, this twenty-five per cent being called the premium, and being altogether distinct from the interest the borrower would pay. The premium was retained out of the sum for which the borrower gave his note, and formed a nucleus for a second loan. In this way the association sometimes made as high as twenty-five per cent. and even fifty per cent, if money was greatly in demand, and the borrower was enabled to build a house, and at the same time at a less cost to him than the payment of ordinary rents. Such was the argument used by Mr. Browning in 1871.

Influenced by such considerations as these thus set forth with such clearness and ability by Mr. Browning, a building and loan association, named the Knoxville Building and Loan Association, was organized in 1872, with W. P. Washburn, president, and John M. Brooks, secretary. After some time C. Aebli became treasurer, serving for a number of years, and J. N. Benziger was secretary for some years.

This association was successful and had a long career, but its business is now in process of liquidation and in the hands of Peter Staub.

The Savings, Building and Loan Association was the next organized, April 23, 1880, and was like the Knoxville, a successful institution. In 1890 its officers were W. W. Woodruff, president; J. W. Fletcher, first vice-president; Peter Kern, second vice-president; H. M. Wilson, secretary; and James E. Hickman, treasurer. Ten series had then been paid in full, and more than five hundred houses built in Knoxville by money borrowed of this association. The business of this association is now in the hands of A. J. Douglas, receiver.

The Covenant Building and Loan Association began business in December, 1889, with an authorized capital of $25,000,000. The shares of stock were $100, and during the first three years of its existence it sold to the people of Knoxville more than $500,000 worth of its stock. It was managed solely by Odd Fellows, but its membership was not limited to them. It loaned to the full face value of the stock, at a premium of six per cent payable monthly. M. P. Hammack was general manager, and W. Boright, manager of the local department. Its affairs are now in the hands of William M. Ashmore and C. R. McIlwaine, receivers.

The Southern Building and Loan Association was organized in Knoxville, January 15, 1889, its charter members being S. B. Luttrell, M. L. Ross, W. H. Collett, S. M. Johnson and Charles Dawes. On October 31 of that year it had outstanding 35,000 shares of stock, each share being $100, and its assets amounted then to $176,020.73. Of this amount $160,624 was in first mortgages on real estate. The association had 188 branches and was selling new stock at the rate of 6,000 shares per month. Its operations extended from Philadelphia, where was located its eastern department, to San Antonio, Texas, and from Louisville, Ky., to Savannah, Ga. It was buying or building for its members an average of forty houses per month, and within the first ten months of its existence it had built thirty houses for its members in Knoxville, and more than 4,000 shares of its stock were held in this city. The profits on its loans had been thirty per cent per annum. S. B. Luttrell was president; Charles Dawes, vice-president; W. H. Collett, secretary; M. L. Ross, treasurer, and S. M. Johnson, general manager. In July, 1890, it had $30,000 income per month and $5,000,000 of its stock subscribed. This was the largest association of the kind in the Southern states, and one of the largest in the entire country. The largest monthly income this company ever had was $92,000. Its affairs are now in the hands of D. A. Carpenter, receiver.

The Citizen's Building and Loan Association began business with an authorized capital of $50,000,000 at 311 Wall street. Its securities were held by the State National bank, the City National bank and the Third National bank. Like all the other associations of this kind it enjoyed a prosperous career until the decision of the supreme court of the state rendered in 1896, which was to the effect that premiums on loans, such as were paid by borrowers from building and loan associations, were usurious and therefore contrary to the laws of the state. Its affairs are now in the hands of A. Y. Burrows, receiver.

Mechanics' Building and Loan Association was organized March 13, 1886, those immediately interested in the organization being R. A. Kellar, C. R. Love, J. W. Caldwell, Frank A. Moses, W. K. Mitchell, W. H. Simmonds and William Epps. This association is not now in existence.

The Equitable Building and Loan Association was organized February 15, 1888, by Frank A. Moses, Petter Ritter, Tully R. Cornick, Jr., John M. Brooks and W. F. Sawyer. This association is now out of existence.

The Perpetual Building and Loan Association was organized in June, 1889. But when it realized that there was a law in the state imposing double taxation on associations of this kind it concluded to disband and went out of existence July 18, 1889.

The Home Building and Loan Association was organized in 1889. It was strictly a home institution. Shares in this association were $100, and the payments sixty cents per month. The first officers were W. H. Simmonds, president; J. H. Scarborough, vice-president; E. H. Scharringhaus, secretary, and the Central Savings bank, treasurer. The affairs of this company have entirely wound up, which is also the case with the Franklin Savings and Loan Company.

The Star Savings and Loan Company was established in 1889 and is now in the hands of William S. Shields, receiver.

The above were all practically home associations, though some of them had, as has been seen, branches in other cities and towns. Besides them there were branches of building and loan associations in Knoxville, the headquarters of which were in other cities, as for example the Southern Home Building and Loan Association of Atlanta, Ga., on January 15, 1890, opened a branch in Knoxville, of which Gaut & Phinney were the managers. But perhaps the most important association of the kind that opened a branch in Knoxville was the Interstate Building and Loan Association of Bloomfield, Ill., with a maximum capital of $20,000,000, which began operations here in October, 1889. On October 14 a meeting of local stockholders was held at the Mechanics' bank, at which a board of directors was elected, consisting of W. H. Simmonds, W. E. Gibbins, Sam House, S. B. Boyd, E. M. Kennedy, W. W. Lee, E. Dean Dow, T. L. Williams and William Rule. W. H. Simmonds was elected president; W. E. Gibbins, vice-president; Sam House, treasurer, and T. L. Williams, secretary. This association claimed to present advantages to its members above any others in operation here, that if a person borrowed money on say ten shares of stock he received $1,000, instead of $1,000 less the premium he gave, the payments being $10.83

per month for 96 months, until the stock matured. The company had no expense fund which required one-sixth of the monthly dues to keep intact. The following illustration was given to the public in order to show the working of this company's plan:

96 months' dues at $6 per month, amounted to....	$576.00
90 months' interest at 6 per cent, $5 per month, amounted to...............................	450.00
90 months' premium at 7 per cent, $5.83 per month, amounted to...............................	524.70
	$1,550.70

Example for Borrower.

Face value of ten shares at maturity..............	$1,000.00
96 payments at $6 per month..................	576.00
Net profit	$424.00

Thus it will be seen that the premium was paid back monthly, instead of being all taken out at the beginning, as was the custom in most of the other building and loan associations. This company, however, did not remain in business long in Knoxville, in 1892 transferring its interests to the Citizens' Building and Loan Association.

Building and loan associations had been in successful operation in Knoxville, as in other cities of the state, for several years before any adverse court decisions were obtained against them. The first came in 1887, by the chancery court in Nashville, which attracted much attention here, as it was seen that if it should be carried to and sustained by the supreme court of the state it would sound the death knell of such associations in the state of Tennessee. This decision was to the effect that the premium paid for the loan, which was altogether separate and distinct from the interest paid by the borrower, was largely in excess of six per cent, the legal rate of interest, and that the device of accepting subscriptions to shares of stock in such associations and making payment in advance was a mere resort to the avoiding of usury laws. "That therefore it is considered by the court that the complainants recover of defendants all sums paid defendants in their two transactions above set out, as dues, principal and interest, in excess of 6 per cent per annum, for the amounts actually borrowed and for the time the loan ran."

At the time this decision was rendered there had been erected several hundred houses in Knoxville by means of money advanced by these associations and there were then several in course of construction. In defense of the association it was said that they were better than anything ever before devised to aid the poor man to acquire a home of his own, for not only did it accomplish this, but it at the same time developed in him a habit of saving a small sum each month, and after his house was paid for he would be likely to continue saving his money for future contingencies.

But the climax came in 1896, in connection with a suit by Mrs. Jane McCauley against the Workingmen's Building and Loan association, the original bill being filed to enjoin the sale of a house and lot under a trust deed executed by the complainant to her husband to secure a debt to the building and loan association. The chancellor refused the injunction and the property was sold to the City National Bank, which held a second mortgage, subordinate to that of the association. The case then went to the court of chancery appeals, which reversed the holding of the chancellor and granted the complainant the relief asked for. The defendants then appealed to the Supreme Court of the state, which sustained the court of chancery appeals. Quoting from the by-laws of the Workingmen's Building and Loan Association the supreme court said:

"The funds of the association as they accumulate in the treasury shall be offered and loaned by the board of directors to the best use and application among the stockholders entitled to borrow the same. The number of shares shall be regulated by the board of directors. * * * No money shall be loaned at a greater premium than thirty per cent nor less than twenty-nine and seven-eighths per cent. The successful applicant at the time of receiving the amount loaned shall pay a premium of thirty per cent on the amount bid for and shall secure the repayment of said loan with legal interest by satisfactory bond or mortgage upon real estate and interest on all loans taken by stockholders, and shall pay from the time of bidding for the same."

The bank paid to the association for the lot $1,258.

The question in this case was as to whether the premium was a fixed premium, and if so whether it made the contract unlawful. The court of chancery appeals had held that the margin of one-eighth of one per cent between the lowest and highest rate was a mere device to avoid trouble that might arise out of an apparently fixed premium, and was too small to be considered except as an attempt at an evasion of the usury laws.

The supreme court therefore held that the by-laws of the association did fix a premium on all loans. The opinion of the court was that competition in bidding for loans was an essential feature of the management of the business of a building and loan association and that this feature was not present in the working of the Workingmen's Building and Loan Association.

When the effect of this decision by the supreme court became fully known and realized there quickly sprang up a general desire on the part of the patrons of building and loan associations to repudiate all excessive forms of interest, and a number of bills looking to that end were filed in the chancery court. Association after association gradually decided to wind up its affairs, each one, however, protecting its interests as well as it could against suits by individual stockholders, each one who had borrowed money seeming to desire to be the first to secure his own individual interests. The Workingmen's Building and Loan Association held a meeting January 8, 1897, at which it was unanimously decided by the board of directors that under the then recent decision of the supreme court it was impossible longer to transact a profitable business, and all the assets of the association were turned over to the secretary with instructions to wind up its affairs, a bill was filed in chancery court under which these instructions could be carried out, and an injunction secured preventing all suits against the association, thus compelling all parties to come in by petition, and be placed on an equal footing. The affairs of the Workingmen's Building and Loan Association are in the hands of Charles M. Funck, receiver.

The Home Building Association was chartered March 17, 1897, with J. E. Willard, president. This association was designed to succeed the Workingmen's Building and Loan Association, and offered to accept the stock of that association. The design in establishing this association was that it should be strictly a home or local concern, and small salaries were to be paid its officers and the by-laws were so arranged as to prevent any difficulty with regard to invalidity or usury. Mr. Willard remained president one year and then was succeeded by Thomas Price. But it appeared that the people had by this time lost confidence in building associations, the business was not profitable, and the association settled up all of its accounts toward the latter part of the year 1898.

The Knoxville Fire Insurance Company was organized in 1879 with a capital of $100,000. On January 1, 1886, it had a surplus of $26,993.10 and a reserve fund of $26,674.98. It carried on a fire insurance business successfully for about fifteen years and throughout the state of Tennessee, having agents in the principal financial centers, and its managers being among the most prominent and successful business men of the city of Knoxville. Upon going out of business it reinsured its patrons in strong Eastern companies.

The Protection Fire Insurance Company was incorporated in 1885, and was under the same management as the Knoxville Fire Insurance Company. In 1887 its assets amounted to $108,093.84, and it continued in business until about 1895, when its business was transferred to Eastern companies.

The East Tennessee Insurance Company was incorporated March 5, 1885, the incorporators being Columbus Powell, Matthew McClung, E. S. Sheppard, C. E. Lucky and R. M. Rhea. Its capital stock was $150,000 and in 1887 it had a surplus of $25,000. This company has also gone out of business.

The Island Home Insurance Company was organized in 1887, with the same officers and directors as the East Tennessee Insurance Company. Its capital stock was $200,000, and it remained in business a few years, when, like the other companies mentioned above, it wound up its affairs and went out of business, the reason for this course in each case being the same, that larger companies in the Northern and Eastern states, having more capital, could secure a large proportion of the patronage that the Knoxville companies naturally sought and depended upon.

The Republic Life Insurance Company of East Tennessee was organized in the rooms of the board of trade, January 21, 1872. The board of directors elected at first was as follows: Col. John Baxter, F. H. McClung, C. W. Coffin, George W. Ross, Joseph Jacques, E. J. Sanford, O. P. Temple, R. C. Jackson, J. W. Gaut, Rev. F. Esperandieu, George H. Smith, David Richards, H. D. Evans, J. B. Hoxsie, Dr. Josiah Curtis, and J. A. Rayl, all of Knoxville, and a few gentlemen of other parts of East Tennessee. R. C. Jackson was elected president; Dr. Josiah Curtis, vice-president; Spencer Munson, secretary; E. P. Bailey, treasurer, and J. M. Thornburgh, attorney. A finance committee, an executive committee and a medical committee were also appointed, and Munson and Bailey were made managers for East Tennessee.

The plan of this company as announced to the public was to invest the funds received in the ordinary course of business and its surplus premiums in real estate securities at reasonable rates, thereby retaining the money invested in life insurance at home, instead of permitting it to go to Eastern or Northern states, which had previously been the case. It was thought that this company would be unusually welcome to the people of the Southern states. In order to encourage those who desired to carry life insurance the stockholders of this company, on February 28, 1872, pledged themselves to take at least $100,000 in life insurance.

This company was in fact a Chicago company, the local organization being merely a branch established by J. E. Jacobs, who was the Knoxville agent. Some of the gentlemen named above took insurance in the company, paying premiums that were very high, a $5,000 policy carrying with it a premium of $111.55. After some years the main company went into the hands of a receiver, Samuel D. Ward of Chicago, who in 1884 notified policy holders that they must prove their claims within one year from August 8, 1884, or be barred from sharing in the distribution of the assets. The company therefore ceased to exist about 1885.

CHAPTER XIV.

TRANSPORTATION.

Charles McClung. the Pioneer Road Builder—Stage-Coach Lines—Progress in Turnpike Roads—The Tennessee River and Tributaries—First Steamboat at Knoxville—Railroad Building—The East Tennessee and Georgia and the East Tennessee and Virginia Roads—The Great Southern System—Roads to Atlanta and Cumberland Gap—Bridges—Street Railways.

THE completion of the Kingston pike in 1894 from Knoxville to Campbell's station. a distance of fifteen miles. was an event of great importance both to Knox county and Knoxville, increasing as it did the trade of the town and the ease with which farmers and others could drive over the road. The time required to drive this distance on the old dirt road was about five hours. while after the completion of the pike two and a half hours was quite sufficient.

In 1792 Charles McClung. from whom the numerous and honorable McClung family of Knoxville have descended. came from the vicinity of Philadelphia. Pa., and by the first county court held in Knox county was engaged to locate a public highway from Knoxville west to Campbell's station. and thence to the western boundary of Knox county. There was already a bridle path following pretty closely after an Indian trail to Sinking creek. but here a divergence was necessary. At Campbell's station there was a block house and a considerable settlement. In this connection it is important to note that the Indian trails usually followed the ridges. in order that the Indians following these trails might overlook the valleys. in which settlements were for the most part made, and thus discover the existence of settlements from the rising columns of blue smoke ascending from the cabins in the nooks and crannies of the forests. Just east of Sinking creek this trail turned abruptly to the south, extending in that direction for a short distance, then ran along the slope of Chestnut or McAnally's ridge to an Indian town on the Tennessee river near the present site of Concord, and thence to the Cherokee country beyond the Little Tennessee.

The road as originally laid out by Mr. McClung was about thirty feet wide, cut the greater portion of the way through the primeval forest. At that time the county of Knox contained only about 2,000 inhabitants, and this undertaking was one of no small magnitude. Many years later the road was widened to fifty feet, every land owner along the way freely giving of his land to the extent made necessary by this widening of the road. Before the beginning of the present century the road reached Kingston, and later on it formed a part of the great national highway from Washington to Knoxville, to Nashville, to Montgomery and to New Orleans.

Along this national highway the means and methods of travel were wonderfully different from those at present in vogue. On that part of it between Knoxville and Washington, in 1842, there was a line of stages, called "The Great Western Line," and in the advertisement of the company owning and operating this line they said that the trip between the two cities could be made in six days and six hours. The line ran by the way of Warm Springs, Asheville, Rutherfordton, Salisbury and Greensboro to Raleigh, a distance of 385 miles, the fare between Knoxville and Raleigh being $25. From Raleigh to Washington the traveler went by rail and steamboat, a distance of 288 miles, making the entire distance 673 miles. From Raleigh to Washington the fare was $19, making the fare between Knoxville and Washington $44, the time, "only six days and six hours," being considered remarkably short, as it in reality was, considering the means of travel. The schedule time now is 19 hours, 50 minutes.

The Kingston Turnpike company was chartered by a special act of the legislature of the state passed May 24, 1866, the company being organized September 17, succeeding a board of commissioners appointed for the purpose by the legislature. This preliminary board consisted of the following gentlemen: Perez Dickinson, Joseph A. Cooper, O. P. Temple, Charles M. McGhee, and Robert H. Armstrong. A board of directors was elected consisting of Robert H. Armstrong, O. P. Temple, Charles M. McGhee, Joseph A. Cooper, and George W. Mabry, the officers of the company being O. P. Temple, president, and Robert H. Armstrong, secretary and treasurer. As fast as the company could raise funds it macadamized the road, and soon after five miles had been thus improved, a toll gate was established and tolls collected which were applied to the further macadamizing and improving of the road. The county of Knox was a stockholder in the company, and in 1892 became by purchase of the remainder of the stock the sole owner of the pike. Soon afterward an order was issued to extend the road to the county line, the work to be done by the convicts of the county, and the pike was completed to Campbell's station by November 1, 1893, at which time the purchase above mentioned was effected, the county paying the other stockholders $20,000 for their stock.

In 1876 Knox county established a workhouse for the punishment of criminals with the view of devoting their labor to the building of roads. Work was begun as soon as practicable, and by January 1, 1892, there had been constructed seventy-seven miles of turnpike roads. During 1892 there were constructed three miles of the Third Creek pike, reaching Beaver ridge, nine miles from Knoxville, and also a mile on a branch of this pike, into Hind's valley. There were also constructed five miles on the Kingston pike, making eight miles in all this year, or nine miles considering the short branch into Hind's valley. The board of pike commissioners built during the year seven and a third miles of pike road, or an equivalent of this length, as follows: On the Sevierville pike, one and one-fourth miles; Pickens Gap pike, one and three-fourth miles; Neubert Springs pike, three-eighths of a mile; Maryville pike, one and one-third miles; Rutledge pike, one-half a mile; Braboson Ferry pike, one and three-fourths miles, and in the Twentieth district, one-eighth of a mile. At the end of 1892 there were about ninety-five miles of turnpike road in the county, which cost in the neighborhood of $300,000.

In addition to the above there was the Tazewell pike, seven miles long, which was owned by a private corporation, and together with this seven miles of Tazewell pike there were about 102 miles of good turnpike road in the county, all of course running into Knoxville and increasing its trade.

At the present time (February 1, 1899), the different turnpike roads leading out from Knoxville are of the following lengths:

The Kingston pike is macadamized to a distance of sixteen miles, and is graded about one and one-half miles further.

Middlebrook pike is macadamized to a distance of eight miles.

Third Creek pike is macadamized seven miles to the forks, from which point Beaver Ridge pike is macadamized five miles, and from the same point Hinds' Valley pike is macadamized two miles.

Clinton pike is macadamized ten miles and is graded one mile further to the county line.

Sharp's Gap pike is macadamized eight miles, and is graded one mile further. Tazewell and Jacksboro pike is macadamized nine miles to Hall's Cross Roads, from which point it takes the name of the Maynardville pike and is macadamized about six miles further to the county line.

Tazewell pike begins at Smithwood four miles out from Knoxville, and is macadamized twelve miles, to the county line.

Washington pike is macadamized twelve miles.

Rutledge pike is macadamized thirteen miles.

Strawberry Plains pike, which runs by the Holston river, is macadamized eight miles.

Thorn Grove pike is macadamized sixteen miles.

Sevierville pike is macadamized to the county line, a distance of nine and a half miles.

Gap Creek pike, which leaves the Sevierville pike about six miles from Knoxville, is macadamized seven miles.

Martin's Mill pike is macadamized nine miles, and Picken's Gap pike branching off from this pike about three miles from Knoxville extends five miles.

Maryville pike extends seven miles to the county line.

Lowe's Ferry pike branches off from the Kingston pike four miles out from Knoxville and extends four miles.

Besides the above pikes which radiate from Knoxville in various directions, there are several cross pikes, connecting the main ones, to the extent in the aggregate of about ten miles. Thus the entire length of turnpike roads in Knox county connecting Knoxville with the country, is 173.5 miles, to which adding the ten miles of cross pikes, makes the total length of such roads in the county at the present time, 183.5 miles.

The Tennessee river, taken as a whole, is a wonderful stream. From the junction of the Holston and French Broad, which of late years has been considered its origin, though formerly the name Holston was applied down to the confluence of the Little Tennessee, the distance to its mouth is 650 miles. Including its tributaries it has more than 1,300 miles of water navigable for steamboats, and when only flat boats are taken into consideration it is navigable for more than 2,200 miles; that is, it and its tributaries together.

In 1820 the government appropriated several thousand dollars for the improvement of the Mussel Shoals, and in 1829 it appropriated $4,000.000 for the construction of a canal round the shoals; but as there was no appropriation ever made either by the government of the United States or by the state of Alabama for keeping the canal in repair, it was neglected and was in use only a few years. And while previous to 1897 there had been considerable money spent in improving the river below Chattanooga, very little had been done in this way above that city.

But the amount of business done on the river showed that

it was worthy of attention. In 1896 there were sixty-four steamboats on the river, with an aggregate capacity of 80,000 tons. During the year these sixty-four steamboats carried more than 20,000 passengers and 20,000,000 tons of freight. About 3,000,000 tons of this freight were carried between Knoxville and Chattanooga. The French Broad is used much more than other of the tributaries of the Tennessee, for the reason that there is but little railroad built up its valley. In 1896 the French Broad carried about forty times as much freight in value as had been expended on the Tennessee in its improvement, including all the appropriations made since the first one mentioned above, in 1820.

The citizens of Knoxville are very much interested in the improvement of this splendid stream. They think that with an expenditure of about $600,000 the channel of the Tennessee could be made three feet deep at low water all the way to Chattanooga, and if this depth were secured the river would become a competing line between these two points. The Tennessee river improvement committee of the Knoxville Chamber of Commerce has this matter constantly under consideration, and is doing all in its power to secure an adequate appropriation.

The first steamboat to arrive at Knoxville was the "Atlas," a small boat which had made its way through "The Suck" in the Tennessee river to Knoxville in 1826, and which greatly astonished the citizens by its movements. The commander of the "Atlas" was Captain Connor, who was greeted on his arrival by a dinner and by speeches and was honorably toasted. The arrival of this little boat suggested to the citizens of Knoxville the possibilities of the navigation of the Holston and Tennessee rivers by means of steamboats, and almost immediately a company was organized with the view of purchasing a steamboat for the purpose. The steamboat thus purchased was designed to run between Knoxville and "The Suck," the place where the Tennessee cuts through the Cumberland mountain range. One of the members of this company

"THE SUCK," TENNESSEE RIVER.

From *Southern Mountain Rambles* - Date Unknown

was sent to Cincinnati to make the purchase, and the steamboat thus purchased was brought to Knoxville and named in honor of the town in which lived the members of the company that thus established the navigation of the Tennessee, for the attempt of the Atlas to so navigate the river was only a suggestion as to what might be done. When this new steamboat, the "Knoxville," arrived at the wharf there was great excitement in the town, for it was looked upon as an event opening up a new era in its history.

In 1848 William Williams and James Williams, the latter of whom was minister plenipotentiary under President Buchanan to Constantinople, began the wholesale grocery business in Knoxville under the firm name of Williams & Co. Their warehouse was located on the river at the foot of Gay street. They purchased the steamer "Cassandra," and a short time afterward built the "Kate Fleming" and the "Chattanooga." The former was in the trade between Louisville, Ky., and Cairo, Ill., in the fall of 1850, until such time as high water in the Tennessee river would permit of her passage over the Mussel shoals; but she was burned to the water's edge just below Louisville in October of that year. The "Chattanooga," however, succeeded in getting over the shoals, and at once went into the trade between Knoxville and Decatur, Ala. This boat was 145 feet long and 23 feet beam, and of 160 tons burden. Her full length cabin was finely fitted up and furnished for carrying passengers, her captain being McMahon and clerk, James E. Williams. This boat was a success in every way, running from and to Knoxville nine months in the year. Then followed in a short time the "Mollie Garth" and the "Lady Augusta." The river traffic was considerable until the completion to Knoxville in 1855 of the East Tennessee and Georgia railroad, and then it was that Williams & Co. closed out their business and the passenger and freight business, until that time enjoyed by the river, was gradually transferred to the railroad, that on the river gradually sinking into insignificance.

In 1895 the following boats were on the Tennessee river, and were more or less intimately connected with Knoxville: The steamer "Telephone," owned by the Union Boat, Store and Warehouse company; the "Flora Swan," owned by the Knoxville, Sevier and Jefferson Steamboat company; the "Lucile Borden" and the "Onega," owned by the Three Rivers Packet and Transportation company; the "Oliver King," owned by Oliver King; the "Bill Tate," owned by the Holston River Packet and Transportation company, and the "City of Knoxville," owned by C. R. Love & Co. The "Onega" was built in 1891, is 106 feet long, and has a net tonnage of 74.77 tons. The "City of Knoxville" is 130 feet long, and has a tonnage of about 100 tons. The "Dixie" is a new boat, built in Knoxville, and is owned by Oliver King of that city. The Three Rivers Packet company has a shipyard, located on the south of the river about 200 yards above the bridge, at which they repair such boats as may need to be repaired. So far they have built no new boats. All of the above-named boats are on the river at the present time.

RAILROADS.

Railroads are one of the most potent factors in modern civilization, and yet it is but seventy years since the first locomotive made its first trip in the United States, that being at Honesdale, Pa., in August, 1829. Horatio Allen was the engineer and the locomotive was named the Stourbridge Lion. It was but six years later, in 1835, when the movement which awakened public interest in Tennessee in the question of railroads began, this being under the new constitution of 1834. This constitution declared that a well regulated system of internal improvements is calculated to develop the resources of the people of the state, and to promote their prosperity and happiness. A general system of public improvements was established in 1836 by an act of the legislature which provided that when two-thirds of the capital stock of any company organized for the purpose of constructing any railroad or macadamized turnpike within the state of Tennessee had been subscribed, the governor, on behalf of the state, should subscribe the remaining one-third, and in payment thereof should issue bonds bearing 5 1-2 per cent interest. Under this scheme the state became subscriber for one-half of the stock of all railroads and turnpike companies, provided that the whole amount of stock taken by the state had not reached $4,000,000. The profits arising from the stock thus subscribed by the state in various companies was set aside to constitute a fund for the redemption of the bonds issued in pursuance of the state's most liberal policy. Under the laws issued by the legislature state bonds were issued to railroads to the amount of $800,000.

But a reaction came against the state's being so extensively engaged in internal improvement schemes, and in 1840 all laws authorizing the governor to subscribe stock in this way to such improvements were repealed; but there was no interference with any work already in progress and being carried on in good faith. No more aid was granted by the state to railroads until 1852, when an act was passed creating a general system of internal improvements. This act provided that when railroad companies had graded a certain amount of track, then bonds not to exceed $8,000 per mile should be issued for the purpose of equipping the road and its franchises, and the road itself to be mortgaged to the state, the mortgage being in the form of a lien on the property. But the state, by reason of the coming on of the war of the Rebellion in 1861, became a great loser through its generosity. The railroads were notwithstanding of great benefit to the people in their commercial and social capacities, and this in all probability much more than compensated for the loss to the state treasury.

After 1867 no bonds were granted by the state to railroad companies, and the constitution of 1870 forbids the loaning or giving of the credit of the state to any corporation or company, and it also prohibits the state from becoming a stockholder in any company. But, notwithstanding this prohibition to the state, counties and incorporated towns may still, as previously, vote to aid railroads and other like companies, under certain limitations.

The year 1835, mentioned in the beginning of this sketch of the railroad history of Knoxville as that in which the spirit of public enterprise manifested itself to such a degree that internal improvements were largely undertaken, is that in which Col. Robert T. Hayne, of South Carolina, paid a visit to Nashville, for the purpose of urging the construction of a railroad from Memphis to Knoxville and thence to Charleston, S. C., on the Atlantic coast. Such a railroad would, if constructed, connect the Mississippi river with the Atlantic ocean. A similar effort was made in 1836 by William Armour, then a representative in the state legislature from Shelby county, to connect the Mississippi with the seaboard by a line "running from the eligible point on that river as near the center of the state as practicable to the Tennessee river, thence near the center of the state to a point on the Virginia line."

For the purpose of discussing the subject of internal improvements, which was still of interest to the public mind, a convention assembled at Nashville, in 1836, at which sixteen counties were represented, and at this convention a resolution was adopted advocating the construction of the above-mentioned road. The legislature, which was then in session, appropriated $15,000 for the survey of a road by the name of the "Central Railroad," and Albert Miller Lea was appointed chief engineer of this road, with authority to survey the line through the state and to estimate the cost of both a single track and a double track road.

During this same year a charter was procured for the Hiwassee railroad, the charter requiring that stock should be subscribed within two years to the amount of $600,000; and on July 4, 1836, a railroad convention assembled at Knoxville composed of gentlemen from many of the states in the Union, of which convention Col. Robert T. Hayne was chosen chairman. This convention adopted measures for the construction of a railroad from Cincinnati or Louisville through Cumberland Gap up the French Broad and on through to Charleston, S. C. Several delegates, however, from lower East Tennessee and Georgia were dissatisfied with this route, and having their attention called to the Hiwassee charter, determined if possible to avail themselves of its privileges and construct a road under them. By the adoption of this route they considered that a railroad could be built from Knoxville through Georgia to Charleston and put in operation before the road by way of Cumberland Gap could be commenced. The McMinn county delegates hastened home and opened subscription books, while the Georgia delegates procured a charter from their state legislature, intending to construct the road in such a way as to meet at the state line. The taking of stock in McMinn county being somewhat slow, six residents of that county agreed to subscribe each $100,000, thus furnishing the entire $600,000 required by the Hiwassee charter, in order to prevent its forfeiture. These six residents were General Nathaniel Smith, Onslow G. Murrell, Ashbury M. Coffey, James H. Tyffe, Alexander D. Keys and T. N. Vandyke. But it was found upon examination of the books that $120,000 had already been subscribed, and thus it was necessary for each of these six gentlemen to subscribe only $80,000.

Upon the organization of the company, Solomon P. Jacobs was chosen president, and Ashbury M. Coffey, secretary and treasurer. As chief engineer, J. C. Trautwine of Philadelphia was selected. This road was surveyed and ground was broken two miles west of Athens, in 1837, and this was the first work on a railroad in the state of Tennessee. The road was soon afterward graded from the state line to Loudon and a bridge erected across Hiwassee river.

After considerable difficulty with the state occasioned by its having subscribed $650,000 to the stock of the road, because of the insufficiency of the original $600,000 already mentioned as having been subscribed, the difficulty taking the form of a lawsuit which was won by the railroad company in the supreme court; and by reason of various difficulties caused by the stringency of the times, several unsuccessful efforts being made to raise money enough to build the road, the company made an agreement with Gen. Duff Green, under which agreement Gen. Green undertook to build the road from Dalton, Ga., to Knoxville, Tenn. But Gen. Green failed and at length was compelled to surrender his contract.

The company then made an agreement with William, Grant & Co., to complete the road from Dalton to the Hiwassee river, and with J. G. Dent & Co. to complete it from the Hiwassee river to Loudon in 1852, and in 1854 it was completed from Loudon to Knoxville. In the chapter on the municipality of Knoxville may be found an account of the proceedings of the mayor and board of aldermen with reference to the location of the depot of this road in the town. But through failures, disappointments and other difficulties the name "Hiwassee" had been changed in 1848 to East Tennessee and Georgia.

In 1852 the East Tennessee and Virginia railroad company was chartered, the road extending from Knoxville to Bristol, on the state line between Tennessee and Virginia. Thus a connecting link was formed between the great railroad systems of the Northeast with the roads of the Southwest, in Georgia, Alabama and Mississippi. This route was completed in 1858, and the two roads mentioned above were afterwards, in 1869, consolidated under the name of the East Tennessee, Virginia and Georgia railroad.

The system of railroads was gradually extended by the construction of new lines and the absorption of other lines, until it became one of the most important systems of the South. The Knoxville & Ohio road was begun before the war, being built as far as Clinton. In 1867 its construction was resumed, and it was completed to Careyville. Still later it was extended through the coal fields to the Kentucky state line at Jellico.

Some time between 1870 and 1880 a line was built from Morristown to Wolf Creek in the Unaka mountains, and while Mr. Thomas was president this line was extended to Paint Rock, connecting with the Western North Carolina railroad, forming with it a through line or connection with the East.

Still later a connection was made between the southwestern terminal of the system at Ooltewah Junction with the Selma, Rome & Dalton to Cohutta, Ga., and a line built thence to Atlanta and Macon, thus making connection with the Macon & Brunswick road and giving a direct line to the sea at Brunswick, which place is still one of the most important ocean terminals of the Southern railway.

A branch road was also built from Johnson City to Embreeville, the road from Emory Gap on the Cincinnati Southern to Oliver Springs was purchased, and the connecting link between the latter point and Clinton on the Knoxville & Ohio was built. Another branch was built from Knoxville to Maryville, Tenn., which is the Maryville branch of the Southern railway. This branch was surveyed in 1876 and completed in 1881, and for the grading of the road from Maryville to the Smoky mountains five hundred Swiss laborers were engaged, but this part of the road has not yet been built. The road from Knoxville to Maryville is known as the Knoxville & Augusta railway.

There was also acquired by the company the road from Rome, Ga., to Meridian, Miss.; the Mobile & Birmingham, from Mobile to Marion Junction, Ala.; and the Memphis & Charleston, and the Blocton branch from Birmingham to Blocton, Ala.

On May 31 and June 1, 1886, the gauge of this system of roads was changed from a five foot to a four foot nine inch gauge, the standard gauge, or nearly so, all the roads in the country at that time, except the Pennsylvania railway, having a gauge of four feet and eight and a half inches.

In 1894 the East Tennessee, Virginia & Georgia railway system comprised 1,780.3 miles, and it was in this year that the organization of the present Southern railway system, which included the Richmond & Danville, the East Tennessee, Virginia & Georgia, the Georgia Pacific, and most of the leased and operated lines of those systems. The Memphis & Charleston and the Mobile & Birmingham were not included, but the former was purchased and absorbed by the Southern Railway Company in February, 1898.

It was in this same year, 1894, that the Louisville Southern railway, extending from Louisville to Lexington, Ky., a distance of eighty-seven miles, was purchased by the Southern, and as it had the Knoxville & Ohio to Harriman Junction, it thus obtained through the Cincinnati Southern railway an outlet to the Ohio river.

The officers of the East Tennessee, Virginia & Georgia Railroad Company elected November 26, 1869, the time of the formal consolidation of the East Tennessee & Virginia with the East Tennessee & Georgia, were Thomas H. Calloway, president; Joseph Jacques, vice-president; James G. Mitchell, secretary and treasurer; R. C. Jackson, superintendent; C. Hodge, master of transportation, and J. R. Ogden, general freight and ticket agent. Among the directors were Thomas H. Calloway, Joseph Jacques, J. T. Grisham, C. M. McGhee, B. M. Branner, William Galbraith, Joseph H. Earnest, Perez Dickinson, J. M. Meek, William R. Sevier and Joseph R. Anderson.

At the time of the consolidation the total owned mileage of these roads was 270 miles, including the line from Bristol, Tenn., to Chattanooga, Tenn., and from Cleveland, Tenn., to Dalton, Ga.

On May 25, 1886, the East Tennessee, Virginia & Georgia Railway Company's property was sold under foreclosure by special master, William Rule, for $10,250,000, and was bought in by interests therein controlled, and the East Tennessee, Virginia & Georgia Railway Company was organized to succeed it. The officers elected under this reorganization were Samuel Thomas, president; Henry Fink, vice-president; L. M. Schwan, secretary, and J. G. Mitchell, treasurer.

In 1891 the mileage of the roads owned, leased and operated by this company, as given by Poor's railway manual, was as follows:

	Miles.
East Tennessee Division.—Bristol, Tenn., to Chattanooga, Tenn.	242
Ooltewah Cut Off.—Ooltewah, Tenn., to Cohutta, Ga.	11.5
North Carolina Branch.—Morristown to Paint Rock, Tenn.	43.5
Walden's Ridge R. R.—Clinton to Harriman Junction, Tenn.	30.6
Tennessee Valley Branch R. R.	4
Tennessee & Ohio R. R.—Rogersville to Rogersville Junction, Tenn.	16
Embreeville Branch.—Johnson City to Embreeville, Tenn.	15.5
	363.1
Atlanta Division.—Cleveland, Tenn., to Rome, Ga.	68
Rome & Decatur Division.—North Rome, Ga., to Attalla, Ala.	61.3
Atlanta Subdivision.—Rome to Macon, Ga.	158.5
	287.8
Brunswick Division.—Macon to Brunswick, Ga.	190
Hawkinsville Branch.—Cockran to Hawkinsville, Ga.	10
	200.00
Alabama Division.—Rome, Ga., to Selma, Ala.	196
Meridian Subdivision.—Selma to Meridian, Miss.	113
Akron Branch.—Marion Junction to Akron, Ala.	53.1
Blockton Branch.—Birmingham Junction to Blockton, Ala.	31.4
Bessemer Branch.—Junction to Bessemer, Ala.	20.6
	414.1

Total length of lines whose operation is included above............1,265.0

Sidings, 252.64 miles. Gauge, 4 ft. 9 in. Rails (steel, 1,087.7 miles, 56 lbs.). Controlled by stock ownership.

	Miles.
Knoxville & Ohio R. R.—Knoxville to Jellico, Tenn., and branches	69.3
Mobile & Birmingham Ry.—Mobile to Selma, Ala.	150
Louisville Southern Railway.—Louisville to Burgin, Ky., and branches	130
Memphis & Charleston.—Memphis to Stevenson, Ala., and branches	330
Alabama Great Southern Railway.—Chattanooga to Meridian, Miss.	295.5
Cin. N. O. & Texas Pacific Railway.—Cincinnati, O., to Chattanooga, Tenn.	336
	2,575.8

Included in the mileage of the Meridian subdivision is a section of the Mobile & Ohio railway from Lauderdale to Meridian, Miss., 18 miles, which was used under trackage contract; and included in the Atlanta subdivision was 17.6 miles from Austell to Simpson street, in Atlanta, which is owned jointly by this company and the Georgia Pacific Railway Company.

The Embreeville branch was opened June 1, 1891, and the Bessemer branch on the same date. In September, 1891, the company purchased a controlling interest in the Chattanooga Union Railway Company. The board of directors of the East Tennessee, Virginia & Georgia Railway Company, elected December 16, 1891, was as follows: Samuel Thomas, New York; Calvin S. Brice, Lima, Ohio; John G. Moore, New York; Samuel M. Felton, Cincinnati, Ohio; John H. Inman, New York; James Swann, New York; T. M. Logan, New York; John Greenough, New York; William L. Bull, New York; R. G. Erwin, New York; E. P. Howell, Atlanta; George J. Gould, New York; C. M. McGhee, New York; George Coppell, New York, and E. J. Sanford, Knoxville, Tenn.

The officers elected were as follows: Samuel M. Felton, Cincinnati, Ohio, president; Calvin S. Brice, vice-president; Henry Fink, New York, second vice-president; J. M. Mitchell, Knoxville, treasurer; William Hawn, Knoxville, auditor; L. M. Schwan, New York, secretary, and C. H. Hudson, Knoxville, general manager.

Henry Poor's manual for 1893 states that plans for reorganization were under consideration. According to the manual in 1892, Charles M. McGhee and Henry Fink of New York were appointed receivers of the East Tennessee, Virginia & Georgia Company. At the election held November 16, 1892, W. G. Oakman of New York became president, and ex-President Samuel M. Felton became vice-president in place of Calvin S. Brice. Samuel Thomas of New York was again chosen chairman of the board. Mr. Brice remained as a director.

The Richmond & Danville railway was sold under foreclosure June 15, 1894, and was purchased by the reorganization committee. The Southern railway was then organized with the following officers: Samuel Spencer, president; A. B. Andrews, second vice-president; W. H. Baldwin, Jr., third vice-president; Francis Lynde Stetson, general counsel; W. A. C. Ewen, secretary; George S. Hobbs, auditor. The new company began to operate the property on June 30, 1894. In

1892, Samuel Spencer, of New York, was added as a receiver of the East Tennessee, Virginia & Georgia Railway Company, in connection with the two former receivers, Messrs. Charles M. McGhee and Henry Fink. The same board elected November 16, 1892, are reported in Poor's manual for the year 1894.

Poor's manual for 1895 gives the following mileage of the Southern at the time of the consolidation:

Washington, D. C., to Richmond, Va., via Danville, Va., and Charlotte, N. C., to Atlanta, Ga. (about)	790.00
Bristol, Tenn., via Knoxville and Chattanooga to Atlanta, Ga., thence via Birmingham, Ala., to Greenville, Miss. (about)	852.00
Rome, Ga., to Lauderdale, Miss.	282.20
Atlanta, Ga., to Brunswick, Ga. (about)	350.00
	2,280.20
Various other lines owned, leased or controlled	2,062.25
Total length of all lines of Southern railway system (December 31, 1894)	4,342.45

The Southern Railway Company was chartered by the legislature of Virginia, February 20, 1894, and the corporation was organized in Richmond, Va., June 18, following. August 1, 1894, the operation of the East Tennessee, Virginia & Georgia railroad was assumed, as was that of the Charlotte, Columbia & Augusta, and the Columbia & Greeneville railroad. Other railroads were acquired September 1, 1894, giving at that date a mileage to the Southern system of 4,429.47 miles.

October 23, 1894, the following board of directors was elected: Aubin L. Boulware, Richmond, Va.; and the following, all from New York: Charles H. Coster, Harris C. Fahnestock, Thomas F. Ryan, Samuel Spencer, Anthony J. Thomas, Samuel Thomas and Skipwith Wilmer. (One vacancy.)

On the same day the following officers were elected: Samuel Spencer, president; A. B. Andrews, Raleigh, N. C., second vice-president; W. H. Baldwin, Washington, D. C., third vice-president; F. L. Stetson, New York, general counsel; W. A. C. Ewen, New York, secretary, and H. C. Ansley, Washington, D. C., treasurer.

288   HISTORY OF KNOXVILLE, TENNESSEE.

At the time of this election the principal office was at Richmond, Va., the New York office being at No. 80 Broadway, and the Washington office, No. 1300 Pennsylvania avenue. Later on other mileage was added to the Southern system and the total mileage, including the Alabama Great Southern, amounting to 5,591.86 miles, was as follows:

MILEAGE BY DIVISIONS.

Washington Division.—Washington to Monroe, Alexandria to Round Hill, Manassas to Harrisonburg, Calverton to Warrenton 338.54
Norfolk Division.—Monroe to Spencer, Greensboro to Goldsboro, Selma to Norfolk (Pinners Point), Franklin Junction to Rocky Mount, University to Chapel Hill, Greensboro to Wilkesboro, Winston-Salem to Mocksville, High Point to Asheboro 655.27
Charlotte Division.—Spencer to Greenville, Biltmore to Spartanburg Junction, Salisbury to Norwood, Charlotte to Taylorsville 327.55
Atlanta Division.—Greenville to Atlanta, Atlanta to Ooltewah Junction, Atlanta to Fort Valley, Toccoa to Elberton, Chamblee to Roswell, Atlanta Belt, Cleveland to Cohutta, North Rome to Attalla 540.04
Richmond Division.—Neapolis to West Point, Keysville to Durham, Oxford to Henderson 284.82
Asheville Division.—Salisbury to Morristown, Asheville to Murphy 350.80
Columbia Division.—Charlotte to Augusta, Columbia to Greenville, Spartanburg to Alston, Hodges to Abbeville, Belton to Anderson, Edgefield to Aiken 422.73
Knoxville Division.—Bristol to Chattanooga, Knoxville to Jellico (K. & O. R. R.), Embreeville Branch, Rogersville Branch, Clinton to Harriman Junction, Coal Branches, Middlesboro Branch 450.54
Memphis Division.—Chattanooga to Memphis and Branches.... 331.70
Macon Division.—Atlanta to Brunswick, Cochran to Hawkinsville, McDonough to Columbus.. 387.18
Birmingham Division.—Austell to Greenville (including Southern Ry. in Mississippi) and branches.. 546.60
Anniston Division.—Atlanta Junction to Meridian, Birmingham Junction to Birmingham, Akron Branch, Blocton Branch, Lauderdale Branch 449.80
Louisville Division.—Southern Railway in Kentucky, Louisville to Lexington, Lawrenceburg to Burgin, Versailles to Georgetown 131.10
Between Knoxville and Maryville (K. & A. R. R.)............ 16.00

   Total 5,232.67
Alabama Great Southern R. R.
 Main Line Chattanooga to Meridian........................... 296.04
 Branches 33.09
 Belt Ry. of Chattanooga (Leased to A. G. S.)............... 30.06

  Grand total 5,591.86

On August 1, 1894, the Southern railway assumed the operation of the East Tennessee, Virginia & Georgia; the Charlotte, Columbia & Augusta and the Columbia & Greenville roads. The mileage at that time as given by Poor's manual was before given.

The Southern railway covers almost the entire South, from the Ohio and Potomac rivers to the Gulf, and from the Mississippi to the Atlantic. There are few important cities which it does not reach, and it gives all points on its lines direct passenger and freight service and facilities scarcely, if at all, surpassed by points on any line.

Since the organization of the Southern railway, the trackage, grades, equipment and service of the roads amalgamated to form it and afterwards added have been greatly improved. Patrons have been given facilities not before enjoyed, and such as are now equal to those given by any railroad line. The administration and policy of the company are progressive and wide-awake. All that is possible is done to build up the country tributary to the lines of the company, and within the past few years a great development in agriculture, horticulture, manufacturing and commerce has been witnessed. That development is still in progress.

The present board of directors is as follows: Hon. Joseph Bryan, Richmond, Va.; Charles H. Coster, H. S. Fahnestock, James T. Woodward and Adrian Iselin, all of New York; S. M. Inman, Atlanta, Ga.; Skipwith Wilmer, Baltimore, Md.; A. B. Andrews, Raleigh, N. C., and William W. Finley, Washington, D. C. The principal officers are: Samuel Spencer, New York city, president; A. B. Andrews, Raleigh, N. C., first vice-president; W. W. Finley, Washington, D. C., second vice-president; Frank S. Gannon, Washington, D. C., third vice-president and general manager; Francis Lynde Stetson, New York city, general counsel; J. F. Hill, New York city, secretary; A. H. Plant, Washington, D. C., auditor; H. C. Ansley, Washington, treasurer; John M. Culp, Washington, traffic manager; W. A. Turk, Washington, general passenger agent, and M. V. Richards, also of Washington, land and industrial agent.

ARTICLE FROM REVIEW.

"KNOXVILLE, July and August, 1897.

"A few years since the East Tennessee, Virginia & Georgia system was reorganized under the name of the Southern railway, under the direction of Samuel Spencer and W. H. Baldwin, Jr., and put upon an advanced basis in point of equipment and management. Standard steel rails, steel and iron bridges, heavy rock ballast and the strongest and handsomest rolling stock obtainable, followed the reorganization. Connections were extended in all directions. The old East Tennessee railroad, with the North Carolina extension, is now known as the branch division of the Southern, with division headquarters at Knoxville. Here are also located the repair shops of the system, a magnificent new establishment costing over $500,000 and employing 1,000 men. Thirty passenger trains daily traverse the East Tennessee lines and the freight business has assumed gigantic proportions. To take one's stand on one of the main lines on any day in the year and watch the incessant outgo and influx of large fast freight trains, laden with coal or slabs and blocks of marble, with iron, lumber, live stock, grain and merchandise, affords a better realization of the great traffic of the valley than any bold figures could produce.

"Along the lines of this system which now penetrate almost every portion of the valley, is found an unparalleled diversity of interests. Agriculturally this division of the Southern reaches an excellent region. The strong upland soils cannot be surpassed, and the abundant water supply, both for power and natural irrigation, affords the first great requisite. Of the 9,000 square miles of territory enclosed in the valley district, a great portion is covered with superb timber, embracing every variety known in the Eastern United States and many species peculiarly indigenous. The manufacturing industries are extensive and growing. The Southern has its headquarters in Washington.

"Scenically the Southern railway is not only unsurpassed but unequaled. The route from North Carolina into Tennessee, where the railroad and the French Broad river pass together through the great mountains, is the most wildly beautiful bit of railway journeying in America. It is an enchanted region."

The Knoxville Southern Railroad Company was organized in 1887, and began the construction of its railroad the same year. On the completion of this line to Blue Ridge station, where it made a junction with the Marietta & North Georgia railroad, which started some years before and was constructed as a narrow gauge to run from Marietta, Ga., north and northeast into the mineral region of northeastern Georgia and northwestern North Carolina, the entire line was made standard gauge, and was taken up under the same management. But the division of the old Marietta & North Georgia railroad from Blue Ridge station to Murphy, N. C., a distance of twenty-five miles, is still a narrow gauge.

At Marietta connection is made with the Western & Atlantic railroad, and in this way solid trains have since been run from Knoxville to Atlanta.

From Knoxville the Knoxville Southern, as it was originally called, but which is at the present time known as the Atlanta, Knoxville & Northern railroad, runs through an agricultural country, until it reaches Louisville, fourteen miles from Knoxville, and six miles further on reaches Friendsville, an old Quaker settlement. Madisonville, the county seat of Monroe county, is forty-four miles from Knoxville. Jellico Junction is sixty-one miles and Wetmore, at the head of navigation on the Hiwassee river, is sixty-seven miles from Knoxville. From this place there is weekly steamboat connection with Knoxville and Chattanooga.

The Knoxville Southern Railroad Company on August 13, 1887, asked the mayor and board of aldermen of the city of Knoxville for a subscription to its capital stock of $275,000, to be paid for in the company's stock, to aid in the construction of the road, under an act of assembly passed February 17, 1887, regulating the manner in which counties and municipalities might subscribe to the capital stock of railroad companies, and upon the submission of the question to the people of Knoxville as to whether they would authorize such subscription, there were cast for the subscription 3,329 votes, to 20 against it. The conditions upon which the bonds thus voted to be issued were that they should be twenty-year, five per cent bonds, to be issued to the company when it should have completed its road from a point within one mile of the city of Knoxville to the state line between North Carolina and Tennessee, where said state line crosses the Hiwassee river, the road to be of the standard gauge, to make connection with the Marietta & North Georgia railroad, and have its trains running from Knoxville to the city of Atlanta.

The railroad was completed within the next three years, and on August 25, 1890, a committee of the mayor and board of aldermen appointed for the purpose, reported that the road began at a point on the south side of the Tennessee river within one mile of the city of Knoxville, that it was a standard gauge, steel railroad, that the southern terminus was at the state line between North Carolina and Tennessee and that the cars had run into the city of Atlanta from Knoxville and into the city of Knoxville from Atlanta. All the conditions having therefore been complied with by the railroad company, an ordinance was passed by the mayor and aldermen of Knoxville, September 2, 1890, that upon the receipt of the stock of the company for $275,000, the bonds of the city should be delivered to W. B. Bradley, president, and George R. Eager, agent and attorney for the company, and the transfer was actually made on September 3, the city receiving certificate No. 176 for 2,750 shares of the stock of the company and the interest on the bonds from July 1, 1890, to September 3, 1890, amounting to $2,367.75, giving the bonds in exchange therefor.

This company was afterward consolidated with the Marietta & North Georgia Railroad Company, the consolidation being authorized by legislation both by the state of Georgia and the state of Tennessee. The first legislation of Georgia on this subject was had December 17, 1892, and this act was amended December 15, 1894, and also December 16, 1895. Under these acts the Atlanta, Knoxville & Northern Railroad Construction Company had become lawful purchasers of the property and franchises of the Marietta & North Georgia Railroad Company through a judicial sale of the same in the city of Marietta, Ga., which sale was confirmed by the circuit court for the northern district of Georgia, January 6, 1896. This company, therefore, filed a petition in the office of the secretary of state of Georgia praying for the formation of a corporation to exist for the period of 101 years with the right to renew the charter, and to be known as the Atlanta, Knoxville & Northern Railroad Company, the petitioners being Charles A. Collier, Eugene C. Spalding, Charles S. Northern, Jacob Haas, Victor L. Smith, William T. Spalding, Edward K. Barnes, Theodore A. Hammond, Jr., Henry L. Smith, and Alexander W. Smith, all of Fulton county, Ga. Their petition was that they be substituted for the original incorporators of the Marietta & North Georgia Railroad Company, that they should have a capital of $3,000,000, to be used for operating the lines of railroad previously owned by the Marietta & North Georgia Railroad Company, between Marietta, Ga., and Knoxville, Tenn., and between Blue Ridge, Ga., and Murphy, Tenn., and the prayer of the petitioners was granted, the company being incorporated by the state of Georgia, and the charter being filed for record in Knoxville, November 6, 1896. Since that time the roads mentioned above have been owned and operated by the Atlanta, Knoxville & Northern Railway Company.

The Knoxville, Cumberland Gap & Louisville railroad was formerly the Powell's Valley railroad, and was begun in 1887, about the same time as the Knoxville Southern railroad, now the Atlanta, Knoxville & Northern. It extends from Knoxville to Middlesboro, Ky., a distance of seventy-three miles, and in an almost exactly northern direction. It passes through Beverly, Corryton, Powder Springs, Lone Mountain, Powell's River and Cumberland Gap, the latter station being three miles from Middleboro.

In order to assist in the construction of this road, the city of Knoxville, upon invitation, subscribed $225,000 to the stock of the company, and agreed to give in exchange therefor the same amount in bonds of the city, the election to determine the will of the voters being held August 13, 1887, at the same time the vote was taken on the subscription to the stock of the Knoxville Southern Railroad Company, and with almost precisely the same result, the vote in case of the Powell's Valley railroad stock being 3,328 in favor to 20 against it. This is a very useful road to the city of Knoxville, as it passes through a rich agricultural and mining country, and almost exactly over the old Cumberland Gap trail, which had for nearly a century been used as a wagon road, and which during the civil war was famous as being the only practicable route from the North into the valley of the Tennessee, and was kept open by the government of the United States at enormous expense. At Knoxville this road connects with the Knoxville Belt railroad, and at Middleboro with the Middleboro Belt railroad, thus increasing its mileage considerably, and it also has short spurs running out from the main line to coal mines at several places.

On August 22, 1889, an excursion party from Knoxville and West Knoxville, being on board a train making a tour of observation over this road, a very serious accident occurred at Flat Creek, Grainger county, Tenn., in which several citizens of the two corporations were either killed or wounded. Those who were killed were Col. Isham Young, chairman of the board of public works of Knoxville, and Alderman F. Hockenjos of the same city; S. T. Powers and Alexander Reeder and Judge George Andrews of West Knoxville. The wounded were Peter Kern and Aldermen Barry and Perry, and Citizens H. H. Ingersoll, H. H. Taylor, A. J. Albers, John T. Hearn, Dr. West, Alexander A. Arthur, Hugh McKeldin, A. M. Wilson, W. I. Smith, C. Aebli, H. Schubert, R. Schmidt, E. W. Adkins and E. S. Kinzel, all of Knoxville, and Hon. George L. Maloney, H. B. Wetzel, Ed. Barker, W. W. Woodruff and Thomas Rodgers, citizens, and Aldermen Park and Ross of West Knoxville.

This accident produced a profound sensation in the two corporations, and the boards of mayor and aldermen of each passed suitable resolutions expressive of sympathy for the families to whom such great calamities had come.

August 30, 1889, Mayor Condon of Knoxville conveyed the information to the board of aldermen that he had been notified by the proper authorities of the Knoxville, Cumberland Gap & Louisville Railroad Company that their road had been completed according to contract as a standard gauge road and that connections had been made at Cumberland Gap with the Louisville & Nashville railroad, and that he had appointed J. C. Anderson and William Park to make an investigation of the condition and quality of the road. September 27, 1889, the railroad company made a demand on the city of Knoxville for the $225,000 in bonds or the same amount in cash, in accordance with the contract with the city, made as above related, their road having been, as they said, completed according to their contract. The entire matter was referred by the board of mayor and aldermen to the finance committee to investigate and report back to the board.

October 12, 1889, two reports were submitted, a majority and minority report, the former signed by George W. Albers and Samuel B. Boyd, Jr., being to the effect that the railroad company had not complied with its contract, but in what particulars the report did not state. The opinion of the majority was sustained by the opinion of Attorney Joseph W. Sneed. The minority report, signed by W. C. Perry, was to the effect that the railroad company had complied with its contract in every particular—that the rails were of steel, the roadbed well tied, the bridges and trestles in good shape, and that connection had been made with the Louisville & Nashville railroad in Claiborne county, 460 feet south of the Tennessee state line. The minority report was adopted by the board of mayor and aldermen. On October 25, 1889, Alderman Perry requested that the city attorney be instructed to draw up an ordinance authorizing the issuance of the bonds of the city for the $225,000 to the Knoxville, Cumberland Gap & Louisville Railroad Company, and on November 8, following, such an ordinance was passed on its first reading by the following vote: Aye—J. D. Selby, Barry, Knaffle, Jones, Horne, Perry and McDaniel; and nays—Boyd and Albers. November 22, 1889, Mr. Templeton and Major T. S. Webb, attorneys for the railroad company, presented the case of the company to the council, asking for the issue of the bonds, and the city attorney expressed his opinion. Alderman Perry called up the ordinance for the issue of the bonds for its second reading, and on motion of Alderman McDaniel the entire matter was referred to a committee of five aldermen, to be assisted by the city attorney, to investigate the financial condition of the company—this committee being composed of Aldermen Selby, Boyd, McDaniel, Knaffle and Albers. December 20 this committee reported to the board that they had investigated the financial condition of the company in connection with the city attorney and Gen. Hood, and had been informed by the company that the stock book was in New York city, which fact from necessity terminated their investigations. They had been informed, however, that the company owned no stock, having turned it over to the construction company, which had disposed of it together with the first mortgage bonds, which this company had sold in order to enable it to build the road.

November 21, 1890, W. P. Washburn, presented an argument to the board in favor of the Knoxville, Cumberland Gap & Louisville Railroad Company, stating that they had completed the road in accordance with their contract to its final connection with the Louisville & Nashville railroad, at Cumberland Gap, and that the company then made application for the issuance of the bonds, or the payment of so much money in cash. The city council replied by passing the following series of resolutions:

"Whereas, The matter of the issuance of $225,000 in bonds of this city to the Knoxville, Cumberland Gap & Louisville Railroad Company has been heretofore fully investigated by a former board with the assistance of expert railroad engineers, of the city attorney and a special attorney employed by the city; and,

"Whereas, The board making the investigation was the one legally existing at the time of the expiration of the railroad company's contract with the city, and was in full possession of all the facts in the case, and after such investigation reached the conclusion adverse to the issuance of said bonds; and,

"Whereas, This board is unwilling to issue bonds of the city which may be subject to the charge or even suspicion of invalidity and believes that any bonds now issued in response to the application at present made by the Knoxville, Cumberland Gap & Louisville Railroad Company, would be subject to such a charge; and,

"Whereas, This board has not the same opportunities of forming correct judgment in the premises as were possessed by its predecessors and does not feel warranted in reversing the action of its predecessors, therefore,

"Be it resolved, That, while this board has the desire and purpose to regard and satisfy all just demands against the city, it declines to comply with the request now made by the Knoxville, Cumberland Gap & Louisville Railroad Company, and to the end that the question may be put at rest, suggests to said company the propriety of securing a determination thereof in the courts of the country, with the purpose of thereby securing a final and indisputable settlement of the rights of the parties and of saving the obligations of the city from attack or suspicion in the event the courts shall adjudge that the city must issue the bonds."

The Knoxville, Cumberland Gap & Louisville Railroad Company thereupon brought suit against the city for the purpose of compelling it to issue the bonds, filing its original bill December 20, 1890, the city filing its answer in January, 1891, setting up more than twenty different defenses—technical and meritorious—the principal one being that the railroad company had not constructed its road within the time and according to the terms prescribed in the contract. Another defense was that Knoxville's subscription had, prior to the suit, been assigned by the railroad company to the Cumberland Gap Construction Company, and that the railroad company had no legal interest in the subscription. The railroad company thereupon amended their bill and alleged the assignment of the subscription to the Cumberland Gap Construction Company and made that company a co-complainant. After voluminous argument on both sides of the case, Chancellor Gibson, on June 19, 1893, held that the terms of the contract had been in all respects complied with by the railroad company, and that the construction company, as assignee of the contract of subscription, was entitled to the city's bonds, and decreed their issuance.

The city appealed the decree to the supreme court, which, on November 20, 1894, held that the railroad company had complied in all respects with the terms of its contract and was entitled to the bonds or to the cash on November 21, 1890, provided the railroad company was then able or was able on November 20, 1894, to deliver to the city the stock subscribed for; but as the court was not satisfied that the railroad company was able to deliver the stock on either date, it ordered and decreed that the cause be remanded to the Chancery court at Knoxville to be there referred to the clerk and master for proof and report on this point.

This decree was presented to the Chancery court December 18, 1894, and on June 27, 1895, the master reported that the railroad company was able to deliver its stock on December 26, 1890, and on November 20, 1894. Exceptions were filed by the city July 6, 1895, and the cause was heard by Chancellor Lindsay on the master's report and on the exceptions, July 30, 1895, the chancellor overruling the exceptions and decreeing that the railroad company was able to deliver the stock on the days given above, and decreed that the city should within ninety days issue its bonds for $225,000 to the railroad company.

The city again appealed to the supreme court, which, after long argument on both sides, decided that it was proven that the railroad company nor the Cumberland Gap Construction Company could deliver the stock to the city at either of the dates mentioned, as all of the stock of the company had been issued to the construction company, which itself had hypothecated all of the stock received from the railroad company, and had actually expended of its own money, $289,500, which amount was to the construction company a total loss. The supreme court decision was made November 16, 1896, the bill of the complainants being deemed invalid, and the unadjudged costs in that court and in the courts below were to be paid by the complainants. And in this way the city of Knoxville was saved from the issue of its bonds. The cost of the road to the construction company was $2,069,560.14. The only cost to the city of Knoxville for being saved from the issuance of these bonds, which, together with the accrued interest at the time the decision was reached, would have amounted to near $300,000, was the fees paid her attorneys, viz.: To John W. Yoe, $10,000, and to Joseph W. Sneed, $15,500, this latter sum being so fixed by the Supreme court of the state of Tennessee, which reduced it from $20,000, as it had been fixed by the court of appeals.

The Knoxville Belt Railway Company was chartered February 28, 1887, by A. L. Maxwell, O. P. Temple, J. W. S. Frierson, Sam House, W. R. Tuttle, William Morrow, A. A. Arthur, Henry B. Wetzel and Charles Seymour, for the purpose of constructing a railway from near the mouth of William's Spring branch, near the Crescent Marble Company's quarries, about one mile above the mouth of First creek on the Tennessee river; thence northwest, passing through or near the fair grounds, crossing the East Tennessee, Virginia & Georgia railway, near the zinc works, and on up the valley of First creek to a point near where the Broad street turnpike crosses said creek, and thence around the city in such a way as to cross the Knoxville & Ohio railway at a point near the Brookside Cotton mills; thence on to the valley of Third creek not far from where the old Clinton road from Knoxville crosses the north prong of the east fork of Third creek; thence down the valley of Third creek, crossing the tracks of the East Tennessee, Virginia & Georgia railway near the car works, and thence on down the valley of Third creek to the Tennessee river; thence up the river along the northern bank to the point of beginning, making a complete circuit of the city, in a line twelve miles in length.

During the years 1887, 1888 and 1889 a portion of this line was constructed, Reps Jones contracting for the construction of three miles of it, and put a number of men to work on the line from a point near the cotton mills down to the mouth of Third creek. In 1889 it was determined that the road should run along the north bank of the Tennessee river to the mouth of Second creek and thence up Second creek to a point where it was designed to erect a union depot. About one-half of the line as originally designed has been constructed.

One of the latest railroad projects in which Knoxville is interested is that of Colonel Boone's Black Diamond system of railways, which it is designed to build from some point or points in a northern state or in northern states through Knoxville to the Atlantic coast at Port Royal, S. C. This route is practically the one selected or favored by John C. Calhoun in 1837, and on which some work was done; but by reason of the breaking out of the war the project had to be abandoned. This dream of Calhoun, therefore, lay dormant until 1893, when a convention of friends of the enterprise met at Knoxville, attended by delegates from South Carolina, North Carolina, Georgia, Kentucky and Tennessee, some of the original directors of the road being present.

Colonel Albert E. Boone of Zanesville, Ohio, having gained considerable reputation as a railroad promoter, was sent for, and has since had charge of the project. The original plan was to construct a road from the Jellico coal fields to the sea, but as there would be great, if not insuperable, difficulties in attempting to financier a local road, Col. Boone insisted that the road be extended to the Ohio river, and later to the capitals of Ohio, Indiana and Illinois, and also that it be a double track road throughout.

Two other points Col. Boone insisted upon: first, that the grades should not exceed sixty-six feet to the mile, which the surveys show has already been accomplished; and second, the colonel interested the people along the proposed route to invest in the franchises and surveys, and they by subscriptions from $5 up to $250 raised enough money to secure the rights of way and to make the necessary surveys of the line, this money to be returned to the subscribers when the road is under construction.

Early in February, 1899, Col. Boone announced that the capital necessary to construct this line of railroad had been secured from English sources, and there the matter rests at the present time, March 1, 1899.

In 1892 there was organized a company which had in view the transfer of persons across the Tennessee river by means of a cable car, the cable extending from the bank of the river on the south side to the top of what was known as Longstreet's Heights on the north side, the car ascending on this side of the river to a height of nearly three hundred feet. This cable line was completed in the latter part of the year, 1893, and in the beginning of 1894 went into operation. It had made several successful trips, when on Sunday, February 18, 1894, the cable broke just as the car had reached the upper end of the line, and was almost ready to land its passengers. The result was that the car slid down the cable at great speed, the broken end of the cable entwining itself about the car, crushing in one end, and stopping it when about half way down the incline, the car being then almost directly over the middle of the river. Here it hung suspended in midair for several hours before a rescue of the passengers could be effected. Those in the car were: Oliver Ledgerwood, who was struck and killed by the cable when it crushed in the end of the car; Miss Alice Wardell, Frank and Fred McBee, George M. Phillips, Henry Hatcher, and Willis Kibley. Mr. J. E. Patten, one of the proprietors of the cable line, as soon as practicable after the accident, procured a cable rope 600 feet in length, and throwing it over the cable supporting the car, slid it down to the car, the ends of this rope being securely held by boatmen below. Then making a loop seat, Mr. Patten was drawn up to the car from the launch Vollette, taking with him block and tackle, which he so fastened to the cable that all the living passengers could readily descend. The body of Mr. Ledgerwood was then taken down, and the excitement, which was very great throughout the city, then subsided. A coroner's jury announced as their verdict that Mr. Ledgerwood came to his death through the breaking of the cable of the cable car which runs from the north to the south side of the river, at what is known as Longstreet's Heights, and that the accident was due to the carelessness of the owners of the cable in not guarding or protecting it, as it evidently had been tampered with. The company had already on that day carried across the river by means of their car 105 persons, and they announced their intention of repairing the cable and going on with the business of transferring people across the river; but this intention was at length abandoned.

Up to 1872 the Tennessee river at Knoxville was crossed by means of ferries, except for a short time during and immediately after the civil war, when there was in use a temporary bridge. On August 3, 1871, a vote was taken on the question of the construction of a bridge across the river at this point, to be paid for by an appropriation from the county treasury. In Knoxville the vote on the proposition to appropriate $75,000 was as follows: For the appropriation, 1,156 votes; against it, 35 votes. Outside the city the vote so far as could be ascertained was 768 in favor of the appropriation and 851 against it, making the affirmative vote 1,919, and the negative vote 886.

This question having been settled in favor of the bridge, a committee was appointed consisting of W. A. A. Connor, John L. Moses, Alfred Caldwell, John Tunnell, Julius Ochs and M. Nelson, to contract for the construction of a bridge, and this committee organized by the selection of W. A. A. Connor, chairman; Julius Ochs, secretary, and John L. Moses, treasur-

SCIENTIFIC AMERICAN

A WEEKLY JOURNAL OF PRACTICAL INFORMATION, ART, SCIENCE, MECHANICS, CHEMISTRY, AND MANUFACTURES.

Vol. LXX.—No. 11.
[Established 1845.]

NEW YORK, MARCH 17, 1894.

[$3.00 A YEAR.
WEEKLY.

THE AERIAL CABLE RAILWAY.

A wire rope tramway for passenger car service over the Tennessee River, at Knoxville, and which is suspended at a height of 350 feet above the water as it reaches the south side of the river, as shown in our illustration, has been in practical use for some time past, passengers being conveyed thereby to a pleasure resort back of the bluff on the other side of the river from the city of Knoxville. The starting point of this suspended railway is only about five minutes' ride by street cars from the center of the city, and here is a power house where are two twenty horse power engines which operate the hauling cable. The tramway cables are each 1¾ inches in diameter, and the length of the span is 1,660 feet. These cables on the Knoxville side are anchored to 12×12 inch oak timbers, 14 feet long, placed behind plank bulkheads. The connecting bars are 12 feet long and 1¼ inches thick, and provision is made for taking up the slack by means of the long threaded screws, as shown in the plan and side view of the anchor. The anchor at the high end, on the opposite side of the river, consists of iron plates fixed in the rock. The supporting cables each have a breaking strain of 60 tons. The cable conveying the motive power is ½ inch in diameter and permanently fastened to the car. The car, empty, weighs 1,260 pounds. It has a 14 foot body and 3 foot platforms, and is 6 feet wide by 6½ feet high. The seating capacity is 16 passengers. The car is provided with automatic brakes, which stop the car in case the propelling cable breaks or slips on the drum. The up trip takes about three and a half minutes. The descent is made in a half minute by gravity.

An accident occurred on this aerial ferry on Sunday, February 18, by which one passenger was killed and two others slightly injured. The hauling cable broke just as the car reached the top of the incline, and struck the car with such force as to damage it somewhat, the car then starting rapidly down the grade until it was stopped by the automatic brakes. When the car was brought to a standstill it was at a point about 300 feet above the water, and the eight passengers it contained were rescued by being let down by ropes into a boat on the river.

PLAN AND SIDE VIEW OF ANCHOR.

THE AERIAL CABLE RAILWAY, KNOXVILLE, TENN., 350 FEET HIGH.

er. The foot of Gay street was selected as the site for the north end of the bridge, and in due time it was constructed, though not without increases in the amount of the appropriation, until finally the cost of the bridge was $163,653.65, the bridge being completed in 1874. This bridge was of the Howe truss pattern, 1,404 feet in length, with a driveway eighteen feet wide, and a sidewalk on each side, five and a half feet wide.

This structure erected at such cost was blown down by a high wind May 1, 1875, being utterly destroyed, and ferries were again resorted to and in use for nearly five years. But in 1879 a contract was made with George W. Saulpaw, by the terms of which he was permitted to use the old piers so long as he should keep open a bridge upon them. Mr. Saulpaw at once began the erection of a bridge on the old piers, which he opened to the public March 2, 1880. Soon afterward S. B. Luttrell purchased a half interest in the bridge, becoming sole proprietor in the year 1881.

This bridge was used until 1898, in July of which year the present fine structure constructed just below the old frame bridge, at the foot of Gay street, was opened to the public. The superstructure of this new bridge is of steel, resting on five stone piers and surmounted by a concrete driveway and sidewalks. Its length is 1,512 feet, width between the sidewalks, 30 feet, the sidewalks themselves being six feet in width and protected on the outer side by an iron railing four and a half feet high. The stone piers rise above low water to a height of fifty feet, and the bridge is 104 6-10 feet above low water. The cost of this elegant structure, which is considered the finest in the Southern states, was $211,000, aside from incidental expenses. The approach at the south end of the bridge is sixty feet long, and at the north end, 127 feet, so that the extreme of the bridge and its approaches is 1,699 feet.

The Knoxville Street Railway Company was the parent company of the street railroads in Knoxville, Tenn. It was chartered December 12, 1875, and secured the first franchise from the city granted to any street railroad, on February 11,

1876. The original directors were M. L. Patterson, Edwin Phelps, Joel J. P. Hargis, Oliver C. Irish and George W. Ross. This company built its first track along Gay street and operated it by mules.

In 1882 the Market Square Railroad Company was organized with C. W. Crozier, D. R. Samuels, W. C. McCoy, John L. Moses, W. H. Simmons, Peter Kern and J. S. Hall as directors, the charter dating February 27, 1882, and they secured a franchise from the city on August 11, 1882. While they had a franchise over all of the streets of the city, they only built from Gay street out Asylum street and made a loop line in that part of the city known as the Ninth ward.

Next the Mabry Street, Bell Avenue and Hardee Street Railway Company was organized by M. E. Thompson, Daniel Cawood, H. H. Taylor, Joseph Meek, Thomas L. Seay and R. N. Hood as directors, the charter being issued on August 12, 1885, and the franchise being granted by the city council on August 25, 1885. This company built a horse car line along Vine and Hardee streets to the cemeteries on the Rutledge pike and along Central avenue to Hardee street, and along that street and Bell avenue to the Rutledge pike and beyond; along several other streets. Afterwards extending to the vicinity of Lake Ottossee.

Early in the nineties the Mabry, Bell Avenue and Hardee Street railroad desired to connect with the Market Square railroad by the construction of a track through Gay street, parallel to the track of the Knoxville street railway. The latter company made a proposition for the use of their tracks and it was accepted.

In January, 1886, the Citizens Railway Company was chartered with John S. Van Gilder, Reps Jones, E. C. Jones, F. H. McClung and Somers Van Gilder as directors, and the city granted a franchise over specific streets on August 10, 1886.

The Knoxville and Edgwood Street Railroad Company was organized March 12, 1887, with William Caswell, N. A. Jackson, J. A. Jackson, S. A. Rogers, F. A. Moses and E. C. Camp named as directors in the charter, and the city gave a franchise on April 1, 1887, for a track through Gay street, Park, Florida, North Fourth avenue, to city line, and from Park through Crozier to Broad and along Central avenue to city line.

On March 15, 1887, the Elmwood Street Railway Company was incorporated with Reps Jones, H. B. Branner, Charles McTeer, A. P. White and H. W. Curtis as directors, and were granted a franchise by the city April 1, 1887, along Main street from the court house to Prince street and along the latter street to Market square and to Gay street; or from the court house along Gay street to White street, now North Gay street, and then along Park street to Elmwood Park, which was outside of the city. This line was constructed from White street to Elmwood Park and operated by dummy engine. In 1890 there was organized by amendment to the charter of the Elmwood street railroad, the Rapid Transit Company, with the following directors: W. G. McAdoo, S. G. Heiskell, M. R. McAdoo, Samuel Hensel and A. P. White, with the right to use either electricity or cable as motive power.

The West End Street Railroad Company was chartered November 10, 1887, with James D. Cowan, R. S. Payne, R. M. Rhea, R. P. Gettys and W. H. Simmonds as directors, and the city granted a franchise over Clinch street from Gay street to the city line, December 23, 1887. The road was erected. It was extended into West Knoxville and operated over Highland avenue, Clinch avenue, Eighth street, Cumberland, Temple, Yale and other avenues.

There was granted a charter to the Middlebrook Railway Company dated October 14, 1889, with Samuel McKinney, T. S. Webb, H. H. Taylor, Hu. L. McClung, S. B. Crawford, W. B. Ragsdale and W. H. Simmonds as directors, and the city granted a franchise April 14, 1893, from Gay street along Fifth avenue and over the Knoxville and Ohio railroad bridge, along University avenue to the city line.

In May, 1893, the Knoxville Electric Railway Company was organized by amendment to the charter of the Knoxville

Street Railway Company (the parent company). W. G. McAdoo, F. K. Huger, Charles E. Bostwick, M. R. McAdoo and Samuel Hensel were the first directors. The city granted a new franchise to this company, recognizing the former grants to the old company and extending the franchise to include other specific streets.

Just prior to the organization of the new company the old company absorbed the Mabry Street, Bell Avenue and Hardee Street Railroad. The new company also consolidated the Market Square Company into the new organization and also the Rapid Transit Company properties, the latter having absorbed the Edgwood Company properties. Then there was installed the system to operate the roads by electricity. The Middlebrook and West End companies remained out of the consolidation.

In 1893, the Knoxville Electric Railway Company having failed to pay interest on its bonds, it was placed in the hands of a receiver, and in June, 1895, the properties were sold to J. Simpson Africa as trustee, representing the Union Trust Company of Philadelphia and other creditors, C. C. Howell acting as agent of the parties at the sale and bidding the same in for the owners of the bonds. This sale included the property of the Rapid Transit Company, and soon after the sale J. E. M. Chamberlain, Jr., as trustee, raised the bid on the Rapid Transit property. The decrees for the sale of these properties were made in two parts. Nine-tenths of the property was confirmed to Africa as trustee and one-tenth (the Rapid Transit line) to Chamberlain as trustee.

Soon after the sale the Citizens' company began to operate the Rapid Transit company line and commenced the construction of lines on Jacksboro, Munson streets and Central and Park avenues. This brought on litigation after litigation and the Citizens' company fought the company operated by C. C. Howell as agent. The city also took a hand in the litigation to protect its rights, and the United States court of appeals decided that a street railroad could only build on streets where the charter specifically named the streets and the municipality specifically granted the franchise. This delayed the Citizens' company and the old company, or Howell's, seemed to have their own way, and through good management obtained possession of all the streets and bridges in and about Knoxville. There seemed to be nothing for the Citizens' company to do.

Mr. Howell organized a new company, known as the Knoxville Street Railway Company. It was chartered November 2, 1896, with W. S. Shields, J. C. Luttrell, T. S. Webb, Hu. L. McClung and C. C. Howell as directors, and the city granted a franchise naming specific streets, including those previously specifically granted to the Knoxville Electric railway and its predecessors and others over which the company desired to build. The Citizens' company enjoined the Knoxville Street Railway Company from accepting the franchise granted as above stated and the injunction held for a year. On being dissolved by the courts, the Knoxville Street Railway Company accepted the franchise. This company was the main or principal company in the city at that time.

The North Knoxville corporation granted to the Citizens' company a franchise over certain streets, and as there had been several extensions and delay after delay, the city by ordinance declared forfeited a deposit of $1,000 made by the company and the track of the Citizens' company within the limits of that city.

On March 1, 1897, the Citizens' company attempted to dig up Depot street, contrary to a city ordinance prohibiting the digging up of streets during winter months. When the police interfered the Citizens' company had the police arrested for interfering with them and the fire department was called out to do police duty, which they did. This brought about additional litigation between the Citizens' company and the city, and the city won every point of the litigation.

In the latter part of 1895 Mr. C. C. Howell, the general manager of the Knoxville Street Railway Company, bought the Middlebrook Railway Company and operated it in connection with the lines managed by him.

The Knoxville Traction Company was organized March 28, 1898, by an amendment to the charter of the Knoxville Street Railway Company. On the same day it acquired by purchase the property and lines of the Knoxville, Middlebrook, West End, and the Citizens' Street Railway Companies. This comprised all of the street railways in the city. On the same day the same company secured by purchase the property of the Knoxville Electric Light and Power Company and the Mutual Light and Power Company. These light and power properties are still held and controlled by the same people. It was a virtual consolidation of all the electric business in Knoxville, which was at that time placed in the charge and management of Mr. C. C. Howell, who had also been in charge of the affairs of the Knoxville Street Railway Company and the Knoxville Electric Light and Power Company and had made them a success.

When the Knoxville Traction Company was organized it chose as directors the following gentlemen: Frank S. Hambleton, John N. Steele and Charles N. Baer of Baltimore, Md.; C. C. Howell, E. E. McMillian, W. S. Shields and R. M. Rhea of Knoxville, Tenn.

Mr. Frank S. Hambleton was chosen as president. He was connected with the Baltimore Consolidated Street Railway Company and his father, T. Edward Hambleton, was the father of rapid transit in Baltimore, Md. Mr. Frank S. Hambleton has been associated with his father for many years and was thoroughly equipped and the proper person to become the head of this important property.

Mr. C. C. Howell was elected vice-president and general manager of the company. Mr. Hambleton first showed his ability and good judgment in placing Mr. Howell at the helm of management of these newly acquired properties, as he was acquainted with the people, who had been watching him since he arrived in Knoxville and knew that he was operating the property of the city well, and in the interest of the people that he represented.

On many occasions when Mr. Howell was in his hardest fight with the city authorities, establishing what he thought was the rights of his company, he would say: "The railway's interest and the people's interest are identical," and his predictions have proved true, as he has the whole community in sympathy with his work. There is not a more thoroughly equipped and better managed property in the country than the Knoxville Traction Company and its allied property, the Knoxville Electric Light and Power Company. The roadbed and the cars are of the best and the service given to its patrons is equal to that of any town of the same size of Knoxville.

Mr. C. C. Howell was born in Jefferson county, New York, March 22, 1848. His father died when he was four years of age and he was compelled to become the architect of his own fortune and in 1861 he apprenticed himself to learn the blacksmith's and machinist's trade in Watertown, N. Y., which he followed until after the war, when he entered the employ of the Watertown Portable Steam Engine Manufacturing Company, remaining for two years, and during that time he attended night school. After working at his trade for seven years in Watertown he went to Utica, N. Y., and remained for one year, following his trade. In the fall of 1868 he left Utica and went to the Michigan State University at Ann Arbor, where he took a special course in chemistry, metallurgy and mechanical engineering.

He has become identified with all the public enterprises of Knoxville and was one of the originators of the annual carnival, each year giving it his strong support. He was one of the principal movers in securing the national camp of volunteers in Knoxville during the Spanish-American war. He identified himself with the women of the city and helped to secure the first funds for the erection of the new city hospital. The Woman's Hospital and Promoting Board entrusted him with the obtaining of the necessary legislation and he secured the passage of an act permitting the city to issue $30,000 of bonds, which sold for $32,000 net. He was selected by the Women's Building and Promoting Board as one of the governors of the new hospital and the city council chose him as one of the building committee of that institution.

CHAPTER XV.

THE PRESS.

The Gazette, Knoxville's First Newspaper—The Register and Its Long Life—The Plebeian, Knoxville's First Daily—Brownlow's Whig and Its Remarkable Career—Recent Ventures in Knoxville Journalism—The Chronicle—The Press and Herald—The Tribune—The Journal and Tribune—The Afternoon Sentinel—The Church Newspapers.

THE first newspaper published in Knoxville, which was also the first in Tennessee and the third west of the Allegheny mountains, began publication in 1791, the year before Knoxville was laid out as a town. Since then more than fifty periodicals have found birth here and all, with the exception of two dailies, with weekly editions, and four with only weekly editions, published at the present time, have also come to their death here. A few of them had comparatively long lives; the life of most of them reached only a few years, in many cases only months. A few, only a small number, of the men who have been connected with these various publications gained considerable fame; most of them have been forgotten, except to a few persons of advanced age and a few others who attempt to gather up the faded facts of unwritten history. It was nearly half a century between the date of the publication of the first Knoxville newspaper and the appearance of the first one issued more than once a week. The first daily paper attempted was in 1851, but it was not a paying enterprise. The first daily that was published for more than a year came out in 1861, and suspended in 1863, as one of the casualties of the Civil war. Since 1866 Knoxville has not been without a daily paper, and at one time had four. At least one Knoxville paper, as will appear further on in this chapter, reached, under all circumstances, a phenomenal circulation, others have had fair success, while many others have printed only small editions, being dependent upon a territory with meager mail facilities.

The first paper published in Knoxville was The Gazette. Its first number appeared on the 5th day of November, 1791. It was the Knoxville Gazette from the beginning; but the first number was printed at Rogersville, where it continued to be published for nearly a year. It was founded by George Roulstone, who, according to a recent article written by Dr. George F. Mellen of the University of Tennessee, and printed in the Knoxville Sentinel, had been connected with an unsuccessful newspaper enterprise at Fayetteville, North Carolina. The Gazette at first and for some time came out only once in two weeks, and its issues were not uniform in size, probably on account of the difficulty in procuring paper upon which to print it. This appears upon examination of a bound file of the paper now in possession of the State Historical Society. In the issue of June 16, 1792, appears the conclusion of Thomas Paine's "Rights of Man," which had been running from the issue of November 5, 1791. The paper was removed from Rogersville in the fall of 1792. The issue that should have appeared on October 6, 1792, did not appear until the 10th, which had the following explanation: "The removal of the printing office from Hawkins C. H. to this place prevented the publication of this paper till this day, by which means we have an opportunity of presenting the public with the following important intelligence." (Here follows an account of a supply of arms and ammunition to the Indians from Pensacola, by the Spaniards, Carondolet and O'Neal.)

Mr. Roulstone had a partner named Ferguson, but in April, 1793, the partnership was dissolved and the publication was continued by Roulstone & Co. In the fall of 1793 a number of issues of The Gazette did not appear on account of the miscarriage of a load of paper. The publisher had troubles common to newspaper men in the earlier days under the credit system, as, in December, 1793, he mentioned outstanding unpaid accounts of two years' standing. The Gazette was a small three-column, four-page paper, not attractive in its appearance, but its appearance was quite an event to the hardy pioneers who were then laying the foundation of the sixteenth of the American Commonwealths. Mr. Roulstone was a printer and came to Tennessee, then the Territory South of the River Ohio, at the suggestion of Governor William Blount, appointed governor of the territory by President Washington in 1790. He was printer afterwards to the territorial and state legislatures and was the clerk of the territorial legislature when it was organized at Knoxville on the 25th day of August, 1794. He continued to publish The Gazette to the date of his death, which occurred in the year 1804. He was doubtless aided in his endeavors by Governor Blount and the authorities in the infant state, who felt the importance of having a medium through which to make known the laws enacted to the people governed. The income of the Gazette was supplemented in that way. The difficulties that confronted the publisher of the Gazette can be easily imagined when it is known that paper and all other material had to be transported hundreds of miles through a country that was without roads except those of the most primitive character. George Roulstone was a man who commanded the respect and enjoyed the confidence of the people of his day, which is attested by the fact that he was elected public printer to the state, held that position at the time of his death, and after he died his wife was elected to fill the office two successive terms.

Mr. Roulstone started two other papers in Knoxville. The Register, a weekly, in 1798, which he published about two years, and then The Genius of Liberty, in connection with John Rivington Parrington. Knoxville then had three weeklies, in every one of which Mr. Roulstone was interested. In 1804, in the month of January, George Wilson became the publisher of Wilson's Gazette, the successor of the Knoxville Gazette. It was a weekly and continued to be published in Knoxville for fourteen years and in the year 1818 Wilson removed to Nashville, that city having then become the capital of the state.

In the year 1816, on the 3d day of August, Major Frederick S. Heiskell and Hu. Brown began the publication of the Knoxville Register, which continued to be published for a longer term of years than any other paper yet published in the city. It suspended publication upon the arrival of General Burnside with the Union army, about the first of September, 1863. Its life was within a few days of forty-seven years, and in the main it was a distinctly honorable career. In this connection a brief sketch of its distinguished founders will be proper and of interest. Major Heiskell remained one of the proprietors of The Register for about twenty-one years, devoting his whole time, energy and ability to its success. He was born in Hagerstown, Maryland, but when yet a child his parents removed to Shenandoah county, Virginia. He learned the printer's trade in the office of his brother, John Heiskell, in Winchester, Virginia, and came to Knoxville in December, 1814. After working as a journeyman printer something less than two years, he, in conjunction with Hu. Brown, whose sister he afterwards married, founded The Knoxville Register, a weekly paper. In 1829 Hu. Brown retired from the paper and Major Heiskell continued its publication until in 1837, when, on account of impaired health, he retired to a farm ten miles west of Knoxville, having sold his interest in The Register to W. B. A. Ramsey and Robert Craighead. While publishing The Register, Major Heiskell was intimately acquainted with Hugh Lawson White, John Bell, Ephraim H. Foster, James K. Polk and other famous men of his time. For years he was a trusted friend of Andrew Jackson, and fought his earlier political battles with characteristic vigor. He also knew Henry Clay well and was one of his earnest, sincere supporters. In 1847 he was elected to the state senate, the only office he ever held, and distinguished himself as an able, conscientious and zealous representative of the people's interests. He was always a gentleman in his habits and deportment, and universally recognized as thoroughly incorruptible. He was a public-spirited man and took a deep interest in the cause of education. He was one of the trustees of the East Tennessee Female Institute and for years up to the date of his death was also one of the trustees of the East Tennessee University, now University of Tennessee. While conducting The Register his counsel and influence was eagerly sought by men in public life and his advice was always received with consideration. His life was long, strenuous and useful. He died in the 94th year of his age at Rogersville, Tennessee, in November, 1882. He remained an omnivorous newspaper reader to the last, and at the time of his death left twenty large scrap-books made up of clippings which he considered of value. His partner and brother-in-law, Hu. Brown, was also a superior man. He retired from The Register in 1829, to accept a professorship in the University of Tennessee. Under their management the power and influence of The Register was second to no paper in the state. It was a credit to its publishers and to the section of the country in which it circulated. Its proprietors took an active part in the politics of the period and made themselves felt by friends and by foes.

In 1836, contrary to the will and wishes of Andrew Jackson, who had been the most influential man in Tennessee politics, and who had decreed that Martin Van Buren should be his successor in the Presidential chair, The Knoxville Register supported Hugh Lawson White for that office. He carried the state, his majority, in spite of Jackson's opposition, being a little more than nine thousand in a total vote of 61,000. In the Eastern division of the state Hugh Lawson White carried every county with the exception of Greene, Sullivan and Washington, most of them by overwhelming majorities. Four years previous to that, in 1832, Andrew Jackson had carried every one of the counties in East Tennessee. This year, against the influence exerted by the Knoxville Register, he could influence but three counties to vote for Martin Van Buren. This is mentioned as showing the influence of The Register in those days. Some of the men who were at times connected with The Knoxville Register office afterwards became prominent in the state. Gen. Felix K. Zollicoffer worked as a printer in the office. He afterwards became, as editor of the Nashville Republican Banner, one of the best-known journalists in the South, was elected state comptroller, served in the lower house of congress, and was killed at Mill Springs, Kentucky, in February, 1862, while gallantly leading a brigade of Confederate soldiers of which he was the commander.

From John E. Helms, one of the oldest newspaper men in the state, it is learned that Major Heiskell, the founder of The Register, was the president of the first meeting of the Tennessee Press Association. It was held in the old Mansion House, an excellent hotel in its day. It stood on the grounds upon which the county court-house now stands. The meeting was held about the year 1838.

In 1840 Thomas W. Humes was the editor of The Register, when it was an earnest supporter of the Whig Presidential ticket and the organ of the Whig party in this section. Mr. Humes afterward took orders in the Protestant Episcopal church, was rector of St. John's church in Knoxville eighteen years and also served eighteen years as president of the University of Tennessee. In 1838 James C. Moses came to Knoxville from Exeter, New Hampshire. He was a practical printer and was first employed as foreman of The Knoxville Times. He afterwards purchased The Register and with his brother, John L. Moses, with whom he was connected for a time, remained with the Register until in 1849, when they retired from the newspaper field and entered mercantile business. For the next ten years The Register was less prosperous. For two or three years its editorial department was conducted by John Miller McKee, who afterwards removed to Nashville and for years was on the editorial staff of the old Union and American. At another time, when quite a young man, with brilliant prospects, Hon. John M. Fleming presided over the editorial department of the paper. About the year 1859 the services of George W. Bradfield were secured as editor and the paper, which had been Whig, espoused the principles of the Democratic party. Mr. Bradfield was a strong partisan and an upright gentleman, universally respected.

Early in 1861 Mr. Bradfield severed his connection with The Register and it passed into the hands of J. Austin Sperry. The Civil war began soon afterwards and the paper became a vigorous, uncompromising advocate of secession. About the time that the Confederate soldiers began to be mobilized in the vicinity of Knoxville in 1861, The Register was issued as a daily, six days in the week, and continued to be so issued until some time in August, 1863, when it suspended publication, and never again resumed. A large majority of the people of East Tennessee were opposed to secession and remained loyal to the Union. These were antagonized bitterly by The Register and Mr. Sperry realized that with the advent of the Union army it would be impossible for him to continue the publication of his paper, therefore upon the approach of General Burnside he fled South and the paper was never afterwards revived. Thus was ended the career of a newspaper that had been published for forty-seven years, a longer period than any of its predecessors or successors. As already shown, its career for the most part was one of which its founders had good reason to feel proud.

In 1823 The Enquirer was started. It was printed in the office of Hiram Barry, who came to Knoxville in 1816, and who carried on the printing business here for more than fifty years. When Mr. Barry was the owner and publisher of The Enquirer it was edited by J. J. Meredith. It lived a precarious sort of life and came to an early death, without having made an impression sufficient to give it a permanent place in local history.

Hon. John R. Nelson, a lawyer of considerable natural ability, combative in disposition, without literary attainments to speak of, but nevertheless a man of marked character, made two ventures in the newspaper world, starting The Republican in 1831, and Uncle Sam in 1834. There was no place for them and they soon disappeared.

In the year 1838, Mr. Heiskell having disposed of his interest in The Knoxville Register, some gentleman of character and influence became dissatisfied with that paper and determined to start another. When the matter was finally settled, all of those who had favored it and had decided to put money into it declined, except Mr. Perez Dickinson. He went to Philadelphia and bought an outfit. He then went to Boston, and while there, James C. Moses was recommended to him as being a good man to take charge of the mechanical department of the new venture. Mr. Dickinson secured his services and he came on to Knoxville. The paper was brought out under the name, The Knoxville Times. Thomas W. Humes was engaged as editor, and tri-weekly editions were printed, it being the first paper printed in Knoxville oftener than once a week. It was published successfully for two years, when its owners bought The Knoxville Register and the name of The Times was dropped, The Register being continued. While it was published The Times was printed on the best paper, was tasteful in its make-up and edited with ability.

In 1841, Capt. James Williams, afterwards United States minister to Constantinople under President Buchanan's administration, started the Knoxville Post. In 1848 The Post was removed to Athens, Tennessee, where it was published to the time of his death by Sam. P. Ivins, who had been employed as a printer in the office of The Post at Knoxville. He was one of the best known newspaper men in the state, and as a writer of editorial paragraphs had few equals. It may be noted here that while the office was conducted in Knoxville a book was published there, of which J. W. M. Brazeale was the author, entitled "Life as It Is," which attracted much attention, and though long out of print is sought after yet. While relating facts of history, it contains comments upon the customs of the early settlers, notable for their freshness and freedom from all restraint. It also relates how two noted murderers, "The Harps," went about the country killing people, for no other purpose than murder. The Post is still in existence and is published at Athens, Tennessee.

A Democratic paper called The Argus was started in 1838, the name of which was changed in 1844 to The Standard. It was continued precariously for a number of years under various managements until 1855, when its light went out. In 1850 The Plebeian was started by John E. and William T. Helms. In 1851 it was published as a morning daily, being the first daily paper published in Knoxville, but it was not a success.

In the year 1839 Brownlow's Tennessee Whig made its appearance at Elizabethton, Tennessee, William G. Brownlow, editor and proprietor. After being published a year at Elizabethton, it was removed to Jonesborough, where it continued to be published for nine years. It was, as its name indicates, a Whig paper and its editor was a remarkable man, fond of controversy, given to the use of vigorous language, and consequently had bitter enemies as well as warm, sincere friends. In 1849 he determined to remove to Knoxville, this city, though then a small town, presenting a more promising field for his enterprise. The first number of the Knoxville Whig was published about the first of the year 1850. It soon won for itself and its editor a national reputation. It was taken and read solely on account of its editorials, and before the end of the decade, although a weekly published in a small town with limited facilities for reaching the outside world, its circulation reached the phenomenal figure of twelve thousand copies weekly. It was common in those days for newspapers to adopt mottoes, or devices, printed at the top of their front pages, meant to be explanatory of the policy of such papers. Among those thus printed in Brownlow's Knoxville Whig were "Cry Aloud and Spare Not," and "Independent in All Things, Neutral in Nothing." These devices very succinctly set forth the general policy of the paper.

While The Whig was a political paper, an enthusiastic adherent of the Whig party, Mr. Brownlow, the first years of whose manhood life had been spent as an itinerant Methodist clergyman, a "circuit rider," engaged actively in the discussion of religious questions, and was an outspoken champion of temperance. Besides preaching frequently, in addition to his duties as editor and publisher of a newspaper, he was often called upon to deliver addresses on temperance, and his denunciations of the liquor traffic were amongst the most scathing that ever fell from man's lips. He also became involved in some very acrimonious controversies on religious questions, once with Rev. Frederick A. Ross, an able Presbyterian divine, and again with Rev. James R. Graves, an able and distinguished Baptist clergyman. He himself, as already stated, being a Methodist, stood up valiantly for his own church and its peculiar doctrines and controverted the doctrines of his antagonists. His style was vigorous, incisive and few men have excelled him in the employment of invective and sarcasm, which he used without stint in dealing with his antagonists, whether the subject of controversy happened to be politics or religion. It is perhaps impossible for men and women of the present day to realize fully the full measure of bitterness with which religious controversies were waged about the middle of the century. In his intercourse with the public, Mr. Brownlow adhered to his motto, "Cry Aloud and Spare Not."

While an outspoken champion of Whig principles, he did not always support the Whig candidates for office, he was "independent in all things, neutral in nothing." A notable exception was in the presidential campaign of 1852, when the Whigs nominated Gen. Winfield Scott for President. Brownlow refused to support him and supported and voted for Daniel Webster instead, although Webster died a few days before the election was held. He also opposed the election of Hon. Horace Maynard, nominated by the Whigs of the district for congress in 1853. Mr. Maynard was defeated by William M. Churchwell, who, by the way, was the last Democrat elected to congress from the Knoxville district from that day to this. Mr. Maynard was afterwards, in 1857, again nominated for congress, was supported by Mr. Brownlow and was re-elected eight consecutive times. He and Mr. Brownlow became fast friends and remained so to the close of their lives, Maynard outliving Brownlow five years. These things are mentioned to show that Mr. Brownlow was never neutral and always independent.

During the years immediately following the removal of The Whig from Jonesborough, the question of slavery became a more conspicuous issue than it had ever been before. In the years 1854-5 a new party arose, called the Know-Nothing, afterwards the American party. Its motto was, "Put None but Americans on Guard," and it sought to extend the period of residence required of foreign immigrants before naturalization. The party also made war upon the Roman Catholic church. Mr. Brownlow warmly espoused this new party, the old Whig party being dead, not only through the columns of The Whig, but also on the stump. He also wrote and published a book about that time, entitled, "Americanism and Romanism Contrasted." In this place it may be remarked that he also wrote a book during the decade here under consideration, entitled, "The Great Iron Wheel Examined, and Its False Spokes Extracted." It was written in reply to a book of which Rev. J. R. Graves was the author, called "The Great Iron Wheel," being an attack on the doctrines and the polity of the Methodist Episcopal church. Brownlow's reply was published by the Book Concern of the Methodist Episcopal Church South, and with the official sanction of that church. It was during the ten years, from 1850 to 1860, when he was from 45 to 55 years old, that he won a national reputation. He was then in his prime, and besides editing The Whig, did a prodigious amount of other work.

Going back to the fierce discussion of the slavery question, precipitated by the repeal of the Missouri Compromise, Mr. Brownlow took the pro-slavery, or Southern, side of the issue. His paper became very popular in this section and had a large circulation in every state in the South. This popularity was increased when in 1858 he held a debate lasting five days, in the city of Philadelphia, with Rev. Abram Pryne. Brownlow defended the institution of slavery and Mr. Pryne attacked it. The joint discussion was published together in a volume soon afterwards. About this time his paper reached a very large circulation for a country weekly. In the campaign of 1861, when the question of secession from the Union was the issue, Mr. Brownlow was an uncompromising Union man, and the secessionists printed extracts from his speeches against Pryne as a campaign document. But they were garbled. He was always a strong Union man. When the nullification movement was inaugurated in South Carolina in 1832, Mr. Brownlow was riding a circuit and preaching in that state. He opposed nullification earnestly and vigorously at considerable personal peril. In his debate with Pryne he indulged in a strong plea for the Union, from which this is an extract:

"Who can estimate the value of the American Union? Proud, happy, thrice-happy America! The home of the oppressed, the asylum of the emigrant! Where the citizens of every clime, and the child of every creed, roam free and untrammeled as the wild winds of heaven! Baptized at the fount of Liberty in fire and blood, cold must be the heart that thrills not at the name of the American Union!"

Two years after this debate, he supported his personal and political friend, Hon. John Bell, of Tennessee, for President on the platform. "The Union, the Constitution and the Enforcement of the Laws." He entered this campaign with all the ardor of his nature, both in his paper and on the stump. He denounced disunion and the men who favored it as a remedy for alleged evils. John Bell carried the state of Tennessee, but Abraham Lincoln was elected President.

South Carolina adopted a secession ordinance a few weeks after the election became known, and other states were preparing to follow. The Knoxville Whig became more and more outspoken for the Union. Many of its subscribers in the Southern states refused to take it from the postoffices and some of them wrote insulting and threatening letters to the editor. But what the paper lost in the South was more than made up from the Northern states. Subscribers poured in from that section, hundreds of them in a day, and The Whig thundered anathemas against secession and disunion. A large majority of his neighbors in Eastern Tennessee stood by him loyally and to the last. In June, 1861, the state voted on the question of secession and ratified an ordinance to that effect that had been proposed by the legislature at an extra session called for that purpose. But the editor of the Knoxville Whig continued to write and print Union editorials. The campaign preceding the June election was one of the most exciting ever seen in this country, and during its progress Mr. Brownlow was busy with his pen and on the stump. His style both in writing and in speaking suited the times, and he was heard by tens of thousands, while his editorials were read by ten times as many. Hostilities had begun and armies were being mobilized. He was considered a public enemy by many. His state had voted to go with the Southern Confederacy; but he kept the flag of the Union floating from his residence while armed soldiers threatened to tear it down. Still he wrote and printed defiant editorials, hurling thunderbolts of epithet and sarcasm at his opponents.

But the end came. He could no longer send his paper to Northern subscribers, for the mails were cut off. The Southern authorities very naturally regarded The Whig as an incendiary paper and it could not be circulated in the South. Finally, in October, 1861, believing that he was about to be arrested on a charge of treason against the Southern Confederacy, Mr. Brownlow decided to suspend the further publication of The Whig, which he did. He announced his purpose in a signed editorial, dated October 24, 1861, more than six months after the beginning of hostilities and more than four months after the ratification of the ordinance of secession in Tennessee. The editorial was printed in the last number of the paper, issued a day or two after it was written. Measured by the influence exerted upon the people in the immediate section in which it circulated, the temporary death of the Knoxville Whig may be compared to the death of a Sampson, the slain outnumbered those of its life. It is quite possible that Mr. Brownlow so intended it. After announcing the information he had, to the effect that he was to be indicted and arrested, he said that under the usages of the courts he presumed he might go free by taking the oath the authorities were administering to other Union men, or that he might enter into bond to keep the peace, but that he should obstinately refuse to do that, and added, "if such a bond should be drawn up and signed by others, I will render it null and void by refusing to sign it. In default of both I expect to go to jail, and I am ready to start upon one moment's warning." In addition to this he said, among other things:

"I shall in no degree feel humbled by being cast into prison, whenever it is the will and pleasure of this august government to put me there; but on the contrary I shall feel proud of my confinement. I shall go to jail—as John Rogers went to the stake—for my principles. I shall go, because I have failed to recognize the hand of God in the work of breaking up the American Government, and the inauguration of the most wicked, cruel, unnatural and uncalled-for war ever recorded in history. I go, because I have refused to laud to the skies the acts of tyranny, usurpation and oppression inflicted upon the people of East Tennessee for their devotion to the Constitution and laws of the government handed down to them by their fathers, and the liberties secured to them by a war of seven long years of gloom, poverty and trial! I repeat, I am proud of my position, and of my principles, and shall leave them to my children as a legacy far more valuable than a princely fortune, had I the latter to bestow!"

A few days after writing the editorial from which the foregoing is quoted, he went into the counties of Blount and Sevier and was the guest of friends. A little more than a month afterwards he returned to Knoxville, under a promise of permission to go North, when he was arrested and put in jail, where he remained a month. He became seriously ill and on the advice of his physician was removed from the jail to his residence, where he was kept under guard by details of armed soldiers. Having recovered sufficiently to travel, in March, 1862, he was sent through the Confederate lines, near Nashville, from which place he went North and remained there, his family being also sent through the lines in the fall of 1862, until the advent of Gen. Burnside in Knoxville in September, 1863. In the month of November of that year he again began the publication of the Knoxville Whig, to which he added, "And Rebel Ventilator." In 1865, when the state government had been reorganized, William G. Brownlow was elected governor, and he was re-elected in 1867. He resigned in 1869, and took his seat on the 4th of March as one of the United States senators from Tennessee. Having retained his connection with The Whig, in connection with his son, Col. John B. Brownlow, and Tilghman Hawes, the paper went into the hands of a joint stock company in 1869, and Rev. Thos. H. Pearne became its editor. After this Gov. Brownlow gave it little attention beyond occasional signed contributions. Later the Whig was controlled by Joseph A. Mabry and it became a Democratic paper, with C. W. Charlton as editor. Still later it was sold to Saunders & Clark. It was published as a daily from early in 1869. Saunders & Clark failed of success and the paper was permanently suspended in 1871. Much space has been given to The Whig and its famous editor, because of its large circulation and because the reputation of its editor was national. Having served out his term in the senate, Governor Brownlow returned to Knoxville and purchased a half interest in the Knoxville Daily and Weekly Chronicle. The name of the weekly edition was changed to The Whig and Chronicle. He became editor-in-chief of this paper, being associated in its publication with Wm. Rule, one of the founders of The Chronicle. Governor Brownlow closed his vigorous, busy, eventful life at his home in Knoxville, on the 29th day of April, 1877, and he rests in Gray Cemetery, where a beautiful granite shaft marks his resting place. And though his life was a stormy one, his death was sincerely mourned, well nigh universally by those who knew him well. He honored his name, his country, his state and the profession in which he won national fame.

There are a number of reasons for the large success of The Knoxville Whig under Governor Brownlow's management. It was published at a time when controversy was rife; he was a born controversialist. He was a master of invective and burning sarcasm, and he flourished in an age when such things were expected of a public journalist. He kept himself well informed concerning the weak as well as of the strong points of men, and that was a day of personal journalism. He was a man of the strictest integrity, and as a newspaper editor never permitted principle to become subservient to expediency, so his friends had in him unlimited confidence. He seldom made mistakes. And in all of his editorial writings there ran a vein of humor that was sometimes exquisite. This was often exhibited at unexpected times, and sometimes troubled his antagonists more than his bitterest words. But it was not always employed in that way, it made him the center of whatever social circle he became a part. He employed it on one occasion when a young preacher, lying, it was thought, at the point of death at Abingdon, Virginia. The venerable Bishop Capers and other ministers, a Methodist conference being then in session at that place, were curious to know how the "eccentric parson" felt in view of a possible exchange of worlds. The bishop called at his room.

read from the Scriptures and prayed with him, and on taking his leave held Brownlow by the hand, looking him in the face, asked him about his prospects beyond the grave. Brownlow replied: "Well, Bishop, if I had my life to live over again, I could improve it in many respects and would try to do so. However, if the books have been properly kept in the other world, there is a small balance in my favor." He didn't die then, but lived to win a very large measure of fame.

In 1855, 1856, and 1857 The Southern Journal of Medical and Physical Sciences was published by Kinsloe & Rice and edited by Dr. Richard O. Currey, a man of much ability. The publication ceased with December, 1857. It was a monthly and in the latter years was the organ of the East Tennessee Medical Society.

In 1857 The Southern Citizen was published in Knoxville for about a year. Its editor was the "Irish Patriot," John Mitchell, whose name was familiar, in his time, to all English-speaking people. He was born at Dungiven, County Derry, Ireland, and was the son of a Unitarian clergyman. He was well educated, and began life as a practicing lawyer, in Dublin. Afterwards he became the editor of The Nation, Dublin, and soon got himself into serious trouble by writing revolutionary articles for his paper and publishing them, for which he was prosecuted and his paper suppressed. Mitchell was sentenced to expatriation for fourteen years. He was deported to Australia, where he remained on parole until 1854, about six years, when he resigned his parole and, escaping from the colony, sailed for New York, landing there on the 29th day of November, 1854. Shortly after his arrival there he founded The Citizen, a weekly journal, which he continued until failing eye-sight induced him to give it up and seek a more congenial climate. It was then that he came to Knoxville, where he associated himself with William G. Swan, then a leading member of the Knoxville bar. Swan was an extreme man, fond of controversy, and it was probably through his influence that Mitchell came to Knoxville. Mr. Swan, besides being extreme was an able and scholarly man, who wielded much influence over his associates and friends. These two started The Southern Citizen in Knoxville, which was a very extreme paper, and soon got its editor into some warm controversies. Among other things advocated by The Southern Citizen was the reopening of the African slave trade. It is a mystery why a paper advocating so extreme a policy in that day should have been published in Knoxville, for there was not a town in the whole South, or a section, where such a policy had fewer sympathizers than in Knoxville, in Eastern Tennessee. There were comparatively few slave-holders in this part of the state, and there were many who were opposed to slavery. Mr. Mitchell went from Knoxville to Richmond, where, during the Civil war, he was editor of The Richmond Examiner. After the war he removed to New York and settled there, where he did some literary work. He visited Ireland in 1874, was elected to parliament for Tipperary in 1875, though disqualified for a seat. Soon afterwards he died in Ireland. He was an able and fluent writer, his editorials combining force, choice English and often great bitterness. They were read eagerly by his enemies as well as by his friends and his journals always attracted widespread attention, both those printed in Ireland and in the United States.

John Miller McKee, whose name has already been mentioned in connection with The Knoxville Register, founded a paper about 1846 called The Tribune, which was published about four years, and was then sold out to the owners of The Knoxville Register and was absorbed by that paper. Mr. McKee becoming the editor of The Register. He is still living in Nashville, where he did many years of active newspaper work and was noted for the painstaking methods and for the completeness and accuracy of his contributions.

The Knoxville Argus was published in this city for some time by E. G. Eastman, who was a prominent man in his day.

He went from Knoxville to Nashville and spent several years in that city in newspaper work.

It was about the year 1854 that John E. Helms founded a Democratic weekly newspaper called The Knoxville Mercury. It was a neat-appearing sheet and a good newspaper, but it suspended after a life of about two years.

In February, 1862, Hon. John Baxter, a leading and able lawyer of Knoxville, who was afterwards appointed a United States Circuit Judge by President Hayes, determined to publish a daily paper in the office in which Brownlow's Knoxville Whig had been printed previous to its suspension. It was called The East Tennesseean. It was a neat paper, but it suspended with its first number. While it was not intended to oppose the Confederate government, its purpose was to defend the Union people of East Tennessee, and to be such a paper as they might read and feel that it was their friend. The paper was started soon after the disastrous defeat of the Confederate forces at Fishing Creek, just beyond the Kentucky border, where the Confederate General Zollicoffer was killed, and its projectors may have anticipated a time coming when they could publish a Union paper. But after mature deliberation it was probably seen that the publication of such a paper as they contemplated would be impracticable and it was at once abandoned. Colonel Baxter remained in Knoxville until the advent of General Burnside and then successfully practiced his profession until in 1877, when he was made United States Circuit Judge of the Sixth Judicial Circuit, composed of the states of Kentucky, Michigan, Ohio and Tennessee, which position he held to the date of his death, which occurred in 1886, at Hot Springs, Arkansas.

The Southern Chronicle was started in 1862, but lived only about a year, suspending publication when General Burnside came to Knoxville in September, 1863. It was conducted with ability, but was not sensational enough to suit the public appetite in such eventful times.

In January, 1865, the end of the Civil war being apparently

near at hand, J. W. Patterson, an Ohio man, came to Knoxville and founded The Daily Commercial, which he continued to publish for something more than a year. It was a paper of merit, sprightly and newsy; but the political policy of its editor, Mr. Patterson, was in opposition to the sentiments of a majority of the people residing in the section in which it was published. It was at a time when the virtue of toleration was a scarce article and The Daily Commercial occasionally found its course a stormy one. For this reason, and for the additional reason, perhaps, that the outlook for reasonable remuneration was not inviting, its publication was abandoned in the year 1866.

The Knoxville Whig having changed its politics under its changed management, there was no Republican paper in Knoxville, and as an overwhelming majority of the voters of Knox county and East Tennessee were Republicans, Wm. Rule and Henry C. Tarwater determined early in the year 1870 to establish a Republican weekly newspaper in the city. An order was made for the necessary material and a press was bought. The old building on South Gay street, opposite the court-house, which had been the office of The Knoxville Whig when it suspended in October, 1861, was secured as the office of publication. The new venture was called "The Chronicle" and it met with much favor from the beginning. Mr. Rule had had some experience in the business, had spent something more than a year as an employe in Brownlow's Whig office before the Civil war, in 1860-61, and had served on the reportorial staff of that paper about three years after the war. The first number of "The Chronicle," weekly, appeared in April, 1870, and a month later a daily edition was printed. Shortly afterwards Mr. Tarwater sold his half interest in the paper to A. J. Ricks, who had been connected with the editorial department, and the firm became Rule & Ricks. By them it was published successfully until in 1875, when Mr. Ricks sold his interest to Senator William G. Brownlow, whose term in the United States senate was about to expire.

Mr. Ricks soon afterwards removed to Ohio, where he engaged in the practice of his profession, the law. In 1878 he was appointed by Judge John Baxter, clerk of the United States circuit court at Cleveland, Ohio. He is now United States district judge for the Northern district of Ohio, having been appointed to that position by President Harrison. It may be said of Judge Ricks that as an editor he was a fluent and vigorous writer and that his knowledge of affairs in general enabled him to write on a wide range of subjects.

Senator Brownlow came in as editor-in-chief in 1875, with Wm. Rule as his associate, and they two published the paper, the name of the weekly edition having been changed to the "Whig and Chronicle" to the date of Mr. Brownlow's death, which occurred on the 29th day of April, 1877. After Senator Brownlow's death his interest in the paper was sold by the administrator of his estate, R. A. Brown becoming the purchaser. Mr. Brown had been connected with The Chronicle from the beginning and at the time he purchased this half interest was in charge of the local news department. He then became business manager, and Mr. Rule had charge of the editorial department. In the month of November, 1882, they sold the paper to a stock company, and this company published the paper nearly four years. The first editor under the new management was Hon. Henry R. Gibson, present representative in congress from the Knoxville district, who had previously published and edited the Knoxville Republican. The name of the weekly was again changed, to the "Republican-Chronicle." Judge Gibson was succeeded by George W. Drake, who had been for some time editor of the Chattanooga Commercial. Hon. L. C. Houk, at that time a representative in congress, served as editor for some months. In the spring of 1886, the paper having become involved financially, went into the hands of a receiver, and in the month of July, 1886, was sold at public sale, and was bid off for Major E. B. Stahlman of Nashville, who was one of its largest creditors. John J. Littleton, afterwards killed in Nashville, edited it a short time, when the establishment, with its good will and franchises, was sold to Wm. Rule and Samuel Marfield, they then being the publishers of the Knoxville Journal. The Chronicle being thus merged with The Journal lost its name, after having been published as a daily and weekly for a little more than sixteen years.

In 1879 Henry R. Gibson started The Knoxville Republican, a weekly, and continued its publication until 1882, when he, with others, purchased The Chronicle and he became its editor.

In June, 1867, a daily paper called The Knoxville Press was started, with John M. Fleming as editor. In politics it was Democratic and its purpose was to support the administration of President Andrew Johnson, who was then engaged in a controversy with congress over the question of the reconstruction of the states in the South that had attempted secession. Mr. Fleming had had some previous newspaper experience and was a graceful and vigorous writer. On the 27th of October, 1867, another Democratic daily, The Herald, made its appearance—Wm. J. Ramage, publisher, and Major Thos. B. Kirby, an ex-Union officer, editor. Soon afterwards Mr. Ramage purchased from M. J. Hughes a weekly paper called The Messenger. In January, 1868, these papers were consolidated, the daily becoming The Knoxville Press and Herald and the weekly The Press and Messenger. In the spring of 1868, Samuel C. Ramage, a brother of William J., came to Knoxville and became associated with Wm. J. Ramage. The services of Col. John M. Fleming were retained as editor of the consolidated paper and Major Kirby was assistant editor. Afterwards Major Kirby went to Chattanooga, where he started the Daily Times, in that city, in December, 1869. The Press and Herald continued to be successfully published under the same management until 1876, when it was sold by Mr. Ramage to John M. Fleming and Samuel McKinney, who had just started another Democratic daily called The Knoxville Tribune, and the name "Press and Herald" disappeared.

William J. Ramage, besides being a good business manager, is a practical printer. He is a native of Philadelphia and learned the printer's trade in the old Johnson type foundry in that city. When a young man he went to Chicago, and was employed as a journeyman printer in the office of The Chicago Democrat, "Long John" Wentworth's paper. He was there at the beginning of the Civil war and enlisted at the beginning in the Nineteenth Illinois infantry volunteers, in which he served three years and was mustered out in July, 1864. In the fall of 1864 he went to Chattanooga, where he worked as a printer in the office of The Chattanooga Gazette for a time, and then started a news stand business. Some Northern gentlemen, about that time endowed with great expectations of Chattanooga's immediate future, had purchased an outfit, expensive and complete enough to run a great metropolitan paper. Their paper was called The American Union. Finding that they had an elephant on their hands, they induced Mr. Ramage to come to their relief. He took hold of the paper, reduced its expenses and continued to publish it until in the fall of 1867, when he came to Knoxville, as above stated, and founded the Herald, acquired The Press and then continued to publish The Press and Herald and The Press and Messenger until he sold out to The Tribune, as before stated, in 1876. Since he retired from the newspaper business he has established a thriving book and stationery business in Knoxville, in which he is still engaged.

Soon after the close of the Civil war M. J. Hughes founded a Democratic weekly called The Messenger, which he published until in the latter part of the year 1867, when he sold out to William J. Ramage, the proprietor of The Daily Herald. It was continued as The Messenger until in January, 1868, at which time Mr. Ramage became the owner also of The Press and the weekly was continued as The Press and

Messenger until in 1876, when it was absorbed by The Tribune.

In December, 1884, Wm. Rule and Samuel Marfield, then a citizen of Circleville, Ohio, determined to publish a daily and weekly paper to be called The Knoxville Journal. Being denied the Associated Press news service, Mr. Rule went to New York and made arrangements for a news service with W. P. Phillips, then with the United Press, and with Mr. Somerville, manager of the press department of the Western Union Telegraph Company, by which a news service was obtained. The service was to be edited and sent out from the Washington office of the United Press, then in charge of two young men, P. V. DeGraw and John Boyle. Mr. Rule visited them, explained the competition he would have to meet and the character of dispatches he wanted. They promised to make the service the best possible under the circumstances and they did, making up in quality very largely for what was lacking in quantity. The first issue appeared on the 26th day of February, 1885. A little later, on the 4th of March, 1885, when Grover Cleveland was inaugurated for a first term as President, its proprietors convinced the public that The Journal was going to be a newspaper. Mr. Marfield took charge of the business, and Mr. Rule of the editorial department of the paper. In June, 1886, The Knoxville Chronicle was sold at public sale and was bid off by one of its creditors, who, after running the paper for a short time, sold it with its good will and franchises, to Rule & Marfield, the proprietors of The Knoxville Journal, after which the combined papers were published under that name. In 1889 Mr. Rule purchased the interest of Mr. Marfield in the paper, and about the same time organized a joint stock company under a charter from the state.

This company was organized with a board of directors, and Mr. Rule was made president and general manager; Henry T. Cooper, vice-president, and James F. Rule, secretary. The paper was then, as The Chronicle had also been for many years, the only daily Republican paper published in the eleven states that seceded and joined the Southern Confederacy. The paper continued under this management for eight years, when, on the 30th day of June, 1898, it was sold at public sale, by a trustee, and E. J. Sanford became the purchaser. In these eight years a Web perfecting press and Mergenthaler Linotype machines had been added to the outfit of the office. On the same day that Mr. Sanford purchased The Journal, he also purchased the good will and franchises of The Knoxville Daily Tribune. A joint stock company was organized at the same time and the two papers were combined under the name of "The Knoxville Journal and Tribune," and it is still so published. The new company was organized with Alfred F. Sanford, president; Edward W. Ogden, secretary, and Samuel L. Slover, business manager. The editorial department of The Journal remained the same as that of The Journal—Wm. Rule, editor; George W. Denney, managing editor. The Knoxville Journal and Tribune is a seven-column, eight-page paper, published seven days in the week, its Sunday issues covering from sixteen to twenty-eight pages, sometimes more. It has a circulation larger than has ever before been reached by any seven-days-in-the-week newspaper published in the city. The editor, William Rule, has been continuously, with an interim of two years and four months, from the date of selling The Chronicle to that of founding The Journal, connected with the Knoxville daily press for more than twenty-nine years. The Journal and Tribune is now the only daily morning Republican paper published in the eleven seceding states. While a political paper, it is thoroughly devoted and loyal to the agricultural, industrial, commercial and educational interests of Knoxville and of the country tributary to Knoxville. It will be seen that it is the legitimate successor to "The Knoxville Tribune," established in 1876; "The Knoxville Chronicle," established in 1870, and "The Knoxville Whig," established in 1839.

The Knoxville Tribune, daily and weekly, began to be published in March, 1876. Its founders were Col. John M. Fleming, who had been editor of The Press and Herald, and Samuel McKinney. It started with an excellent outfit and presented a fine typographical appearance. It was Democratic in politics. It was published for about two years by Fleming and McKinney, when it passed into the hands of Col. Moses White and Frank A. Moses, a son of James C. Moses, who some forty years previous to that time had published The Knoxville Register. Colonel White had charge of the editorial and Mr. Moses of the business department. The paper was continued under their management until 1880, when it suspended for a short time, and was then sold to Joseph H. Bean, James W. Wallace and Alexander Summers, who revived The Tribune. Mr. Bean is a practical printer, and four years previous to this date had been publishing a weekly paper at Sweetwater called The Monroe Democrat. In 1888 Mr. Wallace retired from The Tribune and the publication of the paper was continued by the remaining partners until, in 1891, it was sold to a stock company and W. C. Tatom became its editor. He continued in that position until in the summer of 1898, when he resigned to accept a commission as major in the Fourth Tennessee volunteers. He is a writer of rare ability and established an enviable reputation as an editor. In June, 1895, the paper was sold to J. B. Pound and R. H. Hart, who, after publishing it for three years, sold its good will and franchises to Col. E. J. Sanford and it was consolidated with The Knoxville Journal on the 1st day of July, 1898. The consolidated paper, The Journal and Tribune, is still being published.

Rev. Charles W. Charlton was at different times connected with the press of Knoxville, including two afternoon dailies, since the Civil war, The Age and afterwards The Dispatch, neither of which were successful, though both were edited with ability. Mr. Charlton was a man of energy and a writer of note on agricultural and industrial topics. His papers were devoted also to politics, he being an ardent champion of the Democratic party. But he never was able to enlist sufficient capital to assure the success of his enterprises.

The Knoxville Sentinel, an afternoon daily, was established in 1886 by Mr. John T. Hearn, a native of Kentucky, who had some experience in newspaper business before coming to Knoxville. He brought the first Web press to Knoxville. The Sentinel was not a success under Mr. Hearn's management and the paper was sold to J. B. Pound of The Chattanooga News, in 1892. Mr. R. H. Hart was put in charge of the paper and remains with it yet, being in charge of the business department. Messrs. Pound and Hart secured control of The Knoxville Tribune in 1894 and from that time to July 1, 1898, The Sentinel and The Tribune were published from the same office, a Web perfecting press and Mergenthaler Linotype machines being added to their outfit. After selling The Tribune, July 1, 1898, Mr. Pound returned to Chattanooga, though he still retains his interest in The Sentinel. George F. Milton became editor of The Sentinel in 1895, and continued in that position until in the summer of 1898, when he resigned to accept a commission as first lieutenant in the Sixth United States volunteers, in the war with Spain. In the fall following he resigned his commission in the army and returning to Knoxville again became the editor of The Sentinel. In February, 1899, Mr. Milton having acquired a controlling interest in the paper, a reorganization was effected and its present managers are: George F. Milton, president; J. B. Pound, vice-president, and R. H. Hart, secretary and treasurer. In the thirteen years of its life The Sentinel has made many substantial improvements and ranks well among the afternoon papers of this section.

The Holston Methodist, published in the interest of the Methodist Episcopal Church South, was first printed at Morristown in 1871. It was founded by Rev. Richard N. Price, a man of learning and ability. Associated with him was Rev. T. P. Thomas. In the fall of 1873 the paper was moved to

Knoxville. Among others concerned in its publication here, at different times, were Rev. J. R. Payne, W. W. Gibson, Thos. A. Lewis, J. H. Bean and Rev. W. L. Richardson. In 1881 the paper was moved to Bristol and Rev. Frank Richardson became its editor, John Slack being its publisher. In 1885 it came back to Knoxville, and again Rev. R. N. Price became its editor. He was the editor of the paper in 1898, and Owen W. Patton was in charge of the business department, having purchased a half interest in the paper in 1890 from John W. Paulett and W. L. Richardson. In March, 1898, the paper was removed to Nashville, where it is now published as The Midland Methodist.

In March, 1898, another paper was started, called The Holston Epworth Methodist, the name of which has been since changed and it is now The Holston Christian Advocate. It is published by The Holston Company and edited by Rev. James I. Cash of the Methodist Episcopal Church, South. It is well on in the second year, is vigorously edited and quite popular.

The Methodist Advocate-Journal is the successor of a paper published first, in Atlanta, Georgia, more than a quarter of a century ago. It was published in Chattanooga for a number of years and removed to Knoxville in 1898. It is the organ of a number of Southern conferences of the Methodist Episcopal church, and is recognized as one of the official papers by the general conference of that church. It is edited by Rev. R. J. Cooke, an able scholar and divine. The business department is managed by Rev. John S. Petty.

Knoxville was the center, during the first half of the present century, of two separate seasons of religious controversy, remarkable for their fierceness and for the substantial ability of some of those who led in them, all of whom have long since been gathered with the fathers. These controversies led to the establishment of church periodicals, the editorial departments of which were conducted by men of marked strength. The first of these was The Holston Messenger, a monthly, of which

Rev. Thomas Stringfield was the editor and publisher. He had previously published a church paper at Huntsville, Ala., called "The Western Armenian and Christian Instructor." He had no other motive in the publication of these journals than the defense of the Methodist Episcopal church, of which he was a member, being at the time an active pastor, for the expense of the publications was borne by himself and little income resulted. He was a man of large ability, good education and wonderful powers of endurance. He was involved in an unusually vigorous controversy, and met it from the pulpit and through his publications. It seems to have been kept up for ten years, though the publication of the Holston Messenger was not continued so long. Mr. Stringfield had for antagonists foemen worthy of his steel, in the persons of three able Presbyterian clergymen, Messrs. Gallaher and Ross, and Dr. Nelson. He acquitted himself to the entire satisfaction of his church and his partisans. Of Mr. Stringfield, Rev. David R. McAnally, for many years editor of The St. Louis Advocate, said in 1859:

"In this struggle for the very existence of the church of his choice, Mr. Stringfield spent not only his time and mental labor, but hundreds, and perhaps thousands, of his worldly means, for which he will never, in this world, be recompensed. Yet, by these labors and sacrifices, he gave an impulse to Methodism, the result of which may be distinctly traced all along her history there, from that day to the present."

Mr. Stringfield was present at Knoxville in 1824, November 27, and participated in the organization of the Holston conference of the Methodist Episcopal church and was that year appointed presiding elder of the Knoxville district, in which capacity he labored for many years afterwards. In 1836 the general conference of the Methodist Episcopal church established the Southwestern Christian Advocate at Nashville, and elected Thos. Stringfield editor, in which position he served four years.

The other period of controversy mentioned was along in

the '40s, and a weekly paper called "The Methodist Episcopalian" was published. The project of starting this paper originated with Rev. Thos. Stringfield and Rev. D. R. McAnally. Estimates were made of the cost and submitted to a number of Methodist preachers in Knoxville, who were on their way to attend an annual conference that was held at Athens in the fall of 1845. The plans were approved, a publishing committee was appointed by the conference, at Athens, proposals were circulated and subscribers obtained. The first number of the paper appeared on the 5th day of May, 1846, with Rev. Samuel Patton as editor. He continued to be the editor of the paper, the name of which was changed in 1850 to "The Holston Christian Advocate," to the date of his death, which occurred at the home of his friend, William G. Brownlow, on the 24th day of August, 1854. Soon after his death the paper was discontinued, or merged with the Nashville Christian Advocate. "The Methodist Episcopalian" and "The Holston Christian Advocate" were devoted to a defense of the doctrines and polity of the Methodist church, and was intended to meet and supply the necessity of such a periodical suited to the wants of the mountainous, and then isolated position of the Holston conference of the church. The paper was conducted with singular ability by Dr. Patton. Its tone was elevating and its editorials evinced on the part of their writer a very high degree of ability. He lived at a time when controversy was rife and while such polemics were probably distasteful to him, he did not shrink from them. The income of the paper was not large enough to remunerate sufficient help to get out and mail its issues. As a consequence the editor had to do much of the drudgery of the office, including work to which he had never been accustomed. This told on his health and physical strength, and doubtless hastened his death, which occurred at the home of W. G. Brownlow in 1854. Dr. Patton was a native of South Carolina, born in Lancaster district, on the 27th of January, 1797. In eulogy of him, immediately after his death, William G. Brownlow said in his Knoxville Whig:

"He was the ablest divine in the Holston conference and a man of the greatest variety. He fervently sought the spirituality of those who attended his ministry, and burned with a holy zeal for his Master's glory. These were the uniform, unvaried objects of his preaching, and, to promote these ends, he was prepared to sacrifice his ease, his health and even his life."

Samuel Patton and William G. Brownlow, both able men, both distinguished as newspaper editors, in their spheres, were very unlike in some respects, but they were lifelong devoted friends, and when Dr. Patton died Mr. Brownlow sincerely mourned his departure as if he had been his own brother. Dr. Patton began the publication of his paper when there were no railroads to carry his mails, and before the modern improvements that have rendered the publication of newspapers less difficult in some respects; the smallness of the revenues coming to him made his remuneration wholly inadequate, but now since nearly a half-century after his death, it may be said of him that a greater man than he has not been connected with the religious press of Tennessee.

A paper was published in Knoxville in 1819, called The Western Monitor. The writer of this chapter has not been able to secure data as to its publisher or editor or to fix its exact character; but through its columns the Presbyterian clergymen reached the public to give information concerning the state of the church in this section.

About the last of the year 1850 or the first part of the year 1851, a weekly church paper was established, called The Presbyterian Witness. It was published by J. B. G. Kinsloe and Charles A. Rice, and edited by an able young man, Rev. Andrew Blackburn. He was born in Jefferson county in 1828, and was consequently less than 23 years old when he accepted this responsible position. The purpose for which The Presbyterian Witness was started was to advocate the doctrines and advance the interests of the church, which it did with signal ability. It was published at a time when there was much controversy over denominational differences and The Witness, with its able young editor and its able contributors, represented their side of the controversy to the satisfaction of their people. It was a paper dignified in bearing and admirable in spirit, commanding the respect of even those whom it failed to convince. Mr. Blackburn's health failed, but the paper continued to be published under his editorial supervision until a short time before his death, which occurred at Maryville in 1859. He was in charge of a church at Bristol, but still the editor of the paper. While in the pulpit of his church at that place, delivering a sermon, his voice suddenly dropped to a whisper, and he never regained it. He removed to Maryville, for treatment and care, where he died about six months afterward and was buried near the place of his birth, at Westminster Church, in Jefferson county, Tennessee. He studied theology with Rev. Wm. Minnis of New Market, Tennessee, who visited him a short time before his death and when taking his leave said to Mr. Blackburn: "My son Andrew (he called him son), you are about to be cut down in your young manhood, but you have a consolation and comfort to know that you have already accomplished more good than many of us who have been in the ministry for forty years and more." This was a tribute from a high source to Mr. Blackburn's worth in the Gospel ministry, and as an editor. He was only about 31 years old at the time of his death, but had conducted an able and influential paper for eight years, besides establishing a solid reputation as a minister of the Gospel. When quite young he was married to Miss Ann E. Gillespy of Blount county, who is still living and resides at Maryville. He was a son of Col. Alexander Blackburn, who was for a long term of years a ruling elder in old Westminster Church in Jefferson county, and a grandson of Rev. Gideon Blackburn, one of the pioneers in the early settlement of the country. While

Mr. Blackburn and William G. Brownlow were wide apart in their theological views, their papers were for a time printed on the same press and they were warm personal friends.

In 1893 George W. Ford began the publication of The Knoxville Independent and is still publishing it. It is a weekly and is devoted chiefly to the interests of organized labor.

The latest venture in Knoxville journalism is The Chilhowee Echo. It is the first and only paper ever published in the city by women, devoted to the interests of women. It began publication in October, 1899. Its editors and proprietors are Mrs. Samuel McKinney and Mrs. W. C. Tatom. It is a handsome weekly, ably edited and has been received with substantial evidence of public favor.

In closing this chapter, the author acknowledges indebtedness to Col. Moses White for much of the information pertaining to the earlier papers published in Knoxville. Colonel White, a number of years ago, delivered an able address before the State Press Association, in which he related much valuable history, which address has been drawn upon for much of the information contained in this chapter concerning the earlier newspapers.

The papers now published in Knoxville are The Journal and Tribune, morning, daily and weekly, Republican in politics; The Sentinel, afternoon, daily except Sunday, and weekly; and The Holston Christian Advocate, Methodist Advocate-Journal, The Independent, and The Chilhowee Echo, all weekly issues.

CHAPTER XVI.

EDUCATIONAL MATTERS.

The Schools of a Century Ago—Rev. Samuel Doak, the Pioneer—Interest Manifested by Governor Blount—Blount College, Now the University of Tennessee—Knoxville Female Academy—Hampden Sidney Academy—Organization and Success of City Schools—University School—Knoxville College for Colored Students—Tennessee Medical College.

THE first school established in Tennessee was named Martin Academy, founded under an act "for the promotion of learning in the county of Washington," which was passed by the general assembly of North Carolina in 1785. The founder and first president of this pioneer institution of learning was Rev. Samuel Doak, who is mentioned at some length in the chapter on religious history in this volume. He was a graduate of what was then known as Nassau Hall, now Princeton College. He was a member of the Franklin Assembly, was a man of great ability, force of character and learning, especially in the classics, as was usual with educated men in those days, and most men in the Presbyterian ministry, even in those days, were educated men. For many years his school was the only seat of classical learning west of the Alleghanies, and for a still longer period it was the principal seat of this kind of learning in that portion of the country. His school-house, a plain log building, which he erected on his farm, was near Jonesboro, a little west of the site afterward selected for Washington Academy, which became Washington College. It was near this academy that Rev. Mr. Doak established Salem Congregation, one of the first, if not the first, church in Tennessee.

Upon being appointed governor of the new territory of Tennessee, William Blount immediately removed his family to his new field of activity, and, as became him in his important position, took the lead in attempting to build up institutions of higher education in Tennessee. After considerable difficulty Blount College was established, having been chartered by the territorial assembly in 1794, the bill incorporating the institution being introduced September 4, by Hon. William Cocke of Hawkins county. On the 10th of the month this bill became a law. At the same session of the legislature Greeneville College was also chartered.

Following is a portion of the act which became a law September 10, 1794, as referred to above:

"Whereas, The legislature of this territory are disposed to promote the happiness of the people at large, and especially of the rising generation, by instituting seminaries of education, where youth may be habituated to an amiable, moral and virtuous conduct, and accurately instructed in the various branches of useful science, and in the principles of ancient and modern languages; therefore,

"Section 1. Be it enacted by the governor, legislative council and house of representatives of the territory of the United States, south of the River Ohio, That the Rev. Samuel Carrick, president, and his Excellency William Blount, the Hon. Daniel Smith, secretary of the territory; the Hon. David Campbell, the Hon. Joseph Anderson, Gen. John Sevier, Col. James White, Col. Alexander Kelley, Col. William Cocke, Willie Blount, Joseph Hamilton, Archibald Roane, Francis A. Ramsey, Charles McClung, George Roulstone, George McNutt, John Adair, and Robert Houston, Esquires, shall be and they are hereby declared to be a body politic and corporate by the name of the president and trustees of Blount College, in the vicinity of Knoxville."

This college was declared open to all denominations in the following language:

"And the trustees shall take effectual care that students of all denominations may and shall be admitted to the equal advantages of a liberal education, and to the emoluments and honors of the college, and that they shall receive alike fair, generous and equal treatment during their residence."

This clause is especially noteworthy because of the fact that it was the first legislation of the kind, establishing as it did a non-sectarian college in the United States. It is also noteworthy because of the fact that such legislation is now almost universally mentioned with commendation, as it tends to develop the minds of youth without bias on subjects connected with religion. Most of the state institutions of learning are now on the same basis. For the use of the trustees of this new college Col. James White donated the town square upon which now stand the First Baptist Church and the Mechanics National Bank, and near the northwest corner of this square was erected a two-story frame building, the money to pay for which being raised by subscription, and the school was opened as soon as pupils enough could be enrolled. Washington and Greeneville Colleges were both under clerical control.

Rev. Samuel Carrick was a native of Pennsylvania, was educated in Virginia, and came to Tennessee in 1787, preaching from the artificial mound near the confluence of the Holston and French Broad rivers. The records of the college begin with 1804, those kept previously, if kept at all, having been lost or destroyed. The institution, however, appears to have been very popular from the first. Among the students in 1804 were C. C. Clay, William Carter, Thomas Cocke, Lemuel P. Montgomery and William E. Parker, the last-named being the first graduate from the institution, his graduation occurring October 18, 1806. Female students were also taken during its early history, the first named being Polly McClung, Barbara Blount, Jenny Armstrong, and Matty and Kitty Kain. Originally this college was dependent for its support entirely on the patronage of the public.

In 1806 an act of congress was passed and approved which provided for the establishment of two colleges in Tennessee, which was in part as follows: "That the state of Tennessee shall appropriate one hundred thousand acres, which shall be located in one entire tract, within the limits of the lands reserved to the Cherokee Indians by an act of the state of North Carolina, entitled 'An act for opening the land office for the redemption of specie and other certificates, and discharging the arrears due the army,' " passed in the year one thousand seven hundred and eighty-three, and shall be for the use of two colleges, one in East and one in West Tennessee, to be established by the legislature thereof."

At its next session after the passage of this act, the general assembly of the state was flooded with memorials and petitions from the people of several counties, and from the president and trustees of each of the colleges in East Tennessee, praying for the grant and setting forth the advantages of their several localities for the establishment of the college. Greeneville College urged in its favor its local situation, extensive library, its philosophical apparatus, its ample funds and numerous other circumstances, and Blount College sent up a resolution offering to unite its funds with those of the college to be established, provided said college should be established within two miles of Knoxville. The people of Blount county desired to have the college located at Marysville, while those of Hawkins desired it at Rogersville.

But it was not until the next session of the legislature, that is the second session after the passage of the act of congress alluded to, that the question of locating the new college was settled. At this session thirty persons were appointed trustees of East Tennessee College, which was to be "located on ten acres of land within two miles of Knoxville, conveyed in trust for the use of said college by Moses White at a place called the Rocky or Poplar Spring." Twenty-three of the trustees were appointed from the several counties of East Tennessee according to their population, as follows: For Hawkins county, Richard Mitchell and Andrew Galbreath; for Sullivan county, John Rhea and James King; for Greene, Augustus P. Fore and John Gass; for Washington. Matthew

Stephenson and John Kennedy; Carter, George Duffield; Jefferson, James Rice and Joseph Hamilton; Grainger, John Cocke and Major Lea; Cocke, Alexander Smith; Sevier, Hopkins Lacy; Blount, Joseph B. Lapsly and Dr. Robert Gant; Claiborne, William Graham; Anderson, Arthur Crozier; Roane, Thomas I. Van Dyke; and Knox, George W. Campbell, John Sevier and Thomas Emmerson. Seven trustees were appointed from men living in the vicinity of the college, in order that they might have a more direct oversight of its workings, as follows: John Crozier, John Williams, Archibald Roane, Francis A. Ramsey, David Deaderick, George Doherty and John Lowry. Until buildings could be erected for the new college the trustees were authorized to use those of Blount College, and the funds of this institution were declared incorporated with those of East Tennessee College.

From 1794 to 1807, the latter year being the time of making the above-mentioned change, the work done by Blount College was practically the same as that done by a classical academy. Both sexes attended, but owing to the limited population of the state, there were in the vicinity of Knoxville but few pupils to attend. The expenses were not heavy nor were the funds of the institution large, for "when Blount College and Greeneville College were chartered, the essential feature of Doak's plan for a Franklin University, namely: that it should be supported by public taxation, was omitted. Blount College neither in its beginning, nor in its subsequent history, at any time, received any grant from the public revenues nor any support from the government; nor did each family contribute either one peck of corn or twelve pence to its support, as the citizens of New England taxed themselves to support Harvard College; it was always dependent for its support upon its tuition fees and voluntary contributions."

The price of tuition at Blount College was $8 per session of five months, and board cost $25 per session; but it should not be forgotten that Washington and Greeneville Colleges were located in the more thickly populated portions of the state, and that therefore they attracted to themselves all the college-going youth from their respective sections of the state, and were naturally more largely attended than Blount could be. This latter institution was attended by those who desired to become familiar with the polite arts and sciences, the only graduate from Blount College being William E. Parker, who graduated October 18, 1806, being examined by President Carrick in Virgil, Horace, rhetoric, logic, the Greek Testament, geography, Lucien, mathematics, ethics and natural philosophy. Thus it will be seen that education given in this institution, like most other institutions of the day, was mainly classical, on the theory perhaps that classical studies give a superior tone and quality to the mind, and also that the students might be better fitted for the study of theology and thus become, if they so desired, ministers of the Gospel.

But if Blount College did not receive any aid from the government, this can not be said of East Tennessee College, chartered, as above narrated, in 1807. Its great difficulty was in connection with securing its patrimony, as perhaps it may be called. This, however, was not the fault of the congress of the United States, which made the grant above alluded to in 1806, of 100,000 acres of land for the benefit of two colleges to be established by the state of Tennessee, and also of 100,000 acres of land for the benefit of the county academies, which the state was also required to establish. The difficulty was in part inherent in the situation, and in part was the fault of the state, which failed to perceive the equities involved in the case.

The act of congress provided that the state of Tennessee should appropriate these lands within the limits of the lands reserved to the Cherokee Indians by the state of North Carolina in 1783; but these lands thus set apart for the benefit of learning were not to be sold for less than two dollars per acre, while lands not thus reserved were to be sold at a minimum price of one dollar per acre. The cession act also contained the provision that the people residing south of the French Broad and Holston rivers and west of Big Pigeon, should be secure in their respective rights of occupancy and pre-emption.

Now it so happened that the people residing south of the French Broad and Holston and west of the Big Pigeon, resided also within the limits of the lands reserved to the Cherokee Indians by the state of North Carolina, and had become quite numerous within these limits, a condition of things which congress did not anticipate when making its grant. These people had in fact invaded and taken possession of this territory against the express orders of congress and in violation of treaties made with the Indians by both state and nation. Notwithstanding this, they remained, and had the state of Tennessee, besides recognizing their "rights" as settlers to purchase these lands as pre-emptioners, at the minimum price of one dollar per acre, doubled the acreage to be sold for the benefit of the two colleges and the county academies, but little if any difficulty would have resulted. But the state provided for the sale at one dollar per acre of all the lands reserved for the institutions of learning, without increasing the number of acres to be sold, which latter it could and should have done, in order to carry out the beneficent spirit of congress, which was to establish a fund of $400,000 for the benefit of higher education, $100,000 for each of the two colleges, and $200,000 for the benefit of the several county academies in the state.

"A simple and just solution of all the difficulties would have been to fix the price of all lands in the district south of the French Broad and Holston at $1 per acre, and to have made the college and academy tracts each to consist of 200,000 acres, instead of 100,000 acres."*

The full name under which this institution was chartered

---

*Edward T. Sanford.

in 1807 was "The President and Trustees of the East Tennessee College," and it was endowed with that portion of the congressional fund designed for East Tennessee. To these trustees the prospect of assured support, as compared with the previous tuition fees, always an uncertain quantity, was exceedingly pleasant. But they were doomed to severe disappointment as the years rolled away. The location of this new institution, "at a place called Rocky or Poplar Spring," was near the old Branner residence in Shieldstown, the buildings of Blount College being temporarily used and the old trustees remaining in control until the new trustees, thirty in number, as above related, took charge of the school.

"At the same time the legislature also began with a flourish of trumpets to provide for the care of the fund to be realized for the support of the colleges, and appointed a commission of six, among whom were James Park and John Overton, to superintend its management and investment." (Edward T. Sanford.)

The trustees of East Tennessee College, in 1808, met and organized, retaining the Rev. Samuel Carrick as president. His term of service was, however, short, for he was stricken with paralysis and died before the dark days of disappointment came to the college which he fondly hoped would be his charge for years. He now lies buried beneath the myrtles and the elms in the historic graveyard of the First Presbyterian Church, where also rest William Blount and James White, President Carrick's headstone bearing the following mysterious inscription: "Samuel C. Z. R. Carrick," no one knowing the meaning of the letters "C. Z. R.," as they were not a part of his name. The inscription in full upon his tombstone may be found in connection with the history of the First Presbyterian Church.

No immediate steps were taken to fill the vacancy in the president's chair, nor was anything done toward the erection of a new college building, from the fact, no doubt, that the trustees had no funds and no immediate prospect of receiving any revenue from the land grant, the reason for which will appear as this sketch proceeds. However, in 1810, in order to aid the institution, the legislature authorized the holding of a lottery, and appointed as trustees to manage the same, Hugh Lawson White, Thomas McCorry, James Campbell, Robert Craighead and John N. Gamble. These trustees put out an advertisement in which they "flatter themselves that the scheme will be satisfactory to all who wish to become adventurers with a view to better their circumstances. When the object to be attained by the lottery is considered, it is believed every individual will become anxious to become an adventurer. It is not designed to retrieve a shattered fortune, nor to convert into cash at an extravagant price property that is of no use; but it is intended to aid the funds of a seminary of education where youth of the present and succeeding generations may have their minds prepared in such a manner as to make them ornaments to their families and useful to their country, as will enable them to understand their rights as citizens and duties as servants of the people."

This scheme, however, did not succeed. There was not sold a sufficient number of tickets, and no drawing was held.

Rev. Samuel Carrick was born in what is now Adams county, Pa., July 17, 1760, was licensed to preach by Hanover Presbytery in 1782, was in 1783 installed pastor of a church in the valley of Virginia, and was dismissed to Abingdon Presbytery in 1891. In this year he took up his permanent residence in Tennessee, and in 1794, when pastor of the First Presbyterian Church in Knoxville, was elected president of Blount College, in which position he served until his death, which occurred August 17, 1809.

The next president of this institution was Rev. David A. Sherman, who graduated from Yale College in 1802, served as tutor in Yale from 1804 to 1810, was principal of Hampden-Sidney Academy in Knoxville from 1817 to 1820, in which year he was elected president of East Tennessee College, remaining thus engaged until 1825, when he resigned, going then to Jackson College at Columbia, Tenn., where he died in 1843.

From 1825 to 1827 the college was again without a president, and it was during this interval, in 1826, that the trustees obtained permission to change the location of the institution, purchasing of Pleasant M. Miller for $600 the present site of the University of Tennessee, which site was then known as Barbara Hill, named in honor of Barbara Blount, daughter of Governor Blount. Upon this hill the trustees proceeded to erect the center college building and three one-story dormitories in the rear of the college, all in such positions as to form a square of the campus. This having been accomplished, the trustees succeeded in securing as president the Rev. Charles Coffin, D. D., of Greeneville College, who was born in Newburyport, Mass., August 15, 1775, and graduated from Harvard College in 1793. In 1800 he went to Norfolk, Va., where he was induced by Rev. Hezekiah Balch to accept a position as professor in Greeneville College, and upon the death of Dr. Balch, Mr. Coffin succeeded to the presidency of Greeneville College, which position he retained until elected president of East Tennessee College in 1827. After six years of hard labor in behalf of this institution, not fully appreciated, he resigned and returned to Greeneville, where he died June 3, 1853.

Dr. James H. Piper succeeded to the presidency in 1833, and served one year, resigning at the end of that time in despair of making the institution a success. Dr. Piper was a graduate of the college, in the class of 1830, and it is said that he was the ambitious youth who aspired to carve his name above that of the father of his country on the Natural Bridge in Virginia. After leaving East Tennessee College, Dr. Piper led a useful life in Virginia as a Presbyterian divine.

The two great difficulties with which the college had to contend up to about this time were these: One which may be considered the cause of the other, the first being the poverty of the settlers on the college lands, who kept up a constant clamor for a postponement of the payment of their interest from year to year, and in some cases of the principal. The legislature, in order to oblige them, yielded to their demands, postponing these payments continually until 1819, and even later. But the settlers were not satisfied even with the payment of the minimum price for their land, and with the continual postponements permitted by the legislature. They knew that payment was likely to be enforced sometime, and that the colleges were to be the recipients of the money. They were thus led to develop a feeling of animosity toward colleges, as is often the case with debtors against their creditors, which feeling, unreasonable and unjust though it was, was continually worked up and practiced upon by demagogues for their own purposes.

In 1819 the legislature provided for the first time for the sale of such lands as were not claimed by occupants and authorized the general taking up of all vacant lands south of the French Broad and Holston at fifty cents per acre, making this rule applicable to all college and academy lands that had not been taken up. This rule amounted to a further reduction in the price of college lands from the former price of one-half of what congress authorized to one-fourth of that price, and to the practical ruin of the college and academy funds; but the assent of congress was provided for in the legislation, and this assent appears never to have been granted. But the spirit of the legislature was manifest just the same.

In this same year, 1819, the payment of the principal due on the lands was again indefinitely postponed, and the time for the payment of the interest again extended. In 1821 the legislature again permitted the postponement of the payment of the principal, and the same policy was again renewed in 1822. The attempt, so far as it was made, still further worked upon the feelings and prejudices of the settlers against colleges and institutions of learning in general, which ambitious politicians well knew how to use, and which they did not scruple to use to further their own ambitious ends.

But at length light shone in upon all this darkness. "The president and trustees of the University of North Carolina, to whom the state of North Carolina had issued warrants for many thousand acres of land in Tennessee, founded upon military services that had been performed by certain officers and soldiers of the Continental line of North Carolina, who had died, leaving no heirs in the United States, had presented a memorial to the Tennessee legislature, praying that grants might issue upon these warrants and that all their lands in Tennessee might be exempt from taxation, offering to give a fair equivalent for such exemption.

"There were, however, grave doubts as to the validity of these warrants, and the legislature directed the appointment of two commissioners to investigate and adjust the claims of the University of North Carolina, authorizing them to enter into an agreement with the university concerning the warrants and exemption from taxation, which, it was provided, should be binding on the state." (E. T. Sanford.)

The commissioners appointed under this authority were Jenkins Whiteside and James Trimble, and they, on August 26, 1822, entered into a compact with the University of North Carolina by which grants should issue upon its warrants and all lands owned or acquired by the university within the state of Tennessee should be exempt from taxes until January 1, 1850; the university agreeing to transfer 60,000 acres of its land warrants to two public seminaries designated by the commissioners—20,000 acres to East Tennessee College and 40,000 acres to Cumberland College, and further agreeing to assign to the two colleges one-half of all military land warrants which might in future be issued to it by North Carolina, all of which gave promise of additional revenue to East Tennessee College, and inspired its trustees with renewed hope and courage. In 1823 the legislature, in order to do something for the colleges and at the same time still further to indulge and favor the settlers, two apparently contradictory projects, remitted one-third of the purchase money remaining due on all lands south of the French Broad and Holston, and vested in the institutions of learning the entire unremitted balance due upon all lands that had been previously sold within the district, whether within or without the college and academy tracts, together with all such lands as might be subsequently resold for default of payments and bid in by the state, or that had been previously sold or should not be redeemed by the owners. This fact, "in consequence of the delays of payment heretofore or hereafter to be sustained by the colleges and academies and in order to make a final appropriation and investiture of the moneys and lands aforesaid, and put it out of the power of the legislature to interfere hereafter by indulging the debtors or in any other way whatever." (E. T. Sanford.)

Not long afterward an act was passed making all of the territory which had been acquired by Tennessee east and north of the Congressional Reservation line, subject to entry at twelve and a half cents per acre, this act including the lands south of the French Broad and Holston, and even those within the college and academy tracts! And such was the sad end of the beneficent provisions of the cession act of 1806, which required these lands to be sold at a minimum price of two dollars per acre!

Considerable payments were made in 1824, but in 1825 the occupants of the lands almost unanimously refused to pay any more. In this year an act was passed by the legislature providing for the appointment of a commission to examine all military land warrants laid before him by the University of North Carolina, East Tennessee College and Cumberland College, which had been issued by the University of North Carolina, and to adjudicate their validity, not exceeding 105,000 acres, upon which adjudication a corresponding amount of land should be sold by the state at certain specified prices;

one-third of the proceeds to be paid to the University of North Carolina, one-third to be appropriated to the use of common schools, two-ninths to be paid to Cumberland College, and one-ninth to be paid to East Tennessee College; all sums paid to Cumberland and East Tennessee Colleges to be considered as made for the relief of the people residing on the college and academy tracts south of French Broad and Holston; and it was further provided that out of the moneys thereafter collected from the college and academy lands the academies should first be paid an amount equal to that received by the two colleges from the proceeds of these warrants, and that East Tennessee College should be equalized with Cumberland College.

The entire matter of the collection of the fund due to East Tennessee College for the Western lands under compact and the act of 1825 is so involved in uncertainty that it is impossible to make any definite statement with reference thereto. But Mr. E. T. Sanford, who has made the most exhaustive study of this whole matter and whose historical address on "Blount College and the University of Tennessee," delivered in 1894, has been the main source of information in the preparation of this sketch, stated that "probably the entire amount was not far from $24,000."

In 1829 the state of Tennessee offered to give one-half a township of land in the country south of the Hiwassee river to which the Indian title had not then been extinguished, to East Tennessee College and the University of Nashville (formerly Cumberland College), provided these two institutions would execute a written instrument releasing all their claims south of the French Broad and Holston rivers, and all rights they had acquired to lands in that section. To this proposition East Tennessee College, through its trustees, gave assent, protesting, however, against anything in the said act being construed to operate as a release to the state from its obligation to pay to the institution the balance of its proportion of the congressional donation. To this proposition neither the University of Nashville nor the Western academies would then consent, considering it wholly inadequate as a substitute for the magnificent gift intended for them by the congress of the United States; but in 1835 the university consented with great reluctance, and in 1838 the legislature directed the setting aside of the one-half township in the Ocoee district for the use of the college and university. Out of this Ocoee lands, which were almost immediately sold, East Tennessee College realized something more than $34,000 in cash.

Rev. James H. Piper has been mentioned. Upon his resignation as president in 1834, he was succeeded by Rev. Joseph Estabrook, who was born in Lebanon, N. H., December 8, 1792, graduated at Dartmouth College in 1815, came to Knoxville in 1828 as president of Knoxville Female Academy, and was elected president of East Tennessee College in 1834. By his ability, energy and wisdom he soon placed the institution on a better foundation than it had been before, and revised the course of study, brought scholarly men into the faculty and so changed the policy and scope of the institution that in 1840 the name was changed from East Tennessee College to East Tennessee University. It was not far from this time that the sale of a portion of the lands belonging to the institution enabled the trustees to make important improvements. Thomas Crutchfield, who had built the main edifice, was now engaged to erect the two three-story dormitories, and the two houses intended for residences for professors on the right and left slopes, but which an increasing demand for room afterward rendered it necessary to appropriate for other purposes. These improvements, which were finally paid for in July, 1848, cost $20,965.18.

In 1850 President Estabrook resigned, his resignation having a tendency to hasten the decline of the institution, which subsequent years proved to have just then set in. This decline was due in part at least to the multiplication of colleges and denominational schools then being established throughout Tennessee and other Southern states.

Appreciating the necessity of having at the head of the institution a man with a great name and of unusual ability, the trustees elected to the presidency Hon. William B. Reese, who had then recently resigned his seat upon the supreme bench of the state. President Reese, notwithstanding his great ability, energy and industry, was unable to arrest the decline of the university, and after graduating just twelve students in three years, resigned at the end of his third year. He died at Knoxville, July 7, 1859.

The next president was Rev. George Cooke, who was born at Keene, N. H., December 26, 1811, graduated at Dartmouth in 1832, was pastor at Amherst, Mass., from 1839 to 1852, in which latter year he accepted the pastorate of the Second Presbyterian church at Knoxville, and was elected president of the East Tennessee University in 1853. A majority of the faculty having resigned at the time of President Reese's resignation, it was necessary to fill the vacancies thus caused, and the opening of the university was necessarily postponed until the beginning of the summer session of 1854. In the following September the cholera prevailed in Knoxville and the students were prevented from returning at the opening of the winter session by reason thereof. An attempt to organize a medical department failed, and a subsequent attempt made in 1858 also failed. President Cooke suggested the establishment of an agricultural department, but before it could be determined whether this were a practical suggestion President Cooke resigned, in despair, in 1857.

March 20, 1858, Rev. William D. Carnes, A. M., a graduate of the university in 1842, and then president of Burritt College, Van Buren county, Tenn., was elected president, and served until 1860, when he resigned, afterward being ordained a minister in the Christian church. But while he was president he procured the adoption of a joint resolution by the legislature, requesting the judges of the Supreme court of the state to report at the next session the facts in reference to the appropriation of the college lands under the act of congress of 1806, and to state their opinion as to the equitable right of the two universities to further compensation on this account. The trustees appointed John H. Crozier and Thomas C. Lyon to present the claim of the university to the Supreme court; but the war came on and this matter is still undecided.

The vacancy caused by the resignation of President Carnes was immediately filled by the election of Rev. J. J. Ridley, of Clarksville, to the position. The first session under his administration opened with a largely increased attendance, owing to the labors of Rev. Mr. Carnes during his incumbency. The first important action by President Ridley was to secure the adoption of a resolution extending gratuitous education to candidates for the ministry, without regard to their denominational preferences. President Ridley remained in his position until February 7, 1862, when he unconditionally resigned, and from that time on until the close of the war the buildings of the university were alternately used by the Federal and Confederate forces, and when needed again for its legitimate purposes the buildings were in no condition to be used.

Succeeding the act of congress of 1806, the next important legislation by that august body which affected the University of East Tennessee, was an act approved by President Lincoln July 2, 1862, entitled "An act donating public lands to the several states and territories which may provide colleges for the benefit of agriculture and the mechanic arts." This act granted to each state a certain amount of the public lands within its borders (thirty thousand acres for each senator and representative to which the states were respectively entitled by the apportionment made under the census of 1860), or if there were not sufficient lands, then land scrip for a corresponding acreage, which lands were to be sold by the states and the moneys derived therefrom to be invested in safe stocks and to constitute a perpetual fund, which should remain forever undiminished, and the interest thereon inviolably appropriated to the endowment and maintenance of at least one college whose leading object should be to teach such branches of learning as relate to agriculture and the mechanic arts.

The Civil war prevented Tennessee from accepting this generous gift until 1865, which, according to the provisions of the act, was too late, as two years from the approval of the act was the limit of time extended within which to accept the gift; but Tennessee having been readmitted to the Union, congress was induced to extend the time specified in the original act in order that Tennessee might avail herself of its provisions, which she did by an act passed February 1, 1868. This act made provision for obtaining and selling the land scrip, which by lack of public lands the state was entitled to receive, and directed that the proceeds should be invested in bonds of the state to await the proper disposition.

In the meantime the trustees of the university unanimously elected Rev. Thomas W. Humes, who was born in Knoxville, Tenn., April 22, 1815, and who graduated from East Tennessee College in 1830, president of the university, a position which he held continuously and successfully until 1883, when he resigned. One of the provisions of the act of congress of 1862 was that each state claiming the benefits of the act should within five years from its approval, July 2, 1862, provide a college to receive the endowment. East Tennessee University was already somewhat of a state institution and was desirous of securing the location of the Agricultural College. Under the leadership of President Humes she made application for the congressional appropriation, offering, if given the fund, to provide the necessary college building. In 1869 the legislature of the state appropriated the proceeds of the sale of the land scrip to East Tennessee University, making it the express duty of the trustees of the university to establish an agricultural college, in such manner as to strictly conform to the congressional enactment. This state law required the trustees of the university to complete buildings for the accommodation of 275 students, and to provide a farm of not less than 200 acres, so that the whole property at a fair valuation should be worth not less than $125,000 before it should be lawful for the governor to issue to the university the scrip; and the university was required to admit three students from each county in the state free of tuition, said students to be nominated by the several representatives from each county.

These conditions having been complied with, the Tennessee Industrial College was organized in June, 1869, and went into operation in September following, and the endowment from the United states was invested in 396 bonds of the state of Tennessee, each bond for $1,000, bearing six per cent interest, the payment of which has been often delayed. The farm purchased is situated about three-fourths of a mile from the university, just west of Third creek on the north bank of the Tennessee river, new buildings were erected and a chemical laboratory was provided and equipped.

The establishment of this industrial department created extraordinary demands upon the teaching force, and while Dr. Humes remained president of the institution and professor of mental and moral philosophy, Prof. J. K. Payne retained the chair of mathematics, to which natural philosophy was added: Prof. W. M. Grace took English language and literature, rhetoric having been dropped; and the new professors were assigned to the following branches of learning: F. H. Bradley, M. A., natural science; R. L. Kirkpatrick, M. A., Latin and literature; E. Dean Dow, M. A., agriculture; I. T. Beckwith, A. B., ancient languages; W. O. Atwater, agricultural chemistry; M. C. Butler, M. A., became principal of the classical preparatory department; and William V. Deaderick, principal of the scientific preparatory department.

Professor Dow not accepting the chair of agriculture, that chair was filled later by Prof. Hunter Nicholson, at which time horticulture was added to agriculture. Professor Atwater did not take possession of his chair until the fall of 1871. Principal Deaderick taught half the year, and his place was then filled by J. V. Bradford. In the classical preparatory department George L. Maloney and W. A. Rice were employed to give instruction.

In this new organization there were, as will have been seen, two preparatory departments, the classical preparatory department being taught for some time in the old "White House," which stood where Agricultural Hall now stands, and the scientific preparatory department was taught at the old Hampden-Sidney Academy on Church street. The design was to dispense as soon as possible with all preparatory work as soon as the educational condition of the people of the state would justify such a course; but this condition of things was slow to arrive, and the preparatory schools did much good work, and though the lack of efficient preparatory schools throughout the state still renders preparatory work in the university necessary, yet no regular class is now maintained.

The class of 1871, containing four members, was the first to graduate after the war. These members were S. A. Craig, T. C. Karns, Albert Setzepand and J. W. C. Willoughby, all receiving the degree of bachelor of arts except S. A. Craig, who received the degree of bachelor of science.

The courses of study at this time were four in number: agricultural, mechanical, classical and scientific, the latter being identical with the classical, except that Greek was supplanted by certain studies of the agricultural and mechanical courses. Prof. Atwater returned from Europe in the fall with a fully supply of improved apparatus for the chemical laboratory. Albert Ruth, A. M., and Levi Van Fossen, Ph. B., were appointed instructors in the preparatory department, and Lieut. T. T. Thornburgh, of the United

States army, in December, 1871, became professor of military science and commandant of cadets.

In the year 1871 the farm was surveyed and laid off into lots, preparatory to the beginning of rotation of crops. The next year crops were planted and considerable preparatory work done; stock was purchased, a barn built, and the teaching of practical farming began, many of the students in this way earning enough to pay for half of their board.

At the time of the establishment of four full courses, as mentioned above, there were also established two shorter courses, viz.: one in agriculture and one in mechanics, for the benefit of such men as were getting somewhat advanced in years, and there had been also for some time a Latin-scientific course, also for the benefit of the same class of men. In 1872 these three short courses were discontinued, and students, or their parents for them, allowed to select one of the other courses, and one year was added to the non-classical course, making it a three years' course.

In 1872 Prof. Van Fossen resigned his position as instructor in the preparatory department, and Rev. Thomas Roberts, M. A., was appointed to the vacancy. F. E. Hacker resigned as instructor in drawing, and Charles Waring, C. E., of the University of Dublin, was appointed to the place, but does not seem to have served.

The next year there were several changes in the faculty. Prof. F. D. Allen resigned the chair of Latin and Greek and was succeeded by Morton William Easton, Ph. D. Rev. F. Esperandieu became professor of French in place of Prof. I. B. Barker, and Prof. Atwater was succeeded in the chair of general and agricultural chemistry by Prof. B. S. Burton, Ph. B. Lieut. Thornburgh having been recalled to the army, was succeeded by Col. S. B. Crawford as professor of military science and commandant of cadets. A special chair of rhetoric was filled by Rev. Thomas C. Teasdale, D. D. The president of the university took evidences of religion instead of mental science, the latter falling to Prof. Kirkpatrick. C. S. Newman resigned as principal of the preparatory department and was succeeded by A. Ruth. Spurrier Howard-Smith, A. B., Eben Alexander, A. B., and William B. Payne, A. B., were elected tutors, and L. W. Philson, A. M., and A. L. Wakefield, B. A., B. S., instructors in the preparatory department.

During the scholastic year 1873-74, the attendance reached 318, of whom 211 were state appointees, fifty-two counties being represented by appointees. And it is somewhat remarkable that while a majority of students were sons of farmers, yet they seldom chose agriculture as their course of study. It may be stated also in this connection that it became necessary to disabuse the public mind at this time that one of the principal objects of the establishment of this department of instruction was to furnish manual labor to the agricultural student, Prof. Hunter Nicholson showing that the successful study of agriculture is based upon knowledge of the physical sciences, and that the student is not prepared to specialize in agriculture until the last years of his course.

In June, 1875, Col. Crawford resigned as professor of military science, and was succeeded by Lieut. A. H. Nave of the United States army. W. B. Payne and A. L. Wakefield were succeeded in the preparatory department by S. B. Crawford, A. B., and T. C. Karns, A. B. Lewis M. Herring was appointed instructor in chemistry in 1876, and Lieut. J. E. Bloom of the United States army became professor of military science in 1876, serving one year.

In the summer of 1877 the entire faculty of the university was reorganized, after which reorganization it stood as follows:

Rev. Thomas W. Humes, S. T. D., president and professor of ethics and evidences of religion.

Richard L. Kirkpatrick, M. A., professor of logic and English literature.

Hunter Nicholson, professor of agriculture and horticulture.

Morton William Easton, Ph. D., professor of modern languages and comparative philology.

Eben Alexander, B. A., professor of ancient languages and literature.

S. H. Lockett, M. A., professor of mathematics and mechanical philosophy.

W. G. Brown, B. S., professor of chemistry and instructor in geology and mineralogy.

David Hunt Ludlow, B. A., assistant professor of mathematics.

W. G. McAdoo, M. A., S. B. Crawford, B. A., and T. O. Deaderick, B. A., instructors in preparatory department.

G. R. Knabe, instructor in vocal and instrumental music.

William E. Moses, assistant in analytical chemistry.

Lieut. George W. Baxter, of the United States army, served a short time as professor of military science, but was succeeded in the fall of 1877 by Col. S. H. Lockett.

In the same year separate colleges were made of the three ancient courses of study—the agricultural course becoming the college of agriculture; the mechanical course becoming the college of engineering and the mechanic arts, and the classical course becoming the classical college. Each had its separate curriculum and corps of instructors, but all were under one government and of equal rank. It was noticeable that more and more students followed a scientific course of study and fewer of them took the classical course as time sped on.

In 1878 Prof. Kirkpatrick took the new chair of history and philosophy, and Edward S. Joynes, A. M., LL. D., then late of Vanderbilt University, became professor of English language and belles-lettres.

By an act of the legislature of the state passed March 24, 1879, it was provided that no further vacancies in the board of trustees should be filled until the number of trustees should be reduced below thirty, and the same act also provided that a board of visitors should be appointed by the governor—three from each of the three divisions of the state—holding their offices for four years, who should visit the university at least once a year, and report upon its condition to the governor. On commencement day, June 18, 1879, the University of Tennessee was inaugurated, and in compliance with the act just referred to, Governor Albert S. Marks appointed the following as the first board of visitors: Ex-Governor James D. Porter, Hon. J. Harvey Mathes, Gen. R. P. Neely, Hon. John C. Gaut, Gen. Lucius E. Polk, Hon. Z. W. Ewing, Perez Dickinson, Hon. James T. Shields, and Dr. E. M. Wight.

In 1879 the name of East Tennessee University was changed to that of the University of Tennessee, and laws were enacted connecting the university more intimately with the state system of public schools.

For four years succeeding the resignation of Dr. Humes the faculty, upon authority of the board of trustees, annually elected one of their own number chairman, such chairman being clothed with the authority and charged with the duties of president; but in 1887, desiring to strengthen the institution in the sciences relating to the industries and in engineering, the trustees elected to the presidency Dr. Charles W. Dabney, Jr., who was born at Hampden-Sidney, Va., June 19, 1855. Dr. Dabney received the degree of bachelor of philosophy at the University of Goettingen, Germany, and previous to his election to the responsible position he now fills, had held several important positions connected with educational institutions in Virginia and North Carolina. In 1893 he was appointed by President Cleveland, Assistant Secretary of Agriculture, and in 1894 he was appointed chairman of the board of managers of the government exhibit at Atlanta, Ga., and in 1897 he was appointed to a similar position at the Tennessee Centennial Exposition. He received the degree of LL. D. from Davidson College in 1889, and is now serving his twelfth year as president of this great state institution, the University of Tennessee.

What afterward became the medical department of the University of Tennessee was organized as the Nashville Medical College in 1876, this college being founded by Drs. Duncan Eve and W. F. Glenn. The first faculty was composed of Drs. Paul F. Eve, T. B. Buchanan, George S. Blackie, W. P. Jones and J. J. Abernethy, taken from the faculties of Nashville and Vanderbilt Universities. The first session of this college opened March 5, 1877, and in the spring of 1879 a dental department was established, the first in the South. During this same year an overture was made by the University of Tennessee to the Nashville Medical College to become the medical department of the university, the overture being accepted.

Following are the names of the members of the medical and dental faculties as they stood in 1891:

Charles W. Dabney, Jr., Ph. D., LL. D., president of the university.

Hon. William P. Jones, M. D., president of the faculty.

Duncan Eve, M. D., A. M., dean of the faculty and professor of the practice of surgery.

John S. Cain, M. D., professor of the principles and practice of medicine, with clinical medicine and general pathology.

J. Berrien Lindsley, D. D., M. D., professor of medical chemistry and state medicine.

J. Bunyan Stephens, M. D., professor of obstetrics and clinical midwifery.

William D. Haggard, M. D., professor of gynæcology and diseases of children.

W. M. Vertrees, M. D., professor of materia medica and therapeutics.

Paul F. Eve, M. D., professor of the principles of surgery, operative and clinical surgery.

William E. McCampbell, A. M., M. D., professor of general, descriptive and surgical anatomy.

CHARLES W. DABNEY, JR.,
President University of Tennessee,

From *The Graphic - An Illustrated Weekly Newspaper* - November 19, 1892, p. 373

GEORGE F. MELLEN, PH. D.,
Professor of Greek.

T. W. JORDAN,
Dean Academic Department.

FRANK M. SMITH,
Principal Teachers Department   Ex-State Supt. Public Instruction.

F. LAMSON-SCRIBNER,
Director of Experiment Station and Professor of Botany.

HENRY H. INGERSOLL, A.M., LL D.,
Dean of Law Department.

From *The Graphic - An Illustrated Weekly Newspaper* - November 19, 1892, p. 373

John A. Witherspoon, M. D., professor of practice of medicine and medical hygiene.

T. Hilliard Wood, M. D., professor of physiology.

William F. Glenn, M. D., professor of venereal diseases.

John G. Sinclair, M. D., professor of clinical diseases of the eye, ear and throat.

William G. Brien, M. D., LL. D., professor of medical jurisprudence.

J. H. Blanks, M. D., professor of clinical medicine.

Haley P. Cartwright, M. D., professor of physical diagnosis.

Charles Mitchell, M. D., professor of microscopy and histology.

James W. Handly, M. D., professor of genito-urinary diseases and demonstrator of anatomy.

Ross Dunn, M. D., demonstrator of anatomy.

The course of medical instruction consists of "didactic lectures, with demonstrations, clinical teaching, examinations or quizzes, and practical teaching in subjects involving manipulation." The candidate for graduation must be 21 years of age, of good moral character, and must have studied at least two years. The first year may be passed at some other reputable college. A graded course of three years is also provided, but it is not obligatory.

The school is located on Broad street and has one of the best equipped buildings in the country. A free city dispensary is located on the ground floor. The fees are: Matriculation, $5; lectures, $75; demonstrator's fee, $10; graduation fee, $25.

The dental course of study embraces "operative, prosthetic and clinical dentistry, lectures on oral and clinical surgery, chemistry, materia medica and therapeutics, regional anatomy, physiology, and microscopy." The requirements for graduation and the fees are similar to those of the medical department.

The degrees that were conferred in 1879 were divided into

collegiate, post-graduate and professional. The collegiate degrees were those of bachelor of arts and bachelor of science. The degree of bachelor of arts was given in the classical college, and included full courses of study in Latin, Greek, English history and philosophy, and partial courses in mathematics, chemistry, natural history and modern languages. The degree of bachelor of science was given in the mechanical college and in the agricultural college. In the former it included full courses of study in mathematics, applied mathematics, chemistry, natural history and partial courses in English history and philosophy and modern languages. In the agricultural college it included full courses in chemistry, including agricultural chemistry, natural history and agriculture, and partial courses in mathematics, applied mathematics, English history and philosophy and modern languages.

The post-graduate degrees were those of master of arts and doctor of philosophy. The master's degree had hitherto been given in course to graduates of three years' standing who had sustained a good moral character and would present to the faculty a satisfactory original thesis. Instead of this, in 1879, there was required one year of postgraduate study, and in order to receive the degree of doctor of philosophy two years of resident postgraduate study under the direction of the faculty were required, thus converting these degrees into degrees of merit instead of degrees of honor.

The professional degrees were those of civil engineer and doctor of medicine, the former requiring two years of special study.

In the summer of 1879 there were made some changes in the faculty. The chair of agriculture and horticulture was divided into two chairs, the one containing natural history and geology, assigned to Prof. Hunter Nicholson, and the other containing agriculture, horticulture and botany, assigned to Prof. John M. McBryde. Prof. S. B. Crawford became professor of military science, and David B. Johnson,

B. A., assistant instructor in mathematics. In July of this year Prof. Kirkpatrick died, and in 1880 Prof. M. W. Easton resigned the chair of modern languages, thus leaving two leading chairs vacant, and modern languages then went to the professor of English and belles-lettres; the instructorship in mathematics was discontinued and the new chair of pure mathematics was filled by Prof. James Dinwiddie, M. A.

In 1880 a surveyor's course of two years, a practical agricultural course of two years and a business course of one year, were established, and in 1881 an arrangement was made with the Knoxville business college by which its professors conducted the business department of the university.

In 1882 Prof. Joynes resigned his chair of English and modern languages, and was succeeded therein by Prof. Rodes Massie, and Prof. John W. Glenn of Georgia succeeded Prof. McBryde in the chair of agriculture and horticulture.

In 1883, upon the resignation of Dr. T. W. Humes from the presidency, the board of trustees decided to elect a chairman who should be in effect president, and Prof. Rodes Massie was chosen. Col. Lockett resigned the chair of applied mathematics and the work was assigned to Prof. Dinwiddie, Lewis C. Carter being elected instructor in applied mathematics. Prof. W. A. Noyes was elected to succeed Prof. Brown in the chair of chemistry and mineralogy. Thomas O. Deaderick became adjunct professor of ancient languages. In the summer of 1885 Prof. Dinwiddie resigned the chair of mathematics, and was succeeded by Prof. W. W. Carson. During the year 1885-86 Prof. E. Alexander served as chairman of the faculty, and at the end of the year was succeeded by Prof. Thomas O. Deaderick. Adjunct Professor W. E. Moses was promoted to the chair of chemistry and mineralogy made vacant by the resignation of Prof. Noyes. Col. S. B. Crawford was chairman of the faculty for 1886-87; Price Thomas, A. M., was chosen instructor in natural history, agriculture, etc.; Charles Walker, A. M., instructor in chemistry and physics, and T. C. Karns, A. M., principal of the preparatory department.

March 3, 1887, Congress passed what is known as the "Hatch Bill," which provided for the establishment of agricultural experiment stations in connection with the various agricultural colleges then already founded in different states. On March 28 the legislature of Tennessee passed an act accepting the gift of $15,000 and bestowed it upon the agricultural department of the University of Tennessee. In the following July the trustees of the University reorganized the agricultural department. President Dabney was made director of the station and entered upon his duties August 4, 1887, and although by an oversight no appropriation clause had been included in the congressional act, Director Dabney added two men to his staff in September, 1887—C. S. Plumb and C. L. Newman, the former being at the same time elected professor of agriculture. During the summer of 1888 a new station building worth $6,800 was erected adjoining Agricultural Hall on the south, and a new mechanical building was also erected during the same summer. At the same time a new residence was erected for the president just east of the experiment station, at a cost of $5,000. Agricultural Hall had not up to this time been completed, and now both it and the new station building were fitted up with the best gas, water, heating and ventilating apparatus. In addition to the improvements for the experiment station and the agricultural department, a new mechanical building was erected in the summer of 1888, being of brick and costing $11,500.

In the summer of 1888 a complete reorganization of the faculty was effected. The board of trustees under which this reorganization was made consisted of the following-named gentlemen: Governor Robert L. Taylor, ex-officio; Hon. John Allison, secretary of state, ex-officio; Hon. Frank M. Smith, superintendent of public instruction, ex-officio; Hugh L. McClung, Hon. O. P. Temple, Frank A. R. Scott, Robert H. Armstrong, S. H. Smith, M. D.; R. P. Eaton,

H. L. W. Mynatt, Hon. D. A. Nunn, Edward J. Sanford, W. A. Henderson, Esq.; Hon. J. M. Coulter, Rev. James Park, D. D.; James D. Cowan, C. Deaderick, M. D.; John M. Boyd, M. D.; Hon. George Brown, J. W. Gaut, Samuel L. McKinney, William Morrow, M. D.; William B. Reese, Esq.; Moses White, Esq.; James Comfort, Esq.; Samuel B. Luttrell, and Robert Craighead.

The officers of the board were Dr. Charles W. Dabney, Jr., president; Robert Craighead, treasurer, and S. H. Smith, M. D., secretary.

The board of control of the agricultural experiment station consisted of O. P. Temple, J. W. Gaut, R. H. Armstrong, James Park, D. D., and Robert Craighead.

The board of visitors, appointed by the governor, consisted of Charles Mason, Jonesboro; John W. Paulett, Knoxville; Rev. George Stuart, Cleveland; J. W. Sparks, Murfreesboro; Clinton Armstrong, Lewisburg; T. B. Harwell, M. D., Pulaski; William Sanford, Covington; J. Harvey Mathes, Memphis, and S. B. Williamson, Trenton.

The officers of government and instruction elected were:

Charles W. Dabney, Jr., Ph. D. (Göttingen), President of the University.

Thomas W. Jordan, A. M. (graduate University of Virginia), Dean of the College.

Kenneth G. Matheson (South Carolina Military Academy), Commandant of Cadets.

The faculty elected, in the order of official seniority, were as follows:

William W. Carson, C. E., M. E. (Washington and Lee University), Professor of Mathematics and Civil Engineering.

Charles W. Dabney, Jr., Ph. D. (Göttingen), Professor of Organic and Agricultural Chemistry.

Charles S. Plumb, B. S. (Massachusetts Agricultural College), Professor of Agriculture.

F. Lamson-Scribner, B. S. (Maine State College), Professor of Botany and Horticulture.

J. S. Coon, M. E. (Cornell University), Professor of Mechanical Engineering and Physics.

Thomas W. Jordan, A. M. (graduate University of Virginia), Professor of Latin Language and Literature.

Charles E. Wait, C. E., M. E. (University of Virginia), Ph. D. (University of Missouri), Professor of General and Analytical Chemistry and Metallurgy.

Charles W. Kent, A. M. (University of Virginia), Ph. D. (Leipsic), Professor of English and Modern Languages.

Edward E. Gayle, first lieutenant, Second Artillery, U. S. A., Professor of Military Science and Tactics.

Theodore F. Burgdorff, passed assistant engineer, U. S. N., Associate Professor of Mathematics and Engineering.

Thomas C. Karns, A. M. (University of Tennessee), Associate Professor of the English Language and of Literature and of History.

Henry E. Summers, B. S. (Cornell University), Associate Professor of Biology and Zoölogy.

Clifford L. Newman, B. S. (Agricultural and Mechanical College of Alabama), Assistant Professor of Agriculture.

Kenneth G. Matheson (South Carolina Military Academy), Assistant Professor of English.

S. N. Smith, A. M. (University of Tennessee), Instructor in Ancient Languages.

Charles Hancock (graduate Miller Manual Labor School of Virginia), Instructor in Mechanics.

David B. Oviatt (Cornell University), Instructor in Drawing.

William R. Ellington (University of Tennessee), Instructor in Mathematics.

J. E. Matheny, Instructor in Bookkeeping.

Dr. J. E. Kennedy, Physician.

Prof. W. W. Camson, Secretary of the Faculty.

Prof. Chas. S. Plumb, Librarian.

Capt. K. G. Matheson, Inspector of Buildings.

Robert J. Cummings, Superintendent of the Farm.

The officers of the agricultural experiment station elected were:

Charles W. Dabney, Jr., Ph. D. (Göttingen), Director.

Charles S. Plumb, B. S. (Massachusetts Agricultural College), Assistant Director, in charge of field and feeding experiments.

F. Lamson-Scribner, B. S. (Maine State College), Botanist and Horticulturist.

Winthrop E. Stone, B. S., Ph. D. (Göttingen), Chemist.

Henry E. Summers, B. S. (Cornell University), Entomologist.

Clifford L. Newman, B. S. (Agricultural and Mechanical College of Alabama), Assistant.

Robert J. Cummings, Foreman of Experiment Farm.

Thomas L. Norwood, A. M. (University of North Carolina), had been elected professor of modern languages and English and also dean of the faculty, but very unfortunately sickened and died before the term opened.

The departments of instruction comprised, first, the academic, which was subdivided into the collegiate and the university, or post-graduate; secondly, the professional, located at Nashville, which was divided into a course in medicine and a course in dentistry.

The collegiate department embraced the following courses of study: 1. Literary-scientific; 2. Latin-scientific; 3. Agriculture; 4. Civil engineering; 5. Mechanical Engineering; 6. Chemistry; 7. Mining engineering. These courses led to the degrees of bachelor of science, bachelor of philosophy, bachelor of agriculture, bachelor of science in engineering, and bachelor of science in applied chemistry.

The university department included courses for the graduate degrees of master of arts, master of science, and doctor of philosophy. The first and second required each one year of study; the third two years. Then there were the professional courses leading to degrees of civil engineer, mining engineer and mechanical engineer. In the third place there were courses for special students in the various departments. University students working for degrees were required to be graduates of the academic department of this or equivalent schools and resident at the university. The degree of master of agriculture was afterward introduced.

The medical department at Nashville conferred the degree of doctor of medicine, and the dental department that of doctor of dental surgery.

The following schools were included in the academic department:

1. School of ancient languages, with one professor and one instructor.
2. School of English and modern languages, with two professors and one assistant professor.
3. School of mathematics, and civil engineering, with two professors and one instructor.
4. School of mechanical engineering and physics, with one professor and two instructors.
5. School of general and analytical chemistry and metallurgy, with one professor.
6. School of agriculture and organic chemistry, with one professor.
7. School of agriculture, with one professor and one assistant professor.
8. School of botany and horticulture, with one professor.
9. School of biology and zoölogy, with one professor.
10. School of military science and tactics.

The preparatory school was abolished, a few subcollegiate classes being retained to meet a present demand.

Four new schools of study had been established, viz.: Mechanical engineering and physics, agriculture and organic chemistry, botany and horticulture, and biology and zoölogy. The library was recatalogued according to the well-known Dewey decimal classification system, and then contained about 6,000 volumes, since increased to ———— volumes.

In 1890 Prof. C. S. Plumb resigned the chair of agriculture

and in 1891 was succeeded by Major C. F. Vanderford; Prof. Stonewall Tompkins became superintendent of shops in place of C. S. Coon, resigned; W. M. Yager became instructor in mechanics, and H. J. Darnall in German; Lieut. E. E. Gayle became professor of military science, and Cooper D. Schmitt, M. A., professor of mathematics. In 1889, in order to accommodate workingmen who could not attend during the day, there was established a night school, aided liberally by the citizens of Knoxville. No tuition was charged, the professors of the university donating their time. The sessions were held in the Mechanical building on Monday, Wednesday and Friday evenings of each week throughout January, February, March and April, the members of the teaching force being: Prof. Stonewall Tompkins, principal; Prof. T. W. Jordan, language; Prof. T. C. Karns, English; Prof. C. D. Schmitt, mathematics; Prof. R. S. Collins (Knoxville Business College), bookkeeping and penmanship; W. R. Ellington, freehand drawing, and W. M. Yager, mechanical drawing. A number of popular lectures on such subjects as chemistry, electricity, and political economy were delivered during the season.

The law department was established in the beginning of the second term of 1889-90, with ex-Supreme Judge Thomas J. Freeman dean and professor in charge. The course was a two years' one and led to the degree of bachelor of laws. During the spring of 1891 Judge Freeman resigned on account of ill health, dying in the fall of that year, and he was succeeded as dean by Judge H. H. Ingersoll, George E. Beers, a graduate of Yale law school being elected associate professor.

On February 2, 1877, a Young Men's Christian Association was organized, with D. B. Johnson, president; James H. Cowan, vice-president; Charles J. Heiskell, secretary, and John M. Allen, treasurer. Meetings were held first in the old chapel, then in a room in the steward's hall, and afterward in East College. February 22, 1890, at a meeting held at the university, a subscription was started for the purpose of erecting a new building for the association, which had by this time become an influential body in East Tennessee. There was raised $3,500 immediately, which amount in a few days grew to $6,000, and then the trustees offered to give $3,000, provided $7,000 were raised outside, which was accomplished, and on June 9, ground was broken for the new building. As the building was in course of erection the ambition of its founders grew, and finally a fine three-story brick building was erected at a cost of $20,000. It stands on the east side of the campus commanding a fine view of the Tennessee river.

In 1890 congress made an additional appropriation to the land grant colleges of the various states, the amount to be taken from the sale of public lands. It began with $15,000, on June 30, 1890, and increased $1,000 each year until the amount reaches $25,000, which sum is to be paid thereafter annually. This fund can go only to instruction in agriculture, the mechanic arts, the English language, and the various branches of mathematical, physical, natural, and economic sciences, with special reference to their applications in the industries of life, and to the facilities to such instruction.

The teachers' department was strengthened in 1890 by the election of Prof. Frank M. Smith as principal. F. R. Jones, M. E., was elected superintendent of shops; P. L. Cobb, instructor in ancient languages; J. R. McColl, in mechanics; E. M. Davis, in English; S. W. McCallie, in geology; P. F. Kefauer in practical agriculture, and R. L. Watts in horticulture.

High schools were designated in 1890, whose preparatory work would be received for entrance at the university. On application the University School at Columbia, Institute at Lewisburg, Memphis Institute, University High School at Knoxville, Wall and Mooney School at Franklin, the Yerkes School at Paris, Ky., and the Bingham School of North Carolina, were added to the list. One free scholar-

Buildings at The University of Tennessee

1. SCHOOL OF MECHANIC ARTS. 2. Y. M. C. A. AND GYMNASIUM BUILDING.
3. AGRICULTURAL BUILDING. 4. SCIENCE HALL.

From *The Graphic - An Illustrated Weekly Newspaper* - November 19, 1892, p. 373

ship was awarded to the best graduate of each school. Afterward were added the High School of Asheville, N. C.; the Peabody High School at Little Rock, Ark.; the University School of Kansas City, Mo.; the University School of Monticello, Ark.; and high schools in Tennessee at the following places: Alexandria, Chattanooga, Clarksville, Cleveland, Clinton, Columbia, Dyersburg, Jonesboro, Knoxville, Lexington, McMinnville, Memphis, Milan, Nashville, Newbern, Pulaski, Rogersville, Trenton and West Knoxville.

Early in 1891 Laurence D. Tyson, first lieutenant, Ninth Infantry, U. S. army, was appointed professor of military science, Lieut. Gayle having been recalled to the army. Prof. George F. Mellen, Ph. D. (Leipsic) was elected associate professor of Greek and French, taking charge in the fall of 1891; J. D. Hoskins was appointed in mathematics.

The foundations for a new science hall were laid in the summer of 1890, and the building completed in 1891, at a cost of about $60,000. The money with which to erect this building was obtained principally from the sale of forty-nine acres of land adjoining the college farm. It was not needed for agricultural purposes, and had then recently so appreciated in value as to readily bring $1,000 an acre.

The constitution of Tennessee provides that there shall be no discrimination against colored persons in any of the public schools. The university being simply the head of the public school system the act endowing the institution with the proceeds of the land grant, sets forth that "no citizen of this state, otherwise qualified, shall be excluded from the privileges of the university by reason of his race or color; but the accommodation and instruction of persons of color shall be separate from the white."

For many years, of course, no colored persons were found qualified to take advantage of the grade of instruction provided by the university. When, later, a few state appointees to scholarships were found qualified, their tuition was paid at Fisk University, at Nashville, and then also at Knoxville

College, Knoxville, Tenn. When the present management took charge of the institution, and the number of colored appointees increased considerably, steps were taken to establish a regular department in the university for the benefit of this class of students. In response to an inquiry addressed to the attorney-general of the state, an opinion was received from him to the effect that all the departments of the university ought to be located at Knoxville, in immediate relation with, and under the direct supervision of, the trustees and faculty. As soon, therefore, as the students then attending Fisk University could be graduated, steps were taken which led to the establishment of such a department at Knoxville. By contract with the trustees of Knoxville College, an excellent institution for the education of colored people, the buildings, grounds, and teaching staff of that institution were made available for the university as its colored department.

The facilities there provided needed, however, to be supplemented along the line of scientific and industrial education. The president accordingly visited some of the friends of this institution at the North, and secured the funds for a new scientific and mechanical building. A tract of land adjacent to the college was provided for practical work in agriculture and horticulture. The new building contains a chemical laboratory, drawing rooms, and shops for instruction in mechanic arts. Three new instructors were provided, and all the new departments were well equipped. The new department is called the industrial department for colored students, and is as immediately under the supervision of the trustees and president of the university as any other department of the institution, all of its teachers being elected by the trustees, and the entire expenses of the department being paid by them. The several professors of the university have supervision of the work there in their respective departments.

It is designed to give colored men in this institution that opportunity for industrial education which they so much need. Students are encouraged and required to work in the shops and upon the farm, and get in this way a practical skill which will be of benefit to them in later life. Twelve apprenticeships, worth $50 per annum each, have been created for the benefit of these students and are available both in the agricultural and mechanical schools.

The holdings and income of the university may be summed up as follows:

RESOURCES.

Tennessee State certificates, Agricultural and Mechanical College fund, which bear interest at 6 per cent...	$396,000
Nine State certificates, which are the university's property, interest 5 per cent...	9,000
Knoxville city bonds (library), which bear 6 per cent interest..	20,000
Turnpike stock...	1,000
	426,000
College Hill property, 36.5 acres, and 12 large buildings...	500,000
College farm of 99.3 acres and improvements...	100,000
Unimproved land, 94.1 acres...	80,000
Equipment, live stock, machinery, etc...	100,000
	780,000

INCOME.

Interest on Agricultural and Mechanical College fund...	$23,760
Interest on 9 State certificates...	450
Interest of Knoxville bonds...	1,200
	25,410
The annual appropriations from the General Government are:	
For experiment station ...$15,000	
Under Morrill act (in 1891)... 16,000	
	31,000
The contingent income is, per annum, about...	8,000
Total income ...	64,000

The following named gentlemen constitute the board of trustees at the present time:

His Excellency, the Governor of Tennessee.....Ex-Officio.
The Secretary of State.......................Ex-Officio.
The Superintendent of Public Instruction......Ex-Officio.
T. F. P. Allison, Nashville,

Frank P. Bond, Brownsville,
John M. Boyd, Knoxville,
Joshua W. Caldwell, Knoxville,
James Comfort, Knoxville,
Hu. L. Craighead, Nashville,
Chalmers Deaderick, Knoxville,
William C. Dismukes, Gallatin,
Z. W. Ewing, Pulaski,
James B. Frazier, Chattanooga,
James W. Gaut, Knoxville,
J. M. Greer, Memphis,
Hal H. Haynes, Bristol,
William A. Henderson, Knoxville,
Hugh G. Kyle, Rogersville,
Samuel B. Luttrell, Knoxville,
James Maynard, Knoxville,
Samuel McKinney, Knoxville,
Hu. L. McClung, Knoxville,
Thomas R. Myers, Shelbyville,
James Park, Knoxville,
James D. Porter, Paris,
Wm. Rule, Knoxville,
Edward J. Sanford, Knoxville,
Edward T. Sanford, Knoxville,
Frank A. R. Scott, Knoxville,
Oliver P. Temple, Knoxville,
Marye B. Trezevant, Memphis,
Xenophon Wheeler, Chattanooga.
Moses White, Knoxville.

OFFICERS OF THE BOARD.

Charles W. Dabney..........................President
James Comfort ....Treasurer
James W. Gaut..............................Secretary

The following-named gentlemen constitute the faculty of this university at the present time:

Charles W. Dabney, Ph. D., LL. D., President of the University.

Thomas W. Jordan, A. M., LL. D., Dean of the College.

Henry H. Ingersoll, LL. D., Dean of the Law Department.

Mrs. Charles A. Perkins, A. M., Acting Dean of the Woman's Department.

ACADEMIC DEPARTMENT.

In Groups—In the Order of Official Seniority.

William W. Carson, C. E., M. E., Professor of Civil Engineering.

Thomas W. Jordan, A. M., Professor of the Latin Language and Literature.

Charles E. Wait, C. E., M. E., Ph. D., F. C. S., Professor of General and Analytical Chemistry and Metallurgy.

A. M. Soule, Professor of Agriculture.

George F. Mellen, A. M., Ph. D., Professor of Greek and History.

John B. Henneman, M. A., Ph. D. (Berlin), Professor of English.

Cooper D. Schmitt, M. A., Professor of Mathematics.

Charles A. Perkins, Ph. D., Professor of Physics and Electrical Engineering.

Andrew H. Nave (Captain Eleventh Infantry, U. S. A.), Commandant and Professor of Military Science and Tactics.

Charles W. Turner, A. M., Acting Professor of Constitutional History.

James Maynard, M. A., Lecturer on International Law.

Joshua W. Caldwell, M. A., Lecturer on the Constitutional History of Tennessee.

Edward T. Sanford, M. A., B. LL. (Harvard), Lecturer on History of Tennessee.

Jay R. McColl, B. S., Assistant Professor of Mechanical Engineering.

H. J. Darnall, Adjunct Professor of Modern Languages.

Ralph L. Watts, B. Agr., Instructor in Horticulture.

Charles E. Ferris, B. S., Instructor in Drawing.
Samuel M. Bain, A. B., Instructor in Botany.
Charles E. Chambliss, M. S., Instructor in Zoölogy.
Edwin M. Wiley, B. S., Instructor in English.
Weston M. Fulton, B. A., Instructor in Meteorology.
Charles O. Hill, B. A., Instructor in Pharmaceutical Chemistry.
J. Bolton McBryde, C. E., Instructor in Organic and Agricultural Chemistry.

LAW DEPARTMENT.

Charles W. Dabney, Ph. D., LL. D., President of the University.
Henry H. Ingersoll, LL. D., Dean and Professor of Law.
Charles W. Turner, A. M., Associate Professor of Law.
James Maynard, A. M., Lecturer on International Law.
Leon Jourolmon, Lecturer on the Law of Real Property.
Joshua W. Caldwell, A. M., Lecturer on Tennessee Law.
James H. Welcker, A. B., B. LL., Lecturer on Torts.
Edward T. Sanford, A. M., B. LL., Lecturer on the Law of Corporations in Tennessee.

MEDICAL AND DENTAL DEPARTMENT.

Charles W. Dabney, Ph. D., LL. D., President of the University.
Paul F. Eve, M. D., Dean of the Medical Faculty and Professor of Principles and Practice of Surgery, Abdominal, Orthopaedic, and Clinical Surgery.
J. Bunyan Stephens, M. D., Professor of Obstetrics and Clinical Midwifery.
William D. Haggard, M. D., Professor of Gynaecology and Diseases of Children.
William E. McCampbell, A. M., M. D., Professor of Theory and Practice of Medicine and Clinical Medicine.
T. Hilliard Wood, M. D., Professor of Diseases of the Eye, Ear, Nose and Throat.

HISTORY OF KNOXVILLE, TENNESSEE. 385

Hazle Padgett, M. D., Professor of Physiology and General Histology.

W. C. Bilbro, M. D., Professor of Materia Medica, Therapeutics, and Nervous Diseases.

James S. Ward, A. B., M. D., Professor of Medical Chemistry and Demonstrator of Laboratory Medical Chemistry.

William D. Sumpter, M. D., Professor of General Descriptive and Surgical Anatomy, Microscopy and Bacteriology, and Demonstrator of Laboratory Microscopy, Bacteriology and Pathology.

John Bell Keeble, LL. B., Professor of Medical Jurisprudence.

Haley P. Cartwright, M. D., Professor of Physical Diagnosis.

John DeWitt, A. B., LL. B., Professor of Dental Jurisprudence.

William D. Haggard, Jr., M. D., Associate Professor of Gynaecology.

James W. Handly, M. D., Lecturer on Genito-Urinary and Venereal Diseases.

W. R. Sifford, M. D., Assistant to Chair of Surgery, Lecturer on Minor Surgery, and Demonstrator of Laboratory Operative Surgery.

W. S. Noble, M. D., Instructor in Ophthalmoscopy, and Assistant to Chair of Eye, Ear, Nose, and Throat.

Llwellyn P. Barbour, M. D., Lecturer on Tuberculosis.

Daniel Cliff, M. D., Assistant to the Chair of Obstetrics.

Charles A. Robertson, M. D., Assistant to the Chair of Materia Medica and Therapeutics and Lecturer on Pharmacy.

J. Herman Feist, M. D., Lecturer on Dermatology.

Frederick R. Sandusky, D. D. S., Demonstrator-in-Chief.

James B. Jordan, D. D. S., Assistant Demonstrator.

George W. Seay, M. D., Demonstrator of Practical Anatomy.

Perry Bromberg, M. D., Demonstrator of Practical Anatomy.

F. C. Williams, D. D. S., Clinical Instructor.

A. Sidney Page, D. D. S., Clinical Instructor.

J. W. Bryan, D. D. S., Clinical Instructor.

The officers of the agricultural experiment station are as follows:

Charles W. Dabney, president; A. M. Soule, secretary; Ralph L. Watts, horticulturist; J. Bolton McBryde, chemist; Samuel M. Bain, botanist; Charles E. Chambliss, entomologist; Charles A. Mooers, assistant chemist; Frederick H. Broome, librarian.

The following statistics pertaining to the attendance of pupils at this university are taken from the catalogue of 1897-98:

Students in the Academic Department:
1. College students 226
2. University and special students.......................... 39

    Total number in the Academic Department............... 265

Professional Departments:
3. Law Department, at Knoxville............................. 53
4. Medical and Dental Departments, at Nashville.......... 290

                                                                                                   608

Counted twice 10

Total number of students in the University of Tennessee.... 598

Hampden-Sidney Academy was established under the provisions of the congressional act of 1806, which has already been referred to under the history of the University of Tennessee. This act gave to the state of Tennessee 100,000 acres of land, the proceeds of the sale of which were to be devoted to the endowment and maintenance of one academy in each county of the state, the name of the academy established in Knox county being as above. This academy was incorporated with the following trustees: Nathaniel Cowan, John Crozier, Thomas Humes, John Adair and George McNutt. To these trustees there were added the next year the following: Isaac Anderson, Samuel G. Ramsey, Robert Houston, Francis H. Ramsey, and John Sawyers. By an act of 1811 the number of trustees was still further increased by the addition of Thomas McCorry, George Wilson, James Park, Thomas Emmerson, Hugh L. White, and John Hillsman. The board of trustees was organized for the first time April 4, 1812, Hugh L. White being elected president; George Wilson, secretary, and Thomas Emmerson, treasurer. At this same meeting steps were taken to procure suitable teachers for the academy, and as William Park was about to go to Philadelphia, he was requested to select a principal and an assistant teacher. His instructions were as follows as to the kind of president he was to select: "A president of the academy is wanted, who must be a good scholar, capable of teaching the Latin and Greek languages and the sciences. He must, moreover, be a man of genteel deportment and unexceptional moral character. A minister of talent and a considerable show of eloquence would be greatly preferred, and especially one who has heretofore taught with success. To an able teacher the trustees propose to give a salary of $800 per annum." As to the assistant he "must be a man of good moral character, capable of teaching reading, writing, English grammar and arithmetic. One who understands surveying and bookkeeping, also, would be preferred. To such a man the trustees will engage to pay a salary of $500 per annum." The reasons for offering these low salaries were given as follows: "The salubrity of the climate and the cheapness of living render the proposed salaries equal to much larger ones in most places to the eastward."

These preliminaries having been taken, everything seemed to be in readiness for the opening of the academy, but for various reasons it was not opened until January 1, 1817, under the principalship of David A. Sherman, a graduate of Yale college. The building used was that of the East Tennessee College, which had been suspended then since 1809, when occurred the death of President Carrick. Some of the original subscribers to the support of this educational enterprise were John Crozier, Thomas Humes, Hugh L. White, Joseph

C. Strong, Pleasant M. Miller and Calvin Morgan, each of whom gave $100.

In October, 1820, when the trustees of East Tennessee College decided to put their institution again into operation, they elected David A. Sherman president, and Hampden-Sidney Academy and East Tennessee College were united, and from that time on until 1830 the academy had no separate existence. In October, 1830, the trustees of the academy reorganized under a new charter granted by the legislature, electing Dr. Joseph C. Strong president, H. Brown secretary, and James H. Cowan treasurer. This reorganized board secured the services of Perez Dickinson as teacher, he being a young man then recently arrived from Massachusetts, and the academy was reopened in the old college building. Mr. Dickinson remained in charge of the academy until 1832, when he resigned. During the following summer a lot was purchased on Locust street, from Hugh L. McClung, upon which a frame, two-story building for the use of the academy was erected; but the academy did not prosper, and in 1834 it was suspended. By an act of the general assembly passed in 1818 there was appropriated $18,000 annually for the use of county academies, and the trustees determined to reopen Hampden-Sidney. The building having been repaired the academy was again opened, in November, 1839, with Rev. N. A. Penland as principal, who remained nearly two years, when he was succeeded by William D. Carnes, who resigned in October, 1842. From that time on until 1846 the principals were W. S. Williams, J. H. Lawrence and M. Rowley, and in May, 1846, the academy was consolidated with a public school which had been established in Knoxville. This arrangement, however, did not prove satisfactory, and at the expiration of one year the two schools were separated. In October, 1847, Rev. Mr. Elwell became the principal, remaining until 1850, when he was followed by John B. Mitchell. In 1850 a new charter was obtained and the board of trustees was reorganized with

William Swan, president; Joseph L. King, secretary, and James H. Cowan, treasurer. In 1852 Mr. Mitchell accepted a position as teacher in the East Tennessee University, and from that time on until the beginning of the Civil war the academy was in session but a short time. At the close of the war a school was opened in the building by J. K. Payne, but he soon went to the university. March 22, 1866, a few of the old trustees met and reorganized by electing William Heiskell president and James Roberts secretary and treasurer. September 3, 1866, the academy was once more opened, this time by M. C. Wilcox, who continued in charge until January, 1868. The property was then leased for one year to the university for the use of the preparatory department. In 1871 the lot and building were sold, and a new lot at the corner of State and Reservoir (now Commerce) streets was purchased at a cost of $2,500, and in 1876 the erection of a three-story brick building was begun and completed in 1877, which was then rented to the city for the use of the public schools, at a merely nominal rent, and has been so used ever since.

The Knoxville Female Academy was established in 1827, an organization being effected on April 26, by a number of enterprising gentlemen, of which Joseph C. Strong was elected chairman and F. S. Heiskell secretary, and committees were appointed to secure a suitable building and teachers for the proposed seminary. The school began operations in the following September, with John Davis principal, and Mrs. Davis, Miss Morse and Miss Littleford, assistants.

In October of the same year the academy was incorporated by the legislature, with the following board of trustees: F. S. Heiskell, William C. Mynatt, William S. Howell, S. D. Jacobs, A. McMillan, Dr. Joseph C. Strong, Hugh L. White, Robert King, Robert Houston, Matthew McClung, Calvin Morgan, William B. Reese, M. Nelson, James King, James McNutt, James Park and Daniel McIntosh. Two lots adjoining each other on Main street were donated for the uses of the academy by Dr. Joseph C. Strong and Matthew McClung, upon which a building was erected at a cost of about $3,000, and which was completed in January, 1829, John Crozier and Charles McClung each contributing $200, and several others contributing $100 each. John Davis having resigned the principalship he was succeeded by Joseph Estabrook, a graduate of Dartmouth College, under whose management the institution was very successful. Principal Estabrook, in 1834, being elected to the presidency of East Tennessee College, Henry Herrick became the principal of the academy, remained in charge until 1838, and was succeeded by Rev. J. B. Townsend.

Holston Conference of the Methodist Episcopal Church having proposed to patronize the school on condition of being permitted to share in its control, a meeting of the trustees was held in September, 1841, to take this proposition under consideration. The arrangement made was that the conference should appoint four of the thirteen trustees, to which number the trustees were raised, and that the conference should also appoint a board of nine visitors, the trustees and the board of visitors to constitute a joint board for the election of teachers, the academy being thus in effect transferred to the conference. Rev. J. E. Douglass of Alabama was elected principal and under his management the academy was reopened September 1, 1842. Rev. Mr. Douglass resigned at the end of one year and was succeeded by Rev. D. R. McAnally, under whose management the institution was unusually prosperous. In 1846 the charter was so amended as to permit the conferring of degrees, the name was changed to the East Tennessee Female Institute, and in 1847 a movement was started to sever the connection of the institution with the Holston Conference, which movement was at length successful, and the institution again placed under the control of the old board of trustees.

The first graduates from the institute were Margaret H. White, Isabella M. White, Theodosia A. Findley, and Harriet A. Parker, each of whom in 1850 received the degree of "Mistress of Polite Literature." In 1851 Rev. Mr. McAnally resigned the principalship, and there was considerable difficulty in securing a successor. J. R. Dean was at length elected, remaining in charge until 1856, in which year he was succeeded by R. L. Kirkpatrick, who remained in charge until the beginning of the war. After the war the institute was again opened, three trustees, Thomas W. Humes, Horace Maynard and George M. White accepting a proposition from John F. Spence to open a school, provided the building were restored to its former uses by the provost marshal. During the spring of 1866 the school was again in session, and Mr. Spence remained two years. From that time until 1881 the school was not in session, and in this year the building was leased by the board of education for a girls' high school, and was used for this purpose until 1885. From that time on until 1888 Mrs. Lizzie C. French conducted therein a flourishing female seminary.

In the years 1889 and 1890 a new building for this institute was erected on Main street, No. 702, which building is one of the finest school buildings in Knoxville. The building is of brick, the main part being three stories high above the basement. The rooms are large, well lighted and ventilated, and are well supplied with apparatus, books and maps for teaching languages, science, art and history. The principal of this institute since 1890 has been Charles C. Ross, the other teachers at the present time being Miss Emma Jane Oram, Miss Cora M. Stearns, Miss Florence Young and Miss Mary Ogden. There are eighty pupils in attendance. The departments of study are as follows: Kindergarten, primary, preparatory, collegiate and modern languages. The trustees of the school at the present time. together with the officers, are as follows: J. F. J. Lewis, president;* H. L. McClung, Jr., secretary; A. P. White, treasurer; C. M. Mc-

---

*Since deceased and vacancy has not been filled.

Clung, James H. Cowan, C. S. Newman, W. W. Woodruff, E. J. Sanford, Lewis Tillman and C. M. McGhee.

Knoxville College, like most other schools for the children of colored parents, traces its origin to the results of the Civil war. In September, 1862, under the auspices of three presbyteries of the United Presbyterian church, Rev. J. G. McKee opened a school for negroes that flocked into Nashville. This school grew and prospered until the death of Rev. Mr. McKee in 1868. The United Presbyterian church had also other schools for colored children in the South, and at this time it resolved to concentrate on one school, and to elevate the character of that one school by adding thereto the normal feature. In carrying out this idea the general assembly of the church in June, 1869, recommended its board of missions to freedmen to proceed as soon as possible to the establishment of a normal school somewhere in the South, and authorized it to draw upon the church for the necessary funds. But the project was not easily realized, and it was not until 1874 that it was revived with hopes of success. Knoxville appearing to be the most promising location, the Nashville school was removed to Knoxville in September, 1875, and was opened in a building which had been used as a freedmen's school.

The new building erected for the use of this school contained nine rooms for teachers and seven for recitations and was dedicated September 4, 1876, the address being delivered by Rev. R. B. Ewing, D. D. The first principal of the school in Knoxville was Rev. J. P. Wright, assisted by Rev. S. B. Reed, Miss Aggie Wallace and Mattie M. Baldridge. The school opened in this new building September 5, 1876. The name of the institution became Knoxville College, and at the end of one year Rev. J. S. McCullough, D. D., became president and has retained the position ever since. Miss Eliza B. Wallace was lady principal from the opening of the school in Knoxville until her death, December 12, 1897. Besides the main building erected as above stated in 1876, other buildings have been erected as required by the growth of the school. In 1887 a Little Girls' Home and in 1890 a Little Boys' Home were erected, in which children from six to thirteen years of age are cared for. In 1891 this college had an enrollment of 313, ten of whom were state normal students. The property consists of 224 acres of land and three main buildings, besides other buildings, enumerated later on in this sketch, and it is all valued at more than $100,000, the chief support of the institution being received through the board of missions to freedmen of the United Presbyterian church, amounting to about $7,000 per annum.

In 1892 this college was made virtually the colored department of the University of Tennessee.

The object of this college is to fit young men and women with a substantial, practical education. The primary school with kindergarten covers three years of study. The training school follows with four years. The normal school occupies four years more and fits a student for college work, and he then has the choice of the literary course, two years; the agricultural course, three years; the mechanical course, four years; the scientific course, three years; the classical course, five years; the theological course, three years, and the medical course, three years. Besides instruction is given in music, art, military science, etc.

The buildings, located on a rise of ground about two miles west of Knoxville on the Clinton pike, are as follows: The college building, 119x75 feet in size, with an extension 61x43 feet, and is two stories high, contains seventeen rooms, besides a chapel, with a seating capacity of 600.

The McCullough Hall, an L, one front of which is ninety feet and the other seventy-five feet, the depth being forty-three feet. It is three stories high, and contains forty-five rooms in addition to laundry and bath rooms.

Elnathan Hall, rebuilt in 1897-98, to take the place of old Elnathan Hall, burned down December 15, 1896. This is a four-story building, with sleeping and study rooms for sixty girls, and kitchen and dining rooms capable of accommodating 200. It is 90x40 feet, with a rear extension 47x58 feet. Each floor of this building has bath rooms with hot and cold water.

The Little Girls' Home, three stories high, is 60x40 feet in size, and contains study rooms, kitchen and dining room accommodations for fifty girls.

The Little Boys' Home is of the same dimensions as the Little Girls' Home. In these two buildings children from six to sixteen years of age are taken care of for an almost nominal sum.

The Industrial building is two stories high, 61x40 feet, and has a one-story rear extension 30x50 feet. It is equipped for instruction in agriculture and mechanics, including printing.

Four cottages afford homes for the families of the president, professors and others connected with the institution. Four of the main buildings are heated by steam, and all except one cottage are lighted by electricity furnished by a dynamo run by the students.

Boarding and tuition cost each student $6.50 per month, and during vacation $1.50 per week. The girls in this college are required to dress alike, in order to prevent any feeling of superiority or inferiority among them and to promote economy. According to agreement with the University of Tennessee all colored students over fifteen years of age have free tuition, provided they are able to enter any class above the second normal year.

As showing the elevation in study to which the colored students attain in the scientific and classical courses, the courses for the senior years are given, as follows:

Senior Scientific—First term: German, Moral Philosophy, and Chemistry. Second term: German, Mental Philosophy and Chemistry. Third term: German, Mental Philosophy, Chemistry, and Church History—one lesson per week through the year.

Senior Classical—Moral Philosophy, Political Economy and Science of Government, Mental Philosophy, History of Philosophy, Geology, Logic, and Evidences of Christianity, Church history—one lesson a week throughout the year.

Knoxville College is under the care of the United Presbyterian Church of North America, and is sustained mainly by contributions from the various congregations through the board of missions to the freedmen.

It welcomes students of good moral character, without regard to sex, color, or denomination.

BOARD OF CONTROL.

Rev. Joseph Kyle, D. D., Allegheny, Pa.
Rev. D. A. McClenahan, D. D., Allegheny, Pa.
J. J. Porter, Esq., Pittsburg, Pa.
Rev. D. W. Carson, D. D., Burgettstown, Pa.
Rev. W. H. McMillan, D. D., Allegheny, Pa.
Rev. D. F. McGill, D. D., Allegheny, Pa.
H. J. Murdoch, Esq., Treasurer, Pittsburg, Pa.
Peter Dick, Esq., Pittsburg, Pa.
Rev. R. H. Park, Valencia, Pa.
Rev. J. W. Witherspoon, D. D., Cor. Sec., Allegheny, Pa.

Following is the faculty of the college at the present time (January, 1899):

Rev. J. S. McCulloch, D. D., President, Professor of Mental, Moral, and Political Science.

Rev. J. R. Millin, A. M., Principal of Theological Department.

Rev. R. J. Love, A. M., Ph. D., Principal Normal Department and German.

Miss E. Belle Kerr, Principal of Training and Primary Departments.

A. G. Boal, A. B., Greek and Latin.

L. M. Wright, A. B., Agriculture and Chemistry.

W. G. Purdy, C. E., Mechanical Arts and Mathematics.

George LeRoy Brown (Captain Eleventh Infantry, U. S. A.), Military Science and Tactics.

Mrs. Ida M. French, English.

Miss Matilda Wishart, B. S., Physiology and Mathematics.

Miss Agnes Wishart, B. M., Music.

Miss M. Irena Kerr, Teacher of Dress Making and Sewing.

Miss Grace D. Long, Training School.

Miss Maude Brooks, A. B., Primary Work.

Miss Jennie McCahon, Bible Reader.

Miss Emma Pinkerton, Matron.

Miss Maggie McDill, Superintendent of Little Girls' Home.

Miss Anna Rutherford, Superintendent of Little Boys' Home.

Mrs. Mary Wallace, Matron McCulloch Hall.

Miss H. A. Kerr, Matron Elnathan Hall.

R. M. Ginter, Director Printing Department.

The faculty of the medical department of this college is as follows: Rev. J. S. McCullough, D. D., president; E. L. Randall, M. D., theory and practice of medicine and surgery; A. C. Edwards, M. D., anatomy and histology; W. H. Moore, M. D., physiology and obstetrics; John C. Clear, M. D., materia medica, therapeutics and gynecology; W. W. Derrick, M. D., chemistry and physical diagnosis, and J. C. Ford, attorney, medical jurisprudence.

The University School was established in 1889, by Lewis M. G. Baker, M. A., and Charles M. Himel, both of the University of Virginia, who came to Knoxville upon the invitation of several prominent citizens of the place upon a guarantee of $2,000 for the first year. During this first year the school was kept in a rented building on Main street, just west of High street, and a three-story brick building was erected on Highland avenue between Third and Fourth streets, which, on March 23, 1893, was destroyed by fire. During this year a new building was erected at the southeast corner of Highland avenue and Fourth street, four stories high, of brick, and at a cost of $12,000, including furniture. A large lot was purchased on the northwest corner of the same streets, on which a large dining hall was erected, and the entire property of the school is now worth $25,000.

The object of the University School is to prepare boys for college, and was established to meet a demand in the South for a larger number of schools of this character. During the first year the school had thirty-three students, the second eighty-six, the third, 104, and the fourth, 120. Since then the number of students in attendance here has averaged about 100. The boarding department had at first four boarders, has averaged about twelve and now has ten. The intention of the authorities is to largely increase the numbers in the boarding department.

To this school there are two departments, the preparatory and the academic. The preparatory department is designed for boys from eight to thirteen years of age, and the academic department is designed to receive pupils who have completed the preparatory course. Students completing the academic course are admitted without further examination to the University of Tennessee, the University of Virginia, and to Harvard and Yale colleges. The reputation of this school has become so extensive that it has attracted students from as far north and east as Illinois and Connecticut and as far south as Louisiana and Texas.

This school was incorporated December 24, 1891, by Lewis M. G. Baker, Charles M. Himel, C. S. Newman, J. W. Caldwell and Jacob L. Thomas. Following is the faculty at the present time (January, 1899): Lewis M. G. Baker, M. A., instructor in Latin and Greek; Charles M. Himel, instructor in mathematics; H. D. Hoskins, instructor in history and modern languages; and R. W. Peatross, instructor in English.

The main building of this institution contains three stories and a basement. In the first story are the assembly hall, the recitation rooms and cloak rooms; in the second story are an assembly room, recitation room, library and dormitories, and in the third story are dormitories, lavatories and a study hall.

The Tennessee Medical College was established in the summer of 1889, securing the use of a building on the corner of Gay and Main streets, which was opened for students September 2 of that year. Dr. C. C. Lancaster was professor of physiology and Dr. Cawood dean, and Dr. R. M. C. Hill professor of materia medica and therapeutics. When the term opened there were present twenty students, the number soon being increased to forty-seven. In March, 1890, eight students received the degree of doctor of medicine. A dental department was early established. At length a lot was secured at the corner of Cleveland and Dameron streets, in the northern part of the city, and in the spring of 1890 the erection of a building was begun on this lot. When completed this building was four stories high above the basement, and it was opened for students December 12, 1890.

This building was burned to the ground December 3, 1897, involving a loss of $40,000, the building being valued at $15,000 and the contents at $25,000, the whole amount of insurance being only $10,000.

The Tennessee Medical College was incorporated May 20, 1898, the incorporators being Michael Campbell, M. D.; Charles P. McNabb, M. D.; S. M. Miller, M. D.; J. L. Howell, M. D., and B. B. Cates, M. D. The capital stock of the corporation was $20,000 at which it still remains. Under its charter the college was authorized to purchase or receive by gift in addition to the personal property owned by the corporation, real estate for the transaction of its business, and also to purchase and accept any real estate in payment of any debt. The special business for which the incorporation was effected was to open and maintain and operate a medical college in Knoxville in which to teach the knowledge, science and business of medicine and surgery, dentistry and kindred professions, to grant diplomas, confer degrees, and to exercise all other powers lawfully belonging to a medical college.

On June 17, 1898, Dr. M. Campbell made application to the board of mayor and aldermen of Knoxville for the use of the Rose avenue school building for the use of the college, which, after the renewal of the application on July 1, by Dr. Miller, was granted, at an annual rental of $250, and occupied October 1, 1898.

In the first class of students in this college there are forty-six students; in the second, twenty-four, and in the third, or highest class, twenty.

Following are the names of the several members of the faculty of the college, together with the chairs which they respectively fill:

Chas. P. McNabb, M. D., Dean.
S. M. Miller, M. D., Registrar.
Michael Campbell, M. D., Professor of Mental Diseases.
Benj. B. Cates, M. D., Professor Anatomy.
S. M. Miller, M. D., Professor Obstetrics and Gynaecology.
Harry K. Wingert, B. S., Ph. D., M. D., Adjunct Professor Ophthalmology, etc.
J. H. Morton, M. D., Professor Physiology.
S. L. Jones, M. D., Professor Hygiene.
Henry R. Gibson, M. A., LL. D., M. C., Professor Jurisprudence.
John L. Howell, M. D., Professor Surgery.
J. W. Slocum, Ph. D., Professor Chemistry.
S. R. Miller, M. D., Professor Materia Medica and Therapeutics.
E. R. Zemp, M. D., Professor Dermatology and Pediatrics.
H. P. Coile, M. D., Professor Clinical Medicine.
Chas. P. McNabb, M. D., Professor Practice of Medicine.
Henry J. Kelso, B. A., M. D., Professor Operative Surgery.
Benj. F. Young, M. D., Professor Ophthalmology, etc.
W. S. Nash, M. D., Professor Regional and Surgical Anatomy.
W. R. Cochrane, M. D., Professor Bacteriology, Histology.
Olof Olofsson, Secretary and College Clerk.

The Slater Training School for the manual training of colored children was opened in 1885 and incorporated with the following board of trustees: Rev. Dr. Thomas W. Humes, president; E. E. McCroskey, vice-president; Miss Isa E. Gray of Boston, Mass., treasurer; Miss E. L. Austin, secretary; W. S. Mead, C. Seymour, A. S. Jones of Washington, D. C., and Rutherford B. Hayes of Fremont, Ohio. The work of raising funds for the erection of a new building was begun, the citizens of Knoxville contributing $1,000 and friends of the cause in the North contributing nearly $5,000. In 1886 a three-story house was erected and furnished with all the modern improvements. In September of that year the school was opened with 200 pupils, three grades of the city schools being taught in the building, these pupils being required to take a course in the industrial department. A carpenter shop and a printing office were fitted up, and the girls were taught sewing, cooking and housekeeping. There were also established in connection with the school a Young Men's Christian Association and a Shakespeare Club, composed of the teachers of the colored school.

The first year of the existence of this school there were four teachers, who were paid $1,385. The total receipts were $2,821.24 and the expenditures $2,398.34. J. B. Williams of Knoxville was the principal; the sewing school was under the control of Jennie McCahen, and the cooking school under Mrs. N. Bedout. The receipts for the year 1886 were $1,534.35 and the expenditures the same. The new building was erected this year, the funds for which were contributed by friends in Knoxville to the amount of $983; by colored people, $97.23; by Boston people, $2,501; Philadelphia, $1,076; New York, $670, a total of $5,327.23. The building was of wood, 40x50 feet in size and three stories above the basement. S. L. Dickson was principal of this school in 1886-87; George W. Deaderick, 1887-88; S. L. Dickson, 1888-91.

The receipts of the treasurer of this school, Miss Isa E.

Gray, for the year ending April 1, 1888, were $3,712.17, and the expenditures $2,625.65; for the year ending April 1, 1889, the receipts were $4,199.67, and the expenditures, $2,873.19; for the year ending April 1, 1890, the receipts were $4,520.87, and the expenditures $3,166.46, and for the year ending April 1, 1891, the receipts were $4,910.05, and the expenditures $4,645.42.

The year 1891 was the last of the Slater Training School.

Miss Emily L. Austin had then been working as teacher among the colored pupils of Knoxville for a little more than twenty years, coming here in 1870. From the nature of the case and the preconceived sentiments and opinions of the people in reference to the education of colored people, her labors for the first few years were not of the most pleasant kind; but she persevered and her devoted and self-sacrificing work was continued until she saw the Austin School a success, and the Slater Training School firmly established. The building in which this latter school was held became, in 1891, the property of the American Missionary Association, which association has carried on the same work so nobly begun by Miss Austin. During the year 1890-91 the little housekeepers' class was under the control of Mrs. Greenwood; the cooking school under Julia A. Williamson, and the carpenter shop was conducted by Mr. Whisenant, who came here from Talladega, Ala. There were also given lessons in vocal music and in drawing.

Miss Austin, in her farewell report on the Slater School, said: "I came a stranger to Knoxville a little more than twenty-one years ago, and many persons there know how it was in those days, and what the feeling was toward the 'Yankee teacher,' but it has been many years since I have felt that any one regarded me in any way different from a native Tennesseean." She spoke very kindly of J. A. Rayl, E. E. McCroskey, Albert Ruth, Charles Seymour, Dr. J. H. Frazee. S. C. Roney and the Young Men's Christian Association for the manner in which they had all aided her and tried to make her labors lighter.

Miss Austin died in Philadelphia, Pa., May 4, 1897. On June 20, 1897, memorial services were held in her honor in Logan Temple, the building filled with colored people who wished to testify their appreciation of her labors for them. The meeting was presided over by Principal J. W. Manning of the Austin School, and addresses were made by Dr. John H. Frazee, E. E. McCroskey, S. C. Roney, Rev. Isaac Emory and J. W. Manning. A series of resolutions was adopted expressive of the loss the colored people had sustained, and it was resolved to place in the Austin building a tablet to her memory inscribed as follows:

In Memory of

MISS EMILY L. AUSTIN.

Born October 1, 1829; died May 4, 1897.

Founder of the Austin School of Knoxville, Tenn., and for thirty years a devoted friend of the freedmen, fearless of criticism, shrinking from no duty, unswerving in fidelity, coveting on Divine approval. She is gratefully remembered by those whose elevation she sought by educating mind and heart.

"She has done what she could."

Knoxville public schools had their origin in 1870, on the 16th of December of which year the mayor and board of aldermen appointed a committee, consisting of W. A. Henderson, J. A. Rayl, and J. R. Mitchell, to take into consideration the propriety of establishing a system of free schools. At the next meeting of the mayor and board of aldermen the committee made a favorable report, and on January 21, 1871, the matter was submitted to the people and was carried by a vote of 433 to 162. A tax of one mill on the dollar was levied for the support of the public schools, and a board consisting of J. A. Rayl, chairman; W. A. Henderson, and Dr. John M. Boyd was appointed to inaugurate the system. Although much pressed with their own private affairs, these gentlemen gave the subject thorough study, and frequently met for consultation, being assisted in their deliberations by John K. Payne, professor of mathematics in East Tennessee University. Aided by Rev. Dr. Thomas W. Humes the committee procured aid from the Peabody fund to the extent of $2,000, and as soon as suitable buildings could be procured the schools were opened September 4, 1871, in nine houses situated in various parts of the city, with about 1,000 children in attendance.

During the first year the schools were in session ten months, fifteen teachers being employed. In the summer of 1872 the Bell House, originally erected for hotel purposes, at 220 Main street, was secured at a cost of $5,500. The necessary repairs and alterations were made, and with greatly improved facilities for grading, the school was opened in this building in September, 1872. Twenty teachers were employed, several of whom had taught during the preceding year. Until December, 1873, the schools were conducted by a committee appointed by the mayor, this committee consisting of members of the city council holding their offices for one year. On the 12th of December of this year the council passed an ordinance creating a board of education, consisting of five persons, to be elected by the city council for a term of five years, one member retiring each year, there being thus at all times a board of education experienced in the management of the schools, and familiar with their needs. The first board consisted of J. A. Rayl, chairman; Charles D. McGuffey, secretary; J. W. Gaut, treasurer; F. A. Reeve and W. W. Woodruff.

On July 24, 1874, F. A. Reeve tendered his resignation as a member of the board of education, and Matthew McClung was elected to fill the vacancy thus caused. September 19, 1874, a petition was received from Catholic citizens calling attention to the fact that they had erected a schoolhouse on Summit Hill, capable of accommodating a large number of children, which building had been erected at great expense, and as they did not expect any aid from the city in the shape of donations or salaries of teachers, fuel, etc., they would ask the board of aldermen to make them a donation from the city funds to aid them in providing furniture suitable for said building. Upon motion of Alderman Albers the board appropriated $400 toward said purpose, and appointed a committee of three—Lewis, Albers and O'Connor—to supervise the disbursement of the money thus donated.

In 1874 a new schoolhouse was erected at 311 Morgan street, at a cost of $6,000, and a school named the Peabody School was established, and in 1877 the trustees of the Hampden-Sidney Academy erected a new building at 304 State street, which they tendered to the board of education for the use of the public schools, in which the next year a school for girls was opened. In 1881, the schools again having become crowded, the trustees of the East Tennessee Female Institute offered their building on Main street to the board of education, and in it a girls' high school was opened. This building was thus used until 1885, when the girls' high school was transferred to a business block at the corner of Church and Gay streets. In 1886 a very fine public school building was erected at 431 Walnut street for the accommodation of girls from the third to the tenth grades inclusive. This is a three-story brick building, well-fitted and furnished, and cost $35,000.

January 1, 1883, when the ninth ward was admitted into the corporation, graded schools were opened therein in a building previously erected, and this is now a part of the system of public schools.

It was doubtless greatly to the advantage to the public school system of Knoxville that they had at the beginning such a clear-headed and broad-minded man as president of the board of education. In his report to the board of mayor and aldermen, submitted August 15, 1874, he presented the following paragraph on the character of the schools:

"From the first day that the schools went into operation it has been an inflexible rule with those having them in charge, and fully endorsed by the people, 'that no teacher shall be allowed to teach sectarian views in religion or partisan or sectional views in politics.'" If any violation of this rule has occurred it has not been with the knowledge or consent of the board of education. On the other hand, while thoroughly in sympathy with the idea that all children should be fully instructed in moral and religious truth, yet the main idea in public free schools is to give to every child the opportunity of getting a good practical secular education, leaving to the parents and the churches the duty of training up their children in the principles of our holy religion, and especially of teaching the peculiar tenets of their denomination. With such teaching the schools can have nothing to do, and it is the sense of every friend of popular education that they should not attempt it. But educate white and black, rich and poor, Catholic and Protestant, exactly alike, giving no advantage to the one that you do not give to the other, and making all conform to exactly the same rules."

The several superintendents of the schools of Knoxville have been as follows: Alexander Baird, 1871-75; H. T. Morton, 1876-77; R. D'S. Robertson, 1877-81; Albert Ruth, 1881-97; J. H. McCallie, 1897 to the present time.

The members of the board of education since the first election, thus recorded, together with the dates of the expiration of their several terms of office, have been as follows: W. P. Washburn, 1877 and 1881; J. W. Gaut, 1878; J. A. Rayl, 1871 to 1874, 1879, 1881, 1883, 1893 and 1896; James Comfort, 1880; J. L. Lloyd, 1881; T. L. Moses, 1879 and 1884; Leon Jourolmon, 1880; E. J. Sanford, 1882 and 1887; E. E. McCroskey, 1885, 1890, 1895 and 1900; H. H. Ingersoll, 1886 and 1891; N. S. Woodward, 1888; J. H. Cruze, 1889,

1894 and 1899; William H. Lillard, 1892; Sam House, 1893; William M. Baxter, 1896; John Williams, 1897; M. J. Condon, 1898 and 1902; William Epps, 1901.

The officers of the board of education have been as follows:

Presidents—J. A. Rayl, 1871-1881; E. J. Sanford, 1881-85; Henry H. Ingersoll, 1885-87; E. E. McCroskey, 1887-99.

Secretary-Treasurer—James Comfort, 1871-76; W. P. Washburn, 1877-81; E. E. McCroskey, 1881-87.

Secretary—H. H. Ingersoll, 1888-89; William H. Lillard, 1889-93; John Williams, 1893-97; W. H. Lillard, 1897-99.

Treasurers—N. S. Woodward, 1887-88; J. A. Rayl, 1888-93; James H. Cruze, 1893-99.

The school known as the John Sevier School, mentioned above, has a seating capacity of 450. The principals there since 1876 have been as follows: S. A. Craig, 1876-77; E. P. Moses, 1877-81; Douglass Caulkins, 1881-82; J. H. Pitner, 1882-83, Mr. Pitner dying July 7, 1883; W. T. White, 1883-86; Miss J. L. Gammon, 1886-92; James A. Andes, 1892-99. This school was named the John Sevier School October 22, 1897, and dedicated January 30, 1898, a new two-story brick building having been erected.

The Peabody School, located at 311 Morgan street, has had the following principals: W. L. McSpadden, 1875-76; Grace Kimball, 1876-77; S. A. Craig, 1877-79; W. T. White, 1879-83; W. M. Rogers, 1883-86; W. B. Carty, 1886-99.

The Hampden-Sidney School, located at 304 State street, has had the following principals: Mrs. C. A. Lancaster, 1877-78; Miss S. A. Hoadley, 1878-80; Miss M. A. Fletcher, 1880-81; Miss Ida M. Lee, 1881-86; W. M. Rogers, 1886-91; John W. Hyden, 1891-97; W. A. Cate, 1897-98, and J. W. Bryan, 1898-99.

The Ninth Ward School, located at the corner of Tulip and Deaderick streets, has had the following principals: A. O. Roehl, 1883, the year in which Mechanicsville was admitted to the corporation of Knoxville, to 1886; J. H. McCallie, 1886-1897, and J. W. Trotter, 1897-99.

Park Street School, located at No. 304 Park street, West, has had the following principals: Miss Sallie J. Mann, 1883-84; Miss Mary Odell, 1884-93; Miss Minnie Lichtenwanger, 1893-99. This school, since October 22, 1897, has been known as the Jesse A. Rayl School, and the building was dedicated November 23, 1897.

The Girls' High School, located at 431 Walnut street, formerly in the East Tennessee Female Institute building, from 1881 to 1885, and then in the Barton block at the corner of Gay and Church streets from 1885 to 1886, when it was transferred to its own new building at 431 Walnut street, has had the following principals: Miss M. A. Fletcher, 1881-83; Mrs. M. A. Bowen, 1883-84; Miss Francis M. King, 1884-85; Mrs. M. S. Cummins, 1885-86; W. T. White, 1886-99.

The numbers graduated from this high school have been as follows: 1882, 17; 1883, 19; 1884, 11; 1885, 9; 1886, 13; 1887, 15; 1888, 16; 1889, 18; 1890, 16; 1891, 14; 1892, 15; 1893, 15; 1894, 13; 1895, 25; 1896, 16; 1897, 22; 1898, 32; 1899, 44.

The Austin School for colored children, named in honor of Miss Emily L. Austin, and located at No. 327 Central avenue, originated in the following manner:

On June 20, 1879, Chairman Rayl of the board of education stated to the board of mayor and aldermen that Miss Emily L. Austin of Philadelphia, Pa., and Miss Isa E. Gray of Boston, Mass., had informed him of the fact that certain generous citizens of Philadelphia, Boston, New York, Newark and other places in the North, had subscribed $6,500 with the view of aiding the citizens of Knoxville in building a schoolhouse for colored children, and that this money was forthcoming as soon as the city had complied with the terms of the subscription. It was therefore resolved by the board of mayor and aldermen that the money be accepted in trust and that the honor of the city be pledged to the donors that the whole amount should be used for the purpose of completing the building already commenced by the city of Knoxville, to be used for a school building for colored children residing within the corporate limits of the city, and that the city would, as previously, furnish the said children free tuition in the same.

This school has had the following principals: J. J. O'Shea, 1876-78; J. S. Fowler, 1878-81; J. W. Manning, 1881-99.

Fairview School, for colored pupils, located at No. 1624 Dora street, has had the following principals: Joshua S. Cobb, 1883-85; Mrs. Blanche V. Brooks, 1885-91; W. H. Hannum, 1891-95; Joshua S. Cobb, 1895-98, and W. J. Causler, 1898-99. A new building was erected on Clinton street for this school in 1897, and the name of the school changed to the Horace Maynard School, in honor of the Hon. Horace Maynard. This new building was dedicated November 18, 1897.

King's Chapel School, for colored children, located at No. 606 Payne street, has had the following principal: S. L. Dickson, 1891-99. A new building was erected for this school in 1897, at the corner of Kentucky and Campbell streets, and named Heiskell School, in honor of Hon. S. G. Heiskell, then mayor of the city. It was dedicated November 11, 1897.

In 1887 it was determined to give such colored pupils as were prepared for it a course of high school study, and in 1888 the first class of such pupils was graduated from the colored high school. The class was composed of four members, viz.: Augustus David Hodge, William Lineas Maples, Priscilla Blount Manning and Mary Lelia Moffet. To this class E. E. McCroskey, president of the board of education of the city of Knoxville, delivered an address, full of historical knowledge and of good advice not only to the class itself, but also to the race to which it belonged. After paying a high tribute to Miss Emily L. Austin, Mr. McCroskey said: "You are indebted to her in an obligation of gratitude you will never be able to discharge. She raised the larger part of the money that is assigned exclusively to your people, and has given much of her time to bring about practical methods of instruction in the line of useful education. Some years ago she established an industrial school, now called the Slater Training School, and although some of your race have said that it was a white man's trick to get a nigger to work, yet it is the place where the young people can learn something that will be of lasting benefit to them." Mr. McCroskey said much that would be of interest to quote, but want of space forbids.

In 1889 there were no graduates from this high school. In 1890 there were 3; in 1891, 1; 1892, 5; 1893, 6; 1894, 5; 1895, 2; 1896, 6; 1897, 5; 1898, 9, and in 1899, 6.

The West Knoxville public schools were organized March 18, 1888, with one principal and six teachers, and 215 pupils, and for the remainder of that school year were under the control of a board of five school commissioners appointed by the mayor and consisting of W. H. Simmonds, William Rule, W. W. Woodruff, J. F. Gallaher, and James H. Cowan. An organization was effected by the election of W. H. Simmonds, president, and James H. Cowan secretary and treasurer. The above-named commissioners were elected a board of education March 16, 1889, but soon afterward Dr. H. P. Coile succeeded W. H. Simmonds as a member of the board, and their respective terms expired as follows, together with their successors: J. F. Gallaher, 1891; William Rule, 1892; W. W. Woodruff, 1893; Dr. H. P. Coile, 1894, and James H. Cowan, 1895; J. F. Gallaher, 1896; Dr. J. M. Masters, successor to James H. Cowan, resigned, 1895; E. H. Flenniken, 1897; F. K. Huger, successor to Dr. H. P. Coile, 1894; E. C. Scaggs, successor to Dr. J. M. Masters, moved out of the city, 1895; J. E. Platt, successor to E. H. Flenniken, deceased, 1897; Leon Jourolmon, 1898; F. K. Huger, 1899.

The officers of the board of education were as follows: Presidents—W. H. Simmonds, as above stated; W. W.

Woodruff, 1889-91; H. P. Coile, 1891-93; Leon Jourolmon, 1893. Secretary-Treasurer—James H. Cowan, 1888-92. Secretary—J. C. Tucker, 1892-93, and Treasurer—J. M. Masters, 1892-93; E. C. Scaggs, 1893.

The superintendents of the schools have been as follows: J. C. Tucker, 1888-94; R. Porter, 1894 to 1897; W. M. Rogers, 1897 to 1899.

These schools were free to all persons between the ages of six and twenty-one years living within the corporate limits of West Knoxville, and were divided into primary, intermediate, grammar and high schools, and also into white and colored schools, during the first full year of their existence there being seven teachers for the white schools and one for the colored school. From September 1, 1889, to June 6, 1890, the entire cost of the schools was $4,193.75, the average salaries paid the teachers being $341.87.

During the second year the schools were kept in a building on Highland avenue, with an overflow school in the old building, the total cost of the schools for this year being $5,118.52, the average wages paid the teachers, of whom there were ten, including the principal of the entire system and the teacher of the colored school, being $338.53. In 1890-91 the Highland Avenue School had six teachers, the Rose Avenue School, four teachers, and the Riverside School (colored), one. The same numbers prevailed during the next succeeding year. In 1891-92 the schools cost $6,492.97, and in 1893-94, $5,946.94.

At the beginning of the year 1893-94 the Riverside School was discontinued, the pupils being sent to the Knoxville City schools and to Knoxville College, thereby effecting a saving to West Knoxville of $200.

North Knoxville public schools were organized in September, 1889, by Prof. Charles Mason, and for most of the first year were taught in three small buildings on Gratz street, which had been turned over to the city by the school commissioners of the Second district of Knox county. In this work of organization Prof. Mason was assisted by Mrs. Kate C. Callaway, Miss Mary McDonough, and Miss Jennie B. Irwin. These three buildings proving too small to accommodate the number of pupils desiring to attend, and hence the board of education purchased two lots on the corner of Alexander and Tennor streets, upon which a new school building was erected and which was used for the schools during the last six weeks of the school year of 1889-90. As this building furnished room for most of the pupils the previous practice of receiving them for half-day sessions only, in order that all might attend during a portion of the day, was abandoned, and the following additional teachers employed: Miss Miriam Cocke, Miss Jennie B. Ramsey, and Miss Josie Stansberry. The twenty colored pupils of the city of North Knoxville were sent to the Austin School in Knoxville.

Prof. Mason having at the close of the first school year resigned was succeeded by Prof. J. M. McCallie, who remained principal of the schools until the close of the school year 1893-94, and was then succeeded by the present principal, Prof. J. R. Lowry.

The several members of the board of education of North Knoxville were as follows, together with the years in which their terms expired: W. L. Welcker, 1891 and 1896; W. R. Cooper, 1892, 1897, and 1902; John W. Ward, 1893 and 1898; Frank A. Moses, 1894; J. S. McDonough, 1895; D. L. Ross, 1896 and 1901; J. P. Haynes, 1898; W. A. Wray, 1899, and J. E. Johnson, 1900. The terms of the several members all terminated upon the consolidation of the three corporations and the consequent consolidation of the schools. December 31, 1897, when the three corporations were about to become one, the board of mayor and aldermen of North Knoxville resolved that the superintendent, teachers and janitor of their schools and other employes of North Knoxville were entitled to receive their salaries and wages for January, 1898, and of course subsequent months, from the corporation of Knoxville, and they urged the board of education of West

412   HISTORY OF KNOXVILLE, TENNESSEE.

Knoxville to unite with them in a demand upon the mayor and aldermen of Knoxville for such compensation.

The officers of the board of education of North Knoxville were as follows: Presidents—J. S. McDonough, 1889-94; W. A. Wray, 1894-97. Secretary-Treasurers—Frank A. Moses, 1889-94; D. L. Ross, 1894-95; W. R. Cooper, 1895-97.

The scholastic population of North Knoxville was as follows for the years given: 1891, 765; 1892, 818; 1893, 831; 1894, 851; 1895, 865; 1896, 982; 1897, 1,110.

The average monthly wages paid the teachers in these schools were as follows: 1890-91, $38.75; 1891-92, $40.56; 1892-93, $45.45; 1893-94, $43; 1894-95, $43.32; 1895-96, $42.37; 1896-97, $38.82.

The following table covering the last twenty years of the public schools, including the statistics for the first year of the consolidated schools, will be found both comprehensive and interesting:

Years.	Scholastic Population.	Boys.	Girls.	Average Number Belonging.	Average Number Attending.	Per cent of Enrolment on Scholastic Population.	Total Cost Per Year of Schools.	Total Cost Per Pupil Belonging.	No. of Teachers.	Average Salaries Paid Teachers.
1878-79..	2,100	684	825	1,009	930	68.00	$13,659.83	$13.54	26	$442.50
1879-80..		786	973	1,328	1,253	64.00	15,701.21	11.25	..	416.65
1880-81..		914	1,070	1,526	1,458	65.00	15,701.21	10.28	26	442.91
1881-82..	3,044	970	1,167	1,590	1,512	70.00	16,134.01	10.12	30	421.67
1882-83..	3,196	1,068	1,197	1,607	1,519	70.87	19,920.69	11.61	34	435.48
1883-84..	4,315	1,314	1,423	2,054	1,953	63.45	24,421.30	11.89	44	442.08
1884-85..	4,817	1,304	1,477	2,216	2,142	57.73	27,753.97	12.52	50	461.21
1885-86..	5,180	1,360	1,427	2,305	2,220	53.80	32,986.78	14.31	57	462.36
1886-87..	5,637	1,363	1,571	2,357	2,250	52.05	31,865.82	13.52	55	469.91
1887-88..	6,239	1,531	1,729	2,586	2,489	52.25	31,929.36	12.35	55	478.18
1888-89..	7,375	1,506	1,722	2,615	2,516	43.76	37,870.14	14.48	60	523.64
1889-90..	8,327	1,517	1,771	2,643	2,540	39.48	40,385.85	15.28	61	507.50
1890-91..	8,408	1,536	1,844	2,699	2,598	40.20	41,892.34	15.52	64	583.65
1891-92..	10,083*	1,653	1,917	2,800	2,697	35.46	46,680.58	16.39	69	556.75
1892-93..	10,232*	1,505	1,697	2,551	2,457	31.29	47,968.54	18.80	68	586.14
1893-94..	8,994	1,366	1,617	2,512	2,442	33.16	45,404.36	15.90	62	592.85
1894-95..	9,112	1,504	1,654	2,583	2,489	34.66	41,120.69	15.91	60	559.55
1895-96..	9,160	1,486	1,606	2,644	2,574	33.75	38,866.36	14.70	58	530.44
1896-97..	9,795	1,564	1,637	2,744	2,670	32.68	39,072.69	14.24	62	505.76
1897-98..	14,272	2,090	2,419	3,906	3,774	33.68	48,265.93	12.25	91	487.69

*Including Tenth Ward.

Jesse Addison Rayl, one of the founders and always a strong friend of the public schools of Knoxville, was born near Russellville, Hamblen county, Tenn., in 1825, and graduated at Tusculum College in 1846. From the time of his graduation until 1849 he was engaged in teaching, and then removing to Knoxville, he entered the mercantile house of Cowan & Dickinson, at the corner of Gay and Main streets. In 1851 or 1852 he formed a partnership with F. W. Vanuxem, under the firm name of Rayl & Vanuxem, they keeping a large stock of miscellaneous books. Mr. Rayl remained in the book business until the beginning of the war, when he went to Lexington, Ky., and was there engaged in the same business as a member of the firm of Rayl & Taylor until the close of the war, when he returned to Knoxville, and here became engaged in the general merchandise business with S. B. Boyd. Selling his interest in this firm, he became part owner of a paper mill at Middlebrook, in which he was interested until 1888, when he sold out and retired.

In connection with a few others, Mr. Rayl secured the first tax levy for the public schools of Knoxville, was a member of the first board of education and was a member of the board for twenty-three years, and served as president of the board ten years. He was also active in the work of the associated charities and for forty years was a ruling elder in the First Presbyterian Church. For six years he was superintendent of the Sunday-school, and in all his work he was enthusiastic and efficient. His death occurred January 13, 1897. When it became necessary, on account of physical inability to longer perform the duties of his position, for him to resign as a member of the board of education, in 1897, the board passed a series of resolutions, of which the following may be copied here:

"Resolved, That the people of Knoxville owe to Mr. Rayl a lasting debt of gratitude for the able and efficient manner in which he has served their interests without compensation, and that he should ever be held in grateful recollection for these services."

CHAPTER XVII.

CHURCH HISTORY.

The Pioneer Presbyterians—Rev. Samuel Doak—Knoxville's First Church—Early Methodists—Bishop Asbury's First Visit—First Baptist Organization—Good Works of Rev. Samuel Carrick—Rev. Isaac Anderson—Knoxville Churches Grow and Multiply—Many Large and Flourishing Churches Now in the City.

THE effects of the religious sentiment and of religious teaching upon the minds of men are often great and occasionally astonishing. These effects are equally astonishing when we contemplate the higher end of the diapason of this sentiment as when we contemplate the lower end. At the lower end of this range of sentiment are seen many persons cruelly beaten, or scourged or burned to death, by their contemporaries, merely for the reason that they entertained opinions and sentiments upon religious and theological subjects that differed from those entertained by their persecutors; while at the other or higher end of the scale are found men and women who so construe the beautiful doctrines of "Peace on earth and good-will toward men," to mean absolute non-resistance to all forms of oppression and wrong against individuals, communities and nations, and to be so thoroughly imbued with this construction as to refuse to defend themselves against any kind of attack, and to believe that war in any of its forms and for any possible purpose is wholly unwarranted because wholly un-Christian.

The fate of the Moravian Indians, so familiar to all students of American history, is a most impressive commentary upon the practical workings of a non-resistance creed. The Quaker religion of peace, which had been taught them by zealous and indefatigable German missionaries, followers of Count Zinzendorff, and which forbade them to play a true man's part in defending themselves against aggressions on the part of the white man, led to the most dire results, which fell not only upon themselves, but also upon their white foe. No greater mistake can be made than to place a good man at the mercy of a bad one, the good man having had it instilled into his mind until the doctrine becomes a part thereof, that he must not on any account defend himself against the encroachments and aggressions of the bad; for entire loss of property, family and friends and even life itself may be the result.

But on the other hand it may be said that if all men were alike indoctrinated and actuated at all times by the spirit of peace and good will toward men, there would be no aggression or wrong of any kind to resist, which is certainly true. To bring about this condition of things is perhaps the great mission of religion and religious institutions. To so teach mankind that there shall be as little aggression as possible, to so develop and build up the character that men will not do unto others as they would not have others do unto them, and to do unto others as they would have others do unto them, is a grand and noble work, but so long as a large portion of mankind, even in those countries which are included within the realm of Christendom, is actuated by what may be termed human and selfish motives, so long as the rights of others are so frequently and flagrantly violated and trampled under foot, just so long must every man, no matter what his theories may be, be ready at all times to defend himself and family, and others that may be suffering from aggression, and to recognize the fact that sometimes in order to act on the defensive he must act on the aggressive. Men can not all live in the world which is to a great extent as it ought not to be, as if it were as it ought to be.

It was about the time of the beginning of the French and Indian war of 1758-60 that the great wave of emigration, which has since then swept over the entire territory of the United States to and even beyond the eastern shores of the Pacific Ocean, first reached the eastern portions of what is now the state of Tennessee. In the chapters devoted to the settlement of that part of Tennessee more immediately tributary to Knoxville, the sources whence sprang the emigration to this state and the character and characteristics of the early settlers have been sufficiently dwelt upon. In this chapter an attempt is made to depict their religious characteristics only. From the time of the beginning of settlements in the then wilderness of Tennessee until the Indian tribes were completely dispossessed, the dangers were numerous and great. Many of the brave and hardy pioneers were killed from ambush and in open warfare; but it is altogether probable that the question of danger was of secondary consideration. It was in 1766 that Col. James Smith made his famous exploration of the valleys of the Cumberland and the Tennessee rivers, and upon his return to his home in Western North Carolina, by his graphic accounts of the beauty and fertility of the valleys which he had visited he excited in the minds of the people of North Carolina, Virginia, Maryland and Pennsylvania an urgent desire to emigrate to this new El Dorado of the West. The settlers who first came to this state were to a considerable extent hardy backwoods pioneers from the four states above named. From the watershed that separates the headwaters of the streams that flow into the Atlantic from those that flow into the Ohio river, the emigrants to a great extent from one state resembled those from another. The backwoodsmen from Pennsylvania had little in common with the peaceful Quakers that lived between the Delaware and Susquehanna rivers; nor had their near kinsmen of the Blue Ridge and Hawks mountains any closer affinity of disposition and manners with the aristocratic planters that lived near the Atlantic coast in Eastern Virginia and Eastern North Carolina. The backwoodsmen above mentioned were by birth Americans, but of mixed race, the dominant strain being that of the Pennsylvania Irish, often called Scotch-Irish, and they were in the main believers in the doctrines of John Calvin and John

Knox. They were in the main descended from the Scotch, yet there were among them Englishmen, a few French Huguenots, and some of the ancient Milesian Irish. Andrew Jackson, Samuel Houston, David Crockett and James Robertson were of Presbyterian Irish ancestry; John Sevier was of French Huguenot descent; Shelby was of Welsh extraction, and Daniel Boone and George Rogers Clarke were of English blood.

The early Presbyterians were extremely obstinate in their views. They despised the Catholics, whom their ancestors had conquered, and had but little affection for the Episcopalians, by whom they had themselves been oppressed. They took especial pride in the warlike renown of their forefathers who had fought under Oliver Cromwell, and who had taken part in the battle of the Boyne. The great fact in connection with the early settlement of East Tennessee and Western North Carolina was this—that the immigrants to those two portions of these two states came principally from Western Pennsylvania and secondarily from the Carolinas, and that they differed essentially from the inhabitants of the seacoast counties of the states in question, Pennsylvania, Virginia and North Carolina. They were in the main Irish Presbyterians. They were related to the Covenanters; they interpreted the Bible to suit themselves, and chose their own clergymen. In the stern warfare of the frontier they may have lost much of their religion, but still they had meeting houses and school houses. The Episcopalians, the Baptists and the Methodists did not begin to appear in these frontier Western settlements until about the time of the breaking out of the American revolution, and when they did appear they were of a different mold from their Presbyterian predecessors, who were often gloomy, zealous and earnest, often narrow-minded and even bigoted, but still they were a great power for good in the communities in which they labored.

Perhaps there was nowhere greater necessity for the exercise of their influence, for in the backwoods there were many lawless people, who hated that which was good because it was approved of by others, and did wrong for the sake of doing wrong. They lived lives of abandoned wickedness, and often formed themselves into half-secret organizations and drove out both magistrates and ministers and killed without scruple those who dared to interfere. Under such circumstances the good men of the communities found it necessary to form similar associations and to put down the wicked with ruthless severity. In such cases had the peaceful principles of the Quakers been allowed by the good people to have full scope, the good people themselves would have been exterminated. But when the true nature of the great majority of these backwoodsmen was discovered it was found that they were at heart deeply religious as well as to a great extent superstitious. Many of their cabins contained Bibles and most of them refrained from labor and even hunting on Sunday. As has been stated, they generally preferred Calvinism to Episcopalianism, and they preferred the latter to Catholicism; but with all of this their hearts were not stirred to the depths until Methodism worked its way into the wilderness.

The early preachers, in common with the other early settlers, tilled their fields, with rifles in their hands, and on Sunday they delivered their discourses with as much earnestness and eloquence, if not with as much scholarship and elegance, as do their successors of the present day. They firmly believed they were carrying out the will of the Lord in dispossessing the Canaanites in the form of the Red Man, and that they were conquering the country for the occupancy of the truly chosen people and the only true believers in the Word.

If we are to follow Phelan, the first minister that came to live in East Tennessee was the Rev. Samuel Doak, who was a son of Samuel and Jane (Mitchell) Doak, who had emigrated from Ireland, settled in Chester county, Pa., removed thence to Augusta county, Va., and who were "old side" Presbyterians. Rev. Samuel Doak was born in 1749, married Esther Montgomery, sister of Rev. John Montgomery, and was for two years tutor in Hampden-Sidney College of Prince Edward county, in which institution he studied theology. Having been licensed by Hanover Presbytery, and having preached for some time in Virginia, he removed to Sullivan county, Tenn., and thence in a short time to Washington county, where he purchased a farm upon which he built a church, which some say was the first church building erected in the state. He founded Salem congregation and preached in the eastern part of the state for many years.

Other early Presbyterian preachers were Rev. Samuel Houston, Rev. Hezekiah Balch and Rev. Samuel Carrick, all of the Hanover Presbytery, and all of them of Scotch-Irish descent.

"In 1788 the Presbytery of Abingdon, formed in 1785, was united with the synod of Carolina. Here we see the first introduction of Presbyterianism into Tennessee, for the Abingdon Presbytery lay almost entirely in this state. It was first upon the ground and in it were leading figures of the state. They were men of strong characters and the minds of men had not yet been turned to spiritual affairs. Besides this they were practical school-teachers. Subsequent events alone prevented the complete ascendancy of Presbyterianism in Tennessee and the Southwest."*

The Rev. Charles Cummins (Cummings) deserved mention earlier in this sketch. His experience was similar to that of other early pioneer preachers. According to Ramsey, it was the custom of Mr. Cummins on Sunday morning to dress himself neatly, put on his shot pouch, shoulder his rifle, mount his horse and ride to church, where he would meet his congregation, each man with his rifle in his hand. Entering the church he would walk gravely through the

---

*Phelan.

crowd, ascend his pulpit, and after depositing his rifle in one corner of it, so as to be ready for any emergency, commence the solemn services of the day.

When Knoxville was laid out a lot was reserved for the site of a church, which church was built in 1810.

In 1788 the members of Abingdon Presbytery were Charles Cummins, Hezekiah Balch, John Cossan, Samuel Houston, Samuel Carrick and James Balch. Rev. Samuel Doak joined in 1793 and Gideon Blackburn in 1794.

One of the first difficulties in connection with religious opinion arose in 1792, when "the General Assembly determined, in answer to a question from the Synod of North Carolina, that those who professed a belief in universal salvation through the mediation of Jesus Christ, should not be admitted to the sealing ordinance." In 1796 great excitement existed in Abingdon Presbytery because of the publication by Hezekiah Balch of certain articles of faith which greatly scandalized many members of the church. The result of this excitement was that Charles Cummins, Edward Crawford, Samuel Doak, Joseph Lake and James Balch withdrew from Abingdon Presbytery and formed an independent presbytery. Later when Hezekiah Balch had been suffered to go without discipline, by merely apologizing for certain abusive epithets, the Independent Presbytery withdrew, but afterward by submission was reinstated.

Abingdon Presbytery was then divided into two, Doak, Cummins, Lake, and James Balch being members of Abingdon, and Hezekiah Balch, Cossan, Carrick, Henderson and Blackburn being members of Union Presbytery.

This division in the Presbyterian church showed that when men had time to think for themselves upon doctrinal points, uniformity of belief on theological subjects is uniformly dispelled, because men are differently constituted and differently educated. It was in this way that the Reformation came, afterward the Presbyterian Covenanters, later the Methodist revival in England, and still later the Cumberland Presbyterian Church in Tennessee. All of these were perfectly natural movements or evolutions of thought in the minds of men, and yet none of them perhaps is the ultimate belief of mankind upon religious or theological subjects.

In 1783 when Holston circuit embraced East Tennessee and a portion of Virginia, Rev. Jeremiah Lambert was appointed thereto, the first Methodist preacher in this state. At the end of his first year he reported seventy-six members. In 1784 Rev. Henry Wills succeeded Mr. Lambert, and although he did not increase the membership, yet he was a useful man. In 1785, the year in which Methodism in America was placed upon an independent footing, Mr. Wills was elder in the district embracing Holston, and Richard Swift and Michael Gilbert were on the circuit. Other early Methodists were Revs. Mark Whitaker and Mark Moore. In 1787 Holston circuit was divided into Holston and Nollichucky circuits, and the next year two more were added.

The general history of the times fully informs us as to the tumult and discord into which the people were thrown over the question of the continued existence of the state of Franklin, and it was in 1788, while these troubles were pending, that one of the great historic characters of the religious world opportunely arrived on the scene. This man was Francis Asbury, who reached the head of Watauga, April 28, and who in his journal says: "The people are in discord about the old and new state, two or three men having been killed," etc. Bishop Asbury arrived at Nelson's, and preached from Hebrews vi:11, 12. Later he reached Owen's, and Huffacre's and Keywood's, holding conference at the latter place for three days. This was the first conference west of the mountains. Ramsey says: "The novelty of such an assemblage in the wilds of Watauga, its mission of benignity and peace, the calm dignity and unpretentious simplicity of the venerable Bishop, all conspired to soothe and quiet and harmonize the excited masses, and to convert partisans and factionists into brothers and friends."

The influence of the Methodist preacher upon the early and later life of the people in Tennessee is thus depicted by Phelan:

"The observant traveler who passes through Mexico and who sees the little shrines along the roadside, the smooth-faced priests, or the mendicant friar with pendent rosary and bare feet upon the streets, need not be told the religious life of the people. In like manner the signs of Methodism, though in a measure now fading away before the incoming tide of a general laxity of faith, are equally apparent to him who studies the history of the present. What the Catholic church is in Mexico, the Methodist church is in Tennessee. To follow its footsteps would be foreign to our purpose, but it would be impossible to understand the inner life of the people and the organization of society unless we know the great instruments which first gave bent to the religious impulses of the early settlers. Perhaps it would be proper to say instrument, for without doing injustice to the able and learned successors of Craighead, and without overlooking the Tennesseeans who added a powerful branch to the already numerous Protestant denominations in America, it may be said that the religious life of the state is to-day the direct outcome of the exertions of the early Methodist itinerants. Other denominations have followed in the wake of civilization. The Methodist circuit rider led it. What the friar, the adventurous padre, was in the early day of Mexican settlement, the circuit rider has been in this state, and the evidences of his work and influence are upon every hand. The Sunday of to-day is the Sabbath which we inherit. The silent theater, the houses from which the sound of music and mirth are banished, the empty streets, the calm stillness of the day, in these things we see the signs of his influence. The career of the circuit rider both individually and collectively renewed in a great measure the romantic memories of the medieval church militant. * * * The circuit rider was the embodiment of a sacred and enthusiastic zeal which held in light esteem both the dangers and allurements of the world. And indeed he was a man whose like has not often been seen. His limitations were decided and palpable, but they were not repulsive. He was bigoted as a Christian, but tolerant as a churchman. He believed in the Bible with a literal faith, which in the present day of Renan and Strauss seems to have disappeared from the face of the earth," etc., etc.

The Baptists were also early on the ground. Rev. Tidence Lane organized a congregation in the eastern part of the state in 1779. But it was not until about 1790 that they began the work of organizing churches in Knox county. The oldest Baptist church in Knox county, still in existence, is Little Flat Creek Church, which was organized in 1796. Among the earliest Baptist ministers in Knox county the following names are given: Revs. William Johnson, Isaac Barton, Richard Wood, Elijah Rogers, Thomas Hudiburgh, Duke Kimbrough, Robert Fristoe, Thomas Hall, Richard Newport and West Walker. These men, like their Methodist brethren, were of limited education; but their religious zeal and fervid eloquence were well adapted to the majority of their congregations, and the numbers in these congregations increased probably more rapidly than they would otherwise have done. In fact, the membership of the Baptist churches, in the aggregate, soon outnumbered that of both the Presbyterians and Methodists, and it is still in the lead.

But as the Presbyterians were first in evidence in East Tennessee, and as they have for this reason been given the preference in treating of the various religious denominations in this work, the history of the individual Presbyterian churches will now be briefly traced, the other churches coming in their regular chronological order.

With reference to the organization of the first Presbyterian church in Knoxville, Ramsey says: "With pious regard and consideration for the church and religion of his fathers, the proprietor of Knoxville designated a lot for the erection of a house of public worship. The barracks, the court house, the grove above the mouth of White creek, on the river bank, were at first substituted for this purpose, and it was not until 1810 that a church edifice was erected on this lot. An adjoining square was afterward designated to a purpose scarcely less important—the instruction and education of youth—the entire square between Gay and State streets, and State and Boundary streets, being appropriated to Blount College."

In 1789 or 1790, Rev. Samuel Carrick preached to a very large congregation at the Indian mound which stood at the fork of the French Broad and Holston rivers. A second sermon was preached there immediately after the conclusion of the first, the second by Rev. Hezekiah Balch. Soon afterward other religious services were held at the same place, and a church was organized there by the Rev. Samuel Carrick, which was named Lebanon-in-the-fork, which name was later abbreviated to Lebanon. Soon after becoming pastor of the Lebanon Church, Rev. Mr. Carrick organized the First Presbyterian Church at Knoxville, most of the first members of this church having been members of the Lebanon Church. The first ruling elders of the Knoxville Church were James White, George McNutt, John Adair, Archibald Rhea, Sr., Dr. James Cozby and Thomas Gillespie. Rev. Mr. Carrick continued pastor of this church until his death, in 1809, and the church was then without a pastor until 1812, when Rev. Thomas H. Nelson was installed. Religious services had up to this time been held in the barracks and in the court house, but during the year 1811, under the inspiration of a sermon preached by Rev. Samuel G. Ramsey, three commissioners were appointed to contract for and superintend the erection of a church edifice, these commissioners or building committee being John Crozier, Joseph C. Strong and James Park. This duty they performed, the work upon the meeting house, which was of brick, beginning in the fall of 1812, and the work upon the building being sufficiently far advanced to permit of the occupancy of it that fall, though it was not completely finished and furnished until 1816. When thus completed there was a debt upon the congregation of $529.17, which was assumed by the three members of the building committee mentioned above. The lot, as stated earlier in this chapter, had been donated by Col. James White.

Rev. Mr. Nelson remained in charge of this church as pastor until his death in 1838, under his ministrations 204 names being added to the rolls. The following elders had been elected during his incumbency: Thomas Humes, James Campbell, John Craighead, Moses White, Robert Lindsey, James Craig, Dr. Joseph C. Strong, James Park and William Bark.

During this long pastorate, however, all had not been peace and harmony in this congregation. Soon after the completion of the house of worship, as above narrated, a disaffection arose among the members, and in 1818 those thus dissatisfied sent up a petition to Union Presbytery for permission to organize a new congregation, giving as a reason the insufficient accommodations of the church building. By the other members of the church this was considered as a mere pretext, the real reason being, as they saw it, the tendency in the minds of those desiring to withdraw being toward "Hopkinsianism."

Hopkinsianism is a peculiar form of Calvinism, which, though it embraces most of the doctrines of Calvin, yet it entirely rejects the doctrine of imputation, both the imputation of the sin of Adam and of the righteousness of Christ. But the fundamental doctrine of Hopkinsianism is that all virtue and true holiness consist in disinterested benevolence, and that all sin is selfishness. That form of self love which leads men to give their first regard to their own eternal welfare is condemned by those who hold to this system as sinful.

The petition for a separate church organization was refused by the presbytery, and it then went up to the synod of Tennessee on appeal. A remonstrance was also sent up, which the synod disregarded, overruled the decision of the presbytery and ordered the petitioners to organize the Second Presbyterian Church. An appeal was taken by the First Presbyterian Church to the General Assembly of 1820, but the decision and order of the synod were allowed to stand.

After the death of Rev. Mr. Nelson, as related above, the pulpit of the First Church was supplied successively by the Revs. Samuel Y. Wyley, Joseph I. Foot, Charles D. Pigeon and Reese Happersett, but none of them remained more than a few months. In 1841 Rev. Robert B. McMullen, at that time a professor in the East Tennessee University, became pastor, and remained with the church until the latter part of 1858, when he resigned to become president of Stewart College at Clarksville. In 1859 the Rev. W. A. Harrison was elected pastor and he remained until February, 1864, when he was sent South by the Federal military authorities.

In March, 1855, a new church edifice, which had been begun in 1852, upon the site of the old building, was completed and dedicated, and this building was used by the United States military authorities from November, 1863, to May 1, 1866, first as a hospital, then as barracks, next as quarters for refugees from upper East Tennessee, and finally for the necessities of the Freedmen's Bureau, by whom it was used as a school house for colored children.

Rev. James Park was invited to preach to this congregation in February, 1866, he having then recently returned from Georgia. Upon his own responsibility he rented the Baptist church building, then vacant, and in this building continued to hold services until the succeeding May, at which time the church belonging to the congregation was restored to it. It is natural to suppose that because of the war the membership of the church had been reduced, thirty-nine being the number that greeted Rev. Mr. Park's return, and the elders at that time were David A. Deaderick, William S. Kennedy and George M. White. Dr. Park was, however, a successful pastor, and under his care the membership steadily increased. The church building was repaired and refurnished in 1869. and the lot was improved, all at a cost of upward of $5,000. Dr. Park was again elected pastor May 21, 1876, and still remains in charge. The membership of this church at the present time is 380, and of the Sunday-school, of which Dr. A. R. Melendy is superintendent, 250.

John H. Crozier wrote as follows of the Rev. Samuel Carrick:

"Rev. Samuel Carrick was the first clergyman who also ministered to one or more churches in the country. He was an accurate Greek and Latin scholar, and was president of Blount College. He was a Calvinistic Presbyterian of the strictest sect; believed in predestination and election, and that infants who died without baptism would suffer eternal perdition on account of this neglect of their parents. * * * He was a brave, honest, upright man and a sincere Christian, and had great influence over his congregation, though many of his tenets would not at the present day be very cheerfully acquiesced in by numbers of his own denomination."

Following is the inscription in full upon the monument erected to his memory: "Sacred to the memory of the Rev. Samuel CZR. Carrick, who died August 17, 1809, aged forty-nine years 1 month. He first planted the Presbyterian religion in the wilds of Tennessee; he was the founder and the first pastor of this church, and the first president of E. T. College."

The Second Presbyterian Church of Knoxville was organized in the manner mentioned in connection with the sketch of the First Presbyterian Church; but in this place it is proper to present more of the details. Near the close of the last century the Rev. Dr. Isaac Anderson, one of the ablest men that ever preached the Gospel in Tennessee, organized Washington Presbyterian Church on Rosebury creek, and he also established a school known as Union Academy, for it was the custom then of the Presbyterian ministers to teach as well as preach. In 1803 Rev. Samuel Carrick resigned the pastorate of Lebanon Church, and from that time on until 1813 Rev. Dr. Anderson preached to both Washington and Lebanon congregations. Rev. Dr. Anderson was the principal agent in establishing the Southern and Western Theological Seminary, which was in 1821 incorporated as Maryville College. Dr. Anderson was one of those in East Tennessee, Rev. Hezekiah Balch being another, who had adopted the peculiar form of Calvinism known as Hopkinsianism, mentioned in the history of the First Presbyterian Church, and under his preaching many of his hearers, not only of his own congregation, but also of the members of neighboring churches, were converted to his belief. By some of the members of the First Presbyterian Church in Knoxville he was invited to preach to them, in 1818, and accepting the invitation, the result was the petition elsewhere referred to, and the organization of the Second Presbyterian Church, which was effected October 24, 1818. The elders chosen at that time were Archibald Rhea, John McCampbell, Thomas Craighead, Joseph Brown and John Taylor. A piece of ground containing one acre was purchased of Gideon Morgan, and the erection of a house of worship immediately begun, and the work was so far completed that the building was dedicated by Dr. Anderson in April, 1820. The walls remained unplastered for nearly ten years.

Dr. Anderson continued with the church until 1829, the membership being increased by the addition of 153 new names. The next regular pastor was the Rev. Jefferson E. Montgomery, who was with the church from 1831 until 1838, and in October, 1840, the Rev. William Mack became pastor, remaining until 1843, when he resigned. In February, 1845, Rev. John W. Cunningham was installed, remaining about one year, when he was succeeded by Rev. J. H. Meyers, who remained until April, 1847. Rev. J. H. Martin was then pastor from July, 1847, until October, 1863, the present church being erected in the meantime at a cost of $14,236.84, the dedication occurring November 11, 1860. During this year a chapel was built from the materials of the old church, for the purpose of holding prayer meetings, Sunday-school, etc.

For two years during the war the church was without a pastor, but in October, 1865, Rev. Nathan Bachman became pastor and remained until 1876, when he was succeeded by Rev. F. E. Sturgis, who, in 1885, was succeeded by Rev. T. S. Scott, who was called here from Rockford, Ill., came and remained about two years. On September 11, 1887, Rev. Dr. R. R. Sutherland began his pastorate here, being installed October 2, and remained nine years, preaching his last sermon March 15, 1896. An incident worthy of note occurred in this church November 4, 1894, when Mrs. Julia Ward Howe addressed the congregation, during her address saying there was once a time when women were obliged to leave the church before the benediction was pronounced, because it was thought they had no souls, but "now they are permitted to remain and pronounce the benediction." After the resignation of Dr. Sutherland several ministers occupied the pulpit with a view of becoming pastor, until at length the present pastor, Rev. Robert L. Bachman, then of Utica, N. Y., a native of Tennessee and a graduate of Union Theological Seminary, was called, preaching his first sermon September 27, 1896, and being installed December 2, following.

The membership of this church is now 425, and of the Sunday-school, of which E. G. Oates is superintendent, 350, including a membership of 100 in the home Sunday-school. The elders of the church are W. P. Washburn, A. A. Barnes, Judge S. T. Logan, Judge T. A. R. Nelson, N. D. Barrows, W. E. Gibbins, John L. Rhea, James Lynn and J. B. Minnis. Among the distinguished Tennesseeans who have in the past been elders of this church are Hon. Horace Maynard, James H. Cowan, Dr. James Rodgers, whose father was also an elder, and Judge T. A. R. Nelson. The property of the church is valued at $200,000.

At a meeting of the Presbytery of Knoxville held at Sweetwater, December 18, 1873, a petition of several members of the First Presbyterian Church and of others not members of that church, was presented, asking that they be organized as the Third Presbyterian Church of Knoxville. A committee was appointed to attend at Knoxville on January 16, 1874, hold a meeting to continue over the 18th of the month, that being Sunday, to organize the new congregation. During the same month the church was constituted with twenty-nine communicants, four ruling elders and four deacons. Services were held in the Caldwell school house until a church edifice could be erected, and in 1876 a fine brick structure on Fifth avenue was completed and dedicated. Rev. J. P. Gammon was stated supply of this church for about eighteen months, when he was succeeded by Rev. W. A. Harrison, who remains pastor even to the present time, though on December 1, 1897, Rev. Dr. J. M. P. Otts reached the city to take the position of associate pastor and was installed November 13, 1898, the two reverend gentlemen still remaining co-pastors of the church. The membership of this church is now 375 and of the Sunday-school, of which George R. Jackson is superintendent, 150. The property owned by the church society is worth about $75,000.

Central Presbyterian Church was the result of a division within the Third Presbyterian Church. After worshiping in several places for some time, one of these places being Patterson's Hall, the Central Presbyterian Church decided to have a church building and a pastor of their own, and on Sunday, July 12, 1891, extended a call to Rev. J. M. La Bach to act as stated supply until the meeting of the synod in the fall. This church was regularly organized November 8, 1891, the membership being mainly from the Third Presbyterian Church. The society procured a lot on the corner of Broad and Jacksboro streets, and on November 15 there was subscribed toward a building fund $4,452.75. November 6, 1892, the church building was dedicated, the sermon being delivered by Rev. Dr. T. H. McCallie of Chattanooga.

Rev. Mr. La Bach remained pastor of this church until March 3, 1895, when his pastoral relations were dissolved. The membership of the church at that time was about 300. After being served by different pastors temporarily, at length on May 10, 1896, Rev. George T. Chandler was installed as pastor, remaining until September 17, 1898, when he resigned, and a few months later became pastor of the First Presbyterian Church at Kosciusko, Miss., in which state he had formerly labored. Rev. Paul F. Brown is the present pastor.

The membership of this church at this time is about 175, and of the Sunday-school, of which J. L. Cooley is superintendent, about the same. The value of the church property is now about $12,000.

The Fourth Presbyterian Church was organized April 25, 1886, in the Edgewood school house, with eighteen members, most of whom had been for some time members of other Presbyterian churches, but wanted a church of their own denomination nearer their homes. The elders chosen at this time were W. O. White, C. E. Lucky and Robert Irvin, and the deacons, Charles Champion and Charles Evans. The sermon on the occasion was preached by Rev. T. S. Scott. A church building was erected during the same year, on the corner of Coleman and Luttrell streets, which cost about $4,000, and was dedicated November 6, 1887, but the first services held therein were held November 7, 1886. The present membership of the church is about 275, and of the Sunday-school, 140. The value of the church property, including the parsonage, is $10,000. Rev. E. A. Elmore has been pastor of this church ever since its organization.

The Cumberland Presbyterian Church was organized in the spring of 1883, and is located on Broad street. The principal movers in the work of organizing this church were

Rev. E. J. McCroskey, J. R. Butt and T. W. Kellar. Rev. Mr. McCroskey undertook the work of raising the amount of money needed to purchase a lot, which he accomplished, and the erection thereon of a church building was soon afterward begun. In the spring of 1885 the work had so far progressed as to permit of the occupancy of the building, and the organization of the church was effected by the election of J. R. Butt and T. W. Kellar as elders, and J. B. Malcolm and T. W. Carter, deacons. Rev. W. H. Baugh was installed pastor, remaining until June, 1886, when he was succeeded by Rev. J. V. Stephens, who remained until 1888, when Rev. A. W. Hawkins became pastor.

The church building begun, as above stated, in 1885, was dedicated February 2, 1890, the sermon being preached by Rev. Solon McCroskey, the society at that time being free from debt. June 14, 1891, Rev. Mr. Hawkins preached his farewell sermon, and left the charge in a very prosperous condition. On May 21, Rev. P. M. Fitzgerald preached his first sermon as pastor of this church and remained until April 10, 1897, when he was succeeded by Rev. James A. McKamey. The Sunday-school was reorganized January 2, 1898, with Walter M. Bonham superintendent. The Florida Street mission of this church was also reorganized, and became a prominent feature of the work of the church. September 30, 1898, Rev. Mr. McKamey left Knoxville to take charge of the Sunday-school department of the Cumberland Presbyterian, published at Nashville, and was followed by Rev. T. A. Cowan, who preached his first sermon October 9, 1898. The membership of this church at the present time is 310, and of the Sunday-school, of which T. W. Carter is superintendent, 180. The property of the church is now worth about $10,000.

The Fort Sanders Presbyterian Church was organized in the Highland Avenue school building, May 19, 1895, with twenty-six members. For about eighteen months the congregation worshiped in various buildings and rooms, the pastors or ministers who preached being Revs. Elmore, Dawson, Wilson, Moore, Newman, Duncan and the present pastor of the church, S. A. Coile, the latter being installed as regular pastor in 1895. The lot upon which the church building stands was purchased in January, 1896, at a cost of $1,700, and active work looking to the erection of a church edifice immediately began. The building stands at the corner of Laurel avenue and Eighth street, and the total cost of the church property, including lot, buildings and furnishings, was $5,240.33. The building was dedicated on Sunday, December 18, 1898, by Rev. E. A. Elmore, D. D., pastor of the Fourth Presbyterian Church, and after the dedicatory sermon was delivered there was raised almost enough money to pay off the indebtedness upon the property, which was $1,514.42. Dr. J. M. P. Otts, pastor of the Third Presbyterian Church, called attention to the memorial window in the west side of the church, given by the soldiers of Camp Poland in memory of the soldiers of both armies that fell in the attack upon and defense of Fort Sanders, November 29, 1863, and said also that it was the first monument to piety and to the fallen of both sides in the Civil war ever erected in the world. Rev. S. A. Coile, the first pastor of this church, was the pastor at the time of dedication and still remains.

The South Knoxville Presbyterian Church was established January 26, 1890, with eleven members, and during the fall and winter of 1890-91 a frame church building was erected at a cost of $4,350, which was dedicated March 29, 1891. The first and only pastor of this church was and has been Rev. W. R. Dawson, who is well equipped for his work. The membership of the church is now 108, and of the Sunday-school, 125. R. E. Jones is superintendent of the Sunday-school, which is in a flourishing condition, and the value of the church property at the present time is $3,500.

Bell Avenue Presbyterian Church was organized September 7, 1890, as the outgrowth of a mission established about

1870 by the Second Presbyterian Church, at the corner of Bell avenue and Bertrand street. Preaching services were held in the chapel of the mission during the summer of 1890 by Rev. J. M. Davies, D. D., synodical superintendent of home missions for Tennessee, and on July 11, of that year, Rev. A. J. Coile came to the city from Mount Bethel Church, presbytery of Holston, and the church was organized, as above stated, with twenty-two members. In 1891 a lot was purchased on the corner of Howard and Olive streets, upon which a commodious frame church building was erected at a cost of $4,000, capable of seating 300 persons, and which was dedicated October 6, 1891, Dr. R. R. Sutherland preaching the sermon. Rev. A. J. Coile was ordained minister of the church April 24, 1892, having up to that time been stated supply. He is still pastor of the church, which now has 150 members, and the Sunday-school, of which A. H. Daily is superintendent, has 150 scholars. The property of the church is now worth $4,500.

Shiloh Presbyterian Church, colored, was organized in the following manner: In May, 1865, at a meeting of the General Assembly of the Presbyterian Church, held in New York, Rev. Henry H. Garnett and Rev. John B. Reeve were appointed to look after the interests of such colored people in the South as might desire to identify themselves with the Presbyterian Church. Rev. Mr. Garnett came to Knoxville, finding here eleven colored communicants connected with the Second Presbyterian Church who were desirous of organizing a separate church. Letters having been granted these eleven colored Presbyterians, they, together with one colored member from the First Presbyterian Church, were organized into the First Colored Presbyterian Church, September 4, 1865, the name being later changed to that given above. The sermon at this time was preached by the Rev. Mr. Reeve. For a short time Rev. Mr. Reeve was pastor of the church, then returning to Philadelphia. Not long afterward Rev. G. W. LeVere, who had been chaplain of the

Twentieth U. S. Colored volunteer infantry, during a portion of the war, accepted a position as missionary to Knoxville, arriving in the city February 9, 1866, and found twelve of the original members of this church, and held services in the First Presbyterian Church (that being still vacant), until the owners again desired it for their own use. For some time it was exceedingly difficult to find a place in which the church could hold services, for there was then a decided prejudice against colored churches, but at length Mr. Perez Dickinson offered Mr. LeVere the use of his rear porch and lawn. Afterward the services were for a time regularly held at the house of William Nelson, until a lot was purchased on Clinch street, upon which a building was erected, the entire cost being $3,300, and the building was completed within the next twenty-two months. The church then kept on with its work regularly and with success, and in 1883 Rev. Job Lawrence became pastor, remaining until 1891, when he was succeeded by Rev. John R. Riley, the present pastor. The membership now is 120, and of the Sunday-school, of which Mitchell Burks is superintendent, is seventy-five. The church property is worth about $3,000.

The First Baptist Church of Knoxville was organized January 15, 1843, in the upper room of the court house, the organization being completed on the 22d of that month. The ministers present on the latter occasion were as follows: Rev. Mr. Kennon, Duke Kimbrough, Mr. Milliken, Mr. Bellue, Mr. Coram and Mr. Ray. The membership at first was quite small, being composed of twenty-six white persons and twenty colored. During the first few months of the existence of this church the membership grew quite rapidly and by August the enrollment reached eighty-five. Thirty had been added by experience and seventeen by letter, seven had been dismissed and one had been excommunicated. This large increase in the membership was due to two revivals, one in the spring and one in the summer, the first having been conducted in the First Presbyterian Church by Rev. Dr.

Baker of Texas, and the other by Rev. Israel Robards, who remained for several successive days and nights, arousing a deep religious interest in the community.

The first pastor of the church was Rev. Joseph A. Bullard, who remained one year. Those most prominent among his successors were the Revs. G. W. Griffin, Matthew Hillsman, L. B. Woolfolk, S. H. Smith, Dr. Brenker, D. D., J. L. Lloyd, J. B. F. Mays, George B. Eager, C. H. Strickland and E. A. Taylor. Rev. E. A. Taylor at the end of a three years' pastorate, lasting from 1885 to 1888, had one of the strongest congregations in the state of Tennessee, and a large, handsome brick church building, with his congregation out of debt. His labors in Knoxville are remembered with pleasure by his former parishioners. The membership at that time amounted to about 650, and the Sunday-school had a membership of more than 500 scholars.

The new brick church above mentioned is 72x88 feet in size, its audience room being 62x65 feet in size, and its spire 176 feet high. The corner stone was laid July 1, 1886, and it was dedicated April 8, 1886. The audience room and the gallery have a seating capacity of from 850 to 1,000 people.

After the retirement of Rev. E. A. Taylor toward the latter part of 1888, a call was extended January 23, 1889, to Rev. Carter Helm Jones, who began his labors here about February 1, 1889, remaining until April 30, 1893, upon which day he preached his farewell sermon, having accepted a call from the McFerrin Memorial Baptist Church of Louisville, Ky. During the four years of his pastorate in Knoxville he baptized 243 persons and admitted to the church 435. On May 14, 1893, Rev. R. R. Acree of Roanoke, Va., preached a sermon for the congregation, was afterward called to the church, and arrived to take charge on September 8, that year. The present pastor is Rev. M. W. Egerton. The membership of this church at the present time is 748, and of the Sunday-school, of which John McCoy is superintendent, 500. The value of the church property now is $40,000.

In November, 1873, a second congregation of Baptists was organized in Knoxville, their church building being erected on McGhee street, but the location did not prove satisfactory, and in November, 1880, the congregation was disbanded. Some time afterward a mission was established in the northern portion of the city and at this mission, in November, 1885, a church was organized which was named Calvary Baptist Church. This church was incorporated March 8, 1886, by W. C. McCoy, G. W. Peters, Lafayette Huddleston, James A. Galyon, John J. Martin, W. A. J. Moore and J. R. Dew. The first pastor of the church was Rev. O. L. Hailey. The church was highly prosperous during the first years of its existence, the membership increasing in one year from fifty-three to 115. On February 6, 1890, the charter of this church, upon the petition of W. C. McCoy, L. Huddleston, J. B. Williams, W. A. J. Moore, W. R. Cooper and J. A. Galyon, was so amended as to permit the change of name of this church to the Second Baptist Church of Knoxville, and the name was changed in accordance therewith. Since Rev. Mr. Hailey's time the Rev. M. D. Jeffries has been the only pastor, he commencing his pastorate March 1, 1893. The church edifice is a two-story pressed brick structure, of the Romanesque style of architecture, having an auditorium capable of seating 700 persons, and ample class rooms, ladies' parlor, etc., and cost $31,000. The membership of the church at the present time is 534, and of the Sunday-school, of which W. A. J. Moore is superintendent, 360. The property of the church is now worth $25,000.

The Third Baptist Church, located south of the Tennessee river, was organized February 17, 1889, with eighteen members, the first pastor being Rev. W. R. Grace, who remained from June, 1889, to June, 1891. Rev. S. E. Jones became pastor in July, 1891, and remained until July, 1893, after which the church was without a pastor six months, during which time Dr. C. C. DeArmond acted as moderator at all business meetings. In January, 1894, Rev. Mr. Lightfoot became pastor, remaining until the following July, from which time until September, 1894, Rev. John M. Anderson acted as supply pastor. Then followed Rev. W. C. McPherson, who remained from October, 1894, until January 1, 1898, on which date the present pastor, Rev. R. M. Murrell, began his labors. On June 11, 1893, when the church building was dedicated by Rev. T. T. Eaton, the membership of the church was 175, while at the present time it is 200. The Sunday school, organized February 24, 1889, has continued without interruption. It had at first forty scholars, while now it has 200. The superintendents have been Dr. C. C. DeArmond and served eight years; W. B. Ford served six months; J. C. Ford, six months; J. G. Johnson, one year, and Dr. T. O. McCallie is now superintendent. The church property is worth about $7,000.

The Centennial Baptist Church was the outgrowth of a mission Sunday-school organized April 6, 1890, at the home of Alexander Meek at 1200 Asylum street, and on the 13th of the same month a meeting was held at a store room on Asylum street at which seventy-seven persons were present and Rev. J. Pike Powers elected superintendent, and served as both superintendent of the Sunday-school and pastor for the people until July 12, 1891. The First Baptist Church took charge of the mission July 15, 1891, and elected Thomas L. Moses superintendent, and engaged Rev. J. K. Pace as pastor. The Sunday-school about this time moved to a store room on Asylum and Clinton streets, and W. W. Woodruff presented to the mission a lot on Deaderick street, upon which a church building was erected by the First Baptist Church, which building is 34x80 feet in size and cost $5,800, and was dedicated free from debt on June 5, 1892. It has a seating capacity of 500 persons, and is a very handsome church edifice, somewhat on the Moorish order of architecture, nicely situated on a fine street. The pastor at the time of dedication was Rev. J. K. Pace, he remaining until October, 1892, when he was succeeded by the present pastor, Rev. J. H. Snow, who has had a very successful pastorate. The value of the church property is about $6,500.

Mount Zion Baptist Church (colored) was organized in 1864, in the basement of the First Presbyterian Church, with three members, by Rev. T. Embry. Soon afterward they removed to M. E. Zion Church, remaining there for some time, and then removed to the colored school house in East Knoxville, remaining there until 1866. Rev. William Howell about this time came down from Ohio, was invited to become pastor of the church, accepted and remained until 1869. In 1873 there were about 150 members in this church, which had previously purchased a lot on Patton street in East Knoxville, and erected thereon a church building at a cost of about $2,000.

The Second (Colored) Baptist Church was organized by Rev. William Howell with eight members from the First Colored Baptist Church, and with Rev. J. P. Jay as pastor. After about four months a lot was purchased on an alley leading off from Cumberland street in East Knoxville, upon which lot a church building was erected at a cost of about $900, in which the congregation still worships. After a one year's pastorate, Rev. Mr. Jay was succeeded by Rev. A. B. Cross, and in 1873 there were 173 members in the church. Succeeding pastors so far as could be ascertained have been as follows: Revs. Bigbee, Robert Howard, Robert Mills, Allen Nickerson, Brown, Bain, John Richardson, Shields, C. J. Reed, W. M. Maskerson, Martin Jones, James Barney, John Richardson, R. P. Rumney, John G. L. Crippins and William Armstrong, the present pastor. The church membership now is 157. This church is now called the Mount Carmel Baptist Church.

In 1897 a division in the church occurred. 76 members withdrawing and forming the Guilfield Baptist Church, purchasing the old Clinton A. M. E. chapel, and worshiping therein. The first pastor of this church was Rev. R. P. Rumney, the second and present pastor being Rev. Mr. Clark, from Kentucky. The membership is about the same as that with which the church was organized.

Other colored Baptist churches are the Central, at 1019 Payne street, and the Second Baptist at 616 Central avenue, North.

The Church of the Immaculate Conception was established in 1851, when the claims of the Roman Catholics settled throughout East Tennessee were presented to the Rt. Rev. Richard Pius Miles, then Bishop of Nashville. In obedience to the command of the bishop, Rev. Father H. V. Brown, a pious and zealous missionary, came to Knoxville and organized the Catholics into a congregation, named as above, and under his supervision a church building was erected on Walnut street near Vine, which was of stone and neat in style and architecture. The Catholics then numbered about one hundred families and with them Father Brown, who was a competent artist, labored until 1855, when he was called to Chattanooga.

Rev. Father J. L. Biemans, noted for his learning and humility, succeeded to the pastorate of this church, and served faithfully until 1857, when he was called back to Europe to receive his mother into the faith of her son. Rev. Father J. Bergrath then filled the pastorate until 1865, when on account of failing health he removed further south. Rev. Father Abram J. Ryan then took charge, and was soon endeared to all denominations in Knoxville, because of his loving care and devoted zeal. The increasing congregation could no longer be accommodated in the little stone church, the capacity of which was tested every Sunday, so much so that on many occasions the Catholics were compelled to stand in the aisles or even outside of the building itself by the open windows, in order to accommodate their non-Catholic friends, who desired to listen to the eloquent words of the poet priest. It was during his pastorate here that Father

Ryan wrote that immortal poem, "The Conquered Banner," which has endeared him to the heart of every Southern man and woman.

Rev. Father Joseph S. Kean was next in charge, but was soon followed by Rev. Father M. J. Finnegan, who was appointed in June, 1868, and it was during his administration that the addition was built to the church.

Rev. Father F. T. Marron, the present incumbent, was appointed pastor in 1872, and finding that his charge was not confined to the city of Knoxville, but that in fact it extended all over East Tennessee, over an area of 180x100 miles, he was at first quite discouraged, but after completing his first pastoral visit, that which seemed almost if not quite impossible of accomplishment, became comparatively easy and a pleasant duty, and his efforts were soon crowned with success. Many of those who lived in the country followed his advice and moved to Knoxville, and such was the increase in the Catholic population of the city that a new church building became a necessity, the present fine brick structure at the southeast corner of Walnut and Vine streets being soon afterward erected, all of Tennessee material and the work all done by Knoxville contractors and workmen. This church has a seating capacity of about 800, and was dedicated September 19, 1886, by Rt. Rev. Joseph Rademacher, bishop of Nashville, assisted by Rev. Father Marron and Rev. Father M. J. Ryan. The membership of this parish at present is about 1,500, and the Sunday-school has about 350 scholars.

(Since the foregoing was written Father Marron has been transferred to Memphis, Tennessee, and has been succeeded by Father Gleason, who came from Nashville.)

Bishop Asbury, on November 1, 1790, while on his way from the Cumberland settlements to North Carolina, paid a visit to Knoxville, being accompanied by Bishops Whatcoat and William McKendree. Here they were entertained by Joseph Greer, a friend of Asbury. The bishop preached in the "State House," to about 700 persons, many of whom, however, could not get inside the building. In the autumn of 1802 Bishop Asbury again visited Knoxville on two separate occasions, but did not preach here in either case. He was entertained by Joseph Greer and Francis A. Ramsey. On November 25, 1802, he preached at the house of Justus Huffaker, a local preacher, living near the Seven Islands in the French Broad river. That year the French Broad circuit was formed, extending westward from the west line of Greene county on both sides of French Broad and Holston rivers, and including Knox county. To this circuit from that year to 1811 inclusive the following appointments were made: Luther Taylor in 1802; John Johnson in 1803; E. W. Bowman and Joshua Oglesby in 1804; Ralph Lotspeich in 1805; James Axley in 1806; Benjamin Edge in 1807; Nathan Barnes and Isaac Lindsey in 1808; James Trower in 1809; William Pattison in 1810, and George Ekin and Josiah Crawford in 1811.

In November, 1812, Bishop Asbury, accompanied by William McKendree, visited Knoxville once more and for the last time, being the guest of Father Wagoner. The conference from which the bishop was returning had established Knoxville circuit and had assigned thereto Samuel H. Thompson. The next year Samuel H. Thompson was succeeded by Richard Richards, a strong and popular man, but who later became addicted to strong drink and was expelled from the church. Still later he reformed and was again received into membership.

James Dixon was assigned to Knoxville circuit in 1814, a man of remarkable intellect, and in that day of controversy over religious doctrines, defended the doctrines of his church with great ability. In a long debate in which he was engaged with Dr. Isaac Anderson, founder of Maryville College, he acquitted himself to the full satisfaction, at least, of his church. He was again sent to Knoxville in 1819 and in 1820 had charge of the church in Greeneville as well as of that in Knoxville. About this time he was afflicted with epilepsy in a most remarkable manner, being helpless and almost unconscious for several weeks. Upon again regaining full consciousness he had forgotten everything he had ever known, and was compelled to learn to read over again.

The Church Street Methodist Episcopal Church, South, was organized early in the present century, but it could not be ascertained that there was a church building erected here previous to 1815. Knoxville was first mentioned as a preaching place at a conference held at Fountain Head, Middle Tennessee, November 12, 1812, with Samuel H. Thompson, preacher in charge, Col. John W. Gaut being authority for this statement, Rev. Mr. Thompson having charge of a circuit. In 1813 Richard Richards was preacher in charge, and in 1814 James Dixon, an Irishman, learned, cultured and eloquent, who engaged in a controversy with Rev. Dr. Anderson of Maryville, a Presbyterian divine. Next came John Henegar, in 1815, the year in which was in all probability erected the first frame church building on Methodist Hill, John Haynie being instrumental in its erection. Up to this time those who had been in this part of the state as circuit riders were James Axley, Thomas Wilkerson, and John Kelly. In 1816 the preacher in Knoxville was Nicholas Norwood; in 1817, Josiah B. Doughty, and in 1818, George Atkin, father of S. T. Atkin, an esteemed member of this church at the present time. In 1819, Robert Hooper; in 1820, David Adams; in 1822, James Axley, with John Doan, assistant; in 1823 Thomas Stringfield was presiding elder, Thomas Madden, preacher in charge, and F. A. Owen, assistant. While the church remained on Methodist Hill the membership was about 100, and in 1834 a new church edifice was erected and known afterward as "The Old Methodist Church."

In 1824 Holston Conference was organized at a meeting held in Knoxville, Bishop Roberts presiding, the new conference comprising Southwest Virginia, East Tennessee,

Western North Carolina, and a small portion of North Georgia. The whole number of white members was 13,443; colored, 1,491, and preachers, 42. George Horn was the preacher in Knoxville. In 1825 the preacher was J. Y. Crawford; in 1826, James Cummings and W. T. Senter; in 1827, Isaac Lewis; in 1828, John Craig and O. F. Johnson; in 1829, John B. Doughty and Harry Cummings; in 1830, Abraham Murphy and J. Nutty; in 1831, David Fleming and R. Birdwell; in 1832, David Fleming; in 1833, David Adams; in 1834-35, Joseph Pryor; in 1836, Timothy Sullins; in 1837, J. M. Kelley; in 1838-39, John Barringer; in 1840, John M. Kelley; in 1841-42, Timothy Sullins; 1843-44, James Atkins; 1845, Samuel Patton; 1846, Miles Foy; 1847, W. G. E. Cunningham; 1848, E. F. Sevier; 1849, C. W. Charlton; 1850, Timothy Sullins and D. R. McAnally; 1851, J. C. Pendergrast; 1852, E. E. Gillenwaters; 1853, William M. Kerr; 1854, Timothy Sullins and W. H. Bates (interchange); 1855-56, E. C. Wexler; 1857, R. M. Hickey; 1858-59, David Sullins; 1860, David Sullins and E. C. Wexler; 1861, W. E. Munsey; 1862, Grinsfield Taylor, and 1863, David Sullins. From this time on for a few years on account of the occupation of the city by Union soldiers, religious services were not regularly held, but in November, 1866, the society was reorganized and as the old church building on Church street had been taken possession of by the members of the Methodist Episcopal Church, the members of the M. E. Church, South, occupied the basement of the First Presbyterian church, remaining there until their own new brick chapel was erected and completed, in 1867.

The first pastor of this church after the cessation of hostilities was Rev. T. C. Carroll, who was followed by Rev. W. H. Bates. Next came Rev. Grinsfield Taylor, in 1869; E. E. Hoss in 1870-71; R. H. Parker, 1872; W. G. E. Cunningham, 1873-74; J. S. Burnett, 1875-77; George C. Rankin, 1878-81; John H. Keith, 1882-83; H. H. Carlock, 1884-85; R. G. Waterhouse, 1886-89; W. W. Hicks, 1890-91; H.

D. Moore, D. D., 1892-94, and the present pastor, Rev. James A. Duncan, D. D., 1895-99.

In 1875 the society regained possession of its church lot, with the old church, and upon this lot, in 1877, the present brick church edifice was completed and dedicated in February, 1878, by Bishop Wightman, assisted by Dr. R. A. Young. In 1886 or 1887 fifty-six feet of land was purchased adjoining the church on the west and upon this land a Sunday-school chapel was erected. In 1893 the parsonage was erected on the front of this lot, and at the present time the property of the church is worth some $40,000.

Broad Street Methodist Episcopal Church, South, was organized in 1871 and a lot was purchased by D. A. Carpenter, M. J. Reams, James Hayley, J. L. Nelson, and A. J. Price, trustees, for its use, the price paid being $500, the owners of the lot at the time being Peter Staub and Lewis Tillman. The location of this lot, on which the church building was erected, is the southeast corner of Fifth avenue and Broad street. The building was dedicated June 5, 1871, Rev. Bishop H. H. Kavanagh preaching the sermon, and on this occasion about $1,200 was raised to apply on the indebtedness. About the time of the dedication of this building Rev. George D. French became pastor and remained until 1873, when he was succeeded by Rev. B. O. Davis, who was himself succeeded by Rev. J. L. M. French. Rev. W. W. Bays became pastor in 1879, and was followed by Rev. J. H. Keith. Then followed Rev. J. F. Frazier, Rev. D. Sullins, D. D., and Rev. J. H. Keith, who this time remained until October 13, 1889, on which day he preached his farewell sermon. In the meantime the first building erected for a church, which was a plain, rectangular structure, in the style of the old-fashioned country meeting-house, became too small, and in 1886 a new and more commodious building was resolved upon, and was erected at the corner of Fifth avenue and Broad street, the first work being done on this new edifice July 22, 1886. The corner-stone was laid September 21, and the building, completed, was dedicated September 9, 1888. It is 72x80 feet in size, has an auditorium 59x75 feet, and a spire 150 feet high. Rev. Dr. J. H. Keith, mentioned above, was succeeded by Rev. T. C. Carroll, D. D., he by Rev. W. M. Dyer, and he by Rev. F. Richardson, who was himself succeeded by Rev. W. S. Neighbors. The present pastor is Rev. J. L. Orr. The present membership of the church is 547, that of the Sunday-school, of which J. E. Johnston is the superintendent, 340, and the value of the property owned by the church is $37,500, including the parsonage, at No. 528 West Fifth avenue.

Highland Avenue Methodist Episcopal Church, South, was organized in 1893, the first pastor being Rev. W. Wisdom Newberry, who remained from 1893 to 1896, and during his pastorate the little frame church building, which was and is still designed for the use of the Sunday-school, was erected. This building was dedicated July 14, 1895, by Rev. Dr. Richardson, and after the regular dedicatory sermon had been delivered Dr. Moore announced that when the remaining debt was assumed he would pronounce the sentence of dedication. Dr. Moore's appeal was almost immediately responded to and the debt assumed, the church building, which cost about $1,500 being then fully dedicated free from debt. This church building stands on a large lot on Highland avenue immediately northwest of the site of Fort Sanders. Since the Rev. Mr. Newberry the pastors have been as follows: Rev. A. B. Hunter, 1896-97; Rev. E. S. Bettis, 1897-98, and Rev. Frank Jackson, 1898 to the present time. The membership of this church on March 1, 1899, was 181, and of the Sunday-school 160, the superintendent of the Sunday-school being Joel Seaton. The entire value of the church property is $3,500.

May 27, 1864, a call was issued for a convention of members and preachers of the Holston conference who were loyal to the government of the United States, the convention to be held in Knoxville July 7 following, by William G. Brownlow, J. A. Hyden, E. E. Gillenwaters, William T. Dowell, James Cumming, Thomas H. Russell, William H. Rogers, and David Fleming. On the day appointed fifty-four delegates assembled in the Episcopal church, organizing by the selection of E. E. Gillenwaters chairman and Robert G. Blackburn secretary. A report was adopted favoring a return to the Methodist Episcopal Church subject to the approval of its general conference, which latter body ratified the action of the Knoxville church. At its next meeting the Holston Conference of the Methodist Episcopal Church was organized at Athens, June 1, 1865.

The First Methodist Episcopal Church of Knoxville was established during this same year, under the pastorate of the Rev. Dr. John F. Spence, the trustees being William G. Brownlow, R. D. Jourolman, E. N. Parham, and C. W. De Pue, and the stewards S. P. Angel, William Rule, H. C. Tarwater, F. W. Wheeler, and J. T. Ambrose. For three years this church organization worshiped in the court-house and in the First Baptist Church, and in 1867 began the erection of a church building on Clinch street, which was completed in 1869. It was a large and commodious brick structure, capable of seating 600 people.

Dr. Spence labored with this congregation, which held services in Temperance Hall, East Knoxville, and afterwards as above stated, for one year, and in June, 1866, was succeeded by Rev. J. B. Ford, who reorganized the society at the court-house with thirty members. In the Baptist church Rev. Mr. Ford then held a protracted meeting and after this came to an end the congregation returned to the court-house. By this time the old Methodist church on Church street was repaired and taken possession of, and it was in this building that the congregation remained until the new building at the corner of Clinch and Prince streets was finished. In 1867 Rev. Mr. Ford was succeeded by Rev. J. S. Petty, who remained one year, and was followed by Rev. J. W. Mann, during whose pastorate the new church building was dedicated by Rev. Dr. Cobleigh. Rev. J. L. Mann next became pastor, remaining one year, when he was succeeded by Rev. J. R. Eads, who was followed by Rev. J. B. Ford. In 1872 the membership of this church was 275. Succeeding pastors were Revs. L. H. Carhart, J. F. Goldman, J. J. Manker, William McKinley, N. G. Taylor, C. B. Sparrow, R. J. Cooke, I. A. Pearce, L. E. Prentiss and T. C. Warner, during whose pastorate the present fine church building was dedicated, the dedicatory services being conducted by Bishops J. N. Fitzgerald and I. W. Joyce, the former preaching the sermon. The old church stood at the corner of Clinch and Prince streets, the new one standing at the southeast corner of Clinch and Locust streets. This new structure is in the Romanesque style of architecture, the plans for which were supplied by Weaver & Kramer of Akron, Ohio. It is 71x130 feet in size, is built of marble, and when the auxiliary rooms are thrown open in connection with the auditorium, has a seating capacity of 1,800. It cost about $50,000, the larger part of which sum was derived from the sale of a house on the lot where the building itself stands ($1,000), and the sale of the property at Clinch and Prince streets ($35,000). The organ in this new building is very fine, consisting of six stops of fifty-eight pipes each; the swell organ having six stops, four of which have each fifty-eight pipes, one forty-six pipes, and one sixty pipes, and the pedal stop, which has twenty-seven pipes, or a total number of 713 pipes. There is a memorial slab in this church upon which is engraved, "William Gannaway Brownlow, born August 29, 1805, and died April 29, 1878." The church was dedicated on Sunday, June 10, 1894.

The trustees of the church at the time of the erection of this fine edifice were E. W. Adkin, W. A. Galbraith, C. A. Benscoter, G. L. Maloney, C. T. Stephenson, S. P. Fowler, William Rule, Eugene Young and L. Godfrey.

After the retirement of Rev. Mr. Warner, who went to the Bethany Methodist Episcopal Church of Baltimore, Md.,

Rev. J. W. Jones became pastor, preaching his first sermon August 30, 1896, and still remains. The membership of the church at this time (March 1, 1899) is about 700, and of the Sunday-school, 350. Of the Sunday-school, C. W. Searle is superintendent, and in all there are thirty teachers and officers. Prof. C. A. Garratt has charge of the orchestra. The library contains 700 volumes, Charles W. Whittle and Frank W. Biddle being librarians. The Woman's Home Missionary Society of the M. E. Church employs Miss Rhoda Sigler as deaconness, she devoting all her time to visiting and assisting the poor, and receiving a regular salary.

Centenary Methodist Episcopal Church was organized in 1884, and as that year was the "centenary" of organic Methodism in America, that name was chosen. This church is the successor to the old Mabry Street Methodist Episcopal Church, the property of which was sold and the proceeds invested in Centenary Church. The present church building was completed in 1885, costing about $2,500. The following pastors have served this church: Rev. J. N. Lotspeich, October, 1884, to October, 1885; Rev. R. G. Waterhouse, October, 1885, to October, 1886; Rev. S. H. Hilliard, October, 1886, to October, 1889; Rev. J. A. Lyons, October, 1889, to October, 1891; Rev. J. A. Burrow, 1891 to 1895; Rev. J. W. Perry, 1895 to 1897, and Rev. W. R. Barnett, 1897 to 1899. The present pastor is Rev. C. W. Kelley.

Centenary Church has two Sunday-schools. The trustees of this church hold a lot in the vicinity of Brookside Cotton Mills, upon which a church is now (February, 1899) being erected, and here for more than a year a Sunday-school has been held, formerly in a tent, but now in the unfinished church building. It is anticipated that during the present year the church building will be completed. Altogether there are 350 Sunday-school scholars. The superintendents of the two Sunday-schools are Crew Webb and W. C. Pope. The entire value of the property owned by the church is about $3,500.

Luttrell Street Methodist Episcopal Church was organized in the summer of 1889, but in the form of North Knoxville Mission Sunday-school, which was established by Rev. L. E. Prentiss of the First or Clinch Street M. E. Church, in Patterson's Hall, at the corner of Broad and Crozier streets, with about twenty-five scholars. Rev. J. S. Jones was pastor about two months, and was succeeded by Rev. H. J. Van Fossen. The church building erected stood at the corner of Luttrell and Walnut streets, and cost about $6,500. The auditorium was 44x44 feet in size, and the pews arranged in a circular form. The class room was 16x30 feet in size and the pastor's study 12x12 feet. The church was dedicated December 21, 1890. Rev. J. S. Jones became pastor of this church in 1894, and remained until 1897, preaching during his pastorate numerous powerful sermons against sin and vice as he saw it in the city, thereby earning the name of the "Knoxville Parkhurst." After Rev. Mr. Jones retired from this pulpit to take charge of temperance work he was succeeded by the present pastor, Rev. J. M. Melear, who preached his first sermon here on October 3, 1897. The membership of the church at the present time is 215, and of the Sunday-school, of which W. C. Bradley is superintendent, is 250. The value of the church property is now $6,000.

The East Main Street Methodist Episcopal Church was established in the following manner: On February 7, 1893, Miss Rhoda Sigler, at the suggestion of Rev. T. C. Warner, went into East Knoxville to seek a place for the establishment of a mission, and found next day a vacant store on Mabry street, which she rented for the purpose. In this store religious services were held for nearly four years, and at the close of protracted services a Sunday-school was organized and also an Epworth League. In 1896 ground was broken for a new church building, on the very spot where Matthias Householder had many a time stood and prayed for the erection of a church thereon for his children and grandchildren, and in this church building religious services were held for the first time July 12 of that year, but in the basement, as the auditorium was not then completed. The new building was dedicated February 7, 1897, by Rev. Dr. Moore and on that day $400 was raised to liquidate the indebtedness of the society. At that time the trustees of the church were J. L. Falconer, John Davis, J. L. Householder, W. D. Sanders, S. H. Scott and Frank Biddle. The pastors of this church have been Rev. J. M. Durham, from 1895 to 1898; Rev. Robert Parham, 1898-99, and Rev. I. H. Miller, 1899 to the present time. The membership of the church is now sixty-four, an increase of twenty-seven in the four months closing March 10, 1899; the Sunday-school has 110 members, an increase of sixty within the same time, the superintendent being Thomas Pettie, and the church property is worth $4,000. On the left side of the altar of this church is a large marble tablet to the memory of Matthias Householder, a devoted Methodist and a religious man, and in the center of the tablet is placed his photograph.

The Asylum Street Methodist Episcopal Church was organized in 1885, with about twenty-five members. A church building was erected on Asylum street and Deaderick street, which cost about $5,500. It is of brick and is often called the "Red Cross Church," because in the roof there are slates painted red in the form of a cross. The pastors of this church have been as follows: Rev. J. J. Robinet, D. D., and Rev. Mr. Holden in 1885 and 1886; Rev. T. W. Salt, 1887; Rev. J. A. Ruble, 1888-89; Rev. J. N. Kendall part of 1890, Rev. Mr. Holden filling out the term; Rev. William C. Miller, 1891-92; Rev. E. C. Avis, 1893-94; Rev. I. H. Miller, 1894-98, and Rev. W. A. Saville, D. D., Ph. D., 1898 to the present time. The present membership of the church is 320, and of the Sunday-school, of which J. C. Roberts is superintendent, is 200. The church property, including the parsonage, which is worth $1,500, is worth $8,000.

Logan Chapel, M. E. Church (colored), was established in 1865 by the Rev. A. E. Anderson, who remained until

1869. His successor was Rev. J. P. Jay, who remained two years, and was followed by Rev. H. De Bose. In 1873 there were 160 communicants in this church. For some years a small building served the purposes of this congregation; but in 1885 a new and larger building became a necessity, and it was begun in December of that year, being completed in September, 1886. It is located on what was then called Reservoir street, now Commerce street, just below State street. It is 54x85 feet in size, and has a seating capacity of nearly 1,000, at the time of its being completed being the third largest in the United States owned by colored people. It was dedicated September 19, 1886, by Rev. A. L. Cowan of Maryville, the pastor at the time being Rev. A. G. Warner. He was succeeded in 1887 by Rev. A. Walters, who remained until succeeded by F. R. White. The succeeding pastors have been Revs. R. T. Anderson, J. H. Manley, F. M. Jacobs, E. D. W. Jones, F. R. White, F. M. Jacobs, F. R. White and W. B. Fenderson, present pastor. The membership of this church at the present time is 600, and of the Sunday-school, 250. The church property is valued at $10,000.

The Clinton Street M. E. Church (colored), located on Clinton near Asylum street, was established in 1881, and a frame chapel building erected at a cost of about $2,000. The pastors of this church have been as follows: Revs. A. L. Green, Lewis Baker, William Walton, A. S. Monroe, B. J. Jones, T. J. Braxton, H. B. Moss, G. W. Brazelton, G. W. Hampton and the present pastor, F. R. White. The membership is now about 450, and of the Sunday-school, 150. The property is worth about $2,000.

Other colored Methodist Episcopal churches are the First, on Mabry street; Little Zion, at 203 McGhee street, and St. Paul's Independent M. E. Church, on Patton street, among the pastors of which have been Revs. R. H. Miles, J. W. Valentine, R. A. Payne, A. Lindsey, and J. W. Randolph, the latter of whom recently resigned, leaving the church without a pastor at the time.

St. John's Protestant Episcopal Church was really established by Rev. T. W. Humes, in March, 1844, who was then a candidate for the ministry, and who began to serve as lay reader on Sunday mornings. On June 9, following, Rev. Charles Tomes of New York, by appointment of the bishop, took charge of the parish, conducting the services at first in a dwelling house, but soon afterward transferred them to a small building at the corner of Gay and Church streets, donated for the purpose by Andrew R. Humes. This building, neatly fitted up as a chapel, was used for about two years, and in the meantime the corner stone of a new church edifice was laid with appropriate and impressive ceremonies by the bishop of the diocese on July 22, 1845. The location of this church is at the southeast corner of Cumberland and Walnut streets. Rev. T. W. Humes about this time became assistant to the rector, Rev. Mr. Tomes, who remained until September 21, 1846, when he resigned, and was succeeded by the Rev. Mr. Humes, who remained rector of the church, with the exception of two years in the early part of the war, until 1869, those two years being filled in by Rev. William Vaux of London. Rev. William Graham succeeded to the rectorship in January, 1869, remaining until the fall of 1870, when he was succeeded by the Rev. John Howard-Smith, who remained nearly four years. Rev. Thomas Duncan was the next rector, and he remained nearly six years. Rev. Mr. Duncan was succeeded by Rev. H. M. Morrell, D. D., who remained until 1887, when the present rector, Rev. S. S. Ringgold, took charge. His has been a very successful rectorship and the present membership is about 425. The Sunday-school contains 200 scholars, and is under the superintendency of James Maynard. The value of the church property is estimated at $100,000.

The Church of the Epiphany, Protestant Episcopal, was organized in the following manner: In 1867 Rev. T. W. Humes, then rector of St. John's Church, invited Rev. William Mowbray to assist him in his church, having in view at the same time the establishment of a mission in North Knoxville. Early in October of this year services were held by Rev. Mr. Mowbray at Gray Cemetery, only a few persons being present. Afterward the use of a brick mill was granted to these few worshipers by Col. C. M. McGhee, the mill standing on Broad street. North Knoxville at that time contained but one Episcopalian, and that a lady, and there was one prayer-book only that could be found. Mr. Mowbray, under the circumstances, experienced considerable difficulty in organizing his church, but by holding meetings in the evening at different houses he succeeded at length in awakening an interest, and on October 22, 1867, at a meeting in the brick mill, a subscription was started for the purpose of building a church. A building committee was appointed, and a contract signed February 27, 1868, the work was begun March 4, the corner-stone was laid March 28, the church was completed June 21, and dedicated June 29, 1868, by Rev. Mr. Mowbray. The first meeting to organize the church was held December 22, 1868, and Rev. Mr. Mowbray was chosen rector. When Rev. Mr. Mowbray went to Chattanooga the church was served by Rev. Dr. Humes, and in July, 1872, Mr. Mowbray returned. He then remained until 1878, when he was succeeded by Rev. A. A. McDonough, who remained about eight years. The rectors since then have been Revs. A. Buchanan, Dr. William Graham, T. J. L. Hynes, W. J. Morton and Henry Easter, the present rector, who came to the church in November, 1896. This church at this time has 126 communicant members, and the Sunday-school, of which William H. W. Lucas is superintendent, has seventy-five scholars. The value of the church property is $10,000.

The First German Evangelical Lutheran Church was organized October 12, 1869. Rev. John Heckel of Mendota, Ill., being induced by Hon. W. A. Passavant of Pittsburg, Pa., to visit Knoxville to look after the spiritual welfare of this class of Christians, and an organization was effected in the hall over the store of Peter Kern, at the corner of Prince and Union streets. A constitution was drawn up and signed by twenty-two members, and the first board of church officers was composed of the following gentlemen: Dr. Goetz, Charles Baum, trustees; J. A. Aurin, Sr., and Stephen G. Fuchs, elders, and Ferdinand Aurin and Peter Kern, stewards. Rev. Mr. Heckel became the pastor and immediately took steps looking toward the erection of a church building, a lot having been already purchased by a few of the Germans of the place, with the object in view of erecting such an edifice. Rev. Mr. Heckel entered upon his duties in December, 1869, services being temporarily held in the "Old Methodist Church," and in Hampden-Sidney Academy. In May or June, 1870, on the day of Pentecost, the congregation for the first time held services in the basement of their new church building, which was completed and dedicated in September following. On the day these services were held a debt of $2,200 was almost entirely canceled by subscriptions among the congregation, and in 1871 the remaining $100 due was paid off by the treasurer of the church. In December, 1872, there were 118 parishioners and 73 communicants. In November, 1873, on the first Sunday after October 31, a peculiar custom of the German Lutheran Church was celebrated, in commemoration of the 31st of October, 1517, on which day Martin Luther nailed on the door of the Castle Church the famous ninety-five declarations in opposition to the rule of indulgences and the power of the Pope or priest to forgive sins, and an historical sermon was delivered by Rev. John Heckel, pastor of the church. Rev. Mr. Heckel remained in charge four years, and about eighteen months after his retirement he was succeeded by Rev. J. George Schaidt, a graduate of the Philadelphia Theological Seminary. Under his pastorate the church greatly prospered, having in 1887 a membership of 180. Rev. Mr. Schaidt remained until 1881, and during his pastorate a pipe organ was purchased. He was succeeded by Rev. John R. Lauritzen.

who remained until 1892, and it was during his pastorate that the unusual scene was witnessed of the admission of a Hebrew into a Christian church, this event occurring July 6, 1890, John M. Wise being on this day received into the church and baptized. In 1892 Rev. J. A. Friedrich became pastor of this church, remaining until the present time.

St. John's English Lutheran Church was incorporated January 13, 1890, by J. A. Henson, J. C. Kinsel, P. C. Ottinger, Uriah Krider, David L. Smith and M. M. Newcomer, "for the purpose of worshiping Almighty God in accordance with the doctrines of the Bible as taught by the English Lutheran Church." The number of members of this church at the time of organization, in December, 1888, was twenty-seven, and a church edifice, together with the lot on which it stood, was purchased from the Methodist Episcopal Church, South, at a cost of $6,000, and since then there has been spent upon the building $2,000 additional. This church building was dedicated June 7, 1890, by Revs. A. J. Brown, D. D., and Edward T. Horn, D. D. The Rev. L. K. Probst was the first pastor of the church and was succeeded by Rev. R. B. Peery, Ph. D., as supply. The next supply was the present pastor, Rev. A. D. R. Hancher, each of these two pastors remaining five weeks. Then Rev. George S. Diven was supply for five months, and then Rev. Mr. Hancher was called to the pastorate, accepting the call May 7, 1893, remaining to the present time. There are now eighty-six communicant members, and in the Sunday-school, of which Prof. Cooper D. Schmitt is superintendent, there are sixty-five scholars.

The First Welsh Congregational Church was organized in this manner: In April, 1866, five Welshmen named Joseph and David Richards, Daniel Thomas, and John and Daniel Jones, paid a visit to Knoxville, and being pleased with the place determined to make it their home. Handing their letters to the Second Presbyterian Church, they became members of that congregation, and in June following their families, together with other Welsh people, came to Knoxville, and also gave in their letters to the same church. In July they formed a prayer meeting of their own, continuing to hold meetings of this kind for about three and a half years, still retaining their membership in the Second Presbyterian Church.

About June, 1869, they decided to organize a church society and erect a building of their own, a lot being donated to them by Col. C. M. McGhee and the Knoxville Iron Company, near the corner of McGhee and Atkin streets. In the basement of their new building erected on this lot, services were held on October 24, 1869, for the first time, and the members then withdrew from the Second Presbyterian Church, forming a congregation of their own under the name given above. The following officers were elected: Trustees and deacons—Joseph Richards, John Jones and Thomas Davis; secretary, David Lewis, and treasurer, William J. Richards. On February 12, 1870, Rev. Thomas Thomas reached Knoxville, having come here direct from Wales, was called to the pastorate, and filled that position for nearly two years, about thirty members being admitted to the church. In April, 1872, Rev. R. D. Thomas came to Knoxville from Pennsylvania and became pastor in September following, at which time there were fifty members. He added thirty members, and had a flourishing congregation; but the building was not completed until 1875. Rev. R. D. Thomas returned to this church in 1877, having been absent two years, and remained pastor the second time until 1882, when he resigned. In November, 1883, he was succeeded by Rev. D. D. Davis, who remained until December, 1885, and was succeeded by Rev. Robert D. Thomas, who this time remained until 1890, when he was succeeded by Rev. L. Lake. In April, 1895, at a meeting of the congregation, it was resolved that thereafter services be held in English only, and that the name of the church be changed to the First Congregational Church. Rev. J. Francis Davies, who had for some time been located in

Lima, Ohio, came to Knoxville and began his labors as pastor of this church on Sunday, July 7, 1895. In January, 1896, the plans for a new church edifice were completed, which was to be erected at the corner of Oak and Atkins streets. Toward the erection of this new building $10,000 was raised by March 15, 1896. Rev. Mr. Davies resigned his pastorate in June, 1896, to accept a call to the First Congregational Church of Springfield, Ill., and was succeeded by Rev. G. James Jones July 12 following. March 5, 1897, this church was received in the Union Presbytery of the synod of Tennessee, and thus became a Presbyterian church, known since that time as the Atkin Street Presbyterian Church. June 27, 1897, Rev. Mr. Jones resigned his pastorate here to accept the presidency of a college and the pastorate of a church in Wisconsin, and was succeeded by Rev. Dr. W. S. Pryse from that state. Rev. Dr. Pryse resigned in December, 1898, to accept a call to a Presbyterian church in Humboldt, Nebraska.

The Pilgrim Congregational Church is somewhat of an exotic in the South, and for this reason it may be permissible to briefly set forth what Congregationalism is and has done for the country. This church at large represents the Pilgrims and Puritans, who came hither from England in the seventeenth century. The Pilgrims landed at Plymouth, Mass., in 1620, the Puritans came in 1628, to Massachusetts Bay. Each sought freedom to worship God, and they soon merged into one body. In 1628 the First Church of Salem was organized, and in 1630 the First Church of Boston. New England thus became the home of Congregationalism. From that source its colonies have gone abroad, carrying along their distinctive doctrines and zeal for personal liberty and generous education. The bravest and best men known among our settlers were among the Pilgrims and Puritans. Congregationalism gave the country the common school, and the most noted among American institutions of learning, viz.: Harvard, Yale, Dartmouth, Williams, Bowdoin and

Amherst, owe their origin to these people. From New England Congregationalism spread to the West and Northwest. Its recognition of individual rights, its vigor in earnest missionary work, its faith in the Bible as the word of God, its harmony with the doctrines on which all evangelical denominations are agreed, its breadth of purpose and readiness to enter upon new work, are all characteristic features of this church.

In the Southern states Congregationalism has as yet but limited representation; but its polity is adapted to the spirit of independency and soundness of faith which are the strongest features of Southern character. And these characteristics would seem to be the strongest prophecy of its future growth and development in this section of the country.

Pilgrim Congregational Church was organized in June, 1886, by Superintendent C. C. Creegan, the organization being the result of a visit to Knoxville of about six weeks' duration of Rev. John H. Frazee, who came here at the request of the Congregational Board of Home Missions. Rev. Mr. Frazee was at the time settled in New York and could not then well come to Knoxville, hence Rev. Lyman E. Hood became pastor of the church, and remained from September, 1886, until March, 1887. In December, 1886, the church was fully organized with twenty-three members. Services were held in the rooms of the Young Men's Christian Association and several other public halls, but at length the society erected a church building at the corner of Vine and Broad streets, the edifice being of brick and having a seating capacity of about four hundred. It is a unique structure, having the modern features of annex rooms for Sunday-school and social purposes. The building was formally opened for services September 27, 1891, and the cost of the building and lot on which it stands was about $15,000, having been erected in "boom" times.

In June, 1887, the present pastor, Rev. J. H. Frazee, returned to the church, and after a short residence in Knoxville the degree of D. D. was conferred upon him by the University of Tennessee. The membership of the church is now (January 1, 1899) nearly one hundred, having been recently reduced somewhat by restrictions in business and removals. The Sunday-school and Bible classes have a membership of about fifty. The superintendent of the Sunday-school is Samuel C. Roney. The value of the church property at the present time is about $12,000.

The Second Congregational Church (colored) is located at 627 Mabry street, where the society owns quite a fine frame church building.

The First Church of Christ had its origin in 1870, when a few people, believing in the doctrines of the Bible as taught by Alexander Campbell, began holding meetings in rooms hired for the purpose and in private dwellings from time to time for Bible study and prayer. Their number having sufficiently increased they united in a covenant to worship God according to the Holy Scripture on September 6, 1874, under the direction of L. H. Stine, a young minister then just out of Bethany College, West Virginia. They became a regularly organized congregation with A. C. Bruce as elder and N. R. Hall and George T. Rhoades as deacons. At this time there were eighteen of them, but this number gradually increased until in 1887 there were seventy-six names on the roll of membership, and their officers were N. R. Hall and Lewis Tillman, elders, and T. P. McDaniel, George T. Rhoades, and M. O. Cooley, deacons. Up to that time they had had but about two years of preaching, owing to the difficulty of supporting regular ministers; but the elders during the other years conducted services and the congregation met almost every Sunday, as did also the Sunday-school. The ministers who had preached to this congregation previous to the last mentioned year were E. F. Taylor, A. S. Johnson and N. G. Jacks.

For some years the congregation met at the corner of Depot and Broad streets, then at their church on McGhee street, and finally, in 1886, they erected a neat frame church edifice at the northeast corner of Gay and Park streets, which has a round tower, cathedral windows in front and a seating capacity of 500. Since the erection of this new building the ministers of this church have been as follows: S. Turner Willis, from June, 1887, to October, 1888; Gilbert J. Ellis, a few months in 1889; Henry W. Stewart, the latter part of 1890; J. B. Briney from April, 1892, to April, 1893; J. B. Mayfield, from June 1, 1893 to February, 1895; R. M. Giddens, from November 1, 1895, to September, 1897, and Robert Stewart, from August 1, 1898, until the present time. When the church was without ministers the elders thereof conducted Sunday services and Sunday-school work. The present membership is about 100 and of the Sunday-school about 50. This church is now known as the Park Street Christian Church.

The Third Christian Church was organized October 13, 1896, with fifty-three members. Rev. J. P. Holmes became pastor at the time of the organization of the church, and has remained ever since. The membership at the present time is 143, and of the Sunday-school, of which T. A. Hays is superintendent, seventy-five. The congregation is worshiping in Prince's Hall, on the corner of Asylum and Arthur streets, and a fund is being collected with which to purchase a lot and build a church, both of which will be done as soon as the fund is sufficiently large.

The Ramsey Memorial Church, unique in its history, was organized in 1889. The movement leading up to the establishment of this church was conducted by A. G. Scott, whose desire was, as was the desire of those associated with him in the movement, to establish a church which should be practically free from doctrinal teaching. In the summer of 1889 a few names were secured to a paper proposing the establishment of a church of this kind, but for some time prominent men hesitated to sign because the name "Southern," or "Northern" was not placed before the name of the proposed church, those approached being in some cases Presbyterians or Methodists or Baptists. At length in the fall of the year mentioned, Rev. R. N. Thompson, D. D., held a series of revival meetings in the Third Presbyterian Church, and a short time before he was to leave the city he was driven over the ground occupied by Fort Sanders during the late Civil war, and remarked: "I see everything here except something for the Lord—schools, electric lights, street cars, etc. Mr. Scott informed Rev. Mr. Thompson of the efforts he had made to establish an undenominational church, and seeing about 100 young men playing base-ball near the Woolen mills, Mr. Thompson offered to remain three weeks in case a suitable room could be secured for holding meetings. The Highland Avenue school-house was secured and meetings were held, during which meetings the money was raised to build a church, which was erected complete in precisely two weeks, and was occupied on the fifteenth day from that on which its construction was begun. This church, used ever since, stands on the corner of Highland and Eighth avenues, in what was formerly West Knoxville.

The church was organized December 24, 1889, and then named Ramsey Memorial Church, in honor of W. B. A. Ramsey, who was secretary of state of Tennessee for eight years, his daughter having donated the lot on which the church building stands. Rev. R. N. Thompson was called to the pulpit and accepted the call, with the understanding that no doctrinal sermon should be preached, this understanding having obtained with each subsequent minister. Members of seven different churches became members of this church at the time of its organization, and hence it is plain that only the essential doctrines of Christian faith can be insisted upon, as faith, repentance, prayer, and the guidance of the Holy Spirit. At the time of Dr. Thompson's retirement, in 1892, there were 155 members. His successor was Rev. Dr. W. L. Richardson, a minister of the Methodist Episcopal Church, South, who remained until 1895, and was succeeded in 1895 by Rev. I. A. Pierce, a minister of the Methodist Episcopal Church, who remained until June, 1898, and on September 1, 1898, Rev. Dr. R. R. Sutherland became pastor, he being from Danville, Ky. At the present time (November, 1898) there are 140 members in this church, and in the Sunday-school, of which W. B. Henderson is superintendent, there are 130 scholars. The church building is capable of seating about 450 persons.

The First Universalist Church of Knoxville was established in 1895, services being held in the Harris building on March 10, that year, by Rev. W. H. McGlauflin of Harriman. At the conclusion of this meeting a committee was appointed to prepare a constitution and by-laws of church government, looking to the organization of a church of this denomination in this city. The committee consisted of Mrs. E. M. Brown, Mrs. Washburn, C. F. Borden, C. A. Greenwood, Mr. Estes, Mr. Heabler and Rev. Mr. McGlauflin, the latter gentleman having been preaching in Knoxville occasionally for those who accepted the doctrine of universal salvation. Arrangements were then made by which the reverend gentleman should in future preach here twice each month. In February, 1896, Rev. O. H. Shinn and Rev. G. S. Weaver, D. D.; conducted a series of meetings with the view and hope of strengthening the society and ultimately erecting a church edifice, which they felt confident would be done. In order to enlighten the people of Knoxville, to whom the doctrines of this denomination were little known, Rev. Mr. Shinn said: "We believe more, not less; we believe in a God of eternal love, not a Father of vindictiveness; we believe in Christ's victory, not defeat." Rev. Mr. Weaver and Rev. Mr. McGlauflin held services in Harris's block. On June 21, 1896, Rev. C. S. McWhorter of Baltimore, an able lay minister of the Universalist Church, addressed the Universalists of Knoxville in Patterson's Hall, one of his subjects being: "Does the Bible teach endless punishment?" Mr. McWhorter answered this question most emphatically in the negative. He said that St. James' version of the Bible was a collation of other translations, and while it is in the main correct, yet it should be remembered that the translators had a preconceived belief in favor of eternal punishment, and that they could not always be depended upon. He gave as instances three words: Everlasting, damnation, and hell, not one of which he said ought to stand in the English Bible, because they are mistranslations, etc.

In July, 1896, Rev. Richard M. Smith preached for this church on the same lines as those mentioned above in connection with the ministrations of Mr. McWhorter. In November following, Rev. Harry L. Veasey became pastor of the church, remaining here until 1898, when he went away, having been the only regular pastor to serve the congregation; but the organization is still maintained.

The Unitarian Church of Knoxville was organized February 17, 1895, by Rev. Henry Westall, though the Unitarians had previously held meetings among themselves, and had listened to sermons delivered by Rev. Seth Saltmarsh; by Mrs. Ednah Dow Cheney, who preached November 4, 1894; by Mrs. Botume; Miss Channing, daughter of the great Channing; Mrs. Bigelow of Massachusetts, and Mrs. L. C. French, at whose home at No. 620 Cumberland avenue, West, meetings were for some time held. When the organization was effected, as above narrated, about twenty members joined, mostly Northern people, and the church continued to prosper for about two years, meeting sometimes in private houses and sometimes in public halls. When their numbers became too few to enable them to hire public halls, they met at the home of Mrs. J. C. Tyler, on West Clinch street, and finally ceased altogether to hold meetings, some time in 1897, after about eighteen months of labor in the city, which is not ready for Unitarian doctrines.

Beth El Congregation (Reformed) was organized about 1866 with twenty-five members, which number is now reduced to fourteen. Religious worship has been conducted in different halls from that time, except since the last Hebrew New Year's day, in September, 1898. Those who have acted as rabbis have been numerous, mostly young men from the Hebrew Union College at Cincinnati, Ohio. While Julius Ochs was a resident of Knoxville he delivered the weekly sermon, but since then there has been no regular pastor. The officers at the present time are E. Samuels, president; J. Spiro, vice-president; F. Heart, secretary, and L. David, treasurer; trustees: A. Arnstein, A. Lobenstein, D. Blaufield.

Haske Hamuna Congregation (Orthodox Hebrew) was organized in September, 1890, by L. Schwartz, and with ten members, which number has increased to thirty. The first Rabbi of the congregation was Rabbi Michaelof, who remained from 1890 to 1891; the second was Louis Tigris, who remained from 1891 to 1894; and the third, Isaac Winnick, who came in 1894, and still remains. The property of this congregation is located on the corner of Mabry and Temperance streets, and consists of a large lot on which is a moderate-sized frame building used as a synagogue and residence for the Rabbi. It cost $2,000, all of which has been paid except $800. It is now the design to build a new synagogue during the year, 1899, to cost, perhaps, $2,000. The officers at this time are as follows: L. Schwartz, president; H. Kreitzman, vice-president; Solomon Kreitzman, secretary; and Mauritz Deutsch, treasurer. The trustees are I. Volinski, B. Jaffa and D. Coplin.

The First Church of Christian Scientists made application for a charter December 21, 1898, the incorporators being Mrs. Harry H. Ainsworth, Emma A. Thurston, Charles A. Ralston, Addie B. Moore and Calvin Humphreys. The charter filed specifies that the organization seeks all the privileges and rights of a religious organization granted under the constitution of the state, its principal object being to heal the sick as Jesus' disciples healed, and as taught in their text book, "Science and Health, with the Key to the Scriptures," by Mary G. Eddy.

CHAPTER XVIII.

THE BENCH AND BAR.

THE COURT OF THE WATAUGA ASSOCIATION.

First Court in Tennessee—First Court in Knoxville, 1792—The Courts of Knox County and Judges who Held Them—Courts of Chancery—Clerks of the Courts—Sketches of Members of the Knoxville Bar in the Past Hundred Years.

THE first ever held in Tennessee consisted of five members: John Sevier, John Carter, Zach Isbell, Charles Robertson and James Robertson. It continued to exercise authority from 1772 until 1777, in April of which year the general assembly of North Carolina established courts of pleas and quarter sessions, and passed laws for the appointing and commissioning of justices of the peace and sheriffs for the several courts in the district of Washington, as the Watauga county was then called. In 1777 the district of Washington was organized into a county. The courts of pleas and quarter sessions had original jurisdiction in all cases when the debt exceeded £5, in all misdemeanors of an inferior nature, etc., and appellate jurisdiction in all cases tried before a single justice. The court was composed of all the magistrates within its jurisdiction, but any three of them were authorized to transact the business of the court.

The first court of this kind in Washington county, then a part of Salisbury district, met in February, 1778. In 1782 the district of Salisbury was divided and the district of Morgan, including Washington and Sullivan counties, established, its first court session being held in August of the latter year, and the Hon. Spence McCay presiding. This court, however, failed to accomplish the purpose for which it was created, and soon afterward the general assembly of North Carolina organized the counties of Washington, Sullivan,

OLIVER P. TEMPLE.

Davidson and Greene into a judicial district, and appointed an assistant judge and an attorney general for the superior court. This court was directed to be held at Jonesboro.

In May, 1788, courts were held under the authority of North Carolina in Greeneville, and the following lawyers admitted to practice: Andrew Jackson, John McNairy, David Allison, Archibald Roane and Joseph Hamilton. In 1792 the governor of the territory removed the seat of his government to White's Fort, now Knoxville, and the first session of the court of pleas and quarter sessions for Knox county was held here July 16, of that year, James White being the chairman, and there being four other justices. The following-named lawyers were admitted to practice: Luke (Lew?) Bowyer, Alexander Outlaw, Joseph Hamilton, Archibald Roane, Hopkins Lacy, John Rhea and James Reese.

When the territory south of the Ohio river was organized, the courts were permitted to remain practically as they had been, while this country was governed by North Carolina, and the two judges of the superior court—David Campbell and John McNairy—were reappointed by the President, and Joseph Anderson was added as the third judge. Judge McNairy, however, does not appear to have taken any active part in administrative affairs, as authorized by the act of congress creating the territory. These three judges held their offices until the state was admitted into the Union, in 1796.

Among the remarkable facts connected with the first constitution of Tennessee one was that it established no courts, leaving that duty to the legislature; and the first general assembly of the state, which assembled at Knoxville March 28, 1796, established a superior court of law and equity and courts of pleas and quarter sessions, defining their jurisdiction and modes of procedure, which did not materially differ from those of the courts previously existing under the authority of North Carolina and the territory.

Congress passed an act January 31, 1797, making the state a judicial district. Under the act of April, 1796, establishing the superior court, John McNairy, Archibald Roane, and Willie Blount were elected judges. Blount declined to serve, and in his stead W. C. C. Claiborne was appointed September 2, 1796. McNairy resigned to accept the federal judgeship, and to succeed him Howell Tatum was appointed in May, 1797. McNairy served as district judge until 1834, and was succeeded by Morgan W. Brown, who served until 1853, being then succeeded by West H. Humphreys. In 1861 Judge Humphreys accepted the office of confederate states judge for Tennessee, was impeached by the house of Representatives at Washington, and was convicted and deposed by the senate. Connolly F. Trigg was appointed by President Lincoln, in July, 1862, serving until his death in 1880, and being succeeded by D. M. Key, appointed in August of that year by the President and holding the position until his retirement January 26, 1894. His successor was Charles D. Clark, the present judge.

November 16, 1809, an act was passed abolishing the superior court, and establishing circuit courts, and a supreme court of errors and appeals. The judges of the superior court were as follows: David Campbell, 1797 to 1807; Andrew Jackson, 1798 to 1804; Samuel Powell, 1807 to 1809; John Overton, 1804 to 1809; Parry W. Humphreys, 1807 to 1809; Hugh L. White, 1801 to 1807; Thomas Emmerson, 1807 to 1809.

The act of November 16, 1809, mentioned above, as establishing circuit courts, established five circuit courts for the state, each court to consist of one judge, and to be held twice annually in each county. The circuit court was given the same jurisdiction in all matters of common law and equity as previously belonged to the superior court; it had exclusive jurisdiction in criminal cases, and appellate jurisdiction in case from the court of pleas and quarter sessions. The judge and solicitor-general were elected by a joint vote of the general assembly. The second circuit was composed of the following counties: Anderson, Bledsoe, Blount, Cocke, Jefferson, Knox, Rhea, Roane and Sevier.

The supreme court of errors and appeals under this act consisted of two judges in error and one circuit judge, and was to be held annually at Jonesboro, Knoxville, Carthage, Nashville and Clarksville. This court had only appellate jurisdiction. The judges of this court were Hugh L. White, 1809 to 1815; George W. Campbell, 1809 to 1811; John Overton, 1811 to 1816; W. W. Cooke, October 19, 1815 to 1816, and Archibald Roane, 1815 to 1818. In 1815 the number of judges of the supreme court was increased to three, Archibald Roane being appointed as the third judge. In 1823 a fourth judge was added, and in 1824 a fifth. Shortly afterward, however, the number was reduced to four, as it remained until 1834, when a new constitution was adopted. Under this constitution there was established a supreme court, of which William B. Turley, William B. Reese and Nathan Greene were elected judges. Judge Reese resigned in 1848, Judge Turley in 1850 and Judge Greene in 1852. Their places were severally filled by the election of Robert J. McKinney, A. W. O. Totten and Robert L. Caruthers, all three of whom were elected again in 1853. Judge Totten, who resigned in 1855, was succeeded by William R. Harris, who, upon his death in 1858, was succeeded by Archibald Wright. Upon the resignation of Judge Caruthers in 1861, William F. Cooper was elected to the vacancy thus caused. During the Civil war no term of this court was held, and when the war ceased Governor Brownlow declared the supreme bench, appointing thereto Samuel Milligan, J. O. Shackleford, and Alvin Hawkins. Judge Shackleford resigned in 1867, Horace H. Harrison holding the office about a year, when Judge Shackleford was reappointed. In 1868 Milligan and Hawkins resigned, their places being filled by the appointment of Henry G. Smith and George Andrews. In May, 1869, George Andrews, Andrew McLain and Alvin

Hawkins were elected judges of this court, serving until the new constitution of 1870 went into effect.

Because of the suspension of this court during the four years of the Civil war and the large accumulation of litigation growing out of the war, the dockets of the supreme court were much crowded when the constitutional convention met in 1870. It was therefore ordered that temporarily there should be six judges of the supreme court, two from each grand division of the state; but that after the first vacancy occurring after January 1, 1873, the court should consist of five members only. The members of the court elected in 1870 were: From East Tennessee, Thomas A. R. Nelson and James W. Deaderick; from Middle Tennessee, A. O. P. Nicholson and Peter Turney, and from West Tennessee, John L. T. Sneed and Thomas J. Freeman. Judge Nelson resigned December 5, 1871, and was succeeded by Robert McFarland. Judge Nicholson, who was chief justice from the establishment of the court, died March 23, 1876, and was succeeded by James W. Deaderick. In 1878 all the members of the court were re-elected except Judge Sneed, who was succeeded by William F. Cooper, and four of these judges served the full term, Judge Deaderick being chief justice. Judge McFarland died in October, 1884, and was succeeded by J. B. Cooke, by appointment.

In 1886 the following court was chosen: Peter Turney and W. C. Caldwell for the state at large; D. L. Snodgrass for East Tennessee; Horace H. Lurton for Middle Tennessee, and W. C. Folkes for West Tennessee. Judge Folkes died in 1890, and was succeeded by W. D. Beard of Memphis, who served until the August election of that year, when B. J. Lea was elected. Upon the death of Chief Justice Lea, in 1894, Judge Snodgrass became chief justice, the former chief justices having been Judge Turney and Judge Lurton. In January, 1893, Judge Turney having been elected governor, his place on the bench was filled by the appointment of John S. Wilkes, and when Judge Lurton accepted the United

States circuit judgeship his place was filled by the appointment of W. K. McAlister, April 1, 1893. Upon the death of Judge Lea in 1894, the vacancy thus caused was filled by the appointment of A. D. Bright.

In 1894 the following gentlemen were elected to the bench of the supreme bench: For East Tennessee, D. L. Snodgrass, who was re-elected chief justice; for Middle Tennessee, John S. Wilkes; for West Tennessee, W. D. Beard, and for the state at large, W. C. Caldwell and W. E. McAlister.

It was soon discovered that even the enlarged supreme court could not dispose of the cases in arrears on the docket, and in 1873 temporary courts with limited powers were created to assist in the work, the first of these courts being the arbitration court of Middle Tennessee, which expired by limitation September 1, 1873. In 1875 and in 1877 the experiment was tried again, in the latter year being extended to West Tennessee. In 1879 a similar court was created for East Tennessee, its members being Henry H. Ingersoll, J. B. Cooke and William V. Deaderick.

In 1883 there were created courts of referees, composed of three members from each grand division of the state, appointed by the judges of the supreme court. These courts were authorized and instructed to report on the facts and the law of each case, except revenue cases filed in the supreme court for their respective divisions before January 1, 1885. The members of the court for East Tennessee were John Frizell, John L. T. Sneed and S. J. Kirkpatrick. The reports of the referees were final unless excepted to in writing with assignments of error within fifteen days after they were filed.

During recent years the appealed cases have steadily grown in number, those of the East Tennessee docket having increased from an average of about two hundred to more than five hundred. The labors of the supreme court, therefore, are constant and incessant, and for this reason it became necessary in 1895 to devise additional means of clearing the dockets.

The court of chancery appeals was therefore created, composed of three members, one from each grand division of the state. This court hears chancery cases such as may be assigned to it by the supreme court, but cannot determine causes affecting state revenue. It has only appellate jurisdiction. Upon all questions of fact its findings are conclusive, but on questions of law an appeal in the nature of a writ of error to the supreme court may be taken within ten days after decree. By every one this court is considered the most satisfactory experiment yet made to relieve the supreme court. In 1895 R. M. Barton, Jr., was appointed from East Tennessee, and was elected in 1896.

The circuit court, as stated elsewhere in this chapter, dates back to 1793, on March 13 of which year Governor Blount established the district of Hamilton, including Jefferson and Knox counties, in which district a superior court of law and equity was held at Knoxville twice each year, beginning on the second Monday of April and October. To trace the succession of judges that have held the circuit court with anything like accuracy would be a very difficult matter, hence it is attempted only to present a tolerably complete and accurate list of the judges that have held court in this district, which was denominated the third judicial circuit at least from 1853 down to 1870, when the criminal court was established. The first judges that held court were John McNairy, David Campbell and Joseph Anderson, and succeeding them have been Edward Scott, who was judge from as early as 1818 and down to 1847; Samuel Powell, from 1823 to 1838; Charles F. Keith, from 1826 to 1850; Robert M. Anderson, 1840 to 1850; S. J. W. Lucky, 1845 to 1847; E. Alexander, 1845 to 1856; William C. Dunlap, 1846; William G. Swan, 1857; Thomas C. Lyon, 1858; George Brown, 1859 to 1863; E. T. Hall, 1865 to 1878; S. A. Rodgers, 1878 till Knox county was made a separate circuit.

In 1885 the judge of the criminal court was authorized by law to hold the circuit court, and as Judge S. T. Logan was then judge of the criminal court he also held the circuit court from 1886 to 1891, but in 1891 the two courts were again separated and Joseph W. Sneed was appointed judge of the criminal court, presiding in this court until he became judge of the circuit court in 1894, succeeding Judge Logan, Judge Sneed's term expiring in 1902.

The clerks of the circuit court have been in part as follows, the records in the early part of the century not giving the names of all the clerks: I. Hamilton, in 1793, and how long is not shown by his record. George M. White was clerk at least from 1838 to 1847 and possibly to 1853, when M. L. Hall was clerk, serving until he resigned April 11, 1864; S. H. Smith, 1864-66; W. R. McBath, 1866-70; E. W. Adkins, 1870-82; William B. Ford, 1882-98, and R. A. Brown, 1898-1902.

The chancery court, first established in what is now Tennessee by an act of the legislature of North Carolina in 1784, was a general law and equity court combined. In 1787 this court was divided and the chancery branch called the court of equity, a clerk and master being appointed for each equity court, but both courts being held by the same judge.

The North Carolina session act of 1790 provided that the laws of North Carolina should remain in force in the territory until changed by the territorial legislature, and the first act of this legislature 1794, chapter 2, section 1, continued the superior court as established by North Carolina, and the same act confirmed the division of the territory south of the River Ohio, into Washington, Hamilton and Mero districts, and conferred upon each district a superior court of law and equity. Knox county was in Hamilton district. The state of Tennessee adopted the same system in April, 1876.

By an act of the legislature passed in 1809 these superior courts were abolished, and a superior court and five circuit courts were established, the circuit courts being invested with all the original equity jurisdiction of the superior courts.

In 1811 this equity jurisdiction was taken away from the circuit courts and conferred upon the supreme court. In 1813 the circuit courts were given concurrent jurisdiction with the supreme court in equity cases, and in 1822 an act was passed to amend the judiciary system of the state, by which it was provided that there should be held by one of the supreme court judges a court of equity in each of the places in which the supreme court was then held in each circuit, said courts to be confined entirely to matters of equity. Under this act the chancery court was held once a year in Rogersville, Knoxville, Chattanooga, Sparta, Nashville and Columbia, sitting two weeks at each place except at Nashville, where it sat six weeks.

In 1824 it was enacted that the chancery court should sit twice a year in each circuit, and finally in 1827 it was enacted that two chancellors should be elected, the state being divided into two chancery divisions, with one chancellor for each, having jurisdiction over the entire state, and the right to interchange.

The first legislature under the constitution of 1834 increased the chancellors to three, since which time the number has been enlarged at the will of the legislature. The first chancellor under the act of 1827 was Nathan Green, who was chancellor of the Eastern district from 1827 to 1831, the second chancellor for this district being William B. Reese, who served from 1831 to 1836. The first record found in the office of the clerk and master of Knox county is of a court held at the court house on Monday, April 16, 1832. for the chancery division, composed of Sevier, Knox, Anderson, and Campbell counties, by W. B. Reese. W. B. A. Ramsey was appointed clerk and master. The next record is dated October 15, 1832, on which day R. H. Hynds. William Swan, Jacob F. Foute, S. R. Rodgers and E. Alexander were admitted to practice.

On April 11, 1839. the court was presided over by Judge Thomas L. Williams, for the sixth chancery district of the

Eastern division of Tennessee, and W. B. A. Ramsey was reappointed clerk and master. Chancellor Williams served from 1836 to 1854, when he was succeeded by S. J. W. Lucky, who held the office until 1865, in which year S. R. Rodgers was appointed and served one year. He was succeeded in 1866 by Oliver P. Temple, who served until 1878, in which year W. B. Staley was elected and served until 1886. Henry R. Gibson was then elected and served until 1894, when the present incumbent, H. B. Lindsay, was elected, his term expiring in 1902. Judge Lindsay's chancery division was abolished by the legislature in 1899.

The clerk and masters of this court have been as follows: W. B. A. Ramsey, April 16, 1832 to 1848; Hu. L. McClung, appointed January 29, 1848; Samuel A. White, appointed October 7, 1857; David A. Deaderick, appointed January 18, 1859; M. L. Patterson, appointed October 3, 1870; S. P. Evans, appointed November 10, 1882; W. L. Trent, appointed November 10, 1888; John W. Conner, appointed November 10, 1894, and J. F. Chumbley, appointed December 31, 1898.

The criminal court for Knox county was established by an act of the legislature in 1870, second session, chapter 100, which provided that there should be a court in the city of Knoxville for the county of Knox, which should "have exclusive jurisdiction for the indictment, or presentment, trial and punishment of all crimes and offenses in said county against the state." This court was also given common law jurisdiction, the practice and pleadings therein to be the same as prescribed for circuit courts.

In 1873 the style of the court was prescribed as "The Criminal court for the District of Knox," and the judge of this court was granted the privilege of interchange with other judges, and the judges of the criminal court were not disqualified from the practice of their profession in other courts. In the same year it was also provided that there should be a district attorney for the district of Knox and a clerk, both of whom should be elected at the regular August election. In 1875 it was enacted that there should be three terms per year, beginning on the first Monday in January, May and September.

The first term of this court was begun on Monday, September 26, 1870, that being the day prescribed by law for the first term of the court. Hon. M. L. Hall was judge of this court, elected in August preceding, and H. C. Tarwater was clerk, he having been elected by a majority of 534 votes. Judge Hall's commission was signed by Governor D. W. C. Senter.

The several judges of this court have been Hon. M. L. Hall, 1870-86; S. T. Logan, 1886-91; Joseph W. Sneed, 1891-94; and T. A. R. Nelson, the present incumbent, elected 1894.

The district attorneys have been as follows: J. M. Thornburgh, 1870-72; John M. Fleming, 1872-73; J. C. J. Williams, 1873-78; D. D. Anderson, 1878-86; T. A. R. Nelson, 1886-94, and E. F. Mynatt, 1894-1902.

The clerks of this court have been as follows: H. C. Tarwater, 1870-73; W. H. Swan, 1873-74; G. L. Maloney, 1874-82; W. F. Gibbs, 1882-94, and A. G. French, 1894-1902.

ARCHIBALD ROANE, second governor of the state of Tennessee, and one of the early lawyers and judges of Knoxville, was born in Lancaster county, Pa., in 1760. He was a thoroughly educated man, and appears to have been admitted to the bar both at Jonesboro and at Greeneville in 1788. He was the territorial attorney-general for the district of Hamilton, comprising originally the counties of Jefferson and Knox, and he was a delegate to the constitutional convention of 1796 from Jefferson county. He was one of the first three judges of the superior court of the state, the other two being John McNairy and Willie Blount. In 1801, John Sevier having served three consecutive terms as governor, the length of time permitted by the constitution,

Archibald Roane was elected, and served one term, became a candidate for a second term, but was defeated by John Sevier. The reason for this defeat is probably to be found in the enmity aroused in the mind of Governor Sevier, who during Roane's term of office had been a candidate for the office of major-general of the militia of the state, against Andrew Jackson. The electors of the major-general were the field officers of the militia, but upon the vote being cast and counted there was a tie as between Sevier and Jackson. The law in this case gave the deciding vote to the governor of the state, who cast it in favor of Andrew Jackson.

The casting of this deciding vote by Gov. Roane was followed directly by his own defeat for re-election, by the election of John Sevier instead, and to the subsequent career of Andrew Jackson, military and civil, fraught with such tremendous consequences to the people of the United States, with which all readers of American history are familiar. Archibald Roane was a most scholarly man, and at one time the tutor of Hugh Lawson White. From 1811 to 1815 he was judge of the Second circuit, and in the latter year he was made one of the judges of the supreme court of errors and appeals, serving in this capacity until his death in 1818.

According to Joshua W. Caldwell, from whose longer sketch of the subject this sketch is condensed, Archibald Roane was, in all probability, with the exception of Haywood and possibly also Felix Grundy, the most cultured man of his time in the state. He was fond of literature, well versed in the classics, of affable manners, and next to Sevier in favor with the people, the superiority of the latter in this regard being because of his services in the war of the Revolution and in Indian wars. Among the common people courage upon the field of battle is more easily appreciated than mere scholarly attainments, and for this reason, in part, Sevier, the determined man of action, the partisan, the inveterate hand-shaker, the lavishly hospitable Sevier, defeated the thoughtful, careful, scrupulous scholar, Archibald Roane.

THOMAS L. WILLIAMS, formerly a chancellor and also a judge of the supreme court of Tennessee, was born in North Carolina, and came to Tennessee early in the present century. He was a skillful and successful lawyer, and in 1826 was made a judge of the supreme court, being appointed to a vacancy by the governor, but the legislature declined to permanently fill the place, thereby reducing the number of judges. From the time of his retirement from the supreme court he practiced law in Knox and adjoining counties until 1836, when he was elected chancellor for the Eastern division, and held the position until 1854, having been twice re-elected. He presided in nineteen counties, holding thirty-eight courts each year, and being absent from home forty weeks of the fifty-two. To all of these courts Judge Williams rode on horseback, there being then no railroads in Tennessee until the fifties, and this riding was over rough roads, in summer and in winter, in all kinds of weather, and he endured hardships which few men now, or even then, could have endured. And it is to this endurance and to the fidelity of Judge Williams that the lawyers of the state attribute in large measure the preservation of the chancery system. Judge Williams was a man of strong convictions and will, and, though not without prejudice, yet he was essentially honest and just, and he holds a prominent and honorable place in the judiciary of the state. His death occurred December 2, 1856, at Nashville, and his portrait hangs in the chancery court room at Knoxville, showing him to have been a dignified, handsome, refined looking man.

JOHN WILLIAMS, one of the pioneer lawyers of East Tennessee, and later a United States senator from this state, was born in Surry county, N. C., January 29, 1778. That he was well educated in his youth appears evident from the fact that he was a man of culture and refinement, as well as strength, and he was admitted to practice law in North Carolina, though he did not enter upon the practice until he came to Tennessee, this date not being certainly known, but it must have been prior to 1813, as in that year he was commissioned colonel of the Thirty-ninth regiment United States infantry, and was in command of that regiment in the Creek war. In this sketch, for want of space, it can only be stated that he came out of that war with great credit, and in 1815 he was elected to the United States senate, to fill the vacancy caused by the resignation of George W. Campbell. At the end of this short term he was re-elected and served until 1823, when he was again a candidate for re-election, but was defeated by Andrew Jackson, the friends of Jackson having resolved to defeat Williams, unless he would promise to support Jackson for the presidency. Mr. Williams had already committed himself to the support of Crawford, and so could not comply with the demands of Jackson's friends. In 1825 he was appointed by President Adams minister to Guatemala, and after returning home he was an active promoter of the projected Louisville, Cincinnati & Charleston railroad, which was intended to extend from the Ohio river through Kentucky, Tennessee, North and South Carolina, to the Atlantic ocean, on substantially the same route now in contemplation for the Black Diamond railway. From this time on until his death, which occurred August 10, 1837, he devoted his time mainly to the law, though twice after coming home he was elected to the state senate.

His son, Colonel John Williams, probably the most intimate friend of Andrew Johnson, was the father of J. C. J. Williams, and Thomas L. Williams, both members of the Knoxville bar, and of Rufus W. Williams, of the New York bar.

HUGH LAWSON WHITE, a man remarkable for the high order of his mental and moral endowments, was for many years one of the most prominent leaders in East Tennessee. He was a son of James White, the founder of Knoxville, and hence whatever pertains to his life is of unusual interest to the people of this city. But in this sketch, as in all others in this chapter, he is treated of mainly as a lawyer and a judge. When he was sixteen years of age, Hugh L. White began the study of the classics under Rev. Samuel Carrick, the first president of what is now the University of Tennessee. Occasionally he was assisted by Archibald Roane, who is described as a "scholar of eminence." Young White was in the battle of Etowah, which closed the career of Governor John Sevier as an Indian fighter, and in this battle he shot and killed the Indian leader, King Fisher, an act which, though committed in open and honorable warfare, yet so overwhelmed him with grief that he would not permit it to be mentioned in his presence, and he even went so far that he forbade Dr. Ramsey to relate it in his "Annals of Tennessee."

About 1794 he went to Philadelphia to study mathematics, and about a year later to Lancaster, Pa., to study law. In 1796 he began the practice of the law in Knoxville, meeting with almost immediate success. In 1801 he was elected a judge of the superior court, then the highest judiciary in the state. In 1807 he resigned to enter the state senate, and in 1809 he was appointed United States district attorney, resigning this office also to go into the state senate. At the close of his second senatorial term he was appointed a judge of the supreme court of errors and appeals, holding this office until 1815. In 1812 he was elected president of the Bank of Tennessee, and he retained this office until 1827, in the meantime having been for the third time elected to the state senate. In 1807 he had compiled the land laws of Tennessee, and in 1817 he prepared and secured the passage of the first effective law against dueling in the state, doing more than any other man to establish the law against, and the public sentiment against, this barbarous custom in Tennessee. Throughout his entire career he was guided by a large and accurate knowledge of the essential principles of the law, and by a strong natural sense of justice. His most distinguished career was terminated by death April 10, 1840. He was United States senator from 1825 to 1839, was for a time president pro tem., and was candidate for presidency of the United States in 1836.

ROBERT J. McKINNEY, one of the great judges who served upon the supreme bench of the state under the constitution of 1834, was born in County Coleraine, Ireland, February 1, 1803. His father, Samuel McKinney, settled not far from the present site of Rogersville, Tenn., and there young Robert J. grew up on the farm, determined to rise in the world. After attending school in the winter months for some years he then went to Greeneville College, leaving, however, without graduating, and began the study of law in the office of his uncle, John A. McKinney of Rogersville, being admitted to practice in 1824. Settling at Greeneville, he there began practice, by riding the circuit, as was the custom in those days. In 1829 the case of Rhea vs. Rhea was tried at Blountville, on an issue of devisavit vel non, McKinney being the junior counsel for the proponents, and when the case was called the senior counsel was ill, and McKinney tried and won it, thereby establishing his reputation and securing a lucrative practice. He was probably the most thorough lawyer in the constitutional convention of 1834.

In 1847 William B. Reese resigned his place upon the supreme bench, and, largely through the instrumentality of Return J. Meigs, Mr. McKinney was elected to the vacancy, his principal competitor being William Henry Sneed. He served continuously until 1861, when he became one of the peace commissioners sent to Washington by Governor Isham G. Harris. After the war, when the state brought suit to enforce its lien against the railroads to which it had given aid, Judge McKinney was one of the commissioners, the other two being Archibald Wright and Francis B. Fogg. He died at his home in Knoxville, October 9, 1875.

While he was in no respect a brilliant or showy lawyer,

yet he was diligent, thorough, accurate and sound, and he had great knowledge of and admiration for the common law. And while as a judge his opinions lack the embellishments and flavor of scholarship, yet they are always definite and clear, and are carefully written in strong, plain English, with the single purpose of expounding the law. So far as the necessities of lawyers are concerned, they are considered equal to the best among those of the judges of the supreme court.

CONNALLY F. TRIGG, the fourth in succession of the United States district judges for Tennessee, was born in Abingdon, Va., March 8, 1810. He entered upon the practice of the law at Abingdon in 1833, lived there until 1856, when he removed to Knoxville, Tenn., bringing with him an excellent reputation as a professional man. This reputation he not only maintained but increased, and when the Civil war came upon the country he was looked upon as one of the ablest lawyers in Tennessee. He was great by nature and possessed a most attractive personalty, was kindly and cordial and made friends wherever he was known. Though a Southerner by birth, relations and sentiment, yet he clung to the Union with unswerving devotion, was outspoken in his opinions, and displayed the highest courage and most positive decision in laboring to prevent Tennessee from seceding, and it was this course, taken at the beginning of the war and maintained steadily all through, that won for him the confidence of Union men everywhere, and secured for him the appointment by President Lincoln in July, 1862, mentioned in the beginning of this sketch. And at the close of the war he was the sole Federal judge in Tennessee to administer the penal laws of the United States. While he had been one of the strongest and most pronounced of Union men, yet when it came to a decision on the constitutionality of the Test Oath act, he declared it unconstitutional, and was the first Federal judge to so decide. He was essentially generous and just in his character, and in the administration of his high office the qualities he displayed, devoid as they were of malice or resentment, cannot be too highly commended. All men of all parties he treated fairly, and the Confederate soldier or sympathizer, while never unduly favored, was always sure of justice in the court presided over by Judge Trigg. More than this need not be said. The memory of Judge Trigg is held in honor and gratitude. He remained upon the bench until his death, which occurred April 25, 1880.

THOMAS C. LYON, formerly of the Knoxville bar, was born in Roane county, Tennessee. December 10, 1810, and was educated at the East Tennessee University under Dr. Charles Coffin, graduating in 1829, his graduating address being an original poem, which "was esteemed by the large audience present and the best critics of the day, a most excellent and creditable production."

He has the reputation of having been an able and successful lawyer, and a thorough and profound jurist. He was an ideal lawyer, and brought honor to the profession, and he was frequently called upon to sit upon the supreme bench as a special judge, his opinions being among the best to be found in the state reports. He was exceedingly careful of the rights and feelings of others, and it is said of him that during a professional career of thirty years there was no instance of his having used a term offensive to the bench or to any member of the bar.

In 1864 he left Tennessee for Richmond, Virginia, with the view of offering his services to the Confederate government, but on the way was attacked by disease, and died at Richmond, October 1, 1864.

JAMES W. DEADERICK was born at Jonesboro, Tenn., November 12, 1812, and began life by farming and keeping a store in Jefferson county, Tenn. After failing in business about 1837, because of the general financial depression of the times and also because of having gone surety for his friends to a considerable extent, he moved to Iowa, where he resided as Indian agent, and afterward returned to Jonesboro, taking up the study of the law. In 1844 he was admitted to the bar, and by persevering industry gradually rose in his profession until he achieved an honorable position. In the Presidential election of 1860 he was a Bell and Everett elector for the first district, but when the state seceded he united his fortunes with the Confederacy and was loyal to that government throughout the war. In 1870, when under the new constitution the judiciary was reorganized, he was elected one of the judges of the supreme court from East Tennessee, and in 1878 he was re-elected, for the state at large. In 1876, upon the death of Judge A. O. P. Nicholson, he was elected chief justice of the court, and continued to hold that position until his retirement from the bench in 1886.

Judge Deaderick was a good man, a good lawyer and a good judge, without pretense of superior learning and yet possessed of great learning. Upon his retirement from the bench in 1886 he repaired to his home in Jonesboro, and there died October 8, 1890. His career is illustrative of the value of industry, perseverance and integrity, which will always win for their possessor the highest position possible for him to attain.

WILLIAM-HENRY SNEED, a prominent member of the Knoxville bar in the period immediately preceding the war, was born in Davidson county in 1812, and soon after attaining his majority began the practice of the law at Murfreesboro. The high standing which he early attained he maintained until the end of his life. In 1843 he was elected to the state senate, and at the end of his term located at Greeneville. He had in 1839 formed a partnership with Judge Charles Ready, his former preceptor, this partnership lasting until he was elected to the senate. After locating in Greeneville he formed a partnership with R. J. McKinney, which lasted about a year, and he then removed to Knoxville, where he was unusually successful in practice until the beginning of the war. In 1855 he was elected to congress as a whig from the Knoxville district, served in that body with distinction and made many friends. At the beginning of the war he was a strong Union man, but said that his conduct with regard to secession would be governed by the action of the state. When Tennessee seceded, he gave his adherence to the Confederate cause. When Burnside occupied Knoxville, he moved his family to Virginia, remaining there until after the surrender of Lee. As soon as conditions would permit he returned to Knoxville, residing here until the time of his death in 1869.

As a lawyer Mr. Sneed was unusually successful, excelling especially as a chancery pleader and practitioner. There is no question that he was one of the most painstaking, laborious and able lawyers of his time in Tennessee, and he was of great force of character, of high social standing and one of the most popular men in the state. His son, Joseph W. Sneed, is judge of the circuit court of Knox county.

HORACE MAYNARD, one of the most brilliant of orators, one of the ablest of lawyers, and one of the best of men, was born at Westborough, Mass., August 30, 1814, and graduated at Amherst college in 1838. During that same year he came to Knoxville, Tenn., and began the study of law in the office of Judge Ebenezer Alexander, at the same time being made tutor in East Tennessee university, and afterward professor of mathematics. Having been connected with the university six years he then began the practice of the law. His means being quite limited he walked the circuit, while other lawyers rode. But he had industry, the first requisite in law as in everything, and was not long in making himself known and felt. While the bar of East Tennessee at that time contained many lawyers of learning and culture, yet Horace Maynard was easily the best read man of them all.

A story is told that at one time the Knoxville lawyers in going to court at Clinton found the Clinch river so swollen that it could be crossed only by swimming. Maynard plunged boldly in and swam across, when the other lawyers told him to attend to their cases, and returned home. From that time on, the story continues, the cases being well attended to, the clients all went to Maynard. As an advocate he was a brilliant and logical speaker, but at times very sarcastic and severe, yet he was at heart one of the kindest of men. He was always regarded, even by his most bitter political antagonists, as a sincere and honest man. A story is told of him that on one occasion a certain prominent Tennessee politician approached him with the suggestion which involved improper rewards. Mr. Maynard took down a copy of the United States statutes, and read to his auditor again and again the law on the offering of bribes to congressmen, at each reading emphasizing a different word in order that the full effect of the statute might be felt. The visitor was thus given every opportunity for becoming familiar with the law on bribery, and is said to have ultimately retired in confusion.

While his speeches always seemed far above his audience yet they were always appreciated by even the common people, and with the possible exception of Judge T. A. R. Nelson he was the most popular public speaker in East Tennessee. As a man, however, he was rather admired and respected than popular, for in manner he was austere and cold except to personal and intimate friends, who alone were able to know and to appreciate his real worth. In 1875, after having served sixteen years in congress, he was appointed by President Grant minister to Turkey, and there served until 1880, when he was recalled by President Hayes and made postmaster-general. This was his last public office, and he died at Knoxville, May 3, 1882.

THOMAS A. R. NELSON, one of the most distinguished men in the history of Tennessee, was born in Roane county, Tenn., in 1812, and graduated at East Tennessee College, now the University of Tennessee, in 1828. Having studied law with Judge Thomas L. Williams, he was admitted to the bar before he attained his majority, and when he became twenty-one he was appointed by Governor William Carroll, state's attorney for the first circuit, in which he then resided. Afterward he was twice elected by the legislature to that office, and held it until 1844. In 1851 he was a candidate before the whig caucus for United States senator, but was defeated by one vote by James C. Jones. In 1859 he was a candidate for congress in the First district, his competitor being Landon C. Haynes, and they two were more capable of affording the people the entertainment they most craved than any other two men in the state. Nelson was elected by a small majority, and it was during his service in the succeeding congress that his famous speech was made, which was declared by the London Times to be the highest product of American oratory.

In 1861 he was again elected to congress, but endeavoring to make his escape across the mountains into Kentucky he was captured by Confederate scouts, taken as prisoner to Richmond, where he was paroled upon the condition that he would not engage in hostilities against the Confederate states so long as they held possession of Tennessee. Returning to his home in Washington county, he there remained until General Burnside took possession of East Tennessee in 1863, when he removed to Knoxville, making that city his home the remainder of his life, dying in 1873.

In 1870, when the supreme court was reorganized, he was elected a member thereof, serving about a year when he resigned for the purpose of attending to his private affairs. In the great impeachment trial of Andrew Johnson, Judge Nelson was one of the counsel of the President. His argument was almost an impromptu one, and so failed to satisfy him that until the day of his death he did not cease to criticise it, and some say with undue severity. But the speech is an admirable one, and will continue to reflect credit on its author.

Judge Nelson was one of the best lawyers Tennessee has produced. His mind was both powerful and quick to act. He was a thorough and profound student of the law, and he was always fond of the rounded verbiage and fine distinctions of the common law. He was his own secretary, and his constant companion was a large portfolio in which he carried carefully prepared briefs and notes for argument in every case. Judge Nelson had a large practice, but was too indifferent to money to secure from his practice adequate returns. His temperament was that of the orator and also of the poet, two rare qualities still more rarely combined, but when so combined giving great strength. For style he went to the old masters, and as a consequence his diction was always imposing and rich. His retirement from the bench was a purely personal matter, for his relations with his associates were pleasant and the work was congenial to his tastes. And after retiring, he spent the remaining two years of his life quietly and happily among his friends.

His son, Thomas A. R. Nelson, is a lawyer of high standing in East Tennessee, and in 1894 was elected judge of the criminal court of Knox county. His court was abolished by the legislature in the spring of 1899.

MAJOR LEAROY HALL was born in Knox county, Tenn., August 16, 1814, and was the eldest of six children born to William and Nancy (Nelson) Hall. He was reared on the farm, and when nineteen years of age began teaching school, which profession he followed a short time after his marriage in 1836, and then began the study of law with Judge Robert M. Anderson. Afterward he studied with Samuel R. Rodgers until January, 1841, when he was admitted to the bar. In 1852 he was elected clerk of the circuit court and held the office until the close of the war, being re-elected in March, 1864, but resigned in April following to accept an appointment by Judge Trigg to the office of clerk of the United States circuit and district courts and United States commissioner, all of which he resigned in August, 1870, to accept the office of judge of the criminal court, created in July, 1870. This office he retained until 1886, when he was defeated, for the first time in his life, by Judge Logan, and he then resumed the practice of the law. Judge Hall wrote a treatise on criminal law.

WILLIE BLOUNT, youngest half-brother of Governor William Blount, was born in Bertie county, N. C., in 1767 or 1768. While still under thirty years of age, he was elected a judge of the superior court of the state, but declined to accept the office. In 1809 he was elected governor, and by successive re-elections served three terms. During his administration occurred the Creek war, and by his personal efforts, and, it is said, on his own responsibility, he raised for General Jackson $370,000, for which he received the thanks of the President and three secretaries of war. He was eminently patriotic, and his vigorous prosecution of the war of 1812 attracted attention throughout the country. He was earnestly devoted to the policy of internal improvements, and as a delegate from Montgomery county to the constitutional convention he urged upon that body the importance of increased facilities for transportation and travel, and it is believed that but for the Civil war events would have proved the soundness of his views. He died September 10, 1835, and the legislature voted him a monument to be erected at Clarksville.

ALFRED CALDWELL, formerly one of the acknowledged leaders of the Knoxville bar, was born in Jefferson county, Tenn., July 5, 1829, and was a son of John Caldwell, pension agent at Knoxville under the administration of

Andrew Johnson. Alfred Caldwell grew to manhood on the farm, and as a school teacher earned the money to pay his way through college, graduating at Maryville College, having taken the junior and senior class studies in one year. Graduating at the Lebanon law school in 1854 he at once entered upon the practice of his profession at Athens, where he formed a partnership with Milton P. Jarnagin, and was at once successful at the bar. Thoroughly educated and possessing a mind of unusual acuteness and power, he found the study and practice of the law entirely congenial, and his great gifts as a speaker made him an exceptionally successful advocate.

After the war he located at Knoxville, and there practiced law until his retirement from active life in 1882. At Knoxville his ability was fully recognized, and he was habitually chosen special chancellor when one was needed. Being thoroughly equipped and efficient in all branches of the law, his practice in the higher class of cases was always large and remunerative. His knowledge of land law was exceptional, and he was one of the counsel on the successful side of the famous Jolly Island case, the most noted land suit in the history of East Tennessee.

As a speaker he was earnest, impressive and often eloquent, and in diction he was copious but accurate, and forcible without exaggeration. He was incapable of inflicting injury or pain, and because of the kindliness of his nature conflicts at the bar were often distressing. A natural diffidence which he could not overcome caused him at times to appear reserved, but he craved the sympathy of and loved his fellow men. In his death the bar and society of Knoxville lost one of their chief ornaments.

RICHARD G. DUNLAP was born in Knoxville some time in 1793, and was the first male child born in the city. He was a student at Ebenezer Academy under the Rev. Samuel G. Ramsey when the war of 1812 began. Being filled with patriotism and martial ardor, he raised a company of cavalry which was accepted by General Jackson. Becoming one of the favorites of General Jackson, he retained his confidence and good will to the end. At the conclusion of the war he located at Knoxville and studied law in the office of John McCampbell, and while the practice of this profession does not seem to have been altogether suited to his tastes, yet, according to Dr. Ramsey, he was a successful practitioner. In 1831 he was elected from Knox county to the legislature, where he appears to have been one of the champions of public improvements, and Dr. Ramsey refers to him as the "father of our system of common schools," though the exact service he performed in connection therewith does not appear. While he was not so conspicuous as some others in the practice of the law, yet he was an energetic and able man, best satisfied when in action, and he was worthy, honest and brave.

JOHN BAXTER, one of the most successful of the lawyers of East Tennessee, was born in Rutherford county, North Carolina, March 5, 1819. He had no opportunities for education except such as were afforded by the old field schools of the neighborhood in which he lived. For a time he followed the occupation of a merchant, but abandoned it for the study of the law, his adaptation to which was speedily shown in the most gratifying manner. In the spring of 1857 he removed to Knoxville, and it was here that his most important professional work was done. During the Civil war he was loyal to the government of the United States, and was always a fearless advocate of its cause. In the constitutional convention of 1870 he was a delegate from Knox county, and was a prominent member of the judiciary committee, and it is worthy of note that the majority of the members of the convention had supported the Confederacy. During the succeeding seven years he conducted what was probably the most lucrative law practice that had ever been acquired in East Tennessee, his ability being acknowledged in all the courts of the state, including the supreme court. In 1877 he was appointed by President Hayes judge of the circuit court of the United States for the Sixth district, which position he filled with great credit. He died at Hot Springs, Ark., April 2, 1886. His distinguishing characteristic was force, and he was independent, self-reliant and firm in all respects. Though sometimes arbitrary and harsh in his language and manner, yet he was essentially just, progressive and liberal, and he was the accepted leader of the East Tennessee bar. Taking him all in all, he was one of the most remarkable men known to the history of Tennessee.

JOSEPH ANDERSON, one of the judges of the superior court of the territory of Tennessee, was born near Philadelphia, Pa., November 5, 1757, and was of German ancestry, his family having come to America in 1656. Joseph, together with five of his brothers, was an officer in the Continental army. Having received a good education he studied law, and in 1775 was appointed ensign in the New Jersey line, was made first-lieutenant in November, 1776; captain in October, 1777, and was regular paymaster from that time until the end of the war, retiring with the rank of brevet-major. Then practicing law in Delaware he removed to the territory southwest of the Ohio river, and became one of the judges of the territorial court, serving throughout the existence of the territory. He was one of the trustees of Blount College and of Washington College, and in the constitutional convention of 1796 was a delegate from Jefferson county. When William Blount was expelled from the United States senate, July 8, 1797, Judge Anderson was elected to the vacant seat, serving continuously until 1815. Upon retiring from the senate in 1815 he was appointed by President Madison comptroller of the United States treasury, serving in that capacity until 1836, and dying in 1837. Anderson county, Tenn., is named in his honor.

Judge Anderson was the father of Alexander Anderson, who was a senator of the United States from Tennessee, and was the grandfather of David D. Anderson of Knox county, who, by virtue of descent from him, is a member of the Order of the Cincinnati. Judge Anderson was a devout man, and of sincere but unostentatious piety. His sister, Margaret, married David Deaderick and became the mother of the late Chief Justice James W. Deaderick.

THOMAS EMMERSON, the first mayor of Knoxville, was one of the lawyers and judges of the early days. He served on the superior bench from 1807 to 1809, was judge of the first circuit from 1816 to 1819, and from 1819 to 1822 was a judge of the supreme court. From these facts it would appear that he was no ordinary man. From 1832 to 1837 he edited at Jonesboro the Washington Republican and Farmers' Journal, an anti-Jackson paper, for the first three years of which period his associate in the enterprise was S. J. W. Lucky.

LEONIDAS CAMPBELL HOUK, one of the most prominent men in East Tennessee for many years, was born in Sevier county, Tenn., June 8, 1836, and died in Knoxville, May 25, 1891. His birthplace was a log cabin located in the mountains, and his early life was passed in obscurity, hardship and poverty. It was as a cabinetmaker that he began the course of self-improvement which made him one of the most notable men in the state. While carrying on this trade he read law at night by the light of a blazing pine knot, and was admitted to the bar shortly before the war. From 1866 to 1869 he served as judge of the circuit court for the Seventeenth circuit; from 1873 to 1875 he was a member of the lower branch of the legislature from Knox and Anderson counties, and was elected to all the congresses from the Forty-sixth to the Fifty-second, inclusive of both, his death occurring in the middle of his seventh term. At the bar he was one of the most successful advocates in East Tennessee, and it was said by a judge of the supreme court that his briefs were not surpassed by those of any other lawyer practicing in that court.

JUDGE EBENEZER ALEXANDER, one of the most popular men that ever lived in Knox county, an able lawyer and a competent, efficient and dignified judge, was born in Blount county, Tenn., December 23, 1805, and died at Knoxville, April 29, 1857. His father, Adam R. Alexander, soon after the birth of Ebenezer, moved his family to West Tennessee. Ebenezer Alexander was educated at Greeneville College, and at East Tennessee College, at Knoxville, now the University of Tennessee. Afterward he studied law with Judge Joshua Haskell at Jackson, Tenn. Having removed to Knoxville he was there married, October 15, 1829, to Margaret White, fourth daughter of Hugh L. White, was a long time a member of Judge White's family, and in charge of his private affairs while the judge was absent on public duties. Mr. Alexander's wife died soon after the marriage, and on January 31, 1833, he married Margaret McClung, youngest daughter of Charles McClung.

In 1838 Mr. Alexander was appointed attorney-general for the second circuit, serving a little less than a year, and in 1844 he succeeded Edward Scott as judge of the second circuit. Judge Alexander remained in this position until his death, and was one of the best judges that ever sat upon the bench in Tennessee, always courteous, upright, pure and without reproach.

SPENCER JARNAGIN, one of the most prominent men and lawyers of his time, was born in Grainger county, Tenn., in 1792. He was a well-educated man, and graduated from Greeneville College in 1813. Four years later he was admitted to the bar, having studied law with Hugh Lawson White. Very early in his career as a lawyer Mr. Jarnagin became connected with litigation growing out of the interpretation of Indian treaties and the cessions of lands made under these treaties. He was connected with the famous Foreman case, which had its origin in the following manner: The legislature had passed an act to extend the jurisdiction of the state in cases of high felony over the territory of the Cherokee nation, and under the provisions of this law Foreman was indicted in McMinn county for a murder committed in the country of the Cherokees. The circuit judge sustained a plea to the jurisdiction, the case was appealed by the state and was heard by Judges Catron, Peck and Green. The state was represented by John H. Crozier, solicitor for the fourth district, and by George S. Yerger, while Foreman was represented by Spencer Jarnagin. Jarnagin's speech before the supreme court has ever since been famous in East Tennessee as a masterpiece of audacity, eloquence, learning and logic, the audacity consisting in its criticisms of the court. Judge Catron's opinion in the case is certainly one of the most learned in the history of Tennessee jurisprudence, and is invaluable to the student of history and of the law.

Until about 1838 Mr. Jarnagin made his home in Knoxville, moving at this time to Athens, attracted to that place, it is thought, by the prospect of litigation under the Ocoee land law. If these were his expectations they were realized, and he was generally the lawyer of the Indians, presumably because of his connection with the Foreman case. Milton P. Jarnagin states that Spencer Jarnagin largely instructed the Federal courts in the law of Indian titles. In 1843 Mr. Jarnagin was elected to the United States senate by the whigs, having been prevented from election to that high office in 1841 by the immortal thirteen, headed by Andrew Johnson. In the senate he took high rank both as a constitutional lawyer and as an orator, being justly regarded as one of the most brilliant and able members of that body. Upon retiring from the senate, being entirely without means, Mr. Jarnagin took up his residence in Memphis, where he continued the practice of his profession with brilliant success. Chancellor Kent is reported to have said of him that he was one of the most intellectual men of the country, and in this high tribute all who were not influenced by prejudice concurred. In July, 1853, while engaged in preparing an argument in an important case, he went to a lake near Memphis to fish, and, having fasted all day, ate so heartily a supper as to cause a violent illness, and his attending physician, thinking he had cholera, resorted to such heroic treatment as to cause his death. It is generally conceded that he was one of the brightest intellectual lights of his time.

GEORGE ANDREWS, one of the best of men and one of the best of lawyers that ever lived in Tennessee, was born at Putney, Vt., December 28, 1826. His father, Rev. Elisha D. Andrews, removed to Macomb county, Mich., in 1840, and there George Andrews was well educated, both in literature and in law. He first established himself in practice in Detroit, and came to Knoxville in 1865, residing here the remainder of his life. In 1868 he was appointed by Governor Brownlow to a vacancy on the supreme bench, holding the office for two years, and proving himself to be a thoroughly competent judge. His opinions rank among the best in the Tennessee state reports, and are, hence, highly esteemed both by the profession and the courts.

After retiring from the bench he was United States district attorney for East Tennessee, and for the last twelve years of his life he was the senior member of one of the most successful law firms in Knoxville. He was one of the unfortunate victims of the great railroad disaster on the Knoxville, Cumberland Gap & Louisville railroad, August 22, 1889, which is fully treated in another chapter of this work. Judge Andrews was a man of extraordinary intellect and versatility, was a most industrious and capable lawyer, and was widely read in the general literature of his profession. For some years before his death he held probably the first place at the Knoxville bar, submitted to interruption and gave assistance to others with marvelous patience and kindness. Judge Andrews was a member of the board of trustees of the University of Tennessee, and for several years was chairman of its executive committee. To this place he was peculiarly adapted, and hence was of great service to the university. He was a devout Christian, and a member of the Presbyterian church.

EDWARD SCOTT, one of the early judges of East Tennessee, was a diligent student and had a tenacious memory, though he was not considered a man of broad and comprehensive mind. Good lawyers seldom trust their memories, even though their memories are good; but in order to make no mistake, carefully look up the law in each case as though they were entirely ignorant of it. This was not the habit of Edward Scott. He prided himself on his ability to cite and quote cases, and on one occasion he made a decidedly original ruling. It was in an assault and battery case, where it appeared in the testimony that the prosecutor had called the defendant a "school-butter," the meaning of which term is not now known, but it certainly was considered one of the most offensive of insults. This was the opinion of Judge Scott, who charged the jury that the use of the epithet was equivalent to striking the first blow, the result being that the defendant was acquitted.

Judge Scott resided at Knoxville from 1815 to 1841, serving during the whole of that period as circuit court judge. This fact alone would seem to indicate that he was well thought of, even if his manners were not pleasant, as is said to have been the case. Goodspeed's History of Tennessee says that he was never partial to young lawyers, but was frequently uncivil and rude, though at heart a man of kind and tender sensibilities.

In 1820 he published his "Revisal" of the statutes of Tennessee, and of the charters and statutes of North Carolina.

a work even now highly valued by the profession. It is a careful, trustworthy and creditable piece of work, and will never cease to be interesting and useful.

PLEASANT M. MILLER, a native of Virginia, removed to Rogersville, Tenn., in 1796, remaining there until 1800, when he removed to Knoxville. In 1801 and 1802 he was one of the commissioners for the government of Knoxville, and in 1809 he was elected to congress from the Hamilton district. About 1824 he removed to West Tennessee, serving as chancellor of that division of the state from 1836 to 1837. He was one of the most successful and prominent members of the Tennessee bar of his time. He married Mary Louisa Blount, daughter of Governor William Blount, and from this marriage are descended many of the best people in Tennessee, especially of the city of Knoxville.

WILLIAM B. REESE, at one time a member of the supreme court of Tennessee, was born in Jefferson county, Tenn., November 19, 1793, and died at Knoxville, July 7, 1859. His father was a lawyer and a prominent supporter of the state of Franklin. William B. Reese was educated at Blount College and at Greeneville College, and was admitted to the bar in 1817. In 1832 he was elected chancellor of the Eastern division to succeed Nathan Green, in which position he displayed ability of the highest order, of the cases appealed from his court to the supreme court only two being reversed. In 1835, when the legislature was called upon to elect judges of the supreme court, Judge Reese was unanimously chosen one of the three, and served the full term of twelve years, but was a candidate for re-election in 1847. Soon afterward he was made president of the East Tennessee University, holding this position until failing health compelled him to retire. With the possible exception of Haywood, Judge Reese was easily the most scholarly of the supreme judges of the state, and his opinions show the results of extensive and thorough research. He could analyze as well as acquire, and he had a clear understanding and a firm grasp of principles, and he was certainly one of the most learned and efficient of the jurists of the state.

His son, William B. Reese, of Nashville, was one of the most learned of the scholars of his time, blest with a wonderful memory, with a sound judgment, with the manners of a gentleman, a profound knowledge of the law, and was highly esteemed by all.

JACOB MONTGOMERY THORNBURGH was a son of Montgomery Thornburgh, a prominent lawyer of Jefferson county, Tennessee, and was born in that county July 3, 1837. He died at Knoxville on the 19th day of September, 1890. He had just been licensed to practice law when the Civil war began. He crossed the mountains into Kentucky in 1861 and joined the Union army. He was afterwards commissioned as lieutenant-colonel of the Fourth Tennessee Cavalry. He made an enviable reputation as a soldier and officer, having for some time been the commander of a brigade. He was mustered out in July, 1865. In 1866 President Johnson tendered him a major's commission in the regular army, which he declined. He was district attorney for the third judicial circuit from 1866 to 1871. In 1872 he was elected to congress and re-elected in 1874 and 1876. After retiring from congress he formed a law partnership with Judge George Andrews, which continued until Judge Andrews' death, which occurred in 1889. He was industrious, popular and a successful lawyer, especially noted for his ability as an advocate.

O. P. TEMPLE, one of the oldest men and one of the oldest members of the bar of Knoxville, was born in Greene county, Tenn., in 1820. He was reared upon the farm and attended Greeneville College when young. In 1838 he went to Tusculum College, remaining three years, and then spent three years at Washington College, graduating in 1844. Soon afterward he began reading law and was admitted to the bar in 1846, settling at Greeneville, Tenn. In 1848 he removed to Knoxville, which place has ever since been his home. Here he successfully followed the practice of his profession until 1880, when he retired. In 1866 he was appointed chancellor, which position he held for twelve years, in 1878 declining to become a candidate for re-election. In 1881 he accepted the position of postmaster of Knoxville, as a convenient method of retiring from the practice of the law, filling the office four years. Since then he has been engaged in attending to his own private affairs and in literary pursuits, to which he is peculiarly adapted. He has recently written and had published two books: "The Covenanters, the Cavaliers and Puritans," and "East Tennessee in the Civil War," which show great research and are valuable volumes.

In the Knoxville bar of to-day there are many men who are an honor to their most honorable profession. Some of them would rank high in the bar of any city in the land. The bar of Knoxville has always been a strong one, as will be seen from the brief sketches of some deceased members, printed in this chapter. There are men in this bar to-day who have had the advantages of a better education than most of those who figured conspicuously in the profession in the earlier days of the city's history. It may be said of them, too, that they take the same pride in sustaining the good name and the honor of their profession that characterizes good lawyers everywhere. Their contests before the courts in which they practice are such as will be seen wherever foemen meet foemen worthy of their steel, and it is a rare thing for one of them to lose a case through ignorance of its strong points, or neglect to avail themselves of them. A Knoxville lawyer who would go into court without having his cases well and fully prepared would soon find that he was losing clients. Those who are leading practitioners owe the fact to their ability, fidelity to their clients, and to untiring industry.

CHAPTER XIX.

MEDICAL HISTORY.

Knoxville's Medical Men Have Honored Their Profession—Dr. J. C. Strong—Fathers Followed by Sons in the Profession—Ramsey the Historian—Sketches of Knoxville Physicians, Past and Present—Some Disastrous Epidemics—Cholera in 1854—Organization of Medical Societies.

THE medical fraternity of Knoxville has always had among its members a large proportion of skillful and conscientious practitioners. At this late day, however, it is quite difficult to adequately present a complete and accurate account of the professional careers of the earliest among them; for the reasons that many valuable records were destroyed during the Civil war, and the memories of those now living do not extend far enough back into the past. Such data and dates as could be collected are briefly presented in the chapter which is to follow, and it should be understood that the omissions which may be noticed are in reality those that were unavoidable, and are regretted more by the writer than they can be by the general reader.

One of the first and at the same time one of the most prominent of the physicians of Knoxville was Dr. Joseph Churchill Strong, who was born in Bolton, Conn., October 3, 1775. His education was obtained from a private tutor, and after being educated in the profession of medicine, whether at a medical school or with a private teacher could not be ascertained, he entered the United States navy as assistant surgeon, which fact of itself would seem to indicate that his medical knowledge and skill were ample. This was during the Presidency of John Adams, and he was called, in the language of the service, a "surgeon's mate." He continued in that capacity until President Jefferson sold the navy, at which time he was on the old frigate Trumbull, and he was often heard to say that he came near being sold when the Trumbull was sold, as the auctioneer offered her together with her contents, to the highest bidder.

In 1804 he came to Knoxville, and here became eminent in his profession, which he continued to follow until his death in 1844. He was one of the founders of the First Presbyterian Church, became a member of it in 1816, and was afterward an elder. He was a man of strong character, was unusually earnest in all that he did, and was a man of deep religious convictions. For several, if not for many years of his professional career it was his custom to give to charitable purposes all his fees for Sunday practice. Besides being a most eminent physician he was a most estimable man, and left to posterity a splendid reputation and a most honorable family, many of his descendants being among the best citizens of this and other states. The residence he erected for himself has been used for years as the Knoxville Hospital. His three sons, Robert Nelson, Joseph Churchill, Jr., and Benjamin Rush, were all educated as physicians, Joseph C., Jr., practicing for many years in the vicinity of McMillan station. Benjamin Rush is the only one of the three now living, his home being at Marietta, Ga.

Dr. Donald McIntosh was another of the early and distinguished physicians of Knoxville. He was born in Inverness, Scotland, in 1797, and was a son of William McIntosh. He graduated in medicine at the University of Edinburgh, in 1818, and almost immediately afterward came to the United States, locating in Knoxville, where he married Miss Marjorie Campbell, who, with her father, James Campbell, had preceded him to this city. Dr. McIntosh practiced in Knoxville and in the surrounding country, going as far away as Kentucky, the remainder of his life, dying, in 1837, a victim to the epidemic which prevailed in that and the preceding year, and which, as stated elsewhere, some called yellow fever. He was a most skillful physician, was very successful and immensely popular. For a short time he was in partnership with a Dr. Wyatt, who left this city for Missouri, Dr. McIntosh then having most of the practice previously belonging to the firm.

Dr. James C. McIntosh, son of the above, was born in 1825, graduated from the University of Pennsylvania in 1846, and then studied medicine in France for two years. Returning to Knoxville he here established himself in the practice of the profession, was for some years a partner of Dr. Frank A. Ramsey, and was held in very high esteem as a physician for some twenty years, since which time he has not been engaged in regular practice. He is still living at the age of seventy-four years.

Dr. John Paxton, also one of the earlier physicians of Knoxville, came here some time previous to 1820. He established a high reputation as a physician, and was one of the most scientific men of his class. He continued to practice here until after the war, and died at a ripe old age, being more than eighty at the time of his death. His son, John W. Paxton, took a course of medicine at each of two medical colleges, but did not to any great extent put into practice the knowledge thus acquired.

Dr. William J. Baker, another of the early physicians, came here about 1830. He was a graduate of Transylvania University, Lexington, Ky., and came here from that state. Besides being a successful physician he was one of the most skillful of surgeons, performing in 1857 one of the first three successful operations of the removal of the womb in the history of the world. He was assisted in this operation by Dr. James Rodgers and Dr. John M. Boyd, both of whom are elsewhere mentioned in this work, the latter being the only one of the three now living. In 1859 Dr. Baker removed to a farm about seventeen miles below Knoxville, there following his profession and also farming until 1863, when he returned to Knoxville, dying in 1866. He was a man of great force of character, and a good man as well as a good physician and most skillful surgeon.

Dr. King, also one of the early physicians, had a fine medical education, secured a large practice, was a man of great dignity, possessed a good character and was of excellent family and social position. He died about 1844.

Dr. J. Morrow came to Knoxville some time before 1840. He was a fine physician, and was noted for surgical skill. He was of excellent family, and was an excellent man. He died about 1845.

Dr. Parmenio Fatio, who came to Knoxville in 1853, was born in one of the French cantons of Switzerland. He was well educated in Germany, and spoke French and German fluently upon arriving in this city. Here he devoted the first year or two to the acquisition of English, after which he followed the profession of medicine until his death, in 1868. He was a man of fine accomplishments, of splendid professional acumen, accurate diagnosis, exceptionally correct treatment of disease, and withal was a strikingly handsome man. His professional reputation was unusually high, and his scholarly attainments were far above those of the average scholar.

Dr. O. F. Hill came to Knoxville about 1855, from the state of Maine, was a graduate of a medical college and practiced in Knoxville and vicinity until his death in 1879. He was possessed of a very earnest and self-sacrificing spirit, was a clean, pure man, a gentleman in every way, and had a very large practice so long as his health remained, which it did until a few years before his death. He was associated with E. J. Sanford in business for some years, and, dying, left a most excellent name.

Dr. Frank A. Ramsey was a half-brother of Dr. J. G. M. Ramsey. He became a practitioner of medicine about 1840, and continued in the profession the rest of his life. When the war came on he joined the Confederate army, and was made medical director for Southwestern Virginia and Tennessee. After the close of the war he practiced in Memphis three or four years, returned to Knoxville, where he lived until his death, which occurred in 1888. He was a most scholarly man, and was the best medical literarian in East Tennessee. But he was somewhat eccentric in his views, often denying the existence of disease when all other physicians and everyone else knew it to exist. On one occasion, when the cholera was present in Knoxville, he posted up a notice to this effect:

"A disease very much resembling cholera prevails in the city, and I would advise every one to be very prudent in his manner of living and in his diet."

His memory was wonderful, and he retained knowledge gained from reading in an extraordinary degree. He was a man of many happy traits. He was not only learned, but also unusually broad-minded in his views and tolerant of every one's opinions, no matter how divergent from his own, whether in scientific matters, politics or religion. In fact he seemed to enjoy the society of those whose opinions were different from and even contradictory to his own. While some other physicians did not wholly respect his judgment, yet they did respect his learning. He was of elegant deportment and majestic bearing, and once seen could never be forgotten. About a year before his death he requested Colonel John L. Moses, if within reach, to make at his funeral any remarks that might seem to him appropriate, with which request Colonel Moses, when the time came, complied, closing his remarks with that famous poem, "Abou Ben Adhem," the last stanza, as follows, being particularly appropriate:

"The angel wrote and vanished. The next night
It came again, with a great wakening light,
And showed the names whom love of God had blest,
And lo! Ben Adhem's name led all the rest."

James Gettys McGready Ramsey, M. D., one of the successful practitioners of medicine of Knox county and in later life of Knoxville, and the most distinguished native historian of Tennessee, was born in Knox county, March 25, 1797.

Reynolds Ramsey, grandfather of Dr. Ramsey, came from Scotland when a child with his parents, the mother being drowned, however, during the voyage. Francis A. Ramsey, father of Dr. Ramsey, was born May 31, 1764, removed from New Castle, Del., early in life, and located in Washington county, N. C., soon afterward moving still further west into Tennessee. April 7, 1789, he married Miss Peggy Alexander of Mecklenburg county, N. C., and settled on Little Loudon creek, where their first son, William B. A., was born, March 26, 1791. They then removed to Knox county, and settled six miles east of Knoxville, where three other sons were born, of these three Dr. J. G. M. Ramsey being the youngest. He remained upon the farm until old enough to attend school, receiving in the meantime the rudiments of an education from a private teacher, and in 1809, together with his brother William B. A. Ramsey, was sent to Ebenezer Academy, where he remained until 1814. Both were next sent to Washington College, at which institution they graduated in 1816. In 1817 young James began the study of medicine with Dr. Joseph C. Strong of Knoxville, and in 1819 entered the University of Pennsylvania, and on August 1, 1820, opened an office for the practice of medicine in Knoxville, remaining there thus engaged until 1823. This year he removed to the forks of the French Broad and Holston rivers, naming his home "Mecklenburg Place," and from that time until the war he was actively engaged in the practice of medicine, in railroad enterprises and in banking, and from 1840 to 1853 was engaged in writing his celebrated work, "Ramsey's Annals of Tennessee," the most authentic work covering the period treated of so far produced. Upon the Federal occupation of East Tennessee his house, together with all its contents, including much valuable manuscript history, was burned, and he was compelled to take refuge within the Confederate lines, and with his wife he remained in North Carolina until 1870, when he returned to Knoxville, opening an office here again on August 1, 1872. His residence and office were near the eastern junction of Main and Cumberland streets, and here he lived until the time of his death, which occurred in 1884.

Dr. James Rodgers, formerly one of the most prominent physicians of Knoxville, was born in this city July 2, 1818. He was a son of Thomas and Annie (Patton) Rodgers, both natives of East Tennessee. Having completed his education at the University of Tennessee, young Rodgers began the study of medicine with Dr. J. Morrow of Knoxville in 1840, and during the years 1842 and 1843 listened to lectures at Transylvania University at Lexington, Ky. Then returning to Knoxville he began the practice of his profession and continued it during the remainder of his life, and for many years enjoyed a very large practice because of his unusual success. His practice in the country was also very large, as well as in the city, and his career both as a man and as a physician was a most honorable one. Dr. Rodgers served for several years as president of the East Tennessee Medical society, which is now the Knox County Medical society, and he was a member of the American Medical association and of the American Public Health association. Besides being a prominent physician he was noteworthy in other respects. Through the influence of W. G. Brownlow and Horace Maynard he was appointed by President Grant postmaster of Knoxville in 1869, holding the office one term, this being the only public office he ever held. At the time of his death, which occurred February 25, 1898, he was the oldest member of the Second Presbyterian church, having united therewith in 1832, and he had been a deacon in the church from 1847 and afterward an elder. He was also one of the oldest members of the order of Odd Fellows in the state of Tennessee.

Dr. John M. Boyd, at the present time the oldest continuous practitioner of medicine in Knoxville, graduated from the University of Pennsylvania in 1856, and immediately began the practice of medicine in Knoxville, where he has ever since enjoyed the confidence of the people, both professionally and otherwise, to an eminent degree.

Dr. John M. Kennedy was born in Knoxville in 1847, and was educated at what is now Washington and Lee University at Lexington, Va. Afterward he studied medicine at the University of Pennsylvania, graduating in 1870, since which time he has been engaged in the practice of his profession with unusual success in Knoxville.

Dr. John M. Gass was born in Jefferson county, Tenn., April 7, 1836, and is a son of Ewing and Parmelia (Scruggs) Gass. Dr. Gass was reared on the farm, and obtained his literary education at Greeneville and at Lebanon, Tenn., and began the study of medicine at the former place with Dr. John R. Boyd. After graduating at the medical department of the University of Nashville, he began the practice of medicine at Greeneville, removing thence to Morristown, and finally in August, 1883, located at Knoxville, where he was one of the most successful among the physicians of the place. He is a member of the Knox County Medical society, and has a fine practice and excellent reputation.

Dr. Samuel P. Hood was born November 9, 1834, at Newport, Cocke county, Tenn., and is a son of Rev. Nathaniel and Isabella W. (Edgar) Hood, both natives of Tennessee, the former of whom was born February 14, 1804, was a minister of the Presbyterian church, and died in 1874; the latter was born April 28, 1807 and died in 1848. Dr. Hood was reared in Jefferson county, and graduated from Maryville College in 1855. He began the study of medicine the next year in Knoxville under Dr. Beriah Frazier, and in 1858 entered Nashville Medical College, was never a graduate. He had served in the Confederate army as assistant surgeon at Knoxville and at Bean Station, Tenn. He also served as surgeon of Rucker's Legion and of Col. James Carter's First regiment of Tennessee Confederate cavalry. The war having come to an end, he located at Mossy Creek, Jefferson county, where he practiced his profession until

1885, when he removed to Knoxville, where he continued to practice his profession for several years. He was a member of the Jefferson and Knox County Medical societies, and was recognized as one of the most successful practitioners of the city.

Dr. John H. Carriger, formerly a physician of Knoxville, was born in Carter county, Tenn., August 18, 1825, and was a son of John and Margaret (Elliott) Carriger, the former of whom was born in Pennsylvania in 1776, and the latter in 1786 in Ireland. John Carriger moved to Tennessee about 1779 and in this state followed farming until his death, in 1848, Mrs. Carriger dying in 1854. Dr. Carriger was reared in Carter county, attended the schools of his immediate neighborhood, then at Elizabethton, next at Jonesboro, and finally went to Washington College in Washington county. April 3, 1846, he began the study of medicine at Tazewell, Tenn., under Dr. Michael Carriger, and in 1848 attended medical lectures at Transylvania University at Lexington, Ky., and afterward graduated from the Jefferson College at Philadelphia, Pa., in 1851. Beginning the practice of his profession in Tazewell, Tenn., he removed thence in 1852 to Columbus, Ohio, where he remained until 1874, locating in Knoxville in December of that year. From that time on until his death, which occurred in ———, he was engaged in the practice of medicine in this place. He was a member of the Knox County Medical society and of the State Medical association.

J. Sterling Carriger, son of the above, began the study of medicine with his father in 1882, attended medical lectures at Bellevue Hospital Medical College, New York, from 1883 to 1886, and then located in Knoxville, where he began the practice of medicine.

Dr. J. C. Hudgings, formerly one of the most successful medical practitioners of Knoxville, was born in Monroe county, Tenn., September 6, 1849, and was a son of Edward and Mary (Carter) Hudgings, the former of whom, born in

Virginia in 1823, removed to Monroe county, this state, and there followed farming the remainder of his life, and the latter was born in Tennessee in 1832, and died in 1886. Dr. J. C. Hudgings acquired his education in Hiwasse College, which was within half a mile of his home, and for some years after graduating from this institution followed farming, in order to accumulate funds with which to pay his way through a medical college. In 1874 he graduated from Jefferson Medical College at Philadelphia, and began the practice of medicine at Strawberry Plains, Jefferson county, Tenn, where he remained until January, 1876, when he removed to Knoxville. In the fall of 1878 he went to Texas, but returned to Knoxville in the spring of 1879, and here followed his profession until ———. In 1881 he was elected city physician, and was re-elected in 1882 and 1883, having charge of all the city smallpox patients during the latter two years. He was a member of the Knox County and the State Medical societies, and was one of the most highly esteemed members of the medical profession in Knoxville.

Dr. Thomas H. Kearney, formerly one of the most successful and prominent physicians of Knoxville, was born November 23, 1832, in Ireland, and was a son of Patrick and Sophia (Apjohn) Kearney, both natives of Ireland. Dr. Kearney, when he came with his parents to the United States, was nearly seventeen years of age, and in 1855 began his medical studies at Cincinnati, Ohio, and graduated from the Ohio Medical College, located there, in 1858. After serving for a year as house physician at the Commercial hospital in the same city, he began the practice of medicine in Cincinnati, remaining there until the spring of 1861, when he entered the medical service of the Union army on one of the gunboats of the Western flotilla. After one year's service on a gunboat he was commissioned surgeon of the Forty-fifth Ohio volunteer infantry, holding this position until the close of the war, when he returned to Cincinnati and there began again the practice of medicine. After serving for some time as assistant physician of Longview Asylum for the Insane at Cincinnati, he was elected to the chair of principles of surgery in the Miami Medical College at Cincinnati in 1872, and some years later, upon the death of Prof. Mussey, was made professor of the principles and practice of surgery in that institution, holding the place until 1884, when he removed to Knoxville. Here he remained in practice until ———. He was a member and president of the Knox County Medical society, and was highly regarded both as a physician and as a citizen.

Dr. James H. Keeling, formerly one of the successful physicians of Knoxville, was born in Shelbyville, Tenn., in 1849, and was a son of James L. and Charlotte (McGrew) Keeling, the former born in Virginia in 1800, and the latter in South Carolina in 1802. Dr. Keeling, reared in Pulaski, Giles county, Tenn., attended the Pulaski High School and also Giles College. In 1869 he began the study of medicine at Elkton, Giles county, under Drs. Bealy & Bowers, attended medical lectures at the Maryland University at Baltimore, graduating from this institution in 1871. In 1872 he graduated from the University of Louisville, Ky., and after spending a few months in hospitals, returned to Pulaski, and there practiced his profession until 1882, when he removed to Knoxville, where he continued his practice until his death, which occurred in ———. In this city his professional standing was among the best, and he was highly esteemed.

Dr. James S. McDonough, a physician of Knoxville, was born in Knox county, Tenn., October 24, 1830, and is a son of John and Araminta (Scott) McDonough, the former of whom was born in Baltimore, Md., May 12, 1803, and the latter in Buckingham county, Va., August 24, 1803, and died in March, 1875. Dr. McDonough attended Ewing and Jefferson College in Blount county, Tenn., began the study of medicine in 1856 under B. B. Lenoir, at Lenoir Station, attended the University of Nashville, and graduated from the Atlanta (Ga.) Medical College in 1860. He began the practice of medicine at Concord, Tenn., but soon afterward entered the Confederate army as surgeon of the Sixty-third Tennessee volunteer infantry, in which capacity he served until the surrender of Lee at Appomattox, April 9, 1865. After practicing his profession a few weeks in Knoxville he removed to Memphis, where he remained about eighteen months, and then returned to Knoxville, where he continued the practice of his profession until the present time.

Dr. John Willard Hill, one of the most prominent of the later class of physicians in Knoxville, was born in Falmouth, Maine, October 15, 1853, and was the third child and oldest son of Dr. Otis F. Hill, who died in Knoxville in January, 1881. When yet a child Dr. John Willard Hill came to Knoxville with his father, and in this city he lived the remainder of his life. Having attended for a time a preparatory school in the town of Gais, Switzerland, he afterward entered the military academy at St. Gall, that country, remaining there some time, and was later a member of the artillery in that country. Being honorably discharged, he became a student at the French academy at Neufchatel.

Having at length decided to become a physician, he matriculated in Emperor William's University at Strassburg, in Alsace, graduating from this institution with the highest honors in July, 1878. For a short time he was employed in a hospital, but in December of the same year he paid a visit to Knoxville, and at the solicitation of friends determined to locate here, established an office and entered upon the practice of his profession. After three years of successful practice, having in the meantime established an enviable reputation as a physician, he went to Glasgow, Scotland, and there attended lectures in the Western and Royal infirmaries. Returning to Knoxville, he here resumed his practice, which he continued until the time of his death, December 4, 1898. In addition to being one of the most accomplished physicians in the state of Tennessee, he was one of the finest scholars in literature and in science, possessed an intellect of rare brilliancy, and was familiar with most of the languages in use in Europe at the present day. He was buried from St. John's Episcopal church on Monday, December 5, 1898, his death being widely and sincerely mourned, as he was yet only in the prime of life, and with apparently many years of usefulness in store.

Samuel B. Boyd, M. D., was born in Knoxville, March 24, 1853, and is a son of Samuel B. and Susan H. (Mason) Boyd, both natives of Virginia. The former, who died in 1855, was a prominent member of the Knoxville bar, and occupied a position on the bench of the chancery court. Dr. Boyd was reared in Knoxville, entered the preparatory department of the University of Tennessee in 1866, graduating from that institution in 1873. For a short time he studied medicine with his brother, Dr. John M. Boyd, in Knoxville, and then entered the University of Pennsylvania, attending there during the years 1873-75, graduating in the latter year. Returning to Knoxville, he at once began the practice of his profession and has so continued until the present time. He has served as secretary, treasurer and president of the Knox County Medical society, and as secretary of the Knoxville board of health, and is considered one of the most successful of the physicians of the place.

Dr. J. L. Price was born at St. Clair, Pa., in 1856, and when twelve years of age was apprenticed to a druggist at Catasauqua, Pa. In 1871 he removed to Knoxville and afterward received an appointment from Hon. L. C. Houk to the East Tennessee University. Still later he received from Hon. Horace Maynard an appointment to the Hospital College at Louisville, Ky., and in 1877 he graduated from this institution with first honors in the special hospital course, and second honors in the collegiate course. At Coal Creek he practiced his profession about a year, and then after a three years' sojourn in the North he returned to Knoxville. Soon afterward, however, he went to Texas, whence he returned to Coal Creek, and remained in this place engaged in the practice of his profession about six years. By President Arthur he was appointed United States examining surgeon, but was retired by President Cleveland and restored by President Harrison, becoming secretary of the board of examining surgeons.

Dr. Charles E. Ristine, a prominent physician of Knoxville, was born in December, 1845, in Abingdon, Va., and is a son of J. C. and Susan (Elliott) Ristine, the former being a native of New Jersey and the latter of Virginia. Dr. Ristine was reared in Knoxville and obtained his early education at the East Tennessee University. In 1866 he began the study of medicine with Dr. L. L. Coleman of Nashville, and in 1867 and 1868 attended the University of Nashville. After attending the University of Pennsylvania a couple of years he graduated from that institution in 1870. In 1880 he established an office for the practice of medicine at Coal Creek, Anderson county, remained there one year, and then removed to Nashville, where he was engaged in practice eleven years, during three years of which time he was professor of physiology in the medical department of the University of Nashville. Then removing to Knoxville, he has been engaged in the practice of his profession here up to the present time.

Dr. F. K. Bailey, who was one of the prominent physicians of Knoxville for some years prior to his death, was born at Rutland, Vt., February 16, 18—. Having studied medicine with Dr. Horace Green of New York, he went to Michigan in 1837, when that was a new state, and sadly afflicted with malarial diseases. From Michigan he went to Quincy and Joliet, Ill., and in 1862 became surgeon in the United States army under Grant, serving in West Tennessee and North Mississippi. In 1867 he located in Knoxville, where he continued the practice of medicine the remainder of his life, and was quite successful and popular. During the cholera season of 1873 he was health officer of the city, and performed his duties well. His death occurred June 18, 1876, funeral services being held in the Second Presbyterian church, and the interment taking place on June 19, 1876, in Gray cemetery.

Dr. A. D. Scruggs was born in Monroe county, Tenn., May 29, 1842, was educated at Mossy Creek College, Jefferson county, Tenn., graduating in 1861, and afterward attended Jefferson Medical College, at Philadelphia, Pa., graduating in March, 1876. Locating then at Mouse Creek, McMinn county, Tenn., he practiced there seven years. Then removing to Cleveland, Tenn., he remained there engaged in practice fifteen years, and then removed to Knoxville, where he has been ever since. He is a member and secretary of the Knox County Medical society, of the East Tennessee Medical society and of the American Medical association.

Dr. Herman G. Bayless, one of the successful medical practitioners of Knoxville, was born in Covington, Ky., March 23, 1854. His parents were John C. and Rosa (Lewis) Bayless, the former of whom was born in Louisville, Ky., and was a prominent preacher in the Presbyterian church. Dr. Bayless received his education at Center college, Danville, Ky., and in 1873 entered the Ohio Medical College at Cincinnati, Ohio, graduating therefrom in 1878. Then passing a year at the Good Samaritan hospital, Cincinnati, he located at Augusta, Ky., and followed there the practice of his profession until 1883, when he went to Europe, spending two years in the hospitals of Vienna and London. Returning to the United States, he located in Knoxville in 1886, and he continued the practice of his profession with abundant success until 1890.

Dr. Charles M. Cawood, formerly a physician of Knoxville, was born in Jefferson county, Tenn., in 1863, and was a graduate of the University of Tennessee. He was a son of Dr. J. C. Cawood, and no sooner had he graduated from the university than he determined to adopt the profession of his father, and by 1894 had acquired an extensive practice.

Dr. Cawood was at one time city physician, but resigned because he had removed from within the corporate limits of the city. He died at his residence, No. 157 Scott street, from the effects of the administration of chloroform to mitigate the pain of an operation on his ankle about to be performed, on April 7, 1894, to the great regret of family, friends and all that knew him.

Dr. Chalmers Deaderick, one of the most prominent and successful physicians of Knoxville, was born in this city August 22, 1847, and is a son of David and Elizabeth J. (Crozier) Deaderick, both of whom were natives of Tennessee, the former of whom was born in 1797 and died in 1873, and the latter was born in 1804 and died April 14, 1887. Dr. Deaderick was educated first at the Tennessee University and graduated from Washington and Lee University, Lexington, Va., in 1869. In this same year he began the study of medicine with Dr. John M. Boyd in Knoxville and in the fall entered the University of Pennsylvania, graduating in 1871. Immediately beginning the practice of medicine in his native city, he has continued to practice here ever since. He is a member of the Knox County Medical society, of the State Medical society, and of the American Medical association, and in 1886 was appointed examining surgeon of the United States Pension office at Knoxville without solicitation on his part. Dr. Deaderick is still engaged in the practice of medicine in Knoxville.

Dr. Charles M. Drake, formerly of Knoxville, was born in Greene county, Tenn., December 20, 1854, and was a son of Dr. W. W. and Amanda (Evans) Drake, the former of whom was born in Rockbridge county, Va., in 1818, and the latter near Russellville, Tenn., in 1824. Dr. Charles M. Drake attended Tusculum College in Greene county, and in 1872 began the study of medicine, entering Jefferson Medical College that year and graduating in 1875. After serving a short time as assistant surgeon of the Philadelphia Charity College, he came to Knoxville and practiced medicine here two years. The next six years he spent as assistant to Profs. Joseph and William H. Pancoast, visiting Europe in the meantime and being assistant demonstrator of anatomy at Jefferson Medical College from 1877 to 1880, and removing to Knoxville in 1883, and here continued to practice medicine until 1896. He was a member of the Knox County Medical society and of the State Medical society, and was a contributor to medical journals. For some years he was chief surgeon of the Southern Railway company and in the spring of 1898 was appointed brigade surgeon in the United States volunteer army, engaged in the war with Spain. He is now with the army in the Philippines.

Among the Knoxville physicians who have honored themselves and their profession is Dr. A. B. Tadlock, who has not been in active practice for a score of years, chiefly on account of impaired health. After retiring he made a trip around the world accompanied by his talented wife, an authoress of note. Ever since that time he has spent his winters in Southern climates. Recently his eyesight failed him, which to one who loves books so well is a great affliction. Dr. Tadlock served as a surgeon in the Union army during the Civil war and won distinction. Since the war he was for some time a member of the Pension Examining Board of Knoxville, and he also served a term as city physician. He is a painstaking, conscientious practitioner and has always been a close student, applying himself assiduously to the study of the branches of science relating to his chosen profession. He has delivered a number of notable addresses and has also been an able contributor to medical publications.

Dr. H. P. Coile, city physician of Knoxville, was born in Jefferson county, Tenn., and is a son of John Leonard and Mary E. (Bettis) Coile. He was educated at Maury Academy, Dandridge, Tenn., and at Jefferson Medical College, Philadelphia, graduating from this institution in 1875. Afterward for twelve years he practiced his profession in Jefferson county, in Dandridge and other towns, and in the fall of

1887 removed to Knoxville, where he has since remained. He is a member of the East Tennessee Medical society and of the Knoxville Academy of Medicine. In 1882 he was appointed by President Arthur a member of the pension examining board, serving until he removed to Knoxville. In 1884 he was appointed a member of the special examining board by the pension department and served with the assistant referee of the pension bureau, who examined some 400 pensioners at one sitting. His third appointment was by President Harrison, and he served throughout Harrison's administration. In 1897 he was elected city physician of West Knoxville, serving until the consolidation of the three boroughs, and was then elected city physician of Knoxville, in which position he still remains. In 1898 he was elected professor of clinical medicine in the Tennessee Medical College, which position he still holds, and during the collegiate year beginning in 1898 he delivered clinical lectures in the Knoxville hospital, the first ever delivered in that institution. In 1898 he was elected secretary of the Knoxville Board of Health, and is still in that office. Dr. Coile was elected City Physician of Knoxville in 1898, for the term of two years.

Dr. Walter S. Nash was born in McComb county, Ill., December 15, 1865, and was educated first at a high school in Winchester, Ky., then at Transylvania University, and later at the University of Michigan, graduating from the medical department of this institution in 1889, after having taken a special course in biology, chemistry and anthropology under Professor Alexander R. Winchell. Later he took a course of study at the New York Post-Graduate school and also in the New York Clinic, and immediately afterward came to Knoxville, and for the last ten years, since 1889, has been engaged here in the practice of medicine. He became a member of the Knox County Medical society in 1890, of the American Medical association in 1893, and is also a member of the East Tennessee Medical society. He is now serving his second term as president of the Tennessee Health Officers' association, and has been connected with the public health service of the state since 1894. From 1895 to the latter part of 1898 he was health officer of the city. He is now lecturer and professor of regional and surgical anatomy in the Tennessee Medical College, the only professor of the kind in the Southern states.

Dr. R. P. Oppenheimer is a native of Virginia, born in 1868, and received his literary education at Virginia Midland College, University School and Richmond College. In 1887 he began the study of medicine and graduated from the Richmond Medical College in 1890, and took a post-graduate course in New York, serving two years in the New York Post-Graduate hospital.

He also practiced in the New York hospital and was in private practice in New York city. In the fall of 1894 he came to Knoxville and has since enjoyed a lucrative general practice.

He is a member of the New York County Medical association, East Tennessee Medical society and Knox County Medical society, is physician for the Knoxville Traction company, Knox County Industrial school and examiner for the Prudential Life Insurance company, the Indemnity company and the Covenant Mutual of St. Louis.

J. L. Howell, M. D., is a native of Morristown, Tenn., was born in 1854 and received his early education at Morristown and Mossy Creek. In January, 1875, he began the study of medicine under Dr. Green T. McGee, and graduated from the medical department of the University of Louisville in 1877. He began practice at Alpha, Tenn., where he remained two years, and then spent one year at Brownsville, Oregon. Returning to Tennessee, he practiced his profession five years at Morristown, and in January, 1885, moved to California and was surgeon for the Southern Pacific railway until 1890, when he located at Knoxville, and has for four years filled the chair of principles and practice of surgery in the Tennessee Medical College. He is a member of the American Medical association, the East Tennessee Medical society and the Knox County Medical society.

Dr. J. H. Morgan, for years one of the most prominent physicians of Knoxville, was born in Manlius, N. Y., September 21, 1834. After attending several medical colleges he graduated in the city of Chicago, and at the breaking out of the war of the Rebellion enlisted at St. Louis, Mo., in the Union army, fighting until the close of hostilities. In 1866 he removed from Michigan to Knoxville, where he continued to reside until his death, which occurred February 16, 1886. Having been educated as an old school physician he practiced in accordance with the principles of that school for some years, but at length turning his attention to homeopathy he made a study of that system and adopted it in his practice and was the first to practice it in Knoxville. Afterward he made a specialty of electric treatment of disease. Dr. Morgan was a member of the State Homeopathic association and of several fraternal orders.

W. W. Tydeman, M. D., a successful and prominent physician of Knoxville, and one of the first to practice homeopathy in this city, was born in England in 1824. He located in Knoxville in 1872, and immediately began practicing his profession, homeopathy being then almost unknown in the place. He at once succeeded in establishing himself in practice, and for some years has been the senior member of the firm of Tydeman & Caulkins, the latter member being Douglas Caulkins, who was born in Duchess county, N. Y., December 15, 1857, and began the study of medicine in Athens, Tenn., in 1879. Having attended Rush Medical College at Chicago in 1882-83, he then attended and graduated from Hahnemann Medical College, Philadelphia, locating in Knoxville in the practice of his profession in 1886. Dr. Tydeman died in 1897 and Dr. Caulkins is still in practice.

Dr. W. L. McCreary, homeopathic physician of Knoxville, was born in Butler county, Ohio, in 1850, and was educated at Wittenberg University, Springfield, Ohio, graduating in 1871. Then attending the Cleveland (Ohio) Homeopathic College, he graduated from that institution in 1873, and immediately located in Greenfield, Ohio, in the practice of his profession, remaining there until 1886, when he came to Knoxville, and has been here ever since. He is a member of the Southern Homeopathic Medical association and of the Tennessee State Medical association, and since 1890 has been a member of the state medical examining board.

Dr. Daniel T. Boynton was born at Athens, in the state of Maine, on the 8th day of February, 1837, and died at his home in Knoxville, Tenn., in 1887, in the 51st year of his age. His parents removed to Ohio when he was a boy, and he was educated in the public schools at Elyria, in that state. He attended the Western Reserve University at Cleveland, from which he graduated and from which he also received his diploma as a doctor of medicine. During the Civil war he was surgeon of the One Hundred and Fourth Ohio infantry, with which he came to Knoxville in the fall of 1863. About the close of the war he was married to Mrs. Sue Brownlow Sawyers, eldest daughter of Governor William G. Brownlow. His home was here from that time to the date of his death. During Governor Brownlow's incumbency in the office of governor of Tennessee, Dr. Boynton was with him in a confidential position. In 1869 he was appointed United States pension agent at Knoxville by President Grant, which office he continued to hold through successive administrations until 1883. He was an invalid in the later years of his life, not very actively engaged in the practice of his profession. He was a brilliant man, skillful physician and estimable gentleman, popular with his profession and with all who knew him. He was thoughtful, progressive and conscientious, and stood in the front rank of his profession.

Dr. John Fouche, "the first and original" dentist of Knoxville, was born in Loudon county, Va., in 1817. He was of both French and English descent, his great-grandfather, a

Frenchman, having married an English woman in England, afterward emigrating to America and settling in Virginia on a grant of land made to him by King George III.

Dr. John Fouche (Fou-che, with the accent on the second syllable) took a course of lectures at a dental college in Philadelphia in 1839, went to Little Rock, Ark., where he practiced his profession about two years, at the same time studying with a competent dentist, and came to Knoxville in 1841, practicing his profession in this city down to 1880, and died in 1898. Upon his arrival in Knoxville he found the town yet quite small and labored with other enterprising citizens to build it up. In his professional work he was far ahead of his time. He was unusually skillful and his work was so well done that it bore an individuality of its own. After some years other dentists, no matter where they might be, who saw his work, recognized it as "Fouche's dentistry." It is even now said by some that there has never been a finer dentist in the state. He was capable, conscientious and conservative, and apparently very desirous of an extended reputation for the excellence of his work, which he certainly achieved, for he placed his work and his reputation among the highest in the land. He performed the first bridge-work in the city, which did much to extend his reputation in Tennessee, and after he gave up traveling to the surrounding country towns, people came to Knoxville from as far away as Abingdon, Va., to have dental work done by him.

Dr. Horine, one of the ante-bellum dentists of Knoxville, came here from St. Louis, Mo., in 1855, and remained in practice until 1860. He was a very fine dentist, second only, if second, to Dr. John Fouche, by whom his work was highly praised. He was a man of pleasing address, elegant manners, one of the most courteous gentlemen to be met with anywhere. In 1860 he returned to St. Louis, where he for some years occupied a high position in his profession.

Dr. Buckwell, another of the early dentists of this city, came here also in 1855. He was an Englishman by birth, and was educated in his profession in Philadelphia. After coming to Knoxville he married here, and later entered the Confederate army in the quartermaster's department, and was killed in the battle of Murfreesboro. He was also an excellent dentist, and for some time was in partnership with Dr. Horine.

Dr. A. P. White, formerly a dentist of Knoxville, is a son of George M. White, who for several years was recorder and treasurer of Knoxville. He began the practice of dentistry about 1869, and was in practice about thirteen years, since which time he has been engaged in the real estate business.

William H. Richards, D. D. S., was born in Salem, Roanoke county, Va., and is a son of Dr. Wm. M. and Sarah M. Harvey Richards, the former of whom was a highly educated and skillful physician and dentist, and his mother was one of the old, aristocratic family of Burwell, who were prominent people of Virginia.

Dr. William H. Richards was a student at Roanoke and the Blacksburg Agricultural Colleges of Virginia, and began the study of dentistry at the old Baltimore College of Dental Surgery in 1873. In 1875 he located in Knoxville and began the practice of his specialty. In 1878 he was graduated from the Baltimore Dental College and has since been continuously engaged in the practice of his profession in this city.

He has been for many years an active member of the dental societies. In 1895 he was made president of the Tennessee State Dental Association, and in 1897 held the highest office which the Southern dentists could bestow, that of president. He was the last president of the Southern Dental association; its first president having been from Memphis and its last from Knoxville. It was during Dr. Richards' administration as president that the American Dental association and the Southern Dental association resolved themselves into a national organization, laying aside on the soil of Virginia, at Old Point Comfort, sectional lines incident to the war.

Dr. Richards was instrumental in organizing the dental department of the Tennessee Medical College of Knoxville and held the position of professor of principles and practice of dental science, dental surgery and mechanism. His contributions to the literature of the profession along original lines of special investigation are worthy of mention, particularly his mode of studying the anatomy of the pulps, which is being introduced in the dental colleges.

Dr. Richards was one of the appointed clinicians at the International Medical and Dental congress, held in Washington, D. C., in 1887, and also a clinician at the Columbian Dental congress during the World's Fair in Chicago, holding the distinction of being the only clinician from Tennessee.

Dr. John Thomas Cazier, dentist, was born in 1833 in Cecil county, Md., and was educated at Elkton Academy in that county. He studied dentistry about five years in Philadelphia with Dr. J. G. White, leaving that city in the spring of 1852. He received a diploma from the St. Louis Dental College, and after traveling two years in the practice of his profession, settled down, in the spring of 1854, to the practice of his profession in Jonesboro, Tenn., where he remained most of the time, with the exception of a few years during the Civil war, until 1878, when he removed to Knoxville and has been here ever since.

B. D. Brabson, D. D. S., was born in Sevier county, Tenn., in 1860, and was educated at the University of Tennessee, taking the academic course. His professional education was received at the dental department of Vanderbilt University, Nashville, Tenn., from which department he graduated in 1887. After practicing for a short time in Greenville, Texas, he removed to Chattanooga, and there practiced eight months in partnership with Dr. S. B. Cook. Then coming to Knoxville in October, 1889, he has been engaged in practice here ever since.

Dr. A. R. Melendy, dentist, was born near Brattleboro, Vt., and moved to Hawkins county, Tenn., with his parents in the fall of 1869. He was educated at the local schools, at McMinn Academy, Rogersville, Tenn., and at the University of Tennessee. He was a student of dentistry with R. R. Freeman of Nashville, attending lectures at Vanderbilt University (Dental College), and leaving college in the spring of 1884, he began practice associated with Dr. S. B. Cook, now of Chattanooga, at Sweetwater, Tenn., under the firm name of Cook & Melendy. In 1890 this firm was dissolved, and in May of that year Dr. Melendy removed to Knoxville, where he opened an office and has been engaged here ever since, and since September, 1893, in the Deaderick building. In 1895 he was elected president of the East Tennessee Dental association, and in 1896 vice-president of the Tennessee State Dental association. At present he is a member of the East Tennessee Dental association, of the Tennessee State Dental association, and of the National Dental association. He is a member of the executive committee of the Southern branch of the National Dental association, and also of the executive committee of the Tennessee State Dental association.

Dr. S. A. Willis, dentist, of Knoxville, was born in Greenville, Tenn., in 1865. He was educated at the University of Tennessee, leaving that institution in 1889. He immediately began the practice of his profession in Newport, Tenn., remaining there one year, going thence to Pana, Ill., in 1890, and remaining there until 1897, when he came to Knoxville and formed a partnership with Dr. William H. Richards, this partnership continuing to the present time.

Among the other dentists of Knoxville may be mentioned Dr. R. Neil Kesterson, Dr. A. A. Francis, Dr. A. J. Cottrell, Dr. J. S. Clements, Dr. S. P. Sharp and Dr. B. R. McBath.

In 1836 and 1837 there was more malaria in the town and more sickness in consequence of this malaria than usual, but not enough of either to cause alarm. In 1838, however, the case was different. Knoxville suffered severely from malarial fever, not yellow fever, as some writers have stated, for the elevation above the sea of the site of Knoxville is sufficient to prevent this disease from originating here, and as the disease is not contagious, it would be impossible for it to spread even if a case or several cases were imported. So safe do the people feel in their security against this disease that they have never quarantined against it, and all sufferers or refugees are welcome to come at any time.

The reason for the prevalence of malarial fever in Knoxville in 1838 was that the mill ponds on the creeks adjoining the town contained large deposits of decomposing matter, which, on account of the long-continued dry weather and the heat of the sun's rays, became much more than ever before exposed to the open air, and freely and fully developed their baneful influences. The fever appeared first in June, reached its height in September, and did not disappear until cold weather came in the fall. It prevailed throughout the town. Very few, if any, families escaped. Country people were afraid to come into the city and even travelers shunned it as far as was practicable. The number of deaths during the season from this calamity could not be ascertained, but one result was that the city council was induced thereby to declare the dams in the creeks to be nuisances and had them abated.

In 1854 the cholera paid Knoxville a visit, the result being that a number of people died therefrom. Among the first to fall a victim to this disease was Col. John McClellan (a brother of Gen. George B. McClellan), of the United States army, who was in Knoxville in charge of some river improvements. It was he who superintended the construction of the retaining dam which extends from the south side of the river just above the bridge at the foot of Gay street, down to the low islands below it, and which raises the water sufficiently to enable boats to traverse the river at low water. Col. McClellan died at the Mansion House on August 30, 1838. After the death of Col. McClellan the Sevier family was attacked, they living on Main street, where the residence of Samuel McKinney now is. Mrs. John White came next on the same street. Hon. James Welcker's home was next visited, and then that of Mr. Van Meter, who died at the Mansion House. The people then began to leave the city in great numbers. "Uncle Lem," the driver of the water tank, then Knoxville's only water works, left the city, but many others remained from a sense of duty and nobly performed such duty to the sick as came to hand from day to day. Prominent among these was Parson Brownlow, and Col. E. J. Sanford, who had resided in the city only a few months. Samuel Newman, then one of the three undertakers in the place, filled orders for seventy-two coffins in six weeks, and it was estimated that there were one hundred deaths in all. As a sanitary measure the streets were covered all over with lime in all directions. The greatest number of deaths in any one day was on Sunday, September 2, when thirteen died.

On November 6, 1848, the physicians of Knoxville were requested to investigate the question as to whether a certain case of sickness in the town was one of smallpox, and they reported that it was not a case of smallpox, but that in their opinion it was a case of varioloid, and the family was requested not to remove from their residence for two weeks.

On January 13, 1849, it being apprehended that Asiatic cholera was soon again to visit the shores of the United States, the citizens were ordered by the board of aldermen to clean up their premises. Two inspectors were on that day appointed for each ward to look after the condition of their respective wards, and it was deemed important that a board of health be appointed, which was done, as follows: Drs. James W. Paxton, William S. Baker and F. A. Ramsey, and Gen. S. D. Jacobs and William G. Givan. The two inspectors in each ward were as follows: First ward, James M. Welcher and William Palmer; second ward, James H. Cowan and Jacob Newman, and third ward, Isaac B. Havely and I. E. S. Blackwell.

On February 10, 1849, the board of aldermen purchased

5,000 bushels of lime for free distribution among the citizens, to be used by them as a disinfectant, and the citizens were required to remove from their premises by the first of March all nuisances, such as manure and filth of every description, decaying vegetable matter and all other material prejudicial to health, and also to cleanse their cellars of all impurities.

But the cholera throughout the country continued to grow worse and by the latter part of July had become quite alarming, so much so that the President of the United States issued a proclamation setting aside a day of fasting and prayer and humiliation, and urged the people to observe it as generally as possible. On the 27th of the month the board of aldermen received a letter from pastors of several of the churches in Knoxville, viz.: Thomas W. Humes, rector of the Protestant Episcopal church; J. H. Myers, pastor of the Second Presbyterian church; E. F. Sevier, pastor of the Methodist Episcopal church; R. B. McMullen, pastor of the First Presbyterian church, and H. Lewis, pastor of the First Baptist church, to the effect that inasmuch as the President of the United States had recommended to the people of the United States, in view of the judgments of God, that were then abroad in the land, that Friday, August 3, be observed as a day of fasting, humiliation and prayer, they were desirous that as general a compliance as possible be had by the people. They urged that so far as practicable with secular occupations that the people assemble in their respective houses of worship and acknowledge the infinite goodness which had watched over our existence as a nation, and to implore the Almighty in full and good time to stay the destroying hand which was then lifted up against this country. On July 30 the board of aldermen urged upon the citizens the recommendations of the ministers.

In June, 1873, because of the existence of cholera in various parts of the United States, there began to be felt considerable uneasiness in Knoxville. Numerous remedies were advertised as sure cures for the disease.

A board of health was appointed, consisting of Drs. John M. Boyd, D. T. Boynton, M. L. Rogers, James Rodgers, F. K. Bailey and C. Deaderick, to have charge of sanitary matters and measures, and this board recommended that in view of the existence of cholera in Nashville, a rigid system of policing the city of Knoxville be carried out, that ponds of standing water be not drained, that mill dams and races be kept as full as practicable, and that as disinfectants dry clay, dry ashes (from mineral coal) and chloride of lime be used.

Dr. Frank A. Ramsey gave to the public a prescription which he said was an almost certain cure for cholera if taken in time:

"Aromatic sulphuric acid, one ounce; laudanum, one-half ounce; compound tincture cardamon, four and a half ounces. Dose, a tablespoonful in water after each movement of the bowels."

The doctor also made the statement that there was then no epidemic cholera in the United States, referring to his letter of 1855 on the subject to the board of mayor and aldermen, and also to the dictionaries.

On June 24 the public prints stated that then there was no cholera in Knoxville, but in view of the possibility of its coming to the city the ministers of eight of the churches of the city, together with a considerable number of the members of each of these eight churches, asked that a day of fasting, humiliation and prayer to Almighty God be set apart, on which day thanks might be offered to the Deity for sparing the city thus far and asking for a continuance of His goodness to Knoxville and for His favor to such cities as were afflicted, believing that the community should recognize the hand of the Lord in the affliction that had come upon other cities, and also in the blessings that had been vouchsafed to all. Mayor Rule thereupon fixed upon May 26 as such day of thanksgiving, humiliation and prayer. Services were held in most of the churches of the city, in accordance with the proclamation of the mayor, and they were in keeping with the spirit of the petition.

The policy of the press through the succeeding seven or eight weeks, during which the cholera afflicted a considerable number of the citizens of Knoxville, was to encourage the people as much as possible, and to minimize the difficulties with which the medical profession had to contend; that is, to make it appear that the disease was as little prevalent as it really was, and that those suffering and dying therefrom were themselves largely if not wholly to blame. This was on the correct principle that the mind has much to do with the health of the body, and it is certainly true that in some cases imprudence had much to do with bringing on the disease. One of the precautionary measures taken was the prohibition by the mayor of the sale of melons within the city limits, though this prohibition was in several cases disregarded, and melons smuggled in. Reports were made from day to day as to the number of cases of cholera in the city and of the number of deaths that had occurred. Up to June 27, the statement was made that there had been but one case, that of Mr. Robert H. Brown, his death having occurred on the 25th of the month. Each case as it occurred was commented upon, the cause of death being shown in many instances to have been imprudence either in eating or drinking, especially in the use of certain vegetables, and in the use of intoxicating drinks.

The deaths as they occurred during the summer were as follows, succeeding that of Mr. Brown: Jacob Easterday, July 1; Mrs. Nancy S. Rutherford, 3; Mrs. Hodge, 5; Mrs. Harris, 5; A. W. Johnson, 12; Mrs. Nelson, 15; Pauline Contourier, 15; Spence Eaton, colored, 16; Caroline Hollihan, 17; Elvina Eaton, colored, 19; George Pearson, 22; Ham Shetterly, colored, 28; Anderson Day, 29; Mrs. Provost, August 3; Ellen Donohue, 4; Miss Floyd, 5; Mrs. Defreese, 18; colored child, 18; Henry White, 22; Hon. T. A. R. Nelson, 24; Joseph Roth, 26. There were also a few other deaths occurring, three of them as late as September 8, these three being of Mrs. Karns and Mrs. Welton, both colored, and Samuel Roberts, white.

During the prevalence of the disease Dr. Frank A. Ramsey suggested to the public that if each person would take from two to five grains of quinine each day, he would be less susceptible to an attack.

In 1897, at a time when there was much suffering in different parts of the South, especially in Memphis, from yellow fever, there were two well developed cases in Knoxville. But the disease did not spread, and the mayor of the city, S. G. Heiskell, the city council and the majority of the citizens took the ground that even if a case of yellow fever should develop here among the natives, there would be no further danger because the city was in fact free from attack, as has been previously explained. Yet it was in that year that the state quarantine was strictly enforced by Dr. W. S. Nash and Dr. S. R. Miller, which fact becoming known had the effect of preventing people who were fleeing from the plague from stopping in the city. Only two persons ventured to brave the violation of the quarantine, and they were promptly imprisoned in a box car until they could be isolated in a house on Black Oak ridge.

On March 9, 1883, Dr. Hudgings, city physician, reported to the council that during the year ending March 1, 1883, he had visited 29 patients suffering with smallpox, of which cases 27 came directly under his care. Of the white persons afflicted 9 were males and 8 females, and of the colored persons, 4 were males and 6 females. Of the white persons that died, 3 were males and 2 females, and of the colored persons, 2 were males and 4 females. Of those that died 5 had been vaccinated, 3 whites and 2 colored. There were 13 persons afflicted with the disease that had never been vaccinated, 3 of whom died, and taking everything into consideration, Dr. Hudgings thought that Knoxville ought to be thankful that this dread disease had been kept so well under control. Eight cases had been visited by him outside the city limits, making 35 cases in all, and there had been in all 12 deaths, 6 white persons and 6 colored.

Another epidemic of smallpox occurred in Knoxville, remarkable particularly because of the success with which it was treated by the city physician. The first case was recognized January 29, 1898, and the last one on or about July 4, that year. During the prevalence of the disease there were in Knoxville eighty cases, only one of which, that of Louis Ninnie, a colored man, proved fatal. In Knox county, outside of Knoxville, there were nine cases, all of which were successfully treated.

During the winter of 1898-9 a peculiar but not widely extended epidemic occurred in Knoxville, which though not necessarily confined to persons of any particular age, was yet really confined mostly to people under middle age. This disease carried off one person, David E. Keegan, in December, 1898, quite a large number in January, 1899, and a few in February, 1899. It was called by the physician cerebro-spinal meningitis. The names of those who died in January together with their ages, were as follows:

Maggie Buchanan, on the 2d, age, 12; on the 3d, Horace Murphy, age, 19; Horace King, age, 21; George Mable, age, 2; 6th, Mary Leming, age, 20; 7th, James B. Sedden, age, 16; E. B. Lane, age, 45; 8th, Kimber Watton, age, 16; John Jett, age, 1 month; 9th, Katie Glasscock, age, 26; 11th, Ralph Simpson, age, 8; 12th, Mrs. W. P. Mitchell, age, 38; Roscoe Shields, age, 13; 13th, Frank Sheets, age, 16; 14th, Robert Crowell, age not reported; 15th, Bessie Bayless, age, 14; Simon Smith, age, 29; 18th, Mes Moore, age, 14; ——— Maxwell, age, 3 months; 19th, Stella Young, age, 18; Albert Storey, age, 2; 29th, Lee Wilson, age, 20; Calloway Proffitt, age, 10; 30th, Edward Tedford, age, 5; 31st, L. G. Roth, age, 31; Fredda May Jett, age, 2; February 5, Henry Wilson, age, 20; 10th, Morse Burnett, age, 14 months; 17th, Eliza Smith, age, 13; John Roddy, age not reported; ———

Smoker, age, 5 months; 18th, George Hackney, age, 7, and 22d, O. V. Monday, age, 49.

This is an infectious disease, and as a rule there was but one case in a family, the only exception during this epidemic being in the family of Mr. and Mrs. John Jett. But the mortality among those affected was very great, about 75 per cent.

The East Tennessee Medical society was organized in 1847 or 1848. The meetings were held at Knoxville, Jonesborough, Athens and Chattanooga. This was before the day of railroads and members traveled to the meetings on horseback. Prominent among the members were Doctors Frank A. Ramsey, J. G. M. Ramsey, B. B. Lenoir and William Baker, of Knoxville. A medical journal, the organ of the society, was published by Dr. Frank A. Ramsey. A public address was delivered at each meeting and the meetings were held every year until interrupted by the Civil war.

The East Tennessee Medical society was reorganized about 1890, with a membership of 150 physicians scattered throughout East Tennessee. This society holds semi-annual meetings in different towns in this part of the state, from Bristol to Chattanooga. Its president is Dr. M. B. Pearce of Bean's Station; it has a vice-president from each county; its secretary is Dr. R. C. Smith of Newport, and its treasurer Dr. Snoddy of Newport. It is a very active society, and has among its members some distinguished physicians and surgeons, and is doing a vast amount of good.

The Knox county branch of the East Tennessee Medical society was organized in 1874, and was in existence ten years. In 1884 the Knox County Medical society was organized under the authority of the constitution of the Medical Society of the State of Tennessee, and held their meetings by authority of that constitution and the by-laws of the state organization. At first there were but few members, but as this was the official medical society of Knox county, the membership steadily grew, until at the present time there are forty-eight members, most of whom are physicians of the city of Knoxville. Their names are as follows: William Bowen, John M. Boyd, S. B. Boyd, F. H. Braymer, C. M. Capps, Michael Campbell, J. C. Cawood, B. B. Cates, W. R. Cochrane, C. Deaderick, C. C. DeArmond, L. W. Davis, W. Delpeuch, H. T. Fisher, J. M. Gass, J. L. Howell, A. R. Horseley, H. A. Ijams, S. L. Jones, H. J. Kelso, J. H. Kincaid, C. E. Lones, M. H. Lee, C. B. Lee, B. B. Lenoir, S. M. Miller, J. M. Masters, W. H. Moore, C. P. McNabb, S. R. Miller, W. A. McCallie, J. A. Mourfield, W. S. Nash, J. W. Norton, R. P. Oppenheimer, C. E. Ristine, E. L. Randall, W. F. Ross, J. F. Scott, A. D. Scruggs, J. Smith, A. B. Tadlock, J. H. Taylor, D. H. Williams, H. K. Wingert, B. F. Young, E. Zion and E. R. Zemp. The officers of this society at this time are as follows: S. M. Miller, president; C. C. DeArmond, vice-president; A. D. Scruggs, secretary, and M. H. Lee, treasurer.

The Knoxville Academy of Medicine was organized January 8, 1896, with the following members: H. P. Coile, John M. Kennedy, John M. Boyd, C. M. Drake, F. B. Bowers, Thomas R. Jones, Benjamin D. Bosworth, J. M. Black, J. W. Hill, J. M. Masters, S. R. Miller, H. W. Bright, S. L. Tillery, E. R. Zemp and William Delpeuch. The first officers were: John M. Kennedy, president; secretary, Benjamin D. Bosworth, and treasurer, H. P. Coile. The object of this society is to promote the progress of medicine and surgery and good fellowship among physicians. It has had a successful career and has accomplished much good. Weekly meetings are held from September to June, on Tuesday nights. The present officers are: H. P. Coile, president; C. M. Capps, vice-president; J. H. Kincaid, secretary, and John M. Kennedy, treasurer. The other members at the present time are as follows: John M. Boyd, S. B. Boyd, Benjamin D. Bosworth, J. M. Black, W. R. Cochrane, William Delpeuch, Thomas R. Jones, J. M. Masters, S. R. Miller, E. R. Zemp, S. L. Tillery and A. G. Matthews.

CHAPTER XX.

PUBLIC INSTITUTIONS.

Provisions Made for the Treatment of Insane Persons—Lyon's View Hospital—School for Deaf Mutes—Lawson McGhee Library—Margaret McClung Industrial Home—St. John's Orphanage—New City Hospital—Home for the Friendless—Other Charitable Institutions—Woman's Building.

WHILE it can not be expected that in a history of Knoxville much space will be devoted to public institutions outside of its boundaries and which are in addition peculiarly state institutions, yet it is deemed appropriate that a few paragraphs at least be devoted to that noble charity, known as the East Tennessee Hospital for the Insane. And in order to set forth the proper place of this institution in the charitable work of the state, it is necessary to briefly cover the ground traveled by previous efforts of the legislature and private individuals.

The first legislation upon this subject appears to have been made October 19, 1832, when a law was passed establishing an asylum in Davidson county, near Nashville, $10,000 being appropriated for the erection of a suitable building. This asylum was not ready for occupancy until 1840, and was located one mile away from the capital of the state. In 1847 Miss D. L. Dix visited the state and through her efforts further legislation was secured by which nine commissioners were appointed, who selected a farm on the Murfreesboro pike about six miles from Nashville, on which a building was erected after the general style of Butler asylum, Providence, R. I. The building is a model in every way, and a vast amount of good has been accomplished through its thorough management. In December, 1884, the whole number of patients there was 412, a few of whom were colored.

The superintendent had for some years urged upon the legislature the necessity of providing more accommodations for the insane, and in 1883 there was appropriated through the efforts of Hon. M. D. Bearden, $80,000 for the East Tennessee Insane asylum, which was to be erected in the vicinity of Knoxville, upon the property known as Lyon's View. Under the provisions of the act making this appropriation the governor appointed as a board of directors the following gentlemen: R. H. Armstrong, J. C. Flanders and Columbus Powell, all citizens of Knoxville, and they, upon effecting an organization, elected W. H. Cusack of Nashville as architect, and Dr. Michael Campbell, of Nashville, superintendent of construction. After visiting the most important and famous asylums in the country, this board of directors adopted a plan embracing the very latest improvements, both architectural and sanitary. The asylum consists of nine buildings, including an administration building, chapel, kitchen, laundry, boiler house and engine house. The main building is 472 feet long, and the wards consist of 174 rooms, capable of accommodating from 250 to 300 patients. In 1885 the legislature granted an additional appropriation of $95,000, to be used for the completion of the buildings, and the asylum was ready for occupancy on March 1, 1886, the patients naturally belonging to East Tennessee being transferred thither. This asylum is about four miles from Knoxville, its situation being on high ground, commanding a full view of the Tennessee river and the adjacent hills and mountains, with their beautiful scenery. No more desirable location could anywhere be found for an institution of this kind, designed as it is for the comfort and care of persons suffering from the diseases which it is especially designed to alleviate if not to cure.

A building for insane colored people was erected here in 1896, suggested first by Dr. Campbell, and a bill providing for an appropriation for this purpose was introduced by Hon. S. G. Heiskell, carrying an appropriation of $20,000. The building is three stories high above the basement, is 63x135 feet in size, the basement being used for heating apparatus and the mechanical department for engineers. On the first floor are two dining rooms, one for males the other for females, each room being 20x50 feet in size, and also on this floor is a fine sitting room and a "strong room" for violent patients.

The second and third stories have cast iron stairways with steel railing, and each story has an assembly room, used for the exercising of patients and is provided with corridors leading into the different cells. There are in this building 250,000 square feet of floor space, all the floors being made of mill flooring and covered with cement, in order that the building may be fireproof. The slate roof covers 100,000 square feet, the building contains 160 windows and 100 doors. The architects of this building were Baumann Bros. of Knoxville, and the contractors, the Galyon & Selden company.

Still another building at this institution was provided for in April, 1898, which was designed to be one of the finest buildings connected with the asylum. The bids for its construction ranged all the way from $23,399 to $19,300, the latter bid being made by J. D. Hunt of Chattanooga. It is to be a fireproof structure, two stories high, and fitted up in the interior with the most modern arrangements necessary for the accommodation and comfort of its inmates. The appropriation made for its construction was $25,000.

Reports on the condition of the asylum are made biennially because the sessions of the legislature are biennial. The last report, for the period from December 19, 1896, to December 19, 1898, inclusive, is as follows:

	Males.	Females.	Total.
Number in hospital Dec. 19, 1896	142	139	281
Number admitted during the term	129	86	215
Total number treated	271	225	496
Discharged during the term	71	52	123
Died during the term	27	14	41
Discharged and died	98	66	164
Number remaining Dec. 20, 1898	173	159	332

Of the seventy colored patients admitted during the term, forty were males and thirty were females.

The expense of maintaining this asylum for the year ending December 19, 1897, was $48,881.84, and for the year ending December 19, 1898, $53,966.46. For the seventh year ending December 19, 1897, the receipts from the farm, garden and dairy were $5,853.44 and the expenditures $3,892.34, and for the year ending December 19, 1898, the receipts were $6,474.45 and expenditures $3,366.16.

The trustees of this asylum are S. G. Heiskell, S. R. Miller, C. D. Clark and George W. Winstead, and the superintendent, Michael Campbell, M. D. The assistant physician is T. F. Fitzgerald, M. D., and interne, Henry M. Childress, M. D. The steward is Edward S. Shepard; receiver, S. M. Drake; and chaplain, W. H. Bates.

The Tennessee Deaf and Dumb School, situated at 629 Asylum street, Knoxville, had its origin in the benevolence of General John Cocke of Grainger county, who was a member of the state senate at the time. It was on December 20, 1843, when a bill providing for the establishment of an institution for the blind in Nashville was on its third reading, that General Cocke moved to amend the bill by adding a section providing for the appropriation of $2,000 for the establishment at Knoxville of a school for the deaf and dumb of the state. After the substitution of $1,000 for $2,000, the amendment was adopted, and then the bill as so amended was rejected by a vote of 11 in its favor to 13 against it. Next day the vote by which the entire bill had been rejected was reconsidered, the vote on General Cocke's amendment being reconsidered by a majority of three, and then adopted by a majority of one. The bill was passed in the senate December 21, 1843, and then went to the house, where it was finally passed as it left the senate, January 29, 1844. The first board of trustees appointed by the governor was composed of the following gentlemen: R. B. McMullen, Joseph Estabrook, and D. R. McAnally, which board met at Knoxville July 27 following, and organized by the election of Mr. McMullen as president, and Mr. McAnally, secretary.

After having held correspondence with officers of similar institutions in other states, and ascertaining the number of deaf mutes in Tennessee, this board selected a suitable building in which to open the school and secured the services of competent instructors. The first principal of the school was Rev. Thomas McIntire, who had been a teacher in the Ohio Deaf and Dumb School, under whom the school was opened in the Churchwell house, in East Knoxville, in June, 1845. On January 31, 1846, the legislature passed an act incorporating the new institution, and added to the first board of trustees Rev. T. Sullins, J. H. Cowan and Campbell Wallace.

The next important step taken was to secure the erection of more suitable buildings for the purpose of the school, and the board issued circulars to the benevolent throughout the state, and made application to congress for a donation of public lands. They also established several local agencies, and placed in the position of manager of a general soliciting and collecting agency, Col. John M. Davis of Knoxville. Through these various agencies and efforts about $4,000 was secured from individuals, which sum, supplemented by an appropriation from the legislature, enabled the trustees to erect a large building, which cost in the neighborhood of $20,000. The main building consisted of a portion three stories high and 25x79 feet, together with two wings, each of the same size, so that the main front of the building, to the south, was 100 feet in length, and the east and west front was 129 feet in length. The original site on which this building was erected consisted of two acres, donated by Calvin Morgan of Knoxville, and the remaining six acres now owned by the trustees of the school were purchased at a cost of about $6,000.

During the first session of this school the attendance was nine. In 1857 the attendance had increased to seventy, and in 1861 the school was among the largest of the kind in the United States. But when the war came on the school was disbanded and the buildings taken possession of by the military authorities, being used in turn as a military hospital by the two contending armies, until at length, in 1866, the buildings were turned over to the trustees in a badly damaged condition; but nevertheless the school was again opened on December 3 of that year. For about seven years the institution had to be managed in the most economical manner, owing to the financial depression felt throughout the state; but in 1873 an appropriation was made by the legislature of $10,000, which again placed the school on a solid foundation, and since then it has prospered in a most satisfactory manner.

In 1882 a new chapel was erected and other needed improvements made, and at the present time the school is capable of accommodating about 200 pupils.

In 1881 a school was opened for colored mutes in a rented building in East Knoxville, about one mile from the main school. At first there were ten pupils, and in 1883 twenty-seven acres of land, upon which there was a brick building, was rented for the uses of the school. In 1884 there were seventeen pupils in the school, at which time there were about 100 in the white school.

The following-named gentlemen have been principals of this school: Thomas MacIntire, 1845-50; C. W. Morris, 1850-53; H. S. Gillet, 1853-56; A. G. Scott, 1856-59; James Park, 1859-61; Joseph H. Ijams, 1866-83, and Thomas L. Moses, 1883 to the present time.

Presidents of the board of trustees: R. B. McMullen, W. D. Carnes, John H. Crozier, James C. Moses, John L. Moses and John M. Boyd, the latter since 1887.

Treasurers: D. R. McAnally, James H. Cowan, Joseph H. Walker, Henry Ault, Abner G. Jackson, Samuel B. Boyd and John S. Van Gilder.

The present officers aside from those named are Miss

Sallie L. Jackson, matron; Calvin A. Gurley, steward, and Mrs. Lizzie Gurley, housekeeper.

In 1897 there were 196 pupils in this school and in 1898, 197. The last legislature made an appropriation for the support of the school of $165 per capita of attendance. For the last ten or fifteen years the expense of conducting the school has amounted to from $165 to $180 per capita. For the year 1897-98 the colored department contained thirty pupils, and for the year 1898-99, twenty-seven.

The Public Library of Knoxville was established April 1, 1879, by changing the old Knoxville Library and Reading Room into a public library, the library and reading room having been in existence for several years. All the property of the library and reading room was transferred to the Public Library under certain conditions. Of the meeting at which this change was effected Perez Dickinson was chairman, and the motion to make the transfer was made by Hon. O. P. Temple. Under the charter then recently obtained each share of stock was worth $3. Judge Temple said that one object of the public library was to collect every book and pamphlet ever published in Tennessee.

On April 20 this library received from Rev. Dr. T. W. Humes a present of 156 volumes, valued at $250, the largest donation received up to that time. Other gifts had been received from Hon. H. R. Gibson, Hon. L. C. Houk, Prof. W. G. McAdoo and wife, Hon. J. M. Thornburgh, Mrs. M. E. Carey, Mrs. Paxton, Moses White, J. W. Paulette, and T. A. R. Nelson, Jr., and then the association had added $250 worth of books during the year.

In May, 1882, an effort was made to pay off the debt upon the library, and in order to encourage the movement, fourteen of the prominent business men of the city offered to give each $100 and two others, $50 each, provided the debts were paid. The debts were paid, and a committee appointed to purchase books, five hundred new volumes being added in the following August, bringing the total number up to

1,200. In 1886 this library was converted into the Lawson-McGhee Library, a new three-story brick building being erected for its accommodation at the northeast corner of Gay and Vine streets, by Col. C. M. McGhee, and so named in memory of a deceased daughter. The building is 50x100 feet in size, and the library room, in the second story, is 50x80 feet in size. On the right side of the library room are the shelves for the books, now numbering 6,000 volumes. Rev. T. W. Humes was the first librarian, holding the position until 1892, when Miss May L. Davis succeeded, serving until July 1, 1896, and at that time Miss Mary M. Nelson became librarian and still retains the position with Miss Sadie McIntosh as assistant librarian. The president of the library at the time of its conversion was Adrian Terry, and treasurer, C. M. McClung. The president at the present time is A. J. Albers; treasurer, Adrian Terry; secretary, William Rule. The library contained 11,432 volumes on February 14, 1899.

The Margaret McClung Industrial Home was founded in 1873 as the Girls' Industrial Home, and it was the pioneer charitable institution in Knoxville. It was supported by the cooperation of the churches and the citizens at large. But like most charitable institutions it sometimes had difficulty to meet its expenses. For this reason it was thought best in 1895 that it should take on larger work and larger responsibilities, and that in order to accomplish these ends the private purse should be relieved of its support and that it should become a county institution. On July 9, 1895, at a meeting held in the Second Presbyterian Church, it was resolved that inasmuch as it was believed that this home should become the foundation for larger work and made more certainly a public institution, that the property, both real and personal be tendered to Knox county or to such reformatory corporation as might be organized under and in pursuance of the act of the general assembly passed May 10, 1895, entitled "An act to establish and provide a system of reformatory institutions for youthful persons," the country to assume the incumbrances of the institution and care for the inmates in a proper manner. A committee was appointed to confer with the county court, the committee consisting of Lewis Tillman, J. M. Meek, Mrs. James Park, Mrs. L. C. French, Mrs. W. W. Gibson and Mrs. S. D. Mitchell, and after several meetings had been held to consider this matter, it was proposed at one of them that if the management could be assured of $2,000 per annum, they would be in favor of maintaining it independently of the county court. At a meeting held August 20, 1895, it was ascertained that $1,000 of the amount had been subscribed, and subsequently the remainder needed was raised, thus enabling the home to remain a private institution.

This home is located east of the main portion of the city of Knoxville, between the Bell avenue and Park street railways, and is a large two-story brick building. Mrs. M. P. Garth and Miss Nannie Anderson have alternated as matrons of the Home since September, 1893. Mrs. Garth holding the position from September, 1893, to June, 1895; Miss Anderson from then about one year; Miss Fleming a few months in 1897; Mrs. Garth from August, 1897, to August, 1898, and Miss Anderson from September, 1898, to the present time. The average number of girls in the Home has been about twenty-five, the number there at present being eighteen.

St. John's Orphanage was organized in the year 1875, as a chartered institution, and is supported by St. John's Protestant Episcopal parish. Property was first purchased on Henley street, between Church and Union. The first president was Mrs. Frank H. McClung, who, after her death, was succeeded by Mrs. William M. Baxter, and she, in 1893, by Mrs. Ringgold, wife of Rev. Samuel Ringgold, rector of St. John's parish, who still serves in that position. In 1887 two acres of land was purchased on Linden street, upon which a handsome and commodious brick orphanage was erected, with a capacity for the accommodation of thirty children. There are now twenty-five in the institution. Children are taken at from three to eight years of age and supported until they are grown, or until suitable permanent homes are found for them. The rector of St. John's Church is the president of the board of trustees, W. S. Mead, treasurer, and Otis A. Brown, secretary. There is an executive board of lady managers, of which Mrs. S. Ringgold is president, Mrs. A. K. Selden, treasurer, and Mrs. Emma Sanford, secretary. The orphanage is free from debt and its property is valued at $10,000. During the year 1898 seven children were admitted to the orphanage and good homes found for two. The expenses for the year were $1,100.

Mount Rest Home, for homeless, aged women, was organized in October, 1893. It is located at the corner of Second street and Forest avenue. Under its charter it provides a home for destitute women of good moral character, not under sixty years of age. Application for admittance must be made to the board of directors, be referred to a committee for investigation, upon the favorable report of which the applicant is admitted by a vote of the board. No admission fee is required. Applicants may be admitted who are under the required age, who may be suffering from physical infirmity; but those afflicted with chronic ailments who require special attention are not received.

The institution is supported largely by the churches and individual contributions, although the county makes annual appropriations of small sums for its benefit. The supporters of the Home elect annually the directors, consisting of fifteen members; from the directors thus chosen the officers for the year are elected. The first officers were: Miss Annie Richardson, president; Mrs. John L. Hudiburg, vice-president; Mrs. M. G. McWilliams, secretary; Miss Mary Richardson, treasurer. The present officers are: Mrs. Charles E. McTeer, president; Miss Annie Richardson, vice-president; Mrs. Andrew P. White, secretary; Miss Alida Rule, treasurer.

Since its organization thirty-three aged women have been

cared for in the Home, as permanent inmates, while temporary shelter has been furnished many others. During the year 1899 the Home family has numbered sixteen members. There have been two deaths in the year, and one admission. Under existing circumstances the capacity of the Home is thirteen.

The Florence Crittenden Home was established in 1896 as the Rescue Mission, after many years of unsatisfactory efforts to do something for unfortunate women by which they might be enabled to lead upright lives. The movement thus started in May, 1896, to establish a rescue home was looked upon as a response to a long-felt need. It was started and maintained by the good women of Knoxville, members of the Woman's Council, a society composed of representatives from a majority of the women's clubs of the city. This council, on May 14, 1896, appointed a rescue board to have charge of the work of establishing the proposed rescue home, this rescue board being composed of one representative from the several clubs of which the Woman's Council was composed, and which had been previously appointed by the respective presidents thereof. The rescue board, designed to be permanent, was composed of fourteen women, who effected an organization May 14, 1896. On June 28, 1896, a public meeting was held at Staub's Theater, presided over by James Maynard, for the purpose of devising plans for the work, many of the clergy of the city, as well as other prominent gentlemen, being present. Rev. Martin Luther Berger delivered an address, as also did Hon. T. A. R. Nelson, Police Matron Right, and Rev. P. M. Fitzgerald, after which S. C. Roney urged that subscriptions be made toward the movement, and in a short time there was subscribed $536.30.

The Florence Crittenden Rescue Home was opened for the reception of inmates August 30, 1896, and was located on the old Branner property, at the corner of Hardee and Florida streets. The building contained ten large rooms and was surrounded by a spacious yard, and when opened was in charge of Miss Carlisle of Baltimore. The formal opening of the Home occurred September 3, 1896. Major E. C. Camp, to whom the property belonged, donated its use to the Home for a year. The Home was managed by a committee of which Mrs. Frank L. Fisher was chairman.

Charles N. Crittenden, on the death of his young daughter, Florence, in 1883, began the work which this mission was designed to carry on, and by January, 1898, when he visited Knoxville, there were fifty-three of such homes in different cities of the United States, which he visited once each year, traveling in his private car, "Good News." February 3, 1898, Mrs. J. C. Tyler resigned as president of the board of directors and was succeeded by Mrs. Barney Braine. The Home was then situated on Central avenue, for which reason the best results could not be obtained. An attempt was therefore made to secure a new building in a more favorable location, the Pastors' Union pledging its support to the erection of a Crittenden Home, and Major Camp, in March, 1898, donated a lot on Fifth avenue, upon which to erect a building, and offered to donate $500, provided the other $1,500 necessary to erect the building should be raised otherwise. This new building has not, however, as yet been erected, and the Home is located in a frame building at the corner of Florida and Hardee streets.

During the year 1898 this Home cared for thirty-three young women, giving them every possible care and attention, and instructing them in every department of housework. And in addition to these thirty-three several girls coming in from the country were lodged, fed and protected until such time as places could be found for them. Of the thirty-three, twelve went out to work and three were sent to their parents or friends, and from all favorable reports have been received. The average number in the Home for the year was thirteen, and the expense of conducting it was $692.12, including matron's salary. The support of the Home comes from voluntary subscriptions. the county of Knox for the year 1898 appropriating $100 and for 1899, $75, which should have been larger, for the reason that there are in the Home several wards of the county. The board of management hopes soon to see a new building erected on the lot so generously donated by Major E. C. Camp, for then they will have a comfortable home for their noble work, in a retired locality favorable in every respect for the work to be done. Of the board of managers Mrs. Frank Fisher is president and Miss Ellen Rhea, secretary and treasurer.

Knoxville Hospital, located at the corner of State and Cumberland streets, and standing flush with each street, was established several years ago. The building was erected for residence purposes and taken for a hospital because that was the best that could be done. The necessity for a new building for this worthy institution has been felt for years; but it was not until 1896 that any determined effort was made to raise money with which to erect such a building, and even since then funds have accumulated slowly. A movement looking to this end took definite form April 1 of the year named, when a board of officers was elected as follows: Mrs. W. M. Ashmore, president; Mrs. W. C. McCoy, vice-president; Mrs. T. ap R. Jones, secretary, and Mrs. W. L. Roberts, treasurer. All favored the erection of a hospital building at as early a day as practicable. Dr. T. ap R. Jones thought a building such as the city needed could be erected for $30,000, and in order to start the ball rolling a committee of ten women was appointed to prepare plans for the future of the organization that day effected, as above related, the committee consisting of the following persons: Miss Pauline Woodruff, Mrs. S. B. Luttrell, Mrs. H. G. Bayless, Mrs. W. A. Henderson, Mrs. W. G. Williams, Mrs. Lucy Finnegan, Mrs. J. M. Black, Mrs. T. J. Peed, Mrs. D. L. Ross, and Mrs. J. H. Frazee.

April 8 following, a constitution and by-laws were adopted, by which the organization was named The Hospital Building and Promoting Board, and the object being to secure funds with which to erect a hospital building in Knoxville. The matter was presented to the city council at its next meeting. July 28, 1896, a meeting of the advisory board was held, this advisory board consisting of the following individuals: S. G. Heiskell, W. L. Welcker, M. L. Ross, James Van Deventer, S. B. Luttrell, Rev. E. A. Elmore, R. S. Hazen, Rev. M. D. Jeffries, S. C. Roney, Rev. Thomas Campbell, W. H. Collett, J. W. Borches, Walter S. Roberts, Dr. A. A. Francis, and Jonathan Tipton.

In order to further this project there was held on September 4, 1896, what was called a "Hospital Day," the cars of both the street car companies being on that day turned over to the ladies or to the hospital board at noon, each car being run by young ladies, Mrs. Frank Post being the treasurer of the day, and the receipts for the afternoon and evening being donated to the hospital fund. In July, 1897, the Southern Railway Company contributed $500 toward the fund, and by November 11 of that year there had been raised $3,402.37.

A hospital Christmas festival was held in December, 1898, for the benefit of this work, which netted $1,000, and in January, 1899, the project was so far along that Baumann Bros., architects of Knoxville, were selected to prepare the plans for the new hospital building. The architects having been selected the following sub-committees were appointed to labor in connection with them, who were instructed to keep within the amount mentioned above as suggested by Dr. Jones:

Committee on General Hospital Arrangements—Drs. W. L. McCreary, T. ap R. Jones, J. M. Black and S. R. Miller.

Committee on Heating, Ventilating and Plumbing—Dr. C. E. Wait and H. O. Nelsen.

Committee on Finance—J. T. McTeer, Mayor William Rule and S. C. Roney.

The hospital building, as it is proposed to be erected, contemplates accommodations for seventy-five patients, a corps of doctors and nurses twenty in number, and all waiting rooms, operating rooms, laboratories and offices that will be needed. The building will be erected on a lot purchased by the Hospital Building and Promoting Board, located on Cleveland place, near Dameron avenue, opposite the ruins of the old Tennessee Medical College building, the cost of the lot having been $2,300. The hospital board has now on hand something more than $2,000.

The state legislature, at its session held in 1899, passed an act authorizing the corporation of Knoxville to issue the bonds of the city to the amount of $30,000, bearing interest at the rate of 4 per cent, the proceeds to be used in the erection of a hospital building. The bonds were issued and sold for $32,000. Thereupon the board of mayor and aldermen elected a building committee of five to take charge of the funds and erect the building. The committee is composed of J. T. McTeer, E. C. McMillan, F. K. Huger, C. C. Howell and Wm. Rule. Mr. Huger afterwards resigned and H. O. Nelsen was chosen to fill the vacancy. Plans prepared by the firm of Baumann Brothers, architects, were adopted, and they were employed to supervise the work. Contracts were let and the work is now going on to completion.

It will be an elegant building, with all modern conveniences, and will stand a splendid monument to the enterprising, public-spirited women of Knoxville to whose efforts the credit of the hospital building is due.

The Children's Mission Home was founded July 10, 1890, by Rev. J. R. Lauritzen, the incentive to found such an institution being in the necessities of six young girls who went to his house on that day and applied for shelter and a home. At that time Mr. Lauritzen was pastor of the German Lutheran Church, but he at once gave up his pastorate and his salary to devote himself to the necessities of poor children, and has had charge of the home ever since. At first he rented a house on Locust street near Union street, the number of inmates increasing rapidly and the necessity for larger quarters was soon apparent, as well as the necessity for the separation of children from older people. The Home of the Friendless was the result of this necessity. The Children's Mission was removed in December, 1891, to the northeast corner of Hill and State street, where it still remains and is still in charge of Rev. Mr. and Mrs. Lauritzen. The Home is supported by private contributions to its necessities, and by a small donation annually from the county court, the amount thus donated by the court for 1899 being $450. Children are taken in at any age up to fourteen and when they reach that age in the Home they are transferred to the Home for the Friendless, if they can do no better. In 1898 there were thirty-eight children in this Home, the average number being from thirty-five to forty.

The Knoxville Home for the Friendless was started in 1894, as a branch of the Children's Mission Home, but it is carried on separately by five members of the Mary T. Lathrop W. C. T. U., and is therefore a total abstinence institution. Up to the time of its annual report made January 13, 1899, this Home had received and cared for 693 inmates, never refusing to receive any one needing aid. The Home is located at 912 State street, and is under the direction of Mrs. J. R. Lauritzen. The year 1898 was begun with eighteen inmates, and during the year there were received 156 others. The classes received are poor, sick and homeless women, widows and women separated from their husbands, and young girls seeking work who have no home. Every one admitted promises to obey the rules of the Home, and to live a useful and Christian life. Rev. Mr. Lauritzen conducts religious services every evening, and there is also a Sunday-school in connection with the Home. The Home is supported by private donations of money, coal, food, clothing and other useful and necessary articles, and at the April term the county court contributed $50 towards its support.

The inmates average about nineteen, and the receipts for the year ending in February, 1899, were $512.43, the expenses being $514.58, showing that the Home is conducted in an economical manner; but the inmates aid to support it by doing any kind of work of which they are capable.

In 1897 the state of Tennessee held a Centennial Exposition at Nashville, to celebrate the one hundredth anniversary of her admission to the Union, which was, however, one year late, owing to the difficulties of preparing for the great event. At first it was the design to have a county exhibit, but, although county centennial commissioners were appointed, and though repeated efforts were made looking to this object, all efforts failed, and the movement was abandoned. This prospective condition of things was not at all satisfactory to the citizens of Knoxville, and those favoring the erection of a building at the exposition by the city of Knoxville appealed to the mayor, and petitions were circulated among the citizens in favor of the city having a building of its own and the council passed a measure in support of the proposition. But as under the charter no appropriation could be made for the purpose, Mayor Heiskell went to the capital of the state and secured a change in the charter, under which an appropriation could be made, the bill being passed by the legislature March 11, 1897, and approved the following day.

Thereupon the mayor of Knoxville was authorized and empowered to appoint nine commissioners to take charge of the movement, to provide for the erection of a city building, and to install the exhibits therein. These commissioners were as follows: Aldermen Alexander Allison, David G. Fuller, and George W. Brown, and citizens John E. Chapman, W. L. Trent, J. M. King, M. L. Ross, J. E. Willard and W. P. Chandler. An organization was effected by the election of John E. Chapman, president, and W. L. Trent, secretary and treasurer. Baumann Bros. of Knoxville, were selected as the architects of the proposed building and Galyon & Seldon, the contractors. James E. Lipscomb was selected as custodian, S. B. Boyd, assistant custodian, and Henry Parker, colored, janitor.

The material for this building was furnished exclusively

by Knoxville men, and the work done on it was exclusively by Knoxville mechanics. The time employed in its erection was fifteen working days, and a conservative calculation is that from the time it was opened on Knoxville day, June 17, 1897, until it was closed, there passed within its doors 372,000 persons, and that from first to last there was distributed advertising literature to the extent of 25,000 pieces.

Among the exhibitors were the Knoxville Woolen Mills, the East Tennessee Stone and Marble Company, the Evans Marble Company, the Tennessee Producers' Marble Company, and C. B. Atkin, dealer in furniture, all of whom received silver medals on their exhibits; H. O. Nelsen, of the Knoxville Valley Forge and Foundry Company, received a bronze medal, and the Knoxville Fire Extinguisher Company received honorable mention.

The building was completed and all exhibits installed by June 17, Knoxville Day, the second floor being used as an assembly hall and picture gallery. The three oil paintings exhibited were those of Mayor S. G. Heiskell, painted by Miss Catherine Floyd Heiskell; of Mrs. Michael Campbell, wife of Dr. Michael Campbell of the Eastern Hospital for the Insane, painted by Mrs. J. E. Lutz, and of President John E. Chapman, painted by Lloyd Branson.

The celebration of Knoxville Day was a pronounced success. Five hundred citizens of Knoxville besides the Knoxville military company were in Nashville, and the Legion Band was present to provide the music. The piano used on the occasion was manufactured in Knoxville by Socin & Company. After music by the band, a prayer by Rev. R. A. Young, D. D., and a second piece of music, Hon. John E. Chapman delivered an address, which was replied to by Hon. S. G. Heiskell. Then Miss Rosalie Gaut performed on the Knoxville piano and was encored; William C. Saunders sang a bass solo: the Legion band played "Poor Jonathan;" Hon. J. W. Caldwell delivered an address on "East Tennessee in the State History;" Mrs. Mary Fleming Meek sang a solo;

Edward T. Sanford spoke on "Knoxville: Her History and Her Destiny;" President John W. Thomas delivered an address, and after another piece of music by the Legion band there was a dress parade by the Knoxville Legion on Capitol avenue, which closed the exercises of the day.

A movement was afterward set on foot for the removal of the Knoxville Centennial building to Knoxville, in order that future generations might have before them the monument placed at Nashville by the people of Knoxville, the ladies of Knoxville taking the matter in hand and forming themselves into the Knoxville Centennial Building Association, with Mrs. L. D. Tyson, president; Mrs. Samuel McKinney, vice-president; Mrs. John Williams, secretary; Mrs. W. H. Hague, treasurer, and Mrs. S. G. Heiskell and Mrs. W. B. Lockett, auditors. The city council presented the building to these ladies on condition that they would return it to Knoxville and there re-erect it. This condition they complied with, and it now stands on Main street, directly opposite the court house, a thing of beauty and a joy forever.

For many years the people of Tennessee felt that the memory of John Sevier, the first governor of the state, was being treated with great disrespect, in that his remains were permitted to lie in an unmarked grave in the state of Alabama. It was even stated by certain writers on historical matters pertaining to the state that no monument had ever been ereced in commemoration of his deeds; but this was not strictly correct, for in the old cemetery at Nashville there stands a shaft erected to his memory, the date of the erection of which is perhaps not now known. But the movement to transfer his remains to Tennessee began at least as early as the first part of the year 1887, and was largely due to Hon. E. F. Mynatt, member of the state senate from Knox county, through whose influence a bill passed that body by a vote of 24 to 4 providing for their removal, after it had been unanimously rejected in committee.

But little was done, however, until the spring of 1889,

when the board of mayor and aldermen of Knoxville was informed by Col. Moses White that the legislature had then recently passed an act appropriating funds for the removal of the remains of the distinguished first governor of the state from Alabama to Knox county for reinterment, and that the county court had agreed that they should be buried in the court-house square at Knoxville. On May 7, 1889, the Sevier Memorial Committee adopted a series of resolutions instructing its chairman, Joshua W. Caldwell, to designate five or more citizens from each county in East Tennessee to aid in raising the funds necessary to erect a suitable monument to John Sevier, with which instructions the chairman complied, those appointed for Knox county being as follows: M. M. Gaines, R. C. Jackson, H. L. McClung, Perez Dickinson, Rev. Dr. T. W. Humes, Rev. James Park, Judge George Brown, John J. Craig, Judge O. P. Temple, Judge S. T. Logan, Robert Armstrong, R. R. Swenson, John M. Fleming, William Rule, Alexander Summers, John T. Hearne, W. P. Washburn, J. M. Thornburgh, George L. Maloney, J. R. McCallum, W. A. Henderson, H. H. Taylor, Alexander Allison, J. C. J. Williams, Martin J. Condon, A. J. Albers, S. B. Luttrell, C. E. Luckey, B. R. Strong, E. E. McCroskey, James D. Cowan, Frank A. Moses, J. M. King, Joseph R. Mitchell, W. W. Woodruff, John L. Rhea, R. S. Payne and Samuel McKinney.

Preparations having all been made a special car left Knoxville June 14, 1889, for Cole's Station, Ala., to transfer the remains to this city, and on its return reached Knoxville at 1:15 P. M., June 19, being met at the station by a large concourse of people, the streets being full of people from all parts of the surrounding country, to the estimated number of 30,000. Col. S. B. Crawford was marshal of the day, and the pall-bearers were the Hons. E. F. Mynatt, W. L. Clapp, J. L. Weakley, H. Clay Jarvis, A. J. Patterson, A. McNabb and J. W. Andes. Hon. Robert L. Taylor, governor of the state, made the first address at the grave, and was followed by W. A. Henderson. J. R. McCallum read a poem composed for the occasion, and the closing religious exercises were conducted by Rev. James Park. The pageant was probably the most imposing ever witnessed in Knoxville, and the occasion was one never to be forgotten by those in attendance.

At a meeting held June 21 at the office of Luckey & Yoe an executive committee was appointed consisting of C. E. Luckey, Frank H. McClung, Hon. O. P. Temple, W. W. Woodruff, and John M. Fleming, to secure the erection of a suitable monument over the remains in the court-house square, and subscriptions came in from all over East Tennessee. Up to the close of June 22 there had been received $1,898, quite a share of the amount being in one dollar subscriptions. Cleveland, Tenn., leading the list with more than fifty subscriptions of this kind.

Frank H. McClung was chairman of the committee appointed to secure the erection of the monument, and by the close of the year 1892 sufficient funds had been subscribed to warrant a contract for the monument. Ground was broken for its erection in the northeast corner of the court-house square December 3, 1893, the remains of the first governor being taken from their resting place temporarily to permit of the laying of solid foundations for the small but elegant monument now standing in the spot indicated. The cost of this monument, according to Mr. James R. McCallum, who was secretary and treasurer of the committee, was $2,200. Appropriate inscriptions were placed on each of its four sides, that on the north side being as follows:

"First Governor of Tennessee, Nolachucky Jack, September 23, 1744; September 24, 1815; Pioneer, Soldier, Statesman, and One of the Founders of the Republic."

The date of the completion of this monument was early in 1893.

CHAPTER XXI.

SOCIETIES.

Tennessee's First Masonic Lodge—Grand Lodge Organized—First Lodge at Knoxville in 1800—Chapter and Templar Masonry—Three Score Years of Odd Fellowship—Various Other Society Organizations.

THE first Masonic lodge in Tennessee received its charter from the Grand Lodge of North Carolina, and was named St. Tammany Lodge, No. 1. The date was December 17, 1796. The Grand Lodge of North Carolina continued its authority over Masonry in Tennessee until 1812. St. Tammany, No. 1, was organized in Nashville. During the period prior to 1812 a lodge in Tennessee was chartered by the Grand Lodge of Kentucky, which was not satisfactory to the Grand Lodge of North Carolina, which requested the Grand Lodge of Kentucky to recall all its charters granted to lodges in Tennessee. This request was not complied with, and then a threat was sent out by the Grand Lodge of North Carolina to the Grand Lodge of Kentucky that unless the charters were recalled, communication between the two Grand Lodges would cease. There appeared no way out of the difficulty except by the establishment of a separate Grand Lodge for Tennessee.

Accordingly, on December 11, 1811, a convention met at Knoxville, composed of representatives from all the Masonic lodges in Tennessee, at which convention resolutions were passed favoring a Grand Lodge for the state, these resolutions being adopted and forwarded, together with an address, to the Grand Lodge of North Carolina. These resolutions and address were received in December, 1812, and a petition asking for a separate Grand Lodge was granted. A convention was thereupon called by Grand Master Robert Williams, to meet at Knoxville on December 27, 1813, at which time a charter was granted by the Grand Lodge of North Carolina to the Grand Lodge of Tennessee. This charter is on file in the Grand Lodge, and is said to be unlike any other charter in the United States.

The officers installed at the first meeting were as follows: Thomas Claiborne, G. M.; George Wilson, D. G. M.; John Hall, S. G. W.; Abraham K. Shaifer, J. G. W.; Thomas McCorry, Grand Treasurer and Senior Grand Warden, and Edward Scott, Grand Secretary and Junior Grand Warden. As originally adopted the constitution provided that the meetings of the Grand Lodge should be held at the capital of the state, but in 1815 this provision was so changed as to provide that they should be held at Nashville permanently thereafter.

Previous to the establishment of the Grand Lodge of Tennessee there were eight lodges in the state, one of which was constituted at Knoxville, November 30, 1800, or very soon afterward, and it is interesting to note that on that very day, according to the records of the Grand Lodge of North Carolina, it was on motion:

"Resolved, That a charter issue to the brothers heretofore working by dispensation in the town of Knoxville, in the state of Tennessee; that they be incorporated into a just and perfect lodge by the name of Tennessee, No. 41; that his Excellency, John Sevier, Esq., governor of the state of Tennessee, be appointed Master, James Grant, Senior Warden, and George Washington Campbell, Junior Warden of said lodge—the Grand Lodge having heretofore investigated and approbated their proceedings."

This was the first lodge organized in East Tennessee. But it appears that after the organization of the Grand Lodge of Tennessee the name thereof was changed to Tennessee, No. 2; but on November 27, 1813, the Grand Master reporting to the Grand Lodge of North Carolina said: "In consequence of a resolution of this Grand Lodge, passed on December 5, 1812, I have caused to be made and signed a Great Charter constituting a Grand Lodge of the State of Tennessee," and in naming the lodges then in the state he mentioned "Tennessee, No. 41." And on December 2, 1811, at a convention of ancient York Masons held at Knoxville, "Tennessee Lodge, No. 2," was represented by George Wilson and William Kelly. At this convention it was resolved that in order to constitute a Grand Lodge it would be necessary for the Masters, Past Masters and Wardens of the different lodges represented in the same, to meet at Knoxville on the second Monday in August next" (August 10) "for the purpose of forming a constitution and by-laws," etc.

Then, on December 27, 1813, the Masonic lodges of the state assembled at Knoxville to constitute the Grand Lodge, "Tennessee Lodge, No. 41," was one of the eight lodges named in the charter. However, in the proceedings of the convention, this lodge is referred to as "Tennessee Lodge, No. 2, Knoxville," and was represented in the convention by "Brothers Geo. Wilson, Thos. McCorry, Jno. Bright, Jno. Anthony and Wm. Kelly."

Thomas Claiborne, who was unanimously chosen Grand Master, appointed George Wilson of Knoxville Deputy Grand Master, and Thomas McCorry Grand Treasurer. A constitution and by-laws were then adopted, which was signed for Tennessee Lodge, No. 2, by the five gentlemen named above as representing the lodge in the convention. Of these five John Bright of Knoxville was the first Grand Tyler of the Grand Lodge of Tennessee.

The meetings of the Grand Lodge having been transferred to Nashville, following the capital of the state, they were not attended for some years by any representative from Knoxville, and "Tennessee Lodge, No. 2," appears to have gone into a decline. George Wilson was present at the meeting held October 4, 1819, though it does not appear from what lodge. He was elected Senior Grand Warden in 1819, 1820 and 1821, and upon the election of Andrew Jackson, Grand

Master. in 1822 and 1823, he appointed George Wilson his Deputy.

Mount Libanus Lodge, No. 59, Knoxville, was working under a dispensation in 1825, and in 1826 William B. Reese received the charter of this lodge, which named him as Master; George W. Churchwell, Senior Warden, and James McBath, Junior Warden. In 1827 George W. Churchwell was elected Junior Grand Warden, and in 1828, chairman of the committee on appeals, in which capacity he brought in a report sustaining the action of Lodge No. 8, in suspending Sam. Houston for fighting a duel with Brother White, the committee, however, saying that they found many extenuating circumstances—a sufficiency, perhaps, for the justification of Brother Houston among men—"but as Masons we do not think him justifiable, and recommend that the sentence of the lodge be confirmed."

October 3, 1826, a charter was granted to Libanus Lodge, No. 59. William B. Reese was appointed first Master; George W. Churchwell, first Senior Warden, and James McBath, first Junior Warden. George W. Churchwell was a prominent Mason for many years. In 1828 the name of Libanus Lodge was changed to Mount Libanus Lodge, this name being still retained.

Among the most prominent of those connected with Mount Libanus Lodge, No. 59, whose names appear in the records of the Grand Lodge of the state between 1830 and 1860 may be mentioned John L. Moses, Grand Senior Warden in 1849, and R. R. Bearden, Grand Junior Warden in 1856. This lodge ceased to work soon after this date.

Master's Lodge, No. 244, F. & A. M., was organized by John W. Paxton, about 1856, but its records have been destroyed. It is now the oldest lodge in Knoxville. Dr. Paxton was the first master, serving as such for twelve years. He was a most devoted Mason and under his fostering care this lodge grew to a membership of 250, and was the largest in Tennessee. Dr. Paxton also served as Deputy Grand Master and Grand Master in 1870.

Maxwell Lodge, No. 433, was organized in 1872 by L. H. Rogan and others.

Oriental Lodge, No. 453, was organized in 1873, with N. S. Woodward, Master; J. V. Fulkerson, Senior Warden, and Alfred Caldwell, Junior Warden. Of this lodge N. S. Woodward has served as Senior Grand Warden, Deputy Grand Master, Grand Master and Grand Treasurer (five years) of the Grand Lodge. He has also served as Grand Treasurer of the Grand Chapter and Grand Council for twenty-five years. Henry H. Ingersoll of this lodge has served in the Grand Lodge on many important committees, and has filled the offices of Senior Grand Warden, Deputy Grand Master and Grand Master. Judge Ingersoll is a recognized leader by all grand Masonic bodies.

H. M. Aiken of Master's Lodge, No. 244, has been greatly honored in Masonry in Tennessee, having served as Grand Master of the Grand Lodge, Grand High Priest of the Grand Chapter, and Grand Commander of Knights Templar.

Pearl Chapter, No. 24, Royal Arch Masons, was organized in 1841 with W. G. E. Cunningham, D. D., as first High Priest.

Coeur De Leon Commandery, No. 9, Knights Templar, was organized May 5, 1868, with John W. Paxton as Commander. This commandery has furnished three Grand Commanders of the state in the persons of H. M. Aiken, N. S. Woodward and S. B. Dow.

Knoxville Consistory, No. 10, S. P. R. S., was instituted July 7, 1884, and

Knoxville Council, No. 75, R. & S. M., was organized September 28, 1891.

Tennessee Lodge, No. 1, Independent Order of Odd Fellows, was instituted at Nashville, June 1, 1839, and was, as its name implies, the first lodge of its order in the state, though it had existed for a short time previously to the date

HISTORY OF KNOXVILLE, TENNESSEE. 561

given above, under another name. A second lodge was organized in Nashville in 1840. The Grand Lodge of Tennessee was instituted under a charter issued by the Grand Lodge of the United States, August 10, 1841, and on August 24 following the constitution and by-laws of the Grand Lodge of Ohio were adopted. New charters were granted to the two lodges mentioned above, and in October of the same year a charter was granted to Columbia Lodge, No. 3, the first granted under the authority of the Grand Lodge of Tennessee.

East Tennessee Lodge, No. 34, of Knoxville, was organized March 20, 1848, with A. A. Barnes, A. R. Crozier, P. M. McClung, William M. Churchwell, and Dr. James Rodgers as charter members. The officers at the present time are: A. R. Miller, N. G.; D. A. Smith, Treasurer, and E. A. Reed, representative to Grand Lodge.

Knoxville Lodge, No. 138, was instituted October 29, 1869, with James M. McAffry, L. C. Shepard, E. G. McClanahan, S. D. J. Lewis, W. H. Parker, and J. C. Ristine as charter members. The officers elected January 1, 1899, were as follows: B. M. Carr, N. G.; J. C. Bearden, V. G.; Samuel Brown, Secretary; J. B. Carty, Treasurer, and W. A. Gage, representative to Grand Lodge.

Golden Rule Lodge, No. 177, was instituted November 21, 1873, with R. Y. Hayes, G. B. Burleson, J. B. Campbell, J. E. Newman, W. R. Stephenson, W. C. Putnam, George W. Roth, P. F. Jenkins, and E. B. Mann as charter members. The officers at the present time are: J. F. Carman, N. G.; J. N. Poe, V. G.; A. G. Mann, R. S.; B. F. Conger, F. S.; E. B. Mann, Treasurer, and J. W. Kirby, representative to Grand Lodge.

Chilhowee Lodge, No. 247, was instituted June 2, 1897, with sixteen charter members. On January 1, 1899, it had 540 members. Its first officers were: S. P. Armstrong, N. G.; G. W. Dunn, V. G.; B. R. McBath, Secretary, and W. C. Frazier, Treasurer. The present officers are: G. T.

Fowler, N. G.; W. E. Moses, V. G.; W. C. Frazer, Treasurer; W. F. Hinton, R. S.; Dr. B. R. McBath, Financial Secretary, and N. N. Osborne, representative to the Grand Lodge.

The Grand Encampment of Tennessee was instituted at Nashville July 21, 1847, the constitution and by-laws of the state of Maine being adopted. At that time there were five subordinate encampments in the state of Tennessee, the first of which was Ridgely Encampment, No. 1, of Nashville. The first encampment organized in Knoxville was

Knoxville Encampment, No. 11, about 1850, with James A. Deery, A. A. Barnes, William M. Churchwell, William Hunt, Daniel Lyons, William Lyons and M. D. Bearden as charter members. This encampment is not now in existence, being succeeded by

John Sevier Encampment, No. 54, instituted December 17, 1889.

Marble City Canton, No. 5, Patriarch Militant, was mustered September 12, 1894, and has forty-four members.

Colfax Rebekah Lodge, No. 43, was organized in 1895, and now has 155 members.

Triumph Rebekah Lodge, No. 59, was instituted September 30, 1896, and has eighty-seven members.

The East Tennessee Mutual Benefit Association of the Independent Order of Odd Fellows was incorporated May 30, 1884, the incorporators being S. D. Bowman, W. M. Householder, R. J. Stephenson, L. W. Scheuermann, E. B. Mann, J. L. Miller, F. A. Dobson, E. Mynderse, W. S. Hilton, C. Kohlhase, A. Todtenhausen, A. Kelly, J. H. Keeling, J. C. Hudgings, G. C. Robertson, D. C. Robinson, Y. K. Robinson, Mrs. R. J. Kelly, Mrs. A. E. McIntire, Mrs. M. A. Bomar, Samuel Redden, S. W. Sheppard and W. H. Dawn. The object for which this incorporation was effected was the meeting more permanently with Odd Fellows who had obtained the third degree and were in good standing in their respective lodges, who were of sound bodily health and between the ages of twenty-one and sixty years, and the establishment of a benefit fund from which to satisfactorily pay out money on the death of members of the association when such members had complied with all the legal requirements of the association, the sum so paid out not to exceed $2,000 in any case.

The Order of Knights of Honor was introduced into Tennessee May 6, 1874, by the organization of Tennessee Lodge, No. 20, at Nashville, and the Grand Lodge of Tennessee was organized at Nashville, July 3, 1875. The constitution and by-laws of the Supreme Lodge were adopted and remained in effect until October, 1875, when a permanent constitution was adopted for the government of the Grand Lodge of Tennessee.

Teutonia Lodge, No. 141, of Knoxville, was organized August 20, 1875, and holds its meetings every Monday night.

The other two lodges in Knoxville are Relief Lodge, No. 163, and Eureka Lodge, No. 3,640.

The Order of Knights of Pythias was instituted during or soon after the close of the Civil war. It was introduced into Tennessee in March, 1872, in the establishment of Holston, No. 1, at Knoxville. The Grand Lodge was organized at Nashville, April 2, 1872, at which time there were present representatives from six lodges in the state. Calvin McCorkle of Knoxville was the first Grand Chancellor. Since that time Knoxville has had another Grand Chancellor in the person of Alexander Allison. At the present time there are in Knoxville the following lodges of this order:

Corona Lodge, which meets every Tuesday; Orient Lodge, No. 68, which meets every Monday, and Queen City Lodge.

The Ancient Order of United Workmen was organized in Meadville, Pa., in October, 1868, and the Grand Lodge of this order was organized February 22, 1877, in Nashville.

Tennessee Lodge, No. 2, the first lodge of the order organized in the state, was organized at Nashville, November 26, 1876. No Lodge No. 1 was ever organized.

Fidelity Lodge, No. 9, was organized in Knoxville, in August, 1876.

Phoenix Lodge, No. 14, was instituted soon afterward, and meets every second and fourth Friday in each month.

Peabody Lodge, No. —, was organized soon afterward, but was united with Phoenix Lodge, No. 14, in December, 1886.

Knoxville Lodge, No. 100, was organized March 1, 1894, and meets every first and third Friday nights in each month.

The Grand Council of the American Legion of Honor was organized at Nashville, August 3, 1882, Frank A. Moses of Knoxville being elected Grand Treasurer.

Pioneer Council, No. 34, of this order was organized at Knoxville, September 10, 1879, and meets every third Thursday night of each month.

The Royal Arcanum originated in Massachusetts, the Supreme Council being incorporated there November 5, 1877.

Nashville Council, No. R. A., was organized May 22, 1878 the first council in Tennessee.

Knoxville Council, No. 110, R. A., was organized in June, 1878, with L. A. Gratz, Past Regent; A. L. Maxwell, Regent, and Julius Ochs, Secretary. This council meets ever second and fourth Thursday in each month.

The other councils of this order in Knoxville are Chilhowee Council, John Sevier Council, Marble City Council, and Unaka Council, No. 1,620, the latter meeting every second and fourth Wednesday in each month.

The United Order of the Golden Cross is peculiarly a Knoxville organization, originating in the following manner: On May 9, 1876, eleven ladies and gentlemen met in the city of Knoxville and resolved to make application for a charter under the laws of Tennessee, under which such an organization might be effected. The names of these eleven persons were as follows: J. H. Morgan, Maggie P. Morgan, J. F. Goldman, C. F. Gschwend, M. H. Emory, E. W. Adkins, R. A. Brown, A. M. Emory, O. T. Roberts, William Wood and D. H. Weaver. On May 16 ten others united with the above, as follows: P. H. Cardwell, W. F. Cummings, Isaac Emory, A. S. Marriner, H. W. Clark, P. A. Marriner, C. L. Marriner, J. A. Weaver, G. W. Weaver, and Mary F. Adkins. May 23 there were added four additional names—H. Clark, Addie Wood, W. R. Cooper, and Florence Clark. During the month of June there were added seventeen other persons, the membership on the 27th of the month reaching forty-three. On June 22, 1876, the following-named fourteen persons made application for a charter of incorporation under the laws of the state, and on July 4, 1876, the Supreme Commandery of the United Order of the Golden Cross was organized. The fourteen persons above referred to as making this application were as follows: J. H. Morgan, Maggie P. Morgan, E. W. Adkins, Mary F. Adkins, William Wood, Addie Wood, Isaac Emory, A. M. Emory, D. H. Weaver, M. E. Weaver, R. A. Brown, Charles F. Gschwend, J. F. Goldman, and W. R. Cooper.

The first subordinate commandery of this order was instituted at Knoxville, July 11, 1876, and named Peace Commandery, No. 1, and on August 1, 1876, the charter of this commandery was closed with forty-six members.

Hope Commandery, No. 2, United Order of the Golden Cross, was instituted August 16, 1876, with the following officers: J. C. Flanders, Noble Commander; Mrs. Kate Dallas, Vice-Noble Commander; George E. Williams, Past Noble Commander; S. P. Angel, Worthy Prelate; W. H. Agnew, Worthy Herald; J. A. Porter, Keeper of Records; F. C. Richmond, Financial Keeper of Records; William De Groat, Treasurer; Mrs. S. C. George, Warder of the Inner Gate, and T. D. George, Warder of the Outer Gate.

During the months that followed the growth in commanderies and membership so increased that by May 1, 1877, it was deemed advisable to organize a Grand Commandery for Tennessee, there being at that time no membership outside of this state. A convention was therefore called, which met in Knights of Honor Hall in Knoxville, May 10, 1877, this convention being composed of representatives from nine subordinate commanderies, representing 307 third degree members, those present being J. H. Morgan, Supreme Commander; Addie A. Wood, Supreme Vice-Commander; Isaac Emory, Supreme Prelate; D. H. Weaver, Supreme Keeper of Records; William Wood, Supreme Treasurer; R. A. Brown, Supreme Herald; C. F. Gschwend, Supreme Warden of the Inner Gate; E. W. Adkins, Supreme Warden of the Outer Gate; Harvey Clark, Supreme Past Commander; W. R. Cooper, Mary F. Adkins, Maggie P. Morgan, M. E. Weaver, and A. M. Emory. An election for officers was held, resulting as follows: E. E. Young, Past Grand Commander; A. J. Baird, Grand Commander; A. M. Emory, Grand Vice-Commander; S. H. Day, Grand Prelate; George W. Henderson, Grand Keeper of Records; E. W. Adkins, Grand Treasurer; J. A. Ruble, Grand Herald; Addie Wood, Grand Warden of the Inner Gate, and W. J. Fagan, Grand Warden of the Outer Gate.

The first annual session of the Supreme Commandery was held at Knoxville, May 15, 1877, performing its work in one day. The second annual session was held at Knoxville, May 21, 1878, remaining in session four days, and the third annual session of the Supreme Commandery was held at Washington, D. C., in 1879.

The first annual meeting of the Grand Commandery was held at Cleveland, Tenn., April 16, 1878, all succeeding meetings, which were annual until 1880, and bi-ennial since that time, have been held in Nashville. No person is permitted to join this order unless pledged to total abstinence from all kinds of intoxicating liquors.

Central Commandery, No. 5, was organized at Knoxville, Tenn., April 5, 1877, and Bethlehem Commandery, No. 6, was instituted at Knoxville, Tenn., July 21, 1877. The first commandery instituted outside of Tennessee was at Huntsville, Ala., and named Eureka Commandery, No. 10.

The officers of Peace Commandery, No. 1, at the present time are as follows: F. C. Keep, Noble Commander; E. B. Ziegler, Vice-Noble Commander; Mary E. Weaver, Worthy Prelate; J. W. Ward, Keeper of Records; E. W. Adkins, Financial Keeper of Records; James B. Brown, Worthy Treasurer; Ellis B. Zeigler, Worthy Herald; Mary L. Reed, Warder of Inner Gate, and John A. Miller, Warder of Outer Gate. The membership of this commandery, January 1, 1899, was 107. There are of this order 607 sub-organizations in twenty-three states, with an aggregate membership of upward of 32,000.

The officers of Hope Commandery, No. 2, at the present time are: J. S. Miller, Past Noble Commander; B. R. McBath, Noble Commander; Mrs. M. E. Crawford, Vice-Noble Commander; Mrs. S. J. Osborne, Keeper of Records; Charles F. Trent, Financial Keeper of Records; R. G. Osborne, Treasurer; Mrs. A. M. Griffin, Worthy Prelate; F. C. Richmond, Worthy Herald; D. A. Giffin, Warder of the Inner Gate, and Frank Attix, Warder of the Outer Gate. The membership of this commandery at this time is sixty-eight. It may be added with reference to the general order that in a period of twenty-two years, ending November 25, 1898, the average number of assessments per annum was thirteen and three-elevenths, and that the order disbursed in the payment of 3,197 death claims, $5,101,760.83.

Fort Sanders Council, No. 576, of the National Union was organized in August, 1891, with about thirty members, and in the same month Cherokee Council, No. 601, of the same Union was organized with about the same membership. Of the latter council C. M. Baumann was President; J. A. Armstrong, Secretary; W. L. McSpadden, Financial Secretary, and John N. Blair, Treasurer. In the early part of 1893 the two councils were consolidated under the former name, and there has been but one council in Knoxville since that time. The National Union is a beneficiary order, established in 1881 at Toledo, Ohio, and it is now very strong, especially in the Northwest. Of the local council the membership on January 1, 1899, was sixty-six, and the officers at the present time are: C. H. Ogden, President; E. W. Adkins, Vice-President; J. A. Armstrong, Secretary; W. L. McSpadden, Financial Secretary, and M. M. Harris, Treasurer. The amount of insurance that may be carried by one member varies from $1,000 to $5,000.

Other beneficiary associations which have one or more branches in Knoxville are the following:

The American Guild of Richmond, Va., of which Knoxville Lodge, No. 485, was organized October 30, 1897, with forty-nine charter members. The Governor of this lodge is Fred R. Purple, and Secretary and Treasurer, John M. Currier.

John Sevier Forum, No. 936, of the Home Forum Benefit Order of Chicago, organized July 2, 1896, with sixty-four charter members. Of this Forum William L. Murphy is President; Orin C. Beaman, Secretary, and John M. Currier, Treasurer.

Knox Lodge, No. 153, of the Fraternal Union of America was organized July 30, 1897, with 159 charter members. Of this lodge William L. Murphy is Fraternal Master; John M. Currier, Secretary, and Orin C. Beaman, Treasurer.

Alhambra Lodge, No. 66, of the National Legion, New York City, was organized September 16, 1898, with forty-one charter members. William L. Murphy is President; Orin C. Beaman, Secretary, and John M. Currier, Treasurer.

Knoxville Lodge, No. 87, of the National Fraternity, Philadelphia, Pa., was organized November 1, 1898, with seventy-three charter members, and with Herbert C. Sanford, Guardian, and John M. Currier, Cashier. This fraternity claims to combine all the leading features of fraternal protection, viz.: death benefits, total disability benefits and surplus benefits. It has a fixed monthly assessment, according to age and class or amount of benefits, and after a period of five years of continuous membership, each member is entitled to an equitable proportion of the surplus remaining in the benefit fund, after the payment of all sick, disability and death claims.

George H. Thomas Post, No. 1, G. A. R., was organized at Nashville, February 27, 1882, with sixteen charter members. The Provisional Department of Tennessee and Georgia was formed May 1, 1883, with four posts and 136 members.

Ed. Maynard Post, No. 14, was organized at Knoxville, December 23, 1883, with the following members: A. S. Prosser, L. A. Gratz, W. R. Carter, W. J. Ramage, W. W. Dunn, W. C. Brandon, Ignaz Fanz, C. H. Brown, W. R. Tuttle, P. D. Roady, S. J. Todd, B. Goodhart, and George L. Maloney. L. A. Gratz was the first commander, and A. S. Prosser was the second. This lodge meets every first and third Tuesday nights in each month.

The Woman's Relief Corps, a most worthy organization, meets every first and third Tuesday afternoon in each month.

W. P. Sanders Camp, Sons of Veterans, meets every second and fourth Tuesday in each month.

Felix K. Zollicoffer Camp, Confederate Veterans, was organized with 135 members, December 10, 1885. The object for which this camp was formed was to perpetuate the memories of those who fell in the Civil war in the Confederate armies, to aid those who had been permanently disabled in the service, and to preserve that sentiment of fraternity born of hardship and danger shared alike by all in the march, the battle, and the bivouac. Alexander Allison was the first commander and P. B. Sheperd the first lieutenant commander. This camp meets every second and fourth Thursday in each month.

The Daughters of the Confederacy meet on the first Tuesday afternoon of each month.

Fred. Ault Camp, No. 5, United Confederate Veterans, meets every second Tuesday in each month, and

Fred. Ault Bivouac, No. 17, United Confederate Veterans, meets also on the second Tuesday in each month.

Sycamore Camp, No. 3, Woodmen of the World, was organized February 1, 1893, and meets every Monday night in the Southern Building and Loan Association building. Woodcraft came in 1882, soon met with favor, rapidly developed, until June 6, 1890, on which day the Woodmen of the World were promulgated. Both orders were founded by Joseph Cullen Root of Omaha, Neb., the new order, unlike the older one, which limited its operations to a few of the states, extended its limits over the entire continent with the view of disseminating its principles throughout the whole civilized world. By February 1, 1898, there had been enrolled more than 110,000 members, giving this order the fifth place in numbers among the 200 fraternal orders in the United States. Mr. Root, who at that time came to Knoxville, delivered an address on the 2d of February, in which he said that fraternalism would in time become so extended and powerful as to establish fraternal arbitration between governments, and war would be thus banished from the earth. The beneficiary feature of each camp was the payment of $3,000 at the death of a member, and in addition the order erected a monument over the grave of each deceased member, which would cost $100.

The officers of Sycamore Camp, No. 3, at the present time are as follows: William L. Murphy, Consul Commander; Edward L. Dearing, Adviser Lieutenant; John M. Currier, Clerk; George K. Preston, Banker; W. A. Trotter, Escort; George W. Turner, Watchman; Henry Hays, Sentry; A. M. King, W. F. Newton and R. A. Keller, Managers, and Drs. J. D. Henderson and C. C. D'Armond, Physicians.

During the eight years of its history more than 3,000 camps have been instituted and upward of 140,000 certificates have been issued to members; three millions of dollars have been paid to beneficiaries, and more than 1,600 monuments have been erected at the graves of deceased members. Every death loss has been paid in full, and in ninety-six months only eighty-seven assessments were called, a trifle more than ten each year. And it may be added that this association is one of the few beneficiary societies that has a reserve fund, established for the purpose of limiting the number of annual assessments, the limit in this case being sixteen.

Post "C," Travelers' Protective Association, was organized March 10, 1894, by W. E. Gibbins, Wylie Brownlee, Joseph H. Broyles, L. M. Ewing, J. E. Chapman, and William Dick. A permanent organization was effected March 17, 1894, by the election of the following officers: President, M. L. Shields; First Vice-President, William Dick; Second Vice-President, L. M. Ewing; Third Vice-President, David A. Giffin; Fourth Vice-President, Robert H. Cate; Fifth Vice-President, Albert A. DuRocher, and Secretary and Treasurer, Wylie Brownlee. November 29, 1894, this post gave a banquet at Schubert's, now Flanders' Hotel, and since then there have been entertainments in the form of lectures, etc., in 1896 securing the attendance of the third annual state convention of the Tennessee division of the association. This convention lasted three days, April 16, 17 and 18, the officers of this association at the time being William R. Johnson, President; G. J. Ashe, First Vice-President; Reuben N. Payne, Second Vice-President; Wood G. Haynes, Third Vice-President; Joseph T. Brownlee, Fourth Vice-President; Edwin R. Wade, Fifth Vice-President; Joseph H. Broyles, Secretary and Treasurer; L. M. Ewing, M. L. Shields, W. E. Gibbins, W. C. Perry and Harry Levy, board of directors.

The national organization was brought into existence as a result of a movement on the part of representatives of the commercial and industrial institutions of the country and was organized at Denver, Colo., June 3, 1890, and was immediately incorporated under the name of the Travelers' Protective Association of America. This organization established its chief office and place of business in St. Louis, Mo., the principal object of the association being a better acquaintance and a more fraternal feeling among traveling men. By 1896 the number of members of the national association had reached 10,538.

The officers of Post "C" at the present time (January, 1899) are as follows:

President, Hazen House; First Vice-President, Herbert W. Hall; Second Vice-President, H. Rogan Briscoe; Third Vice-President, R. H. Cate; Fourth Vice-President, John Bane; Fifth Vice-President, Simpson Little; Secretary and Treasurer, James A. Hensley; Chaplain, Rev. C. W. Duncan, and Surgeon, Dr. L. W. Davis.

On February 1, 1899, the membership of this order was 275, and increasing rapidly. The post meets regularly every Saturday night in the third story of the Branner building, on the southeast corner of Gay and Vine streets, the rooms being well fitted up with desks, writing materials, pool and billiard tables, everything being free to members.

The benefits under the constitution of this order are as follows: In case of death by accident, $5,000; in case of injury by accident, $25 weekly, not to exceed fifty-two weeks; loss of both arms or both legs, $2,500; loss of one arm and one leg, $2,500; loss of one hand or one foot, $1,000; loss of one arm or one leg, $1,000; loss of both eyes, $5,000, and loss of one eye, $1,000. To join the organization cost $2 membership fee, and $10 dues per year. The amount paid to members and their beneficiaries up to January 1, 1899, was $364,649.60.

Knox Council, No. 91, United Commercial Travelers, was organized in October, 1897, with ten members. The number at this time (February, 1899) is forty-four. The officers of this council at the present time are F. M. Hambright, Senior Counsellor; C. W. Duncan, Junior Counsellor; Charles Murphy, Conductor; Frank Preston, Secretary and Treasurer, and G. W. Murphy, Past Counsellor.

This order was established at Columbus, Ohio, in 1888, under the laws of that state. It is exclusively for the benefit of commercial travelers, and none but active travelers who have been so engaged for at least a year. Its insurance benefits are as follows: For accidental death, $6,300; loss of both eyes, $5,000; loss of hands, $5,000; loss of both feet, $5,000; loss of one hand and one foot, $2,500; loss of one hand, $1,250; loss of one foot, $1,000, and loss of one eye, $650. In cases of accidental injury resulting in total disability, $25 per week is paid. There is also a widows' and orphans' fund, out of which, if a traveler's family is left without means, the widow draws $250 per year, and each child the same.

Knoxville Senate, No. 1068, Knights of the Ancient Essenic Order, was organized May 8, 1895. As is well known to readers of Jewish history the Essenes were one of the three principal sects of the Jews, they being first mentioned about the middle of the second century before Christ, at which time they were classed with the Sadduces and Pharisees. They were remarkable for their strictness and abstinence. The mission of the Essenes was to restore a man's soul to that state whence it had fallen, as from its native seat of perfection. The order became very popular, even kings and princes being anxious to identify themselves therewith. So much for its nature before the beginning of the Christian era.

Of this Knoxville order there were eighty-five charter members, of whom sixty-four were present at the time of organization, at which time the following officers were elected: Dr. William Bowen, Excellent Senator; Dr. G. C. Childress, Senior Senaschal; J. C. Ford, Jr., Junior Senaschal; Rev. M. D. Jeffries, Sarcedras; L. S. Hull, Treasurer; and A. Y. Burrows, Secretary.

Company A, First Regiment of the Essenic Army, was organized March 31, 1896, with the following officers: Captain, A. Y. Burrows; First Lieutenant, Albert M. Ross; Second Lieutenant, Joe E. Borches, and by appointment, First Sergeant, W. P. Chandler, and Second Sergeant, P. J. Williams. This company meets every first and third Friday night in each month.

The Essenes observed Sunday, June 28, 1896, as the

2906th anniversary of their ancient order, that being the first Sunday following St. John's day, which that year came on the 24th of June. The Essenes were taught to honor and revere the memory of the holy St. John as the forerunner of Christ, remembering also that St. John the Baptist was a member of the ancient Essenic order.

The Young Men's Christian Association was first organized in 1854 by a few earnest gentlemen and a constitution was adopted April 7, 1855. One year later this constitution was revised and under it anyone was permitted to become a member who was in good standing in any one of the evangelical churches. The association was helpful to young men living in Knoxville and also to strangers visiting the city. But it remained in existence only a portion of two years. From November, 1854, to April, 1856, it had two presidents, viz.: J. B. G. Kensloe and M. C. Butler.

In June, 1865, a new organization was effected, but it continued in existence only until March 27, 1866, L. C. Trowbridge being president during this period.

On August 16, 1874 the present organization was effected, and under the present constitution any young man or other man is eligible to membership, without regard to religious opinions. A steady growth and development have been manifest and it has had a successful and useful career. From one small rented room it has come to occupy in the third story of the Borches building a large suite of rooms, and the association now owns a fine lot, on which it will in due time erect a building. Since 1874 the presidents of this association have been as follows: Samuel McKinney, 1874-76; J. A. Rayl, 1876-78; James Somerville, 1878-80; Charles Armstrong, 1880-81; James H. Cowan, 1881-82; R. W. McBryde, 1882-83; James Cowan, 1883-84; W. E. Gibbins, 1884-89; John M. Allen, 1889-91; Frank Barker, 1891-93; John M. Allen, 1893 to date.

Secretaries—A. S. Bixby, 1880-83; C. H. Mills, 1883; P. A. Walling, 1883-84; E. M. Cook, 1884-87; W. E. Henderson, 1887-88; J. J. Frater, 1888-90; A. K. Perkins, 1890-93; H. A. Baldwin, 1893 to date.

The Young Men's Christian Association of Knoxville was incorporated April 7, 1884, the incorporators being James H. Cowan, W. E. Gibbins, John M. Allen, John B. Clothworthy, W. P. Washburn, J. A. Rayl, Joseph A. Porter, B. A. Jenkins, John T. Roundtree, Alfred L. Young, Charles Armstrong, Samuel B. Boyd, William Rule, William C. Everett and P. Augustus Weiting. The object of this association was and is to improve the spiritual, social, mental and physical condition of the young men of Knoxville, by the support and maintenance of lectures and such other means and services as might conduce to the accomplishment of the object and to support public worship, the building of churches and chapels, and the maintenance of missionary undertakings.

The Ladies' Auxiliary to the Y. M. C. A. was organized in 1883, for the purpose of aiding that association in their work and to render the social side of it more attractive to the members. The first president of the auxiliary was Miss Cinnie Boyd, 1883-91, and since then Mrs. John M. Allen and Mrs. I. E. Barry have been presidents, and since 1893 the president has been Mrs. S. C. Roney. In 1897 a constitution and by-laws were adopted and since May, 1898, Mrs. Ainsworth has been secretary. The auxiliary meets in the rooms of the Y. M. C. A. on the first Tuesday of each month.

The Knoxville Woman's Christian Temperance Union was organized in 1883 by Miss Frances E. Willard, who, during that year and the year previous made a tour of the United States, speaking in every city of ten thousand population and upward, and in many smaller places. Miss Willard was introduced to her first Knoxville audience by William Rule, the present mayor of Knoxville, as she had been previously introduced to her first Southern audience by Bishop Stevens, who, as Colonel Stevens, commanded the battery that fired the first shot on Fort Sumter in 1861. Among the many good works this Union has done to help the city of Knoxville and the state of Tennessee was its work in attempting to secure a prohibition amendment to the constitution of the state, and it is stated to be an historical fact that wherever the womanhood of the state was at the polls, there there was a majority in favor of said amendment. This Union was instrumental in creating and in keeping in existence the office of police matron for the city of Knoxville. When it discovered that the law of the state did not protect the girls as long as it protected her inherited property this Union immediately began to add its influence to that of other unions to get the age of protection raised, and succeeded in getting the age of consent raised from ten years to sixteen and a half years. The Woman's Christian Temperance Union, under the leadership of Mrs. Mary Hunt of Boston, had introduced into all territories and into nearly all the states, legislation requiring the study of the natural effect of alcoholic drinks on the human system in all schools supported in whole or in part by public money. The women of Tennessee had labored long with their legislators to get them to see the necessity of this kind of instruction, but they would not, because they could not, or they could not because they would not, understand it.

And after ten long years of failure the women of the state still had faith in their ultimate ability to make it apparent to their law-makers that the laws of the state should be changed in this respect, the real difficulty being discovered by the Knoxville W. C. T. U., and in the Woman's edition of the Knoxville Tribune, issued March 15, 1895, appeared a map of the United States, on which those states which had passed scientific temperance laws were shown in white, while those which had not yet enacted such laws were shown in black! Immediately afterward the woman's edition of the Clarksville Chronicle published the same map, and then came the woman's edition of the Nashville American, showing to the readers thereof how black Tennessee appeared amid her white sister states: and when the law-making body of the state were thus made to see how "black" their state looked among the states of the Union, with reference to this matter of temperance, they immediately changed the laws of the state in such a manner as to make scientific temperance instruction in the public schools compulsory.

This organization has also directed the thought of many ministers and church officials to the question of using unfermented wine at the communion table, noting the fact that the Scriptures mention two kinds of wine, condemning one and commending the other. In the mothers' meetings of this Union mothers have learned that it is easier to form character than to reform it, and they have also learned much about the laws of heredity. The Knoxville Union also lends its influence in trying to reclaim fallen men as well as fallen women, believing that the greatest good can be done by beginning at the root of the difficulty, and that an ounce of prevention is better than a pound of cure. For the past three years this Union has conducted a free kindergarten, the good done by which can not be estimated, much less computed. The Union has done much in aiding congress to see the evils of the "army canteen," and in many other ways that can not in this short history thereof be even mentioned. The members of this Union, together with the other W. C. T. U.'s in Knoxville, are doing all they can to hasten the day which they hope will soon come, when it can not be truthfully said:

> "Out from the hearthstone
> The children fair,
> Go forth from the breath of a mother's prayer,
> And the father's vote on the crowded street,
> Consent to the snares for their thoughtless feet."

The Mary T. Lathrop Branch of the W. C. T. U of Knoxville was organized January 2, 1895, by Mrs. L. Lauritzen, who was chosen President; Miss Nannie McCormick, First Vice-President; Miss Hannah Price, Second Vice-President, and Mrs. M. Kiser, Treasurer. Miss McCormick being also

Secretary. At the time of organization there were fifteen members. One of the conditions of membership is that every one uniting with the organization must sign the temperance pledge. On January 1, 1899, there were forty-four members, and the officers were: Mrs. L. Lauritzen, President; Miss Mary Vance, First Vice-President; Miss J. L. Kinzel, Second Vice-President; Mrs. M. Skillman, Third Vice-President; Miss Nannie McCormick, Corresponding Secretary; Mrs. Hannah Price, Recording Secretary, and Mrs. M. Skillman, Treasurer. This branch of the W. C. T. U. works in eleven departments.

The Frances E. Willard Branch of the W. C. T. U. was organized in the spring of 1898, with Mrs. J. Baker, President; Mrs. Mary Bowers, Corresponding Secretary; Mrs. L. Lauritzen, Recording Secretary, and Mrs. Lucy E. Gray, Treasurer. The Union meets at the residence of Mrs. Lucy E. Gray, who is the President now, has a large membership, and works in twelve departments. The three branches of the Union work in twenty-four departments. The Corresponding Secretary at the present time is Mrs. L. Lauritzen.

Ossoli Circle, named in honor of Margaret Fuller Ossoli, was founded in 1885 by Mrs. L. C. French, for the mutual benefit of women of literary taste and ability. Its object was to stimulate intellectual growth and moral development and it has been of great usefulness along these lines. The number of members at first was thirteen and at the first meeting of the general federation held in New York in April, 1890, the only ladies present from the Southern states were Miss Mary B. Temple and Mrs. Samuel McKinney, Miss Temple being made Corresponding Secretary. By 1893 the membership had increased to seventy-five and there were then numerous other clubs of the kind in the state. On February 14, 1896, an important meeting was held in the parlors of the Young Men's Christian Association in Knoxville, for the purpose of forming a state federation, sixteen women's clubs, located in various parts of the state, being present by representation. Of this meeting Mrs. J. M. Greer of Memphis was elected President; Mrs. Charles A. Perkins of Ossoli Circle, Secretary, and an enrollment committee appointed, consisting of Mrs. Thorndike of Harriman, Mrs. Burger of Maryville, and Mrs. A. P. White of Knoxville. This committee having reported to the meeting the names of those present, several speeches were made by the women from several of the clubs represented, and a committee was appointed to frame a constitution and by-laws for the proposed federation, consisting of Mrs. C. E. McTeer of Knoxville; Mrs. J. G. Richardson of Chattanooga; Mrs. J. Wilkes of Pulaski; Mrs. J. H. Kirkland of Nashville; Mrs. Grace H. Watkins of Memphis, and Mrs. L. C. French. In this constitution the organization was named the "Tennessee State Federation of Women's Clubs," the object being to bring the women's clubs in the state into communication for acquaintance and mutual help and to develop and strengthen interest along all lines of growth. Under this constitution Mrs. William D. Beard of Memphis was elected President; Mrs. J. G. Richardson of Chattanooga, Vice-President; Mrs. Charles A. Perkins of Knoxville, Recording Secretary; Mrs. Thorndike of Harriman, Corresponding Secretary, and Mrs. Joseph Burger of Maryville, Treasurer, and Mrs. Romine of Pulaski, Auditor.

The Presidents of Ossoli Circle have been as follows: Miss Mary B. Temple, 1885-90; Mrs. W. G. McAdoo, 1890-91; Miss C. M. Woodbury, 1891-92; Mrs. Henry R. Gibson, 1892-94; Mrs. Charles E. McTeer, 1894-95; Mrs. C. J. McClung, 1895-96; Mrs. Charles A. Perkins, 1896-97; Mrs. Samuel McKinney, 1897-98; Mrs. A. P. White, 1898-99.

Under the auspices of Ossoli Circle the Woman's Council of Knoxville was formed in 1895, for the purpose of awakening a greater interest in all kinds of good work. This council is composed of representatives from all women's clubs in the city, and there are now about twenty-one of these different clubs belonging to it. The Presidents have been Mrs. Frank L. Fisher and Miss Alida Rule.

The Woman's Educational and Industrial Union was organized January 1, 1890, by Mrs. L. C. French, who was its first President, the other Presidents having been Mrs. C. S. Frazee and Mrs. C. J. McClung. The object of this organization, as its name implies, is both educational and industrial. Its charity is of the broadest kind, believing in the principle of helping others to help themselves. Largely through its influence the office of police matron in Knoxville was established, the first instance of a woman being placed in such an office in the Southern states. Through the Woman's Exchange, the first in East Tennessee, established through the influence of this Union, much good has been done to the poor and needy, work having been supplied to many women in need who were of the best character, perfectly willing to work, but often without the aid of this exchange, unable to find anything to do. It was also through the influence of this Union that women have become eligible to a position on the school board of Knoxville, though up to the present time no woman has been elected to the board. It was through the suggestion of this Union that the Knox county industrial school was established in 1896 or 1897, and the first strong stand taken in this city in the social purity movement was by this Union through the influence of Mrs. C. M. McClung, by whose death, which occurred September 1, 1898, Knoxville lost one of the noblest women who ever lived here. It was she who brought to Knoxville Mr. Aaron M. Powell of New York city, to speak to the young men of this city and others on the subject of social purity, and through whose labors much good has been accomplished. The Union holds regular monthly meetings and has in all probability accomplished as much good as any other one organization in Knoxville. Its officers at the present time are Mrs. C. J. McClung, President; Mrs. David Ross, Vice-President; Mrs. A. M. Pitman, Secretary; Mrs. J. W. Slocum, Treasurer, and Miss Mabel Mitchell, Corresponding Secretary.

The Knoxville Lyceum was organized November 4, 1898,

in the directors' room of the Holston National Bank, for the purpose of bringing to Knoxville the leading authors and lecturers of the United States and of England. Those present were J. W. Caldwell, Dr. J. B. Henneman, Joseph Gaut, William Rule, Rev. J. A. Duncan, George F. Milton, Hugh L. McClung, Prof. W. T. White, Junius Parker, Miss Lucy Crozier, and Miss Laura McAdoo. The following officers were elected: Hugh L. McClung, President; Miss Lida Rule, Vice-President; Prof. W. T. White, Secretary, and Joseph Gaut, Treasurer. Directors were elected as follows: J. W. Caldwell, George F. Milton, James Park, Junius Parker, J. B. Henneman, J. H. McCallie, R. R. Acree, William Rule, H. H. Ingersoll, James Maynard, J. A. Duncan, Mrs. J. Y. Johnston, Mrs. William Lockett, Mrs. S. McKinney and Miss Lucy Crozier. An executive and lecture committee was elected, consisting of the officers and J. B. Henneman, Mrs. S. McKinney, and George F. Milton. The membership fee was fixed at $5, to be paid when three hundred names were enrolled, and on this basis each member was to be given two season tickets for ten entertainments. Should four hundred names be enrolled, then two season tickets for twelve entertainments were to be given, and if five hundred names should be enrolled, then two season tickets for fifteen entertainments. The requisite number of subscriptions, three hundred, was secured by December 2, 1898, and the first entertainment of the series for that winter was given Wednesday evening, December 21, by the Mozart Symphony Club, in the Woman's building, Market Hall, the second being a lecture by Henry Watterson, January 4, 1899; the third by Dr. James Hedley, January 17; the fourth by Harry Stillwell Edwards, January 23; the fifth by Alexander Black, January 30; the sixth by Hamilton W. Mabie, February 11; the seventh by Frank Beard, February 15, the eighth being by the Pasquali Opera Company, February 21; the ninth by George Kennan, February 28.

CHAPTER XXII.

CEMETERIES.

The Oldest, That of the Presbyterians—Gray Cemetery—The Confederate or Bethel Cemetery—The National Cemetery—Soldiers' Monument—Catholic Cemetery—Woodlawn Cemetery—The Hebrew Cemetery.

THE oldest and perhaps the most interesting cemetery in Knoxville is that of the First Presbyterian Church, containing as it does the remains of some of the most prominent characters of the early history of the state. Among those who were thus prominent and who were buried in this cemetery were Governor William Blount and his wife Mary, the inscription on the tombstone of the former being: "William Blount, died 21st March, 1800, aged 53 years." The tombs of these two people, not only on account of the memories they serve to perpetuate, but also on account of their peculiar form, are notable, though there are others in this cemetery of the same form. They consist of four low brick walls, capped with a large marble slab lying flat upon them, the inscription being engraved on the flat top, and being thus easily read. These peculiarly formed tombstones are reminders of the fact that in the ages that have passed as well as in the present, monuments of different forms were erected and are erected to recall to mind the services and virtues of individuals to their families or to their race. Tombs of this particular form were common in India, among the North American Indians, in England, and in France, though the form now seen in the cemetery of the First Presbyterian Church, known as dolmens, from "Daul," a table, and "Maen," a stone, are more common in France than in England, in which latter country the cromlech, from "crom," a circle, and "lech," a stone, is more common than in France.

Some of those buried in the cemetery of this church, over

whose remains have been erected tombstones of this kind are the following: William and Mary Blount, as above noted; James Scott, Margaret Elizabeth Colhoun, Mrs. Maria Lea, Rev. Thomas H. Nelson, Mrs. Sarah Jacobs and Mrs. Catharine Strong, Rev. Samuel Carrick, Hugh Lawson White, Col. John Williams, and other notables of the pioneer days.

Gray Cemetery is located in the northern part of the city, between Jacksboro street on the west and Broad street on the east. Many years ago, when Knoxville was quite a small place, what is now the southeast corner of this cemetery was laid out as a burying ground, but the location was not satisfactory to all, it being, as they thought, too far away. People having relatives buried there could not get to their graves, the most of Knoxville being then south of Clinch street. Still the cemetery continued to be used, and finally the city extended out to and even beyond the cemetery, as it does now to a considerable distance both toward the north and toward the west. Then, too, there was for a long time a difference of opinion as to what would be an appropriate name for this last repose of the dead, some favoring "Greenwood," some "Woodlawn," others "Greendale," still others, "Fairview," and others other names. At length a lady present at one of the meetings of the association having charge of the cemetery suggested that it be called "Gray Cemetery," in honor of the author of Gray's Elegy, and the suggestion was instantly acted upon, hence the name of this now beautiful place of sepulture. To the north of it is the National Cemetery, the two being separated by a stone wall four and a half feet high.

The original company which made application for a charter for this cemetery was composed as follows: William B. Reese, Marcus D. Bearden, James C. Moses, James M. Welcker, Joseph L. King, John H. Crozier, and Perez Dickinson. Their application was made February 9, 1850. In 1889 the ground was purchased for New Gray Cemetery, the trustees were W. P. Washburn, H. H. Taylor, A. J. Albers, S. B. Boyd, Rev. James Park, James Craighead and Hugh

McClung, Sr. There are eighty acres in the new plot, and it is two and a half miles from the city on the Clinton pike. At the time of the purchase it was owned by J. C. Flanders, the price paid being $9,601.51. A superintendent of the new cemetery was employed in the person of William Hall, formerly manager and gardener for Perez Dickinson's Island Home farm.

In May, 1890, A. J. Albers proposed to erect in the old Gray cemetery, on certain conditions, "The Ella Albers Memorial Fountain;" the conditions were accepted and the fountain erected. On July 25, 1896, at a meeting held in the rooms of the chamber of commerce, it was decided to set apart $6,000, which should be invested and the income devoted to the preservation and care of the old cemetery grounds. The two cemeteries are under the same management. At this meeting the trustees elected for two years were Dr. James Park, W. P. Washburn, A. J. Albers, H. H. Taylor, James Van Deventer, C. M. McClung, and W. W. Woodruff. W. P. Washburn was chosen President and Lewis Tillman, who had been Secretary since 1886, was re-elected.

One peculiar feature in connection with the management of this cemetery is: that there are not in the ordinary sense of the term any stockholders; each owner of a lot is a proprietor and has one vote and no more. Among the prominent people buried in this cemetery are Horace Maynard, Judge John Baxter and W. G. Brownlow.

The Confederate or Bethel Cemetery is located about one mile east of Gay street on the Rutledge pike, and includes four acres of land, two acres of which was purchased in 1862 of Knox county, and two acres of Joseph Mabry. Ever since it was established it has been in charge of the Ladies' Memorial Association. More than 1,600 Confederate dead lie buried in this cemetery, and according to the present sexton, W. D. Winstead, an old Confederate soldier, there were buried here in the southeast corner, three hundred bodies of soldiers killed in the charge on Fort Sanders, immediately after the battle, which, if correct, when added to the ninety-two buried in neat pine boxes under the direction of S. T. Atkins, would make three hundred and ninety-two killed in that disastrous attack.

Previous to 1884 there was no regular sexton in charge of this cemetery, but in that year P. Johnson was engaged, serving until 1886, since which time W. D. Winstead has been the sexton.

The monument to the Confederate dead in Bethel Cemetery was erected through the efforts of the Ladies' Memorial Association, and was unveiled May 19, 1892, that being the day usually observed for the purpose of decorating Confederate soldiers' graves. On the occasion of this unveiling there were present Gen. E. Kirby Smith, Gen. William B. Bate, Rev. Dr. James Park, and Col. James E. Carter. The address of welcome was delivered by Hon. H. H. Taylor, and the monument, designed to be unveiled by Miss Moody McTeer, was really unveiled by the strong wind then blowing, and the figure of the Confederate soldier on top of the monument was thus exposed to view, standing at parade rest on top the high marble column. General Bate delivered the dedicatory address, and there were other appropriate exercises. The monument is inscribed to the memory of soldiers that had bravely fought for the principles which they believed were right.

The National Cemetery at Knoxville is situated on a slight eminence in the northwestern portion of the city, the principal entrance being on Jacksboro street, which passes along the western side of the cemetery. There are also entrances on the eastern side, one for carriages and one for people on foot. This cemetery was established in 1865, and laid out according to plans furnished from Washington. In the center of the cemetery is a mound, upon which stands a flag staff, from the top of which the national emblem floats while the sun is above the horizon. Surrounding the central mound is a driveway, and from this driveway radiate driveways to the circumference of the graves of the dead, which are arranged in circles, and at the head of each grave is a stone bearing the name of the dead soldier, when known, and a number, and in case the soldier were not known, then only a number is on the headstone. Around the cemetery is a stone fence, 2,650 feet long, 4 feet high and 18 inches wide, which was built by Patrick McNamara, as a subcontractor under M. D. Bearden. The building of this wall was begun in November, 1872, and finished in May, 1873. The wall on the south side of this cemetery separates it from Gray Cemetery, mentioned elsewhere in this chapter.

The number of graves in this cemetery at the present time is 3,238, and contain the bodies of 2,191 soldiers whose names are known and 1,047 whose names are unknown. Among the known are thirteen bodies of soldiers that died in camp at Knoxville during the year 1898.

On May 26, 1873, Mayor Rule received the following telegram:

HEADQUARTERS SEVENTY-NINTH HIGHLAND REGIMENT.

New York, May 26, 1873.
His Honor the Mayor of Knoxville, Tenn.:

Please decorate the graves of the Seventy-ninth Highland New York volunteers killed in the defense of Fort Saunders at Knoxville. Their living comrades still keep their memories dear. Letter by mail.

C. E. STETSON,
Lt.-Col. Commanding.

This request was handsomely complied with and the entire ceremonies on May 30 were impressive and satisfactory to all. Gen. Joel A. Dewey was orator of the day.

The superintendents of this cemetery have been as follows: Thomas Ridge, November, 1865, to October, 1887; James McCauley, October, 1887, to March, 1891; Thomas Ridge, March, 1891, to November, 1896; W. Clayton Hart, November, 1896, to July, 1898, and Thomas Ridge, July, 1898, to the present time.

The incomplete monument standing in this national cemetery, to the Union soldiers of East Tennessee, is the result of a movement begun at Athens, Tenn., in 1892. A committee was appointed at the encampment held there that year to have charge of the raising of funds and of overseeing the erection of the monument, the committee consisting of Captain William Rule of Knoxville, late of the Sixth Tennessee infantry; Samuel W. Hawkins of Huntington, late captain of Company I, Seventh Tennessee infantry; John Ruhm, Nashville, late lieutenant and assistant adjutant-general, Fourth United States infantry; A. J. Gahagan, Chattanooga, late lieutenant Company G, First Tennessee cavalry; H. C. Whitaker, New Market, late private Company A, Second New York cavalry; W. E. F. Milburn, Greeneville, late sergeant Company B, Twelfth Tennessee cavalry; L. M. Jarvis, Sneedville, late captain Company E, Eighth Tennessee cavalry; John C. Smith, Elizabethton, late private Company F, Second Tennessee infantry.

On July 4, 1893, an address was issued by the monument committee in which all comrades were urged to aid the committee in their work of raising funds. A few days previously Ed. Maynard Post, No. 14, G. A. R., of Knoxville, had pledged itself to contribute $1,000 to the fund, and said that it would give $1,000 additional if the monument were placed in Knoxville.

The custodians of funds raised for the monument, in 1896, consisted of G. L. Maloney, H. T. Cooper, and G. W. Peters. The corner-stone was laid October 15, 1896. The oration on this occasion was delivered by Gen. Gates P. Thurston of Nashville, and an historical address was delivered by Capt. William Rule. The entire height of the monument when complete will be about fifty feet. On the base of it, all that has so far been erected, is the following inscription:

TO THE TENNESSEE MEN WHO LAID THEIR LIVES, A
VOLUNTARY SACRIFICE, ON FREEDOM'S ALTAR; WHO
ENDURED WITH FORTITUDE TEMPORARY BANISH-
MENT FROM THEIR MOUNTAIN HOMES; WHO FOL-
LOWED THE FLAG THEY LOVED ON SCORES OF
BATTLEFIELDS, AND WHO FELL CONSCIENTIOUS-
LY AND VALIANTLY CONTENDING FOR NA-
TIONAL UNITY, THIS MONUMENT IS LOV-
INGLY ERECTED BY THEIR SURVIVING
COMRADES AND FRIENDS. THEY CHOSE
THEIR IDEAL OF THE RIGHT WITH
INVINCIBLE RESOLUTION, CHEER-
FULLY BORE THEIR BURDENS
AND UNFALTERINGLY MET
DEATH FOR THE SAKE
OF HOME AND
COUNTRY.

The Catholic Cemetery is situated on the Rutledge pike about one mile east of the principal part of the city, and immediately west of the Confederate cemetery. It was purchased July 5, 1869, and contains six acres of land, for which $855 was paid. The ground at the time of purchase was so rough that it was feared by many people it would prove a failure; but by hard work it has been so far beautified that it is now in good condition and in time will be very beautiful. There are numerous monuments in this burial place that tower above the young trees, yet there is one monument that is especially noteworthy, a tall and massive shaft of fine granite, erected to the memory of Thomas White, father of Professor W. T. White, principal of the Girls' High School. The cemetery is well kept, and is growing more and more beautiful every year.

The Woodlawn Cemetery was established in 1893 by I. L. and C. M. Ford. It is situated three miles southeast of the city on one of nature's loveliest spots. The Ford brothers have had built an excellent turnpike road, well macadamized to the cemetery. The plat embraces thirty acres, which has been laid off with driveways and upon which grows a luxuriant crop of blue grass. They have also planted a large number of ornamental trees and shrubbery. The Ford brothers have made a special study of driveways and lawns. To the thirty acres, the owners also have 100 acres adjoining, which they will convert into cemetery property when necessary. The present plat is about to be enclosed with an iron fence. The first interment made in the cemetery was James M. Whittle, December 23, 1893. The officiating clergyman was Rev. Thomas Corwin Warner, who has died since and also sleeps in Woodlawn. There have been something over three hundred interments made in the cemetery.

Early in the Civil war Mr. A. Schwab brought home the body of his young son, who had enlisted in the Confederate army and had fallen in one of the engagements in Virginia, or had succumbed to disease. There were then but few Israelites in Knoxville, and they possessed no burial ground. One of their number, Solomon Lyons, offered a lot 50x120 in what was then called Shieldstown for this purpose, which was accepted, and young Schwab was laid to rest there. Several interments were made in 1862-63, one among them, Isaac Stern, also a soldier in the Southern army.

In August, 1864, the first organization among Knoxville Israelites was formed, called "The Knoxville Hebrew Benevolent Association," the names recorded as joining being Solomon Lyons, D. March, Edward Stern, Moses Stern, Joseph Lyons, Louis David, Joseph David, Isaac Hooman, Sampson Hirsch, Isadore Fishel, J. Solomon A. Gosdorfer, G. Gottlieb, Samuel Guggenheim, Jacob Spiesberger, B. W. Wise, David Marks, M. Heart and F. Heart. To this organization the firm of Mayer, Lyons & Co., who did business here before the war, then conveyed the lot above mentioned. Several years afterwards it was ascertained that the lot in which the interments had been made belonged to Hon. Peter Staub, and that the lot adjoining it on the west side had been conveyed to the Hebrew Benevolent Association. The association then purchased from Mr. Staub the lot in which the interments had been made. Some twenty-five interments had been made, when Congregation Beth-El (the successor of the Knoxville Hebrew Benevolent Association) came to the conclusion that the ground was not suitable for a burial ground, and purchased five acres near the present terminus of the Middlebrook car line. The ground was surveyed and platted by Professor John K. Payne, Civil engineer. When the new cemetery was purchased it was the intention to remove the bodies from the old, but opposition was developed, and families that had relatives buried there have continued to inter their dead in the old cemetery.*

---

*For information concerning the Hebrew Cemetery the author is indebted to Mr. Frank Heart.

INDEX

ABINGDON PRESBYTERY 80, 352, 419
ABRAHAM, Old 31
ACREE
  R. R. 581
  Rev. R. R. 436
ACT OF ASSEMBLY 48
ADAIR
  James 30
  John 41, 47, 48, 49, 57, 59, 72, 77, 81, 91, 92, 345, 386, 424
  John, House of 59
ADAIR'S STATION 41
ADAMS
  David 443, 444
  John 479, 501
ADKINS
  E W 294, 448, 473, 564, 565, 566, 567, 568
  Mary F 565, 566
ADKINSON
  Capt J W 160
  Lt. W. W. 160
AEBLI, C 262, 294
AFRICA, J Simpson 306
AGNEW, W H 565
AGRICULTURAL COLLEGE 361, 362
AGRICULTURAL COLLEGE LIBRARY 107
AGRICULTURAL EXPERIMENT STATIONS 372
AGRICULTURAL HALL 363, 372
AGRICULTURAL IMPLEMENT TRADE 240
AGRICULTURAL IMPLEMENTS 197
AGRICULTURE 11, 16
AIKEN
  H M 125, 257, 560
  Thomas 95
AINSWORTH
  Mrs. Harry H 465
  Mrs. 575
ALABAMA 12, 182, 275
  College of 375
ALABAMA GREAT SOUTHERN RAILWAY 288
ALBERS 296

A J 192, 232, 246, 247, 255, 294, 542, 554, 583, 584
  Alderman 404
  Ella Memorial Fountain 584
  George W 114, 260, 295, 296, 404
ALDERMEN 94, 105, 109, 110
  1889 296
  1897 551
  1898 125
  Board of 95
  Salaries 118
ALEXANDER
  Adam R 494
  Col 164, 179, 180
  Dicks 150
  E 472, 474
  Prof E 371
  Eben 365
  Judge Ebenezer 485
  Ebon 366
  Gen 176
  Margaret McClung 494
  Margaret White 494
  Peggy 506
ALEXANDER ALLISON, Steam Fire Engine 132
ALEXANDRIA, TN 379
ALGER, Secretary of War 185, 189, 191
ALHAMBRA LODGE #66 568
ALLEGHANIES 27, 30, 344
ALLEGHENY, PA 395
ALLEN
  Prof F D 364
  Horatio Engineer First Locomotive 278
  John M 221, 258, 377, 574, 575
  Mrs. John M 575
ALLEN, STEPHENSON, & COMPANY 238
ALLISON
  Alderman 115, 117
  Alexander 158, 551, 554, 563, 569
  David 49, 467

John	139, 372
R D	151
T F P	381
ALPHA, TN	519
AMBROSE, JT	447
AMERICAN GUILD, Richmond, VA	568
AMERICAN HANDLE COMPANY	221
AMERICAN LEGION OF HONOR, Grand Council	564
AMERICAN MEDICAL ASSOCIATION	507, 515, 520
AMERICAN MISSIONARY ASSOCIATION	401
AMERICAN PARTY	321
AMERICAN PUBLIC HEALTH ASSOCIATION	507
AMERICAN SETTLEMENTS	62
AMERICANISM AND ROMANISM CONTRASTED	321
AMHERST COLLEGE	459, 485
AMICUS, Gazette Correspondent	82
AMIS, Thomas	49
ANCIENT ORDER OF UNITED WORKMEN	563, 564
ANDERSON	90
Rev. A E	451
A W	140, 142
Alexander	493
D. D.	476
David D	493
Gen G T	174
Isaac	386
Dr. Isaac	442
Rev. Dr. Isaac	427
J C	295
James	151
James A	257
Rev John M	438
Joseph	345, 467, 472
Judge Joseph	56, 90
Joseph R	254, 284
Joseph, bio	492
Judge	49
Margaret	493
Nannie	543

    Rev. R T 452
    Ref. Dr. 428, 443
    Robert M 472
    Judge Robert M 488
ANDERSON & McNULTY 231
ANDERSON COUNTY, TN . 13, 19, 112, 209, 241, 250, 348, 469, 492, 493, 514
ANDERSON, LITTLEFIELD, & STEERE 239
ANDES
    J W 554
    James A 406
ANDREW, Rev. Elisha D 496
ANDREWS
    A B 286, 287, 289
    George 144, 469
    Judge George 116, 294, 499
    George, bio 496
    J M 243
    Judge 499
ANDREWS & COMPANY, Chicago 259
ANGEL, S P 447, 565
ANGIER E A 180
ANNALS OF TENNESSEE, JGM Ramsey 480
ANNAPOLIS ACADEMY (US Naval Academy) 185
ANNISTON, AL 193
ANSLEY, H C 287, 289
ANTHONY, John 558
APPALACHIAN RANGE 13, 29
APPOMATTOX (Court House, Battle, VA) 512
ARCHITECTS 537, 548
ARCHITECTURE, tallest buildings 249
ARECIBO (Puerto Rico) 189
ARMOUR, William 280
ARMSTRONG, S P 561
ARMSTRONG
    "Trooper" 44
    Charles 574, 575
    Clinton 373
    F W 255, 259
    J A 567, 568

   James 44, 48
   James E 181
   James M 160
   Jenny 346
   M A M 260
   R H 166, 373, 536
   Robert 554
   Robert H 273, 372
   S P 561
   Rev William 439
ARMSTRONG DIVISION 170
ARMSTRONG HOUSE 167, 177, 179
ARMSTRONG RESIDENCE 180
ARMY OF TENNESSEE 169
ARMY POST 59
ARNOLD
   M D 233, 236
   Gen Thomas D 153
ARNOLD, HENEGAR, DOYLE, & COMPANY 236
ARNOLD, HENNEGAR, DOYLE, & COMPANY 248
ARNSTEIN, A 465
ART WORK OF KNOXVILLE 38, 39
ARTESIAN WELL 220
ARTHUR
   A. A. 299
   Alexander A 294
   President 514, 518
ASBURY
   Bishop 441, 442
   Francis 421
   ASHE, G J 571
ASHEVILLE, NC 27, 272
ASHMORE
   Mrs. W M 547
   William M 262
ASSOCIATED BANKING & TRUST COMPANY 260
ASSOCIATED PRESS NEWS SERVICE 334
ASYLUMS, TN, History of 535
ATCHLEY, William D 160

ATHENS
  GA 191
  TN 149, 225, 281, 318, 319, 340, 490, 495
ATHENS, TN, medicine 520
ATKIN 109
  Alderman 117
  C B 201
  C B & Company 201
  C B Furniture 552
  F S 201
  F S &Company 201
  Frank S 201
  George 443
  S T 175, 201, 208, 585
  S T & Company 201
  Samuel T 109, 117, 200, 443
ATKINS, James 444
ATKINSON, Matthew A 49
ATLANTA, GA 19, 180, 283, 367
ATLANTA MEDICAL COLLEGE 512
ATLANTA, KNOXVILLE, & NORTHERN RAILROAD 220, 291, 292, 293
ATTIX, Frank 567
ATWATER, Prof W O 362, 363, 364
AUGUSTA, GA 19, 27, 132
AUGUSTA COUNTY, VA 418
AULT
  Fred Bivouac #17 569
  Fred Camp #5 569
  H T 247, 255
  Henry 106, 228, 246, 540
  Henry T 260
AURIN
  Ferdinand 455
  J A Sr. 455
AUSTIN
  Miss E L 400
  Emily L 401, 407, 408
  Emily, death of 402
  R W 186

AUSTIN SCHOOL 401, 402, 407, 411
AVIS, Rev E C 451
AXLEY, James 442, 443
BACHMAN
   Rev. Nathan 429
   Rev Robert L 429
BAER, Charles N 308
BAILEY
   E P 246, 269
   F K 112
   Dr. F K 514
BAIN
   Rev 439
   Samuel M 384, 386
BAIRD
   A J 566
   Alexander 405
BAKER
   C H 153
   Mrs. J 578
   Rev Lewis 452
   Lewis M G 396, 397
   Mr. 435
   Rev Dr 436
   William 533
   William J 98, 102, 503
   William S 527
BALCH
   Hezekiah 82, 420
   Rev Hezekiah 353, 419, 424, 428
   James 420
BALDRIDGE, Mattie M 392
BALDWIN
   H A 575
   W H 287
   WH Jr. 286, 290
BALER, Mrs. J 578
BALTIMORE, MD 57, 205, 226
BALTIMORE CONSOLIDATED STREET RAILWAY COMPANY 308

BANE, John 572
BANK OF TENNESSEE BUILDING 250, 255
BANKS 88, 250
    Associated Banking & Trust Company 260
    Bank of East Tennessee 88, 252
    Bank of Knoxville 252
    Bank of Tennessee 181, 250, 253, 480
    Central Savings 264
    Citizen's Building & Loan 263, 265
    City National Bank 257, 263, 266
    Covenant Building & Loan Association 262
    Equitable Building & Loan Association 263
    Exchange & Deposit Bank 252
    Farmers & Traders Bank, Safe Deposit, and Trust Co 259
    Farmers Bank 252, 253
    First in Knoxville 250
    First National Bank 253
    Franklin Savings & Loan Company 264
    Holston Banking & Trust Company 257
    Holston National Bank 257, 581
    Home Building & Loan Association 263, 264
    Home Building Association 268
    Knox County Bank & Trust Company 258
    Knoxville Banking Company 256
    Knoxville Building & Loan Association 261
    Market Bank 260
    Mechanics 264
    Mechanics Building & Loan Association 263
    Mechanics National Bank 253, 255
    Ocoee Bank of Cleveland, TN 253
    Perpetual Building & Loan Association 263
    Savings, Building, & Loan Association 262
    Second in Knoxville 251
    Southern Building & Loan Association 262
    Southern Home Building & Loan Association, Atlanta 264
    Star Savings & Loan Company 264
    State National Bank 263
    Third National Bank 258, 263
    Workingmens Building & Loan Association 266, 267, 278

BAPTISTS 417, 423, 425, 462
BARBARA HILL 353
BARBOUR, Llwellyn P 385
BARGER, John P 160
BARKER
   Ed 294
   F 221
   Frank 145, 574
   Prof I B 364
   J H 221
BARKER MANUFACTURING COMPANY 221
BARNES
   A. A. 429, 561, 562
   Edward K 293
   Nathan 442
BARNETT, Rev W R 449
BARNEY, Rev. James 439
BARRACKS 88
BARRINGER, John 444
BARROWS, N D 429
BARRY
   Alderman 294, 296
   Hiram 97, 317
   Mrs. I E 575
BARRY & McDANIEL 106
BARTER, John 252
BARTERING 226
BARTON
   A 119
   Alvin 129, 189
   Rev Isaac 423
   R M Jr. 472
   R W 202
BARTON BLOCK 407
BATE, Gen. William B 585
BATES, W H 444, 446, 538
BATTLE OF CERRO GORDO, MEXICO 151
BATTLE OF FISHING CREEK, KY 329
BATTLE OF MOWERY 151

BATTLE OF TALLADEGA 149
BATTLE OF THE BOYNE 417
BATTLE OF TOHOPEKA 150
BATTLE OF THE WAHOO SWAMP 149
BATTLESHIP MAINE 182
BAUGH, Rev. W. H 432
BAUM, Charles 455
BAUMANN BROTHERS 259, 537, 548, 549, 551
BAUMANN, C M 567
BAXTER
   Lt. George W 366
   John 152, 252, 329
   Col. John 269
   Judge John 331, 584
   John, bio 491
   William 131
   Dr. William J 503
   William M 406
   Mrs. William M 543
BAYLESS
   A G 132
   Bessie 532
   Mrs. H. G. 547
   Dr. Herman G 515
   J C 160
   John C 515
   Rosa Lewis 515
BAYS, Rev. W. W. 445
BAYS MOUNTAIN 9
BEACH, John P 205
BEALS, James F 260
BEALY, Dr. 511
BEAMAN
   George M 106
   John R 106
BEAMANN, Orin C 568
BEAN
   Alonzo 157
   D B 244, 248

Index - 11

J H	338
Joseph H	336
William	30
BEAN'S STATION	508, 533
BEARD	
Frank	581
John	64
Capt John	73
W D	470, 471
Mrs. William D	579
BEARDEN	109
J C	561
M D	106, 125, 138, 160, 196, 562, 586
Hon M D	536
Marcus D	583
R. R.	559
BEAUMONT RIDGE	132
BEAVER, Gen James A	191
BEAVER CREEK	70
BEAVER RIDGE	14, 273
BEAVER VALLEY	14
BECK, J C	234
BECKWITH, I T	362
BEDOUT, Mrs. N	400
BEERS, George E	377
BELFOUR	
Andrew	48
J	48
BELL	137
J A H	217
John	314, 322
Samuel	124, 151
Samuel W	136
BELL HOUSE	403
BELLUE, Mr.	435
BENGE, Bob	69, 70
BENJAMIN, Lt.	168, 176
BENNETT	
David	153

Rufus M 160
BENSCOTER, C A 448
BENTON, Thomas 149
BENZIGER, J N 262
BERGER
   Charles 235
   Rev Martin Luther 545
BERGRATH, Rev Father J 440
BERRY
   James M 160
   James O 159
BESSEMER BRANCH 286
BEST YET SOAP 217
BETHANY COLLEGE, WV 460
BETHEL CEMETERY 175, 584, 585
BETHLEHEM COMMANDERY #6 566
BETTIS, Rev E S 446
BEVERLY, TN 293
BEYLAND, Capt S E 187
BIDDLE
   Frank 451
   Frank W 449
BIEMANS, Rev Father J L 440
BIG CREEK GAP 163
BIG LIMESTONE CREEK 33
BIG PIGEON RIVER 38, 43, 350
BIG SEVEN, stove 213
BIGBEE, Rev 439
BIGELOW, Mrs. 464
BILBRO, W C 385
BINCE, R 160
BINGHAM SCHOOL OF NORTH CAROLINA 378
BIRD, Capt A. 86
BIRDWELL, R 444
BIRMINGHAM, AL 22
BIRTH AND DEATH RECORDS 119
BIXBY, A. S. 574
BLACK
   Alexander 581

J M	534, 548
Dr J M	126
Mrs. J M	547
BLACK DIAMOND COAL COMPANY	240, 242
BLACK DIAMOND RAILWAY	300, 479
BLACK OAK RIDGE	14, 531
BLACK TROOPS	191
BLACK WARRIOR RIVER, AL	12

BLACKBURN
Col Alexander	342
Mrs. Andrew	3
Rev Andrew	341, 342
Gideon	420
Rev Gideon	342
John	72
Robert G	447

BLACKIE, Dr. George S	368
BLACKS, education	426
BLACKSMITH	194
BLACKSMI TH SHOPS	195
BLACKSTONE MEMORIAL LIBRARY, CT	206

BLACKWELL
I E S	527
J E	158

BLAIR
A. A.	157
John N	567

BLANC SPRING	131
BLANG, Joseph A E	160
BLANKS, J H	369
BLAUFIELD, D	465
BLEDSOE COUNTY, TN	13, 19, 250, 469
BLOCKHOUSE, Knoxville	91, 92
BLOCTON, AL	283
BLOOM, Lt. J E	365

BLOUNT
Barbara	92, 346, 353
Mary Grainger	84
Mary Grainger, burial place	582

Mary Louisa 498
Mrs. 51
Gov William 35, 41, 42, 43, 44, 45, 46, 48, 50, 51, 52, 53,54, 56, 61, 63,
. 72, 73, 75, 77, 83, 85, 87, 89, 90, 91, 148, 149, 313, 344, 351, 353, 468, 472,
.... 489, 492, 498, 583
   Gov William, death date 582
   Gov William, home 56
   Willie 345, 468, 476
   Willie, bio 489
BLOUNT COLLEGE 55, 75, 81, 85, 345, 347, 348, 351, 352, 357, 424,
.... 427, 492, 498
   Only graduate 349
   Tuition 348
BLOUNT COUNTY
   Establishment 77
   TN 13, 19, 195, 204, 207, 250, 325, 342, 347, 348, 469, 494
BLOUNT FAMILY 51
BLOUNT MANSION 87
BLOUNTVILLE 481
BLUE RIDGE MOUNTAINS 416
BLUE RIDGE STATION (NC?) 291
BOAL, A G 395
BOARD OF EDUCATION 1871 – 1899 .... 127, 405, 406
BOARD OF HEALTH 98, 103, 112, 119, 126, 527, 529
BOARD OF PUBLIC WORKS 120, 127
BOARD OF TRADE 245
BOLTON, CT 501
BOMAR, Mrs. M A 562
BOND, Frank P 382
BONHAM, Walter M 432
BONNER, J W 183
BOOK CONCERN (PUBLISHERS),
   Methodist Episcopal Church, and South 321
BOONE
   Col Albert E 300
   Col 301
   Daniel 30, 417
BOONE'S CREEK 30
BOOTS & SHOE MANUFACTURERS 197

BORCHES
- J W 548
- Jacob W 229
- Joe E 573

BORCHES & COMPANY 229
BORCHES BUILDING 574
BORDEN, C F 463
BORIGHT, W 262
BOSTON, MA 131, 407
BOSTWICK, Charles E 306
BOSWORTH
- Benjamin D 534
- Nathaniel 195

BOSWORTH'S DAM 99
BOSWORTH'S FACTORY 196
BOTUME, Mrs. 464
BOUGH, Rev W H 432
BOULWARE, Aubin L 287
BOUNDARIES 98
BOUNDARY STATES 12
BOUNDS, Francis H 160
BOUNTY LANDS 35
BOWDOIN COLLEGE 458
BOWEN, Mrs. M A 407
- William 534
- Dr William 186, 187, 573

BOWERS
- Dr. 511
- F B 534
- Mrs. Mary 578

BOWLING, A H 244
BOWMAN
- E W 442
- John 218
- S D 562

BOWYER, Luke 54, 467
BOY, S B 254
BOY'S HOME 393, 394
BOYCE, George 156

BOYD 296
    Alderman 117
    Benjamin S 296
    Cinnie 575
    J L 243
    John 94
    John M 373, 382, 534, 540
    Dr. John M 403, 503, 507, 513, 516, 529
    Dr. John R 508
    Judge 89
    S B 56, 115, 221, 246, 413, 534, 551, 583
    Dr S B 113
    S B Jr. 221, 295
    Samuel B 102, 124, 238, 513, 540, 575
    Samuel B, Jr. 295
    Susan H mason 513
    William 49
BOYD & CASWELL 238
BOYD, ALLEN, & COMPANY 221, 238
BOYD'S CREEK 31
BOYER, Luke (Lew?) 467
BOYLE, John 334
BOYNTON
    Dr. D T 529
    Daniel T 181
    Dr. Daniel T 521
BRABSON, BD, Dentist 524
BRABSON FERRY PIKE 274
BRADFIELD, George W 317
BRADFORD
    J V 363
    William 157
BRADLEY
    F H 362
    T J 214
    W B 292
    WC 450
BRADLEY COUNTY, TN 13, 17
BRAGG, Gen. 169, 174

BRAINE, Mrs. Barney 546
BRANDAU, Henry 199
BRANDON
   Capt 185
   Mel 184
   W C 159, 569
BRANNER
   B M 284
   Benjamin 253
   George M 253
   H B 116, 117, 125, 258, 259, 260, 305
   John R 253
   Joseph 253
   William A 253
BRANNER BUILDING 572
BRANNER PROPERTY 545
BRANNER RESIDENCE 351
BRANSON
   H M 186, 248
   Lloyd 552
BRASS FOUNDRY 195
BRATTLEBORO, VT 524
BRAXTON, Rev T J 452
BRAYMER, F H 534
BRAZEALE, J W M 318
BRAZEALTON
   G W 452
   William 157, 254
BRAZELTON'S BATTALION 157
BRECKENRIDGE, Gen 169
BREESE, James L 245
BRENKER, Rev. Dr. 436
BREWERY 212
BRICE, Calvin S 286
BRICE MILL 454
BRICEVILLE, TN 244
BRICK MANUFACTURING 200
BRICK MILL 199

BRIDGE
- Church Street ... 133
- East Knoxville ... 137
- First Creek ... 133
- 5th Ave. ... 133
- Gay Street ... 113
- Hill Street ... 133
- Main Street ... 99
- Oak Street ... 133
- Pontoon ... 164
- Railroad ... 220
- Temporary ... 302
- Tennessee River ... 302

BRIDGES ... 134, 197, 303
- G W ... 151

BRIDLE PATH ... 271

BRIEN, William G ... 369

Bright
- A D ... 471
- H W ... 534
- John ... 558

BRINEY, Rev J B ... 461

BRISCO
- Daniel ... 186, 254
- Daniel, Brothers & Company ... 233, 238
- H Rogan ... 572
- J Earnest ... 233
- P J ... 233
- Philip J ... 233

BRISCOE BLOCK ... 248

BRISTOL, TN ... 284, 338, 342, 382

BRISTOW, J L ... 136

BROAN, W H ... 187

BROCK, HUDDLESTON, & COMPANY ... 235

BRODEN, C F ... 463

BROMBERG, Perry ... 385

BROOKS
- Alderman ... 118
- Blanche V ... 408

  J M 129
  John M 113, 117, 118, 262, 263
  Capt John M 117
  Maude 396
BROOKSIDE MILLS 190, 211, 212, 215, 217, 299, 499
BROOME, Frederick H 386
BROWN
  Rev A J 456
  C H 569
  Carrie 243
  Charles H 198, 569
  Mrs. E M 463
  George 234, 373, 472
  Judge George 554
  George Leroy 187, 396
  George W 125, 551
  H 388
  Rev Father H V 439, 440
  Hu 314, 315
  Jacob 33, 49
  James B 567
  Col John 149
  John S 234
  Joseph 428
  Mary J 243
  Morgan W 468
  O A 210
  Otis A 544
  Rev Paul F 431
  Prof 371
  R A 331, 473, 564, 565, 566
  Robert H 530
  Dr. S G 121
  Samuel 561
  T G 236
  W G 366, 371
  W H 184, 187
BROWN, PAYNE, DEAVERS, & COMPANY 236
BROWNING, W H 261

BROWNLEE
  J T & COMPANY 236
  Joseph T 571
  Wylie 571
BROWNLEE, CHUMBLEY & COMPANY 236
BROWNLOW
  Gov 469, 496
  James O 138
  James P 159
  Col John B 325
  William G .. 138, 152, 153, 156, 253, 319, 320, 321, 322, 323, 324, 325, 326,
  .... 330, 331, 340, 341, 343, 446, 447, 448, 469, 496, 507, 521, 527, 584
  William G, death of 326
  William G, memorial 448
  William G, on slavery 322
BROWNSVILLE, OREGON 519
BROYLES, Joseph H 571
BRUCE, A C 460
BRYAN
  J W 386, 406
  Joseph 289
BUCHANAN
  Rev A 454
  Maggie 532
  President 277, 318
  Dr T B 368
BUCKEYE COKE COMOPANY 240, 241
BUCKNER
  Gen 163, 169, 179
  Gen S B 162
BUCKWELL
  Dr 522
  E G 234
BUFFAT, E 234
BUILDINGS
  Government 261
  Insurance building on Gay Street 196
  Knoxville Centennial Building 553
  McNulty 236, 248

Sedgwick	225
Skates Furnace buildings	212
Tallest in Knoxville	249
BULKLEY, Charles H	242
BULL, William L	286
BULL RUN CREEK	14
BULL RUN VALLEY	14, 15
BULLARD, Rev. Joseph A	436
BUNCH	
McD J	152
Samuel	150
BURDETT, George M	260
BURGDORFF, Theodore F	374
BURGER	138
Alderman	117
Joseph	259
Mrs. Joseph	579
Mrs.	579
Victor & Son	106
BURGETTSTOWN, PA	395
BURIAL OF SOLDIERS	175
BURKHART, M T	159
BURKS, Mitchell	435
BURLESON, G B	561
Burnett	
David	153
J S	444
Morse	532
Dr Swan M	112
BURNS	
A. M.	140
Mary	186
BURNSIDE	170, 174
Gen 163, 164, 165, 166, 168, 169, 174, 176, 314, 317, 325, 329, 485, 487	
BURRITT COLLEGE, Van Buren County, TN	359
BURROUGH'S BATTERY	158
BURROUGHS	
J. J.	158
W H	158

BURROW, Rev J A 449
BURROWS, A Y 263, 573
BURTON
   Alvin 227
   Prof B S 364
BUSINESS HOURS, Sabbath 110
BUSINESS LICENSES 104
BUTCHERS 58
BUTLER, M C 362, 574
BUTLER ASYLUM, Providence RI 535
BUTT, J R 432
BUTTERFIELD, J G 245
CABINET MAKERS 195
CABLE CAR, Tennessee River 301
CAIN, John S 368
CAIRO, IL 277
CALDWELL
   Alderman 117
   Alfred 4, 302, 560
   Alfred, bio 489
   J W 193, 263, 397, 552, 581
   John 181, 489
   Joshua 3, 39, 180, 382
   Joshua W 393, 394, 477, 554
   S A 140
   Samuel 117
   W C 470, 471
CALDWELL SCHOOL HOUSE 430
CALHOUN
   Elizabeth 583
   John C 300
   Margaret 583
CALLAWAY
   Kate C 411
   Mr. 70
CALLOWAY, Thomas H 241, 253, 284
CALVIN, John 416
CALVINISM 418

CAMP

- E C 242, 247, 259, 304
- Maj. E C 546, 547
- H N 242
- CAMP BOB TAYLOR 189, 190
- CAMP CREEK 33
- CAMP GARBER, KY 159
- CAMP NEW BOSTON 60
- CAMP POLAND 190, 191, 192, 433
- CAMP WILDER 189, 190
- CAMPBELL 90
  - Alexander 460
  - David 49, 54, 56, 90, 94, 250, 345, 467, 468, 472
  - George W 348, 469, 479
  - George Washington 557
  - J B 561
  - James 352, 425, 502
  - James "Scotch Jimmy" 252
  - James W 102, 136
  - Judge 49
  - Dr. M 399
  - Marjorie 502
  - Merchants 227
  - Michael 398, 399, 534, 538
  - Dr Michael 536, 552
  - Mrs. Michael 552
  - Mrs. 65
  - Patrick 93
  - Rev Thomas 548
- CAMPBELL COUNTY, TN 19, 20, 160, 241, 245, 250
- CAMPBELL'S STATION 41, 55, 66, 69, 165, 170, 271, 273
- CAMSON, W. W. 374
- CANNON, Elbert J 159
- CANNON COUNTY, TN 15
- CANTONMENT SPRINGS 92
- CAPERS, Bishop 326
- CAPITAL 91
- CAPITOL AVE 553
- CAPPS, C M 534

CAR WORKS 197
CARDING MACHINE 196
CARDING MACHINES 195
CARDWELL
   Joshua W 382
   P H 565
CAREY, Mrs. M E 541
CAREYVILLE, TN 244
CAREYVILLE GAP 27
CARHART
   H B 259
   H B & Company 230, 231
   Rev L H 448
   W B 230
   W E 230
CARLISLE, Miss 546
CARLOCK, H. H. 444
CARMAN, J F 561
CARMICHAEL
   Alexander 58
   Dr John W 186
CARMICHAEL'S TAVERN 76
CARNES
   W D 540
   William D 360, 388
   Rev William D 359
CARNIVAL, annual 309
CARONDOLET & O'NEAL 312
CARPENTER
   D A 198, 218, 219, 263, 445
   Daniel A 125, 181
   M L & Company 232
   Ross & Company 230, 232
CARPER, Jacob 49
CARR
   B M 561
   Capt 59

CARRICK
  Rev Samuel . 49, 51, 73, 80, 81, 82, 85, 91, 345, 346, 351, 352, 387, 419, 420, ... 424, 427, 428, 480, 583
    Samuel C Z R 351
    Rev Samuel, bio 352
    Rev Samuel, death date 427
CARRINGER, J Sterling 509
CARROLL
  Gen 162
  T C 444
  Rev T C 446
  Gen W H 156
  William 252
  Gov William 487
CARSON
  Rev D W 395
  Prof. W. W. 371
  William W 373, 383
CARSON-NEWMAN COLLEGE 185
CARTER
  E R 188
  J D 157
  J W 157
  Col James 508
  James E 157
  Col James E 585
  John 49, 466
  Lewis C 371
  Gen S P 169
  S V 254
  T W 432
  Rev T W 432
  W R 144, 569
  William 346
CARTER COUNTY, TN 13, 16, 21, 22, 33, 198, 250, 348, 509
CARTHAGE 469
CARTWRIGHT, Haley P 369, 385
CARTY
  J B 561

John B 260
  T L 125
  Thomas L 260
  W B 406
  W J 260
CARUTHERS, Robert L 469
CASH, Rev James I 338
CASUALTIES
  Burial of Soldiers 175
  Civil War 170, 176
CASWELL
  William 221, 304
  William & Company 220
  William R 151
CATAWBA INDIANS 32
CATE
  A. M. 161
  R H 572
  Robert H 571
  W A 406
CATES
  B. B. 398, 534
  Benjamin B 399
  W A 406
CATHOLIC CEMETERY 588
CATHOLIC SCHOOL 404
CATHOLICISM 417, 418
CATRON, Judge 495
CAULKINS
  Douglas 520
  Douglass 406
CAUSLER, W J 408
CAVET'S STATION 65, 66, 69, 70
CAWOOD
  Dr Charles M 515
  Daniel 304
  Dr 398, 516
  J C 258, 534
  Dr J C 515

CAZIER, Dr John Thomas 524
CECIL COUNTY, MD 524
CELEBRATIONS 84
CENSUS 77
    1795 90
CENTENNIAL EXPOSITION 551
CENTER COLLEGE, KY 515
CENTRAL COMMANDER #5 566
CENTRAL MARKET STATION 132
CENTRAL RAILROAD 280
CENTRAL SAVINGS BANK 264
CENTRAL STATION 132
CEREBROSPINAL, Meningitis 532
CESSION
    Act of 1806 356
    North Carolina 87
CHADWICK, Capt 183
CHAMBER OF COMMERCE 247, 276
CHAMBERLAIN
    H S 200, 208, 210, 232, 246
    J E M Jr. 306
    W P 210, 232, 242, 247
CHAMBERLAIN & ALBERS 232
CHAMBERLAIN BROTHERS & VANGILDER 232
CHAMBERLAIN, RICHARDS, & COMPANY 208
CHAMBLISS, Charles E 384, 386
CHAMPION, Charles 431
CHAMPION MANUFACTURING COMPANY 211
CHANCERY COURT 298, 472, 473
CHANDLER
    Rev George T 431
    Joseph 245
    W P 551, 573
CHANNING, Miss 464
CHAPMAN
    E R 242
    J E 192, 571
    John E 232, 257, 552
    Thomas 54

CHAPMAN, WHITE, LYONS & COMPANY 232
CHARLESTON, SC 27, 280, 281
CHARLOTTE, COLUMBIA & AUGUSTA RAILROAD 287, 289
CHARLTON
    C W 325, 444
    Charles W 136
    Rev Charles W 336
CHATTANOOGA
    Battle of 171
    TN .. 34, 116, 164, 169, 187, 225, 275, 276, 284, 333, 379, 382, 440, 454, 474
CHATTANOOGA UNION RAILWAY COMPANY 286
CHAVENNE, A 258
CHENEY, Mrs. Ednah Dow 464
CHEROKEE CHIEFS 90
CHEROKEE COUNCIL #601 567
CHEROKEE COUNTRY 272, 495
CHEROKEE LAND 52
CHEROKEE LOWER TOWNS 34, 61, 76
CHEROKEE NATION 29, 44
CHEROKEE NATION OF INDIANS 29
CHEROKEE UPPER TOWNS 63
CHEROKEES 33, 38, 42, 61, 62, 64, 66, 75, 87, 88, 150, 347, 349
    Christian Expedition 34
    Dispossession of Land 32
CHESTER COUNTY, PA 418
CHESTNUT RIDGE 13, 272
CHICKAMAUGA 185, 190
    Battle of 157, 169, 185
CHICKAMAUGA INDIANS 34
CHICKAMAUGA PARK 187, 189
CHICKASAWS 62, 63, 85, 88
CHILDRENS MISSION HOME 549
CHILDRESS 138
    Dr G C 573
    Henry M 538
    M J 139
CHILHOWEE COUNCIL, Royal Arcanum 564
CHILHOWEE LODGE #247 561

CHILHOWEE PARK 123
   Spanish-American War Reception 188
CHILSHOLM
   Ignatius 49
   J 49
CHISHOLM, John 49, 50, 58
CHISHOLM'S TAVERN 56, 89
CHOCTAWS 62
CHOICE, Flour 213
CHOLERA 526
   Asiatic 527
   Causes of 530
   Day of Observance 528, 529
   Deaths from 527
   Prescription 529
   Recommendations against 529
CHOLERA SEASON, Knoxville 514
CHOLERA, 1854 359
CHRISTIAN, Expedition 34
CHUMBLEY, J F 236, 475
CHUQUILATAGUE 90
CHURCH, H A 118
CHURCH STREET BRIDGE 133, 134
CHURCHES
   Asylum Street Methodist Episcopal Church 451
   Atkin Street Presbyterian Church 458
   Bell Avenue Presbyterian Church 433
   Bethany Methodist Episcopal Church of Baltimore, MD 448
   Broad Street Methodist Episcopal Church South 445
   Calvary Baptist Church 437
   Castle Church 455
   Centenary Methodist Episcopal Church 449
   Centennial Baptist Church 438
   Central Baptist Church ("colored") 440
   Central Presbyterian Church 430
   Church of the Epiphany Protestant Episcopal 453
   Church Street Methodist Episcopal Church South 443
   Church Street Methodist Church 447
   Clinch Street Methodist Episcopal Church 450

Clinton A M E Chapel 439
Clinton Street Methodist Episcopal Church ("colored") 452
Cumberland Presbyterian Church 420, 431, 432
East Main Street Methodist Episcopal Church 450
English Lutheran Church 456
Episcopal Church 450
First Baptist Church 346, 435, 438, 447, 528
First church building in Tennessee 419
First Church of Salem, MA 458
First Church of Christ 460
First Church of Christian Scientists 465
First "colored" Baptist Church 439
First "colored" Presbyterian Church 434
First Congregational Church 457
First German Evangelical Lutheran Church 454
First in Tennessee 344
First Methodist Episcopal Church 447, 450
First Methodist Episcopal Church ("colored") 452
First Presbyterian Church 39, 80, 81, 351
First Presbyterian Church, site of 423
First Presbyterian Church, building 424
First Presbyterian Church, controversy 425
First Presbyterian Church ... 427, 428, 430, 431, 434, 435, 439, 444, 502, 528
First Presbyterian Church, cemetery 582
First Universalist Church 463
First Welsh Congregational Church 456
Fort Sanders Presbyterian Church 432
Fourth Presbyterian Church 431, 433
German Lutheran Church 454, 455, 549
Guilfield Baptist Church 439
Highland Avenue Methodist Episcopal Church, South 446
Immaculate Conception Church 440
Lebanon Church 424, 428
Lebanon-in-the-Fork 81
Lebanon-in-the-Fork Presbyterian Church 424
Little Flat Creek Baptist Church 423
Little Zion Church 452
Logan Chapel Methodist Episcopal Church ("colored") 451
Logan Temple 402

Luttrell Street Methodist Episcopal Church 450
Mabry Street Methodist Episcopal Church 449
McFerrin Memorial Baptist Church, KY 436
Methodist Episcopal Church 166
Methodist Episcopal Church, attack on 321
Methodist Episcopal Church South, Book Concern 321
Methodist Episcopal Church South 337, 338
Methodist Episcopal Church 339, 390
Methodist Episcopal Zion Church 439
Methodist Episcopal Church 447, 449
Methodist Episcopal Church South 456
Methodist Episcopal Church 462
Methodist Episcopal Church South 462
Methodist Episcopal Church 463, 528
Mount Bethel Church 434
Mount Carmel Baptist Church 439
Mount Zion Baptist Church ("colored") 439
Park Street Christian Church 461
Pilgrim Congregational Church 185
Pilgrim Congregational Church History 458
Protestant Episcopal Church 316, 528
Ramsey Memorial Church 461, 462
Red Cross Church 451
Roman Catholic 321
Saint Johns Church 316
Saint Johns English Lutheran Church 456
Saint Johns Protestant Episcopal Church 453, 513, 543, 544
Saint Paul's Independent Methodist Episcopal Church 452
Salem Congregation 344
Second Baptist Church 437
Second Baptist Church ("colored") 439, 440
Second Congregational Church ("colored") 460
Second Presbyterian Church 99, 166, 359, 428, 434, 456,507, 515, 528, 542
Second Presbyterian Church, formed 426
Second Presbyterian Church, established 427
Shiloh Presbyterian Church 434
South Knoxville Presbyterian Church 433
The Old Methodist Church 443, 455
Third Baptist Church 437

Third Christian Church 461
Third largest black 452
Third Presbyterian Church 430, 433, 462
Undenominational 462
Unitarian Church of Knoxville 464
United Presbyterian Church 392, 393, 395
Washington Congregation 428
Washington Presbyterian Church 427
Westminster Church, Jefferson County 342
CHURCHWELL
  George W 559
  William 457
  William M 103, 252, 321, 561, 562
CHURCHWELL & HARRIS 200
CHURCHWELL HOUSE 539
CINCINNATI
  OH 27, 253, 277, 280
  Order of the 493
CINCINNATI SOUTHERN RAILROAD 19, 27, 283, 284
CIRCUIT COURT 469, 472, 473, 474
  Established 468
CISTERNS 105
CITICO 31
CITIZEN'S BUILDING & LOAN 263
CITIZEN'S COMPANY 306
CITIZEN'S RAILWAY COMPANY 304, 307
CITIZEN'S STREET RAILWAY COMPANY 308
CITIZENS BUILDING & LOAN 265
CITIZENS RAILROAD COMPANY 304
CITY, Error in Plots 93
CITY ATTORNEY 125
CITY CHARTER 126
CITY COMMISSIONER, Payment of 93
CITY COMMISSIONERS, First 92
CITY COUNCIL, Building for the 106
CITY ELECTRICIAN 132
CITY ENGINEER 125
CITY HALL 120
CITY NATIONAL BANK 257, 263, 266

CITY PHYSICIAN 113, 126
CITY RECORDER, Building for the 106
CIVIL DISTRICTS 140, 144
CIVIL WAR 136, 148, 152, 178, 1190, 196, 279
    Casualties 170, 176
    Confederate Authorities in Knoxville 207, 311, 317, 328, 329,
    . . . . 330, 361, 389, 392, 462, 482, 491, 501, 589
    Fort Sanders Casualties 174
    Maryland Campaign 178
    Mississippi Troops 168, 174
    Secession, Middle Tennessee 154
    Siege of Knoxville 167
    Use of churches 426
    Veterans Reunion 180
CLAIBORNE
    Thomas 557, 558
    W. C. C. 468
CLAIBORNE COUNTY, TN 13, 19, 160, 250, 295, 348
CLAPP
    James 160
    Russell A 245
    W L 554
CLARK
    C D 538
    Charles D 468
    Florence 565
    H 565
    H W 199, 565
    Harvey 198, 246, 566
    Rev 440
CLARK FOUNDRY & MACHINE COMPANY 199
CLARK FOUNDRY COMPANY 198
CLARK, QUAIFE, & COMPANY 198
CLARKE, George Rogers 417
CLARKSVILLE, TN 251, 379, 469, 489
CLAY
    C. C. 346
    Henry 314
    Henry, tribute to 102

CLEAGE, Samuel E 125
CLEAR, John C 396
CLEARINGHOUSE ASSOCIATION OF KNOXVILLE 260
CLEMENTS, Dr. J S 525
CLEVELAND
   Pres. Grover 334, 367, 514
   TN 225, 284, 373, 379, 515
CLEVELAND OHIO HOMEOPATHIC COLLEGE 521
CLEVELAND PLACE 549
CLIFF, Daniel 385
CLIMATE 16, 23
CLIMATE AND DISEASE 23
CLINCH MOUNTAIN 41
CLINCH RIVER 14, 55, 486
CLINTON, TN 15, 225, 232, 283, 379, 486
CLOTHWORTHY, John B 575
CLOUD, J A & Company 129
CLOUD'S CREEK 33, 34
COACH MAKERS 195
COAL 18, 19, 20, 21, 22
COAL BUSINESS 240
COAL CREEK 208, 209, 245, 513, 514
   TN 243
COAL CREEK COAL COMPANY 241, 242
COAL CREEK MINING & MANUFACTURING COMPANY 241, 242, 243
COAL MINING 209, 210, 211
COAL MINING COMPANY, first 241
COBB
   Joshua S 408
   P L 378
   William 42, 51
COBLEIGH, Rev Dr 448
COCHRANE, W R 399, 534
COCKE
   Gen 148
   James R 106
   John 348
   Gen John 149, 538
   John Jr. 181

   Miriam 411
   Thomas 346
   Walter M 134
   William 75, 345
   Col William 345
COCKE COUNTY, TN 13, 19, 250, 348, 469, 508
COCOA CASTILE, Soap 217
COEUR DE LEON COMMANDERY, No 9 560
COFFEY, Ashbury M 281
COFFIN
   Alderman 100
   C H 227
   C W 269
   Dr Charles 483
   Rev Charles 353
   D L 227
   David L 100
   Hector 129
COFFIN FACTORY 200
COFFIN, MARTIN & COMPANY 230
COFFIN, WILSON & MARTIN 106
COFFMAN
   D M 187
   Lt Col D M 193
   William 113
COHUTTA, GA 283
COILE
   Rev. A J 434
   H P 131, 399, 410, 534
   Dr H P 126, 409, 517
   John Leonard 517
   Mary E Bettis 517
   Rev S A 433
COLD SPRING ADDITION 124
COLEMAN
   Banner 244
   James H 160
   Dr. L. L. 514
COLEMAN HOUSE 103

COLES STATION, AL 554
COLFAX REBEKAH LODGE #43 562
COLHOUN, Margaret Elizabeth 583
COLLEGE, first non-sectarian 346
COLLEGE HILL, Civil war 163
COLLETT, W H 144, 223, 262, 263, 548
COLLIER, Charles A 293
COLLINS, R S 377
"COLORED" HIGH SCHOOL 408
"COLORED" TROOPS 191
COLUMBIA, TN 251, 279, 474
COLUMBIA & GREENEVILLE RAILROAD 287, 289
COLUMBIA LODGE #3 561
COLUMBIAN DENTAL CONGRESS 524
COLUMBUS IRON WORKS 204
COMFORT, James 373, 382, 495, 406
COMMONS 48
COMPTROLLER OF THE CURRENCY 254
CONCORD, TN 512
CONCORD, TN, site of Indian Town 272
CONDON
    M. J. 247, 406
    Martin J 125, 554
    Mayor 295
    Michael J 230
    Stephen P 230
CONDON BROTHERS 230
CONE, SHIELDS, & COMPANY 230
CONFEDERATE CEMETERY 175, 584, 588
CONFEDERATE GOVERNMENT 200
CONFEDERATE STATES 153, 154, 161
CONFEDERATE TROOPS, forming of 156
CONFEDERATE VETERANS 569
CONGDON, Samuel 241
CONGER, B F 561
CONGREGATIONAL BOARD OF HOME MISSIONS ... 459
CONGRESS, U. S. 35, 37, 62, 73, 74, 75
CONGRESSIONAL LIBRARY BUILDING 206
CONGRESSIONAL RESERVATION 356

CONNER, John W 475
CONNOR
    James 39
    Capt of "Atlas" 276
    W. A. A. 302
CONQUERED BANNER by Father Ryan 441
CONSOLIDATION 139, 142
CONSTABLE, First 94
CONSTANTINOPLE
    Minister to 277
    US Minister to 318
CONSTITUTION, Tennessee 77
CONSTITUTION 91
CONSTITUTIONAL CONVENTION 77, 91
CONTINENTAL ARMY 492
CONTINENTAL LINE 35
CONTINENTAL MONEY 226
CONTOURIER, Pauline 530
CONVICT LABOR 209, 273
COOK
    E M 574
    Judge J B 116
    Dr. S B 524, 525
COOK & MELENDY, DENTISTS 525
COOKE
    Rev George 359
    J B 471
    Rev R J 338, 448
    S E 119
    W. W. 469
COOLEY
    C M 259
    J L 122, 431
    James L 257
    M O 460
COOLEY BROTHERS CONTRACTORS 222
COON
    C S 377
    J S 374

COOPER
- Al 225
- H T 587
- Henry T 334
- Joseph A 161, 273
- W R 192, 411, 412, 437, 565, 566
- William F 469, 470

COOSA RIVER, AL 12
COPLIN, D 465
COPPELL, George 286
COPPER RIDGE 14
CORAM, Mr. 435
CORNELL UNIVERSITY 374, 375
CORNETT VS WINTON'S LESSEE 31
CORNICK
- Simpson 199
- Tully R 260
- Tully R., Jr. 263

CORPORATE LIMITS 104
CORPORATION BOUNDARIES 98
CORRYTON, TN 293
CORSO 124
COSSAN, John 420
COSTER, Charles H 287, 289
COTTON CROPS 195
COTTON GIN 195
COTTON MILLS 300
COTTON SPINNIN 195
COTTRELL
- Dr A J 525
- Adam T 160

COULTER, J M 373
COUNCIL, Capt Jordan T 151
COUNCIL OF WAR 169
COUNTY COMMISSIONERS 51
COUNTY COURT 195
COURT CLERKS 473
COURT OF PLEAS & QUARTER SESSSIONS 54, 56

COURTHOUSE 88, 98, 305
   Building of 55
   Description 76
COURTS
   Established 75
   First Session 54
   History of 3, 4
COVENANT BUILDING & LOAN ASSOCIATION 262
COVENANT MUTUAL OF ST LOUIS 519
COVENANTERS 417
COVENANTERS, CAVALIERS, AND PURITANS 500
COWAN
   A G 150
   Rev A L 452
   George & Company 237
   J D 246
   J H 539
   James 574
   James D 129, 216, 246, 305, 373, 554
   James H 124, 227, 237, 258, 377, 388, 389, 392, 409, 410, 429, 527,
   . . . . 540, 574, 575
   Nathaniel 49, 56, 57, 59, 60, 68, 83, 89, 227, 386
   Samuel 50, 56, 57, 59, 60, 83, 92, 227
   Rev T A 432
COWAN & DICKINSON 227, 252, 413
COWAN, McCLUNG & COMPANY 106, 227, 228, 233
COX
   T B 260
   William 49
COYATEE 61
COYTOY 31, 34
COZBY
   James 48, 49, 64
   Dr James 83, 424
CRAB ORCHARD 61
CRAIG
   David 54
   David, Mill 55
   J. J. & Company 205

James 425
John 444
John J 152, 205, 258, 554
John J Company 205
John J Jr. 205
Mr. 138
S A 363, 406
William 138
CRAIGHEAD 422
  Hu. L 382
  I P N 98
  James 583
  John 213, 425
  Robert 93, 314, 352, 373
  Thomas 428
CRAIGHEAD'S [CORNER] 89
CRAWFORD
  Presidential Candidate 479
  Col 365
  Edward 420
  J Y 444
  John 77, 91
  Josiah 442
  Mrs. M E 567
  S B 305, 365, 366
  Col S B 364, 371, 554
  Prof S B 370
CRAWFORD'S BRANCH 144
CREEGAN, C. C. 459
CREEK INDIANS 150
CREEK WAR 479, 489
CREEKS 13, 14, 61, 62, 64, 66, 74, 88
  See individual names
CRENSHAW, W B 122
CRESCENT MARBLE COMPANY 299
CRESSWELL, Andrew 65
CRIMINAL COURT 472, 475
CRIPPENS, Rev John G L 439

CRITTENDEN
  Charles N 546
  Florence 546
  Gen G B 156
CRITTENDEN HOME 546
CROCKETT
  David 91, 417
  Joseph H 151
CROMWELL, Oliver 417
  Crops 11
CROSS
  Rev A B 439
  Charles W 161
CROSS MOUNTAIN COAL 211
CROWELL, Robert 532
CROZIER 57
  A R 561
  Arthur 348
  C W 304
  Capt 89
  E W 193, 228
  John 89, 93, 94, 136, 250, 348, 386, 387, 390, 424
  Col John 228
  John H 228, 360, 427, 495, 540, 583
  Col John H 102
  Lucy 581
CRUDGINGTON, J W 147
CRUTCHFIELD, Thomas 358
CRUZE
  C. C. 234
  J H 234, 405
  James H 406
CRUZE & BUFFAT 234
CRUZE, BUFFAT & BUCKWELL 234
CRYSTAL ICE COMPANY 203
CUBA 188
CUBA INDEPENDENCE 184
CULLEN, John M 94
  Cullen & Newman 235, 248

CULP, John M 94
CUMBERLAND COLLEGE 355, 356, 357
CUMBERLAND COMPACT 74
CUMBERLAND COUNTY, TN 15, 19, 59
CUMBERLAND GAP 156, 174, 280, 281, 293, 295, 296
CUMBERLAND GAP CONSTRUCTION COMPANY 298
CUMBERLAND GAP TRAIL 294
CUMBERLAND GUARDS 41
CUMBERLAND MOUNTAIN COAL & LAND COMPANY 241
CUMBERLAND MOUNTAINS 12, 17, 18, 19, 23, 27, 90, 169, 195, 249, 276
CUMBERLAND RIVER 61, 416
CUMBERLAND SETTLEMENTS 41, 52, 62, 441
CUMBERLAND TABLELAND 15, 20
CUMMING, James 447
CUMMINGS
   D H 157
   Harry 444
   James 444, 447
   Robert J 374, 375
   W F 565
CUMMINS
   Charles 420
   Rev Charles 419
   Mrs. M S 407
CUNNINGHAM
   Alexander 55
   Rev John W 428
   Paul 47, 48, 49, 92
   W G E 444, 560
CURREY, Dr. Richard O 327
CURRIER, John M 568, 570
CURTIS
   H W 305
   J R 147
   Dr Josiah 269
CUSACK, W H 536
CUSTOM HOUSE 107, 112, 246

Index - 43

D'ARMOND
  CC 570
  Dr. C. C. 438, 534
DABNEY
  Charles W 382, 383, 384, 386
  Dr Charles W 193
  Charles W Jr. 367, 368, 373, 375
  Dr Charles W Jr. 373
  President 372
DAILY, A H 434
DALLAS, Mrs. Kate 565
DALTON, GA 284
DAM, foot of Gay Street 256
DAMS 196
DANA, Charles A 164
DANDRIDGE, TN 225
DANIEL BRISCOE BROTHERS & COMPANY 233
DANIEL, BRISCOE & COMPANY 238
DANNER, W C 158
DANVILLE, KY 463
DARDIS, James 94, 250
DARNALL, H J 377, 383
DARTMOUTH COLLEGE 358, 390, 458
DAUGHTERS OF CONFEDERATE VETERANS 569
DAUGHTERS OF THE AMERICAN REVOLUTION ... 192
DAUGHTERS OF THE CONFEDERACY 192
DAVID
  Joseph 589
  L 465
DAVIDSON, William 48
DAVIDSON COLLEGE 367
DAVIDSON COUNTY, TN 467, 484
DAVIE, William R 82
DAVIES
  D J 239
  E J 243, 244, 245
  Rev J Francis 457
  Col John M 539
  Rev Mr. 458

DAVIES FURNITURE COMPANY 239
DAVIS
   Capt Alex M 190
   Rev B O 445
   Rev. D. D. 457
   E J 243, 244
   E M 378
   Evan J 241
   Hywell 243, 244
   J L 236
   J L & COMPANY 236
   Rev J M 434
   James 250
   John 389, 389, 451
   John M 389, 539
   L W 260, 534
   Dr L W 572
   Louis 589
   May L 542
   Mrs. 389
   Thomas 457
   Thomas A 188
DAVIS, CHUMBLEY, & COMPANY 236
DAWES, Charles 260, 262, 263
DAWN, W H 562
DAWSON, Rev W R 433
DAY
   A B 212
   Anderson 530
   J N 184
   S H 566
DAYTON, TN 225
DEADERICK
   C 373, 534
   Chalmers 382
   Dr Chalmers 516
   Chalmers, see also EC
   David 348, 493, 516
   David A 97, 181, 426, 475

Dr E C	147
E C, see also Chalmers	
E Chalmers	529
Elizabeth J Crozier	516
George W	400
J C	213
James W	470
Chief Justice James W	493
James W, bio	483
Margaret Anderson	493
Principal	363
T O	366
Thomas O	371
William V	362, 471
DEADERICK BUILDING	205, 525
DEADERICK, George W	400
DEADRICK, Dr. C	529
DEAN, J R	391
DEARING, Edward L	570
DEARMOND	
C. C.	534
Dr. C. C.	438
DEATON, Spencer	160
DEAVERS, J L	236
DEBATE, secession	322
DEBOSE, Rev H	452
DEBT	135
DECATUR	
AL	277
TN	227
DECHERD, Gen	174
DEERY, James A	562
DEFREESE, Mrs.	530
DEGRAW, P V	334
DEGROAT, William	565
DELAWARE INDIANS	29
DELAWARE RIVER	416
DELPEUCH, W	534
DEMOCRATIC PARTY	317, 321

DEMPSTER
  James 211
  John 122, 214
DEMPSTERS MACHINE SHOP 211
DENBY, Col Charles 191
DENISON, Joseph 150
DENNEY, George W 335
DENT, J G & COMPANY 282
DENTIST, first in Knoxville 521
DEPOT, union 300
DEPUE
  C W 447
  E H 258
DERRICK, W. W. 396
DEUTSCH, Maruitz 465
DEW, J R 437
DEWEY, Gen Joel A 586
DEWITT, John 385
DEWITT'S CORNERS 34
DICK
  Peter 395
  William 571
DICK, McMILLAN & COMPANY 229
DICKINSON, Perez 227, 246, 253, 273, 284, 318, 367, 388, 435, 541, 554, 583, 584
DICKSON
  Alderman 117
  S L 400, 401, 408
DINWIDDIE, Prof James 371
DISEASE
  Electric treatment of 520
  Outbreak 525, 526, 527
DISMUKES, William C 382
DISTRICT OF WASHINGTON 466
DIVEN, Rev George S 456
DIVINE, Paul E 188
DIVISION HOSPITAL 192
DIX, Miss D L 535
DIXIE WAGON 202

DIXON, James 442, 443
DOAK
  H M 157
  Jane Mitchell 418
  Rev Samuel 344, 348, 418, 419, 420
  Doan, John 443
DOBSON, F A 562
  Doherty
    Col 63
    George 348
    Gen George 149
DONAHUE, Ben N 229
DONALDSON, William 72
DONELSON, Stockley 75
DONOHUE, Ellen 530
DOOLEY, I E 236
DORTCH, N 150
DOUBLEHEAD 66, 70
DOUGHTY
  Capt 168
  John B 444
  Josiah B 443
DOUGLAS, A J 262
DOUGLASS, Rev J E 390
DOW
  E Dean 264, 362, 363
  Samuel B 230, 231, 560
DOWELL, William T 447
DOYLE, James S 236
DOZIER, Alderman 138
DRAGGING CANOE 31
DRAGOONS 151
DRAKE
  Amanda Evans 516
  C M 534
  Dr. Charles M 516
  George W 331
  S M 538
  Dr. W. W. 516

DUCHESS COMPANY, New York 520
DUCLOUX, Charles 243
DUDDLESTON, T L B 161
DUELING 559
   Law against 480
DUFFIELD, George 348
DULANEY, J E 157
DUMPLIN CREEK 34, 38
DUNCAN
   Rev C W 572
   Rev J A 581
   Rev James 433
   Rev James A 444
   John G 239
   Joseph C 225
   S & I Company 57
   Rev Thomas 453
DUNLAP
   Hugh 47, 56, 57, 59, 227
   R G 149
   Richard G 4
   Richard G, bio 490
   William C 472
DUNN
   G W 561
   Ross 369
   W. W. 160, 569
DUPONT
   B 244
   C 244
DURHAM
   Benjamin F 223
   Rev J M 451
   John A 223
   William J 223
DUROCHER, Albert A 571
DYER
   C M 184
   Calvin M 159

Rev W M	446
DYERSBURG, TN	379
DYESTONE REGION	19
EADS, Rev J R	448

EAGER
Rev George B	435
George R	292

EARNEST
Felix W	136
Joseph H	254, 284

EAST COLLEGE	377
EAST KNOXVILLE	218
Annexation	38
Cumberland	439
Debts	107
Incorporated	137
Wards	137
EAST TENNESSEE & GEORGIA RAILROAD	99, 109, 277, 282, 284
EAST TENNESSEE & VIRGINIA RAILROAD	99, 100, 107, 284
EAST TENNESSEE & VIRGINIA RAILROAD COMPANY	282
EAST TENNESSEE COAL COMPANY	241, 244
EAST TENNESSEE COLLEGE	65, 96, 347, 348, 349, 351, 352, 353, 355, 356, 357, 361, 387, 388, 390, 427, 487, 494
Becomes East Tennessee University	358
Funding	349
Monetary debt	354
Unified w/ Hampden-Sidney Academy	388
EAST TENNESSEE COLLEGE LOTTERY	352
EAST TENNESSEE CONVENTION	154
Resolutions of	155
EAST TENNESSEE DENTAL ASSOCIATION	525
EAST TENNESSEE FEMALE INSTITUTE	315, 390, 404, 407
EAST TENNESSEE HOSPITAL FOR THE INSANE	535, 536, 552
EAST TENNESSEE IN THE CIVIL WAR	500
EAST TENNESSEE INSANE ASYLUM	536
Statistics	537
EAST TENNESSEE INSURANCE COMPANY	269
EAST TENNESSEE IRON & COAL COMOPANY	241
EAST TENNESSEE LODGE #34	561

EAST TENNESSEE MEDICAL SOCIETY 327, 507, 515, 518, 519, 520, 533
EAST TENNESSEE MUTUAL BENEFIT ASSOCIATION 562
EAST TENNESSEE NATIONAL BANK 254, 255
EAST TENNESSEE NATIONAL BANK BUILDING 255
EAST TENNESSEE STONE & MARBLE COMPANY 206, 552
EAST TENNESSEE TELEPHONE COMPANY 224, 225
EAST TENNESSEE UNIVERSITY 24, 95, 315,
    Name change 367, 389, 403, 426, 483, 485, 487, 498, 513, 514
    Naming of 358, 359
    Medical Department 359
    Agricultural Department 359
EAST TENNESSEE UNIVERSITY BUILDINGS, Civil War 360
EAST TENNESSEE VALLEY, size 12, 14
EAST TENNESSEE, VIRGINIA & GEORGIA RAILROAD 14, 27, 113, 123,
.... 124, 140, 144, 196, 199, 206, 216, 290
    Mileage 284
EAST TENNESSEE, VIRGINIA & GEORGIA RAILROAD COMPANY
    282, 284, 286, 289
EAST TENNESSEE, VIRGINIA & GEORGIA RAILWAY 283, 299, 300
EAST TENNESSEE, VIRGINIA & GEORGE RAILWAY COMPANY .. 286, 287
EASTER, Rev Henry 454
EASTERDAY, Jacob 530
EASTERN HOSPITAL FOR THE INSANE 552
EASTMAN, E G 47, 328
EASTON
    Prof M W 371
    Morton William 364, 366
EATON
    Elvina 530
    R P 372
    Spence 530
    Rev. T. T. 438
EBENEZER ACADEMY 490, 506
EDDY, Mary 465
EDGE, Benjamin 442
EDGEWOOD SCHOOL HOUSE 431
EDGEWOOD COMPANY 306

EDINGTON
  J M 205
  Thomas D 160
EDUCATION 79
  Blacks 379, 394, 408, 410,
  Curriculum 349
  Description of 80
  Equal 405
  Industrial Department for "colored" Students 380
  Night school established, 1889 377
  Secular 405
EDWARDS
  A C 396
  Harry Stillwell 581
EGERTON, Rev M W 436
EICKS, C H 242
EKIN, George 442
ELDORADO OF THE WEST 416
ELECTRIC LIGHT 128
ELECTRICITY, RAILWAYS 306
ELIZABETHTON, TN 186, 193, 319, 509, 587
ELK FORK VALLEY 20
ELKTON, TN 511
ELLINGTON
  W R 377
  William R 374
ELLIOTT, Gen 174
ELLIS
  Dr. G Manning 187
  Rev Gilbert J 461
  J H 160
ELMORE
  E A 548
  Rev E A 431, 433, 548
ELMWOOD PARK 189, 305
ELMWOOD STREET RAILWAY COMPANY 305
ELNATHAN HALL 393
ELWELL, Rev 388
ELY, Mr. S W 18

EMANCIPATION ... 87
EMBREEVILLE, TN ... 283, 286
EMBREEVILLE BRANCH ... 286
EMBRY, Rev T ... 439
EMMERSON
    Thomas ... 4, 94, 124, 348, 387, 468
    Thomas, bio ... 493
EMORY
    A. M. ... 564, 565, 566
    Isaac ... 565, 566
    Rev Isaac ... 402
    M H ... 564
EMORY GAP ... 27, 208, 283
EMORY RIVER ... 27
ENGINEER POE ... 165
ENGLISH, settlers ... 417
ENOLCHI ... 90
ENTERPRISE FOUNDRY COMPANY ... 212
ENTERPRISE MACHINE WORKS ... 212
ENTERTAINMENT ... 84, 85
EPISCOPALIANS ... 417, 418
    First in area ... 454
EPPS, William ... 263, 406
EPWORTH LEAGUE ... 450
EQUITABLE BUILDING & LOAN ASSOCIATION ... 263
ERWIN, R G ... 286
ESPERANDIEU, Rev F ... 269, 364
ESSENIC ARMY FIRST REGIMENT, Company A ... 573
ESTABROOK
    Joseph ... 390, 538
    Rev Joseph ... 358
ESTERS, Mr. ... 463
ETOWAH, Battle of ... 480
EUREKA COMMANDERY #10 ... 566
EVANS
    C R ... 206
    Charles ... 431
    H E ... 269
    S P ... 244, 255, 475

W H 206
  W H & Son 205
EVANS MARBLE COMPANY 552
EVE
  Dr. Duncan 368
  Paul F 384
  Dr. Paul F 386
EVERETT
  W C 232
  William C 575
EWEN, W A C 286, 287
EWING
  L M 571
  Rev R B 392
  Z W 367, 382
EWING AND JEFFERSON COLLEGE 511
EXHIBITION, 1871 261
EXPORT LAGER 220
FAGAN, W J 566
FAHNESTOCK
  H S 289
  Harris C 287
FAHNESTOCK HILL 114, 115
FAIR, J B 2121
FAIRGROUNDS 157
  Old 156
FAIR, DAY & DEKLYNE FOUNDRY & PATTERN SHOP 211
FAIR-DAY FOUNDRY 212
FAIRVIEW CEMETERY 583
FAIRVIEW SCHOOL 408
FALCONER, J L 451
FAMOUS, Flour 213
FANZ, Ignaz 161, 203, 569
FARMER, W T 144
FARMING, COURSE OF STUDY 364
FATHER OF COMMON SCHOOLS 491
FATIO, Dr. Parmenio 504
FAYETTEVILLE, NC 312
FEDERAL ARMY 200

FEIST, J Herman 385
FELLOWS, Lt, death of 163
FELTON, Samuel M 286
FENDERSON, Rev W B 452
FENNEGAN, Lucy 547
FENTRESS COUNTY, TN 15, 19
FERGUSON 312
FERRERO, Gen 164, 165
FERRIS, Charles E 384
FERRY CROSSINGS 55, 302, 303
FIAT, Justinia 82
FIDELITY LODGE #9 564
FIFTH AVENUE BRIDGE 133
FINDLEY
   John 30
   Theodosia A 390
FINK, Henry 284, 286, 287
FINLEY
   H F 243
   William W 289
FINNEGAN
   Mrs. Lucy 547
   Rev Father M J 441
FIRE
   1855 213
   1886 . . . . 215, 221, 224
   1897 248
FIRE ALARM 132, 133
FIRE ARMS 194
FIRE BRIGADE STATION, North Knoxville 132
FIRE CHIEF 111, 113
FIRE COMPANY 94, 97, 98
FIRE DEPARTMENT 111, 120, 132
   On police duty 307
FIRE ENGINE 97, 112
   Building for the 107
   Chemical 141
   First steam in Knoxville 132
   JC Luttrell 106

Steam	105
FIRE ENGINES	104
FIRE FIGHTING	96
FIRE HOUSE	98
FIRE PROTECTION	94, 97, 133
FIRST CREEK	39, 43, 96, 103, 109, 123, 133, 137, 165, 167, 171, 194, 195, 196, 200, 213, 214, 249, 299
FIRST NATIONAL BANK BUILDING	254
FISH HATCHERY	92
FISHEL, Isadore	589
FISHER	
Frank L	254, 255, 260
Mrs. Frank L	546, 547, 579
H T	534
FISHING CREEK, Battle of	329
FISK UNIVERSITY	379, 380
FISKE, Mr.	252
FITZGERALD	
Garret	72
Bishop J N	448
Rev P M	432, 545
T F	538
Capt Walter M	188
FITZPATRICK, J. J.	113
FIZER, W H	219
FLAG POND	103, 167, 196
FLAGG, Henry G	159
FLANAGAN, Sister Mary Elizabeth	192
FLANDERS, J C	536, 565, 584
FLANDERS HOTEL	228, 571
FLAT CREEK, Railroad Accident	294
FLAT CREEK, GRAINGER COUNTY, TN	294
FLEMING	
David	444, 447
John	332
John M	153, 316, 332, 336, 476, 554, 555
FLENNIKEN	
Alexander	120
E H	145, 409

W P ... 260
FLETCHER
   J W ... 247, 262
   Miss M A ... 406, 407
FLINT RIDGE ... 9, 13
FLORENCE CRITTENDEN RESCUE HOME ... 545
FLORIDA STREET MISSION ... 432
FLOYD, Miss ... 530
FOGG, Francis B ... 481
FOLKES, W C ... 470
FOOT, Rev Joseph I ... 426
FORD
   C M ... 588
   George W ... 343
   I L ... 588
   Rev J B ... 447, 448
   J C ... 396, 438
   J C Jr. ... 573
   W B ... 438
   William B ... 473
FORE, Augustus P ... 347
FOREMAN MURDER CASE ... 495
FORST, Earthwork ... 171
FORT BUCKNER ... 167
FORT CHISWELL, VA ... 38
FORT DEPOSIT ... 148
FORT LOUDOUN ... 32, 170, 172
FORT MEYER ... 192
FORT MIMMS ... 148
FORT SANDERS ... 132, 167, 168, 171, 180, 433, 446, 462, 584, 586
   Assault on ... 168, 171
   Battle of ... 137, 172
   Casualties ... 174
   Confederate flags on ... 168
   Description of ... 171, 175
   Development of area ... 177
   Ditch surrounding ... 176
   Movement to ... 178
   Naming of ... 170

Orders for 172
Supplies 167
FORT SANDERS COUNCIL #576 567
FORT SOUTHER 149
FORT SUMPTER 152, 575
FOSTER
Ephraim H 314
Gen 169, 174
H 138, 139
Prof Stephen 65
FOUCHE
Dr. John 521
Dr John, first dentist 522
FOUNDRY 197, 198
FOUNTAIN CITY 190
FOUNTAIN HEAD 443
FOURTH OF JULY 84
FOUTE, Jacob F 474
FOWLER
G T 562
J S 408
S P 126, 448
FOY, Miles 444
FRANCIS
Dr. A. A. 525, 548
Col Miller 70
FRANKLAND CONSTITUTION 75
FRANKLIN, State of 31, 34, 35, 37, 39, 43, 74, 75, 421, 498
FRANKLIN ASSEMBLY 344
FRANKLIN BUILDING 225, 243, 244, 245
FRANKLIN COUNTY, TN 19
FRANKLIN UNIVERSITY 348
FRATER, J. J. 575
FRATERNAL UNION OF AMERICA 568
FRAZEE
Mrs. C S 580
Mrs. J H 547
John H 184, 185, 192, 193, 401, 402, 459
FRAZER, W C 562

FRAZIER
- Dr. Beriah 508
- Rev J F 445
- James B 382
- W C 561

FREEDMEN'S BUREAU 426

FREEMAN
- R. R. 525
- Thomas J 470
- Thomas J, death of 377

FRENCH
- A G 476
- Rev. George D 445
- Ida M 396
- J Baird 188, 189
- Rev J L M 445
- L C 578
- Mrs. L C 464, 543, 579, 580
- Lizzie Crozier 391
- William B 229, 254

FRENCH & INDIAN WAR 32, 415
- French Broad and Holston, Land 354

FRENCH BROAD RIVER 10, 17, 27, 34, 35, 38, 39, 43, 50, 52, 167, 168, 204, 275, 276, 281, 290, 346, 350, 357, 442
- Fork 424, 506

FRENCH HUGUENOTS 417
FRIEDRICH, Rev J A 456
FRIENDSVILLE, TN 291
FRIERSON, J W S 193, 247, 299
FRISTOE, Rev Robert 423
FRIZELL, John 471
FRYAR, merchants 227
FUCHS, Stephen G 455
FULCHER, William C 125

FULKERSON
- A 157
- J V 560

FULLER
- David G 551

>   F E 224

FULTON
>   Hugh 49
>   Weston M 384

FULTON COUNTY, GA 293

FUNCK
>   C M 206
>   Charles M 268

FURNITURE FACTORY 200

FYFFE, J P 187

G A R
>   Post 14 587
>   Provisional Dept TN & GA 569

GAGE, W A 125, 561

GAHAGAN, A J 587

GAINES
>   Lt Edmund 92
>   M. M. 554
>   Mary 134
>   Matthew M 124, 134

GALBRAITH
>   W A 448
>   William 284

GALBREATH, Andrew 347

GALE, Justin E 216

GALLAHER 339
>   J F 409

GALLATIN, TN 382

GALYON
>   James A 437
>   R F 144

GALYON & SELDEN COMPANY 537
GALYON & SELDON CONTRACTORS 551

GAMBLE
>   A. M. 160, 161
>   John N 352

GAMBLES STATION 63
GAMEWELL, Fire Alarm 133

GAMMON
  Miss J L 406
  Rev J P 430
GANNON, Frank S 289
GANT
  J W 373
  Dr Robert 348
GAP CREEK – see also "Streets, Gap Creek Pike" 275
GAPS 27
GARNETT, Rev Henry H 434
GARRATT, Prof C A 449
GARTH, Mrs. M P 543
GAS LIGHTING, uses of 129
GAS LIGHTS 103, 128
GAS OFFICE, site of 232
GAS WORKS 103
GASS
  Ewing 508
  J M 534
  John 347
  John M 508
  Parmelia Scruggs 508
  W H 125, 256
GATLIFF, Dr A 243
GAUT
  J W 118, 121, 136, 246, 269, 373, 382, 403, 405, 443
  John C 367
  Joseph 581
  Joseph P 258
  R F 257
  Rosalie 552
GAUT & PHINNEY 264
GAY STREET BRIDGE 113, 302
  Destroyed 303
GAYLE
  E. E. 374, 377, 379
  R H 244
GAYNOR, Fire Alarm 133
GAYNOR FIRE ALARM COMPANY 135

GAZETTE 312
GEARS, W S 242
GEERS, W H 257, 258, 260
GEHON, John 49
GEIGER, C 203
GENERAL HOSPITAL, Committee on Arrangements 548
GENIUS OF LIBERTY [THE] 313
GEOGRAPHY, Gaps 27
GEOLOGICAL SURVEY OF TENNESSEE 18, 23
GEORGE
    Albert 237
    Calvin 212
    Edgar 237
    Len 212
    Mrs. S C 565
    S H 237, 257
    S H & COMPANY 238
    T D 565
GEORGE & BRISCOE 233
GEORGIA PACIFIC RAILWAY 283
GEORGIA PACIFIC RAILWAY COMPANY 285
GETTYS, R P 216, 217, 246, 258, 305
GETTYSBURG 169, 174
GIBBINS, W E 186, 233, 429, 571, 574, 575
GIBBONS, W E 192, 264, 571
GIBBS, W F 476
GIBSON
    Chancellor 298
    Henry R 181, 298, 331, 332, 399, 475, 541
    Mrs. Henry R 579
    Lt. S L 160
    W. W. 338
    Mrs. W. W. 543
    Gen William H 180
GIDDENS, Rev. R M 461
GIFFIN
    D A 567
    David A 571
GILBERT, Michael 421

GILES COLLEGE 511
GILLENWATERS, E. E. 444, 447
GILLESPIE 134
   Mrs. 65
   Thomas 424
GILLESPY, Ann E 342
GILLET, H S 540
GILSON, S L 160
GINTER, R M 396
GIRLS HIGH SCHOOL 407, 588
GIRLS HOME 393, 394
GIRLS INDUSTRIAL HOME 542
GIRLS RELIEF SOCIETY 192
GIST, Joshua 72
GIVAN, William G 527
GIVINS, Dr. G C 187
GLASS 109
GLASS WORKS 165
GLASSCOCK, Katie 532
GLEASON
   John 128
   Father Patrick J 441
GLENN
   Prof John W 371
   William F 368, 369
GLOBE FOUNDRY COMPANY 224
GLOVER, J L 254
GODFREY, L 448
GOETZ, Dr 455
GOFORTH
   Alexander 157
   H R 215
      GOLDEN RULE LODGE #177 561
GOLDMAN, J F 448, 564, 565
GOLDSMITH 194
GOOD NEWS 546
GOODALL, T. T. & Company 203
GOODHART, B 569
GOSDORFER, A 589

GOSSETT
  Calvin 151
  V F 132, 160
GOTTLIEB, G 589
GOULD, George J 286
GOVERNMENT BUILDING 261
GRACE
  Prof W M 362
  Rev W R 437
GRAHAM
  L B 156
  William 55, 348, 453, 454
GRAINGER COUNTY, TN 13, 17, 250, 348, 494, 538
GRAND ARMY OF THE REPUBLIC – see "GAR"
GRAND ENCAMPMENT 562
GRAND LODGE FOR TENNESSEE 556
GRAND LODGE OF TENNESSEE 557
  Order of Knights of Honor 563
GRANT
  Gen 165, 169, 174
  James 557
  President 486, 507, 514, 521
GRASSY VALLEY 14, 38, 57
GRATZ, L A 140, 142, 564, 569
GRAVES, James R 320, 321
GRAY
  Isa A 407
  Isa E 400, 401
  Lucy E 578
GRAY CEMETERY 326, 454, 515, 583, 584, 586
GRAY'S ELEGY 583
GREAT IRON WHEEL 321
GREAT IRON WHEEL EXAMINED ... FALSE SPOKES EXTRACTED 321
GREAT SOUTHERN MARBLE COMPANY 205
GREAT WESTERN LINE 272
GREDIG, A 233, 234
GREDIG & CRUZE 234
GREEN
  Rev A L 452

Andrew 49
 Gen Duff 282
 Dr Horace 514
 John W 256
 Judge 495
 Nathan 469, 474, 498
GREENDALE CEMETERY 583
GREEN COUNTY, TN 9, 13, 22, 33, 155, 250, 315, 347, 442, 467, 499
GREENEVILLE COLLEGE 55, 75, 345, 346, 347, 348, 349, 353, 481,
 ..... 494, 498, 499
GREENEVILLE CONVENTION, Civil War 155
GREENOUGH, John 286
GREENSBORO, NC 272
GREENWAY, James 49
GREENWOOD
 C A 463
 Mrs. 401
GREENWOOD CEMETERY 583
GREER
 Andrew 150
 J M 225, 382
 Mrs. J M 579
 J M & Company 239
 Joseph 50, 89, 441, 442
 W O 239
GREER MACHINERY COMPANY 238
GREERS, W H 257, 258, 260
GRIFFIN
 Mrs. A M 567
 Rev G W 436
GRIFFIN SPRING 131
GRIFFITH, Fred D 147
GRINSTEAD, W E 243
GRISHAM, J T 284
GROCERY BUSINESS 230, 240
GROTON BRIDGE COMPANY 133
GROVE, Arthur 244
GROVES, David 243
GRUNDY, Felix 477

GRUNDY COUNTY, TN 15
GSCHWEND, C F 564, 565, 566
GUGGENHEIM, Samuel 589
GURLEY
    Calvin A 541
    Lizzie 541
HAAS, Jacob 293
HACKER, F E 364
HACKETT, John 49
HACKNEY, George 533
HAGGARD, William D 368, 384, 385
HAGUE, Mrs. W H 553
HAHNEMANN MEDICAL COLLEGE, Philadelphia 520
HAILEY, Rev O L 437
HALE, N W 236
HALEN, R S 231
HALL
    A. M. 188
    E T 472
    H W 126, 147
    Herbert W 572
    J S 304
    John 159, 557
    Maj. Learoy, bio 488
    M L 138, 473, 476
    N R 460
    Nancy Nelson 488
    Rev Thomas 423
    William 488, 584
HALL & HAWKINS 201
HALLS CROSS ROADS 274
HAMBLEN COUNTY, TN 413
HAMBLETON
    Frank S 308
    T Edward 308
HAMBLIN, Daniel 49
HAMBRIGHT, F M 572
HAMILTON
    Alexander 72

I 473
   Joseph 54, 55, 82, 345, 348, 467
   Samuel 156
HAMILTON COUNTY, TN 13, 19
HAMILTON DISTRICT 72, 473, 476, 498
   Established 472
   Superior Court judges 472
HAMMACK, M P 262
HAMMOND, Theodore A Jr. 293
HAMPDEN-SIDNEY, VA 367
HAMPDEN-SIDNEY ACADEMY 39, 227, 352, 363, 386, 404, 406, 455
   Reopens 388
   Unified w/ East Tennessee College 388
HAMPDEN-SIDNEY COLLEGE, Prince Edward County 419
HAMPDEN-SIDNEY SCHOOL 406
HAMPTON, G W 452
HANCHER, Rev A D R 456
HANCOCK, Charles 374
HANCOCK COUNTY, TN 13
HANDLEY, Samuel 61, 65
HANDLY, James W 369, 385
HANGING MAW 34, 61, 63, 66
HANNA, R H 222
HANNA MANUFACTURING COMPANY 222
HANNAH
   Harvey H 187
   Samuel 49
HANNUM, W H 408
HANOVER PRESBYTERY 80, 352, 419
HAPPERSETT, Rev Reese 426
HARDEE, Gen 169
HARDEE STREET RAILWAY COMPANY 304, 306
HARGIS, Joel JP 304
HARPE BROTHERS 86, 319
HARRILL, G M 204
HARRIMAN JUNCTION 284
HARRIS
   George W 136
   H S 255

Gov Isham G	481
M. M.	568
Mrs.	530
William R	469
HARRIS BLOCK	463

HARRISON

A P	225
Horace H	469
President	331, 514, 518
Rev W A	426, 430

HART

Gen	166
J E	206
R H	336, 337
W Clayton	586
HARTRANFT, Gen	164
HARVARD COLLEGE	348, 353, 397, 458
HARVEY, R B	150
HARWELL, T B	373
HASCALL, Gen	164
HASKELL, Judge Joshua	494
HAT RACK MANUFACTURER	201
HATCH BILL	372
HATCHER, Henry	301
HATTERS	195
HAUN, William	286
HAVELY, Isaac B	527
HAWES, Tilgham	325

HAWKINS

Rev A W	432
Alvin	469, 470
C H	312
John B	132
Samuel W	587
Senator	44
HAWKINS COUNTY, TN	9, 13, 17, 47, 155, 204, 205, 207, 250, 345, 347, 524
HAWKS MOUNTAIN	416
HAWN, William	286
HAWS, T & Company	16

HAYES
    R Y 561
    President Rutherford B 329, 400, 486, 492
HAYLEY, James 445
HAYNE, Col Robert T 280
HAYNES
    Col 163
    Hal H 382
    J P 238, 257, 411
    Landon C 487
    Wood G 571
HAYNES, HENSON & COMPANY 238
HAYNIE, John 443
HAYS
    Henry 570
    John 48
    T A 461
    William 139
HAYWOOD, Judge John 46, 477, 498
HAZEN
    Asa 234
    Gideon M 99, 124, 196
    R S 230, 548
HAZEN & LOTSPIECH 229, 231
HEABLER, Mr. 463
HEALD, T H 242, 243, 246, 247, 256
HEALTH, vaccination 98
HEALTH OFFICER 112, 126
HEARN, John T 294, 337, 554
HEART
    F 465, 589, 590
    M 589
HEATH, W L 243
HEBREW BENEVOLENT ASSOCIATION 589
HEBREW CEMETERY 590
HECKEL, Rev John 454, 455
HEDLEY, Dr James 581
HEISKELL
    Catherine Floyd 552

Charles J	377
Frederick S	152, 316, 318, 389, 551
Frederick S, bio	314
John	314
Mr.	318
S G	125, 193, 305, 408, 531, 536, 538, 548, 551, 552
Mrs. S G	553
William	253, 389

HEISKELL SCHOOL 408
HELLNER, J G 256
HELMS
   John E 136, 316, 319 328
   William T 319
HENDERSON 420
   George W 566
   J D 570
   James 151
   Richard 33, 35
   W A 180, 373, 382, 402, 403, 554, 555
   Mrs. W A 547
   W B 144, 146, 463
   W E 574
HENEGAR
   Edward 236, 257
   John 443
HENNEMAN, John B 383, 581
HENRY, William 49
HENSEL, Samuel 305, 306
HENSLEY, James A 144, 231, 572
HENSON, J A 238, 456
HERRICK, Henry 390
HERRING, Lewis M 365
HICKEY
   James 95
   R M 444
HICKMAN
   James E 262
   John C 233
HICKORY CREEK 14

HICKS, W. W. 444
HIGHLAND AVENUE SCHOOL HOUSE 410, 432, 462
HILL
    Charles O 384
    J F 289
    J W 512, 534
    James 72
    Dr Otis F 232, 504, 512
    Dr R M C 398
HILLIARD, Rev S H 449
HILLSBORO, NC 38
HILLSMAN
    John 250, 387
    Rev Matthew 436
HILTON, W S 562
HIMEL, Charles M 396, 397
HINDS VALLEY 14, 15, 273
HINTON, W F 562
HIRSCH, Sampson 589
HIWASSEE CHARTER 281
HIWASSEE COLLEGE 510
HIWASSEE RAILROAD 280
HIWASSEE RIVER 281, 291, 292, 357
HOADLEY, Miss S A 406
HOBBS, George S 286
HOCKENJOS
    Alderman 117
    F 294
HODGE
    Augustus David 408
    C 284
    Mrs. 530
HODGES, James 49
HOLDEN, Rev 451
HOLEMAN, J H 113
HOLLIHAN, Caroline 530
HOLLOWAY, Thomas C 244
HOLMAN, J H 107, 204
HOLMES, Rev J P 461

HOLSTON, rivers called 275
HOLSTON CIRCUIT 421
HOLSTON COMPANY 338
HOLSTON CONFERENCE 339, 390, 443, 444, 446, 447
HOLSTON METHODIST 337
HOLSTON PRESBYTERY 434
HOLSTON RIVER .. 13, 33, 34, 35, 38, 39, 42, 43, 44, 45, 50, 52, 61, 66, 82, 87,
    . 88, 108, 137, 139, 167, 168, 196, 204, 274, 275, 346, 350, 357, 424, 442, 506
HOLSTON RIVER PACKET & TRANSPORT 278
HOLSTON SETTLEMENTS 62
HOLSTON STEAMBOAT 241
HOME BUILDING ASSOCIATION 268
HOME OF THE FRIENDLESS 549, 550
HOMEOPATHY 520
HOOD
    Isabella W Edgar 508
    Dr J P 147
    Rev Lyman E 459
    Rev Nathaniel 508
    Gen R N 164, 166, 180, 219, 225, 255, 258, 259, 296, 304
    Dr Samuel P 508
    W P 259
    William 235
HOOKER, LITTLEFIELD & STEERE 239
HOOMAN, Isaac 589
HOOPER, Robert 443
HOPE, J W 256
HOPE COMMANDERY #2 .... 565, 567
HOPEWELL TREATY 43
HOPKINS
    Lacy 54, 82, 467
    Richard 248
HOPKINSIANISM 425, 428
HORACE MAYNARD SCHOOL 408
HORINE, Dr 522
HORN
    Rev Edward T 456
    George 444
HORNE [William] 296

HORNSBY, W J 242, 243
HORSE CAR LINES 304
HORSELEY, A R 534
HOSKINS
   HD 397
   J D 379
   William P 260
HOSPITAL 310
   Black 536
   City 309
   Division 192
   Smallpox 112
HOSPITAL BUILDING AND PROMOTING BOARD 547, 549
HOSPITAL COLLEGE, KENTUCKY 513
HOSPITAL COMMITTEES 548
HOSPITAL DAY 548
HOSPITALS, Woman's Hospital and Promoting Board 309
HOSS, EE 444
HOTEL KNOX 248
HOUK
   EE 188
   Leonidas Campbell 4, 331, 513, 541
   Leonidas Campbell, bio 493
HOUSE
   Hazen 572
   Sam 255, 264, 299, 406
HOUSEHOLDER
   J L 451
   Matthias 138, 450, 451
   William 562
HOUSTON 75
   Robert 54, 67, 345, 386, 389
   Samuel 150, 417, 419, 420, 559
HOUSTON'S STATION 65
HOWARD, Rev Robert 439
HOWARD-SMITH
   Rev John 453
   Spurrier 365
HOWE, Julia Ward 429

HOWE BROTHERS 220
HOWE TRUSS PATTERN, bridge 303
HOWELL
   Alderman 109
   C. C. 102, 306, 307, 308, 549
   C. C. (photograph) 271
   C. C., bio 309
   E P 191, 286
   J L 398, 519, 534
   John L 399
   John W 260
   Rev William 439
   William S 389
HOXIE'S HALL 246
HOXSIE, J B 114, 168, 269
HUBBARD, James 31
HUDDLESTON
   Lafayette 437
   T L B 161
HUDENBURG, John L 125
HUDGINGS
   Edward 509
   J C 509, 510, 531, 562
   Mary Carter 509
HUDIBURG
   A. S. 106
   Alderman 105, 117
   John L 125, 128, 136
   Mrs. John L 544
HUDIBURGH, Rev Thomas 423
HUDSON
   C H 131, 286
   Henry 260
HUFF'S FERRY 164, 170
HUFFACRE [PLACE] 421
HUFFAKER, Justus 442
HUGER, F K 144, 193, 306, 409, 549
HUGHES, M J 332, 333
HULL, L S 573

HUMES
- Andrew R ... 453
- James W ... 157
- Merchants ... 227
- Rev Dr Thomas W ... 47, 94, 153, 166, 316, 318, 361, 362, 365, 367, 371, 386, 387, 391, 400, 403, 425, 453, 454, 528, 541, 542, 554

HUMPHREYS
- Calvin ... 465
- Parry W ... 468
- West H ... 468
- Hunt
- J D ... 537
- Mrs. Mary ... 576
- W M ... 161
- William ... 562

HUNTER
- Rev A B ... 446
- John ... 194
- Robert ... 194

HUTCHINSON, Anderson ... 94
HUWALD, G A ... 158

HYDEN
- Rev J A ... 166, 447
- John W ... 406

HYNDS, R H ... 474
HYNES, Rev T J L ... 454
HYWEL-DAVIS COAL COMPANY ... 244

IJAMS
- H A ... 534
- Joseph H ... 540

IMMIGRANTS ... 416
IMMIGRATION ... 29, 30, 35
IMPERIAL HOTEL ... 39
INDEMNITY COMPANY ... 519
INDEPENDENCE DAY, 1793 ... 84, 85
INDEPENDENT ORDER OF ODD FELLOWS, Golden Rule Lodge ... 177, 560
INDEPENDENT PRESBYTERY ... 420
INDIAN CREEK ... 61, 62, 64, 66, 74, 88
INDIAN MOUND, French Broad & Holston ... 424

INDIAN TOWN, Concord 272
INDIAN TRAILS 271
INDIAN WARS 62, 148, 149, 181, 477
INDIANS
    Expedition 76, 79
    Fighters 73, 74
    First treaty with United States 35, 72
INDUSTRIAL BUILDING 394
INDUSTRIAL EXHIBITION, 1871 261
INDUSTRIAL HOME 542
INGERSOLL, Henry H . 116, 121, 129, 294, 377, 383, 384, 405,406, 471, 560, 581
INGLES, W C 218
INMAN
    John H 286
    S M 289
INSURANCE BUILDING 196
INTERIOR DEPARTMENT, Treasury Department 181
INTERNATIONAL MEDICAL AND DENTAL CONGRESS 524
IREDELL COUNTY, NC 39
IRELAND 327, 328, 418, 481
IRISH, Oliver C 304
IRISH PATRIOT 327
IRON 19, 20, 212
IRON MANUFACTURING 200, 207
IRON ORE 198
IRON WORK 197
IRVIN, Robert 431
IRWIN
    Alderman 117
    Jennie B 411
    Robert 140, 142, 431
ISBELL, Zach 466
ISELIN, Adrian 289
ISH'S STATION 69
ISLAND FLATS 31
ISLAND HOME FARM 584
ISLAND HOME INSURANCE COMPANY 269
IVINS, Sam P 318
J C LUTTRELL, Steam Fire Engine 132

JACK, Jeremiah 54, 72
JACKS, N G 460
JACKSBORO, TN 225
JACKSON
   Abner G 228, 540
   Andrew 91, 148, 149, 150, 167, 314, 315, 417, 467, 468, 477, 479, 489, 491, 558
   Rev Frank 446
   George R 430
   J A 304
   Joseph S 150
   N A 304
   Richard C 129, 241, 254, 269, 284, 554
   Sallie L 541
   TN 494
JACKSON COLLEGE, Columbia, TN 353
JACOBS
   Rev F M 452
   S D 389, 527
   Mrs. Sarah 583
   Solomon D 124, 281, 389, 527
JACQUES, Joseph 114, 125, 265, 269, 284
JAFFA, B 465
JAIL 88
   Building of 55
JARNAGIN
   Milton P 257, 490, 495
   Spencer 4, 495, 496
   Spencer, bio 494
JARNIGAN, John 158
JARVIS
   H Clay 554
   L M 587
JAY, Rev J P 439, 452
JEFFERSON, Thomas 46, 77, 501
JEFFERSON COUNTY, TN 13, 17, 72, 155, 188, 250, 341, 342, 348,
                    469, 472, 476, 483, 489, 492, 498, 499, 508, 515
JEFFERSON COUNTY MEDICAL SOCITY 509
JEFFERSON MEDICAL COLLEGE 516, 517
JEFFRIES, Rev M D 184, 437, 548, 573

JELLICO, TN	225, 243, 244
JELLICO, TN, Coal	245
JELLICO COAL FIELDS	300
JELLICO COAL MINING COMPANY	241, 243
JELLICO JUNCTION	291

JENKINS
B A	575
J	243
P F	561
William	244

JENNY LIND FURNITURE	105
JESSE A RAYL SCHOOL	407

JETT
Freda May	532
John	532

JEWELERS	58, 194
JOHN, Z T	218
JOHN SEVIER COUNCIL, Royal Arcanum	564
JOHN SEVIER ENCAMPMENT #54	562
JOHN SEVIER FORUM	568
JOHN SEVIER SCHOOL	406

JOHNSON
A. S.	460
A W	530
Alderman	138
Andrew	113, 152, 154, 332, 479, 490, 495, 499
Andrew, impeachment	487
David B	370, 377
H M	256
J E	411, 446
J G	438
J R	147
John	442
John B	210
O F	444
P	585
Robert	159
S H	144
S M	262, 263

    V. Q. 157
    Rev William 423
    William R 571
JOHNSON CITY, TN 188, 283
JOHNSON COUNTY, TN 13, 16, 33
JOHNSTON
    H M 256
    J E 446
    Mrs. J Y 581
    Dr. Robert 84
JOLLY ISLAND 490
JONES 128, 296
    A. S. 400
    Rev B J 452
    Rev Carter Helm 436
    Daniel 456
    Dr 548
    E C 304
    Rev E D W 452
    Lt Col F B 191
    F R 378
    Rev G James 458
    J B 205
    Rev J S 450
    Rev J W 449
    James C 487
    Job 244
    John 150, 456, 457
    John H 208
    Rev Martin 439
    Moses 244
    Rev R E 433
    R G 243
    Reps 128, 219, 300, 304, 305
    Rev S E 437
    S L 399, 534
    Gen Sam 162, 167
    Tap R 548
    Dr Tap R 547

Mrs. Tap R	547
Thomas R	534
William P	358
JONES BRICK COMPANY	219
JONESBORO, TN	56, 57, 58, 251, 319, 321, 344, 373, 379, 467, 469, 483, 484, 493, 509, 524
Jordan	
James B	385
Thomas W	373, 374, 377, 383
JOUROLMAN, R D	447
JOUROLMON	
Leon	214, 384, 405, 409, 410
R D	98
JOYCE, Bishop I W	448
JOYNES	
Edward S	366
Prof	371
KAIN	
Kitty	346
Mary	346
W C	102, 158
KAISER BROTHERS	229
KARNS	
Charles	258
Charlton	125, 258
J C	258
Mrs.	531
T C	363, 365, 372, 374, 377
W C	258
KAVANAUGH, Rev Bishop H. H.	445
KEAN	
John	72
Rev Father Joseph S	441
KEARNEY	
Patrick	510
Sophia Upjohn	510
Dr Thomas	510
KEARNS, L J	214
KEEBLE, John Bell	385

KEEGAN, David E 532
KEELING
   Charlotte McGrew 511
   Dr J H 511, 562
   James L 511
KEENER, W Bruce 233
KEEP, F C 567
KEFAUVER, P F 378
   KEITH
   Charles F 472
   John H 444, 445, 446
KELLER
   R A 202, 217, 263, 570
   T W 217, 260, 432
KELLEY
   Alexander, Mill 55
   Rev C W 449
   John M 444
KELLY
   A 452
   Alexander 73, 345
   John M 443
   Lt 63
   Mrs. R J 562
   William 558
KELSO, Henry J 126, 399, 534
KENDALL
   Rev J N 451
   Maj. W P 190, 192
KENNAN, George 581
KENNEDY
   Alderman 106
   E 264
   Dr J E 374
   Mrs. J H 99
   James, Mill 213
   Jane H 39, 99
   John 348
   Dr John M 508, 534

   Mr. 96
   Samuel B 150
   W T 236
   William S 426
   William, Mill 213
KENNON, Rev 435
KENSLOE, J B G 574
KENT
   Chancellor 496
   Charles W 374
KENTUCKY 37, 74, 158, 161, 162, 163, 178, 487
   Secession 154
KEPHART, W H 248
KERN
   Peter   106, 115, 116, 125, 128, 186, 193, 203, 223, 255, 256, 262, 294, 304, 455
   Peter, store 455
KERR
   Capt 59
   E Belle 395
   Miss H A 396
   M Irena 396
   William M 444
KERSHAW, Gen J B 172, 179
KESTERSON, Dr. R Neil 525
KEY, D M 468
KEYS, Alexander D 281
KEYWOOD 421
KIBLEY, Willis 301
KIDD, S A 217
KIMBALL
   Frank C 131
   Grace 406
KIMBROUGH, Rev Duke 423, 435
KINCAID
   J G 218
   J H 126, 534
   J W 218
KING
   A. M. 237, 570

   Dr 504
   Miss Francis M 407
   Horace 532
   J M 551, 554
   James 50, 124, 228, 347, 389, 504
   John, Sr. 49
   John T 181
   Joseph L 92, 124, 389, 583
   Lt 192
   M L 551
   Oliver 278
   Robert 181, 250, 389
   S L 159
   Thomas 49
KING & CROZIER 57
KING FISHER, death of 480
KING IRON & BRIDGE COMPANY 133
KING, OATES, & COMPANY 236
KING'S CHAPEL SCHOOL 408
KING'S MOUNTAIN 32
KINGSTON, TN 38, 90, 155, 162, 164, 165, 225, 272
KINGSTON CONVENTION, Civil War 155
KINGSTON PIKE 170, 271, 273, 274, 275
   Description of 272
   Improvements 271
   Name change 145
   Travel time 271
KINGSTON TURNPIKE COMPANY 272
KINSEL, J C 456
KINSLOE, J B G 138, 341
KINSLOE & RICE 327
KINZEL
   E S 294
   G J 218
   Miss J L 578
KIRBY
   J W 561
   Maj. Thomas B 332
KIRKLAND, Mrs. J H 579

KIRKPATICK
  R L 366
  R L, death of 371
KIRKPATRICK
  R L 362, 365, 366, 391
  S J 471
KISER, Mrs. M 577
KNABE
  G R 366
  William A 188
KNAFFL, Rudolf 231, 256
KNAFFL & LOCKE 229, 231
KNAFFLE 296
KNIGHTS OF HONOR, Order of 563
KNIGHTS OF HONOR HALL 566
KNIGHTS OF PYTHIAS 563
KNIGHTS TEMPLAR 560
KNOBBY REGION 10
KNOW NOTHING PARTY 321
KNOX
  Henry 9, 50, 52
  James 49
  John 416
  John L 254
KNOX COUNCIL #91 572
KNOX COUNTY
  Cession of 35, 51, 54
  County Court 271
  Courts established 54, 72, 73, 75, 77, 80, 90, 91, 93, 112, 140, 149, 150
  Criminal Court 475
  Established 9, 13, 17, 18, 54
  Marble 204, 207, 271, 273
  Workhouse 273, 275, 348, 467, 469, 472, 473, 476, 485,
  .... 491, 493, 584
KNOX COUNTY INDUSTRIAL SCHOOL 519, 580
KNOX COUNTY MEDICAL SOCIETY .. 507, 508, 509, 511, 513, 515, 519, 520
KNOX LODGE #153 568
KNOXVILLE
  Altitude 23

Army post ... 59
Black population ... 137
Blockhouse ... 88
Board of Health established ... 119, 126
Bonds ... 96, 100
Capital of Tennessee ... 78
Charter ... 126
City limits ... 123
City physician ... 510
Commons ... 48
East, incorporated ... 137
Established ... 50, 75, 90
Fire protection ... 94, 96, 111, 112, 113, 114, 120, 307
Fire, 1893 ... 201
Fire, 1897 ... 248
First bank ... 250
First buildings ... 46
First building ... 106
First church ... 81
First government troops ... 89, 92
First legislature ... 73
First male child ... 490
First mayor ... 493
First people ... 37
First railroad ... 136
Founder ... 42
Founding of ... 46
Gas lights ... 128
Gas works ... 103
Incorporation ... 94
Indebtedness ... 134
Jail ... 55, 88
Location of ... 50
Naming of ... 50, 51
Night watchmen ... 95
North ... 135
Old ... 135
Planned attack upon ... 66
Police department ... 120

Public library of 541
Second bank 251
Semi-centennial 47
Siege of 158, 167, 174
Tallest buildings 249
West 135
KNOXVILLE & AUGUSTA RAILROAD BRIDGE 220
KNOXVILLE & AUGUSTA RAILROAD 283
KNOXVILLE & EDGEWOOD STREET RAILROAD COMPANY 304
KNOXVILLE & KENTUCKY RAILROAD 101, 105, 112
KNOXVILLE, & LEXINGTON RAILROAD 100
KNOXVILLE & OHIO RAILROAD 19, 20, 21, 100, 133, 199, 205, 208,
. . . . 211, 212, 217, 241, 282, 283, 284, 299
KNOXVILLE & OHIO RAILROAD BRIDGE 305
KNOXVILLE ACADEMY OF MEDICINE, organized 534
KNOXVILLE BAR 82, 327
KNOXVILLE BELT RAILWAY 294, 299
KNOXVILLE BOARD OF HEALTH 513, 518
KNOXVILLE BOARD OF TRADE 246
KNOXVILLE BOUNDARIES 123
KNOXVILLE BOX & KEG COMPANY 221
KNOXVILLE BREWING COMPANY 219
KNOXVILLE BRICK COMPANY 218
KNOXVILLE BUGGY WORKS 203
KNOXVILLE BUILDING & LOAN ASSOCIATION 261
KNOXVILLE BUSINESS COLLEGE 371, 377
KNOXVILLE CAR WHEEL COMPANY 198, 199
KNOXVILLE CENTENNIAL BUILDING, moved 553
KNOXVILLE CENTENNIAL BUILDING ASSOCIATION 553
KNOXVILLE CITY MILLS 213, 215
KNOXVILLE CITY SCHOOLS 410
KNOXVILLE CITY WATER COMPANY 129
KNOXVILLE COFFIN COMPANY 217
KNOXVILLE COLLEGE 131, 379, 392, 395, 410
KNOXVILLE CONSISTORY #10 560
KNOXVILLE CONVENTION, Civil War 155
KNOXVILLE COUNCIL #75 560
KNOXVILLE DAY 552
KNOXVILLE DIRECTORY 228

KNOXVILLE DIXIE, stove	213
KNOXVILLE ELECTRIC LIGHT AND POWER COMPANY	308
KNOXVILLE ELECTRIC RAILWAY COMPANY	305, 306
KNOXVILLE ELECTRIC RAILWAY	307
KNOXVILLE ENCAMPMENT #11	562
KNOXVILLE FEMALE ACADEMY	358, 389
KNOXVILLE FIRE DEPARTMENT	223
KNOXVILLE FIRE EXTINGUISHER COMPANY	552
KNOXVILLE FIRE INSURANCE COMPANY	268
KNOXVILLE FOUNDRY	199
KNOXVILLE FURNITURE COMPANY	221
KNOXVILLE GAS LIGHT COMPANY	128
KNOXVILLE HEBREW BENEVOLENT ASSOCIATION	589, 590
KNOXVILLE HOME FOR THE FRIENDLESS, est. 1894	550
KNOXVILLE HOSPITAL	502, 518, 547
KNOXVILLE ICE COMPANY	203
KNOXVILLE IRON COMPANY	200, 208, 241, 457
KNXOVILLE LEATHER COMPANY	197
KNOXVILLE LIBRARY AND READING ROOM	541
KNOXVILLE LODGE #100	564
KNOXVILLE LODGE #138	561
KNOXVILLE LODGE #485	568
KNOXVILLE LODGE #87	568
KNOXVILLE LYCEUM	65, 580
KNOXVILLE MANUFACTURING COMPANY	197
KNOXVILLE MARBLE COMPANY	204
KNOXVILLE PARKHURST	450
KNOXVILLE PROVISION & SUGAR COMOPANY	231
KNOXVILLE PUBLIC SCHOOL	402
KNOXVILLE SENATE #1068	573
KNOXVILLE SOUTHERN RAILROAD	291, 293, 294
KNOXVILLE STORAGE COMPANY	231
KNOXVILLE STREET RAILWAY COMPANY	303, 305, 307, 308
KNOXVILLE SUPPLY COMPANY	199
KNOXVILLE TRACTION COMPANY	308, 309, 519
KNOXVILLE VALLEY	14
KNOXVILLE VALLEY FORGE & FOUNDRY COMPANY	552
KNOXVILLE WATER COMPANY	119, 129
KNOXVILLE WATER WORK	93, 189

KNOXVILLE WOOLEN MILLS 131, 216, 223, 552
KNOXVILLE, CUMBERLAND GAP, & LOUISVILLE RAILROAD
 .... 131, 206, 293, 295, 296, 297, 496
KNOXVILLE, MIDDLEBROOK, WEST END RAILWAY COMPANY 308
KNOXVILLE, SEVIER, & JEFFERSON STEAMBOAT COMPANY 278
KOHLHASE, C 562
KRAG-JORGENSEN RIFLES 191
KREITZMAN
   H 465
   Solomon 465
KRIDER, Uriah 456
KUERT, Col 191
KUNOKESKIE 90
KYLE
   Hugh G 382
   Rev Joseph 395
LABACH, Rev J M 430, 431
LACKEY
   James W 48
   Capt. W. W. 156, 157
LACY, Hopkins 54, 82, 348, 467
LADIES MEMORIAL ASSOCIATION 584, 585
LAFOLLETTE, TN 218
LAHR, A P 248
LAKE
   Joseph 420
   Rev L 457
LAKE OTTOSSEE 304
LAMAR, G B 241
LAMAR HOUSE 166
LAMBERT, Rev Jeremiah 421
LAMSON-SCRIBNER, F 373, 375
LANCASTER
   Mrs. C A 406
   Dr. C. C. 398
LAND, French Broad and Holston River 354
LAND LAWS, Tennessee 480
LAND LOTTERY 47, 48, 50

LANE
  E B 532
  Moses 115, 118, 119 130
  Rev Tidence 423
LANGFORD, N C 158
LAPSLY, Joseph B 348
LATHROP
  Mary T 550
  Mary T Branch 577
LAUDERDALE, David 150
LAURITZEN
  Rev John R 455, 549, 550
  Mar L 577, 578
  Rev Mr. and Mrs. 549
LAVENDER, John 194
LAW SYSTEM 224
LAWRENCE
  F M 118, 119
  J H 388,
  Rev Job 435
  Mr. 119
LAWSON McGHEE LIBRARY 542
LAWSON McGHEE LIBRARY BUILDING 236
LAWYERS 54
LEA
  Albert Miller 99, 134, 280
  B J 470
  James 49
  Luke 70, 181, 250
  Major 348
  Mrs. Maria 583
  W 49
  William 72
  William L 160
LEACH, Dr A D 129
LEAR, James 49
LEBANON, TN 424, 508
LEBANON LAW SCHOOL 490

LECTURE
    "East Tennessee in the State History" 552
    "Knoxville: Her History and Her Destiny" 553
LEDGERWOOD
    J L 160
    Oliver 301, 302
    W L 160
LEE
    C B 534
    Miss Ida M 406
    M H 534
    Robert E 485, 512
    W. W. 264
LEE COUNTY, VA 161
LEGION ARMORY 184
LEGION BAND 552
LEGION FLAG FUND 186
LEGIT, Robert 49
LELAND, F J 221
LEMING, Mary 532
LENOIR, B. B. 511, 533, 534
LENOIR CITY 38
LENOIR CITY CAR COMPANY 199
LENOIR STATION . . . . 162, 163, 164, `65, 511
LEVERE, Rev G W 434, 435
LEVY, Harry 571
LEWIS 109, 404
    David 457
    H 528
    Isaac 181, 444
    J F J 136, 391
    S D J 109, 111, 404, 561
    Thomas A 338
    Thomas D 208
    W T 241, 245
    William 158
LEWIS & CARHART 230
LEWISBURG, TN 1953

LEXINGTON
  KY 195, 413
  TN 379
LEYDEN, Col 164
LIBERTY HALL 55, 80
  Library
    Agricultural College 107
    Public 541
    University of Tennessee 376
LICENSING FEES 104
LICHTENWANGER, Minnie 407
LIFE AS IT IS 318
LIGHTFOOT, Rev 438
LILLARD
  J W 254, 255
  William H 406
LIME, distribution of 528
LIMESTONE 14
LINCOLN, President Abraham 322, 360, 468, 482
LINCOLN PARK 190
LINDSAY
  Chancellor 298
  H B 259, 298, 475
LINDSEY
  Rev A 452
  Isaac 442
  Moses 425
  Robert 194, 425
LINDSLEY, J Berrien 169, 368
LINOTYPE MACHINE 335, 337
LIPSCOMB, James E 551
LIQUOR LAWS 103
LITERATURE 83
LITTLE, Simpson 572
LITTLE BOY'S HOME 393, 394
LITTLE GIRL'S HOME 393, 394
LITTLE LOUDON CREEK 506
LITTLE RIVER 34, 45
LITTLE TENNESSEE RIVER 13, 27, 34, 272, 275

LITTLE VALLEY FAMILY, Flour 213
LITTLEFIELD, H E 240
LITTLEFIELD, STEERE & SANDERS 239
LITTLEFORD, Miss 389
LITTLETON
   John J 332
   Sanford N 125, 128, 186
LLOYD J L 405, 436
LOBENSTEIN, Anton 257, 465
LOCKE, E C 231, 242, 243
LOCKETT
   A Percy 230
   Edward 230
   S H 130, 366, 371
   W B & Company 229, 230, 231
   William B 230, 247
   Mrs. William B 553, 581
LOGAN
   Judge S T 429, 472, 476, 289, 554
   T M 286
LONAS
   Henry 67
   Joseph 66
LONDON, TN 162
LONE MOUNTAIN 293
LONES
   C E 534
   Jacob K 159
LONG
   Grace D 396
   John B 150
LONG ISLAND ON THE HOLSTON 33
LONGMIRE, E. E. 161
LONGSTREET
   Gen . 158, 164, 165, 166, 167, 168, 169, 179, 171,174, 175, 176, 177, 178, 180
   Gen's Official Report 179
LONGSTREET'S HEIGHTS 301
LONSDALE 131, 190
LONSDALE MILL COMPANY 214

LONSDALE-BEAUMONT WATER COMPANY 131
LOOKOUT MOUNTAIN 15
LORD & McCOY 194
LOTS 47, 48, 49, 50, 51
LOTSPEICH
  Rev J N 449
  J O 230 231
  Ralph 442
LOTTERY, East Tennessee College 352
LOUDON, TN 164, 169, 170, 208, 225, 281, 282
LOUISVILLE, KY 27, 123, 132, 263, 277, 280
LOUISVILLE & NASHVILLE RAILROAD 19, 245, 295, 296
LOUISVILLE BRIDGE & IRON COMPANY 113
LOUISVILLE SOUTHERN RAILWAY COMPANY 284
LOUISVILLE, CINCINNATI, & CHARLESTON RAILROAD 479
LOVE
  C R 255, 259, 260 264
  C R & Company 278
  John 49
  Rev J R 395
  Robert 38, 254
LOWEREE, F M 129
LOWRY
  Prof J R 411
  John 348
  William 49
LUCAS, William H W 454
LUCKEY, C E 218, 219, 225, 269, 431, 554, 555
LUCKEY & YOE 555
LUCKY, S J W 472, 475, 493
LUDLOW, David Hunt 366
LURTON, Horace H 470
LUTTRELL
  James C 104, 124, 125, 136, 158, 233, 247, 307
  James C, JR. 125
  James L 136
  John M 145, 147
  Mrs. 67
  S B & Company 232, 233

Samuel B . . . . 125, 129, 217, 223, 233, 243, 247, 255, 262, 263, 303, 373, ... 382, 548, 554
  Mrs. Samuel B 547
LUTZ, Mrs. J E 552
LYMAN
  E P 243
  H W 132
LYNN
  H W 204, 256
  James 429
LYON
  Thomas C 4, 360, 472
  Thomas C, bio 483
  William 115, 181, 562
LYONS
  Daniel 562
  Rev J A 449
  Joseph 589
  Louis David 589
  Lt. 150
  Solomon 589
  Thomas C 150, 241
  W L 232
LYONS VIEW 536
M E THOMPSON, Steam Fire Engine 132
MABIE, Hamilton W 581
MABLE, George 532
MABRY 123
  George W 283
  James 54
  Joseph A 102, 105, 325, 584
MABRY HILL 114, 115
  Civil War 163
MABRY STREET, BELL AVENUE, & HARDEE STREET RAILROAD . 304, 306
MABRY TRACT 123
MACHINE SHOP 197
MACINTIRE, Thomas 540
MACK, Rev William 428
MACON, GA 19, 132, 192, 283

MACON & BRUNSWICK
  Railroad 283
  Road 283
MADDEN, Thomas 443
MADISON, President 492
MADISONVILLE, TN 92, 225, 291
MADLE, George 532
MAGNETO SYSTEM 224
MAGNOLIA Flour 213
MAIN JELLICO MOUNTAIN COMPANY 244
MAINE STATE COLLEGE 373, 375
MALARIA 525, 526
MALCOLM, J B 432
MALONEY
  Frank 188
  George L 144, 160, 294, 363, 448, 554, 569, 587
MANKER, Rev J. J. 448
MANLEY, Rev J H 452
MANLIUS, NY 520
MANN
  A G 217, 561
  E B 561, 562
  Mrs. George 65
  Rev J L 448
  J W 447
  Miss Sallie J 407
MANNIER, P A 242
MANNING
  J W 402, 408
  Priscilla Blount 408
MANSION HOUSE 316, 526, 527
MANUFACTURERS, Domestic 195
MANUFACTURING 16, 194, 240
MAP [Tatham's] 83
MAPLES, William Lineas 408
MARBLE 16, 17, 18, 204, 205, 207
MARBLE CITY, Stove 213
MARBLE CITY CANTON #5 562
MARBLE CITY COUNCIL 564

MARBLE CITY FIRE EXTINGUISHER COMPANY 223
MARBLE CITY HAT COMPANY 248
MARBLE MILL 199, 206
MARCH, D 589
MARFIELD
    Samuel 199, 332, 334
    William T 257
MARIETTA, GA 502
MARIETTA & NORTH GEORGIA RAILROAD 291, 292, 293
MARION COUNTY, TN 13, 19
MARION JUNCTION, AL 283
MARIX, Lt 183
MARKET BANK 260
MARKET CROPS 11
MARKET HALL 193, 581
MARKET HOUSE 94, 102
MARKET SQUARE 102, 129, 305
    Paving of 134
MARKET SQUARE RAILROAD COMPANY 304, 306
MARKET WAGONS 98
MARKS
    Gove Albert S 367
    David 589
MARRINER
    A. S. 565
    C L 565
    P A 565
MARROW, Rev Father F T 441
MARSHALL, John 144
MARTIN
    J E 258
    Rev J H 428
    John J 437
    Maj. Joseph 66
    William 158
MARTIN ACADEMY 344
MARYLAND UNIVERISTY 511
MARYVILLE, TN 164, 170, 225, 283, 342, 347, 443, 452
MARYVILLE COLLEGE 428, 442, 490, 508

MARYVILLE RAIL ROAD TRACK 211
MASKERSON, Rev W M 439
MASON, Charles 373, 410
MASONIC LODGES – see individual names
MASONRY, Exposition of 92
MASONRY IN TENNESSEE 556
MASSIE, Prof Rodes 371
MASTERS, J M 409, 410, 534
MASTERS LODGE #244 F & A M 559
MATAMORES 151
MATHENY, J E 374
MATHES, J Harvey 367, 373
MATHESON, Kenneth G 373, 374
MATSON, Thomas E 188
MATTHEWS, A G 534
MAURY, Gen 162
MAURY ACADEMY, DANDRIDGE 517
MAXWELL
   (unknown name) 532
   A L 197, 198, 241, 252, 299, 564
   J L, Jr. 260
MAXWELL LODGE #433 560
MAXWELL, BRIGGS, & COMPANY 197
MAY, Francis 93
MAYER, LYONS & COMPANY 589
MAYFIELD, Rev J B 461
MAYNARD
   Ed Post 569, 587
   Edward 161, 186, 587
   Horace 4, 152, 161, 185, 253, 320, 391, 408, 429, 507, 513,584
   Horace, bio 485
   James 193, 216, 382, 383, 384, 453, 545, 581
   Capt Washburn 185
MAYOR & ALDERMEN 98
   Board of 96
   Compensation 117, 118
   Election 1860 104
MAYORS 146
   First 94

  List of 124
  Vote for 95
MAYS Rev J B F 436
McADOO
  Laura 581
  M R 305, 306
  W G 102, 305, 306, 366, 541
  Mrs. W G 579
McAFFRY
  James M 117, 561
  Thomas 151
McALISTER
  W E 471
  W K 471
McANALLY, Rev David R 339, 340, 390, 391, 444, 538, 539, 540
McANALLY'S RIDGE 272
McARTHUR
  F E 237
  W R 237
McARTHUR SONS & COMPANY 237
McBATH
  Dr B R 525, 561, 562, 567
  James 559
  W R 473
McBEE
  Frank 301
  Fred 301
McBRYDE
  J Bolton 384, 386
  Prof John M 370, 371
  R W 574
McCAHEN, Jennie 400
McCAHON, Jennie 396
McCALLIE
  J H 405, 406, 581
  Prof J M 411
  S W 378
  Rev Dr T H 431
  Dr T O 438

W A 534
McCALLUM
  J R 157, 180, 219, 554, 555
  J W 219, 222
  R N 157
McCALLY, George W 260
McCAMMON, Samuel 137
McCAMMON TRACT 123
McCAMMON'S SPRING 137
McCAMPBELL 109
  John 428, 491
  William E 368, 384
McCAMPBELL'S SPRINGS 94
McCAULEY
  James 586
  Mrs. Jane 266
McCAY
  Spence 466
  Spruce 82
McCLANAHAN, E G 561
McCLANNAHAN, J G 145
McCLANNAHAN MILL 211
McCLELLAN
  Gen George B 178, 526
  M S 234
  M W 150
McCLELLAND, Col John 526
McCLENAHAN, Rev D A 395
McCLUNG
  C J 128, 228
  Mrs. C J 579, 580
  Mrs. C M 580
  C M & Company 228, 233, 234
  Calvin M 233, 254, 391, 542, 584
  Charles 47, 47, 54, 57, 77, 89, 91, 92, 114, 115, 158, 216,
  .... 227, 233, 271, 272, 345, 390, 494
  Charles J 114, 115, 216, 227
  Charles J, Jr. 233
  Charles, illus 72

   E S 158
   Frank H 129, 227, 228, 254, 269, 304, 555
   Mrs. Frank H 543
   H L, Jr. 391
   H L W 158
   Hugh, Sr. 584
   Hugh L 229, 252, 258, 305, 307, 372, 382, 388, 475, 554, 581
   Margaret 494
   Matthew 122, 219, 227, 229,269, 389, 390, 403
   Matthew G 233
   Col. Pleasant M 561
   Col Pleasant M, death of 163
   Polly 346
   Rufus M 254
McCLUNG, BUFFAT & BUCKWELL 234
McCLUNG, MARGARET, Industrial Home 542
McCLUNG, POWELL & COMPANY 233
McCLUNG, WALLACE & COMPAN 227
McCLURE, J F 245
McCOLL, J R 378, 383
McCOMBS, Dr Thomas 84
McCOOK, Maj. Gen Alexander MC D 191
McCOREY, Thomas 558
McCORKLE, Calvin 563
McCORKLE & BROWN 234
McCORMICK
   C R 256
   Nannie 577, 578
McCORRY, Thomas 94, 352, 387, 557
McCOWN, Gen J P 162
McCOY
   John 154, 436,
   W C 304, 437
   Mrs. W C 547
McCREARY, Dr W L 520, 548
McCROSKEY
   Alderman 117
   E. E. 245, 400, 401, 402, 405, 406, 408, 554
   Rev E J 432

Rev Solon 432
McCULLOCH
  Mr. 196
  Thomas 72
McCULLOUGH, Rev J S 392, 395, 396
McCULLOUGH HALL 393
McDANIEL
  Alderman 296
  T P 460
McDILL, Maggie 396
McDONALD, William 72
McDONALD, SHEA, & COMPANY 141
McDONOUGH
  Rev A. A. 454
  Arminta Scott 511
  J S 411, 412
  James S 511
  John 511
  Mary 411
  W B 113
McDONOUGH & COMPANY 116
McDOWELL, James P 155
McELROY
  Col, death of 174
  Col 176
McEWEN, Margaret 65
McFARLAND
  John 68
  Robert death date 470
McFARLANE, George 98
McGAUGHEY, Samuel 49
McGEE, Dr. Green T 519
McGHEE, Charles M 106, 129, 216, 241, 253, 255, 259, 273, 284, 286, 287, 392, 454, 457, 542
McGILL, D F 395
McGLAUFLIN, Rev W H 463
McGRYDE, R W 574
McGUFFEY, Charles D 403
McILWAINE, C R 262

McINTIRE
  Mrs. A E 562
  Rev Thomas 539
McINTOSH
  Daniel 389
  Dr Donald 124, 502
  Dr James C 503
  Sadie 542
  William 502
McINTYRE
  D S 131
  D T 131
McKAMEY, Rev James A 432
McKEE
  Brig Gen 190, 191
  Rev J G 392
  John Miller 316, 328
McKELDIN
  Hugh 294
  J A 217, 258
McKENDREE, William 441, 442
McKINLEY
  President 184, 185
  Rev William 448
McKINNEY
  John A 481
  Robert J 4, 469, 485
  Robert J, Bio 481
  Samuel 114, 115, 166, 201, 254, 305, 332, 336, 373, 382,
  .... 481, 526, 554, 574
  Mrs. Samuel 343, 553, 578, 579, 581
  Samuel, residence 526
McLAIN, Andrew 469
McLAWS, Gen 164, 166, 168, 169, 170, 171, 172, 173, 179
McLEMORE
  Alderman 117
  Mr. 109, 118
McMAHAN, M B 197
McMAHON, Capt. Of "Chattanooga" 277

McMALLIN, David T 144
McMILLAN
    A 389
    Alexander 132
    Dick & Company 229
    E C 549
    E. E. 234, 259, 308
    H P 229
    Robert E 125
    Rev W H 395
McMILLAN STATION 502
McMILLAN, HAZEN & COMPANY 234, 235
McMILLEN, David 150
McMINN, Gov 251
McMINN ACADEMY, Rogersville 525
McMINN COUNTY, TN 13, 17, 216, 281, 495
McMINNVILLE, TN 379
McMULLEN
    R B 426, 528, 538, 540
    W B 205, 207
McMULLIN PROPERTY 107
McNABB
    A 554
    Charles P 398, 399, 534
McNAIRY, John 467, 468, 472, 476
McNAMARA, Patrick 586
McNAMEE, Peter 49, 58
McNULTY
    A C 147
    F 229, 234
    Frank 255, 259
McNULTY & BORCHES 229
McNULTY & KNAFFL 231
McNULTY BUILDING 236, 248
McNULTY GROCERY STORE 229
McNUTT
    George 47, 48, 49, 72, 82, 92, 345, 386, 424
    James 389
    S H 218, 257, 258

W J	233
McPHERSON, Rev W C	438
McSPADDEN, W L	406, 567, 568

McTEER

Charles E	235, 305
Mrs. Charles E	544, 579
J C	235
J T	129, 235, 255, 548, 549
Miss Moody	585
Will A	3
McTEERS, HOOD & COMPANY	235
McWHORTER, Rev C S	463, 464
McWILLIAMS, Mrs. M G	544
MEAD, William S	210, 216, 259, 400, 544
MECHANICS ASSOCIATION	261
MECHANICSVILLE, Corporation of Knoxville	406
MECK, J M	543
MECKLENBURG PLACE	506
MEDICAL INSTRUCTION	369
MEDICINE, Homeopathic	520

MEEK

Adam	72
Alexander	438
James M	144, 255, 284, 543
Joseph	304
Mary Fleming	552
MEIGS, Return J	481
MEIGS COUNTY, TN	13, 17
MELEAR, Rev J M	450
MELENDY, Dr A R	427, 524
MELLEN, George F	4, 312, 379, 383
MEMPHIS, TN	19, 86, 123, 132, 151, 152, 280, 373, 379, 382, 441, 470, 495, 496, 504, 512
MEMPHIS & CHARLESTON RAILWAY	283, 284
MEMPHIS INSTITUTE	378
MERCHANT LICENSES	98, 104
MERCHANTS, early	227
MEREDITH, J. J.	317
MERGANTHALER LINOTYPE MACHINE	335, 337

MERIDIAN, MI 283, 285
MERO DISTRICT 40, 42, 45, 87, 473
METEOROLOGICAL RECORD 24
METER, Van 527
METHODIST HILL 443
MEXICAN WAR 148, 194, 150, 151, 181
MEXICO CITY 151
MEYER, William 220
MEYERS, Rev J H 428
MICHAELOF, Rabbi 465
MICHAELS, Alderman Hugh 117
MIDDLE RIDGE COAL COMPANY 241
MIDDLEBORO BELT RAILROAD 294
MIDDLEBROOK 196, 413
MIDDLBROOK RAILWAY COMPANY 305, 306, 308
MIDDLEBROOK STREE CAR LINE 207, 590
MIDDLETON, L H 122
MILAN, TN 379
MILBURN, W E F 587
MILES
    Rev H 452
    Rt Rev Richard Pius 440
MILESIAN IRISH 417
MILITARY ANNALS OF TENNESSEE 169
MILITARY HOSPITAL 540
MILITARY UNITS
    Anderson's Brigade 176
    Armstrong's Division 170
    Army, 23rd Corp 164, 165, 178
    Army, 3rd Corp 187
    Barksdale Brigade 168
    Benjamin's Battery 176
    Brazelton's Battalion 157
    Bryan's Brigade 172, 176
    Buckley's Battery 176
    Burnside's 9th Corp 164
    Burrough's Battery 158
    Cameron's Brigade 165
    Cavalry Regiments 159

FL, 6th	163
GA, 1st Regiment	190
Hart's Division	166
Hartranfts Division	165
Hascall's Division	165
Highlander Regiment	180
Hood's Division	174
Humphrey's Brigade	172, 176
Huwald's Battery	158
IL, 112th Mounted Infantry	162
IL, 112	180
IL, 19th Volunteer Infantry	333
IN, 58th Regiment	190
IN, Light Artillery	179
Kain's Battery	158
Knox County Regiments	151, 155, 158, 193
Knoxville Dragoons	151
KY, 1st Cavalry	162
KY, Cavalry	179
KY, 5th Cavalry	178
KY, Mounted Infantry	179
KY, Regiments	158, 180
Law's Howitzer Battery	179
Light Artillery	158
Martins Division	170
McLaw's Division	164, 165, 168
MI, 20th Infantry	176
MI, Cavalry	179
MI, 2nd Infantry	176
MI, 31st Regiment	190
MN, 14th Regiment	190
MN, 14th Regiment	191
MS, 13th	174
NC "colored" Troops	191
NY, 2nd Cavalry A Company	587
NY, 79th Infantry	176
NY, 79th Volunteer Infantry	180
NY, 79th Highland Volunteers	586
NY, 8th Regiment	187

OH, 104th Infantry 521
OH, 2nd Cavalry 162
OH, 2nd Regiment 190
OH, 44TH Mounted Infantry 162
OH, 45th 180
OH, 45th Volunteer Infantry 510
OH, 6th Regiment 190, 191
OH, 7th Cavalry 162
OH, Infantry 179
OH, Konkle's 1st Artillery 162
PA, 100th Infantry 176
PA, 1st Regiment 190
Ransom's Cavalry 174
SC, Infantry 179
SC, Regiments 179
TN, 12th Cavalry B Company 587
TN, 14th Volunteer Cavalry 151
TN, 19th Confederate 156
TN, 19th Infantry Company E 156
TN, 19th Regiment 157
TN, 19th Infantry Company E 157
TN, 1st Battalion 184, 186
TN, 1st Cavalry Company E 158
TN, 1st Cavalry Company C 158
TN, 1st Cavalry 159
TN, 1st Confederate Cavalry 508
TN, 1st Cavalry Company G 587
TN, 1st Mounted Infantry 162
TN, 1st Regiment 159
TN, 1st Union Infantry 159, 162
TN, 2nd Cavalry 157
TN, 2nd Cavalry Company I 158, 159
TN, 2nd Infantry F Company 587
TN, 2nd Regiment Volunteer Cavalry 151
TN, 2nd Regiment 159
TN, 31st Infantry 157
TN, 37th Confederate Regiment 161
TN, 3rd 187
TN, 3rd Confederate 156

Index - 107

TN, 3rd Cavalry 159
TN, 3rd Infantry 159
TN, 3rd Infantry Company D 159
TN, 3rd Infantry Company F 160
TN, 3rd Infantry Company H 160
TN, 3rd Infantry Company I 160
TN, 4th Confederate Infantry 151, 156
TN, 4th Cavalry 159
TN, 4th Infantry Company D 152
TN, 4th Infantry 157, 159
TN, 4th Regiment 151, 190
TN, 4th Volunteers 187, 336
TN, 6th Infantry 159, 160, 587
TN, 7th Infantry Company I 587
TN, 7th Mounted Infantry 161
TN, 8th Cavalry E Company 587
TN, 8th Infantry 159
TN, 63rd Volunteer Infantry 512
TN, 65th Infantry Company D 157
TN, see also Knoxville Knox County
US, 20th "colored" Volunteer Infantry 435
US, 39th Regiment Volunteers 149
US, 3rd Cavalry 185
US, 4th Infantry 487
US, 5th Artillery 185
US, 6th Volunteers 188, 191, 192, 337
US, 7th Cavalry 190
Union Regiments 158
VA, 54th 163
VT, 1st Regiment 187
Wheeler's Cavalry 174
Wheelers Division 164
Whites division 165
Wofford's Brigade 172, 173, 174, 176
WV, 1st Regiment 190
Wyly's Battery 163
MILL 212, 215, 216
   Craig's (David) 55, 195, 213
   Flour 199, 213

    Grist 195, 213
    Kelly's (Alexander) 55
    Kennedy's 213
    Kennedy's (James) 213
    Marble 206
    McClannahan's 211
    Morgan's (Rufus) 213
    Oil 197
    Paper 196, 413
    Planing 222
    Saw 13, 195, 200, 204, 220
    Scott's (James) 213
    Tub 213
    White's (James) 213
    White's (Moses) 213
    White's tub 41
MILL DAMS 195
MILL MACHINERY 199
MILL PONDS 196
MILL SPRINGS, KY 316
MILLER
    A J 147
    A R 561
    Dr. 399
    Rev. I H 451
    J L 562
    J S 567
    James 49, 56, 57, 68
    John 156
    John A 567
    Pleasant M 93, 353, 388
    Pleasant M, bio 498
    S M 186, 398, 399, 534
    S R 186, 399, 531, 534, 538, 548
    Samuel 57
    William C 451
MILLER MANUAL LABOR SCHOOL OF VIRGINIA 374
MILLIGAN, Samuel 469
MILLIKEN, Mr. 435

MILLIN, Rev J R 395
MILLS
   C H 574
   Rev Robert 439
   Maj. Stephen C 191
MILTON, George F 188, 337, 581
MIMS, D A 259
MINERALS 11, 15, 17, 19, 22
MINGO COAL & COKE COMPANY 241
MINING 19, 20, 21
MINNIS
   J B 429
   Rev William 342
MIRO DISTRICT 40, 42, 45, 87
MISSIONARY RIDGE 169
MISSISSIPPI RIVER 29, 34, 37, 62, 85, 150, 169, 280
MISSOURI COMPROMISE 322
MITCHELL
   [John] 328
   Charles 369
   J M 286
   J R & Co 253
   James G 284
   John 437
   John B 388
   Joseph R 109, 253, 402, 554
   Mabel 580
   Richard 347
   S 82
   Mrs. S D 543
   W K 263
   Mrs. W P 532
MIZNER, H S 220, 222, 257, 258
MOBILE & BIRMINGHAM RAILWAY 283, 284
MOFFET
   H P 161
   Mary Lelia 408
MOFFETT, John S 241
MOLTON, M C 150

MONDAY
- J S 146, 147
- O V 533

MONROE, Rev A S 452
MONROE COUNTY, TN 13, 17, 19, 22, 156, 291, 509, 510, 515
MONSERRAT, Maj. G H 162
MONTGOMERY
- Battle of 151
- Esther 419
- Rev Jefferson E 428
- Rev John 419
- Lemuel P 150, 346
- Mrs. M L 234
- Maj. 150

MONTGOMERY COUNTY, TN 489
MONUMENT, Union soldiers 588
MOOERS, Charles A 386
MOORE 31
- Addie B 465
- D Weiley 243
- Dr 446
- G R 239
- H D 444, 445, 446, 451
- John G 286
- Rev Mark 421
- Mes 532
- Rev 433
- Rev Dr 451
- W A J 437
- W H 396, 534

MORAVIAN INDIANS 414
MORGAN 96
- C & Son 228
- Calvin 94, 96, 99, 196, 250, 388, 389, 539
- District of 466
- Franklin 228
- Gideon 428
- J H 520, 564, 565, 566
- John 178, 243

Maggie P 564, 565, 566
Rufus 94
Rufus, Mill 213
William 92
MORGAN COUNTY, TN 19, 161
MORGAN DISTRICT 466
MORRELL
   Rev H M 453
   N B 186
MORRIS
   C W 540
   John 63
MORRISON, W. W. 146, 147
MORRISTOWN, TN 168, 188, 225, 282, 337, 508, 519
MORROW
   Dr James 150, 504, 507
   Robert 241
   Samuel 138, 191, 252
   William 194, 299, 373
MORSE
   E R 207
   Miss 389
   William 195
MORTON
   H T 405
   J H 399
   Rev W J 454
MOSELEY 96
MOSES
   E P 406
   Frank A 193, 247, 248, 253, 263, 304, 336, 411, 412, 554, 564
   James C 316, 318, 336, 540, 583
   John L 252, 302, 316, 318, 336, 540, 559
   Thomas L 405, 438, 540
   William E 140, 142, 144, 366, 371, 562
MOSES SPRING 203
MOSS, H B 452
MOSSY CREEK 18, 185, 186, 508, 519
   Civil War 163

MOSSY CREEK COLLEGE 515
MOUNT ISABELLA 123
MOUNT LIBANUS LODGE #59 559
MOUNT REST HOME 544
MOUNTAIN ASH, KY 243
MOUNTCASTLE, Ralph H 233
MOURFIELD, J A 534
MOUSE CREEK, McMinn County 515
MOWBRAY, Rev William 453, 454
MOXLEY, John 120
MOZART SYMPHONY CLUB 581
MULLETT, A B 107
MUNSEY
   Thomas 125, 128
   W E 444
MUNSON, Spencer 109, 246, 269
MUNSON & BAILEY 269
MURDOCH, H J 395
MURFREESBORO, TN 98, 169, 373, 484
MURPHY
   A E 161
   Abraham 444
   Charles 572
   Frank E 188, 189
   G W 238, 572
   Horace 532
   Alderman John P 118
   NC 291
   TN 293
   William L 568, 570
MURPHY & ROBINSON 238, 248
MURRELL
   Onslow G 281
   Rev R M 438
MUSICAL INSTRUMENTS 237
MUSSEL SHOALS 229
   Canal 275
   Improvements 275
MUSSEY, Professor 511

MUSTARD, J C 203
MUTUAL LIGHT AND POWER COMPANY 308
MYERS
   J H 99, 528
   Thomas R 382
MYNATT
   E F 476, 553
   H L W 373
   William C 124, 389
MYNATTE, E F 554
MYNDERS, E 562
NAIL FACTORY 209
NASH, Dr. Walter S 399, 518, 531, 534
NASHVILLE
   TN 17, 19, 90, 103, 112, 169, 186, 228, 251, 265, 272, 280,
                          314, 328, 379, 382, 392, 469, 474, 499
   TN, State Capital 313
NASHVILLE COUNCIL 564
NASHVILLE GAS LIGHT COMPANY 128
NASHVILLE MEDICAL COLLEGE 3368, 508
NASHVILLE UNIVERSITY 368
NASSAU HALL, now Princeton College 344
NATIONAL BANKING LAW 254
NATIONAL CEMETERY 583, 585
NATIONAL FRATERNITY 568
NATIONAL HIGHWAY 272
NATIONAL LEGION 568
NATIONAL UNION 567
NATURAL BRIDGE, Virginia 353
NAVE, Lt. Andrew H 365, 383
NEELY, Gen R P 367
NEIGHBORS, Rev W S 446
NELSON
   [place] 421
   C. C. 125
   David 94
   Dr. 339
   H O 211, 5548, 549, 552
   J L 224, 445

John R ... 317
Judge ... 154
M ... 302, 389
Mary M ... 542
Mr. ... 118
Mrs. ... 530
Rev ... 425, 426
Susan ... 123
T A R ... 4, 118, 152, 153, 154, 156, 161, 429, 430, 470, 476, 486, 530, 545
T A R Jr. ... 541
T A R, bio ... 487, 488
Rev Thomas H ... 424, 425, 426, 583
William ... 435
NEMTOOYAH ... 90
NETHERLAND, John ... 155
NEW KNOXVILLE BREWING COMPANY ... 219
NEW GREY CEMETERY ... 583
NEW MARKET
   TN ... 342, 587
   Civil War ... 163
NEW ORLEANS, LA ... 151, 228, 272
NEW YORK, NY ... 92, 118, 187, 189, 191, 197, 224, 286, 327, 407
NEW YORK CLINIC ... 518
NEW YORK COUNTY MEDICAL ASSOCIATION ... 519
NEW YORK HOSPITAL ... 519
NEW YORK POST-GRADUATE HOSPITAL ... 519
NEWARK, NJ ... 407
NEWBERN, TN ... 379
NEWBERRY, Rev. W Wisdom ... 446
NEWCOMER, M. M. ... 456
NEWELL, Samuel ... 54
NEWHOUSE, Lewis ... 49
NEWMAN
   Alderman ... 105
   C S ... 365, 392, 397
   Clifford L ... 372, 374, 375
   D ... 120
   J E ... 561
   Jacob ... 527

    James 158
    Rev 433
    S B & Co 248
    Samuel B 105, 106, 527
    Tazewell 151
    William 120
NEWMAN & MAXWELL BUILDERS 102
NEWPORT
    Rev Richard 423
    TN 38, 225, 508, 533
NEWSPAPERS
    Brownlow's Knoxville Whig 155, 319
    Brownlow's Tennessee Whig 319
    Brownlow's Whig, publication suspended 323
    Brownlow's Whig and Rebel Ventilator 325
    Clarksville Chronicle 576
    Democratic 319, 329, 333
    First 311
    First daily 311
    First tri-weekly 318
    The Age 336
    The American Union 333
    The Argus 319
    The Chattanooga Commercial 331
    The Chattanooga Daily Times 443
    The Chattanooga Gazette 333
    The Chattanooga News 337
    The Chicago Democrat 333
    The Chilhowee Echo 343
    The Chronicle 326, 330, 332, 335
    The Citizen 327
    The Daily Commercial 330
    The Daily Herald 333
    The Dispatch 336
    The East Tennessean 329
    The Enquirer 317
    The Herald 332, 333
    The Holston Christian Advocate 338, 340, 343
    The Holston Epworth Methodist 338

The Holston Messenger 338, 339
The Independent 343
The Journal 164
The Journal & Tribune 336, 343
The Knoxville Argus 47, 328
The Knoxville Chronicle 334, 335
The Knoxville Daily and Weekly Chronicle 326
The Knoxville Daily Tribune 335
The Knoxville Gazette 46, 47, 51, 57, 58, 59, 60, 72, 74,
 .... 75, 81, 82, 83 84, 85, 86, 93, 312, 313
The Knoxville Independent 343
The Knoxville Journal 332, 334, 335
The Knoxville Journal & Tribune 335
The Knoxville Journal and Tribune consolidation 336
The Knoxville Mercury 329
The Knoxville Post 318
The Knoxville Press 332
The Knoxville Press & Herald 332
The Knoxville Register 65, 314, 316, 318, 328, 336
The Knoxville Republican 331, 332
The Knoxville Sentinel 312, 336
The Knoxville Times 316, 318
The Knoxville Tribune 333, 335, 336, 337, 576
The Knoxville Whig 155, 319, 320, 321, 322, 323, 324, 325, 326, 329,
 .... 330, 335, 341
The Messenger 332, 33
The Methodist Advocate-Journal 338, 343
The Methodist Episcopalian 340
The Midland Methodist 338
The Monroe Democrat 336
The Nashville American 576
The Nashville Christian Advocate 340
The Nashville Republican Banner 316
The Nation [Dublin] 327
The Plebian 319
The Post 319
The Presbyterian Witness 341
The Press & Herald 333, 336
The Press and Messenger 332, 333

    The Register 313, 315, 317
    Republican 317, 330, 335
    The Republican 317, 318
    The Republican-Chronicle 331
    The Richmond Examiner 328
    The Saint Louis Advocate 339
    The Sentinel 343
    The Southern Citizen 327, 328
    The Southern Chronicle 329
    The Standard 319
    The Times 318
    The Tribune 328, 333, 334, 335
    The Uncle Sam 318
    The Union and American 316
    The Western Armenian and Christian Instructor 339
    The Western Monitor 341
    The Whig 317
    The Whig and Chronicle 326, 331
    The Witness 342
        Wilson's Gazette 313
NEWTON W F 570
NICHOLAS, D. D. 243
NICHOLSON
    A O P 484
    A O P Death date 470
    Hunter 363, 365, 366, 370
NICKELL, F B 160
NICKERSON, Rev Allen 439
NICKOJACK 76
NICOLL, Edward 221
NIGHT WATCHMEN 95
NINE MILE CREEK 55
NINNIE, Louis 532
NINTH WARD 304
NINTH WARD SCHOOL 406
NISONGER, James A 203
NOBLE, W S 385
NOEL, O F 224
NOLLICHUCKY CIRCUIT 421

NOLLICHUCKY RIVER 33
NORFOLK, VA 27, 353
NORTH CAROLINA 31, 32, 34, 35, 37, 38, 56, 57, 182, 188, 253, 347, 349,
. . . . 416, 417, 467, 473
   Ceded Tennessee Territory to U S 42, 43, 87
   General Assembly 344, 466
   Statutes of 497
NORTH CAROLINA STATE GAZETTE 41
NORTH KNOXVILLE 130, 132, 135, 139 140, 141, 142, 143, 144
   Boundaries 140
   History of 139
NORTH KNOXVILLE CORPORATION 307
NORTH KNOXVILLE MISSION SUNDAY SCHOOL 450
NORTH KNOXVILLE PUBLIC SCHOOLS 410
NORTHERN, Charles S 293
NORTON, J W 534
NOYES, Prof W A 371
NUNN, D A 373
NUTTY J 444
OAKMAN, W G 286
OATES, E G 255, 260, 429
OCHS, Julius 302, 465, 564
OCOEE DISTRICT 358
OCOEE LAND LAW 495
OCONNOR
   Alderman James 118, 404
   Thomas 158, 255
OCONOSTOTA 31
ODD FELLOWS 262, 507
   East Tennessee Mutual Benefit Association 562
ODELL, Mary 407
OFFICIAL RECORDS OF THE WAR OF THE REBELLION 175
OGDEN
   C H 568
   Edward W 335
   J R 284
   James R 210
   Mary 391
   S R 144

Titus	57, 83
OGLESBY, Joshua	442
OHIO DEAF AND DUMB SCHOOL	539
OHIO STATE CAPITOL	17
OIL MILL	197
OKEEFE, John	159
OLD ABRAHAM	31
OLD GRAY CEMETERY	584
OLD KNOXVILLE	135
OLD POINT COMFORT, VA	523
OLD TASSEL	31, 34
OLDHAM, William	96, 195
OLIVER SPRINGS, TN	188, 283
OLOFSSON, Olof	399
ONEAL, Howard	229
OOLTEWAH JUNCTION	283
OPERA HOUSE	92
OPPENHIEMER, Dr. R P	519, 534
ORAM, Emma Jane	391
ORDER OF CHICAGO, Home Forum benefit	568
ORDER OF CINCINNATI	493
ORE, James	57
ORIENT LODGE #68	563
ORIENTAL LODGE #453	560
ORR, Rev J L	446
OSBORNE	
N. N.	562
R G	567
Mrs. S T	567
OSHEA, J. J.	408
OSSOLI, Margaret Fuller	578
OSSOLI CIRCLE	578
Presidents of	579
OTHERS, Campbell	227
OTTINGER, PC	456
OTTS, Dr. J M P	430, 433
OUTLAW, Alexander	54, 467
OVERTON, John	86, 351, 468, 469
OVERTON COUNTY, TN	15, 19

OVIATT, David B 374
OWEN
  [place] 421
  F A 443
OWENS, John 49
PACE, Rev J K 438, 439
PADGETT, Hazle 385
PAGE, A Sidney 386
PAINE, Thomas, Rights of Man 312
PAINT ROCK 282
PALACE HOTEL 39, 135
PALMER, William 98, 527
PANCOAST
  Joseph 517
  William H 517
PANIC OF 1893 207
PAPER MILL 196
PARHAM
  E N 447
  Rev Robert 451
  Thomas 160
PARK
  Alderman 294
  J Welcher 188
  James 92, 94, 95, 124, 134, 228, 250, 351, 373, 382, 387,
                389, 424, 425, 426, 427, 540, 554, 555, 581, 583, 584, 585
  Mrs. James 543
  Payne Circle 145
  Rev R H 395
  Wallace 228
  William 94, 295, 387, 425
PARK STREET RAILWAY 543
PARK STREET SCHOOL 407
PARK'S CORNER 89
PARKE, Gen John G 164
PARKER
  D W 161
  Harriet A 390
  Henry 551

   Junius 581
   R h 444
   W h 561
   William E 346, 349
PARKS (public) 145
PARRINGTON, John Rivington 313
PARRY, Alderman 296
PARSONS, Capt. 151
PASQUALI OPERA COMPANY 581
PASSAVANT, W A 454
PASTORS UNION 546
PATE, J F 219
PATH DEED 33
PATHS 271
PATRIARCH MILITANT 562
PATRICK
   James 204
   William 204
PATTEN, J E 301, 302
PATTERSON
   A J 554
   A P 224
   J W 330
   M L 304, 275
   Mr. 253
PATTERSON BLOCK 258
PATTERSON'S HALL 430, 450. 463
PATTISON, William 442
PATTON
   James O 138
   Owen W 338
   Samuel 340, 341, 444
PAULETT, John W 338, 373, 541
PAXTON
   Dr. 503, 560
   James W 527
   John 156
   John W 98, 503, 559, 560
   Mrs. 541

PAYNE
- J K 362, 389
- Rev J R 338
- John K 362, 389, 403, 590
- R 109
- Rev R A 452
- R S 235, 254, 305, 554
- R S & Company 234
- R S, Jar 236
- Reuben N 235, 571
- Reuben S 125
- Simpson 150
- William B 365

PAYNE CIRCLE PARK 145
PEABODY FUND 403
PEABODY LODGE 564
PEABODY SCHOOL 404, 406
PEACE COMMANDERY #1 .... 565, 567
PEARCE
- Rev I A 448
- Dr. M B 533

PEARL CHAPTER #24 560
PEARNE, Rev Thomas H 325
PEARSON, George 530
PEASE, B L 207
PEATROSS, R W 397
PECK
- Adam 49, 72
- Judge 495

PEED, Mrs. T J 547
PEERY, Rev. R B 456
PENDERGAST, J C 444
PENLAND, Rev N A 388
PENNEBAKER 170
PENNSYLVANIA 224, 417, 457
PENNSYLVANIA IRISH 416, 17
PENSION EXAMINING BOARD 517

PENSIONS	180
Money paid	182
Statistics	181
PEOPLES TELEPHONE COMPANY	225
PEOPLES' BANK	253
PERICLES OF TENNESSEE	42
PERKINS	
A K	575
Charles A	383
Mrs. Charles A	193, 383, 579
Nicholson	49
W T	253
PERPETUAL BUILDING & LOAN ASSOCIATION	263
PERRY	296
Alderman	294
Rev J W	449
R B	456
William C	294, 295, 296, 571
PETERS, George W	144, 214, 437, 587
PETERS-BRADLEY MILL	214
PETTIE, Thomas	451
PETTY, Rev John S	338, 447
PHAGAN, John	150
PHELAN [James, Historian]	51, 422
PHELPS, Edwin	304
PHILADELPHIA	
Debate in	322
PA	45, 57, 62, 72, 118, 226, 263, 271, 407, 480
PHILADELPHIA CHARITY COLLEGE	516
PHILADELPHIA THEOLOGICAL SEMINARY	455
PHILIP, Francis	243
PHILLIPS	
George M	301
W P	334
PHILSON, L W	365
PHOENIX BUILDING	248
PHOENIX LODGE #14	564
PHOENIX MARBLE COMPANY	215

PHYSICIANS
  City 113, 518
  West Knoxville City 518
PIAMINGO 85
PICKENS, William C 161
PIERCE, Rev I A 463
PIGEON, Rev Charles D 426
PIKE COMMISSIONERS 273
PIKES . . . . see 'streets'
PILLOW, Gen 151
PINKERTON, Emma 396
PIONEER COUNCIL #34 564
PIPER
  A M 125
  James H 353, 358
PITMAN
  Mrs. A M 580
  Charles 205
PITNER
  J H 406
  John M 220
  William A 220
PITTSBURG, PA 229, 395, 454
PLANT, A H 289
PLATT, J E 409
PLOTS, error in 93
PLUMB, Charles S 372, 373, 374, 375, 376
POE
  J N 561
  O M 165, 166, 167 170, 171
POLAND, Brig Gen J S, bio 190
POLICE 120
  Arresting of 307
POLICE CHIEF 120
POLICE MATRON 545, 576, 580
POLK
  James K 150, 314
  Gen Lucius E 367
POLK COUNTY, TN 13, 16

POLL TAX 140
POLLARD, E A 174
PONTOON BRIDGE 164
POOR, Henry 286
POOR VALLEY 14, 15
POOR'S RAILWAY MANUAL 284, 285, 287, 288, 289
POPE, W C 449
POPLAR CREEK COAL & IRON COMPANY 242
POPLAR SPRING a.k.a. Rocky Spring 347, 351
POPULATION
    Blacks in Knoxville 137
    Of Knoxville 137
    Scholastic 412
    West Knoxville 145
POPULATION CENSUS 77
    1795 90
PORT HUDSON 169
PORT ROYAL 27
PORTER
    J. J. 395
    James D 367, 382
    Joseph A 565, 575
    R 410
PORTO RICO 189
POST
    Mrs. Frank 548
    Frank H 202
    Frank H & Company 202
    S T 202
    S T & Son 202
POST & KELLER 202
POST MASTERS 136
POST OFFICE 107
POST, SIMMONS & COMPANY 202
POST-GRADUATE DEGREES 370
POSTAL SERVICE 58, 229
POSTMASTER 58
POTTER, Gen 164
POUND, J B 247, 336, 337

POWDER SPRINGS 293
POWELL
  Aaron M 580
  Columbus 233, 269, 536
  George L 105
  Samuel 468, 472
  Thomas J 124
POWELL STATION 218
POWELL'S RIVER 293
POWERS
  J Pike 257, 438
  S T 294
POWERS, LITTLE & COMPANY 235
POWERS, LITTLE & McCORMICK 235
PRENTISS, Rev. L E 448, 450
PRESBYTERIAN, settlers 317
PRESBYTERIAN CHURCH, controversy 420
PRESBYTERIAN CHURCH, General Assembly of 434
PRESBYTERIAN CIRCUITS 421
PRESBYTERIAN IRISH 417
PRESBYTERIANS 79, 80, 419, 423, 462
PRESBYTERY OF ABINGDON 419
PRESBYTERY OF HOLSTON 434
PRESBYTERY OF KNOXVILLE 430
PRESIDENT, DIRECTORS & CO .. BANK OF THE STATE OF TENN, act .. 250
PRESTON
  Frank 572
  George K 570
PRICE
  Abram J 222, 445
  Hannah 577, 578
  Dr. J L 513
  Rev. Richard N 188, 337, 338
  Thomas R 222, 268
  William N 160
PRICE CONTROLS 102
PRICHARD, M B 241
PRINCE EDWARD COUNTY, VA 419
PRINCE'S HALL 461

PRINTING PRESS 82
PRISON 56
PROBST, Rev L K 456
PROCTOR COAL COMPANY 243
PROFFITT, Calloway 532
PROHIBITION 576
PROSSER
   A S 569
   Mrs. L B 234
PROTECTION FIRE INSURANCE COMPANY 268
PROVISIONAL DEPARTMENT OF TENNESSEE AND GEORGIA 569
PROVOST, Mrs. 530
PROVOST MARSHALL 256
PRUDENTIAL LIFE INSURANCE COMPANY 519
PRYNE, Rev Abram 322
PRYOR, Joseph 444
PRYSE, Rev Dr W S 458
PUBLIC HIGHWAY 281
PUBLIC LIBRARY, established 541
PUBLIC PRINTER, established 75
PUBLIC WORKS, Board of 120
PULASKI, TN 373, 379, 382, 511
PURDY, W G 396
PURPLE
   Capt 185
   Fred R 568
   W H 184, 185
PUTNAM, W C 561
PUTNAM COUNTY, TN 19
QUAKER RELIGION 414
QUAKER SETTLEMENT 291
QUAKERS 416, 418
QUARANTINE, State 531
QUARLES, R 150
QUARRIES 17
QUEEN CITY LODGE 563
QUINCY, M 203
QUINCY CARRIAGE COMPANY 203
RACOON MOUNTAIN 15

RADEMACHER, Rt Rev Joseph 441
RAGSDALE
    E L 214
    J F 214
    W B 214, 305
RAHT, J E 254
RAILROAD, bond issue 100
RAILROAD ACCIDENT, Flat Creek 294
RAILROAD DEPOT 99
RAILROADS 12, 22, 136, 249, 281, 478, 479
    Bonds for 278
    Destruction of 163
    Development of 278
    See also name of individual railroad
RALEIGH, NC 272
RALSTON, Charles A 465
RAMAGE
    E C 184, 186, 187
    Samuel C 332
    William J 246, 248, 332, 333, 569
RAMSEY
    Francis A 38, 102, 345, 348, 386, 442, 506, 527
    Dr Frank A 503, 504, 529, 531, 533
    G B 158
    James Gettys McGready 46, 419, 421, 423, 480, 491, 504, 505, 506 533
    Jennie B 411
    Reynolds 506
    Samuel g 386, 424, 490
    William B A 95, 124, 314, 462, 474, 475, 506
RAMSEY'S ANNALS OF TENNESSEE 506
RANDALL
    E L 396, 534
    Gen G M 191
RANDOLPH, Rev J W 452
RANKIN, George C 444
RANSOM, Gen 174
RAPID TRANSIT COMPANY 305, 306
RAY, Mr. 435

RAYL
    Jesse Addison 118, 254, 269, 401, 402, 403, 405, 406, 574, 575
    Jesse Addison School 407
    Jesse Addison, bio 314
RAYL & BOYD 106
RAYL & TAYLOR 413
RAYL & VANUXEM 412
READY, Judge Charles 484
REAMS, M J 445
RECORDER
    City 97, 98
    First 94
RED ASH JELLICO COAL 243
RED CROSS SOAP 217
REDDEN, Samuel 562
REED
    Rev C J 439
    E A 242, 561
    J. J. 244
    Mary L 567
    Rev S B 392
REEDER, Alexander 294
REESE
    James 54, 55, 82, 467
    William B 4, 102, 359, 373, 389, 469, 474, 481, 559, 583
    William B, bio 498
REEVE
    F A 104
    Rev John B 434
    Rev 434
REEVES, Hart 187
REGISTER OF DEEDS 51
RELIEF LODGE #163 563
RELIGIONS, settlers 417
RENSHAW, James H 175
REPUBLIC LIFE INSURANCE COMPANY 269
RESCUE MISSION 545
RESERVOIR 114
RESERVOIR HILL 130

REVIEWERS [THE], Gazette correspondents 82
REVISAL OF STATUES OF TENNESSEE 497
REVOLUTIONARY WAR 32, 33, 35, 37, 42, 477
REYNOLDS, God John 80
RHEA
    Archibald 428
    Archibald Sr. 424
    Ellen 547
    John 49, 54, 55, 347, 467
    John L 429, 554
    Robert M 218, 219, 227, 257, 269, 305, 308
RHEA COUNTY, TN 13, 19, 152, 155, 250, 469
RHEA VS RHEA 481
RHOADES, George T 460
RHODE, W O 225
RICE
    Charles A 341
    James 348
    W A 363
RICHARD, Rev John 439
RICHARDS
    A T 212
    D 208
    D C 244
    D C & Sons 212
    David 200, 208, 210, 269, 456
    David C 212
    J 208
    Joseph 209, 210, 456, 457
    M V 290
    Richard 442, 443
    Roger P 212
    Sarah M Harvey 523
    W P 212
    William 208
    William H 523, 525
    William J 457
    William M 523

RICHARDSON
    Annie 544
    Rev Rank 338, 446
    Mrs. J G 579
    James 49
    Rev John 439
    Mary 544
    Rev. Dr 446
    W L 338, 462
RICHMOND
    F C 241, 243, 245, 565, 567
    VA 58, 161, 328, 483, 487
RICHMOND & DANVILLE RAILWAY 283, 286
RICHMOND COLLEGE 519
RICKARD, William 59, 60, 84, 85
RICKS, A J 330
RIDGE, Thomas 586, 587
RIDGE REGION 10
RIDGELY ENCAMPMENT #1 562
RIDLEY, J. J. 360
RIFLE PITS 171
RIFLES, Krag-Jorgensen 191
RIGHT, Police Matron 545
RILEY, Rev John R 435
RINGGOLD
    Rev S. S. 453
    Mrs. Samuel 543, 544
RISTINE
    Charles E 514, 534
    J C 514, 561
    Susan Elliott 514
RITTER, Petter [sic] 263
RIVER FERRIES 55
RIVERSIDE SCHOOL 410
ROAD COMMISSIONERS 273
ROAD IMPROVEMENTS 141, 145
ROADS 41, 294
    Macadamization 273
    Public 95

See also 'Streets'
  Toll 273
  Turnpike 273
ROADS & HIGHWAYS 55
ROADY, P D 569
ROANE
  Archibald 4, 54, 55, 80, 82, 345, 348, 467, 468, 469, 480
  Archibald, bio 476
ROANE COUNTY, TN 13, 17, 19, 22, 250, 348, 469, 483, 487
ROANE IRON COMPANY 208
ROANE MOUNTAIN 345
ROBARDS, Rev Israel 436
ROBERTS
  Bishop 443
  E C 160
  G W 147, 248
  J C 451
  J G 160
  James 389
  John 159
  Lewis P 136
  O T 140, 142, 564
  R Z 145, 206
  Samuel 531
  T P 142
  Rev Thomas 364
  Mrs. W L 547
  Walter S 548
ROBERTSON
  Charles A 385, 466
  G C 562
  James 30, 37, 41, 51, 87, 417, 466
  R D 405
ROBINET, Rev J. J. 451
ROBINSON
  Charles E 118
  D C 562
  W B 238
  W C 159

Index - 133

Y K	562
ROCK FORMATIONS	15, 16, 17, 18
ROCKFORD, TN	164
ROCKWOOD, TN	187
ROCKY SPRING, a.k.a. Poplar Spring	347, 351
RODDY, John	532
RODDYE, James	72

RODGERS
- Alderman . . . 100
- Annie Patton . . . 507
- James . . . 136, 137, 138
- Dr James . . . 429, 503, 507, 529, 561
- S A . . . 472
- S R . . . 474
- Samuel R . . . 488
- Thomas . . . 294, 507

ROEHL, A O . . . 406
ROGAN, L H . . . 560

ROGERS
- Rev Elijah . . . 423
- Dr Fayette . . . 92
- Jesse L . . . 186, 258
- John . . . 324
- Dr M L . . . 529
- S A . . . 304
- S R . . . 88, 89, 100, 152, 474, 475
- Dr W A . . . 153
- W M . . . 406, 410
- William H . . . 152, 447

ROGERSVILLE, TN . 51, 56, 57, 58, 234, 312, 315, 347, 379, 382, 474, 481, 498
ROLLER, mill machinery . . . 199
ROMAN CATHOLIC CHURCH . . . 321
ROMAN CATHOLICS . . . 440
ROME, GA . . . 71, 283
ROMINE, Mrs. . . . 579

RONEY
- Sam C Shoe Company . . . 238
- Samuel C . . . 233, 237, 401, 402, 460, 545, 548
- Mrs. Samuel C . . . 575

RONEY, ARNOLD & COMPANY 238
ROOSEVELT
   [Theodore] 52
   Theodore, quote 76
ROOT, John Cullen 570
ROSE
   D M & Company 220
   Daniel M 220
   James G 257
   Thomas H 220
ROSE AVENUE SCHOOL 410
ROSEBURY CREEK 427
ROSECRANS, Gen 169
ROSENTHAL, D A 258
ROSS
   Albert M 573
   Alderman 294
   Charles C 391
   D L 214, 411, 412
   Mrs. D L 547
   Mrs. David 580
   Elmer D 225
   Rev Frederick A 320, 339
   George W 107, 129, 204, 269, 304
   John M 205
   M L & Co 248
   M L & Company 229, 230, 231
   Martin L 129, 144, 146, 230, 231, 247, 255, 262, 263, 548, 551
   Martin L, photograph 226
   W F 534
ROTACH, John 248
ROTH
   George W 561
   Joseph 531
   L G 532
ROTHMANN, A. A. 220
ROULSTONE, George 49, 50, 51, 58, 75, 82, 83, 93, 136, 312, 313, 345
ROULSTONE & COMPANY 58, 312
ROUNDTREE, John T 575

ROWAN, Andrew S 188, 192
ROWAN COUNTY, NC 39
ROWLEY, M 388
ROY & ARMSTRONG 212
ROYAL ARCANUM 564
ROYAL ARCH MASONS 560
RUBLE, J A 451, 566
RUCKER'S LEGION 508
RUFF
    Col., death of 173
    Col. 176
RUHM, John 587
RULE
    Alida 544, 579
    James F 334
    Lida 581
    William 106, 112, 125, 135, 136, 161, 181, 193, 264, 284,
    . . . . 326, 330, 331, 332, 334, 355, 382, 409, 447, 448, 529, 548,
    . . . . 549, 554, 575, 581, 586, 587
RULE & MARFIELD 334
RULE & RICKS 330
RUMNEY, Rev R P 439, 440
RUNKLE, William 118, 119
RUNNING WATER (Indian town) 76
RUSSELL
    Thomas H 447
    W L 219
RUSSELLVILLE, TN 413, 516
RUTH, Albert 363, 365, 401, 405
RUTHERFORD
    Anna 396
    C 160, 258
    Griffith 75
    Nancy S 530
RUTHERFORD & WHITE 194
RUTHERFORD COUNTY, NC 491
RUTHERFORD EXPEDITION 34
RUTHERFORDTON, NC 272
RUTLEDGE, TN 275

RYAN
- Father Abram J 440, 441
- Father M J 441
- Thomas F 287

SABBATH, Observation of 110
SADDLER SHOP 194
SADDLERS 195
SAFFORD, James Merrill 10, 11, 18, 20, 23
SAINT JOHNS ORPHANAGE 543
SAINT LOUIS, MO 228
SAINT MARY RIVER 74
SAINT TAMMANY LODGE #1 556
SALARIES 412
SALEM CONGREGATION 334, 419
SALISBURY, NC 59, 272
SALISBURY DISTRICT 466
SALMON, W H 132, 144
SALMUN, W H 147
SALOONS 104
SALT, Rev. T W 451
SALTMARSH, Rev Seth 464
SAMPSON, Capt. 183
SAMUEL
- D R 221, 260, 304
- W B 221

SAMUELS, E 465
SAN ANTONIO, TX 263
SAN JUAN 189
SAN JUAN DE ULLOA 151
SANDERS,
- W D, Jr. 240
- W D 451
- W P Camp, Sons of veterans 569
- William H 188
- Gen William P 162, 163, 164, 165, 166, 167
- Gen William P, bio 178
- Gen William P, death of 166, 170, 178
- Gen William P, Kentucky Division 170
- Gen William P, site where mortal wound occurred 177

SANDUSKY, Frederick R 385
SANFORD
   Alfred F 219, 335
   E J & Company 232
   Edward J 114, 210, 216, 219, 242, 254, 255, 269, 286, 335,
                               336, 373, 382, 392, 405, 406, 504, 527
   Edward T 131, 351, 355, 356, 357, 382, 383, 384, 553
   Emma 544
   Herbert C 568
   McMinn County 216
   William 373
SANFORD, CHAMBERLAIN & ALBERS COMPANY 232
SAULPAW, George W 303
SAUNDERS
   E H 129
   William C 552
SAUNDERS & CLARK 325
SAVAGE, W J 199
SAVAGE & TYLER 199
SAVILLE, Rev W A 451
SAVINGS, BUILDING, & LOAN ASSOCIATION 262
SAWYER, W F 263
SAWYERS
   John 386
   Sue Brownlow 521
SAXTON, H N Jr. 221
SAXTON & COMPANY 221
SAXTON TRACT 123
SAYLOR, J W 125
SCAGGINS, Henry 30
SCAGGS, E C 409, 410
SCALES, Alderman 114, 115
SCARBROUGH, J H 264
SCATES, George R 223, 224
SCATES FURNACE COMPANY 223, 224
SCHAIDT, Rev. J George 455
SCHARRINGHAUS, E H 264
SCHENK, Herman 132
SCHEUERMANN, L W 562

SCHMALZRIED, O	239
SCHMIDT, R	294
SCHMITT, Cooper D	377, 383, 456
SCHOLASTIC POPULATION	412
SCHOOL BUTTER	497
SCHOOLS	409, 410
Black	540
Black children	426
Catholic	404
First in Tennessee	344
Girls	404
Girls High School	391, 588
Public	402, 404
SCHRADER, C Gustavo	221
SCHUBERT, H	294
SCHUBERTS HOTEL	571
SCHWAB, A	589
SCHWAN, L M	284, 286
SCHWARTZ, L	465
SCIENCE AND HEALTH, WITH THE KEY TO THE SCRIPTURES	465
SCOTCH JIMMY	252
SCOTCH-IRISH	79, 416, 419
SCOTT	
A G	144, 15, 146, 461, 462, 540
David D	214
Edward	472, 494, 557
Edward, bio	497
Frank A R	197, 213, 214, 372, 382
J F	186, 534
James	196, 214, 583
James, Mill	213
Nancy	79
S H	451
Rev T S	429, 432
Gen Winfield	151, 320
SCOTT BROTHERS & COMPANY	214
SCOTT COUNTY, TN	15, 19, 241
SCOTT MILL COMPANY	214
SCOTT, DEMPSTER & COMPANY	213

SCOTTISH CAROLINA TIMBER & LAND COMPANY 220
SCRUGGS, A D 258, 515, 534
SEARLE
  C W 449
  G W 144
  W F 243
SEATON, Joel 446
SEAV, William F 137
SEAY
  George W 385
  Thomas L 304
  William F 138
SECESSION 152, 322
  Counties 155
  Opposition to 153
  Voting results 154
SECOND CREEK 39, 50, 98, 99, 105, 108, 109, 121, 122, 144,
.... 146, 165, 166, 167, 171, 194, 195, 196, 197, 199, 211, 249, 300
SECOND WAR FOR INDEPENDENCE 140
SECRETARY OF WAR 43
SEDDEN, James B 532
SEDGWICK BUILDING 225
SELBY, J D 296
SELDEN, Mrs. A K 544
SELMA, ROME, AND DALTON RAILROAD LINE 283
SEMINOLE WAR 150
SENN, Mathew 220
SENTER
  Gov. D W C 476
  W T 444
SEQUATCHIE COUNTY, TN 13, 19
SETZEPAND, Albert 363
SEVEN ISLANDS, French Broad River 443
SEVIER
  E F 444, 528
  John 31, 40, 63, 69, 70, 71, 75, 86, 87, 91,l 345, 348,
.... 417, 466, 476, 477, 480, 555, 557
  John Jr. 54
  John, Memorial 553, 554

John, School 406
William R 284
SEVIER COUNTY, TN 13, 220, 325, 348, 469, 493, 524
SEVIER FAMILY, fever in 526
SEVIER MEMORIAL, Nashville 553
SEVIER MEMORIAL COMMISSION 552
SEVIER MONUMENT, inscription 555
SEVIERVILLE, TN 225
SEWER ENGINEER, Office of 122
SEWERS 112, 120, 122, 123
   West Knoxville 145
SEXTON 123
SEYMOUR, Charles 299, 400, 401
Shackleford
   Gen J M 164
   J O 469
SHAIFER, Abraham K 557
SHAKESPEARE CLUB 400
SHARP, Dr. S P 525
SHARPSHOOTERS 171
SHAWNEES 29, 61
SHEA, John 134, 142
SHEETS, Frank 532
SHELBY, Isaac 417
SHELBY COUNTY, TN 280
SHELBYVILLE, TN 382, 511
SHENANDOAH COUNTY, VA 314
SHEPARD
   Edward S 269, 538
   L C 106, 109, 200, 208, 246, 561
SHEPARD, LEEDS & HOYT 197
SHEPERD, P B 569
SHEPHERD & SHELESS 252
SHEPPARD
   E S 269
   S W 562
SHERIDAN, Richard B 203
SHERIDAN & QUINCY 202

SHERMAN
  David A 352, 387, 388
  Gen William T 168, 174
SHETTERLY, ham 530
SHIELDS
  J S 230
  J T Jr. 257
  James T 367
  John 241
  M L 571
  Rev 439
  Roscoe 532
  William S 132, 257, 260, 264, 307, 308
SHIELDS BROTHERS 231
SHIELDSTOWN 351, 589
SHILOH 169
SHINN, Rev O H 463
SHIPMAN, R. R. 212
SHOEMAKERS 195
SHORT MOUNTAIN 15
SIDEWALKS 101
SIENKNECHT, J T 222
SIFFORD, W R 385
SIGLER, Rhoda 449, 450
SIGSBEE, Capt. 183
SILER, J W 243
SILK WORMS 57
SILSBY & COMPANY 106
SILSBY ENGINE 132
SILVER LEAF, flour 213
SIMMONDS, W H 144, 217, 218, 263, 264, 304, 305, 409
SIMMONS
  C N 202
  W H 304
SIMPSON
  Ralph 532
  Ruth 532
SINCLAIR, John G 369
SINKING CREEK 271

SIX NATIONS 29
SKATE'S FURNACE BUILDINGS 212
SKILLMAN, Mrs. M 578
SLACK, John 338
SLATER TRAINING SCHOOL 400, 401, 409
SLAVERY 87, 101, 110, 152
  Knoxville 328
SLOCUM
  J W 399
  Mrs. J W 580
SLOVER, Samuel L 335
SMALL, William 49
SMALL POX 29, 527, 531, 532
SMALLPOX HOSPITAL 112
SMITH
  Alexander 348
  Alexander W 293
  B L 231, 259
  Bartow 219
  Burton 159
  D A 120, 561
  Daniel 59, 71, 345
  David L 456
  Gen E Kirby 162, 585
  Eliza 532
  Frank M 372
  Prof Frank M 378
  George H 269
  Guy 150
  Henry G 469
  Henry L 293
  J 534
  J Allen 215, 247
  Jackson 258
  James 30, 49
  James H 159, 416
  John C 587
  Nathaniel 150, 281
  O T 125

Dr R C	533
Rev Richard M	464
S H	138, 372, 373, 436, 473
S N	374
Simon	532
Thomas	49
Thomas A	160
Victor L	293
W B	233
W I	294
W P	144, 145
SMITH & BONDURANT	231
SMITH, HUDDLESTON, POWERS & COMPANY	235
SMITHWOOD	274
SMOKER	533
SMOKY MOUNTAINS	18
SNAPP, J K	150
SNEED	
J W	135
John L T	470
Joseph W	123, 139, 143, 295, 299, 473, 476, 485
William Henry	4, 481, 485
William Henry, bio	484
SNEEDVILLE, TN	587
SNOODY, Dr	533
SNODGRASS, D L	470, 471
SNOW, Rev J H	439
SNYDER, Gen Simon	191
SOCIAL LIFE	84
SOCIN & COMPANY	552
SOIL	10
SOLOMON, J	589
SOMERVILLE	
James	574
Mr.	334
SOMMERVILLE, John & Company	57
SONS OF VETERANS	569
SORREL, Lt. Col. Moxley	176
SOULE, A M	383, 386

SOUTH CAROLINA 32, 33, 34, 168, 174, 182, 300, 340
SOUTH CAROLINA MILITARY ACADEMY 373, 374
SOUTH KNOXVILLE 222
SOUTHERN [R R] CAR SHOPS 131
SOUTHERN AND WESTERN THEOLOGICAL SEMINARY 428
SOUTHERN BUILDING & LOAN ASSOCIATION 262, 570
SOUTHERN CAR COMPANY 199
SOUTHERN DENTAL ASSOCIATION 523
SOUTHERN HOME BUILDING & LOAN ASSOCIATION, Atlanta 264
SOUTHERN HOMEOPATHIC MEDICAL ASSOCIATION 521
SOUTHERN JOURNAL OF MEDICAL AND PHYSICAL SCIENCES 327
SOUTHERN PACIFIC RAILWAY 519
SOUTHERN RAILWAY 196, 217, 223, 245, 283, 284, 286, 287,
. . . . 289, 290, 517, 548
   Mileage 288
SOUTHERN RAILWAY SHOPS 131, 190
SOUTHERN TRUNK COMPANY 217, 218
SOUTHWEST POINT 38
SOUTHWEST TERRITORY 41, 42, 47
SOUTHWESTERN CHRISTIAN ADVOCATE 339
SPALDING
   Eugene C 293
   William T 293
SPANISH-AMERICAN WAR 148, 182, 183, 184, 517
   Mustering Out 193
   Reception 193
   Volunteer Camp 309
SPANISH-AMERICAN WAR RECEPTION, Chilhowee Park 188
SPARKS, J W 373
SPARROW, Rev C B 448
SPARTA, TN 474
SPENCE
   Cary F 188
   John F 391, 447
   Shirley E 188
SPENCER, Samuel 286, 287, 289, 290
SPERRY, J Austin 317
SPIESBERGER, Jacob 589
SPILMAN, L H 129

SPINNING	195
SPINNING FACTORIES	195
SPIRO, J	465
SPREEN, J H	239
SPRINGS - see individual names	
SQUOLLECUTTAH	90
STAFFORD, Prof	10, 11, 18, 20, 23
STAGE COACH	
Fares	272
Travel	272
STAHLMAN, Maj. E B	331
STALEY, W B	475
STANDARD COAL & COKE	245
STANDARD HANDLE COMPANY	221
STANFIELD, A	150
STANSBERRY, Josie	411
STATEHOOD, vote for	91
STATUTES OF TENNESSEE, "Revisal" of	497
STAUB	
Jacob	147
Peter	115, 116, 118, 119, 125, 129, 262, 445, 589
STAUB & COMPANY	106
STAUBS THEATER	545
STEAM DRILLS	204
STEAM FIRE ENGINE	132
STEAMBOAT	
"Atlas"	277
"Atlas" (first at Knoxville)	276
"Bill Tate"	278
"Buena Ventura"	185
"Cassandra"	277
"Chattanooga"	277
"City of Knoxville"	278
"Dixie"	278
"Flora Swan"	278
"guide"	228
"Harkaway"	229
"Holston"	241
"Kate Fleming"	277

"Knoxville" 277
"Lady Augusta" 277
"Lucile Borden" 278
"Mollie Garth" 277
"Oliver King" 278
"Onega" 278
"Telephone" 278
STEAMBOATS
  List of 278
  Statistics 276
STEARNS, Cora M 391
STEELE
  C W 260
  John N 308
STEERE, A H 240
STEIN, Albert 96
STEPHENS
  J. Bunyan 368, 384
  Rev J V 432
STEPHENSON
  B J 109, 111, 138
  C T 206, 448
  Matthew 347
  R J 562
  T I 210
  W R 561
STERCHI
  J C 125, 147, 236
  J G 236
STERCHI BROTHERS 236
STERCHI BROTHERS BLOCK 248
STERN
  Edward 589
  Isaac 589
  Moses 589
STETSON
  C E, telegram 586
  F L 287
  Francis Lynde 286, 289

STEVENS, Bishop Colonel 575
STEVENSON, R J 221
STEWART
    LG A P 169
    Rev Henry W 461
    Jackson L 203
    Rev Robert 461
STEWART COLLEGE, Clarksville, TN 426
STINE, L H 460
STOCKS 56
STOKELY, J E 188
STONE
    John 49, 54, 76, 243
    Winthrop 375
STONE'S TAVERN 89
STOREY, Albert 532
STOURBRIDGE, Lion 278
STOVE FACTORY 197
STRAWVERRY PLAINS, Civil War 163
STREET CARS 303
STREETS 88, 92, 95, 98
    6th Ave 204, 217
    Academy 108, 109
    Alexander 411
    Altavia 145
    Arthur 461
    Asylum 144, 146, 211, 304, 438, 451, 452, 461, 538
    Atkin 200, 443, 457, 458
    Beaver Ridge Pike 274
    Bell Ave 304, 306, 434, 543
    Bertrand 434
    17th street 207
    Boundary 105, 424
    Brabson Ferry Pike 273, 274
    Branner 133
    Brick 134
    Broad 48, 197, 213, 214, 229, 258, 305, 369, 430, 431,
    . . . . 445, 450, 454, 459, 460, 583
    Broad Ave 214

Broad Street Turnpike 299
Campbell 408
Cavalier 123
Central Ave 43, 92, 203, 229, 239, 258, 304, 305, 306, 407, 440, 546
Chamberlain 212, 219, 222
Cherry 124
Church 88, 95, 146, 195, 201, 218, 228, 249, 363, 404, 407, 444, 447, 453
Churchwell 195
Cleveland 398
Clinch 95, 108, 109, 114, 146, 194, 204, 305, 435, 447, 448 464, 583
Clinton 408, 438, 452
Clinton Pike 131, 166, 214, 274, 299, 393, 584
Clinton Road 170, 299
Cobblestone 134
Coleman 431
College 95
Commerce 39, 132, 135, 225, 235, 237, 238, 248, 389, 452
Commissioners 95
County Road 124
Crooked 88, 94
Crozier 92, 109, 121, 135, 252, 450
Crozier Ave 305
Cumberland 89, 92, 94, 101, 103, 105, 108, 145, 194, 195,
.... 199, 200, 201, 203, 252, 439, 453, 507, 547
Cumberland Ave 145, 305
Cumberland West 464
Dameron 398
Dameron Ave 549
Dandridge Pike 123
Deaderick 406, 438, 451
Depot 135, 222, 241, 307, 460
Dora 408
Eighth 305, 433, 462
Fifth Ave 121, 305, 430, 445, 446, 546
Florida 305, 545, 546
Forest 544
Front 56, 88, 112
Gap Creek Pike 275
Gay 88, 89, 95, 98, 99, 101, 103, 105, 108, 113, 114, 132,

Index - 149

.... 164, 196, 200, 201, 218, 225, 227, 228, 229, 230, 231, 233,
.... 234, 235, 236, 237, 238, 239, 248, 249, 251, 254, 255, 258 259,
.... 277, 303, 304, 305, 398, 404, 407, 413, 424, 453, 461, 526, 542, 584
Gay Street paved 102
Gay, gas lighting 128, 129
Gay, laying of brick 134, 135
Grainger 204
Grand Ave 229
Gratz 410
Hardee 198, 199, 304, 545, 546
Hardin Hill 124
Henley 543
High 396
Highland Ave 305, 396, 410, 432, 446, 462
Hill 132, 133, 550
Hinds Valley Pike 274
Howard 434
Hume 199
Jacksboro 129, 198, 211, 241, 306, 430, 583
Jacksboro Pike 274
Jacksboro Turnpike 140
Jackson 218, 230, 231, 233, 235, 239
Kentucky 408
Kingston Pike 145, 165
Kingston Road 170
Knoxville Turnpike 140
Knoxville, Tazewell & Jacksboro Turnpike 140
Laurel Ave 433
Linden 543
Locust 129, 388, 448, 549
Lowes Ferry Pike 275
Luttrell 431, 450
Mabry 108, 167, 213, 304, 306, 450, 452, 460, 465
Macadamized 101, 139
Main .. 59, 88, 89, 94, 95, 98, 99, 101, 102, 105, 134, 139, 146, 200, 201, 211,
.... 213, 227, 249, 251, 305, 388, 389, 391, 396, 398, 403, 413, 507, 526, 553
Maintenance 101
Market 94
Martins Mill Pike 275

Maryville Pike 273, 275
Maynardville Pike 274
McGhee 219, 222, 437, 452, 457, 460
Middlebrook Pike 274
Middlebrook Street Car Line 207
Morgan 404, 406
Morse 140
Munson 129, 205, 206
Murfreesboro Pike 535
Nelson 123
Neubert Springs Pike 273
North Broad 229
North Fourth Ave 305, 396
Oak 133, 458
Olive 434
Orange 123
Park 189, 407, 461
Park Ave 305, 306
Patton 439, 452
Payne 408, 440
Pearson Ave 140
Pickens Gap Pike 273, 275
Pine 459
Prince 88, 94, 95, 112, 134, 305, 447, 448, 455
Prince Street paved 102
Public Highway 271
Reservoir 389, 452
Ricker 140
River 89
Rose Ave 399
Rutledge Pike 108, 273, 274, 304, 584, 588
Scott 516
Second 544
Seventeenth 207
Sevierville Pike 273, 274, 275
Sharps Gap Pike 274
Sixth Av 204, 217
State 56, 83, 94, 95, 103, 132, 201, 202, 235, 237, 389, 404,
. . . . 406, 424, 452, 547, 550

Strawberry Plains Pike 274
Sutherland Drive Railroad 463
Tax 95
Tazewell Pike 94, 140, 167, 274
Temperance 465
Temple Ave 305
Tennor 411
Third Creek Pike 273, 274
Thorn Grove Pike 274
Tulip 406
Turnpikes 275
Union 39, 241, 248, 254, 260, 455, 542, 549
Union Ave 305
University Ave 207, 305
Vine ... 108, 109, 165, 203, 223, 225, 236, 237, 238, 304, 440, 441, 459, 542
Wall 260, 263
Walnut 88, 94, 404, 407, 440, 441, 450, 453
Washington Pike 274
Water 88, 89, 92, 94, 99, 109, 139
West Boundary 105
West 5th Ave. 446
White 305
Yale Ave 305
York 216
STRICKLAND, Rev C H 436
STRIKES 209
STRINGFIELD, Thomas 339, 340, 443
STRONG 124
  A N 257
  Benjamin Rush 98, 247, 254, 255, 502, 553
  Mrs. Catharine 583
  Joseph Churchill 124, 387, 388, 389, 390, 424, 425, 501, 506
  Joseph Churchill, JR. 502
  Robert Nelson 502
STUART
  Rev George 373
  Thomas 150
STURGIS, Rev F E 429

SULLINS
  David 157, 444, 445
  Timothy 444, 539
SULLIVAN
  Michael D 109, 114, 115, 118
  W B 255
SULLIVAN COUNTY, TN 13, 33, 58, 250, 315, 347, 419, 466
  TN, courthouse 58
SUMMERS
  Alexander 336, 554
  Henry E 374, 375
SUMMIT HILL 225, 404
  Civil war 163
SUMPTER, William D 385
SUN LIFE INSURANCE COMPANY 239
SUNDAY LAW 110
  Exceptions to 111
SUNRISE FLOUR 215
SUPERINTENDENT OF INDIAN AFFAIRS 42
SUPERINTENDENTS OF SCHOOLS, Knoxville 405
SUPERIOR COURT 468, 473
  Hamilton District, Judges 472
  Washington District 40
SUPREME COUNCIL 564
SUPREME COURT 299, 468
SUPREME COURT OF ERRORS AND APPEALS 469
SUPREME LODGE 563
SURGERY [notable] 503
SURRY COUNTY, NC 478
SUSQUEHANNA RIVER, PA 12, 416
SUTHERLAND, Dr. R. R. 429, 434, 463
SWAN
  J D 89, 152
  M D 109
  W H 476
  William 137, 138, 389, 474
  William G 102, 103, 124, 327, 328, 472
SWANN, James 286
SWEETWATER, TN 336, 430

SWEPSON, R. R. 129, 211, 230, 233, 236, 253, 554
SWIFT, Richard 421
SWISS, Railroad Laborers 283
SYCAMORE CAMP 570
SYKES, Adj. Gen. 185
SYNAGOGUES
    Beth-el Congregation (reformed) 464
    Beth-el Congregation 590
    Haske Hamuna Congregation (Orthodox Hebrew) 465
SYNOD OF NORTH CAROLINA 420
T HAWS & COMPANY 16
TADLOCK, A B 113, 517, 534
TAILORS 58
TALLADEGA, Battle of 149
TALLAPOOSA RIVER 149
TALOHTUSKI 90
TAMPICO 151
TANNERS 58
TANNERY 197
TANYARDS 194, 195
TARWATER, Henry C 330, 447, 476
TATE
    J O 150
    Oscar M 260
TATHAM, William 82, 83
TATHAM'S HISTORY 83
TATOM
    W C 188, 336
    Mrs. W C 343
TATUM, Howell 468
TAVERNS 58
TAX, property 97
TAX ASSESSORS, First 94
TAX BILL 76
TAX COLLECTOR 97
TAX LIST 107
TAXATION 56, 77, 97, 104, 105, 107, 140
TAYLOR
    Rev. E A 436

   E F 460
   F W 254
   Gen 151
   Grinsfield 444
   H. H. 193, 294, 304, 305, 554, 583, 584, 585
   J D 157
   J H 534
   John 428
   Luther 442
   Rev N G 448
   Parmenas 75, 86
   Robert L 181, 372, 554
TAZEWELL, TN 188, 509
TEACHERS, wages 412
TEASDALE
   R L 247
   Rev Thomas C 364
TEDFORD, Edward 532
TELEPHONE COMMUNICATION, Law System of 224, 225
TELLICO IRON WORKS 22
TEMPERANCE HALL 152, 447
TEMPERANCE PLEDGE 578
TEMPLE
   Mary B 578, 579
   Oliver P 92, 136, 152, 153, 155, 156, 193, 269, 273, 299, 372,
      .... 373, 382, 475, 500, 541, 554, 555
   Oliver P (photograph) 466
   Oliver P, bio 499
TEMPLETON, Mr. 296
TENNESSEE
   Constitution 379, 467
   First brick house, Webb House 92
   First school 344
   Settlement of 30, 53, 74, 78, 86, 90, 92, 95, 148
TENNESSEE CENTENNIAL EXPOSITION 367
TENNESSEE COAL COMPANY 241, 244
TENNESSEE COAL MINING COMPANY 244
TENNESSEE CONSTITUTIONAL CONVENTION 77
TENNESSEE DEAF AND DUMB SCHOOL 538

TENNESSEE GENERAL ASSEMBLY 152, 153
    Civil War 155
TENNESSEE HEALTH OFFICER'S ASSOCIATION 518
TENNESSEE INDUSTRIAL COLLEGE 362
TENNESSEE LODGE #1 560
TENNESSEE LODGE #2 . . . . 557, 558, 563
TENNESSEE LODGE #20 563
TENNESSEE MEDIAL COLLEGE 398, 518, 519, 520
    Dental department 524
TENNESSEE MEDICAL COLLEGE BUILDING 549
TENNESSEE PRESS ASSOCIATION 316
TENNESSEE PRODUCERS MARBLE COMPANY 207, 552
TENNESSEE RIVER 10, 12, 13, 27, 45, 105, 114, 144, 170, 219,
    . . . . 229, 241, 277, 280, 299, 300, 416
    Bridge 302
    Cable car across 301
    Crossing 301
    Description 275
    Ferries 303
    Improvements 275
    Temporary bridge 302
    The Suck 276
TENNESSEE STATE CAPITOL 17, 91
    Nashville 314
TENNESSEE STATE DENTAL ASSOCIATION 523
TENNESSEE STATE FAIR GROUNDS 123
TENNESSEE FEDERATION OF WOMEN'S CLUBS 579
TENNESSEE STATE HISTORICAL SOCIETY 312
TENNESSEE STATE HOMEOPATHIC ASSOCIATION 520
TENNESSEE STATE HOUSE 442
TENNESSEE STATE LEGISLATURE 92
TENNESSEE STATE MEDICAL ASSOCIATION 521
TENNESSEE STATE PRESS ASSOCIATION 343
TENNESSEE STATEHOOD 78
TENNESSEE UNIVERSITY 516
TERRITORIAL LEGISLATION 47
TERRITORIAL LEGISLATURE 46, 72, 73, 74, 75, 77, 81
TERRITORY OF THE UNITED STATES SOUTH OF THE RIVER OHIO
    . . . . 41, 42, 47, 50, 87, 313, 345, 467, 473

TERRY, Adrian 115, 128, 246, 247, 254, 542
TEST OATH ACT 482
TEUTONIA LODGE #141 563
THATCHER
   Cary 94
   Capt. S. S. 96
THE REVIEWERS, gazette Correspondent 82
THIRD CREEK 131, 144, 299, 30, 362
THOMAS
   Col., death of 173
   Anthony J 287
   Daniel 208, 456
   Ellis 150
   George H Post #1 569
   J E 151
   Jacob L 227, 259, 397
   President John W 553
   Lt. Col. 176
   Mr. 282
   Price 371
   Rev R D 457
   Samuel 284, 286, 287
   Rev. T P 337
   T R 243
   Rev Thomas 457
   William 243
THOMPSON 124
   Capt B T 180
   M E 121, 122, 125, 134, 304
   ME, engine 132
   Rev R N 462
   S. S. 138
   Samuel H 442, 443
THOMPSON & STRONG ADDITION 124
THORNBUGH, Russell 159
THORNBURGH
   Jacob Montgomery 4, 144, 269, 476
   Jacob Montgomery, bio 499
   Jacob Montgomery 541, 554

T. T. 161, 363, 364
THORNDIKE, Mrs. 579
THREE RIVERS PACKET & TRANSPORT 278
THURSTON
    Emma A 465
    Gen. Gates P 587
TIGRIS, Louis 465
TILLERY, S L 534
TILLERY SPRING 131
TILLMAN, Lewis 245, 392, 445, 460, 543, 584
TIMBER 22
TINNER 195, 200
TIPTON, Jonathan 548
TODD, S J 569
TODTENHAUSEN, A 562
TOHOPEKA, Battle of 149
TOMBSTONES, Description of 582
TOMES, Charles 453
TOMPKINS, Stonewall 377
TOPOGRAPHY, Knox County 9, 10, 11
TOTTEN, A W O 469
TOWNSEND, Rev J B 390
TRACY, William R 159
TRAFFIC, Control 98
TRAILS 271, 294
TRANSYLVANIA UNIVERSITY, KY 503, 507, 509
TRAUTWINE, J C 281
TRAVEL
    Fares 272
    Means of 272
    Time needed to 272
TRAVELORS PROTECTIVE ASSOCIATION 571
TREASURER
    City 97
    First 84
TREATIES, with Cherokee 32, 42
TREATY OF FORT STANWIX 32
TREATY OF HARD LABOR 32
TREATY OF HOLSTON 44, 57, 61, 64, 87, 90

TREATY OF HOPEWELL 35, 37, 41, 43, 52, 90
TREATY OF LOCHABER 33
TREATY OF LONG ISLAND IN THE HOLSTON 33, 35
TREATY OF SYCAMORE SHOALS 31
TREES 11, 22
TRECK, Gazette Correspondent 82
TRENT
    Charles F 567
    William L 136, 247, 475, 551
TRENTON, TN 373, 379
TREZEVANT, Marye B 382
TRIGG
    Connally F 4, 152, 153, 156, 468, 489
    Connally F, bio 482
    Joseph M 125
TRIMBLE, James 355
TRIO MILL 213
TRIUMPH REBEKAH LODGE #59 562
TROLLEY, Horse drawn 304
TROLLEY ROUTES 305
TROOPS, black 191
TROTTER
    J W 406
    W A 570
TROWBRIDGE, L C 574
TROWER, James 442
TROY, John 49
TRUEBLOOD, W D 222
TRUMBULL (frigate) 501
TUB MILL 41, 213
TUCKER, J C 410
TUITION, Industrial Building 394
TUNNELL, John 153, 302
TUNSTALL, T B 150
TURK, W A 289
TURKEY, Minister to 486
TURLEY, William B 469
TURNER
    Charles W 383, 384

E A	187
George W	570
J L	160
TURNER PARK	192
TURNEY, Peter	470
TURNPIKES	
Miles of	275
see also "Streets"	
TUSCULUM COLLEGE	413, 499, 516
TUTTLE	
S. S.	242
W R	208, 210, 216, 247, 259, 299, 569
TYDEMAN, W. W.	520
TYDEMAN & CAULKINS	520
TYFFE, James H	281
TYLER	
J C	199
Mrs. J C	464, 546
TYSON	
Laurence D	188, 191, 192, 379
Mrs. Laurence D	553
U S ARMY	92
U S PENSION AGENT	521
UNACATA	63
UNAKA COUNCIL #1620	564
UNAKA MOUNTAINS	12, 282
UNAKA SOAP COMPANY	217
UNCLE LEM, water works	527
UNICOI COUNTY, TN	33
UNION ACADEMY	427
UNION BANK	252, 260
UNION BOAT, STORE & WAREHOUSE COMPANY	278
UNION COUNTY, TN	13
UNION OF CONFEDERATE VETERANS	569
UNION PRESBYTERY	425
UNION PRESBYTERY SYNDOD OF TENNESSEE	458
UNION STRONGHOLD	152
UNION THEOLOGICAL SEMINARY	429
UNION TRUST COMPANY, Philadelphia, PA	306

UNIONISTS
  Meeting of 152
  Resolutions 152
  Sentiment 156
UNITED COMMERCIAL TRAVELORS 572
UNITED CONFEDERATE VETERANS 17, 569
UNITED ORDER OF GOLDEN CROSS 564, 565
UNITED PRESS 334
UNITED STATES BARRACKS 59
UNITED STATES BUILDING 107
UNITED STATES CIRCUIT JUDGE 329
UNITED STATES PENSION OFFICE, Knoxville 516
UNITED STATES TROOPS 59, 92, 112, 133, 177
UNIVERSITY
  Courses of study 363
  Land for 355
UNIVERSITY HIGH SCHOOL, At Knoxville 378
UNIVERSITY HILL 56
UNIVERSITY OF LOUISVILLE 511, 519
UNIVERSITY OF MICHIGAN 518
UNIVERSITY OF NASHVILLE 357, 358, 508, 511, 514
UNIVERSITY OF NORTH CAROLINA 355, 356, 357, 375
UNIVERSITY OF PENNSYLVANIA 503, 506, 507, 508, 513, 516
UNIVERSITY OF TENNESSEE 81, 131, 187, 312, 315, 316
  Site of 353
  Medical Department 368
  Dental Department 368, 372, 374
  Library 376
  Science Hall 379
  Black attendance 379
  Resources 381
  Board of Trustees 381
  Officers 382
  Academic department 383
  Law department 384
  Medical and dental department 384
  Attendance 386
  "Colored" department 393, 394, 397, 460, 480, 487, 494, 497, 507, 513
UNIVERSITY OF VIRGINIA 373, 374, 395, 397

UNIVERSITY SCHOOL 396, 397
    Arkansas 379
    Columbia 378
    Kansas City 379
    Virginia 519
UNTOOLA 31
UPPER CHEROKEE TOWNS 63
UTAH CAMPAIGN 178
UTILITIES 129, 145
VACCINATION 98
VALENTINE, Rev J W 452
VALLEY FORGE FENCE WORKS 211
VALLEY OF TENNESSEE 12
VALLEY OF VIRGINIA 12
VALLEY REGION 10
VAN, Chief 66
VANBENSCHOTEN, W H 210
VANBUREN, Martin 315
VANBUREN COUNTY, TN 15, 19, 359
VANCE, Mary 578
VANDERBILT UNIVERSITY 366, 368, 524
VANDERFORD, Maj. C F 377
VANDEVENTER
    Horace 188
    James 259, 548, 584
VANDEWATE, C F 224
VANDYKE
    T N 281
    Thomas I 348
VANFOSSEN
    Rev H J 450
    Levi 363, 364
VANGILDER
    Albert 255
    John S 105, 109, 114, 115, 116, 121, 122, 125, 129, 138, 139, 143, 197,
    . . . . 232, 246, 255, 304, 540
    Somers 304
    T I 232
VANMETER, Mr. 527

VANUXEM, F W 413
VARIOLOID 527
VAUX, Rev William 453
VEASEY, Rev Harry L 464
VERA CRUZ 151
VERTREES, W M 368
VESTAL Lt. 189
VICKSBURG 169
VIRGINIA 30, 34, 37, 38, 74, 136, 156, 416, 417, 419, 485, 498
   Natural Bridge 353
VIRGINIA & GEORGIA RAILROAD 14
VIRGINIA MIDLAND COLLEGE 519
VOLINSKI, I 465
WADE, Edwin R 125, 571
WAGNER, Joseph H 181
WAGON & CARRIAGE MANUFACUTRER 202
WAGON MAKERS 195
WAGON ROAD 41
WAGONER, Father 442
WAGONS 98
WAHOO SWAMP 149
WAIT, Charles E 374, 383, 548
WAKEFIELD, A L 365
WALDEN'S RIDGE 15, 20
WALKER
   Charles 371
   F M 157
   Joseph H 252, 540
   Dr. Thomas 30
   Rev West 423
   William 150
WALKER, O'KEEFE & COMPANY 228
WALL & MOONEY SCHOOL, Franklin 378
WALLACE
   Aggie 392
   Campbell 241, 539
   Eliza B 392
   James W 336
   Mary 396

WALLEN, Explorer 30
WALLER
   H A 156, 157
   J L 156
WALLING, PA 574
WALTERS, Rev. A 452
WALTON, William 452
WALTZ, A D 125
WAR COMMITTEE 186
WAR OF 1812 . . . . 148, 490
WAR PENSIONS 180
WARD
   J W 140, 567
   James S 385
   John W 411
   Samuel D 270
WARDELL, Alice 301
WARDROPE, W P 147
WARDS 95, 104, 107, 124
   Description of 108
   East Knoxville 137
WARING, Charles 364
WARM SPRINGS 272
WARNER
   Rev A G 452
   Rev Thomas Corwin 448, 450, 589
WARREN COUNTY, TN 19
WARTBURG, TN 162
WASHBURN
   Mrs. 463
   W P 262, 296, 405, 406, 429, 554, 575, 583, 584
WASHINGTON
   D C 17, 178, 191, 192, 272, 481
   George 9, 32, 42, 44, 46, 72, 75, 313
WASHINGTON ACADEMY 344
WASHINGTON AND LEE UNIVERSITY 55, 373, 508, 516
WASHINGTON COLLEGE 344, 346, 349, 492, 500, 506, 509
WASHINGTON COUNTY
   NC 506

TN 13, 33, 155, 157, 250, 315, 344, 347, 419, 466, 487, 509
WASHINGTON DISTRICT 40, 42, 45, 58, 87, 466, 473
WASHINGTON MONUMENT 17
WASHINGTON REPUBLICAN AND FARMERS JOURNAL 493
WATAUGA 421
WATAUGA ASSOCIATION 31, 33, 74, 82
WATAUGA COUNTY, NC 466
WATAUGA FORT 31
WATAUGA RIVER 30, 33, 42
WATER POWER 196
WATER SUPPLY 27, 103
WATERHOUSE
   Euclid 241
   R G 444, 449
   Richard 151, 152
WATERTOWN [NY] PORTABLE STEAM ENGINE MANUFACTURING CO . 309
WATERWORKS 93, 96, 98, 112, 114, 115, 116, 118, 119 527
   Bonds destroyed 116
   Bonds for 116
WATKINS, Mrs. Grace H 579
WATTERSON, Henry 581
WATTON, Kimber 532
WATTS
   John 31, 61, 70
   Ralph L 378, 383, 386
WEAKLEY, J L 554
WEAR, Samuel 72
WEATHER 24, 25, 26
WEAVER
   D H 565, 566
   Rev G S 462
   G W 565
   J A 565
   Mary E 565, 566, 567
WEAVER & KRAMER, Akron, OH 448
WEB PRESS 335, 337
WEBB
   Crew 449
   John 194

T S 296, 305, 307
T S, Jr. 214
WEBB HOUSE 92
WEBS RIDGE 15
WEBSTER
   Daniel 320
   S D 161
WEEKS
   A E 248
   Maj. 186, 187
WEIGHTMAN, Richard 191
WEITING, P Augustus 575
WELCH, L B 243
WELCHER, James M 527, 583
WELCKER
   J M 98
   James H 384
   John M 102
   W L 142, 143, 144, 225, 260, 411, 548
WELL-DIGGERS 58
WELLNER, S M 206
WELLS, Thomas P 145
WELSH 417, 457
WELTON, Mrs. 531
WENTWORTH, "Long John" 333
WERTING, P A 574
WEST, Dr. 294
WEST END STREET RAILROAD COMPANY 305, 306, 308
WEST KNOXVILLE 131, 132, 135, 139, 294, 305, 410, 462
   Annexation 147
   Consolidation 146
   Incorporation, boundaries 144
WEST KNOXVILLE PUBLIC SCHOOLS 409
WESTALL, Rev. Henry 464
WESTERN & ATLANTIC RAILROAD 291
WESTERN NORTH CAROLINA RAILROAD 282
WESTERN RESERVE UNIVERSITY 521
WESTERN UNION TELEGRAPH COMPANY 334
WETMORE, TN 291

Index - 166

WETZEL, Henry B 294, 299
WEXLER, E C 444
WHATCOAT, Bishop 441
WHEELER
  Elbert 131
  F W 447
  Gen 164, 170
  William 131
  Xenophon 382
WHEELERS GAP 20
WHIG PARTY 316, 320, 321
WHISENANT, Mr. 401
WHISTLE COAL AND COKE COMPANY 241
WHISTLE CREEK COAL COMPANY 245
WHITAKER
  H C 587
  Rev Mark 421
  Spears 188
WHITE 63
  A P 218, 305, 391, 523
  Mrs. Andrew P 544, 579
  Brother 559
  D W 218
  F R 452
  Gen 149, 150, 164
  George M 102, 106, 124, 218, 252, 391, 427, 473, 523
  Henry 530
  Hugh A M 227, 252
  Hugh L 158
  Hugh Lawson 40, 80, 149, 150, 164, 250, 314, 352, 387, 388,
  . . . . 468, 469, 477, 494, 583
  Hugh Lawson, bio 479
  Hugh Lawson, presidential candidacy 315
  Isabella M 390
  J C 122
  Dr. J G 524
  J O 239
  James 37, 38, 40, 41, 42, 46, 47, 48, 50, 51, 53, 54, 57, 64, 67, 76, 77, 81,
  . . . . . . 86, 88, 89, 90, 91, 92, 93, 157, 213, 345, 346, 351, 424, 425, 467, 479

   James M 124
   James, fort 39
   Mrs. John 526
   Margaret H 390
   Moses 161, 213, 336, 343, 347, 373, 382, 425, 541, 554
   Samuel A 124, 475
   Thomas 588
   W O 140, 142, 232, 246, 431
   W T 406, 407, 581, 588
WHITE COUNTY, TN 19
WHITE CREEK 424
WHITE HOUSE, Tennessee Industrial College 363
WHITE ROSE FLOUR 215
WHITE SPRING 114
WHITE'S FORT 37, 39, 41, 88, 467
WHITE'S MILL 41
WHITE'S POND 196
WHITESIDE, Jenkins 93, 355
WHITLEY COUNTY, KY 243, 244
WHITTLE
   Charles W 449
   James M 589
   O H 218
   R D 218
   W O 256
WHITTLE TRUNK COMPANY 218
WHOLESALE TRADE 240
WIGHT, Dr. E M 367
WIGHTMAN, Bishop 444
WILCOX
   C. C. 242
   M C 242, 389
WILDER, John T 22, 181, 189, 193
WILEY
   E F 242, 243
   Edwin M 384
   Henry H 242
WILHITE, H R 224
WILKERSON 37

Thomas 443
WILKES
  Mrs. J 579
  John S 470, 471
WILLARD
  Frances E 575
  Frances E Branch 578
  J E 206, 268, 551
WILLIA, Dr. S A 525
WILLIAM, GRANT & COMPANY 282
WILLIAM'S GROVE 99
WILLIAM'S SPRING 299
WILLIAMS
  Gen "Cerro Gordo" 167
  Col 150
  Cornelius 188
  D H 534
  Etheldred 68
  F C 386
  George E 565
  J B 400, 437
  J C J 476, 479, 554
  J L 243
  James 229, 277
  Capt. James 318
  James E 277
  Jennie 243
  John 4, 149, 152, 348, 406, 583
  Mrs. John 553
  John, bio 478
  M N, Mill 213
  M W 241
  P J 573
  Robert 68, 556
  Rufus W 479
  W E 248
  T L 264
  Thomas L 4, 474, 475, 479, 487
  Thomas L, bio 478

    Mrs. W G 547
    W S 388
    William 229, 277
WILLIAMS & COMPANY 277
WILLIAMS & ZIMMERMAN 230
WILLIAMS COLLEGE 458
WILLIAMS, MOFFETT & COMPANY 197
WILLIAMSBURG, section of Knoxville 105
WILLIAMSON
    Julia A 401
    S B 373
WILLIAMSON EXPEDITION 34
WILLIS
    E D 160
    S A 525
    Rev S Turner 461
WILLNER, S M 206
WILLOUGHBY, J W C 363
WILLS, Rev Henry 421
WILMER, Skipwith 287, 289
WILMINGTON, NC 27
WILSON 105
    A M 294
    Col 164
    George 313, 387, 557, 558, 559
    H M 245, 262
    Henry 532
    J L 157
    John L 244
    BG John M 191
    Lee 532
    Rev 433
    William 104
WINCHELL, Prof Alexander R 518
WINCHESTER, James 75
WINGERT, Harry K 399, 534
WINNICK, Isaac 465
WINSTEAD
    George W 538

W D 584, 585
WINTERS GAP 208
WINTHROP, Capt. 180
WISE
  B W 589
  John M 456
WISHART
  Agnes 396
  Matilda 396
WITHERSPOON
  Rev J W 395
  John A 369
WITTENBURG UNIVERSITY, OH 521
WOLF CREEK 282
WOLF VALLEY 15
WOLFORD, Gen. 166
WOMAN'S BUILDING 581
WOMAN'S BUILDING AND PROMOTING BOARD 310
WOMAN'S COUNCIL 545
WOMAN'S EXCHANGE 580
WOMAN'S HOME MISSIONARY SOCIETY 449
WOMAN'S HOSPITAL AND PROMOTING BOARD 309
WOMEN'S CHRISTIAN TEMPERANCE UNION 550, 575, 576, 577, 578
WOMEN'S COUNCIL OF KNOXVILLE 579
WOMEN'S EDUCATIONAL AND INDUSTRIAL UNION 580
WOMEN'S RELIEF CORP 192, 569
WOOD
  Addie 565, 566
  Addie A 566
  Gen 150
  John 58
  Rev Richard 423
  T Hilliard 369, 384
  Col W B 156
  William 564, 565, 566
WOOD WORKING 200
WOODBURY
  C M 221
  Miss C M 579

E P	191
WOODCRAFT	570
WOODLAWN CEMETERY	583, 588
WOODMEN OF THE WORLD	570
WOODRUFF	
Pauline	547
W N	129
W. W.	106, 114, 122, 129, 144, 245, 246, 247, 254, 262, 294, 392, 403, 409, 410, 438, 554, 555, 584
W. W. & Company	233, 248
WOODS, R D & Company	118
WOODWARD	
James T	289
N S	189, 247, 405, 406, 560
WOODWORK	200
WOOL CARDING MACHINES	195, 196
WOOLDRIDGE, J	4
WOOLEN MILLS	462
WOOLFOLK, Rev. L B	436
WORKHOUSE	105
Established	273
WORKINGMEN'S COOPERATIVE COAL COMPANY	241
WORKINGMENS BUILDING & LOAN ASSOCIATION	266, 267
WORLD'S FAIR, Chicago	524
WRAY, W A	142, 411, 412
WRIGHT	
Archibald	469, 481
J	51
J C	146, 187, 193
Rev. J P	392
L M	395
Will D	193
WYATT, Dr.	503
WYLEY, Rev. Samuel Y	426
X. X. PALE	220
YAGER, W M	377
YALE COLLEGE	352, 387, 397, 458
YELLOW FEVER	23, 525, 531
YERGER, George S	495

YERKES SCHOOL, Paris, KY ... 378
YOE, John W ... 144, 146, 299
YORK MASONS ... 558
YOUNG
  Alfred L ... 575
  Benjamin F ... 399, 534
  D K ... 232, 257
  E. E. ... 566
  Eugene ... 448
  Florence ... 391
  Col. Isham ... 128, 294
  R A ... 445, 552
  Robert ... 129
  Stella ... 532
YOUNG MEN'S CHRISTIAN ASSOCIATION
  Organized ... 377, 400, 401, 459, 574, 575
  Ladies Auxiliary ... 575, 578
YOUNGBLOOD, William ... 181
ZACHARY, C ... 160
ZEIGLER
  Ellis B ... 567
  I B ... 217
ZEMP, E R ... 399, 534
ZINC ... 18
ZINC WORKS ... 299
ZINZENDORFF, Count ... 414
ZION, E ... 534
ZOLLICOFFER
  Gen. Felix K ... 156, 162, 316, 329
  Gen Felix K Camp ... 569